WHO'S WHO OF
WEST HAM UNITED

by
TONY HOGG

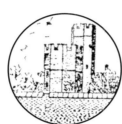

1904-2004
100 YEARS
The Boleyn Ground

Published by:
Profile Sports Media
5th Floor, Mermaid House
2 Puddle Dock, London EC4V 3DS
T: +44 (0)20 7332 2000
F: +44 (0)20 7332 2001
ISDN: +44 (0)20 7236 2467
www.profilesportsmedia.com

Printed in the UK by:
Butler and Tanner, Ltd. Frome, Somerset.

Pictures:
Action Images, Empics, Kieran Galvin, Steve Bacon,
Topps Cards, Panini

CONTENTS

1904-2004

100 YEARS

The Boleyn Ground

FOREWORD

I was delighted and honoured when author Tony Hogg invited me to provide the foreword to this, the third edition now of his labour of love, *Who's Who of West Ham United FC.*

Published to celebrate our famous club's 100 years playing at the Boleyn Ground, Tony has completely updated and revised the previous works and has included a full biog of every player who has joined the Hammers since the Centenary Edition published in 1994.

I had just left the club then after ten years as a Hammer and, looking back, it's amazing how much the game has changed over the intervening decade. In my day, if you referred to a foreign element among players you would be, with occasional exception, referring to Scottish, Welsh or Irish team-mates. But shortly after I left Upton Park and following the advent of Harry Redknapp's inspired "Foreign Legion" of stars, players began arriving from all over the world to claim the honour of playing for West Ham United, and the dressing room resembled the United Nations.

But far from detracting from the unique flavour created at the Boleyn, these multinational stars from far-flung lands with different languages and cultures have actually enriched it further with their own blends of colourful customs and have added their own spice to the land of pie and mash.

But one condition I did make when agreeing to write this foreword was that it should remain in English, or better, Cockney-English!

So when you are having a good butcher's hook at the start of this captain's hook, you have me to thank that it has been written with plenty of Plymouth Argyle!

Returning to the topic of how much the game has changed in the past decade, it suddenly struck me that no less than nine of the team-mates I shared a dressing room with at Upton Park between 1984 and 1994 were awarded a testimonial year in recognition of ten years or more service to West Ham United FC.

The total is ten, including me, and must constitute something of a record. Certainly it's a situation unlikely ever to be repeated in these days when so many clubs operate a "revolving door" policy of transfer activity. Let's have a look at these long-serving stalwarts in the positions they played and their total appearances in brackets: in goal was, of course, Phil Parkes (436); full-backs, Ray Stewart (431), Steve Potts (505) and George Parris (290); centre-backs, Alvin Martin (600), Paul Hilton (65) and myself (367); and midfield, Alan Devonshire (448); Billy Bonds (793) and Geoff Pike (367). And it's worth remembering that Alvin and Bonzo actually had two testimonials – surely another record.

They were all great club men, but to me the most endearing feature of this encyclopedic history of the players of West Ham is the way it represents every player. Whether you are looking for Billy Bonds who played 793 times or Lee Boylan who took the Upton Park stage at senior level for only a few moments, they are all here between these pages.

I'm sure when you flick through you will discover one or two players you never even realised had pulled on the famous claret and blue shirt with the crossed hammers motif.

In these cosmopolitan times, the club enjoys support from all over the world but even in this time of corporate football, the Boleyn Ground still has a working class feel about the place and jealously retains its unique East End atmosphere.

Footballers come and go, as this book amply portrays. But the supporters remain, come sun or rain and this book, although about the players, is for you – the best supporters in the land.

Enjoy,

Tony Gale

Tony Gale

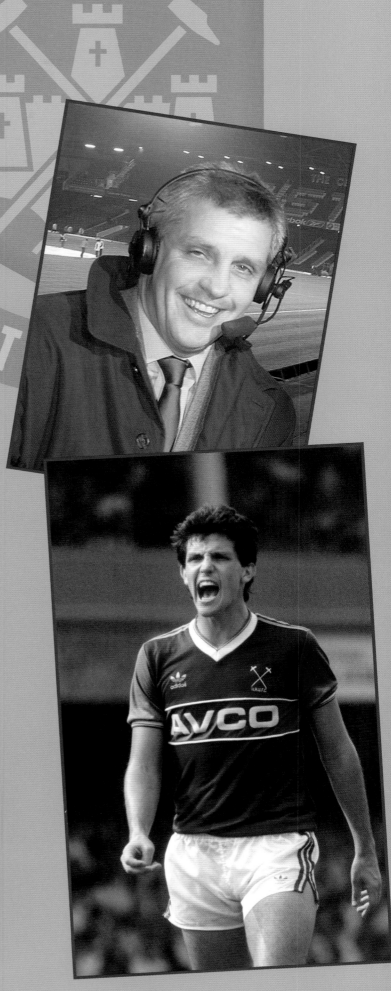

1904-2004
100 YEARS
The Boleyn Ground

INTRODUCTION

When Bobby Zamora raced away to celebrate his winning goal for West Ham United in the Championship Play-off Final against Preston in May 2005, the striker quickly found himself carrying a passenger on his back in the shape of his young colleague Mark Noble.

The 18-year-old midfielder was first on the scene to share in the euphoria, despite having yet to take the field as one of the team's substitutes on that memorable occasion at the Millennium Stadium in Cardiff. Noble's passion is typical of hundreds of players who have recognised how much of an honour and privilege it is to add their names to the list of those who have represented the Hammers.

"All I ever wanted to do when I was growing up was go on to wear the West Ham shirt and I can't believe that I'm now playing for the club," he said as his first season as a squad member came to a close.

The 1-0 victory against Preston at the end of that 2004/05 campaign saw West Ham reclaim their place in the Premiership, and it's impossible to ignore such glorious games and magical moments when reflecting on the club's compelling history.

Triumphs and trophies are usually the criteria by which a club's success is judged and it is over such historical highlights that, generally speaking, any story telling is draped.

Hammers have enjoyed many highs and endured almost as many lows during their existence but their contribution to football cannot be valued purely in terms of results and League tables.

The club has fashioned an image and reputation for playing the game with style and flair, often sacrificing the consistency required to win prizes for the sake of adhering to their traditional philosophy of trying to entertain.

The theory, certainly among many supporters, is that when somebody wears the West Ham crest, they're not merely representing the club but subscribing to a precise set of playing principles.

Ultimately, then, it's the profiles of the players themselves that combine to tell the club's real story.

Accordingly, the *Who's Who of West Ham United* includes a biographical account of every man to have pulled on a claret and blue shirt since the club was formed in 1900, in addition to many of the earlier pioneers of the Thames Ironworks team that began life in 1895.

Sir Trevor Brooking MBE, so elegant as a footballer and an even greater ambassador for the sport since his retirement, in many ways personifies the culture and class of Hammers at their very best.

The former England international midfielder (scorer of the winning goal in the 1980 FA Cup Final, of course) remained a one-club man for his entire playing career and his loyalty to the east London club, even after relegation, was always appreciated by its supporters who themselves remained devoted to the cause – and still are.

Other long-time servants of the club include Dick Walker, John Bond, Ernie Gregory, Ted Hufton, Noel Cantwell, Ronnie Boyce, Pat Holland, Alan Devonshire, Alvin Martin and Steve Potts, while there are those –

among them Syd Puddefoot, Bryan "Pop" Robson, Tony Cottee, Julian Dicks, and, most recently, Shaka Hislop – whose affections for life at the Boleyn Ground saw them return for second periods.

Then there are those players whose family names have more than one association with the club – the Barretts, the Browns, the Lansdownes, the Sealeys, the Lampards and the Ferdinands.

When talking of real claret and blue blood, however, they come no more iconic than the late, great Bobby Moore OBE who, along with brilliant club colleagues Sir Geoff Hurst MBE and Martin Peters MBE, took England to World Cup Final success in 1966.

This book makes no excuses for allocating five pages to the legendary Moore, whose achievements as captain and defender will surely always see him considered as West Ham's greatest ever player.

There are other names that will always be synonymous with the club's trophy successes, with Alan Sealey scoring twice in the 1965 European Cup Winners' Cup Final victory against TSV 1860 Munich and Alan Taylor doing likewise against Fulham in the 1975 FA Cup Final.

Other forwards such as Vic Watson, Jimmy Ruffell, Johnny Dick, David Cross, Trevor Morley and Teddy Sheringham made significant contributions to help Hammers enjoy successful promotion campaigns or, in the case of Frank McAvennie, attain the club's best ever League finish (third place in 1986).

Record signings include Phil Parkes (the world's most expensive goalkeeper when he left QPR to sign for West Ham in a £565,000 deal in 1979), midfielder Don Hutchison (who twice set the club's highest transfer fee paid when booking in at the Boleyn) and Czech international defender Tomas Repka.

Heroes and headline-makers come in the shape of contrasting characters, with twice FA Cup-claiming captain (and later manager) Billy Bonds MBE displaying battling and buccaneering qualities as he became the club's record appearance holder and Italian hitman Paolo Di Canio, undoubtedly one of the game's most mercurial mavericks.

As vital as all these players' contributions were, this book is just as much about the mechanical midfielders such as Geoff Pike and Peter Butler, whose low-key labouring ensured Hammers' engine kept chugging away, and the diligent defenders such as Paul Brush and Tim Breacker.

There are also the one-game wonders, the bad boys, the bad buys and players such as Paul Ince and Jermain Defoe whose attempts to leave the club saw their reputations with supporters irrevocably damaged.

All in all, there are about 800 men to have made first-team appearances for West Ham, with this latest edition of the *Who's Who* – 11 years on from its predecessor and coinciding with the club having surpassed a century of residency at the Boleyn Ground – featuring about 140 new player entries with an additional 100 having been revised. Also included are a handful of individuals who, although never making an official first-team appearance, went on to establish themselves in the game, either in another capacity at Upton Park or as a player with another club (Tony Carr and Harry Cripps being two examples).

The statistics are complete until the very end of the 2004/05 season, with the book also featuring a

Two-goal 1965 European Cup Winners' Cup Final hero Alan Sealey dives for a header against Nottingham Forest at Upton Park in 1961

OGDEN'S CIGARETTES.

G. KAY,
WEST HAM UNITED.

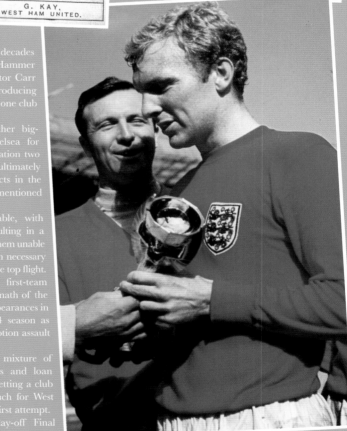

summary of the club's summer signings in preparation for the Premiership.

Promotion to the top tier now represents a financial windfall, with the face of football having changed immeasurably since the early 1990s and the advent of the Premier League.

With the Sky media organisation pouring multi-millions into the game for exclusive live television rights, England's top clubs have been able to invest heavily in new players and stadium development in the quest for success.

West Ham were missing from the first Premiership programme as a result of relegation in 1992 but they stepped up a year later to begin a ten-season stay among the big boys and one that would see a huge increase in turnover of players at the club.

This trend was partly fuelled by the impact of the Bosman ruling that came into effect in the second half of the decade and which allowed players freedom of movement on the expiry of their contracts, with the European Union lifting restrictions on foreign imports within member states.

Whereas the arrival of Belgian attacker Francois Van der Elst was something of a novelty in 1982, such a signing became very much the norm with the likes of Paulo Futre and Hugo Porfirio making brief excursions to the East End in the late 1990s.

The transfer market witnessed a global explosion, with Hammers recruiting players born in territories such as Eastern Europe, Israel, Chile, Costa Rica, Guinea, the United States and Australia.

Cameroon international Marc-Vivien Foe became the club's then record signing when he arrived in a £4.5 million deal from Lens in 1999, as West Ham's training ground became a multi-cultural environment. Slaven Bilic and Eyal Berkovic made a huge impact before earning the club a huge profit when sold.

The revolving door for arrivals and departures became something of a blur, with the increased transfer activity in the 1990s reflecting then-manager Harry Redknapp's wheeler-dealer approach to team rebuilding. Some 35 players represented West Ham at first-team level during 2000/01 – Redknapp's final season in charge – as the manager looked to bolster his squad following the £18 million sale of defender Rio Ferdinand.

As his boss had been, as a player, three decades earlier, Ferdinand was a homegrown Hammer and under Redknapp and academy director Carr the club's youth scheme flourished, producing arguably the greatest crop of talent at any one club for a period.

Frank Lampard junior became another big-money departure when he joined Chelsea for £11 million in 2001 and the club's relegation two years later, under manager Glenn Roeder, ultimately enforced the sales of more youth products in the form of Joe Cole, Glen Johnson, the aforementioned Defoe and Michael Carrick.

Their departures were sadly inevitable, with relegation from the Premiership now resulting in a huge drop in revenue for clubs and leaving them unable to sustain the large wage bills that had been necessary for them to try and remain competitive in the top flight.

The mass exodus saw 13 men with first-team experience depart in the immediate aftermath of the drop, with a total of 36 players making appearances in the claret and blue during the 2003/04 season as Hammers endeavoured to mount a promotion assault amid much trauma and turbulence.

Incredibly, 24 of those players – a mixture of bargain buys, free transfers, youngsters and loan signings – made their debuts that term (setting a club record) so it was perhaps asking too much for West Ham to return to the Premiership at the first attempt.

Thankfully, the memories of the Play-off Final defeat by Crystal Palace in 2004 were erased a year later as the club secured promotion with victory against Preston, allowing a new group of players to establish themselves as Hammers heroes.

The likes of Matthew Etherington, Nigel Reo-Coker, Marlon Harewood and Play-off winner Zamora all played significant roles while, in Anton Ferdinand, Elliott Ward and the aforementioned Noble, supporters could be reassured that the youth academy was producing yet more fine talent.

Such is the ever-growing difference in quality between the top two divisions, that promotion now brings new pressures to drastically improve squads and Hammers were no different, with manager Alan Pardew making a host of signings – including Israeli international Yossi Benayoun – in a bid to improve the club's chances of retaining its top-flight status.

The new Who's Who includes a special section devoted to the new arrivals in the summer of 2005. Supporters are always excited by the prospect of seeing new faces in a West Ham shirt, hoping they will add to the club's legacy as we dream of the bubbles flying high once again.

Whatever the future holds, there's no doubt that the new boys are joining a very select group of players, as the Who's Who of West Ham United testifies.

Kirk Blows

100 YEARS

1945

1944

1957

1940

WEST HAM UNITED

1947

1904-2004

100 YEARS

The Boleyn Groun

1963

1967

1994

WEST HAM UNITED

1904-2004

The Boleyn Groun

NEW SIGNINGS

ALIADIERE, Jeremie   2005-

Born: Rambouillet, France, 30.3.83

AFTER AN UNHAPPY loan spell at Glasgow Celtic, Arsenal's French Under-21 international striker signed another loan deal that will keep him at Upton Park until at least the end of 2005/06, making his Hammers debut against Bolton Wanderers in late August 2005. Having failed to start at Parkhead, Jeremie is keen to impress with West Ham and claimed: "When I heard they wanted me I had no hesitation in signing. They are a very ambitious club and I was very impressed with the whole set-up." Despite never being able to lay claim to a regular first team spot at Highbury, the player had stockpiled an impressive array of honours during his short time in north London including an FA Youth Cup winners' medal in 2001, when he equalled Michael Owen's record of nine goals in the tournament, and Community Shield winners' medals in 2002 and 2004 in addition to his coveted Barclays FA Premiership winners' medal gained earlier the same year. A graduate of the famous Clairefontaine academy, Jeremie was also a winner with France in the 2004 Toulon Tournament, and scored nine times in 37 League and Cup outings for the Gunners, the vast majority of which were made off the bench. In 2003/04, he excelled when hitting four goals in three games during the Reds' run to the Semi-final of the Carling Cup and his signing is regarded as something of a coup by boss Alan Pardew. He has had Champions League experience with both Arsenal and Celtic but enthused: "I cannot wait to play in the Premiership again with West Ham."

Jeremie Aliadiere

BELLION, David   2005-

Born: Sevres, France, 27.11.82

THIS FRENCH UNDER-21 international striker was the subject of an acrimonious £2 million transfer from Sunderland (one goal in 24 League and Cup apps) to Manchester United in July 2003 after making a name for himself in Le Championnat with AS Cannes. First team starts were few and far between at Old Trafford, however, and after scoring nine times in 40 League and Cup games for the Reds, David jumped at the chance to kick-start his Premiership career with a year's loan spell at West Ham in August 2005. Bearing in mind his Champions League experience with United, his signing could prove to be a shrewd move by Irons boss Alan Pardew. Made a scoring debut in 4-2 League Cup win at Sheffield Wednesday.

BENAYOUN, Yossi   2005-

Born: Dimona, Israel, 5.5.80

THIS HIGHLY-RATED ISRAELI international midfielder turned down offers from Everton and Bolton to sign for Hammers at a cost of £2.5 million from Spanish Primera Liga Racing Santander in July 2005, following advice from ex-Hammer and fellow Israel star Eyal Berkovic. A graduate of the renowned Ajax Youth Academy, "The Diamond" as he is nicknamed in his native country, returned to Israel after becoming homesick in the Netherlands and scored 55 goals in four seasons with Maccabi Haifa before his move to Spain. In 2004/05 Yossi hit nine goals in 35 Primera Liga games for Racing to alert a host of European clubs to the potential of the debt-ridden Spaniards' hottest property. But it was Irons boss Alan Pardew who secured his signature ahead of his rivals to claim: "We're delighted to have signed Yossi and I'm sure he'll be a great asset to our squad. He's a creative player who brings an educated discipline to the attack. But he's also a diligent player who hardly misses a game and has improved year-on-year. He's a player with flair who will be able to open the door for us when teams sit deep. We needed a player like that and at 25 he's a great signing for the club." Altogether he scored 19 times in 98 Primera Liga matches for Racing Santander – a superb return for someone who is not recognised as an out-and-out striker and probably the clinching factor of his four-year contract. Bolton boss Sam Allardyce was less enamoured of the player, following Yossi's decision to make Upton Park his new home: "I think he went for the money. The answer is, if he didn't want to come to a club like ours, which is a great club, then he went to West Ham for more money. We are an established Premier League club now and we have achieved a UEFA Cup spot. So I think it was very stupid, a big mistake." Time will tell.

CARROLL, Roy   2005-

Born: Enniskillen, Northern Ireland, 30.7.77

THIS TOWERING NORTHERN Ireland international goalkeeper was Alan Pardew's first signing following Hammers' return to the Premiership in June 2005. Released as a free agent by Manchester United,

Clive Clarke

Roy Carroll

COLLINS, James 2005-

Born: Newport, Wales, 23.8.83

LIKE FELLOW WELSH international central-defensive partner Danny Gabbidon, James was signed from Championship strugglers Cardiff City in July 2005 for a combined fee of £3.2 million. A towering presence at the heart of the Bluebirds' defence, he won his first full cap for the Principality against Norway in May 2004, to become the first player to represent Wales at Schoolboy, Youth, Under-18, Under-21 (seven caps) and full international level. He scored six times in 86 League and Cup games for the Ninian Park club. With Gabbidon, Gavin Williams and Carl Fletcher, he completes a quartet of Welsh caps at the Boleyn. James made his first appearance for Hammers in the 3-1 victory over Swedish First Division side Falkenbergs. Young Welsh Player of the Year (October 3, 2005).

GABBIDON, Danny 2005-

Born: Cwmbran, Wales, 8.8.79

WEST HAM MANAGER Alan Pardew returned to the city that bore witness to his team's Play-off Final victory to sign Cardiff City's talented, 19-times capped Welsh international central-defender Gabbidon and his Wales and Bluebirds team-mate James Collins from the cash-strapped Ninian Park outfit. Having scored ten times in 219 League and Cup appearances during his five years in the Welsh capital after signing from West Brom (27 League and Cup apps) for a £175,000 fee in August 2000, Dan was valued at over £2 million in the double deal transaction. A Welsh Youth and Under-21 international (17 caps), he formed a solid central-defensive partnership with his team-mate James at City, which the pair will be hoping to continue at Upton Park at the expense of Anton Ferdinand and Elliott Ward. Voted Welsh Footballer of the Year (October 3, 2005).

KONCHESKY, Paul 2005-

Born: Barking, Essex, 15.5.81

A FULL ENGLAND international who also appeared at Youth level and won 15 Under-21 caps for his country, Paul is most comfortable at left-back, but has also appeared in midfield – most notably during his 15-match spell on loan from Charlton Athletic at London rivals Spurs in 2003/04. Returning to the Valley for the second part of that campaign, he won back a regular slot in the Valiants rearguard and had scored five times in 179 League and Cup games for the south Londoners between 1998 and 2005 until his £1.5 million transfer to Hammers in July 2005. A dead-ball expert and a strong, resolute tackler, he is expected to be a valuable addition to West Ham's defence. The tough-tackling defender who made his Hammers debut in the 3-1 victory over Swedish First Division side Falkenbergs, during the pre-season tour, has vowed to be the "new Julian Dicks" albeit with a less hot-headed approach! "Remember, I played here as a youth team player with Bobby Zamora and it's a great feeling to pull on the West Ham shirt as a first teamer at last!" Paul is no stranger to Upton Park, having been a West Ham fan all his life and had the honour of winning his first England cap there in the 3-1 defeat to Australia in 2003. Making his League debut for Charlton Athletic at the age of just 16 years and 93 days to become the Addicks' youngest ever player, he is indeed a young veteran in the true sense of the word, 2005/06 being his eighth season as a first team player while still only 24 years of age.

MIKOLANDA, Petr 2005-

Born: Czech Republic, 12.9.84

WHEN THIS CZECH Under-21 international striker completed his "fairytale" move to West Ham he declared, "I am very happy to have signed at West Ham. Teddy Sheringham was my hero growing up. I remember watching his goal against Bayern Munich in the Champions League Final. I never dreamt I would meet him, let alone play in the same side as him." Mikolanda scored 13 goals for Prague's Viktoria Zizkov last season and made a big impression on Hammers' tour of Sweden, scoring twice and notching another in the 2-2 draw at Yeovil Town.

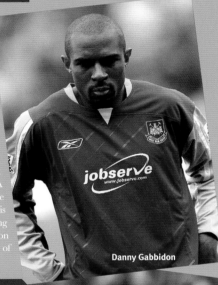
Danny Gabbidon

Paul Konchesky

James Collins

Roy turned down a move to Sunderland after being promised the first-team jersey at Upton Park. Formerly with Hull City, where he made 49 League and Cup appearances from 1995-97; Wigan Athletic (169 apps from 1997-2000); and then United, whom he joined for £2.5 million in July 2001 and made 82 League and Cup appearances with. The holder of 16 full caps for Northern Ireland, Roy also won a Premiership title and an FA Cup winners' medal with United in 2003 and 2004 respectively. He duly made his West Ham debut in the last game of Hammers' pre-season tour of Sweden in the 3-0 victory over Vastra Frolunda.

CLARKE, Clive 2005-

Born: Dublin, Republic of Ireland, 14.1.80

THIS VERSATILE REPUBLIC of Ireland international turned down the opportunity of a transfer to Premiership rivals Sunderland to sign for Hammers for a £275,000 fee in August 2005. Captain of his former club Stoke City, Clive is mainly recognised as a left-back, but can also operate with equal effectiveness at centre-half and midfield and is a welcome addition to manager Alan Pardew's squad. Having amassed 262 League and Cup appearances for the Potters (ten goals), the well-built Dubliner has so far won two full caps for the Republic and played 11 times for the Under-21 side. An Associate Members Cup winner with City in 2000, the 25-year-old defender made his Hammers debut in the 1-1 pre-season friendly draw with Dutch side Den Haag in the Hague on August 2, 2005.

A

ABOU, Samassi
ADAMS, William
ALEXANDERSSON, Niclas
ALLAN, Robert
ALLEN, Clive
ALLEN, Martin
ALLEN, Paul
ALLEN, Percy

ALLEN, Robert H
ALLISON, Malcolm
ALLISON, Tommy
ALVES, Paulo
AMBLER, Charles
ANDERSON, Edward
ANDREW, George
ANDREWS, Jimmy

ARMSTRONG, Eric
ARNOTT, John H
ASHTON, Herbert
ASKEW, Leslie Walter
ATKINS, C
ATTEVELD, Ray
ATWELL, Reg
AYRIS, John

Paul Allen (right) and Geoff Pike parade the
FA Cup at Wembley in 1980

ABOU, Samassi — 1997-2000

Born: Gagnoa, Ivory Coast, 4.4.73
League apps: 22 (5 goals)
Cup apps: 9 (1 goal)

ONE OF THE most popular players ever to don the claret and blue, French Under-21 international striker Samassi quickly became a cult figure at Upton Park following his £400,000 transfer from Cannes (where he scored five goals in 37 League games) in October 1997. Previously with FC Martigues and Lyon, he was fleet of foot and skilful on the ball, and upon signing him manager Harry Redknapp predicted: "He's big, strong and sharp and I'm sure he will prove a useful acquisition for the club." Hammers fans and Samassi hit it off instantly – even if opposition fans were confused by the chorus of "boos" that seemed to accompany his every

move. Samassi knew better – the Boleyn faithful were simply making a play on his surname. It seemed that Redknapp had unearthed another gem as his unpredictable style gave Hammers extra attacking options and provided cover for John Hartson, Paul Kitson and Trevor Sinclair – even if his goal celebrations often made Upton Park resemble scenes from Rorke's Drift as the fans chanted "Aboouu! Aboouu!" with Zulu-like intensity and hailed their new hero. But almost as quickly as his star rose, it began to wane as a consequence of a deteriorating relationship with his manager. After turning down £800,000 moves to first Bradford City then Hearts – which would have realised the club a 100 per cent profit – the six foot striker was ostracised and shipped off to Ipswich Town and then Walsall. Abou insisted all he wanted to do was "make or score goals for West Ham" but the damage had been done. Returning to the club in the autumn of 1999, after a spell on loan at Troyes in France, he found himself banished to reserve team football and then sent on loan again to SPL Kilmarnock where the Scottish tabloids billed him "Abou Samassi"! Released at the end of 1999/2000, Abou returned to France playing for Corsican side Ajaccio and then FC Lorient in 2002/03.

ADAMS, William — 1936-37

Born: Tynemouth, Tyneside, 3.11.1902
League apps: 3 (1 goal)

BILL ADAMS MADE a sensational start in West Ham's colours when he scored against his old club, Southampton, in Hammers' 2-0 victory at the Dell on November 21, 1936 – quite a feat for a right-half! He had begun his career with Sunderland Colliery and then Guildford City before transferring to Southampton. After making his Saints debut in August 1927, he had to wait over three years until his next first team outing. But once in the side, he went on to make 205 League and Cup outings and was appointed captain before joining West Ham. However, he had only a brief stay at Upton Park, transferring to Southend United in January 1937. Bill returned to Hampshire in 1937 and ran the Half Way Inn at Chandlers Ford until his death in March 1963.

ALEXANDERSSON, Niclas — 2003

Born: Halmstad, Sweden, 29.12.71
League apps: 8

A SWEDISH INTERNATIONAL who had played 68 times for his country before signing on a one-month loan deal from Everton in September 2003. Equally comfortable in midfield or on the right wing, Niclas showed a willingness to track back and help his defence when not delivering crosses or marshalling the midfield. Caretaker boss Trevor Brooking was happy to involve the six foot two inch Swede during much of his second spell in the hot seat and the former IFK Gothenburg star didn't let him down. A product of south Sweden's Halmstads BK, Niclas made 114 First Division appearances (18 goals) for his home-town club (1990-96) and gained a Cup winners' medal in 1995 before joining the country's premier club IFK in 1996. An ever-present in his two seasons at the Gamla Ullevi Stadium (52 League apps, 13 goals) and with two Champions League campaigns under his belt, he transferred to Premiership side Sheffield Wednesday in December 1997 for £750,000. After 88 League and Cup appearances for the Owls, Niclas moved to Everton for £2.5 million in July 2000 as Wednesday began their descent through the divisions. Despite a respectable 58 appearances (seven goals) during three years on Merseyside, the Swede's first team outings dropped to only seven in 2002/03 and it seemed he still had a lot to prove to new Goodison supremo David Moyes when he returned to Liverpool with "some wonderful memories of my time at Upton Park".

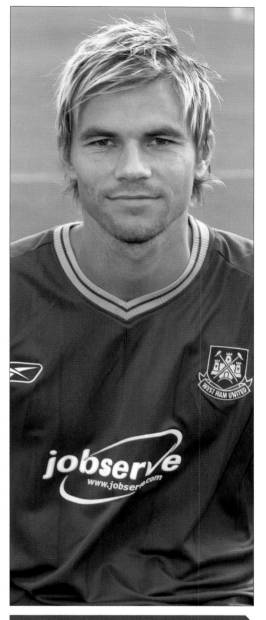

ALLAN, Robert — 1889-1903

Born: Dundee, Scotland, date unknown
League apps (TIW): 21 (1 goal)
SL apps (WHU): 52 (1 goal)
Cup apps: 5

BOB MADE HIS TIW debut in a 3-1 reverse at Southampton in December 1889 at outside-right. He held that position on all but two occasions during Hammers' last campaign under the Ironworks banner, switching to inside-left against Sheppey United and trying out the right-half berth he was later to fill with such distinction in a victorious Hermit Road encounter with Gravesend. His time on the wing prompted a glowing testimonial in a 1900/01 club handbook: "Shows excellent judgment in everything he does, and can take hard knocks and play on as game as ever. Centres on the run, and occasionally contributes a long shot with plenty of steam behind it. Doesn't neglect his inside man and, although weighty, can show a rare turn of speed when necessary." A letter sent to West Ham's former public relations officer, the late Jack Helliar, from an old supporter, reveals that Bob Allan often used to have breakfast at Tom Robinson's house in Benledi Street, Poplar, where hospitality was also extended to other Hammers stars of the day including Hughie Monteith, Roddy McEachrane and Billy Grassam. Happy days!

ALLEN, Clive   1992-94

Born: Whitechapel, London, 20.5.61
League apps: 38 (17 goals)
Cup apps: 6 (1 goal)

ONE OF THE game's most prolific goalscorers, Clive joined his sixth London club when he was transferred from Chelsea for £250,000 in March 1992. The son of former Tottenham and QPR star Les Allen, and the third member of the family to wear claret and blue, Clive first proved his appetite for goals as a young star with Havering, Essex and London Schools teams. Although West Ham was the nearest club to his Hornchurch home, and he trained with Spurs, Clive signed apprentice for QPR in 1976 and turned pro two years later. In the summer of 1980, aged only 19 and after one full League season, Clive became the youngest million-pound player when he moved from Rangers to Arsenal for £1.25 million but, having played only three friendlies for the Gunners, moved on to Terry Venables's Crystal Palace before the following season started, swapped for Kenny Sansom in another deal valued at £1.25 million! Within eight weeks of signing Clive, Venables moved to QPR and after a difficult ten months at Selhurst Park, the striker followed the manager to Loftus Road, for £700,000. His first season back in west London brought him an appearance in the 1982 FA Cup Final against Spurs, but Clive withdrew through injury after only ten minutes and was forced to miss the replay, which Spurs won. Tottenham was his next port of call, in 1984, at a cost of £700,000. A spate of injuries hampered him but in the third of his four seasons at White Hart Lane Clive reached his peak. In 1986/87 he broke Jimmy Greaves's club record by scoring 33 League goals and 49 overall, including one in the 1987 FA Cup Final against Coventry City after just two minutes. Clive had to settle for a second loser's medal, but there was an immediate tonic as he collected both the Football Writers' Association and PFA's Player of the Year awards. In addition to youth and Under-21 caps, Clive made five full appearances for England. His debut came as substitute against Brazil in the Maracana Stadium in 1984. His turbulent spell at White Hart Lane ended in March 1988, when, ironically, Venables sold him to French club Bordeaux for £1 million, although he remained with the north Londoners until the end of that season. He stayed in France for only a year before yet another £1 million deal – his fourth – brought him back to England to play for newly-promoted Manchester City. Despite maintaining an impressive scoring record, he returned to London in December 1991 to join another of his father's former clubs, Chelsea, for £250,000. The same fee took him to Upton Park 14 months later when Clive celebrated his debut with a goal – at Stamford Bridge! Unfortunately, injury restricted Clive to just three more outings that season and he could not save Hammers from relegation from the old First Division in May 1992. A year later, though, Clive was a hero again, as he netted the crucial second goal, as substitute, in the final home game against Cambridge United. That 2-0 victory ensured Hammers pipped Portsmouth for the runners-up spot behind Newcastle United, and automatic promotion to the newly-named Premier League, by a single goal! Although Clive made only two substitute appearances between January and the promotion party, his 12 goals before Christmas proved crucial. Clive's third season with Hammers was also marred by injury, but his ratio of almost a goal every other game continued. He did all his work in the penalty area, where he had the knack of being in the right place at the right time. Clive's farewell game for Hammers was as sub in the goalless FA Cup Quarter-final tie against Luton Town at Upton Park on 14 March, 1994. Millwall – Clive's seventh London club – paid £75,000 for him on transfer deadline day, March 1994. Honoured by the Football League against The Rest Of The World in 1988, he uncharacteristically failed to score in 12 appearances for the Lions and bowed out of League soccer at the New Den in 1995, moving on to a new career as a TV pundit.

ALLEN, Martin   1989-95

Born: Reading, Berkshire, 18.8.65
League apps: 190 (25 goals)
Cup apps: 46 (9 goals)

THE MOST SUCCESSFUL midfield goalscorer since Martin Peters, Martin became the second member of the Allen family (cousins Paul and Clive completed the trio) to play for Hammers when Lou Macari paid £660,000 to make him his first signing. The former QPR midfielder scored on his debut in the 3-1 Second Division home win against Plymouth Argyle (August 26, 1989) and added another ten that season. He earned the nickname "Mad Dog" for his tenacious ball-winning efforts, yet Martin's surging runs from deep, and eye for the long-range strike, yielded many goals. He was particularly effective in Hammers' 1992/93 promotion-winning campaign when he forged a fearless partnership with Peter Butler and netted ten times. An impressive spell that produced five goals in six games near the end of the 1993/94 campaign placed him third in the team's goalscoring chart, behind Morley and Chapman. The return to the top flight also marked an improvement in Martin's disciplinary record – just three bookings compared to the previous season's 13, which resulted in an FA fine and five-match suspension. Martin first showed his competitive strength as captain of

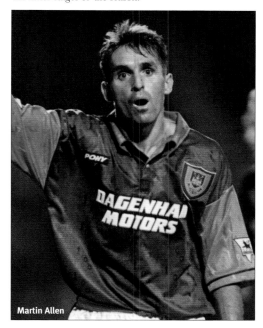

Martin Allen

Career record

Played	League		FAC		LC		Europe		Total	
	App	Gls	App	Gls	App	Gls	App	Gls	App	Gls
1989-90	39	9	1	0	6	2	0	0	46	11
1990-91	40	3	6	0	3	2	0	0	49	5
1991-92	19	0	2	2	2	0	3	0	26	2
1992-93	34	4	2	0	2	0	6	0	45	0
1993-94	26	6	6	2	3	1	0	0	27	0
1994-95	29	2	1	0	3	0	0	0	46	3
1995-96	3	1	0	0	0	0	0	0	41	4
TOTAL	**190**	**25**	**18**	**4**	**19**	**5**	**9**	**0**	**236**	**34**

England Schoolboys in 1980, the year he signed apprentice forms for QPR. Terry Venables gave him his first pro contract three years later, although it was Alan Mullery who called up Martin for his debut, in a UEFA Cup First Round tie against KR Reykjavik (Iceland) at Highbury in September 1984 (the game was switched because UEFA banned the use of Rangers' plastic pitch). He made his League debut as a sub, at Luton, in March 1985. A year later, Martin was sub at Wembley when QPR were beaten 3-0 by Oxford United in the Milk (League) Cup Final. An intense, demonstrative character at times, Martin liked to celebrate his goals – especially the spectacular ones – by running towards the corner flag. His father Dennis – who played for Charlton Athletic, Reading and AFC Bournemouth – used to travel all over the country to watch his son before his death in 1995. After that, Martin decided to leave the Boleyn and all its memories, joining Portsmouth for £500,000. In three seasons at Fratton Park he scored four goals in 45 appearances before a loan spell at Southend United where he played under Alvin Martin along with ex-Hammer Mike Marsh. Having set up the Martin Allen Soccer Schools for youngsters, it was a natural progression for him to join the coaching staff at Pompey, but he was sacked for alleged sexual discrimination. To prove his innocence he took the club to court, cleared his name and won a reported six-figure sum in compensation. Martin was with his home-town club Reading as assistant manager to Alan Pardew until moving to Conference outfit Barnet and taking over as boss from Peter Shreeve in March 2003. He has since taken over at Second Division Brentford whom he successfully steered clear of relegation in 2003/04. In 2004/05, he took the Bees to within a whisker of a lucrative FA Cup Sixth Round clash with Manchester

United, and remained in contention for promotion until the latter stages of the season.

ALLEN, Paul   1979-85

Born: Aveley, Essex, 28.8.62
League apps: 149 (6 goals)
Cup apps: 43 (5 goals)

AT THE TIME of his shock transfer to Tottenham Hotspur for a fee set at £425,000 by the Football League Tribunal during the summer of 1985, this little midfield dynamo was the proud holder of two national football records. In May 1980 he became (at 17 years and 256 days) the youngest player ever to appear in an English FA Cup Final, collecting a winners' medal to boot. He also overtook Bobby Moore's long-standing record of 18 England Youth caps the following year. Before joining his cousin Clive Allen at White Hart Lane, Paul had signed apprentice forms for West Ham in July 1978 and as a pro in August 1979 – after a spell at QPR, where his uncle, Les Allen (a former Spurs star) was once manager. A one-time Essex and Thurrock Boys starlet, Paul returned to West Ham's First Division side in 1984 after a long lay-off through injury and made a major contribution towards the club's successful fight against relegation, displaying the kind of form that made him one of the finest midfield players in the country and led to Liverpool battling Spurs for his signature. The eventual winners later paid Hammers 50 per cent of the profit on his £550,000 move to Southampton in September 1993, because of a clause in his contract. Paul appeared in both the 1987 and 1991 FA Cup Finals for Spurs and amassed a total of 376 League and Cup games while at White Hart Lane, scoring 28 goals. An England Under-21 international, Paul was the first of the "Allen Dynasty" to play for Hammers, being followed by cousins Martin and Clive Allen. After 43 outings for Saints, Paul had a four-match loan stint at Luton Town in 1994/95 and finished the campaign with a more extensive 17-game sojourn with Stoke City. Then followed a two-season contract with Swindon Town where he made another 37 League appearances before moving on at the end of 1996/97 to play 14 times for Bristol City. Another 28 outings under his old skipper Billy Bonds at Millwall the following season allowed the then veteran midfielder to finish his career on a massive total of 587 appearances, yielding 32 goals plus 121 Cup outings during his time at West Ham and Spurs with five goals for each in the various Cup competitions. He now works for the PFA alongside his ex-Hammers team-mate Bobby Barnes.

ALLEN, Percy   1919-23

Born: West Ham, London, 2.7.1895
League apps: 80 (5 goals)
Cup apps: 6

JOINING FROM LOCAL amateur soccer for West Ham's initial League season of 1919/20 (after serving in the Army during World War I), Percy made his Second Division debut at outside-right in a 2-1 home defeat to Birmingham on November 1, 1919. Although he was tried at centre-forward, it wasn't until he converted to right-half that he found his true role to become an ever-present in the 1921/22 campaign and prompted the club handbook of that period to comment: "A class player who would do admirably in First League Football." Unfortunately, he was never put to the test in the higher grade, as he was transferred to Northampton Town before Hammers' promotion to Division One in 1923, later seeing service with Peterborough, Lincoln City, Weymouth and Stamford Town before retiring. He then worked for West Ham Corporation, continuing to support their footballing counterparts at Upton Park. After running a newsagents in Barking Road, East Ham, Percy passed away at the age of 74 in October 1969. His son Don kept the family name alive at the Boleyn Ground as a sports reporter with the South Essex Recorder newspaper group.

ALLEN, Robert H   1919-20

Born: Tynemouth, Tyneside, 3.11.1902
League apps: 1 (1 goal)

FEATURED JUST ONCE in Hammers' first League season. His moment of glory came on November 1, 1919, when he netted from the centre-forward position in the 2-1 home defeat against Birmingham.

Left to right: Jimmy Andrews, Dave Sexton, Noel Cantwell, Malcolm Allison, Phil Cassetarri, John Bond, Frank O'Farrell and Malcolm Musgrove

ALLISON, Malcolm   1951-57

Born: Dartford, Kent, 5.9.27
League apps: 238 (10 goals)
Cup apps: 17

SIGNED FROM CHARLTON Athletic in February 1951 after seven seasons at The Valley, Malcolm's influence on West Ham United cannot be underestimated. During manager Ted Fenton's reign, it was Malcolm who – with Ted's blessing – took charge of the coaching sessions that helped pave the way for aspiring youngsters such as Bobby Moore, who, ironically, went on to replace Malcolm in the heart of defence. A master tactician and innovator, Malcolm was years ahead of his time in his coaching and fitness routines, some of which were based on continental ideas. Fellow pro and former England youth coach John Cartwright once said of Mal: "He should be revered. They should have a statue to him at West Ham... he laid the foundation for the success of the club – not by what he did on the field, but the knowledge he gave to other people." Widely recognised as the founder of the so-called West Ham Academy, which met regularly in the afternoons, after training, at Cassetarri's Cafe in the nearby Barking Road and at local dog tracks, his successes as a leading coach have tended to eclipse his fine career as a centre-half in the 1950s. But Malcolm's ambition to play in the First Division was shattered when he was struck down by tuberculosis eight games into the club's 1957/58 promotion season. Malcolm's last-ever senior appearance for the Hammers came at Sheffield United on September 16, 1957. He was taken ill after the game and had a lung removed in hospital. Although he battled tremendously hard to beat TB, making a steady comeback in the reserves, Malcolm's first-team days were

over. The night he finally realised this (a home game against Manchester United on September 8, 1958) will forever remain etched on the memories of all those who were present. Fenton had to make a choice for the number 6 shirt: Allison, having fought his way back to fitness; or Bobby Moore, the young pretender hungry for his first big chance. It was Malcolm's great friend and team-mate, Noel Cantwell, who, when asked for his opinion by Fenton, nominated Moore for his debut. Moore told the story of that emotional night, and more, to Jeff Powell in his biography, Bobby Moore, *The Life And Times Of A Sporting Legend*: "I'd been a professional for two and a half months and Malcolm had taught me everything I knew. For all the money in the world I wanted to play. For all the money in the world I wanted Malcolm to play because he'd worked like a bastard for this one game in the First Division. It would have meant the world to him. Just one more game, just one minute in that game. I knew that on the day Malcolm with all his experience would probably do

a better job than me. But maybe I'm one for the future. It somehow had to be that when I walked into the dressing room and found out I was playing. Malcolm was the first person I saw. I was embarrassed to look at him. He said, 'Well done. I hope you do well.' I knew he meant it but I knew how he felt. For a moment I wanted to push the shirt at him and say, 'Go on, Malcolm. It's yours. Have your game. I can't stop you. Go on, Malcolm. My time will come.' But he walked out and I thought maybe my time wouldn't come again. Maybe this would be my only chance. I thought: you've got to be lucky to get the chance, and when the chance comes you've got to be good enough to take it. I went out and played the way Malcolm had always told me to play. Afterwards I looked for him back in the dressing room. Couldn't find him. When Malcolm was coaching schoolboys he took a liking to me when I don't think anyone else at West Ham saw anything special in me. Just for that, I would have done anything for him. Every house needs a foundation and Malcolm gave me mine. It went beyond that. He was the be-all and end-all for me. I looked up to the man. It's not too strong to say I loved him. Malcolm said one simple thing, which was to stay in my life forever. We sometimes used to get the same bus from the ground and we were sitting upstairs one day when Malcolm said very quietly: 'Keep forever asking yourself: If I get the ball now, who will I give it to?' He told me that was Di Stefano's secret at Real Madrid." Malcolm shunned medical advice to continue his playing career with Romford in the Southern League, then became a coach at Cambridge University and Toronto before taking his first step on the managerial ladder with Bath City. From there he moved to Plymouth Argyle, followed by a successful period (1965-71) with Joe Mercer at Manchester City, where he became known as "Big Mal" and continued for two seasons on his own after Mercer semi-retired. The pair won all the game's major domestic honours. After those days Big Mal's career took him to Crystal Palace (where his flamboyance was characterised by his fedora, kingsize cigars and champagne lifestyle), Man City again, FC Sporting Lisbon (whom he steered to championship success), Middlesbrough, non-League Durham side Willington and Kuwait – coaching the national side. He was briefly back in the big-time in 1992/93 as boss of Bristol Rovers who gained a shock FA Cup draw at Aston Villa and a 4-0 victory over deadly rivals Bristol City under his management. Mal was dismissed but bounced back to boss little London Docklands club Fisher Athletic where he applied the same principles as he'd employed on his colourful career's more glamorous points of call. Namely play to win – but do it with style!

Career record

	League		FAC		LC		Europe		Total	
Played	App	Gls	App	Gls	App	Gls	App	Gls	App	Gls
1950-51	10	0	0	0	0	0	0	0	10	0
1951-52	38	0	3	0	0	0	0	0	41	0
1952-53	39	2	1	0	0	0	0	0	40	2
1953-54	42	0	3	0	0	0	0	0	45	0
1954-55	25	0	2	0	0	0	0	0	27	0
1955-56	40	3	6	0	0	0	0	0	46	3
1956-57	39	4	2	0	0	0	0	0	41	4
1957-58	5	1	0	0	0	0	0	0	5	1
TOTAL	238	10	17	0	0	0	0	0	255	10

ALLISON, Tommy　1903-09

Born: Edinburgh, Scotland, 1875
SL apps: 156 (7 goals)
Cup apps: 9

TOM BEGAN HIS career with New Brighton Tower, a Second Division club, between 1888 and 1901. When they folded he transferred to Southern League Reading and, after two good seasons with the Berkshire club, he and three others from the Biscuitmen's playing staff joined Hammers for the last campaign at the old Memorial Grounds. By far the most successful of the quartet, he became a regular and was appointed vice-captain – and awarded the proceeds of a Western League match against Portsmouth in recognition of his services. From a scoring debut against Kettering Town in September 1903, until his last appearance against Watford in April 1909, he never gave less than his best, and could consider himself unfortunate in not adding senior recognition to the Scottish junior cap he won with Strathclyde. He died on March 4, 1961.

PROMINENT FOOTBALLERS.

T. ALLISON.
WEST HAM UNITED

ALVES, Paulo　1998

Born: Mateus Villareal, Portugal, 10.12.69
League apps: 4

AN EXPERIENCED PORTUGUESE international striker who had scored eight goals in 13 games for his country, Paulo came to the notice of West Ham when he scored against them for Sporting Lisbon in the Centenary match friendly in May 1996 at Upton Park. Paulo – a fully qualified electrical engineer – was given a glowing report on life at Hammers by Hugo Porfirio, who also played in the Centenary clash, before embarking on a three-month loan spell. First coming to prominence as a member of the Portugal side that won the fifth World Youth Championship Final in 1989, he'd begun his club career with his local team SC Villa Royal before transferring to FC Porto as a 17-year-old. In 1992, he joined Maritimo in Madeira where he formed a dual strike-force with ex-Hammer Alex Bunbury as his new team qualified for the UEFA Cup two years in a row. Then in 1995, after finishing third top scorer on 14 goals, the sparks began to fly as Portugal's biggest club Benfica began a tug-of-war for his services. With the clubs unable to agree on a cash-plus-player arrangement, the deal broke down and the player ended up at Sporting Lisbon instead. Denied the luxury of starting a match at the Boleyn Ground, the striker made just four substitute appearances and failed to match the impression made previously by his fellow countrymen Porfirio, Dani or even the injury-plagued Paulo Futre. But back in Portugal, Alves proved he was far from finished and, after a successful spell at Uniao Leiria, Paulo moved on to Gil Vicente FC for 2001/02 and was the club's top scorer with 11 goals in 27 games.

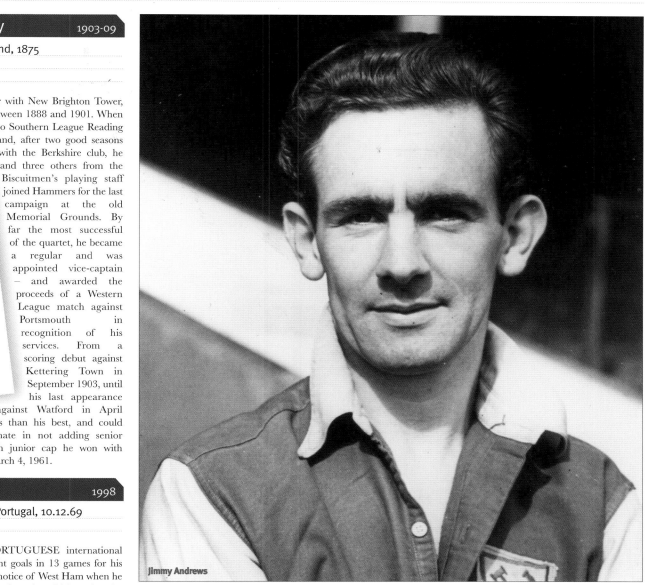
Jimmy Andrews

AMBLER, Charles　1901-02

Born: birthplace unknown, 1869
SL apps: 1
Cup apps: 1

A RESERVE GOALKEEPER who won his lone place in the limelight after an administrative error saw Hammers playing host to Spurs in a Southern League clash at the Memorial Grounds as well as receiving Leyton for an FA Cup third qualifying match in November 1901. With the prospect of larger gate receipts from the meeting with Tottenham, Hammers solved the problem by conceding home advantage in the Cup and sending a second XI to Leyton, where Charlie kept a clean sheet in a 1-0 victory. Back at the Memorial Grounds the first team lost by the same margin – a result which prompted the West Ham management to rest the great Hughie Montieth. So Charles duly made his Southern League debut the following week against QPR. There was to be no fairy-tale ending, however, as West Ham went down 2-1 at Rangers' Latimer Road, North Kensington home after having to change in the Latimer Arms pub and run down the road to the pitch. So ended Charles Ambler's less-than glamorous taste of first-class football. Charlie had begun his career with Bostal Rovers and signed pro for Royal Arsenal in 1891. He moved to Clapton (where he reverted to amateur status) in 1892; Dartford, 1893; Luton Town, 1894; and, after making 133 first team appearances for Spurs between 1894 and 1900, moved again to Gravesend and New Brompton in 1900.

Charlie Ambler

After leaving the Irons he joined Millwall in the summer of 1902. Charles passed away in 1952.

ANDERSON, Edward　1933-35

Born: Durham, County Durham, 17.7.11
League apps: 26
Cup apps: 2

A BROAD-SHOULDERED RIGHT-HALF signed from Torquay United, Ted made 24 Second Division appearances during the 1933/34 season after making his debut on the opening day against Bolton Wanderers at Upton Park. The following season he lost the first team spot to Ted Fenton, and was subsequently transferred to Chester after only two more League outings. Ted played for Jarrow before joining Wolves and Tranmere Rovers.

ANDREW, George　1967

Born: Glasgow, Scotland, 24.11.45
League apps: 2

JOINED WEST HAM from Glasgow junior side Possilpark YMCA, in September 1963. One of several players tried at centre-half as a replacement for Ken Brown, he made the first of only two League appearances at home to Sunderland in February 1967. After a short spell at Crystal Palace, he found his true niche at Southern League Romford. He later became a teacher in Cornwall where he played in the County League with St Blaizey. George died in July 1994.

Eric Armstrong, Bill Nelson, Noel Cantwell, Jimmy Andrews and Dave Sexton

at five foot nine inches – was relatively short for a centre-half but was an ever-present in the Southern League team in 1913/14 and was absent on only two occasions the following campaign after the outbreak of World War I. He turned out 28 times in the London Combination during wartime and underlined the seriousness with which he regarded even this makeshift competition by getting himself sent off twice! Before joining Norwich in 1909, Walter had played for Xylonite FC, Tottenham Gothic Works FC, Chadwell Heath, Finchley FC and Southend United. When at Chadwell Heath, he was banned from football for a lengthy period. He died in 1955.

Leslie Askew

ANDREWS, Jimmy — 1951-55

Born: Invergordon, Scotland, 1.2.27
League apps: 114 (21 goals)
Cup apps: 6

A LEFT-WINGER SIGNED from Dundee FC for £4,750 in November 1951 – quite a substantial fee in those days! Jimmy gave the club great service before leaving for neighbours Leyton Orient (35 League apps, eight goals) in 1956. After ending his player career at QPR (82 League apps, 15 goals), he gained a fine reputation as a coach and later managed Cardiff City after another ex-Hammer – Frank O'Farrell – vacated the post. He later scouted for Southampton, but has now retired.

ARMSTRONG, Eric — 1946-53

Born: Hebburn-on-Tyne, Northumberland, 25.5.21
League apps: 1

WHOLE-HEARTED WING-HALF WHO rarely played in the first XI, but inspired everyone with his devotion. Signed from Cramlington Welfare FC after service in the Royal Navy during World War II, he had played for East Northumberland Boys before progressing to senior soccer. A member of the Combination championship side of 1947/48, he turned his attention to coaching Hammers' junior sides then spent over a decade as coach of Harwich and Parkeston FC from 1954. He died in 1969.

John Arnott

ARNOTT, John H — 1953-55

Born: Sydenham, London, 6.9.32
League apps: 6 (2 goals)

PLAYED FOUR LEAGUE games as an amateur, but made only two further first XI appearances after turning pro for 1954/55. Later had spells with Shrewsbury Town, AFC Bournemouth and Gillingham, ending his playing days (well into his forties) with Dover.

ASKEW, Leslie Walter — 1912-15

Born: Marylebone, London, 1886
SL apps: 104 (2 goals)
Cup apps: 8

ORIGINALLY AT ASTON Villa, for whom he made two Football League appearances, and Norwich City, Walter –

ASHTON, Herbert — 1908-15

Born: Blackburn, Lancashire, 1887
SL apps: 224 (23 goals)
Cup apps: 25 (1 goal)

WITH 224 SOUTHERN League outings, "Tiddler" Ashton holds Hammers' all-time appearance record in that competition, totalling nine more than his nearest rival – team-mate and fellow Blackburn lad, the aptly named Fred Blackburn. He joined Hammers from Accrington in 1908, after helping them win the Lancashire Combination in 1905/06. As his nickname would indicate, Herbert was small in stature, but the diminutive winger had plenty of fans ready to help him out when the going got rough, a section of whom took their protective instincts too far when they invaded the pitch to do battle on their hero's behalf in a particularly tough Upton Park encounter with Syd King's old team, New Brompton. Luckily West Ham chairman Bill White was able to placate the fans and order was restored. The incident seemed to underline the fact that Ashton could do little wrong in Hammers fans' eyes. Herbert joined the Royal Flying Corps during World War I as a mechanic, but still managed to turn out on 63 occasions in the old London Combination. He was also chosen to represent the Southern League versus the Irish League in 1915.

ATKINS, C — 1908-09

SL apps: 2 (1 goal)

THIS CENTRE-FORWARD'S BRIEF flirtation with first XI football saw him among the scorers in a 4-0 Boleyn Castle romp over Southern League rivals Southend United. The following week's 3-1 reverse away to Coventry City was his only other outing.

ATTEVELD, Ray — 1992

Born: Amsterdam, Netherlands, 8.9.66
League apps: 1
Cup apps: 2

RAY MADE A slice of Hammers history when, on February 22, 1992, he became the first Dutchman to play for the club. But apart from that outing, a 2-1 defeat at Sheffield Wednesday, the midfielder's only other appearances during his month's loan from Everton were in the two FA Cup Fifth Round clashes against Sunderland – a 1-1 draw at Roker Park (February 15) and the Upton Park replay 11 days later, which

Career record										
	League		**FAC**		**LC**		**Europe**		**Total**	
Played	App	Gls	App	Gls	App	Gls	App	Gls	App	Gls
1908-09	27	1	2	0	0	0	0	0	29	1
1909-10	42	4	5	0	0	0	0	0	47	4
1910-11	37	6	4	0	0	0	0	0	41	6
1911-12	33	3	5	0	0	0	0	0	38	3
1912-13	36	6	4	0	0	0	0	0	40	6
1913-14	35	3	4	1	0	0	0	0	39	4
1914-15	14	0	1	0	0	0	0	0	15	0
TOTAL	**224**	**23**	**25**	**1**	**0**	**0**	**0**	**0**	**249**	**24**

Ray Atteveld

John Ayris

Reg Atwell

Hammers lost 3-2. After 51 League games for Everton, he joined two former Hammers, Nicky Morgan and Leroy Rosenior, at Bristol City.

ATWELL, Reg   1938-46

Born: Oakengates, Wellington, Shropshire, 23.3.20
League apps: 4

SON OF A former Shrewsbury Town player, this tough-tackling wing-half signed from Denaby United. He served with the Essex Regiment through World War II, and guested with Burnley who he joined after the war ended. Reg played over 250 games for the Lancastrians (including a 1947 Cup Final appearance) before moving to Bradford City in 1954.

AYRIS, John   1970-76

Born: Wapping, London, 8.1.53
League apps: 57 (1 goal)
Cup apps: 8 (1 goal)

SIGNED AS A full professional in October 1970, this right-winger made his League debut in the same month against Burnley, and went on to be selected for the England Youth team seven times during 1971. But injury problems blighted his early promise and he was granted a free transfer at the end of 1976/77. He went on to play for Wimbledon and later Brentford.

B

BAILEY, Dan
BAILLIE, David
BAINBRIDGE, Ken
BALL, John
BAMLETT, Tommy
BANKS, Steven
BANNER, Arthur
BANTON, Dale
BARNES, Bobby
BARNES, William
BARRETT, Jim Jnr
BARRETT, Jim Snr
BASSILA, Christian
BEALE, Robert
BEESLEY, Mick
BELL, Dick
BELL, George
BENNETT, Les
BENNETT, Peter
BERKOVIC, Eyal
BEST, Clyde
BETTS, Eric
BICKLES, Dave
BICKNELL, Charles
BIGDEN, James
BIGGAR, William
BIGGIN, Horace
BILIC, Slaven
BING, Doug
BIRCHENOUGH, W
BIRNIE, Alexander
BISHOP, Ian
BISHOP, Sydney
BLACK, Robert
BLACKBURN, Alan
BLACKBURN, Fred
BLACKWOOD, John
BLOOMFIELD, Jimmy
BLORE, Vincent
BLYTH, James
BLYTHE, Joe
BOERE, Jeroen
BOND, John
BONDS, Billy MBE
BOOGERS, Marco

BOURNE, Stanley
BOURNE, W
BOVINGTON, Eddie
BOWEN, Mark
BOWYER, Lee
BOYCE, Ronnie
BOYLAN, Lee
BRABROOK, Peter
BRADFORD, T
BRADSHAW, Harry
BRADSHAW, Tom
BRADY, Liam
BRANDON, Tommy
BREACKER, Tim
BREEN, Gary
BRETT, Frank
BRETT, Ron
BREVETT, Rufus
BRIDGEMAN, Billy
BRIGNULL, Phil
BRITT, Martin
BROOKING, Sir Trevor MBE
BROWN, Ken
BROWN, Kenny Jnr
BROWN, William
BROWN, William
BRUNTON, Fred
BRUSH, Paul
BUNBURY, Alex
BURGESS, Daniel/Dick
BURKETT, Jack
BURNETT, Dennis
BURRILL, Frank
BURROWS, David
BURTON, Frank
BURTON, John H
BURTON, Stan
BUSH, Robert
BUTCHART, J
BUTCHER, George
BUTLER, Peter
BYRNE, Johnny
BYRNE, Shaun
BYWATER, Stephen

Ken Brown (right) watches as Liverpool's Wallace beats Jim Standen to score at Anfield in the 2-2 Charity Shield draw in August 1964

BAILEY, Dan
1912-21

Born: East Ham, London, 26.6.1893
SL apps: 49 (13 goals)
Cup apps: 4 (3 goals)
League apps: 35 (9 goals)
Cup apps: 3 (1 goal)

SIGNED FROM CUSTOM House FC, Dan took over Danny Shea's inside-right position when the latter transferred to Blackburn Rovers in 1913. Bailey was a member of the side that went from January 1 to September 16, 1913 without defeat in the Southern League. World War I disrupted his career, but he returned from service in Egypt to take part in Hammers' entry into League football. Later had a spell with Charlton Athletic before transferring to Clapton Orient (now Leyton) before finishing his career at Margate FC. He died aged 74 in April 1967.

BAILLIE, David
1925-29

Born: Ilford, Essex, 1906
League apps: 16
Cup apps: 1

A GOALKEEPER SIGNED from Coryton FC, David spent most of his six seasons as understudy to the great Ted Hufton. Nevertheless, a 1920s club handbook said of Baillie: "There are few goalies in the country who can hold and field a wet ball like him." He transferred to Chester in 1929, but returned to the Boleyn when he retired from playing to become assistant groundsman. Died in November 1967, aged 61.

BAINBRIDGE, Ken
1946-49

Born: Barking, Essex, 15.1.21
League apps: 79 (16 goals)
Cup apps: 4 (1 goal)

THIS SPEEDY WINGER was a handful for his opponents and not averse to having a crack at goal. Ken holds the record for scoring the quickest goal at Upton Park – in the Second Division 2-1 win over Barnsley on August 29, 1949 – timed at nine seconds. The goals continued after he was transferred to Reading and later Southend United, where he ended his League career.

BALL, John
1929-30

Born: Stockport, Cheshire, 29.9.1899
League apps: 15 (9 goals)

AS A MINER, John played for Silverwood Colliery FC in the Sheffield Association League where his goals got him signed to Sheffield United. There, a bad injury forced him back into non-League soccer for a season with Wath Athletic before his career underwent a remarkable transformation when he signed for First Division Bury and was subsequently chosen to play for England against Northern Ireland in Belfast in 1927. Also lining-up for England that day were two future West Ham team-mates-to-be, Stan Earle and Ted Hufton. Keeper Hufton sustained a broken arm but – in those pre-substitute days – played on for a while before Ball gave a creditable performance as makeshift keeper as England's ten men went down 2-0. Ball later played inside-left for Hammers, joining Coventry City after a short but prolific spell at the Boleyn.

BAMLETT, Tommy
1904-05

Born: Newcastle, date unknown
SL apps: 18
Cup apps: 1

ALONG WITH GOALKEEPER Matt Kingsley and full-back partner Dave Gardner, Tommy made up a trio of former Newcastle United defenders who were on duty for Hammers' inaugural Upton Park match against Millwall on September 1, 1904. A Geordie by birth, he signed for Newcastle from local League side Kibblesworth but made only two appearances in the famous black and white stripes before his move south. Also known as Herbert, the left-back's 18 Southern League outings for Irons in 1904/05 represented his best spell of first XI football before his return to non-League soccer with West Stanley in the north-east.

BANKS, Steven
1992

Born: Hillingdon, Middlesex, 9.2.72
Cup apps: 1

A YOUNG GOALKEEPER who represented Berkshire Schools before progressing through Hammers' youth ranks and making his Reserve team bow at Fulham (October 11, 1989). He played only one game for Hammers – in a low-key 2-2 draw with Bristol Rovers in the Anglo-Italian Cup, preliminary round, at Upton Park (September 2, 1992) – then spent a while on loan at non-league Wokingham, under the watchful eye of former mentor and Hammers keeper Phil Parkes. He was then given a free transfer in May 1993 and joined Gillingham. He later played for Bolton Wanderers, Rochdale (on loan), then joined Wimbledon in 2003/04 where he subsequently turned out against his former Hammers team-mates in a 1-1 draw at the Dons' new base at the National Hockey Stadium in Milton Keynes in November, 2003. In February 2005, he failed to prevent Hammers winning 1-0 at his new club, Gillingham. In October 2005, he was with SPL Heart of Midlothian.

BANNER, Arthur
1938-47

Born: Sheffield, Yorkshire, 28.6.18
League apps: 27

A STRONG, STURDY full-back who played for the club before, during and after the war. Signed from Doncaster Rovers before hostilities broke out, he served in the Essex Regiment and the Royal Artillery, attaining the rank of sergeant. He moved to Leyton Orient (where he became one of the O's most popular signings) in 1948, became player-manager of Sittingbourne in Kent, and later coached Ilford to the Amateur Cup Final in 1958. Arthur died at his home at Thorpe Bay in April 1980.

BANTON, Dale
1979-80

Born: Kensington, London, 15.5.61
League apps: 5
Cup apps: 1

A PROMISING FORMER Middlesex Schools midfield star who never quite made the grade with West Ham. At his next club, Aldershot, he made headlines when scoring five goals in one match at the end of the 1982/83 season. From there he moved to York City (1984) then, after brief stays at Walsall and Grimsby Town, returned to Aldershot in August 1989.

BARNES, Bobby
1980-85

Born: Kingston, Surrey, 17.12.62
League apps: 22 (3 goals)
Cup apps: 7 (1 goal)

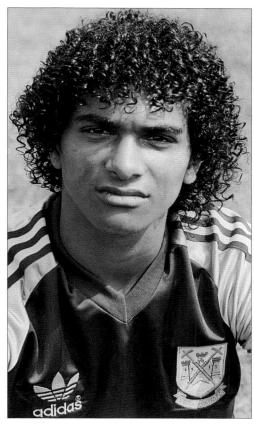

A FAST, SKILFUL winger with the ability to take on and beat opponents, Bobby scored on his League debut against Watford in September 1980. He won an extended run in the first team during Hammers' injury crisis of 1983/84, and featured often in 1984/85. A member of the Youth Cup-winning team of 1981, he also had England Youth honours. Had a spell on loan to Scunthorpe United in 1985/86 before leaving West Ham for Aldershot for £15,000 in March 1986. After Aldershot, Bobby moved to Swindon Town (in 1987), then Bournemouth (March 1989), Northampton Town (October 1989), Peterborough (for whom he played against West Ham – in February 1992) then tried his luck north of the border with Scottish Premier Partick Thistle. As a Thistle player Bobby trained with Ipswich Town, under his old Upton Park bosses John Lyall and Mick McGiven on Mondays and Tuesdays, before jetting off from Stansted Airport, flying home after each match on Saturday! After winding down his career with a spell in Hong Kong and one last League appearance with Third Division Torquay United in 1995/96, he retired. Now works for the PFA dealing with player's contracts and giving financial advice. Still active with the West Ham vets team, which competes in the Carling Masters.

BARNES, William — 1902-04

Born: Yorkshire, date unknown
SL apps: 48 (5 goals)
Cup apps: 5

BILLY JOINED HAMMERS in the summer of 1902 from Sheffield United where he had been a hero in the FA Cup Final replay of that year – a late replacement at outside-right who scored the decisive goal in a 2-1 victory over Southampton at Crystal Palace. After two years regular service in West Ham's Southern League XI, Billy moved to Luton and then across London to Queens Park Rangers, then playing at Park Royal. He later became something of a pioneer in his role as a trail-blazing coach with Spanish club Bilbao, pre-dating ex-Hammer Malcolm Allison by many decades. Hammers met Billy's club on their first-ever continental tour in 1921 and set a good example by winning 2-0. While Billy was finding fame in international football circles, his brother Alfred made a name for himself as Labour MP for East Ham South, later attaining Cabinet rank.

BARRETT, Jim Snr — 1925-38

Born: West Ham, London, 1907
League apps: 442 (49 goals)
Cup apps: 25 (4 goals)

J. BARRETT

A NAME INEXTRICABLY entwined in Hammers' heritage. A larger than life character, "Big Jim" first played at Upton Park as a member of the West Ham Boys team that met Liverpool in the English Shield Final of 1920/21. The then Duke of York (later King George VI) was among the crowd that broke the existing attendance record. A team-mate of Jim's that day was Billy "Bubbles" Murray, so-called because of his uncanny resemblance to the boy in the famous painting by Millais entitled "Bubbles" that used to advertise Pears Soap – hence the origin of Hammers' theme song. Although Billy Murray had no connection with West Ham United, he had been a colleague of Jim's in the renowned Park School side, to which Jim had transferred from Abbey School because the latter had no football team. Also involved with Jim's early development was the Fairbairn House Boys' Club, which also produced other players of Football League standard such as Ted Fenton, Jack Townrow, George Barber (of Chelsea fame) and Alf "Snowball" Barrett of Fulham. Jim's namesake had also played for Park School and was a member of the West Ham Boys team that won the 1916/17 English Shield Final. Signing professional forms in Hammers' Cup Final year of 1923 at the age of 16, Jim had to wait two years to make his League debut against Spurs at White Hart Lane on March 28, 1925. It was the first of a total that stood for many years as the seventh highest appearance record in the club's history. Big Jim's solitary international appearance against Ireland in 1928 constituted a record at the other end of the scale. His four minutes on the field, before injury ended his aspirations, remains the shortest recorded international career. He continued to be an invaluable asset to his club, however, not least because of his remarkable versatility that had seen him perform in every position for the first and second XIs. His ability to switch from defence to attack was borne out by his tally of more than 50 League and Cup goals as a Hammer. As well as being prolific, he was also deadly accurate – during a Hammers' tour of Holland he aimed at a clock behind the goal and hit the target to put it out of action! In 1945/46 Jim was in charge of the "A" team, and played in the same side as his son, Jim Barrett Jnr. After retirement he had the satisfaction of seeing "Young Jim" carry on the family tradition in the League side. His later life was beset with ill-health, and following a long stay in hospital he passed away on November 25, 1970 at the age of 63.

Career record

Played	League App	Gls	FAC App	Gls	LC App	Gls	Europe App	Gls	Total App	Gls
1924-25	5	0	0	0	0	0	0	0	5	0
1925-26	42	6	1	0	0	0	0	0	43	6
1926-27	42	1	3	0	0	0	0	0	45	1
1927-28	34	5	0	0	0	0	0	0	34	5
1928-29	22	1	2	3	0	0	0	0	24	4
1929-30	40	7	4	1	0	0	0	0	44	8
1930-31	40	4	1	0	0	0	0	0	41	4
1931-32	38	3	2	0	0	0	0	0	40	3
1932-33	40	8	6	0	0	0	0	0	46	8
1933-34	38	5	2	0	0	0	0	0	40	5
1934-35	41	5	2	0	0	0	0	0	43	5
1935-36	40	2	2	0	0	0	0	0	42	2
1936-37	11	1	0	0	0	0	0	0	11	1
1937-38	8	1	0	0	0	0	0	0	8	1
1938-39	1	0	0	0	0	0	0	0	1	0
TOTAL	**442**	**49**	**25**	**4**	**0**	**0**	**0**	**0**	**467**	**53**

BARRETT, Jim Jnr — 1949-54

Born: West Ham, London, 5.11.30
League apps: 85 (24 goals)
Cup apps: 2 (1 goal)

SIGNED FROM THE Juniors in February 1949 he was the son of the illustrious "Big Jim" Barrett. Jim Jnr made a good impression at the Boleyn in the early 1950s before being sold for a substantial fee to Nottingham Forest at Christmas 1954. He was their top scorer in 1956/57 and played a big part in their rise to the First Division. After a short spell with Birmingham City, he returned to the fold as player-manager of Hammers' "A" team until 1968, when he left again to serve under another ex-Hammer, Ben Fenton, at Millwall. Later became a publican at the Napier Arms in Halstead, Essex.

BASSILA, Christian — 2000-01

Born: Paris, France, 5.10.77
League apps: 3
Cup apps: 1

THIS WAS THE signing that proved one too many for Harry Redknapp and ultimately cost him his job as West Ham manager. Contracted on a one year's loan from French First Division side Rennes, the former French Under-21 international was previously a team-mate of Freddi Kanoute at Olympique Lyonnais and it was the Hammers' French ace who recommended Bassila to Redknapp (comparing him favourably with Patrick Vieira) having known him since the pair were trainees at the Lyon Academy as 11-year-olds. The tall midfielder made his debut in the electrifying atmosphere of the Premiership clash with Manchester United at the Boleyn Ground in August 2000 when he came off the bench in the 67th minute of the 2-2 draw. He lost no time in making his presence felt when he clattered David Beckham to the approval of the home fans and managed to escape a booking as well. He wasn't 100 per cent fit, having injured his knee the day before, but chose to play the injury down. It was to prove an expensive decision as, after just three further substitute appearances, he had to return to France for an operation. His lucrative contract meant he was paid £720,000 for only 85 minutes playing time! In August 2005, he returned to the Premiership with Sunderland.

BEALE, Robert — 1913-14

SL apps: 1

GEOFF HURST ONCE said that one bad game at the beginning of a career can prove disastrous for future prospects. For a goalkeeper, the dangers are heightened and Beale's debut proved to be a perfect example of this pitfall. Spending most of the 1913/14 season as understudy to regular first XI keepers Hughes and Lonsdale, the ill-fated custodian was given his Southern League baptism in the final match of the campaign against Portsmouth at Fratton Park, where West Ham lost 5-1.

BEESLEY, Mick — 1960-62

Born: High Beech, Essex, 10.6.42
League apps: 2 (1 goal)

DESPITE SCORING HEAVILY for the reserves, winning London and FA Youth honours while with Hammers and scoring on his League debut against Everton at Goodison Park in September 1960, this inside-forward failed to win a regular place in the League side. Transferred to Southend United in July 1962, where he joined up with former Hammers manager Ted Fenton, and moved on to Peterborough United in 1965. He returned to Roots Hall, two years later, where he ended his career.

BELL, Dick — 1938-39

Born: Aberdeen, Scotland, date unknown
League apps: 1 (1 goal)

THIS SCOTTISH INSIDE-FORWARD scored on his League debut for Hammers against West Bromwich Albion at Upton Park on April 15, 1939 – his only first team appearance. He is one of the few to be able to claim such a 100 per cent scoring record. Signed from Sunderland (for whom he also made only one appearance) in 1937, he joined the Essex Regiment TA in April 1939 and served with the Royal Artillery in World War II. Known to his Army mates as "Brindie", he made guest appearances for Clapham and Southend United during the war.

BELL, George — 1911-12

SL apps: 2

IN AN AGE when centre-forwards were expected to average a goal a game, George was given two opportunities wearing the number 9 shirt – against Swindon and Northampton Towns respectively. Both matches ended in defeat for Hammers, with George failing to make an impression on the scoresheet. An amateur from the Barking club, he sustained a serious knee injury in an Amateur Cup tie against Ilford that ended his career in 1913.

BENNETT, Les — 1954-56

Born: Wood Green, London, 10.1.18
League apps: 26 (3 goals)
Cup apps: 2 (1 goal)

THIS POPULAR PLAYER made a big impact during his brief stay at Upton Park. Formerly with Spurs (for whom he signed pro in May 1939), he was skipper for many of his appearances in the claret and blue, and was a frequent member of the side that narrowly missed promotion in 1954/55. Made his debut for Hammers against Derby County at Upton Park on Christmas Day 1954. Became player-manager of Clacton Town and later joined up briefly with Malcolm Allison at Southern League Romford. Later held a business post at the University of Essex.

BENNETT, Peter — 1964-70

Born: Hillingdon, Middlesex, 24.6.46
League apps: 42 (3 goals)
Cup apps: 5

AN ADAPTABLE INSIDE-FORWARD who nevertheless found it difficult to hold a regular place in the senior side. A member of the FA Youth Cup-winning team of 1963, he signed pro forms that summer after two years of apprenticeship, and made his League debut against Bolton Wanderers at Upton Park (April 4, 1964). He joined Orient in 1970 in the deal that brought Tommy Taylor in the opposite direction. Peter now has a thriving cabinet-making business while his son Warren plays on the international golf circuit.

BERKOVIC, Eyal — 1997-98

Born: Nahrya, Israel, 2.4.72
League apps: 65 (10 goals)
Cup apps: 14 (2 goals)

IF BEACHAMP, BOOGERS and Bassila were the signings from hell, then this sublimely gifted playmaker was definitely from the other place. Transferred from Maccabi Haifa in June 1997 (following a season's loan at Southampton) for what proved to be a bargain £1.75 million, Eyal had already been capped 45 times by his country when he arrived at Upton Park after walking out on the Saints when his long-time mentor Graeme Souness quit the Dell. At one stage Spurs were favourites to sign the impish midfielder, but after talks with both sides Berkovic opted to join the Hammers. "All Israel wanted me to go to Spurs, but I preferred West Ham and I had to decide what was best for me – not the country," he insisted. He then rubbed salt into Tottenham's wounds by scoring against them on his home debut in a thrilling 2-1 win. At ten years of age, Eyal had begun training with his local club Haifa and went on to win Championship and Cup winners' medals with them in successive seasons. After two years' National Service he was voted Israel's 1994 Player Of The Year after his ten goals helped unbeaten Haifa to their fifth League title. Souness then signed him on loan. He was a player the Saints manager had long admired (having scored 25 goals in 128 League matches in Israel) and the midfielder repaid the faith shown with some scintillating performances during his 28 appearances in 1996/97. Never were his skills more evident than in his second start when scoring twice in a 6-3 victory against his boyhood idols Manchester United at the Dell. He went on to score six in 35 League and Cup games to prove the Premiership was his rightful stage. He certainly proved the point in his two full seasons at the Boleyn. In a classic example of Redknapp's wheeling and dealing skill in the transfer market, Souness allegedly tipped off H that Berko was not contracted to Saints and so Redknapp got his man. Making his Hammers debut in the 2-1 opening day win over Barnsley at Oakwell (August 9, 1997), the diminutive Israeli never looked back after H handed him the number 29 shirt and the influential midfield role – where everything went through him. Operating just behind the front two – any of Hartson, Di Canio, Wright, Kitson or Abou – the result was always the same: goal-scoring chances galore! Hartson, in particular, thrived – scoring 24 League and Cup goals. Ironically, it was an unsavoury training ground assault on Berkovic by the big Welshman that led to Eyal's departure the following close season, and saw Glasgow Celtic buy him for £5.75 million. A lot of money, but the more discerning among the Boleyn Ground patrons would have preferred to have seen the Welsh international on his way instead and were less than happy with Redknapp's handling of the incident, which was caught on camcorder by a fan and broadcast on national TV. Up to the end of 2004/05 Eyal had made 28 appearances and scored three goals for new club Portsmouth.

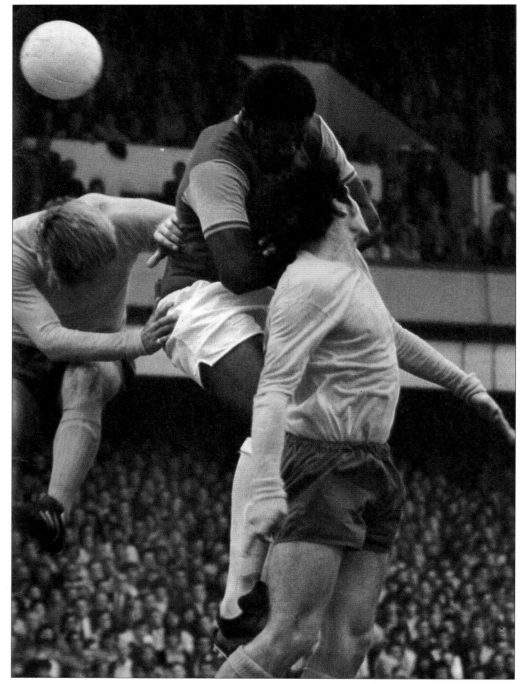

BETTS, Eric   1950

Born: Coventry, Warwickshire, 27.6.25
League apps: 3 (1 goal)

SIGNED FROM WALSALL in April 1950 after service with Mansfield, Coventry and Nuneaton. Eric, an outside-left, made his first appearance in West Ham's colours in a 5-0 win over Watford Reserves at Upton Park (April 22, 1950). Scoring a goal in that match which also featured Hammers' subsequent chief executive-secretary Eddie Chapman (another scorer), he went on to make a trio of Second Division appearances for the club before continuing his transfer travels with Rochdale, Crewe, Wrexham and Oldham where he ended his League career in 1956.

BICKLES, Dave   1963-67

Born: West Ham, London, 6.4.44
League apps: 25

A TALL, COMMANDING pivot. First blooded in the senior side during the American Soccer League Tournament in 1963, he made his initial League appearance in September of that year versus Liverpool at Anfield – the last occasion, incidentally, Hammers managed to win there. Transferred to Crystal Palace in October 1967, he later had a spell with Colchester United before becoming player-manager of the now defunct Romford FC in the Southern League. He was managing Havering side Collier Row in the Spartan League in the 1982/83 season. For the last two decades Dave's main vocation had been PE teacher at Brampton Manor School in East Ham, from where he recommended pupil Lee Hodges, the Essex, London and England schoolboy international midfielder, to Hammers. As well as running Newham District schools team, Dave was employed on a part-time basis with West Ham United, supervising the under-16s at Chadwell Heath. The club held an emotive minute's silence for Dave prior to the Steaua Bucharest UEFA Cup tie at Upton Park following his tragic death from cancer in October 1999.

BEST, Clyde   1969-75

Born: Somerset, Bermuda, 24.2.51
League apps: 186 (47 goals)
Cup apps: 32 (11 goals)

BERMUDA'S MOST FAMOUS footballing son, this striker with the build of Sonny Liston was the highest profile black player involved in English football in the late 1960s and early 1970s. Looked after by the late Hammers full-back John Charles when he arrived in London as a shy and not a little lost 17-year-old in 1969, Clyde made a dramatic impact on the First Division after making his debut against Arsenal in August the same year. A modest return of six goals in 25 League and Cup games was one more than he managed in the same number of matches the following campaign, but it was in the 1971/72 season that he began to fully fulfil his undoubted potential with 23 goals in 56 games in all competitions. His haul included four in the titanic League Cup run, which culminated in an epic four-match marathon with Stoke City in the Semi-final, and ended in the second replay at Old Trafford when Hammers lost 3-2. It proved to be the high-water mark of his Upton Park career as his goalscoring ratio returned nearer to the levels of the first two seasons and by the time of Hammers' Cup winning campaign of 1974, he began to fade from the first team action following the introduction of Alan Taylor, Billy Jennings, Bobby Gould and Keith Robson. He went Stateside to play in the North American Soccer League with Tampa Bay Rowdies and Pele, Moore, Best, and Beckenbauer et al in the summer of 1975, before returning to play a handful of games for Hammers in 1975/76. Missing out on another major triumph as West Ham reached the Final of the European Cup Winners' Cup against Anderlecht in Brussels, big Clyde left to join the rapidly emerging Feyenoord in Holland for two seasons before returning to the States with Portland Timbers armed with the tactics he'd learned from Dutch masters like Wim Jansen, Ari Haan and Ruudi Krol in Rotterdam. A qualified coach, Clyde realised a personal dream when he took charge of the Bermudan national side between 1997 and 2000 as technical director. Although he hasn't ruled out a return to coaching, Clyde is now a prison officer at the Westgate Correction Centre in his native Bermuda.

BICKNELL, Charles · 1936-47

Born: Pye Bridge, Chesterfield, 6.11.1905
League apps: 137
Cup apps: 12

A STRONG, POWERFUL full-back who had made 244 consecutive appearances for Bradford City when Hammers signed him in March 1936. Continued his ever-present record by playing in every match except one until the outbreak of World War II – by which time he had been appointed club captain. Served in the Police Specials during the war, and played many games in regional football. Skippered Hammers in the 1940 War Cup Final at Wembley, when they beat Blackburn Rovers 1-0. He managed a further 19 Second Division appearances after the resumption of normal League activities in 1946/47. Given a free transfer at the end of that campaign, he then became manager of Southern League Bedford Town. Affectionately nicknamed "Wag" at his first club, Chesterfield, for whom he made 85 League and Cup appearances before his £600 transfer to Bradford in May 1930. He died in Cambridgeshire on September 6, 1994, aged 88.

BIGDEN, James · 1901-04

Born: London, date unknown
SL apps: 91 (3 goals)
Cup apps: 5

JAMES MADE HIS first appearance in West Ham colours in the opening game of the 1901/02 season, which was won 2-0 vs Bristol Rovers at Eastville thanks to goals from Grassam and Corbett. A product of local football, he made the majority of his near 100 Southern League and FA Cup appearances at wing-half, although he sometimes played at inside-forward. By 1906, Jim had moved across London to serve Woolwich Arsenal, then playing at the Manor Ground, Plumstead, and with the assistance of two other ex-Hammers in MacEachrane and Satterwaite, helped the Gunners to oust his former club from that year's FA Cup in the first round proper.

BIGGAR, William · 1902-03

Born: Blaydon-on-Tyne, Newcastle, 1877
SL apps: 8

BILL BEGAN THE 1902/03 season as Hammers' first-choice keeper following his transfer from Sheffield United, along with winger Billy Barnes. But a 5-1 reverse in his third match at Wellingborough Town saw him lose his place to Welsh international Fred Griffiths, and although he regained it at the tail-end of the season, he was on his way at the end of the campaign. He joined Fulham for 1903/04 and then Watford for 1904/05. Moved from Watford to Rochdale in 1910 where he won a Lancashire Combination medal in 1910/11. Stayed with the Lancastrians up to World War I.

BIGGIN, Horace · 1919

League apps: 2

EMBARKED ON HIS League career in an infamous 7-0 defeat at the hands of Barnsley at Oakwell (September 7, 1919) from the inside-right position;

BILIC, Slaven · 1996-97

Born: Split, Yugoslavia, 11.9.68
League apps: 48 (2 goals)
Cup apps: 6 (1 goal)

COOL, CLASSY CROATIAN international defender who signed from Bundesliga members Karlsruhe Sport-Club for a then Hammers record fee of £1.65 million in January 1996, having previously established himself with his home town club, Hajduk Split. A member of the Croatian national side which reached the Quarter-finals of the European Championships in England in 1996, Bilic was an instant hit with West Ham fans following his debut at Spurs in January of that year. Rarely allowing an opponent to get goal side of him, the qualified lawyer always provided a strong defence and had the Bobby Moore Lower in particular, eating out of his hand with his skilful displays. A great one for playing to the gallery, he often hoodwinked the fans and referee in equal measure with his theatrical injury-feigning antics, but remained popular regardless as his undoubted star quality shone through. But "Super Slav" went from hero to villain when Everton invoked a little publicised clause in his West Ham contract that stipulated that he could leave Upton Park if £4.5 million or more was offered for his services. Although he eventually stayed long enough to play his part in Hammers' successful fight to preserve their Premiership status, the defender bowed out of the Boleyn proclaiming, "I know I have made the right choice because Everton are a big club and we can go on to win things." The fee? £4.5 million! Bilic had to eat humble pie at the end of the following 1997/98 season as his new team avoided relegation on goal difference and finished 16 points adrift of Hammers and ten places below them in the table. Although he again proved his worth in Croatia's surprise third place finish at the 1998 World Cup Finals, a persistent hip injury picked up in France restricted him to just four League appearances in 1998/99 and following an unsuccessful operation to rectify the problem, the downcast defender was allowed to rejoin Hajduk at a big loss to draw a line under his time at Goodison after making just 28 League and Cup appearances. His return to his native country, for whom he'd made 43 full international appearances, saw him add nine League appearances to the 109 he'd made in his first spell with his local club. Slaven scored 20 goals during his top class career at club level – not a bad total for a defender – including five in 54 matches for Karlsruhe, but how he must rue his decision to leave homely Hammers.

---

switched to the right-wing for his only other first team appearance in a 1-1 draw with Stoke City at Upton Park on October 4 the same year. Previously with Nottingham Forest.

BING, Doug · 1951-55

Born: Broadstairs, Kent, 27.10.28
League apps: 29 (3 goals)

SIGNED FROM MARGATE on New Year's Day 1951 on the recommendation of former Hammer Almer Hall, the Seasiders manager at that time. Doug was originally an inside or wing-forward, but was successfully converted to half-back at the Boleyn. Although never a first team regular, he was a capable deputy when called upon. Making his League debut against Hull City at Boothferry Park in 1951/52, he enjoyed four happy years as a Hammer until returning to his former club in the summer of 1955 – where he was medically advised to give up the game four years later.

BIRCHENOUGH, W · 1933-35

Born: Crewe, Cheshire, date unknown
League apps: 1

A GOALKEEPER WHO made a solitary Second Division appearance in a 2-1 defeat against Nottingham Forest at the City Ground (April 5, 1920). Later transferred to Burnley.

BIRNIE, Alexander · 1903-04

Born: Aberdeen, Scotland, 11.1.1884
SL apps: 1
Cup apps: 1

ALEX MADE HIS solitary Southern League appearance in the inside-right position in a 1-0 defeat at the hands of Brentford at the Memorial Grounds. His only other senior appearance also came against opponents from west London, Fulham, and ended in another 1-0 reverse in that season's intermediate round of the FA Cup. A regular with the reserve team, he went on to play for Norwich City, Maidstone United and Southend United (1908/09), and Bury (1909-11) for whom he scored three times in 86 League games. Alex's daughter Elsie Saunders is still a regular customer at Rob Jenkins' physio clinic in Green St.

BISHOP, Ian 1989-98

Born: Liverpool, Merseyside, 29.5.65
League apps: 254 (12 goals)
Cup apps: 45 (4 goals)

A LONG-HAIRED MIDFIELD creator who achieved the notable distinction of playing in all four divisions of the Football League when Manchester City signed him from Harry Redknapp's AFC Bournemouth for £465,000 in the summer of 1989. But by the following Christmas, popular "Bish" was back in Division Two – valued at £650,000 when he arrived at Upton Park with Trevor Morley in the exchange deal that took unsettled Mark Ward to Maine Road. The classy midfielder began his pro career close to home, at Everton, who he joined straight from school. After four League outings on loan to Crewe Alexandra towards the end of 1982/83, Ian made his only first team appearance for the Toffees, as sub versus Manchester United at Goodison in May 1983, before resuming his battle to make his mark in the lower divisions. He was sold by Howard Kendall to Carlisle United for £15,000 in October 1984 at the age of 19 and played 132 League games for England's most northerly club, enduring two consecutive relegation campaigns, before moving to the south coast club Bournemouth for £35,000 four years later. He played 44 League games in his one and only season for the Cherries. Although he was at Manchester City for only 19 games in a four-month spell, Bish quickly established himself as a firm favourite with the fans who appreciated his silky skills and ability to spray accurate passes all over the field. He and Morley starred in a memorable 5-0 victory over arch rivals United but when manager Mel Machin was sacked, the arrival of Kendall (who released him at Everton), in December 1989, spelled the end of the City line for this talented youngster with the long, flowing mane. At West Ham, Ian proved equally popular with the fans, although he was not always an automatic choice after Billy Bonds succeeded Lou Macari. He made his debut, along with Morley, at Leicester City (December 30, 1989) and capped his first full season in claret and blue by captaining Hammers to promotion in May 1991, having taken over the skipper's armband from the injured Julian Dicks. A few days later, he gained an England B cap versus Switzerland at Walsall. Ian's turbulent career took another twist a year later when he found himself back in Division Two. And his frustration further increased in December 1992 when, along with several other players, he was placed on the transfer list as the club tried to cut its wage bill in the wake of the ill-fated bond scheme. The likable Scouser maintained that he had no wish to leave and his loyalty was rewarded when he returned to the side and played an influential part in clinching promotion back to the top flight in May 1993. Even so, he remained unsettled during that summer and it was only after Ian had been on the brink of joining Southampton that West Ham reacted by signing him on a new three-year contract in September 1993. With his future happily settled, Bish celebrated his, and Hammers', first season in the Premiership by claiming an automatic first team place and playing consistently with all the style and grace of so many of his illustrious midfield predecessors. Ian effectively held his position until the beginning of 1997/98 when the signing of Eyal Berkovic severely limited his first team opportunities and restricted him to just four appearances in League and Cup before his free transfer back to Manchester City in March 1998. Bish asserted his influence on back-to-back promotions from the Second Division to the First in 1998/99 and then returned to the Premiership in 1999/2000 and altogether logged up 88 League and 14 Cup appearances in his second sojourn at Maine Road before an ill-fated move to Major League side Miami Fusion in Florida, USA. Ian's dream ticket to the sunshine state turned into a nightmare when the American club went bust in January 2002 and left him high and dry. He had one last shot at the big-time, however, when former Hammers team-mate and manager of Welsh National League Barry Town, Kenny Brown, sent him an SOS to play for the Welsh minnows in the preliminary round of the European Cup against Latvians Skonta Riga. Bish gladly swapped South Beach, Florida for Barry Island, South Wales for the honour of playing in his first European tie at the age of 37. But there the fairy tale ended as the would-be giant-killers were roundly defeated. Bish then signed for Third Division Rochdale following a trial period at Spotland and went on to make eight League appearances in 2002/03. Bish was assistant manager to old team-mate Mike Marsh at UniBond Premier outfit Burscough FC in his native Lancashire early in 2003/2004.

BISHOP, Sydney 1920-26

Born: Stepney, London, 10.2.1900
League apps: 159 (8 goals)
Cup apps: 14

AFTER A HUMBLE beginning as a forward with Isthmian League Ilford and a spell with Crystal Palace reserves, Sydney Macdonald Bishop, to give him his full title, rose to the pinnacle of his profession after signing for West Ham United in 1920 and playing for the RAF during World War I. Born at the turn of the century in Stepney, during the very year of the formation of West Ham United, he was affectionately nicknamed "Sticks" by the Boleyn crowd in recognition of his slender frame. A member of the side that gained near immortality by appearing in the first Wembley Cup Final of 1923, Syd was one of the few utility players of his generation, playing in nearly every position for Hammers – including goal when Ted Hufton was injured on one occasion! It has been often said that the best half-backs are those who have had experience in the forward positions, gaining first-hand knowledge of the type of service the men up front need in the process. Syd's career certainly benefited from this drill. Well known as a big occasion player, he was named as reserve for England versus Ireland at Liverpool in 1924, but was destined to wait until after he had left Upton Park before gaining full international recognition. His departure from the Boleyn to Leicester City was regretted by his many admirers long after he had left, but there could be no denying that this great player had lost form during his last season with Hammers. He even reverted to his old positions in the forward-line in a desperate effort to regain his lost sparkle. All this changed with his move to Filbert Street, however. Although he continued to live in London (a decision that must have brought its own difficulties in the days before motorways), his form improved to such an extent that he won four full caps for his country in 1927 – versus Scotland, Belgium, Luxembourg and France. This success was followed by disappointment the next year when he had to cry off through illness after being named England's captain versus Scotland – yes, the side that was to become famous throughout the world of football as the "Wembley Wizards" with their 5-1 victory in 1928. Whether or not Syd would have been able to stem the Scottish tide, we will never know, but his former Hammers team-mate in goal for England that fateful day – Ted Hufton – would have doubtless been happier with him playing in front of him, and it is doubtful that Alex James and Co would have had it quite so much their own way had Sticks played. It was a more mature Syd Bishop who returned to his beloved London to sign for Chelsea in 1928 for £4,000, with brain rather than brawn being the hallmark of his play. Some of his thoughts of those days are worth repeating some half-century later: "I think it is a mistake to enter into a game with fixed ideas on tactics. If you are a half-back the first thing you should try to find out is what sort of form each front-line man happens to be in, and see to it that the fellows on top of their game see most of the ball." It would be interesting to hear the comments of some of the coaches of today on such a refreshingly simple approach. Syd Bishop was in the Chelsea team that won promotion to the First Division in 1930, and came back to Upton Park as a member of the Blues side that knocked Hammers out of the FA Cup in a fourth round tie in 1933. A subsequent report in a West Ham match programme opined that Syd looked "as good as ever". Injuries forced him to give up the game soon afterwards, and at the sadly premature age of 49 he died at his Chelsea home in 1949.

BLACK, Robert 1937-38

Born: Washington, County Durham, 17.7.15
League apps: 2

A RUGGED RIGHT-HALF, Bobby made his Second Division debut for Hammers against Nottingham Forest (February 2, 1937). He made one more first team appearance the following season before moving on to near-neighbours Clapton Orient, where he was an ever-present during the second half of the 1938/39 season for O's in the Third Division South to make 23 appearances. Bobby appeared in 81 regional wartime matches for O's but was not retained when League football resumed after the war.

BLACKBURN, Alan 1954-57

Born: Pleasley, Mansfield, Nottinghamshire, 4.8.35
League apps: 15 (3 goals)

A FORMER BARNARDO'S Boy, he was discovered playing in Hertfordshire junior soccer. A centre or inside-forward, he caused a sensation by scoring 13 goals for the Hammers in the FA Youth Cup during the 1953/54 season. A prolific scorer for the reserves, too, he was a member of the Combination championship team of 1954 and made his first team debut against Derby County in December of the same year. After National Service from March 1955 he transferred to Halifax Town, later seeing service with non-league Margate and Wellington Town.

BLACKBURN, Fred   1905-13

Born: Blackburn, Lancashire, 1879
SL apps: 217 (24 goals)
Cup apps: 20 (4 goals)

F. BLACKBURN,
WEST HAM UNITED.

FRED BEGAN HIS first-class career as an outside-left with his home-town club, Blackburn Rovers. He won three Lancashire Cup medals with Rovers and was playing in their First Division team at the age of 17. He represented the English League against the Scottish League and also played in a North versus South fixture. Fred was first capped for England against Scotland in 1901, the first of three appearances at that level. He came south to join Hammers in the summer of 1905. A switch to wing-half during the later stages of his time at Upton Park undoubtedly helped him to establish the second highest total of Southern League appearances for Hammers and in doing so gain a well-deserved benefit match against Coventry – shared with goalkeeper George Kitchen – in 1911. He had another couple of seasons in the claret and blue after that but did not re-sign for the 1913/14 season. Fred joined the merchant navy when he finished playing, but later returned to the game as coach to Barking.

BLACKWOOD, John   1904-05

SL apps: 4 (1 goal)

JOHN HAD THE unfortunate experience of making his first XI baptism in the middle of one of Hammers' worst ever losing runs, in the initial campaign at the Boleyn Ground. He began promisingly enough with his side's only counter in a 4-1 defeat at Portsmouth, after taking over the number 9 shirt from Billy Bridgeman, but failed to score in his next three outings (all defeats). His lack of further success led to the recall of Bridgeman and the end of his Southern League opportunities with West Ham. An experienced player, John had seen service with Queens Park Rangers, Partick Thistle, Glasgow Celtic and Reading (1902/03), before joining Irons.

BLOOMFIELD, Jimmy   1965-66

Born: Kensington, London, 15.2.34
League apps: 9
Cup apps: 4 (1 goal)

A FORMER BRENTFORD (where he played with Ron Greenwood), Arsenal and Birmingham City inside-forward, he was signed by Hammers in October 1965, after a second spell at Griffin Park. Jimmy left Upton Park to continue his playing career with Plymouth Argyle and became player-manager of Leyton Orient in 1968. He took over from fellow ex-Hammer Frank O'Farrell as boss at Leicester City after guiding O's out of the Third Division. Later returned to Brisbane Road as manager until serious illness forced him to relinquish the post. He was still actively involved in the scouting business for Luton Town almost right up to his tragically premature death in April 1983.

BLORE, Vincent   1935-36

Born: Uttoxeter, Staffordshire, 1908
League apps: 9

HAMMERS SIGNED THIS acrobatic goalkeeper from Derby County in the summer of 1935 and he contested the first team spot with Herman Conway the following season. With the arrival of Jack Weare from Wolves effectively relegating Vince to third choice keeper, he didn't hesitate when Crystal Palace offered him the opportunity of first team football, and he did well with the Glaziers up to the outbreak of World War II.

BLYTH, James   1906

SL apps: 3

NOT MUCH IS known about this defender who played against Norwich City, Crystal Palace and Gillingham early in 1906/07 at right-back, right-half and left-half in that order of appearances.

BLYTHE, Joe   1902-04

Born: Berwick on Tweed, 1881
SL apps: 52
Cup apps: 5

A LEFT-HALF OF average height and weight, Joe joined Hammers from Everton (35 apps, one goal) during the close season of 1902/03 and made his debut against Reading in the opening fixture of the ensuing campaign at the Memorial Grounds. Strictly a defender, he never managed to get on the scoresheet during the two troubled seasons leading up to the move to the Boleyn Ground, but nevertheless proved to be a stubborn fixture in Irons' often beleaguered defence. Joe left to join Millwall in August 1904 and it was while at the Den that he came to the fore. A hard working, tough-tackling defender, he played his first game for the Lions against West Ham in the first ever match at Upton Park in September 1904. He went on to win two Western League championship medals together with a London Challenge Cup winners' medal in 1909. In seven seasons with Millwall he played in a total of 341 games scoring three goals. Moving on to Watford in 1911 he finished his playing career there playing in 29 League games. He returned to the North East in 1913 where he became manager at Blyth Spartans. He had previously played for Blyth between 1895 and 1897, having joined them from Delaval Villa. Joe then played for Jarrow from August 1897 before joining Everton in January 1899. He made an impressive start to his Everton career, playing his first game in February 1899 against Bolton, having signed after impressing for Jarrow in the FA Cup against the Blues in an earlier game. He appeared in all three half-back positions for Everton, always giving 100 per cent.

John Bond

BOERE, Jeroen   1993-95

Born: Arnhem, Netherlands, 18.11.67
League apps: 25 (6 goals)
Cup apps: 4 (1 goal)

FOLLOWING THE SHOCK departure of boss Billy Bonds on the eve of the 1994/95 season, the Dutch striker was recalled from a loan spell at West Bromwich Albion and given an extended run in the Premiership by new manager Harry Redknapp. Tony Cottee, who hadn't scored for 12 games, began to feed off the big target man and regained his scoring touch. Jeroen also hit some vital goals as the Hammers, early favourites for the drop, climbed clear of the relegation zone. In September 1995, the six foot three inch striker was used as cash-plus-player bait to bring striking counterpart Iain Dowie to Upton Park for his second ill-fated spell in east London from First Division Crystal Palace. Just six games and one goal later, the Flying Dutchman was on his travels again in a £150,000 move to Southend United on March 1, 1996. Although he scored 25 goals in 81 League and Cup games at Roots Hall, back-to-back relegations in 1996/97 and 1997/98 saw Jeroen become a target for supporter unrest. "There was a website that listed their Top 100 most hated people – Adolf Hitler was number seven and I was number six!" he recalled. In 1998, he left England to join NTT in Japan where, after 14 successful months, disaster struck when he was stabbed in the left eye outside a Tokyo nightclub in an unprovoked attack. Jeroen lost the sight of the eye and his career ended. With typical resolve, he has carved out a new career for himself and his second wife Ann as landlords of the Half Moon public house in Epping, Essex.

BOND, John   1951-65

Born: Colchester, Essex, 17.12.32
League apps: 381 (33 goals)
Cup apps: 47 (2 goals)

A GREAT CHARACTER and first class full-back signed as an amateur from Colchester Casuals in 1950. He made his League debut in 1951/52 and became known as a penalty and dead-ball expert. Bondy represented the Football League on two occasions – against the Irish League in 1957 and Scottish League in 1958. He was in West Ham's Second Division championship-winning team of 1957/58 and the FA Cup-winning side of 1964 before being transferred to Torquay United in 1965. He managed 130 League appearances for Torquay between 1966 and 1969 to bring his career total to almost 600 when he retired from playing at the age of 37 and began his second career as coach of Gillingham. He managed AFC Bournemouth, Norwich City, Manchester City, Burnley (where one of his first purchases was Hammers centre-back Joe Gallagher), Swansea City, Birmingham City and – until the end of the 1992/93 season – Shrewsbury Town, where his assistant was fellow ex-Hammer Mal Musgrove. Now retired from the game, "Muffin", as he was nicknamed for his mule-like kicking, was one of the founder members of West Ham's much-vaunted Academy and one of the leading lights of a group that broke into management after learning the basics at Upton Park (see also: Malcolm Allison, Frank O'Farrell, Mal Musgrove, Noel Cantwell, Dave Sexton, George Petchy, Ken Brown and Jimmy Andrews). Despite his success as a colourful and outspoken manager (he took both Norwich City and Manchester City to Wembley finals) John is most fondly remembered at Upton Park where his unconventional style kept the fans on the edge of their seats as he always tried to play his way out of trouble – saving the "big boot" for speciality free-kicks and penalties. Living in the Manchester area, he has also had the satisfaction of watching his son Kevin play for two of the teams he managed – Norwich and Manchester City.

BONDS, Billy MBE   1967-88

Born: Woolwich, London, 17.9.46
League apps: 663 (48 goals)
Cup apps: 130 (11 goals)

AN UPTON PARK legend, Billy Bonds spent 27 years with the club as player and manager. In a playing career spanning an incredible 21 seasons, "Bonzo" played a record 793 senior games. Billy's first appearance in claret and blue, following his £49,500 move from Charlton Athletic, was in Ken Brown's testimonial at Upton Park (May 15, 1967) against a Select XI, with his League debut following on August 19 that year against Sheffield Wednesday. Ron Greenwood's purchase of the swashbuckling right-back proved one of the greatest bargains of all-time. He cost the club the equivalent of about £62 a match – a paltry sum. Billy played for Kent Schoolboys before signing for Bob Stokoe at Charlton, making his League debut against Northampton Town (February 20, 1965). He went on to make 95 League appearances for Charlton before his transfer to Upton Park on May 13, 1967. A tremendously loyal servant who never gave less than 100 per cent, Bill always led by example on the field. Courageous in the tackle, he grafted hard for possession and would often defy painful injuries, slog it out in the heart of midfield or – in his latter playing days – the centre of defence and always let the opposition know they had been in a match. Yet he used the ball more intelligently and effectively than perhaps he was sometimes given credit for and weighed in with many goals, including a hat-trick against Chelsea in March 1974, on his way to topping the scorechart with 13 that season. In 1974 he succeeded Bobby Moore as captain and led the club to FA Cup Final victories in 1975 and 1980, the 1976 European Cup Winners' Cup Final, and in 1981 the League Cup Final and Second Division championship. He won two England Under-23

caps and was poised for his full England debut against Brazil at Wembley (May 12, 1981), when a rib injury, sustained in a collision with keeper Phil Parkes in Hammers' last match of the season, cruelly ruled him out. But the nearest Bonzo got to a full cap was as non-playing sub for a World Cup qualifier against Italy at Wembley (November 16, 1977). After joining West Ham, Billy quickly established himself as a crowd favourite with his surging forward runs, which is reflected in the fact that he was voted Hammer of the Year four times – a distinction he shares with Moore. This Peter Pan of football was still playing in the First Division at the age of

41 – a remarkable feat recognised by The Queen with an MBE in January 1988, and by his fellow pros, who presented him with the PFA Merit Award in April of the same year. He officially retired on the same day as Trevor Brooking, in May 1984, but Bill's astonishing playing career had not run its course. It was not until the summer of 1988 that, nursing a knee injury that forced him to miss the last two games of that season, he finally decided to hang up his boots. His 663rd, and final, League game for the club came in the First Division match at Southampton (April 30, 1988). Including European, Charity Shield and Full Members' Cup fixtures, Billy

Career record

Played	League		FAC		LC		Europe		Total	
	App	Gls	App	Gls	App	Gls	App	Gls	App	Gls
1967-68	37	1	3	0	2	0	0	0	42	1
1968-69	42	1	3	0	2	0	0	0	47	1
1969-70	42	3	1	0	2	0	0	0	45	3
1970-71	37	0	1	0	2	0	0	0	40	0
1971-72	42	3	4	0	10	2	0	0	56	5
1972-73	39	3	2	0	2	0	0	0	43	3
1973-74	40	13	2	0	1	0	0	0	43	13
1974-75	31	7	8	0	3	2	0	0	42	9
1975-76	18	1	0	0	5	1	9	2	32	4
1976-77	41	3	2	0	3	0	0	0	46	3
1977-78	29	1	3	1	0	0	0	0	32	2
1978-79	39	4	1	0	1	0	0	0	41	4
1979-80	34	1	5	0	9	0	0	0	48	1
1980-81	41	0	3	0	8	1	6	1	58	2
1981-82	29	1	2	1	4	0	0	0	35	2
1982-83	34	3	1	0	4	0	0	0	39	3
1983-84	27	0	1	0	2	0	0	0	30	0
1984-85	22	3	0	0	4	0	0	0	26	3
1985-86	0	0	0	0	0	0	0	0	0	0
1986-87	17	0	4	0	3	0	0	0	24	0
1987-88	22	0	2	0	0	0	0	0	24	0
TOTAL	**663**	**48**	**48**	**2**	**67**	**6**	**15**	**3**	**793**	**59**

Bonds made 795 official matches for West Ham. John Lyall was eager to make use of Billy's experience and influence and appointed him youth team manager in June 1988. Gillingham offered Bill the position of manager, and he applied (unsuccessfully) for the first team manager's job at Upton Park when Lyall was sacked in July 1989. Instead, the Hammers' board opted for "outsider" Lou Macari. Macari resigned just seven months after arriving from Swindon and the ever-popular Bonzo was again the people's choice to take charge of the first team. His eventual appointment, on February 22, 1990, heralded a new wave of optimism and a resurgence of fortunes that saw the Hammers finish just one place off the play-offs in Division Two. Bill marked his first full season in charge by taking Hammers back to the top flight, as runners-up to Oldham Athletic in 1990/91. He made history again on November 12, 1990 when he became the first person to be awarded two testimonials by the club, Spurs providing the opposition. Bonzo experienced a series of highs and lows in his managerial career. Following the euphoria of his first full season, he faced a season-long battle at the foot of the First Division that culminated in relegation at the end of 1991/92. His efforts to produce results on the field were undermined by events off it, where irate fans waged war on the club's ill-conceived bond scheme. Bill's helter-skelter career took another twist a year after the drop when, having been joined by his old mate Harry Redknapp, Hammers bounced straight back as First Division runners-up to Newcastle United. Despite being the bookies' favourites to go straight back down again in 1993/94, Hammers proved many wrong by attaining a respectable 13th place in their first Premiership campaign. Many thought it impossible to imagine West Ham without Billy Bonds, yet on August 10, 1994 the legend stunned the fans by announcing his resignation, just ten days before the start of the new season. Bonds turned down the offer to become a paid director of the club after the board indicated their preference for Redknapp to take over the manager's job. Few saw Bonds as manager long-term, and he himself admitted the demands of modern-day management could never compare with the pleasure he got from playing. So, when he sensed that circumstances were changing at Upton Park, it was hardly surprising that he didn't wish to hang around. The club paid up the remaining three years of his contract (said to be worth £500,000) and duly installed Redknapp. As a player, Bonds was the rock on which the team was built, a magnificent leader. Yet his wholehearted commitment on the field contrasted with his off-field nature – a private man who shied away from the bright lights. At the end of a match day Bill would not hang about the players' bar for long, but would grab a four-pack of beers and head south to Kent through the Blackwall Tunnel to what he has always enjoyed most – time spent at home with his wife and two daughters. Clearly bitter about the events surrounding his departure from the Boleyn, Bill was in no hurry to return to the game, but was appointed youth team manager at Queen's Park Rangers in January 1995 where he was assisted by former team-mate and management colleague Ronnie Boyce. Then in 1997, Bill took charge of Second Division Millwall in an appointment that was always going to be a difficult task for a man steeped in the traditions of their biggest rivals. Unwisely commenting that one of the reasons he'd accepted the post was because of its handy location to his Chiselhurst home, Bill got off on the wrong foot at the New Den and stayed on it as Lions fans vented their prejudice against the ex-Hammers in the struggling side, Paul Allen and Kenny Brown, just as they had done in previous years to Paul Goddard and Clive Allen. Unsurprisingly, Bill's tenure didn't last long and he now seems far more relaxed with life as a summariser for Capital Gold sports football coverage, in which role he communicates his typically honest views on the game in a way that the ordinary fan can relate to. Still playing for Charlton Athletic's vets team in 2004.

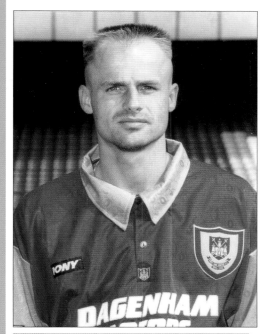

BOOGERS, Marco   1995

Born: Dordrecht, Netherlands, 12.1.67
League apps: 4

WITH THE ARGUABLE exception of the Joey Beachamp debacle, the £1 million transfer of Marco Boogers from Sparta Rotterdam in July 1995 represents the most disastrous signing in Hammers history. Although the club's management was criticised for relying on video evidence when deciding to buy the six-foot-plus striker, the player's record in Dutch football actually bore close scrutiny. In ten seasons for Dutch First Division sides DS 79 Dordrecht, FC Utrecht, RKC Waalwijk, Fortuna Sittard and Sparta Rotterdam he had scored 103 goals in 278 games – including a couple of hat-tricks and one four-goal haul against Go Ahead Eagles. Although there was no evidence of Boogers getting on the scoresheet against those yardsticks of Dutch footballing excellence, Ajax or Feyenoord, it seems the failure of his move to the Premiership was due to his mental state rather than any lack of prowess. The first signs came one game after making his Upton Park debut as sub against Leeds on the opening day of 1995/96 – he was sent off after a high tackle on Manchester United's Gary Neville at Old Trafford. He made only two more first team cameos (both as sub) before he fled back to Holland in December claiming he'd suffered a mental breakdown to spark "Barmy Boogers" headlines in the red tops, with *The Sun* delighted to report he'd gone to live in a caravan. In 2003, this was revealed to be no more than urban mythology by former Hammers' DJ and PA announcer Bill Prosser: "I used to organise all the travel for the West Ham team and because I was a fan I ended up sponsoring Marco Boogers' socks. When he fell out with Harry Redknapp and decided to leave, the chap from West Ham's Clubcall rang to ask if I had organised his travel home. I told him: 'Marco has decided not to fly, he may have gone by train again!' Unfortunately, the line was not clear and the Clubcall man thought I said: 'He's gone to his caravan.' He put it on the Clubcall and *The Sun* then picked it up..." It was a good story the eight years it lasted! Hammers eventually managed to loan their unwanted star to Groningen. In 1997/98, a seemingly sane Boogers was back among the goals again as top scorer for FC Volendam with nine strikes in 20 appearances. His efforts failed to save the side from relegation, but 2002/03 saw the Dutchman back in the bosom of his hometown club FC Dordrecht in the split role of technical director and player-coach. It should suit his personality!

BOURNE, Stanley   1906-12

Born: East Ham, London, date unknown
SL apps: 13
Cup apps: 3

A DISTINGUISHED AMATEUR left-back whose commitment to the non-paid ranks resulted in only a somewhat meagre total of appearances for Hammers spread over six seasons. Making his initial appearance for West Ham in a 1-1 draw against Watford at Upton Park in December 1906, he was noted in a 1947 history of the club as: "the only footballer, other than goalkeepers, to wear spectacles in professional football matches." Stan made his final appearance in a 2-2 draw with Norwich at their former ground, The Nest, in April 1912. He later turned out occasionally for Arsenal during World War I.

BOURNE, W   1913-14

Born: Sittingbourne, Kent, date unknown

THIS OUTSIDE-LEFT PLAYED only one match in Hammers' Southern League side – a 0-0 draw at Reading's Elm Park (March 23, 1914). First played for Sittingbourne, in the Kent League.

BOVINGTON, Eddie   1960-67

Born: Edmonton, London, 23.4.41
League apps: 138 (1 goal)
Cup apps: 45 (1 goal)

AN ABRASIVE, DEPENDABLE wing-half in the Andy Malcolm mould signed from the Juniors in May 1959. His reinstatement to the side after the Boxing Day 1963 debacle against Blackburn Rovers did much to bring about the improved form and stability that led to the team's Cup Final triumph. He made his League debut against Manchester United at Old Trafford in 1960 and his performance against the Red Devils in the 1964 FA Cup Semi-final clash at Hillsborough, when he man-marked Bobby Charlton, was the highlight of his career. Eddie retired early from the game, resisting the temptation of playing in the lower leagues to go into the rag trade at 28. He soon owned a trio of successful clothes shops in Aldgate, Edmonton and Wood Green, which he ran with wife Pauline until her death in 2000 when he sold the business. Eddie still works in the trade for a friend and keeps himself fit as a member of Woodford Green Athletics club and has run a number of London Marathons, clocking up a personal best time of 2 hrs, 56 mins, and 10 secs in 1990.

Ron Greenwood and Eddie Bovington

Mark Bowen

BOWEN, Mark — 1996-97

Born: Neath, Wales, 7.12.63
League apps: 17 (1 goal)
Cup apps: 2

A VASTLY EXPERIENCED Welsh international defender signed on a free transfer from Norwich City. When he was chosen to represent his country for the 56th occasion against San Marino at Cardiff on August 31, 1996, Mark became the first Hammers player to be picked for the Principality since Phil Woosnam played against Brazil in 1962. Although he represented Aberavon District in South Wales as a scrum half, soccer was always his first love and he signed apprentice forms for Tottenham Hotspur in 1980 after starring for Afannedd and Welsh schoolboys. Youth and Under-21 honours followed before his Spurs debut in August 1983, but the tenacious tackler found it hard to break into the first team on a regular basis and was allowed to leave for Norwich at a bargain £90,000 fee in July 1987. He enjoyed ten seasons at Carrow Road, appearing in two FA Cup Semi-finals and helping the Canaries to a best ever third spot in the old First Division in 1992/93. Mark showed his versatility in the subsequent UEFA Cup campaign when playing sweeper in the shock knock-out of Bayern Munich. As at Spurs, Bowen made his Hammers debut versus Coventry – in August 1996 – and a few weeks later was on the scoresheet in a 2-0 ten-man win over Forest at the City Ground, but the Trent men's 1-0 revenge victory at Upton Park on New Year's day 1997 signalled the Welshman's last show in the claret and blue. After being given a free transfer to Shimuzu where he spent six months in Japan's J-League, he returned to the capital with Charlton for 1997/98 and, following the Addicks play-offs success, was also back in the Premiership the following campaign to make one last appearance at the Boleyn as a sub in Charlton's surprise 1-0 win on Easter Monday, 1999. Made 45 League and Cup appearances for Charlton before retiring in May 1999.

BOWYER, Lee — 2003

Born: Poplar, London, 3.1.77
League apps: 10
Cup: 1

THE SIGNING OF Lee Bowyer from Leeds United represented the most controversial transfer transaction in the club's history. From a purely footballing standpoint the signing made perfect sense – how often is it possible to acquire a player who nearly signed for Liverpool five months earlier for £9 million, for nothing? But his capture certainly underlined the naivety or desperation – or perhaps both – of the West Ham management in their efforts to stop the rot during the transfer window in January 2003. For his part, Bowyer behaved impeccably during his time at the

Boleyn – even when under extreme provocation from defenders hoping to get him sent off. On the field, Bowyer seemed only a shadow of the player he was supposed to be and was largely anonymous in his 11 appearances for the club he'd supported as a boy – an allegiance that didn't stop him insisting on a clause in his contract allowing him to leave if Hammers were relegated and another entitling him to a £1 million bonus if they survived the drop. It seems there could be only one winner – Lee Bowyer. Formerly with Charlton Athletic, for whom he made 53 League and Cup appearances scoring 14 times, he joined Leeds for £2.6 million (a record fee for a teenager) in July 1996. At Elland Road he racked up 250 appearances in all competitions and scored 25 goals. Bowyer teamed up with Jonathan Woodgate at Newcastle on a four-year contract that would reputedly earn him £35,000 a week at the start of 2003/04. After giving his image a public boost when becoming involved with the Kick Racism Out Of Football campaign, Lee again found himself making the headlines for all the wrong reasons when he was involved in an unsavoury on-field fracas with team-mate Kieron Dyer. Given a seven-match ban by the FA and fined £228,000 by Newcastle and £30,000 by the FA, to cap it all the unfortunate Bowyer then found himself with the unwanted distinction of being the first ever player to be summoned to appear in court, by Northumbria Police.

BOYCE, Ronnie — 1960-72

Born: East Ham, London, 6.1.43
League apps: 282 (21 goals)
Cup apps: 57 (8 goals)

THE ENGINE ROOM of the successful cup sides of the mid-1960s, Ronnie was known as "Ticker" because he was the heartbeat of the team. He played the game simply, feeding the likes of Hurst, Byrne and Sissons with accurate passes. He guaranteed himself a permanent place in Upton Park folklore with his two goals against Manchester United in the 1964 FA Cup Semi-final at Hillsborough and his Wembley headed winner against Preston North End – the same side he had made his League debut against at Upton Park, aged 17, on October 22, 1960. That was a year after manager Ted Fenton gave the East Ham Grammar School kid his first senior game for the club in a Southern Junior Floodlit Cup tie against Millwall. It was not until 1962/63 that the unselfish and hard-working Ronnie gained a regular first team place, but from then on he became one of the stalwarts for eight years (although injury kept him out for a while in 1965/66). A year after experiencing the thrill of scoring his injury-time winner in the FA Cup Final, Ronnie was back at Wembley celebrating Hammers' 1965 European Cup Winners' Cup triumph over TSV Munich 1860. Ronnie had played a big part in getting the team to Wembley and, in what many described as his best-ever game for the club, took over the skipper's role from the injured Bobby Moore away to Sparta Prague in round one, and steered the side to a brilliant 3-2 aggregate win. Team-mate Geoff Hurst once said of Boyce: "He is a players' player – a tremendous worker but people do not appreciate his value to the team." Manager Ron Greenwood, who saw Ronnie as the perfect replacement for Phil Woosnam, added: "In other people's eyes he was a most underrated player, but to us he was invaluable. The thing that impressed me most about his play was his

Ronn[ie]

Career record

	League		FAC		LC		Europe		Total	
Played	App	Gls	App	Gls	App	Gls	App	Gls	App	Gls
1960-61	3	0	0	0	0	0	0	0	3	0
1961-62	4	1	0	0	0	0	0	0	4	1
1962-63	27	3	5	2	1	0	0	0	33	5
1963-64	41	6	7	3	7	2	0	0	55	11
1964-65	41	4	2	0	1	0	9	1	53	5
1965-66	16	2	1	0	2	0	4	0	23	2
1966-67	37	4	1	0	5	0	0	0	43	4
1967-68	38	0	1	0	3	0	0	0	42	0
1968-69	39	0	3	0	3	0	0	0	45	0
1969-70	20	1	1	0	1	0	0	0	22	1
1970-71	13	0	0	0	0	0	0	0	13	0
1971-72	1	0	0	0	0	0	0	0	1	0
1972-73	2	0	0	0	0	0	0	0	2	0
TOTAL	**282**	**21**	**21**	**5**	**23**	**2**	**13**	**1**	**339**	**29**

Ronnie Boyce **scores West Ham's first goal in the 1964 FA Cup Semi-final against Manchester United**

ce clears with Peters and Moore in attendance

ability to do the simple things quickly and efficiently." Ron played schoolboy soccer for East Ham, London, Essex and England, and also won England Youth honours. The closest he came to a full cap was as reserve for an Under-23 fixture. West Ham awarded him a well-earned testimonial in November 1972, when George Best's Manchester United were the opponents. Although not renowned as a goalscorer, Ron scored one of the most bizarre and spectacular goals of all time at Maine Road in March 1970 (Jimmy Greaves' debut), when he volleyed home from the centre circle following keeper Joe Corrigan's drop-kick! That was typical Boyce – a quick reader of the game. His last League appearance for the Hammers was as sub at Leicester City on December 30, 1972. After serving John Lyall and Billy Bonds as first team coach, "Boycie" took charge of one game as caretaker manager in February 1990 – between the resignation of Lou Macari and the appointment of Billy Bonds. A popular, loyal, one-club man, Ronnie still had his heart and soul in Hammers, having succeeded Eddie Baily as chief scout in September 1991, until his departure in October 1995.

BOYLAN, Lee
1997-99

Born: Chelmsford, Essex, 2.9.78
League apps: 1

ONE OF THE rich cache of young talent unearthed by Tony Carr's West Ham youth academy in the mid-1990s along with Frank Lampard, Rio Ferdinand, Lee Hodges and Manny Omoyinmi, Lee made only one breakthrough into the first team, despite being rated as high as any of his contemporaries. A top scoring member of the Hammers team that reached the 1996 FA Youth Cup Final, Lee was never able to impress Harry Redknapp enough to add to his meagre one minute of first team duty when coming on for the final moments of the 5-1 home win over Sheffield Wednesday in May 1997 – despite finishing as reserve team top scorer in 1997/98 and 1998/99. A Republic of Ireland Youth international, Lee was nicknamed "Buzz" because he was always buzzing around defenders like a fly they couldn't swat. Lee's quest for regular first team football took him to Swedish First Division side Trelleborgs FF, but he'd made just five appearances for them when he was diagnosed with Crohn's syndrome and was out of the game for 18 months. Luckily, Lee recovered his health and after spells with Kingstonian, Hayes and Heybridge Swifts joined Ryman Premier club Canvey Island in 2001. Forty-four goals in 2001/02 won him the

Islanders' Player of the Year award and earned himself a new nickname – "Lightning" – after scoring in just 38 seconds in a 6-1 romp over St Albans when he grabbed a four-goal haul. Not content with that one, the free-scoring front man shaved 11 seconds off his own record when he scored after 27 seconds in Canvey's 3-0 victory over Billericay Town three days later in April 2003! In 2003/04, Lee became the club's record goalscorer with a grand total of 57 in all competitions. His goals were the main reason for the Gulls' promotion to the Conference and he was rewarded with an England call-up against the USA in Charleston, Carolina in June 2004.

BRABROOK, Peter
1962-68

Born: Greenwich, London, 8.11.37
League apps: 167 (33 goals)
Cup apps: 47 (10 goals)

THIS BRILLIANT WINGER slipped through the club's scouting net after he had played schoolboy soccer for East Ham, Essex and London. Nine years later, it cost £35,000 to sign him from Chelsea, with whom he scored 47 goals in over 250 League games and won England Youth and full caps. Even so, it was money well spent. He played in the 1964 FA Cup-winning team and won a League Cup runners-up medal in 1966. He ended his League career at Orient where he made 72 League appearances and was a vital member of the side that won

the Third Division championship in 1970 in company with Hammer-to-be Tommy Taylor under the managership of another ex-Iron, Jimmy Bloomfield, before appearing for Southern League Romford. Peter relinquished his post as coach to Essex Senior League side Ford United in 1985, but was still involved with local football with Billericay Town from where he recommended striker Steve Jones to West Ham. He was also employed as a scout by Hammers. Initially part time, he was appointed on a full-time basis in charge of the Under-17 side in 1995. During his seven years with the youth section he saw the youngsters reach the Semi-finals of the FA Premier Youth Academy Play-offs in 2000 and as assistant to Tony Carr contributed to the Under-19s' triumphs as South-East Counties League Champions (1998) and the FA Premier Youth Academy Play-off Final win over Arsenal in 2000. Peter hasn't cut all ties with the club, however, and trawls the London and south east area, helping to assess forthcoming opposition and future prospects.

BRADFORD, T
1911-12

SL apps: 1

THIS OUTSIDE-RIGHT MADE his solitary Hammers appearance in a Southern League fixture, the 0-0 draw with Stoke City at the Victoria Ground that took place on May 20, 1912.

BRADSHAW, Harry
1919-20

Born: Lancashire, 1896
League apps: 14
Cup apps: 1

ORIGINALLY A WINGER, he converted to wing-half with the Irons. Harry was awarded the Military Medal while serving as a brigade runner in France during World War I. Signing pro for the 1919/20 season, he was also a member of the club's relay-team that won the Professional Footballers' 4 x 440 yards at Stamford Bridge, in an era when such races were a popular part of the entertainment at sports meetings. An active member of the Old Players' Association, he was living at Hockley Avenue, East Ham at the time of his death in October 1967, at the age of 71.

BRADSHAW, Tom
1889-1900

Born: Liverpool, 24.8.1873
SL apps (TIW): 5

A FAST, DIRECT left-winger who began his career with Northwich Victoria and was a regular member of Liverpool's Second Division championship-winning teams of 1894 and 1896. Bradshaw played on two occasions for the Football League in addition to winning an England cap against Ireland in February 1897. Joining Spurs in May 1898, he scored on his debut – against Thames Iron Works – and was an ever-present during their 1888/89 Thames & Medway League campaign. After making 69 appearances in all competitions for Spurs that season, he transferred to TIW in the summer of 1899 along with team-mates Kenny McKay and Bill Joyce in a transfer coup masterminded by Irons secretary George Neil. The highlight of Tom's all too short Irons career was destined to be his four goals in an 11-1 Thames & Medway Combination thrashing of Grays United for, tragically, both Tom Bradshaw and the man who signed him, George Neill, were dead before they had reached the age of 30. Tom died on Christmas Day 1899 of consumption resulting in a Spurs and Ironworks match on April 2, 1900 to raise funds for his dependents.

BRADY, Liam
1987-90

Born: Dublin, Republic of Ireland, 13.2.56
League apps: 89 (9 goals)
Cup apps: 26 (1 goal)

REGARDED BY MANY as the Republic of Ireland's greatest-ever player, Brady's record of 72 Irish caps was finally overhauled by Pat Bonner in June 1994. Although Liam was in the twilight of his illustrious career when he ended his seven-year reign in Italy to join the Hammers in March 1987, he is still recognised as one of the most accomplished players ever to perform in claret and blue. Yet Liam made his name with London rivals Arsenal, who he joined as an apprentice in the summer of 1971 after starring in his homeland for St Kevin's Boys. He made his debut at Highbury as a 17-year-old sub against Birmingham

City on October 6, 1973 and went on to play 235 League games for the Gunners, appearing in three consecutive FA Cup Finals. He was on the losing side against Ipswich Town (1978) and West Ham United (1980), but gained a winners' medal against Manchester United in between. Also in the Gunners side beaten by Valencia (after penalties – Liam missed the first one!) in the European Cup Winners' Cup Final of May 1980. It was a sad British farewell for the Irish genius but he had so many more big games to look forward to as, aged 24, he broadened his horizons with Juventus in Italy's Serie A. Liam's reputation as a creative midfielder, with an exquisite left foot and eye for goal, was enriched by his Italian experience. He ended his first campaign as the team's leading scorer and a championship medal-winner. The Turin club pipped Fiorentina for the title a year later after Brady scored the match-winning penalty in their final game at Catanzaro but, for Liam, the celebrations were muted. Three games prior to that dramatic finale, he had been devastated to learn that he would be replaced as Juve's second foreigner the following season by French superstar Michel Platini. But it was a measure of Liam's character that instead of turning his back on Italy, he stayed and went on to play for Sampdoria and Inter Milan (a season each), and half a season with Ascoli before deciding to return to England. West Ham stole a march on their rivals by snapping him up for £100,000. Liam made his debut at home against Norwich City (March 14, 1987) and scored the first of his ten West Ham goals in a 3-1 home win over Arsenal (!) on April 8. His second season was marred by a knee ligament injury sustained at Derby in February 1988, forcing him to miss the rest of the term and the following summer's European Championship finals. When Liam decided to quit playing at the end of 1989/90 many thought he had retired prematurely. But he went out in a blaze of glory – scoring a spectacular goal in the dying seconds of his farewell game against Wolves at Upton Park on May 5. Eleven days later the Football Association of Ireland honoured Liam with a testimonial against Finland in Dublin. It was the last of his 72 caps – the first was against USSR at Dalymount Park (October 30, 1974) – and during his stint with Hammers, Liam played for his country 11 times. After a break of a year, Liam returned to football as manager of Glasgow Celtic in July 1991 but boardroom wrangles undermined his efforts and, as the team slipped further into the shadow of rivals Rangers, he resigned in November 1993. A month later, he returned to management, at Brighton, steering the Seagulls safely clear of the Second Division relegation zone. After a spell as a players agent, Liam was appointed Head of Youth Development at Arsenal in August 1996.

Irish caps while with West Ham:
1987 vs Bulgaria (twice), Belgium, Brazil, Luxembourg (twice); 1989 vs France, Hungary (twice), West Germany; 1990 vs Finland (11).

BRANDON, Tommy
1913-20

Born: Blackburn, Lancashire, 1893
SL apps: 34
Cup: 3

ESSENTIALLY A RIGHT-BACK, Tommy began his career with his home-town Blackburn Rovers at the age of 16, in 1909. The son of Scottish international, Tom Brandon Snr, Tommy represented Lancashire in inter-county matches and played for South Liverpool until joining up with Hammers in the close-season of 1913. Playing his first game for West Ham in a fine 2-1 win over Bristol Rovers at their former Eastville ground (September 13, 1913), he went on to make 31 Southern League appearances that season, his best by far. With only three outings the following campaign, Tom had to wait until the tail-end of the last wartime season in the old London Combination to make his final appearances in the home and away clashes with Fulham. Unable to command a first team place after Hammers' elevation to the Second Division of the Football League, he went back north to serve Hull City in June 1920, and made 56 appearances (some at inside-right), transferring to Bradford in June 1922, and then on to Wigan Borough in 1925. He died on May 1, 1956.

BREACKER, Tim
1990-99

Born: Bicester, Oxfordshire, 2.7.65
League apps: 240 (8 goals)
Cup apps: 49

A POWERFUL, ATTACKING right-back, Tim became Billy Bonds's first signing, in October 1990, when he joined from Luton Town in a £600,000 deal. Hammers were in Division Two at the time but so confident was Tim that he would soon be returning to the top flight, he had no hesitation leaving the club he joined as a schoolboy and made 208 League appearances following his League debut at Ipswich Town in March 1984. His Hammers' debut came as sub at Swindon Town on October 10, 1990 when he took over the right-back role, allowing Steve Potts to switch to central defence. Tim has also played at centre-back as cover, but it is as an overlapping full-back that he is best known. A placid, unassuming man, Tim was nevertheless a tough, though fair, opponent and was unlucky to be sent off for the first time in his career, after two bookable offences, at Everton in December 1991. Tim was involved in many vital cup ties, having played for the Hatters in their 1988 League Cup Final victory over Arsenal, their reverse at the hands of Nottingham Forest in the corresponding

match a year later. (Ironically, Luton returned to Wembley after beating West Ham in the 1989 Semi-final.) In the FA Cup, he endured the heartbreak of three Semi-final defeats – twice with Luton (against Everton in 1985 and Wimbledon in 1988), and once with West Ham (against Forest in 1991). He won two England Under-21 caps – both against Italy – in Pisa on April 9, 1986 and at Swindon 14 days later. He nearly left the Boleyn in 1993, but a double transfer involving himself and Ian Bishop to Southampton fell through at the last minute. Tim went on to give the club almost ten years' sterling service. He made a telling contribution to the two promotion campaigns of 1990/91 and 1992/93. Having transferred to QPR in 1999, Tim showed the same qualities at Loftus Road where he teamed up with former Hammers Iain Dowie, Keith Rowland and Ludek Miklosko. In three seasons with the West Londoners he added 47 League and Cup appearances and two goals to his impressive career record. The holder of a first class honours degree in Sports and Science, Tim took over the management of the Rangers second string when he retired from playing in 2001.

BREEN, Gary 2002-03

Born: Hendon, Middlesex, 12.12.73
League apps: 14
Cup apps: 4

SIGNED BY VIRTUE of his excellent performances for the Republic of Ireland during their gallant 2002 World Cup in Japan and South Korea, the six-foot-plus defender inexplicably endured a torrid time in his only season as a Hammer. Allegedly a transfer target of Barcelona, Inter Milan and a host of Premiership clubs, Gary chose Hammers because he'd been under the tutelage of Glenn Roeder during the early stages of his career at Third Division Gillingham in 1992. Previously with Maidstone United, Breen made 19 appearances for the Kent club before they went bankrupt. His move to the Gills saw him play 29 times as the Priestfield outfit narrowly avoided going out of the League by finishing just four points above Halifax Town in Roeder's first stab at management. At the end of 1993/94, Gary moved up a rung and joined Second Division Peterborough United where, after 81 League and Cup appearances in two seasons, he attracted a £250,000 bid from First Division Birmingham City in 1995. He was given the captain's armband at St Andrews, and after 45 games he was Premiership-bound in a £2.5 million transfer to Coventry City. He played 171 times in six seasons for the Sky Blues, attained cult status and established himself in the Republic of Ireland side. West Ham released him in May 2003 and he subsequently joined Sunderland.

BRETT, Frank 1898

Born: birthplace unknown, 1877
SL apps (TIW): 1

CAME FROM SWANSCOMBE and played in the first-ever TIW professional match at inside-right in a 3-0 win at Shepherds Bush on September 10, 1898.

BRETT, Ron 1959-60

Born: Stanford-le-Hope, Essex, 4.9.37
League apps: 12 (4 goals)
Cup apps: 1

A STRONG, OLD-FASHIONED type of centre-forward who joined West Ham from Crystal Palace in an exchange deal that sent Malcolm Pyke to Selhurst Park. After nearly three seasons at Upton Park, Brett rejoined Palace on a similar basis, this time being valued at £7,000 in the record-breaking transaction that made Johnny Byrne a Hammer. Ron died only five months after his transfer when his car collided with a lorry in Clerkenwell. Poignantly, the last match he played was a reserve fixture between Hammers and Palace at Upton Park on the Saturday before his tragic and untimely death.

BREVETT, Rufus 2003-05

Born: Derby, Derbyshire, 24.9.69
League apps: 25 (1 goal)
Cup apps: 4

AN INSPIRED SIGNING by Glenn Roeder during the January 2003 transfer window from Fulham, his arrival at Upton Park – together with the emergence of fellow defender Glen Johnson – coincided with a distinct tightening up of the team's previously shaky defence and an improvement in form that almost staved off relegation. Ferocious in the tackle, fast on his feet and 100 per cent committed, "Brev" could be the template for a typical West Ham crowd favourite. A talented and dreadlocked left-back, he soon won the hearts of the Boleyn faithful with his all-action displays in what had been a problem department. After failing to make the grade with his home-town club Derby County, Rufus thought about a career outside football before persevering and making his League debut for Third Division Doncaster Rovers versus Sunderland in August 1987. Tasting relegation in his first season at Belle Vue, he went on to make 118 appearances (scoring three goals) before stepping up two divisions to join Queen Park Rangers for a £250,000 fee in February 1991. Initially, he found it hard to gain a regular first team place at Loftus Road, and by the time he did he ironically again endured relegation as the west Londoners slipped out of the Premiership in 1995/96 with Andy Impey, Trevor Sinclair and Les Ferdinand among the ranks. After notching up 170 games (and one goal) he made the short journey across west London to join Kevin Keegan's Fulham for £375,000 – even though it meant dropping down another grade into the Second Division. But promotions in 1998/99 and 2001/02 saw his gamble pay dividends as the defender found himself back in the Premiership (and back at Loftus Road as Fulham opted to ground share with QPR). With the Cottagers he won an Inter-Toto Cup medal and sampled UEFA Cup football in 2002, making 203 appearances (scoring twice) before moving to West Ham on a two-and-a-half year contract for an undisclosed fee. Ruled out of almost the entire 2003/04 season with an ankle injury, he was sorely missed as Hammers lost in the Play-off Final to Crystal Palace at Cardiff where he remained on the bench. Rufus is now playing with Plymouth Argyle.

BRIDGEMAN, Billy 1903-06

Born: Bromley-by-Bow, London, 1884
SL apps: 71 (19 goals)
Cup apps: 3 (1 goal)

A PUPIL OF Marner Street School where he played in the school XI with another legendary figure, George "Gatling Gun" Hilsdon, he joined the Irons from Adam & Eve FC. Legend has it that Bill scored a hat-trick in West Ham's emphatic 3-0 victory over arch rivals Millwall during the first Southern League fixture to be staged at Upton Park in September 1904 – although contemporary newspaper reports credited Jack Flynn with one of the goals. He did, however, score three in the opening public trial match at Upton Park a few days prior to the meeting with Millwall, a fact that probably helped to blur memories. But wherever the truth of the matter lies, one thing can't be denied: Bridgeman scored West Ham's first-ever goal at Boleyn Castle – in that match against Millwall – and served Hammers well as they struggled to establish themselves in the Southern League and so deserves his niche in the club's history. Mostly a centre-forward with Hammers, he was also tried briefly as a right-winger, a position he was destined to fill with even more distinction at his next club, Chelsea, most notably in helping the Pensioners to promotion back to the First Division in 1912. After making more than 150 senior appearances for the West Londoners, Bill saw out the remainder of his career with Southend United after joining them in 1915.

Rufus Brevett

BROOKING, Sir Trevor MBE 1965-84

Born: Barking, Essex, 2.10.48
League apps: 528 (88 goals)
Cup apps: 106 (14 goals)

ONE OF THE true greats in Hammers Hall of Fame. Having signed as an apprentice after leaving Ilford County High School in July 1965, Trevor turned pro in May 1966 and made his debut at Burnley on August 29, 1967. Moore, Hurst and Peters were Hammers' scorers in a 3-3 draw that day and the shy, 19-year-old Brooking would not have expected he would go on to join the famous trio among the ranks of West Ham legends. Indeed, Trevor took his time to establish himself in the first team, playing initially as a centre-forward. He did not start more than 30 League games in a season until after Peters' transfer to Tottenham in March 1970. In fact, he was so disillusioned after being dropped and then left out for a long period by Ron Greenwood, that he went on the transfer list at the end of 1970/71. During the 1972/73 campaign Derby County manager Brian Clough offered £400,000 for Bobby Moore and Trevor, but Greenwood blocked the move. Derby's loss was certainly Hammers' gain, as the tall, elegant Trevor emerged as one of the classiest midfield players in the world. He was regularly outstanding even when the team performance was way below par, and West Ham came to rely heavily upon the man many once doubted would ever make the top grade. A marvellous reader of the game, Trevor bemused opponents and enthralled Hammers fans with his silky skills in the heart of midfield. He passed accurately with both feet, threaded through-balls into gaps that did not appear to exist and also scored his fair share of spectacular goals from distance. Although he was creator much more than ball-winner (Billy Bonds did much to complement him in this respect), Trevor's tall, strong physique still enabled him to hold off his marker – he was expert at shielding the ball and turning his opponents, having already glanced over his shoulder to assess the scene. His speciality was letting the ball run on the blind side of his opponent when receiving a throw-in. His control of the ball was incomparable and he was as immaculate off the pitch as he was on it. A real gentleman of football, Trevor was nicknamed "Hadleigh" by his team-

mates after a TV character of similar status. First voted Hammer of the Year by the fans in 1971/72, Trevor is the only player to win the award in three consecutive years (1975-78). Brooking had to wait eight years to win a major honour with his club, leading them to victory in the FA Cup Final against Fulham on May 3, 1975. Ironically, a major influence on the younger Trevor had been his schoolboy favourite, the former Fulham great Johnny Haynes. He collected a runners-up medal in the 4-2 European Cup Winners' Cup Final defeat by Anderlecht in May 1976, then returned to Wembley – scoring the FA Cup Final winner against Arsenal on May 10, 1980. Although never renowned as a particularly effective header of the ball, he stooped low to guide Stuart Pearson's shot past Pat Jennings and into the Gunners' net after only 13 minutes. Within a year, he was back at Wembley again to face Liverpool in the 1981 League Cup Final, which was drawn 1-1 before the Reds took the replay at Villa Park 2-1.

These big occasions,

Career record

Played	League		FAC		LC		Europe		Total	
	App	Gls	App	Gls	App	Gls	App	Gls	App	Gls
1967-68	25	9	3	0	0	0	0	0	28	9
1968-69	32	7	2	0	3	1	0	0	37	8
1969-70	21	4	0	0	2	0	0	0	23	4
1970-71	19	2	0	0	1	0	0	0	20	2
1971-72	40	6	4	0	10	1	0	0	54	7
1972-73	40	11	2	0	2	0	0	0	44	11
1973-74	38	6	0	0	2	0	0	0	40	6
1974-75	36	3	8	1	3	1	0	0	47	5
1975-76	34	5	1	0	4	1	7	3	46	9
1976-77	42	4	2	0	2	0	0	0	46	4
1977-78	37	4	2	0	0	0	0	0	39	4
1978-79	21	2	1	0	0	0	0	0	22	2
1979-80	37	3	7	2	8	1	0	0	52	6
1980-81	36	10	3	0	7	0	5	0	51	10
1981-82	34	8	2	0	5	1	0	0	41	9
1982-83	1	0	0	0	0	0	0	0	1	0
1983-84	35	4	3	0	5	2	0	0	43	6
TOTAL	**528**	**88**	**40**	**3**	**54**	**8**	**12**	**3**	**634**	**102**

England caps: 1974 vs Argentina, Portugal (twice), East Germany, Bulgaria, Yugoslavia, Czechoslovakia (sub); 1975 vs Portugal; 1976 vs Wales, Brazil, Italy (twice), Finland (twice), Republic of Ireland; 1977 vs Holland, Northern Ireland, Wales, Italy; 1978 vs West Germany, Wales, Scotland (sub), Hungary, Denmark, Republic of Ireland; 1979 vs Northern Ireland (twice), Wales (sub), Scotland, Bulgaria, Sweden (sub), Austria, Denmark; 1980 vs Argentina (sub), Wales, Northern Ireland, Scotland, Belgium, Spain, Switzerland; 1981 vs Spain, Romania, Hungary (twice); 1982 vs Scotland, Finland, Spain (sub) (47).

1904-2004

the record-breaking 1980/81 Second Division promotion campaign and his award of the MBE, were appropriate reward for Trevor's admirable loyalty. While many people outside Upton Park expected the England star to move on after Hammers were relegated from Division One in May 1978, he stayed faithful to the club he supported as a kid and went on to enjoy the biggest highlights of his long and illustrious career. England manager Ron Greenwood – the very man who signed Brooking as a schoolboy to Upton Park – reassured the midfield maestro that his international future would not be affected by his club's slide into Division Two. Capped once at Under-23 level, Trevor went on to win 47 full England caps. The high spot came during the World Cup qualifying match with Hungary in Budapest in 1981, when his two goals took England to Spain for the 1982 finals. By now recognised as a world-class performer, Trevor was bitterly disappointed that a long-term groin injury virtually ruled him out of the tournament. He and Kevin Keegan – who had an almost telepathic understanding – were both introduced as subs late in the dramatic match against Spain in Madrid but, still nursing injuries, not even these two England greats could save Greenwood's side from elimination. Trevor missed all but the penultimate match of the 1982/83 season due to recurring injury problems, but returned in 1983/84 – his final season – for 43 League and Cup appearances. Although many believed that he could have continued at least a couple more seasons, Trevor decided to quit at the top and it was an emotional Upton Park crowd that saluted their hero on a lap of honour following the game against Everton on May 14, 1984. That was his 528th League match for Hammers – only Billy Bonds, Frank Lampard and Bobby Moore have played more times for the club. A shrewd and intelligent businessman with a number of directorships, Trevor put his school qualifications to full use. Even while still playing at his peak, he built up business interests outside the game. He has maintained a strong involvement with football, as a successful BBC radio and television pundit and a newspaper columnist, often returning to Upton Park in these capacities. And he had not yet finished playing the game. Within months of retiring as a pro at Upton Park, Trevor signed for Havering Nalgo and in 2004 entered his tenth season with the club! Away from the Brentwood Sunday League, Trevor was once more in the national spotlight again when he "volunteered" to act as caretaker manager for the vital last three games of 2002/03 following the illness of Glenn Roeder. History records that his short, enforced stewardship ended in relegation, but not before his animated touchline encouragement brought two wins and a draw that saw his charges come agonisingly close to saving the day. Those who witnessed Brooking's three-year chairmanship of Sport England were not surprised at the passion and commitment he'd shown holding the managerial reins at Upton Park. The Brooking they knew was no appeaser as he illustrated in 2002 when he criticised Sports Minister Richard Caborn with what has been described as "controlled anger" over the Labour government's lack of funding for sport. He is now seen in a new light by the public, his press room and television studio colleagues alike – and there can be little doubt that he fully deserved the knighthood bestowed on him in the summer of 2004. As if Trevor's amazingly varied and successful career hadn't followed enough paths, he was sent in yet another direction when appointed the Football Association's Director of Football Development in 2004. His new post is one of the most prestigious in the game, encompassing every level of the sport from grass roots parks football to Sven Goran Eriksson's national squad. It represents a fitting role for someone so universally respected as a perfect ambassador for the beautiful game and perhaps goes some way to explaining why he was reluctant to take up the managerial reins at the Boleyn Ground on a permanent basis.

BRIGNULL, Phil — 1979

Born: Stratford, London, 2.10.60
League apps: 1

A DEFENDER WHOSE sole first team appearance was made as sub against Cardiff City at Ninian Park in May 1979. Transferred to AFC Bournemouth in 1981, where his cousin, former Chelsea star David Webb, was then assistant manager. Brignull later moved to Wrexham, Cardiff City and his third Welsh club, Newport County, where he played three times before they left the League.

BRITT, Martin — 1963-65

Born: Leigh-on-Sea, Essex, 17.1.46
League apps: 20 (6 goals)
Cup apps: 6 (1 goal)

A FORMER ENGLAND youth international who had been apprenticed in July 1966, this centre-forward faced stiff competition for a place in the free-scoring West Ham attack of the mid-1960s. He made his Hammers debut against Blackburn Rovers in May 1963 – and it was Rovers who later paid £25,000 to take him to Ewood Park in 1965. It was not a happy move, though, as his career was cut short by injury after only six appearances. Britt had earlier scored four goals in a sensational 5-2 win against Liverpool in the second leg of the 1963 FA Youth Cup final at Upton Park – all with his head! He also scored in the 3-1 first leg defeat at Anfield to give the young Hammers hope in a clash that left manager Ron Greenwood singing their praises, but Liverpool legend Bill Shankly reportedly branding them "animals"!

BROWN, Ken — 1952-67

Born: Forest Gate, London, 16.2.34
League apps: 386 (4 goals)
Cup apps: 69

A CENTRE-HALF SIGNED from Dagenham-based Neville United in October 1951, he made his first team debut in 1952/53 and played until 1967 – with a break for National Service with the army from 1952-54. Brown was a stalwart in the promotion season of 1957/58, and won one full cap for England against Northern Ireland at Wembley on November 18, 1959 where he gave a good account of himself in a 2-1 victory. One of nine new caps tried in a three-match spell, Ken was unfortunate to be overlooked in the future as manager Walter Winterbottom continued his search for a successor to Billy Wright. With West Ham, he later collected winners' medals at Wembley in the 1964 FA Cup and 1965 European Cup Winners'

Cup Finals, where he played alongside Bobby Moore in the heart of defence. A crowd of 14,695 turned out at Upton Park on May 15, 1967 to pay tribute on the night of his well-deserved testimonial (in which Billy Bonds made his Hammers debut) against a Select XI. He then joined fellow ex-Hammer John Bond at Torquay United and gained the unusual distinction of drawing wage packets from two clubs as he continued to manage the pools promotion at Upton Park! After that he moved into management, first at Norwich City where he led them to victory over Sunderland in the 1985 Milk (League) Cup Final, although that success was diluted by relegation to Division Two at the end of the same season. But a smile is never missing from Ken's face for long and within a year he led the Canaries back into the top flight, playing the entertaining brand of football he had been involved in at Upton Park for so long. But after a shaky start to the 1987/88 season, Norwich made the shock decision to dismiss Ken. He bounced back as manager of Plymouth Argyle where he had his good friend and former Hammers winger, Malcolm Musgrove, as assistant. He relinquished the Home Park post in 1991 and is now director of Lakenham Leisure Centre, near Norwich, but he can often be seen at Upton Park with his son, Kenny Brown Jnr (see over). Brown senior – along with fellow ex-Hammers and Academy originators Dave Sexton and Noel Cantwell – is part of Sven Goran Eriksson's scouting and match assessment team. Sexton, as chief scout, recommended Brown and Cantwell assist with the England set-up and Ken's duties have included a spying mission to Turkey to run the rule over England's main Group Nine Euro 2004 qualifying rivals as they took on Georgia at Trabson.

Career record										
	League		FAC		LC		Europe		Total	
Played	App	Gls	App	Gls	App	Gls	App	Gls	App	Gls
1952-53	3	0	0	0	0	0	0	0	3	0
1953-54	0	0	0	0	0	0	0	0	0	0
1954-55	23	0	0	0	0	0	0	0	23	0
1955-56	2	0	0	0	0	0	0	0	2	0
1956-57	5	0	0	0	0	0	0	0	5	0
1957-58	41	0	3	0	0	0	0	0	44	0
1958-59	42	0	1	0	0	0	0	0	43	0
1959-60	40	0	2	0	0	0	0	0	42	0
1960-61	42	0	2	0	2	0	0	0	46	0
1961-62	38	0	1	0	2	0	0	0	41	0
1962-63	40	2	5	0	2	0	0	0	47	2
1963-64	36	0	7	0	6	0	0	0	49	0
1964-65	33	1	2	0	1	0	9	0	45	1
1965-66	23	1	3	0	9	0	6	0	41	1
1966-67	18	0	0	0	6	0	0	0	24	0
TOTAL	**386**	**4**	**26**	**0**	**28**	**0**	**15**	**0**	**455**	**4**

BROWN, Kenny Jnr 1991-97

Born: Barking, Essex, 11.7.67
League apps: 63 (5 goals)
Cup apps: 12 (1 goal)

FOLLOWED IN THE footsteps of his father Ken (see previous) and completed the third father and son pairing (following the Barretts and Lansdownes) to play for the Hammers. Kenny initially joined the club, from Plymouth Argyle in August 1991, as a stop-gap following a spate of pre-season injuries. He proved to be a tenacious right-back who, after making his League debut at home against Luton Town on August 17, 1991, demonstrated a fierce shot. Indeed, it was a super-strike against Aston Villa, under the Upton Park lights just a month after his arrival, that prompted the Hammers to make his signing permanent. The West Country club collected a down payment of £175,000, plus £60,000 after Kenny's 50th appearance. Even before establishing himself as a first team regular, Kenny – who could also operate effectively in midfield – scored some important goals. It was his winner at Upton Park against Manchester United on April 22, 1992 that shattered Alex Ferguson's title dream that season, while his goal in a 3-1 win at Swindon (May 2, 1993) proved vital as Hammers clinched promotion ahead of Portsmouth by one goal's difference! Kenny began his career at Norwich City, who were managed by his father at the time, making his debut as sub in November 1986. He made 25 League appearances for the Canaries without scoring, then moved on a free transfer to join his father at Plymouth Argyle in August 1988 where he played 138 League and Cup matches, scoring four times, before joining West Ham. But by the start of the 1995/96 season it became evident that Kenny wasn't part of Harry Redknapp's Premiership plans, and he went out on loan to Huddersfield Town, Reading, Southend United and Crystal Palace (for whom he appeared at Wembley in the Division One Play-off Final defeat against Leicester City). Kenny went back to Reading on loan in September 1996 before finally severing his ties with Hammers in a £75,000 transfer to Birmingham City in December 1996. He made just 11 appearances at St Andrew's, then returned to London to sign for Millwall and Billy Bonds in a £40,000 deal in August 1997. But like many with claret and blue connections before him, Kenny struggled at the New Den and found himself frozen out following the sacking of Bonds and his assistant Patsy Holland. Gillingham boss Tony Pulis then signed him at the end of the 1998/99 campaign. It nearly paid off as the Gills narrowly missed out to Manchester City. His four appearances at Priestfield turned out to be his last in the League as, after an unsuccessful trial at Wigan Athletic, he joined non-League Kingstonian in December 1999 before moving on to League of Ireland Portadown the following year. Following in his father's illustrious footsteps again, Kenny moved into management and was appointed assistant player-manager of Welsh Premier Barry Town in July 2000. The fully professional South Wales club won the League and Cup double three times on the trot and became the first team from the Principality to win a European Champions League tie when they overcame Shankir of Azerbaijan 3-0 on aggregate in July 2001. The next round saw them go out to Portuguese giants FC Porto 9-3 on aggregate, but not before the Dragons had treated the Jenner Park crowd to a 3-1 second-leg victory and a cameo appearance from Brown! Number one at Barry since Peter Nicholas's departure to Swansea City early in 2001/02, Kenny was in charge under chairman John Fashanu until the Welsh club hit financial trouble on the eve of 2003/04. Facing an untenable situation, Kenny returned to his roots to play with Ryman League Division One side North Tilbury. In August 2004, Kenny joined Spanish non-League club FC Torrevieja.

Kenny Brown Jnr

BROWN, William 1907-09

Born: Newmilnes, Ayrshire, date unknown
SL apps: 19 (4 goals)

ALTHOUGH MOST AT home in the inside-left position, Billy appeared in all the forward berths for West Ham following his transfer from Vale of Leven, who were founder members of the Scottish League as well as being among the earliest contestants for the Scottish Cup. He made his debut against Swindon Town at the County Ground in the third fixture of 1907/08, but had to wait until the later stages of the campaign to become a regular. His four goals came as two pairs, his first earning a 2-2 draw at the then professional Leyton, and his second helping towards a 4-2 home victory over Southampton. There was little success for him the next season, however, his two Southern League outings reflecting a sad fade-out.

BROWN, William 1921-24

Born: Hetton-le-Hole, County Durham, 22.8.1900
League apps: 60 (15 goals)
Cup apps: 11 (5 goals)

A PLAY-ANYWHERE UTILITY man when West Ham plucked him from local football in his native North-East with Hetton, Billy eventually settled down in the inside-right position to partner Dick Richards in the 1923 FA Cup Final and promotion side. He made his Hammers debut at South Shields in the final fixture of 1920/21. It wasn't until 1922/23 that he won a regular first team place and, a month after appearing in Hammers' losing Wembley XI, gained England honours as a reserve against France. A year later he won his solitary full cap against Belgium at the Hawthorns. Transferring to Chelsea shortly afterwards, he later played for Fulham, Stockport and Hartlepool United. Kept in trim in later life as a bath superintendent at Easington Colliery and as a cricket umpire. He died at Easington, County Durham in January 1985.

BRUNTON, Fred 1904-05

League apps: 1

FREDERICK MADE HIS only appearance for Hammers in the 4-1 Southern League defeat at Portsmouth on Boxing Day, 1904. He played at right-half in front of the biggest crowd to watch West Ham that season, 16,000.

BRUSH, Paul 1977-85

Born: Plaistow, London, 22.2.58
League apps: 151 (1 goal)
Cup apps: 34

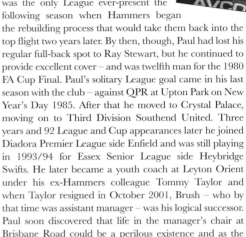

A HIGHLY VALUED member of Hammers' senior squad who proved invaluable during the 1984/85 injury crisis. Paul made his League bow against Norwich City on August 20, 1977 and was the only League ever-present the following season when Hammers began the rebuilding process that would take them back into the top flight two years later. By then, though, Paul had lost his regular full-back spot to Ray Stewart, but he continued to provide excellent cover – and was twelfth man for the 1980 FA Cup Final. Paul's solitary League goal came in his last season with the club – against QPR at Upton Park on New Year's Day 1985. After that he moved to Crystal Palace, moving on to Third Division Southend United. Three years and 92 League and Cup appearances later he joined Diadora Premier League side Enfield and was still playing in 1993/94 for Essex Senior League side Heybridge Swifts. He later became a youth coach at Leyton Orient under his ex-Hammers colleague Tommy Taylor and when Taylor resigned in October 2001, Brush – who by that time was assistant manager – was his logical successor. Paul soon discovered that life in the manager's chair at Brisbane Road could be a perilous existence and as the team continued to struggle to avoid relegation to the Conference, he was sacked early in 2003/04. Paul was assistant manager at Southend United in 2004/05.

Paul Brush

BUNBURY, Alex 1992-93

Born: British Guyana, 18.6.67
League apps: 4
Cup apps: 1

A GAMBLE THAT turned out to be rather expensive, Canadian international Alex cost £200,000 when signed by Billy Bonds from Montreal Supra in December 1992. He was leading scorer in their qualifying bid for the 1994 World Cup Finals that only just failed in a decisive clash with Mexico, but could not reproduce this form for Hammers. He made his debut as sub at Brentford on December 20, 1992 and appeared as sub in two other first team games. But, apart from one Anglo-Italian Cup outing (against Pisa), his only first team starts were at home to Bristol City on January 27, 1993 and at Sunderland on February 27. Then, after struggling to gain a place even in the Reserves, he was sold to Portuguese club Sporting Maritimo for just £50,000 in November 1993. He scored 59 goals in 165 League matches during his six years there and although forced to retire by an ankle injury in 2000 (by which time he was back playing in Canada) he remains one of his country's most famous players – with 65 caps (six of them while with West Ham) and the awards of Canadian Player of the Year (1993) and Portuguese Foreign Player of the Year (1995) to his name.

BURGESS, Daniel/Dick 1922

Born: Goldenhill, Staffordshire, 23.10.1898
League apps: 2

AFTER TWO SEASONS with Arsenal this inside-right opted to follow his friend and former Gunners team-mate George Pattison to Upton Park. He was quickly given a chance in the first team, and made his two Second Division appearances against Bradford City at Valley Parade on September 2, 1922 and Derby County at the Baseball Ground two days later. Dick then joined Welsh club Aberdare Athletic in 1922, who staged Football League fare at the Athletic Ground, Ynis 1921-27, after which they were replaced by Torquay United. Later played for Queens Park Rangers.

BURKETT, Jack 1962-67

Born: Edmonton, London, 21.8.42
League apps: 142 (4 goals)
Cup apps: 39

A QUICK, TENACIOUS full-back signed from the juniors in July 1958. Jack liked nothing better than to join attacks, his speed enabling him to get back to his defensive duties without being stretched. He collected medals with the Cup-winning side of 1964/65. Transferred to Charlton Athletic for £10,000 in 1968, and later saw service with Millwall and Southend United before embarking on a spell as a player-manager with St Patrick's Athletic in the League of Ireland. He returned to the UK in 1976 for a short spell as player-coach back at Southend, then managed Saudi Arabia's Under-18 side and Norwegian Third Division side Orsta (in 1980) before moving to Southend for a third time in 1982 as youth coach under his old skipper Bobby Moore. In 1984 he took up a similar position at Fulham and now has a full-time job in charge of the YTS boys in the South of England on behalf of the PFA. He won England Youth honours while with Hammers.

BURNETT, Dennis 1965-67

Born: Bermondsey, London, 27.9.44
League apps: 50
Cup apps: 16 (3 goals)

A DEFENDER SIGNED from the juniors in October 1962. Dennis always performed capably when drafted into the side and enjoyed 24 League outings in 1965/66, the most he managed in any one season. Made his League debut against Fulham at Craven Cottage in October 1965 and won a League Cup runners-up medal the following year. He joined Millwall for £15,000 in 1967 and had a second spell at The Den after two seasons at Hull City, before finishing his League life with Brighton & Hove Albion. He now runs a painting and decorating firm in the south coast town where he lives with his wife and two daughters. Still plays amateur soccer and is assistant manager of Sussex side Lancing FC.

BURRILL, Frank 1911-14

Born: Manor Park, London, date unknown
League apps: 17 (2 goals)

A PUPIL OF Fourth Avenue school in Manor Park, Frank was signed from local junior football. Frank's 17 appearances for Hammers were spread over three seasons prior to World War I. He made his Southern

League debut at centre-forward against Queens Park Rangers on March 12, 1912 in a 3-0 win at "Boleyn Castle", as Hammers' midden was often called then. It was a remarkable match: the Irons scoring three times in the last 12 minutes to defeat the visitors after Burrill had swapped positions with the great Danny Shea. His six other outings that season were made from the inside-right berth when he deputised for the injured Shea. His two appearances the following campaign saw him in the number 10 shirt, scoring his first goal in a 4-3 reverse at Northampton Town. 1913/14 saw him back at inside-right and scoring his second – and final – goal in a 3-1 win over Gillingham at Upton Park on November 22. Mostly a reserve, he played two further matches in the Supplementary Tournament of the London Combination in 1915/16 against Spurs and Millwall, then transferred to Southend United for 1919/20 and became their leading scorer before being signed by Wolves for £800 to form a triumvirate of ex-Southend players at Molineux, with Maurice Woodward and George Marshall, who all played for Wolves in the 1921 FA Cup Final against Spurs at Stamford Bridge. Frank returned to London in 1923 to join Charlton Athletic, before moving to Walsall the following summer, where he became their leading scorer with 14 goals in 38 appearances.

BURROWS, David 1993

Born: Dudley, West Midlands, 25.10.68
League apps: 25 (1 goal)
Cup apps: 6 (1 goal)

DAVID'S QUALITIES AS a tough-tackling left-back instantly won him the approval of the Upton Park crowd despite replacing their former hero, Julian Dicks. Black Country lad "Bugsy" arrived from Liverpool in September 1993, along with Mike Marsh, in the £2.5 million swap deal that took Dicks to Anfield. He made his debut in the 2-0 win at Blackburn Rovers on September 18 and netted his first goal in the live televised match against Manchester City on November 1. Although hampered by a knee injury during his first season, David settled in quickly and also showed his versatility by covering in the centre of defence when required. A good dead-ball kicker with a ferocious shot – just like the man he replaced. His pro career began at his local club, West Bromwich Albion, in November 1986 where he played 46 League games before his £550,000 move to Liverpool in October 1988. Capped at Under-21 and B levels, and a member of previous full England squads, David enjoyed five successful seasons with the Reds. Played 192 matches and collected medals for the First Division championship (1990) and FA Cup (1992), as well as the Charity Shield (1989 and 1990). But after only a year at West Ham Harry Redknapp's need to sign a new striker saw Burrows return to Merseyside when swapped for Everton's Tony Cottee in September 1994. He moved to Coventry for £1.1 million in March 1995 and stayed for five years and 129 games. After that, a free transfer in July 2000 took him to Birmingham City in Division One, and another fee-less move to Sheffield Wednesday followed in March 2002. He couldn't prevent the Yorkshiremen falling into Division Two in 2002/03, however, and was not retained at Hillsborough at the end of the campaign.

BURTON, Frank 1912-21

Born: Luapanso, Mexico, 1891
League apps: 64 (2 goals)
Cup apps: 5

FRANK WAS A long-legged full-back whose loping gait and extraordinary on-field contortions earned him the nickname "Bronco" because of his supposed likeness to a cowboy's horse! Despite this unorthodox

Jack Burkett

approach, he was popular with the fans and formed a fine partnership with Jim Rothwell and later Billy Cope. He served with the Royal Fusiliers in World War I and was hospitalised at Whitchurch in 1916, suffering from shrapnel wounds. He still managed to turn out in 36 war-time matches for the Hammers and was a regular member of the team in the club's first two League seasons. He was succeeded by Jack Hebden after making the journey across the Thames to join Charlton Athletic in 1921, from where he joined Grays in 1925 to become player-coach.

BURTON, John H 1908-09

Born: Normanby, Yorkshire, 31.7.1885
SL apps: 15 (3 goals)

THANKS TO THE help of the subject's granddaughter, Helen Burton of Hanley Swan, Worcestershire, we have been able to rectify several errors in the player's entry in the 1994 Centenary Edition of the *Who's Who Of West Ham United* when his career details were mixed up with another John Henry Burton who played for Derby, Spurs and Preston at the same time our "Jack" Burton was plying his trade elsewhere. His details have also been confused with the previous entry here – Frank "Bronco" Burton, so let's put the record straight: Jack began his career in earnest with Grangetown Athletic in the north east of England circa 1904/05 when he was the club's top scorer and spotted by First Division giants Blackburn Rovers playing in an Amateur Cup tie. He duly joined Rovers but played just four times in three seasons between 1905 and 1908 when he moved south to join Hammers. He made his debut at home to Queen's Park Rangers in the season's opening fixture and four days later opened his account against Brighton from his favourite position of inside-left. This was his only season at West Ham United during which he appeared in four FA Cup ties – against QPR, Leeds City (twice, including a replay) and Newcastle United – and the same number in the Western League in which he hit three goals. Jack also appeared in London League and London Senior Cup games on at least two occasions and scored a further three times. At the end of 1908/09 Jack was awarded a medal for West Ham winning the Premier Division London Football League. In September 1909 he joined Second Division Birmingham and kept up his high goals per games ratio with three in only four League appearances, but the Blues were relegated at the season's end and he moved to Nelson FC, followed by Cardiff City for 1911/12 when

John H Burton

he was a leading goalscorer and captain as they won the Welsh Cup and were promoted to the First Division of the Southern League. In 1913 he represented the Southern League against the Irish League at Millwall. It is thought that Jack then moved to Southend United for 1913/14 (although there is no mention of him in Peter Mason's excellent club history published in 1993). The last definite record we have of him is making four appearances for Hammers as a wartime guest in the London Combination Principle Tournament in the exalted company of such West Ham luminaries as Syd Puddefoot and Danny Shea. He wasn't upstaged, getting on the score sheet with "Puddy" in the 2-1 win over QPR at Boleyn Castle in September 1915 and with record transfer Shea in the 5-2 win over Clapton Orient at the same venue the following month.

BURTON, Stan   1939

Born: Wombwell, Yorkshire, 3.12.12
League apps: 1

SIGNED FROM WOLVES five days after playing for them in the 1939 FA Cup Final against Portsmouth at Wembley, he became the first player in history to appear in a Final and play for another club before the end of the season. He made his Hammers debut along with Cliff Hubbard against Manchester City at Upton Park in the final match of 1938/39, but that was destined to be his last officially recognised appearance – although he did play a handful of games at the beginning of the following season before League Football was scrapped because of World War II. He began his career with Thurnscoe Victoria, joining Doncaster Rovers in 1932, from where he transferred to Wolves. A dashing winger, he was affectionately nicknamed "Dizzy" by the Wolves crowd. He passed away in Sheffield in 1977.

BUSH, Robert   1902-06

Born: West Ham, London, 1879
SL apps: 20 (1 goal)
Cup apps: 1

DISCOVERED PLAYING SUNDAY morning football for Britannia FC on the pitch adjoining the Boleyn Ground, Robert scored on his Southern League debut for Hammers in a 1-1 draw at Kettering Town on April 28, 1903 from the outside-right position. But he didn't play for the first team for the next two seasons, before reappearing on a more permanent basis in the 1905/06 season at left-half. He played 18 times in the Southern League side that campaign, in addition to an FA Cup tie against Woolwich Arsenal at Plumstead, which was drawn 1-1. A pupil of Abbey Road Board School, he played his first football with West Ham Football Club (no connection to WHUFC) which won the Woodford & District Football League. Transferred to Chelsea in the close season of 1906.

BUTCHART, J   1903-04

Born: birthplace unknown, 1882
SL apps: 3

A SCOTSMAN WHO joined Hammers from Greenock Morton. Although listed in the club's 1903/04 handbook as a centre-forward, J Butchart made his three appearances in the Irons Southern League side in the inside-right position. He figured in two consecutive Memorial Ground victories against Kettering Town (4-1) and Queens Park Rangers (1-0), followed by a 2-0 reverse at Plymouth Argyle.

BUTCHER, George   1910-20

Born: St Albans, Buckinghamshire, 5.10.1890
SL apps: 62 (9 goals)
Cup apps: 9 (3 goals)
League apps: 34 (8 goals)
Cup apps: 4 (2 goals)

A FAMOUS NAME from the old Southern League days, George was signed from St Albans City and scored on his debut at Watford on March 2, 1910. He went on to make over 70 senior appearances up to the outbreak of World War I. Adding another handful of appearances during the conflict, he notched up 33 Second Division outings during Hammers' initial Football League season of 1919/20, but played only once in the following campaign. His weight of 11 stone and height of five foot eight inches was just right for a nippy inside-forward, and also stood him in good stead when he became amateur lightweight boxing champion of Hertfordshire. George left the club in January 1921 for Luton Town, and had five years with the Hatters before retiring to take over the family business of building Artesian wells. He died on January 11, 1970 at the age of 79.

BUTLER, Peter   1992-94

Born: Halifax, West Yorkshire, 27.8.66
League apps: 65 (3 goals)
Cup apps: 7

A TENACIOUS YORKSHIREMAN who brought steel and grit to Hammers' 1992/93 promotion campaign, Peter completed a long journey through all four divisions when he made his Premiership bow in August 1993. This industrious midfielder proved a bargain £175,000 signing from Southend United where "Butts" had established his reputation. In four seasons at Roots Hall, the diminutive midfielder featured prominently in two consecutive promotion-winning successes, making 142 League appearances. After beginning his career with Huddersfield Town in 1984, he played on loan with Cambridge United at the start of 1986, then moved on free transfers to Bury at the start of 1986/87, and Cambridge United in December 1986. He played 55 League matches for them in two years before joining Southend in February 1988. His first game in claret and blue was in Frank Yallop's testimonial at Ipswich Town on August 9, 1992 and his First Division debut came a week later at Barnsley. Unfortunately, Butler was plagued by recurring knee problems in his second season and an operation caused him to miss the last month of the Premiership term. But not before he'd impressed at Upton Park on December 11, 1993, in a Man of the Match display against Coventry City. Butler moved to Notts County in October 1994 for £350,000, had a short loan spell at Grimsby Town in 1995/96, then joined West Bromwich Albion for a £175,000 fee in March 1996. At the Hawthorns he won back his form and became a regular under Alan Buckley and later Ray Harford. After 66 League and Cup appearances for the Baggies, the player returned home to Halifax to join his home town club in Division Three (63 League apps, one goal) before becoming manager there.

BYRNE, Johnny   1962-67

Born: West Horsley, Surrey, 13.5.39
League apps: 156 (79 goals)
Cup apps: 34 (28 goals)

ONE OF THE most revered of all Hammers' big-money signings, Byrne was an inside-forward blessed with great skills, a fine shot and an impressive strike ratio. His transfer from Crystal Palace in March 1962 for £58,000 (plus Ron Brett, valued at £7,000) broke the existing record between English clubs. (The man who first brought Byrne to the attention of the then Palace manager Cyril Spiers was himself a pre-war player with both clubs – goalkeeper Vincent Blore.) Byrne made his debut for Palace against Swindon Town while still on National Service and played in the same Army XI as Alan Hodgkinson (Sheffield United), Bill Foulkes (Manchester United) and the great Duncan Edwards. Already a full England international when he arrived at Upton Park as one of the few Third Division players to win a full cap, "Budgie" (nicknamed thus because of his constant chattering on and off the field!) chalked up another 11 appearances for his country while with West Ham. This included a hat-trick in a game against Portugal in 1964, the same year he enjoyed a starring role in and collected a winners' medal at the FA Cup Final. Unfortunately, he was forced to miss the 1965 European Cup Winners' Cup Final due to a knee injury

Johnny Byrne

Byrne, Moore and Greenwood

sustained while playing for his country against Scotland a few weeks earlier. However, he did play in the 1966 League Cup Final defeat by West Bromwich Albion. His last League appearance (in the number 9 shirt) came against Sunderland at Upton Park on February 11, 1967 when he and Geoff Hurst both scored in a 2-2 draw – his third goal in three games. Called the "English Di Stefano" by manager Ron Greenwood, he was sold back to Palace in 1967 for a staggering £45,000, giving Hammers five years' distinguished service for a total cash outlay of only £13,000! He left Selhurst Park for Fulham a little over a year later for a vastly deflated fee of £18,000, and spent only a year with the Cottagers before being given a free transfer. He then emigrated to South Africa where he became manager of Durban City and later Greek side Hellenic, where he was voted Coach of the Year in 1993 and won a free trip back to the UK to see the Arsenal vs Sheffield Wednesday FA Cup Final! He was back in the country again in March 1994 to pay tribute to his former West Ham and England skipper and great friend Bobby Moore at the memorial match against an FA Premier League side in his honour. All too soon we were mourning the passing of Budgie as well, following the news that he'd died of a heart attack at his home in Cape Town on October 27, 1999. Such was his legendary status the club ordered a minute's silence prior to the UEFA Cup tie versus Steaua Bucharest (both for Budgie and team-mate Dave Bickles) as well as a special service at St Margaret's church, Barking where his old scoring partner, Sir Geoff Hurst gave a eulogy reflecting on his achievements and the qualities that marked his private life. Johnny's ashes are now buried behind the goal by the Bobby Moore stand. The Byrne family were reportedly amazed at the lengths West Ham went to commemorate his passing after he'd been in South Africa for over 30 years but it was well deserved.

England caps: 1963 vs Switzerland; 1964 vs Scotland, Uruguay, Portugal (twice), Republic of Ireland, Brazil, Argentina, Wales; 1965 vs Scotland (10).

BYRNE, Shaun   2000-04

Born: Chesham, Buckinghamshire, 21.1.81
League apps: 2

A REPUBLIC OF Ireland Under-21 international on ten occasions, Byrne was plagued with injuries during his first two seasons but put in some impressive displays and scored some important goals for the reserves towards the end of 2002/03. He made his first team debut as a sub in Hammers' first match of the 21st century on January 3, 2000 against Newcastle United at St James's Park. Also played one game for Bristol Rovers on loan in January 2000 and got on at Goodison in September 2001 in the 5-0 thrashing by Everton. Was on loan at Swansea from January to March 2004 (ten apps).

BYWATER, Stephen   2000-

Born: Manchester, 7.6.81
League apps: 61
Cup apps: 5

A GOALKEEPER SIGNED on a four-year contract from Third Division Rochdale in February 1998 for a £300,000 fee, which could rise to over £1 million depending on progress made. For a player who had yet to break into the first team on a regular basis until 2003/04, this promising youngster has had a wealth of experience at both domestic and international levels. Capped for his country at youth, Under-18 and Under-21 levels, Stephen has played League football for four other clubs on a loan basis, making two appearances for Second Division Wycombe Wanderers (1999/2000), four for Third Division Hull City (1999/2000) and reserve outings for both Wolves and Cardiff City (2001/02). One of the youngest players to appear in all four divisions, having made his Premiership debut in the 5-4 home victory over Bradford City in February 2000. Although he was deemed to be at fault for two of City's goals that day, he showed great resilience when returning to first team duty for the last three games of 1999/2000 and put in sound displays against Sunderland, Arsenal and Leeds United. Only one senior call materialised in 2000/01, however, in the 2-1 win over Bradford City at Valley Parade in February 2001 and his cause was not helped by a persistent wrist injury that cut short his loan spell at Wolves. He recovered in time to be among the record number of West Ham youngsters to be selected for the England Under-21 squad in the company of Jermain Defoe, Michael Carrick, Joe Cole and Glen Johnson. Having made the first-team jersey virtually his own, Stephen was in fine form in 2004/05, but lost his place to Jimmy Walker in the promotion run-in only to regain it in the final moments of the dramatic Play-off Final victory over PNE at Cardiff when he replaced the injured Walker. In early August 2005 Stephen was sent on loan to Coventry until the end of the year.

C

CADWELL, Albert
CALDWELL, Tommy
CALLADINE, John
CAMARA, Aboubacar
"Titi" Sidiki
CAMPBELL, Greg
CAMPBELL, John
CAMPBELL, John
CANNON, Frank
CANTWELL, Noel
CARNELLY, Albert
CAROLE, Sebastien
CARR, Franz
CARR, James
CARR, Tony
CARRICK, Christopher
CARRICK, Michael
CARROLL, Johnny
CARTER, George
CARTER, Henry
CARTWRIGHT, Johnny
CASEY, Jack
CATER, Ron
CATON, Harold
CHADWICK, Luke
CHALKLEY, Alfred
CHALKLEY, George
CHAPMAN, Eddie
CHAPMAN, Lee
CHARLES, Clive
CHARLES, Gary
CHARLES, John
CHARLTON, William
CHISWICK, Peter
CHURCH, William
CISSE, Edouard
CLARK, Alexander
"Sandy"

CLARKE, David
CLARKE, Simon
COCKROFT, Joe
COKER, Ade
COLE, Joe
COHEN, Chris
COLEMAN, Keith
COLLINS, Jimmy
CONNOLLY, David
CONWAY, Herman
CONWELL, Larry
COOPER, Fred
COPE, Billy
CORBETT, David
CORBETT, Fred
CORBETT, Norman
COSHALL, John
COSTELLO, Frank
COTTEE, Tony
COTTON, Charles
COURTOIS, Laurent
COWELL, Herbert
COWIE, George
COWPER, Peter
COX, Chas William
COYNE, Chris
CRAIG, Charles
CRAWFORD, Ian
CRIPPS, Harry
CROSS, David
CROSS, Roger
CROSSLEY, Charlie
CROWTHER, George
CUMMING, James
CURBISHLEY Alan
CURTIS, Frank
CUSHLEY, John

Tony Cottee

CADWELL, Albert — 1923-33

Born: Edmonton, London, 1.11.1900
League apps: 272 (1 goal)
Cup apps: 25

AN UNSUNG HERO who served West Ham United consistently well for ten seasons. Signed from Nunhead during Hammers' initial season in the First Division, Albert eventually took the place of that other great West Ham left-half, Jack Tresadern. Although small in stature, his superb ball control, allied to his tenacious tackling and work-rate, won him a fine reputation. Representative honours, however, were few and far between, although he did play for the Football League against the Irish League in 1930 and was honoured by Surrey and London. Quiet and unassuming, Albert was a keen motorist in his off-field moments. He died July 13, 1944 aged only 43.

CALDWELL, Tommy — 1909-12

Born: birthplace unknown, 1886
SL apps: 84 (12 goals)
Cup apps: 12 (2 goals)

A SPEEDY LEFT-WINGER signed from Southend United, having previously been with Clapton Orient, in time for Hammers' opening fixture of 1909/10 against Exeter City at Upton Park. Caldwell then proceeded to make 32 consecutive Southern League appearances before injury forced him out. His finest achievement during that run of success was a hat-trick in a 5-0 win over Bristol Rovers at the Boleyn, for which he was feted by the fans. Although his goalscoring output fell by half the next season, he was an ever-present throughout and scored a vital goal in a 2-1 FA Cup Third Round win over Manchester United in east London. After scoring his last Southern League goal for the Hammers against Queens Park Rangers on March 2, 1912, he made his final appearance in a 5-1 defeat at Millwall for a somewhat inglorious ending to what had been a successful three years in the claret and blue. Later with New Brompton.

CALLADINE, John — 1921

League apps: 1

THIS RIGHT-WINGER MADE his solitary League appearance in a 0-0 draw in the last game of the 1920/21 season, away to South Shields.

CAMARA, Aboubacar "Titi" Sidiki — 2000

Born: Conakry, Guinea, 17.11.72
League apps: 7
Cup apps: 1

A GUINEA INTERNATIONAL striker who seemed a good buy when signed in December 2000 for £1.7 million from Liverpool, where he'd been pushed out of first team contention by Emile Heskey. Although never a prolific scorer in the French First Division, his nine goals in 33 Premiership games for the Reds in 1999/2000 was largely the reason Hammers decided to take a gamble. But combined with those of Christian Bassila, Gary Charles and Davor Suker, his signature led to manager Harry Redknapp's ultimate demise at West Ham. Titi coming to prominence with St Etienne (1990-95), First moved to Lens, and then Marseille in 1997 for two seasons before leaving for Gerard Houllier's Liverpool in 1999 for a fee of £2.5 million. That move made him the first Guinean to play in the Premiership where he became a Kop favourite due to his direct style and pace, which saw him finish 1999/2000 as the Reds' second highest marksman behind Michael Owen. After West Ham he joined Saudi Arabian club Al Ittihad on loan.

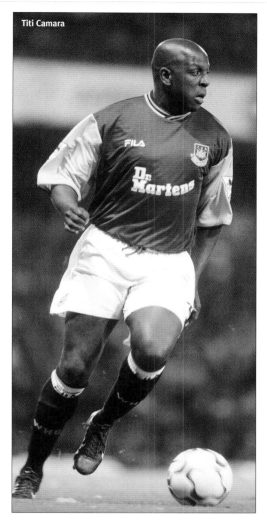

Titi Camara

CAMPBELL, Greg — 1984

Born: Portsmouth, Hampshire, 13.7.65
League apps: 5

A STRIKER SIGNED as an apprentice in July 1981 after trials at Manchester United. The son of former Portsmouth and Liverpool star Bobby Campbell, young Greg's advancement at senior level suffered a big blow when he broke his jaw against Watford in September 1984 after only two appearances at the sharp end of Hammers' attack. Greg went on loan to Brighton in February 1987 where he made two sub appearances before transferring to Plymouth Argyle in November 1988. The following year he gained experience playing for Sparta Rotterdam in Holland, but returned to the UK for 1990/91 to join Northampton Town where he teamed up with ex-Hammer Bobby Barnes and scored seven times in 45 games in that campaign.

CAMPBELL, John — 1902-03

Born: birthplace unknown, 1878
SL apps: 18 (1 goal)

A JINKING SCOTTISH right-winger, Campbell joined Hammers from Scottish League champions Glasgow Rangers, part of the Gers' sale of players to raise funds to help pay for damage following the Ibrox disaster of April 15, 1902. Just five foot five inches tall and weighing only ten stone, he made his debut in the opening game of the 1902/03 season against Reading at the Memorial Grounds. He was tried in all the forward positions – with the exception of centre-forward – and his single goal while in the Hammers' employ came in a 2-1 defeat at Watford on January 24, 1903. He was released at the end of that season.

CAMPBELL, John — 1924-29

Born: South Shields, County Durham, 12.5.1901
League apps: 28 (8 goals)

A SCHOOLBOY GOALKEEPER who turned centre-forward with some success for his local works team, before continuing his career north of the border with Berwick Rangers. Jarrow soon stepped in to bring him back south and it was from the north-easterners that he joined Hammers for the 1923/24 season. Although he was never a first team regular, he was a valued member of the Upton Park playing staff during the 1920s. His finest feat in claret and blue came in a reserve fixture – scoring five goals against Fulham in December 1928 in a 13-2 victory that still stands as a West Ham record in a Football Combination match. John transferred to Clapton Orient in 1929. He died in January 1983 at the age of 81.

CANNON, Frank — 1909-10

Born: Hertfordshire, 8.11.1885
SL apps: 3 (1 goal)

THIS FORMER QUEENS Park Rangers inside-left was never on a losing side during his three-match run in Hammers' Southern League side at centre-forward, and he got on the scoresheet in a 5-0 Upton Park romp over Norwich. He began his career at 15 with Hitchin Town in 1900 and spent seven seasons there before his move to QPR. Cannon had worked as a solicitor's clerk in Hitchin and continued in that capacity after turning pro with Rangers. Described as a "dashing player and good dribbler with a fine shot", he scored a hat-trick against West Ham for QPR in a 4-0 Southern League win in April 1908 at The Park Royal Ground – a performance that prompted Irons to sign him, although he spent part of a season with New Brompton before coming to Upton Park in 1909. Frank assisted Fulham in the early part of World War I, but in February 1916 became one of the many players with West Ham connections to perish in that conflict.

CANTWELL, Noel — 1952-60

Born: Cork, Republic of Ireland, 28.2.32
League apps: 248 (11 goals)
Cup apps: 15

A SWASHBUCKLING, ATTACK-MINDED full-back whose 17 international appearances for the Republic of Ireland while with Hammers bore testimony to his skill. Signed from Cork United in 1952, Noel joined a veritable colony of fellow countrymen at Upton Park. His classic partnership with John Bond formed one of the best full-back pairings ever seen at the club and was a major factor in the promotion-winning team of 1957/58. He made his last League appearances for Hammers at Everton on September 24, 1960 before a transfer to Manchester United for £29,500 (a record at that time for a full-back). Noel, of course, went on to even greater triumphs with United, captaining their 1963 FA Cup-winning side and then in the European Cup Winners' Cup against holders Spurs the following season. He also showed that his skills were not merely confined to the field of play when he took over the chairmanship of the Professional Footballers' Association where he honed the administrative skills that later stood him in good stead with First Division Coventry City and Peterborough United, whom he had two spells with as manager and led into Division Three. He later broadened his horizons with the Boston Tea Men in the North American Soccer League. Noel made a total of 36 appearances for the Republic of Ireland and captained them on many occasions. He was also player-manager of the Republic towards the end of his international career but had to relinquish the post of manager when the dual

responsibilities of the national side and Coventry City proved incompatible. Noel and his wife Maggie ran the New Inn public house at Lincoln Road in Peterborough for over ten years and Malcolm Allison and Bobby Moore were among the many frequent visitors – they even turned out as guest players for the pub's darts team on occasions! Since retired from the trade, Noel became involved with football once again on a national level as part of Sven Goran Eriksson's scouting and match assessment team with fellow ex-Hammers Ken Brown and Dave Sexton. The football world was in mourning in September 2005 following the sad news of Noel's death. West Ham honoured their former captain with an emotive minute's silence before the Premiership clash with Aston Villa (September 12, 2005).
Republic of Ireland caps: 1953 vs Luxembourg; 1955 vs Spain; 1956 vs Holland, Denmark, West Germany; 1957 vs England (twice), Denmark; 1958 vs Austria, Poland (twice); 1959 vs Czechoslovakia (twice), Sweden; 1960 vs Chile, Sweden, Norway (17).

CARNELLY, Albert 1899-1900

SL apps (TIW): 27 (8 goals)
Cup apps: 6 (5 goals)

A MUCH TRAVELLED inside/centre-forward who joined the Irons from Bristol City having previously seen service with Notts County, Loughborough, Nottingham Forest and Leicester Fosse. Albert was a consistent scorer who missed only one Southern League match and one FA Cup tie in his solitary season with the club. He was an instant hit with the Memorial Ground crowd when he scored twice on his home debut against Chatham who succumbed 4-0. He also scored four goals against Grays United in a Thames and Medway Combination match in November 1899. The Irons enjoyed a strong run in the FA Cup that season where Carnelly scored in four of the five rounds played. Moved on to Millwall, then Ilkeston Town in October 1901.

CAROLE, Sebastien 2004

Born: Pontoise, France, 8.9.82
League apps: 1

AN EXTREMELY GIFTED, two-footed player who can operate equally as well at right or left-back or on either flank in central midfield, Sebastien joined Hammers on loan from French first division high-flyers AS Monaco in February 2004 after making over 20 senior appearances and scoring five goals in his three seasons there. He quickly impressed with two stunning goals for West Ham reserves against Chelsea and Nottingham Forest before making his first team bow as a late substitute versus Crewe Alexandra at Upton Park in March 2004. That was his only outing, however, and he was allowed to return to Monaco early to take part in their preparations for the European Cup Final against FC Porto. After a spell at Marseille he signed for Brighton in August 2005.

CARR, Franz 1991

Born: Preston, Lancashire, 24.9.66
League apps: 3

SPEEDY RIGHT-WINGER WHO started just one League game, at Oxford United on March 13, 1991 and came on as sub in two others while on a month's loan from Sheffield United. England Youth and Under-21 international Franz's best days were under Brian Clough at Nottingham Forest, who signed him for £100,000 from Blackburn Rovers. After failing to make it in loan stints at West Ham and Sheffield United, Franz moved to Newcastle United in a £250,000 deal in the summer of 1991. He then joined Leicester City (1994/95), Aston Villa (February 1995) Italian side Reggiana (October 1996), Bolton

NOEL CANTWELL
West Ham United and
Republic of Ireland

Noel Cantwell (left) with Stephanie Moore and Malcolm Allison

Wanderers 12 months later and West Bromwich Albion (February 1998), where he ended his professional career.

CARR, James 1914-15

Born: Maryhill, Glasgow, Scotland, 19.12.1893
League apps: 5 (1 goal)

THIS OUTSIDE-LEFT BEGAN his Football League career at Watford as a 16-year-old and had a spell at Clapton Orient. He made his initial Southern League appearance for West Ham in a 0-0 draw against his former club Watford at Cassio Road on November 28, 1914. He scored on his Boleyn baptism the following week in the 2-0 win over Plymouth Argyle. His last appearance saw him on the opposite flank in the 1-1 draw at Swindon on January 30, 1915. During World War I he guested for Portsmouth and Kilmarnock in between his duties in the army. His career really took off when he formed an exciting partnership with Len Andrews – first at Reading whom he joined in 1919, then again at Southampton from June 1923. He was a valued member of the side that progressed to the FA Cup Semi-finals in 1924/25. After the Saints he joined Swansea Town (May 1926) then took the unprecedented step of placing an advertisement in *Athletic News*, stating that he would "assist a club outside the League in exchange for a business". It worked, because he was soon playing for Southall and running The Red Lion Hotel in the Middlesex town! He died on June 26, 1980.

CARR, Tony

Born: Bow, London, 5.9.50

A PROLIFIC CENTRE-FORWARD who attended St Paul's Way school and was captain of the East London Boys' side that won the English Trophy. He had three years as an apprentice with Hammers and two seasons as a pro, playing in the reserves. He then moved to Barnet in the Southern League for a season before breaking a leg and being out of the game for 18 months. Meanwhile he qualified as a PE instructor and sports master. He returned to West Ham to serve as a part-time coach with the youth squad under John Lyall in 1980 and guided the youth side to their first-ever South East Counties League title in 1985. Tony Cottee, Paul Ince and Alan Dickens are among the youngsters who emerged as stars under Tony's management. Appointed manager of the reserves in 1988, Tony reverted to youth team management duties at the start of 1992/93 and now has considerable responsibility for youth development, through the school of excellence, at Upton Park. In 1996 Tony was responsible (with the help of fellow coaches Peter Brabrook, Dave Bickles and Paul Heffer) for bringing on players such as Frank Lampard, Rio Ferdinand, Joe Cole and Michael Carrick. Now Youth Academy director after nearly 30 years of unbroken service at Upton Park, Tony led the youngsters to the South East Counties title again in 1995/96 and 1997/98 and the Under-19s to FA Premier Academy titles in 1998/99, 1999/2000 (when the Under-17s won their respective League, too) and 2003/04. In 1997 Tony was co-author of a training techniques and tactics book entitled: *Youth Soccer Coaching*, a tome now recognised as an essential work of reference.

CARRICK, Christopher 1904-05

Born: Stockton, Teesside, 8.10.1882
SL apps: 18 (6 goals)

CARRICK'S INCLUSION IN the side at outside-left helped to halt a disastrous nine-match losing run that included a home FA Cup defeat by Brighton. It all came right when Chris scored a timely hat-trick in a 6-2 win over Luton to spark off a revival that saw Hammers find the net 30 times in their last 15 matches, compared with

Sebastien Carole

CARRICK, Michael 1999-2004

Born: Wallsend, Tyne & Wear, 28.7.81
League apps: 139 (6 goals)
Cup apps: 19

A GIFTED MIDFIELDER who at 16 years and 58 days became the youngest player to sign professional forms for West Ham United since Billy Williams in 1921. Similar in pedigree and style to another great home grown utility player, Martin Peters, who was signed at a similarly young age. A Geordie by birth and a Newcastle fan from an early age, Michael was signed in the teeth of fierce competition from Newcastle and Sunderland. He recalls watching the Brazilian striker Francisco Mirandinha and Paul Gascoigne play at St James's Park and later admiring the skills of his hero Peter Beardsley from the Gallowgate End. Initially a striker and a product of Newcastle's Wallsend Boys' Club, he was at Middlesbrough until the age of 13 when he was approached by two West Ham scouts who lived close to his home. He decided soon after to join the famed West Ham Youth Academy and, after signing as an apprentice in July 1997, made rapid progress through the ranks of youth team football. He was handed his first XI debut just two years later in the 1-1 draw with FC Jokerit in the Intertoto Cup in Finland. Two months earlier he'd had his first taste of glory as a member of the Hammers Under-19 team that defeated Coventry City 6-0 in the second leg of the 1999 FA Youth Cup Final at a packed Upton Park to complete a 9-0 aggregate win. In August 1999, he made his Premiership bow when coming on as a sub in the 3-0 victory over Bradford City at Valley Parade and in Hammers first match of the new millennium realised a boyhood dream when making his full debut against Newcastle United at St James's Park in a 2-2 draw televised live on Sky (January 3, 2000). Although disappointed with his own display ("I wanted to score the winner!") it was obvious to both sets of fans and neutral observers alike that they'd witnessed the emergence of an exciting new talent who would soon be receiving international recognition.

It wasn't long in coming as he was called up for the England Under-18s in the company of West Ham team-mates Joe Cole, Stephen Bywater and Izzy Iriekpen for the matches against San Marino at Victoria Road, Dagenham and Cyprus at Brisbane Road when he was presented with the Man of the Match award. He had been loaned out earlier in 1999-2000 to First Division strugglers Swindon Town, to gain first team experience, and had a further loan spell at First Division Birmingham City in February 2000. An ankle injury after just two games for the Blues saw him return early but he recovered in time to make a handful of Premiership outings in April of which the 5-0 win over Coventry at the Boleyn saw him score his first goal. His remarkable season ended on further highs as he helped the Hammers Under-19s win the Youth Academy Play-off Final in a thriller against Arsenal, won the Young Hammer of the Year award and received a call up to the England Under-21 squad for the European Championship challenge in Slovakia. Benefiting from his youth team collaborations with Joe Cole, Carrick's stock began to rise as the pair's linking in Hammers' midfield began to bear fruit in a run to the FA Cup Sixth Round after beating Manchester United at Old Trafford two rounds earlier. Although the season fizzled out and led to the departure of manager Harry Redknapp, Carrick was a revelation on the left side of midfield as his ability to hit accurate passes with both feet over long and short distances and his vision and willingness to tackle back contributed to a series of impressive displays.

His form was noted by a regular visitor to the Boleyn – Sven Goran Eriksson – who called him up for his first ever squad for the friendly against Spain in February 2001 and then awarded him his first full cap as a substitute in the 4-0 win over Mexico in May, and a further sub appearance against Holland in August. Had it not been for groin surgery in February 2002, he would surely have joined colleagues Trevor Sinclair, Joe Cole and David James on the plane to Japan and South Korea for the 2002 World Cup Finals. In November he'd shown his willingness in stepping down a level when his goal gave England's Under-21 side a 1-0 win and 3-2 aggregate triumph against Holland to book a place in the European Championship Finals in Switzerland in May 2002. Cruelly, during a senior European Championship qualifier against Portugal on March 28, 2003, he sustained a further groin injury that kept him out of Irons' last seven Premiership matches before relegation. Now all eyes will be on the popular young "veteran" as he battles to put his injury problems behind him to resume his promising career. In August 2004, he joined former team-mates Jermain Defoe and Freddi Kanoute in a £2.5 million move to White Hart Lane. Up to the end of 2004/05 Michael had made 39 League and Cup appearances for Spurs.

---

only 18 in the first 19 games. In April 1905, he transferred to Southern League rivals Spurs, but it was only around the middle of the 1905/06 season that he was able to command a regular place. However, in March 1906, Spurs played away at Bristol Rovers and Plymouth Argyle and between the two matches Carrick and a team-mate were involved in a misdemeanour that led to the pair being suspended. Carrick never played for Spurs again, transferring to fellow Southern League club Reading. He later served Bradford City and Glentoran in Ireland where a journalist called him "a parcel of strength and muscle. Sturdy little winger who is quick off the mark and has the rare gift of taking chances". He died at Middlesbrough in 1927, aged 44.

CARROLL, Johnny 1948-49

Born: Limerick, Republic of Ireland, 11.5.23
League apps: 5

A CENTRE-FORWARD WHO joined the club at the same time as compatriots Danny McGowan and Fred Kearns. Signed from Limerick, he made only five Second Division appearances in season 1948/49 without getting on the scoresheet.

CARTER, George 1919-27

Born: West Ham, London, 1900
League apps: 136 (1 goal)
Cup apps: 19

AN EAST ENDER born and bred, who first came to notice as a member of the West Ham Boys team that contested the Final of the Schools Shield with Sheffield Boys in 1914. He then progressed to his works team, where he combined his duties as an apprentice engineer with playing under the unlikely banner of Green Silley Weir in the London Munitions League. Before the end of World War I he became one of the early members of the RAF Officer Training Corps, joining Hammers for their initial season of League Football in 1919/20. Equally at home in any of the half-back positions, he proved to be an invaluable deputy for Syd Bishop, George Kay or Jack Tresadern. A keen tennis player in his off-field moments, George was granted a well deserved benefit by the club in 1925 after falling victim to a bad knee injury in a match with Blackburn Rovers at Ewood Park. Despite having a cartilage operation and bravely signing on for the 1927/28 season, the incident effectively ended his first-class football career although he did have a brief spell with Fulham in 1928 and then Grays Thurrock. Hiding his disappointment, George found employment with Tate & Lyle, for whom he also acted as a soccer coach. He went on to organise the West Ham six-a-side tournament and was honorary secretary to the East Ham Memorial Hospital competition.

CARTER, Henry 1912-14

Born: Bristol, Gloucestershire, 1889
SL apps: 10

WHILE NOT BEING particularly big for a goalkeeper – just five foot nine inches – Henry joined West Ham as a 23-year-old from Barrow in 1912 and proved good enough to have never been on the losing side in any of his senior appearances while a Hammer. As this might well constitute a club record we list those match by match: February 7, 1913 Plymouth (h) W 2-0; February 15, Southampton (h) D 1-1; March 24, Brighton (a) D 0-0; March 29, Brentford (h) W 2-1; April 5, Millwall (a) W 3-1; April 12, Bristol Rovers (h) W 3-1; April 19, Swindon (a) D 1-1; April 23, Reading (a) D 1-1; April 26, Portsmouth (h) W 2-1; November 22, Gillingham (h) W 3-1. Despite his record, Carter was not retained at the end of the 1913/14 season. He later became a team-mate of Arthur Winterhalder and Harold Halse in the Wanstead XI of 1904/05.

CARTWRIGHT, Johnny 1959-61

Born: Northampton, Northamptonshire, 5.11.40
League apps: 4
Cup apps: 1

AN INSIDE-FORWARD WHO rose from the juniors and turned pro in November 1957. His first team opportunities were limited, though, by the signing of Phil Woosnam and the emergence of Ron Boyce so he was subsequently transferred to Crystal Palace. Cartwright later played for Bath City and Wimbledon in the Southern League and later managed the England Youth team and gained further coaching experience in Kuwait. He became assistant manager of Arsenal in 1985, but resigned – together with Don Howe – in March 1986. Now youth team manager at Charlton Athletic.

CASEY, Jack 1912-15

Born: Liverpool, Merseyside, date unknown
SL apps: 74 (12 goals)
Cup apps: 9 (1 goal)

JACK WAS SIGNED from Bromley, where he had played a prominent role in the Kent club's run of success between 1908 and 1911 when they won the Spartan League championship, the Isthmian League (twice) and the FA Amateur Cup. He proved an invaluable asset at West Ham too, as the regular outside-left up to World War I. Casey made a further 30 appearances during the conflict, scoring six times, before becoming a schoolmaster in West Ham.

CATER, Ron 1946-49

Born: Fulham, London, 2.2.22
League apps: 63
Cup apps: 7

A UTILITY DEFENDER who joined the groundstaff as a 15-year-old before World War II, and was in the Essex Regiment and Royal Artillery from April 1939. Cater played as an amateur for Leytonstone before joining Hammers and, although born in west London, turned out for East Ham Boys as well as the London side as a youngster and was also a member of the same army team as 16 other West Ham players. He took the same short journey as so many other former Hammers when he left the club to join Leyton Orient, where he made 13 Third Division (South) appearances and one in the FA Cup in 1951/52.

CATON, Harold 1912-15

Born: Berkshire, date unknown
SL apps: 14

AN AMATEUR WITH the Barking Curfew club, Harry made his Hammers debut in a 6-2 defeat at Merthyr Tydfil in January 1913. But the right-winger was given another chance to shine in an altogether more fruitful journey the next month, as a member of the side that won at Plymouth Argyle. A switch to the left flank enabled him to more than double his appearance total in the last peacetime season, although he enjoyed his best campaign during the first wartime season, making 18 outings in the London Combination and Supplementary Tournament, in which he also scored his only goal at senior level.

CHADWICK, Luke 2004-

Born: Cambridge, Cambridgeshire, 18.11.80
League apps: 32 (1 goal)
Cup apps: 4

SADDLED WITH THE unenviable task of understudying David Beckham during almost the whole of his Manchester United career, Chaddie got off to an inauspicious start at Upton Park after being introduced as "Luke Chapman" in manager Alan Pardew's ghosted programme notes! But Pards was only too aware of the credentials of the wide midfielder having taken him on loan at Reading in 2002/03 where he scored on his debut and went on to feature in 15 First Division outings for the Berkshire club and two Cup appearances. Luke had gained considerable experience during an earlier loan spell with Belgian First Division club Royal Antwerp where he scored in successive matches against K Lierse SK and KAA Gent and went on to make eight appearances there. He seemed to have secured a regular subs role when he returned to Old Trafford later in 2000/01 when playing in 16 Premiership matches and scoring twice, but could only manage half that amount in 2001/02. Just one League outing in 2002/03 convinced the England Youth and Under-21 international that his future lay elsewhere and Hammers were more than happy to take him on a free transfer to reinforce their diminished first team squad in August 2004. In March 2005 Luke signed a new two-year contract with Hammers but failed to break into the team that returned to the Premiership. In August 2005 he joined Stoke City on loan.

CHALKLEY, Alfred 1931-37

Born: Plaistow, London, date unknown
League apps: 188 (1 goal)
Cup apps: 14

THE PRODUCT OF a well-known footballing family – both his brothers played the game; George being an early century Hammers centre-half, while Charlie played left-back for Dartford. A goalscoring outside-left in schools soccer, young Alf was capped for England Boys against Scotland at Liverpool in 1917. There was to be a long gap between that early success and his signing for West Ham United in 1931, with army duty in the artillery and his trade as a steel erector taking

up much of the intervening years. After impressing in a trial game, Alf played one League match as an amateur before signing pro forms for 1931/32. By now converted to the full-back position, his solitary goal for Hammers was a remarkable one. It came in a League match against Manchester City at Upton Park on March 2, 1932. In a fixture that also marked the return of Syd Puddefoot after a ten-year absence, Alf kicked the ball from near his own penalty area, and his intended clearance sailed over the head of City goalkeeper Langford for the only goal of the game. Although major honours passed him by, Alf did represent the London Combination on three occasions and was also honoured by the London FA against Diables Rouges of Belgium.

CHALKLEY, George 1908-09

SL apps: 7
Cup apps: 4

A CENTRE-HALF WHO joined West Ham as an amateur from Custom House FC. Chalkley played the first game of his seven-match run in a 1-0 Christmas Day 1908 win over Southampton at Upton Park. His final outing was in a 1-0 reverse at Luton on January 30. He later played for Hastings and Southend United. Not to be confused with FC Chalkley who came to TIW in August 1896 from Park Grove FC and later played for Clapton Orient.

CHAPMAN, Eddie 1937-56

Born: East Ham, London, 3.8.23
League apps: 7 (3 goals)

CHAPMAN JOINED WEST Ham as an amateur in 1936 before signing on the groundstaff in 1937 and played for Romford until signing pro in 1942, eventually becoming one of the longest-serving members on the club payroll. He took up the position of club secretary when he retired from playing in 1956, and added the title of chief executive in 1979. Blooded in wartime soccer by Charlie Paynter when he was only 16, Eddie made one guest appearance for Spurs during World War II but had to wait until 1948 before making his League debut in the Second Division after being de-mobbed by the army (where he served in the Royal Engineers). Chapman once scored five goals in a 7-0 victory over QPR in a Combination fixture just after the war, and was the recipient of the Football League long-service award in 1978. Retired from West Ham in June 1986 after an astonishing 49 years of service, Eddie was awarded a testimonial by the club and he is still a regular visitor to Upton Park. Had it not been for the intervention of Eddie Chapman, you probably wouldn't be reading this book now – in his role as Club Secretary he introduced the author to Public Relations Officer Jack Helliar and set the ball rolling back in 1986. His death in October 2002 severed one of the last remaining links of those with associations with the club before the last war and "Mr Ed", as he was fondly known, probably witnessed more changes, both playing wise and behind the scenes, than anyone connected with the long history of West Ham United FC.

Eddie Chapman challenges Spurs' Ted Ditchburn

CHAPMAN, Lee — 1993-95

Born: Lincoln, Lincolnshire, 5.2.59
League apps: 40 (7 goals)
Cup apps: 10 (4 goals)

WHEN LEEDS UNITED released their veteran striker Chapman at the end of 1992/93, he stepped down a division to join Portsmouth. But "Chappie" soon missed the big-time and within a month of the new season joined West Ham, despite failing to agree terms with the club when they first tried to sign him in the summer! He enjoyed a fairy-tale debut, scoring in a 2-0 victory at Blackburn Rovers on September 18. In his next appearance, his home debut against Chesterfield in the Coca-Cola (League) Cup, Lee scored twice but after that goals were less frequent and fans often grew impatient. In truth, Chapman's strength was as a target man and West Ham's lack of wingers did not help his cause. Nevertheless, his headed goals that carried Hammers through successive FA Cup ties against Notts County and Kidderminster Harriers and into the Quarter-finals must have helped recoup the £250,000 he cost from Pompey. Yet he struggled to win the fans' approval and, as the season neared its end, he was relegated to the subs bench. At 35 his best years were clearly behind him. His career began in 1978 at Stoke City for whom he scored 34 goals in 99 League appearances. After a four-match loan spell at Plymouth Argyle, Lee made what he described in his autobiography, *More Than A Match*, as a "disastrous" move to Arsenal (four goals in 23 games) and hardly enjoyed himself any more at Sunderland in 1982 (three goals in 15 games). His career was revitalised under Howard Wilkinson at Sheffield Wednesday (63 goals in 149 appearances) in 1984 before struggling at French club Niort in 1988. He enjoyed greater success at Nottingham Forest and – in the most successful chapter of his career – back under Wilkinson's wing with Leeds United (scoring 63 times in 137 appearances), winning Second and then First Division Championship medals. After Lee's goalscoring touch deserted him in his last season at West Ham (as he failed to find the net in 11 games in early 1994/95) he continued his wanderings with spells at Southend United (loan), Ipswich Town (£75,000), Leeds again (loan) and finished up with Swansea City in 1995/96 from where he was given a free in March 1996.

CHARLES, Clive — 1972-73

Born: Bow, London, 3.10.51
League apps: 14
Cup apps: 1

A FULL-BACK, AND the younger brother of John, Clive was a competent performer who went on to play and eventually make a big name for himself in the USA. Clive was a product of Newham Boys who joined Hammers' youth section and went on to play four times for England Youth. He signed pro forms in 1968 and made his first team debut against Coventry City at Highfield Road in March 1972. Clive was never able to call a first place his own owing to the claims of Frank Lampard and John McDowell (his fellow pupils at Star Lane and Pretoria schools). The signing of Keith Coleman from Sunderland further limited his prospects and in 1973 he was transferred (initially on loan) to Cardiff, who were coached by Hammers Academy founder member and former West Ham winger Jimmy Andrews. With the Bluebirds fighting relegation to the Third Division, Charles played in the final eight games of the season and helped secure their safety. Andrews duly signed Charles and the new Cardiff manager, Frank O'Farrell – former West Ham half-back and captain in the 1950s – made him the first black player to captain a League side. Clive had had a taste of life across the Atlantic in 1970 when he was loaned out by West Ham to Montreal Olympics in the North American Soccer League and when he received a

bad injury at Cardiff he answered the call of former Bristol Rovers manager Don Megson to join him at Portland Timbers. After serving Portland in the number 3 shirt between 1978 and 1982, and 17 years as a player, Charles embarked on a new career in coaching, starting up by driving around in an old Volvo opening clinics and camps. In 1986, he was appointed as University of Portland soccer director and saw his Portland Academy grow from 20 youngsters to (in 2003) in excess of 400 families. His coaching career eclipsed his achievements as a player and he was appointed manager of the US Under-23 national side and then assistant manager of the US World Cup squad before taking the US men to the Sydney Olympics in 2000 and the women towards the World Championships. Fighting cancer, he later guided his University of Portland Pilots women's team to the NCAA title and was invited to the White House by President Bush in recognition of his team's achievement. Clive finally succumbed to cancer on August 26, 2003 at the age of 51 at his home in Portland, Oregon. In a final mark of respect, Portland Timbers retired his famous number 3 shirt and planned to build a clubhouse to be named The Clive Charles Soccer Complex.

Clive Charles

Gary Charles

CHARLES, Gary — 1999-2000

Born: Canning Town, London, 13.4.70
League apps: 5
Cup apps: 1

AFTER AN INITIAL loan spell, manager Harry Redknapp agonised long and hard over whether to sign this classy right-back/wing-back on a permanent basis from Portuguese giants Benfica. The player's pedigree was never in doubt, but his fitness sadly was. Charles had began his career, in 1987, as an apprentice for the legendary Brian Clough at Nottingham Forest and after a loan spell at Leicester in 1989 he was transferred to Derby for £750,000 following Forest's relegation. After two years he was signed by Premiership side Aston Villa. Three years and over 100 appearances later, Benfica manager Graeme Souness signed him for £1.5 million to take him to the famous Eagles of Benfica. But there he twisted his ankle in training and was out for six weeks. The season was nearly over by the time he was fit and he only made four first team outings while in Lisbon. Then in October 1999, Redknapp agreed to pay £1.2 million for the former east London schools player and hand him a four-year contract. But Gary made just six appearances before accepting medical advice to retire from the game in May 2002 to conclude an episode that cost the club £4.4 million in salary and transfer payments. Charles made his first appearance in a Hammers shirt in a 3-2 League Cup success in November 1999 and his Premiership debut in a 2-1 defeat at Southampton in February 2000 as a sub. He started the following week's 5-4 Upton Park thriller versus Bradford City but was substituted and appeared in only one more League match that season – the 2-1 win at his former club Derby County. His substitute appearance in the first home match of 2000/01 – a 1-0 defeat by another of his previous clubs, Leicester City – proved to be his last for the Hammers. Three games on loan at Birmingham City proved to be his last in the League. A sad postscript in January 2004 saw Gary back in the headlines for all the wrong reasons when he was jailed for four months by Derby magistrates after pleading guilty to dangerous driving and failing to provide a specimen. It resulted in the fallen star pledging to seek help at Tony Adams' Sporting Chance clinic.

CHARLES, John — 1963-70

Born: Canning Town, London, 20.9.44
League apps: 118 (1 goal)
Cup apps: 24 (1 goal)

ONE OF THE first black players to really break through in London soccer, "Charlo" was a good full-back and always strove to live up to one of the most famous names in football. He captained West Ham's Youth Cup-winning side, won England Youth honours and made his League bow in a 1-0 home defeat by Blackburn Rovers on May 4 – all in 1963. John played his Hammers career in the same defence as Bobby Moore and his final appearance was in a 2-2 draw with Leeds United at Upton Park on April 2, 1970. John's solitary League goal came against Manchester United on the day (May 6, 1967) that Best, Charlton, Law and co clinched the First Division title with a 6-1 victory at Upton Park. John was released by West Ham in the summer of 1971, still only 26, when he turned down the chance to join Orient to run a greengrocery market stall. After successfully overcoming psychological problems in later life, in April 2001, John was the unknowing "victim" of a surprise *This Is Your Life* party thrown in his honour and set up by his wife Carol and family. Former team-mates who turned up were Eddie Bovington, Peter Grotier, Mick Beesley, Dennis Burnett, John Cushley, Trevor Hartley, Alan Dickie, John Dryden and the late Derek Woodley in addition to his old pals Boyce, Peters and Dear. It was a turnout that clearly underlined the popularity of one of West Ham's best-loved sons. John had been diagnosed with lung cancer in 2000 and succumbed to it in August 2002, following a courageous fight. Charlo was given a traditional East End send-off by family, friends and former team-mates at his Canning Town birthplace, which included Sir Trevor Brooking, Martin Peters, Brian Dear, Ronnie Boyce, Frank Lampard, Harry Redknapp, Ernie Gregory, Lawrie Leslie and many more who came to pay their respects to a great friend and colleague. John Charles had received a poignant last visit from his brother Clive before he died, making the transatlantic journey from his Oregon home. In a cruel twist Clive died of cancer just over a year later.

CHARLTON, William — 1922

Born: Sunderland, County Durham, 10.10.1900
League apps: 8

THIS DASHING FORMER England Schoolboy international was signed from South Shields on the strength of several impressive displays against Hammers in their formative League seasons. The brother of former Fulham and Carlisle full-back Edward Charlton, Bill made his West Ham debut on the opening day of the 1922/23 season against Bradford City at Upton Park, and played in the first eight matches at outside-right before being superseded by Welsh international Dick Richards. He later played for Newport and Cardiff. Bill died in his home town in the spring of 1981.

CHISWICK, Peter — 1954-56

Born: Dagenham, Essex, 19.9.29
League apps: 19

THIS FINE GOALKEEPER signed pro forms during the summer of 1947 after he had appeared as an amateur with Colchester United as well as Hammers. He had to wait until February 1954, though, before making his League debut at home to Leeds United. He moved on to Gillingham in 1956 and later joined the ever-growing colony of ex-Hammers under Almer Hall at Southern League Margate, before being appointed manager-coach to Barking, where his experience as a PT teacher in the RAF and a fully-qualified FA coach stood him in good stead. Peter died, aged only 32, in August 1962 after being struck down with a throat infection.

CHURCH, William — 1904

SL apps: 2

BILL MADE HIS Southern League debut in a 1-0 defeat at Swindon Town from the outside-left position on March 12, 1904. His only other first team fixture at the Memorial Grounds came seven days later in the 2-0 reverse against London rivals Spurs. A local amateur who played mostly for Leytonstone, but Clapton Orient also made use of his services.

John Charles

William Charlton

Edouard Cisse

CISSE, Edouard — 2002-03

Born: Pau, France, 30.3.78
League apps: 25
Cup: 3

CLASSY MIDFIELDER SIGNED on a year's loan from Paris Saint Germain in 2002. As a French Under-21 international he had been a team-mate of Freddi Kanoute and it was there that he attracted the attention of Glenn Roeder on a cross channel scouting mission in the summer of 2002. A deal was struck with PSG that would have led to a permanent transfer had the player made a sufficient impact. Alas it was not to be as Hammers became embroiled in a fight for survival and Cisse's undoubted skills were sacrificed to the bench and he had to watch players employing more basic battling skills. He reflected: "The football in the Premiership is fast and furious with lots of goals, whereas French football is like the game in Italy – boring." The financial realities of relegation, however, meant that the Frenchman was just one of 16 players either sold or not retained to stave off liquidation and cut the wage bill in the aftermath of losing Premiership status, rejoining PSG in May 2003. Prior to signing for the Paris giants from his home town team Pau in 1997, he had played for French First Division Stade Rennais FC (on loan in 1998/99). In 2003/04 his career took an upturn when he joined Monaco with whom he gained a Champions League runners-up medal as a member of the side that lost to FC Porto in the Final after disposing of Chelsea in the Semi-finals.

CLARK, Alexander "Sandy" — 1982-83

Born: Airdrie, Scotland, 28.10.56
League apps: 26 (7 goals)
Cup apps: 8 (3 goals)

SCOTTISH STRIKER WHO cost £200,000 from Airdrie in 1982. A prolific scorer north of the border, "Sandy" was faced with the daunting prospect of trying to replace popular David Cross in the number 9 shirt. His partnership with Paul Goddard got off to a promising start as he scored five times in a five-match winning spell in September/October 1992, but managed to add just two more to that tally before being replaced by Dave Swindlehurst and the emerging Tony Cottee. His final outing came against Southampton at Upton Park on February 26, 1983. He clearly found the transition from part-time Scottish football to the much more physically demanding First Division difficult to make but he had been named Scottish Footballer of the Year. After West Ham, he returned to Scotland with Glasgow Rangers then Hearts. Sandy also had brief spells with Dunfermline Athletic and Partick Thistle in 1989/90 before finally hanging up his boots. He later became manager at Tynecastle but was sacked when new chairman Chris Robinson took over in June 1994. Sandy took over as boss of Hamilton Academicals for four seasons before being appointed manager of St Johnstone in 1998. Leaving the Perth club in 2002, Sandy now works for the SFA, on whose behalf he trains future coaches through their UEFA and pro licence courses. Ever grateful to Hammers boss John Lyall who inspired him to take up coaching, Sandy also acts as a match summariser for BBC Scotland.

CLARKE, David — 1906-09

League apps: 17

AS THE UNDERSTUDY goalkeeper to George Kitchen, David made his debut in the London derby match against Spurs at the Boleyn on December 29, 1906. Hammers won 4-2 but he was back in the reserves the following week and had to wait until the next season before being given an extended run in the side, after Kitchen was injured at Newcastle, in the last 15 games of the 1907/08 season. Deputising for Kitchen again (on February 27, 1909) Clarke was in goal for a 6-0 drubbing at Northampton in what proved to be his final first team appearance for West Ham. He previously played with Bristol Rovers and Glossop, and moved to Bradford Park Avenue with James Dyer for the start of 1909/10. Later on with Southend United.

CLARKE, Simon   1991-93

Born: Chelmsford, Essex, 23.9.71
League apps: 3

A TALL, LEAN striker who represented Chelmsford Schools before making his mark for Hammers' youth and reserve teams. Simon's first team debut was as a sub for the last minute of the Second Division match at Watford on January 12, 1991. He later played the full second half at Manchester City on April 18, 1992 and the last 18 minutes at Millwall on November 15, 1992 – his final appearance. He joined non-League Kettering Town on loan in December 1992 and was freed by Hammers in May 1993. He then joined Kettering Town permanently before signing for Hendon in 1995 where he went on to become the club's longest serving player with over 400 first team appearances. Joined Dr Martens Premier League side Chelmsford City in June 2002.

Simon Clarke (left)

COCKROFT, Joe   1933-39

Born: Barnsley, Yorkshire, 1911
League apps: 151 (3 goals)
Cup apps: 12

WING-HALF JOE WAS an ever-present in West Ham's Second Division side for four consecutive seasons and probably the finest uncapped player of his generation. At Upton Park he was often involved in a ploy instigated by Charlie Paynter, in which he switched roles during a match with Len Goulden to confuse the opposition; it worked well by all accounts. After seeing service with Yorkshire Paper Mills, Barnsley Old Boys, Ardsley Athletic and Wombwell, Cockroft was signed at the end of 1932/33 on a month's trial from Midland League Gainsborough Trinity. He was pitched into the first XI after playing just four reserve matches when injuries to Albert Cadwell and Joe Musgrave left Hammers short of a left-half. Although Chesterfield won that Good Friday 1933 clash 1-0, Joe held his place in a side that managed to win its next four matches and, in doing so, avoided relegation to the Third Division by one point. He missed only three League matches up to the outbreak of World War II, and played in the 1940 League War Cup win over Blackburn Rovers at Wembley. Direction of labour regulation during the early part of hostilities saw him sent back north to do his bit for the war effort at Edgar Allen's Steelworks, Sheffield. While there he guested for Sheffield Wednesday and joined the Hillsborough club when the war was over. In 1949 he moved to Sheffield United and played in the First Division for the first time at the age of 37 – but only had a year with the Blades before accepting an offer to manage Wisbech Town. After three years with the Cambridgeshire club he retired from the game to run a pub but later became a printer.

J. COCKROFT

Career record

	League		FAC		LC		Europe		Total	
Played	App	Gls	App	Gls	App	Gls	App	Gls	App	Gls
1932-33	6	0	0	0	0	0	0	0	6	0
1933-34	42	0	2	0	0	0	0	0	44	0
1934-35	42	0	2	0	0	0	0	0	44	0
1935-36	42	1	2	0	0	0	0	0	44	1
1936-37	42	1	2	0	0	0	0	0	44	1
1937-38	38	0	1	0	0	0	0	0	39	0
1938-39	39	1	3	0	0	0	0	0	42	1
TOTAL	**251**	**3**	**12**	**0**	**0**	**0**	**0**	**0**	**263**	**3**

COKER, Ade   1971-73

Born: Lagos, Nigeria, 19.5.54
League apps: 10 (3 goals)
Cup apps: 1

A LIVELY STRIKER who was spotted by legendary West Ham talent scout Wally St Pier playing for Henry Compton School and for West London District and London Schoolboys, Ade turned down his local team Fulham to come to Hammers. His first appearance for Hammers caused a sensation. A late replacement for the injured Geoff Hurst against Crystal Palace at Selhurst Park (October 30, 1971), he stunned the opposition with his close-ball skills and sent the fans into raptures by scoring in a 3-0 victory. English winters were not conducive to his style, however, and he never fully recaptured that form. His last outing was as a sub against Leicester City at Upton Park on September 22, 1973. After being loaned to Lincoln City, he played in the North American Soccer League for Boston Minutemen (where he played with former West Ham colleague Alan Wooler), Minnesota Kicks, the San Diego Sockers, and others. Gradually, he became a big name in the USA where he carved out a new life for himself between 1974 and his retirement from the game in 1988. Now working at Home Depot, the largest home improvement company in the US, Ade hopes to return to watch a match at Upton Park when he eventually retires.

COHEN, Chris   2003-

Born: Norwich, Norfolk, 5.3.87
League apps: 18
Cup apps: 3

A STRONG LEFT-SIDED defender, discovered playing schoolboy football by former Under-17 coach and player Peter Brabrook, Chris has been with the club since the age of 12 and has played for England at both Under-16 and Under-17 levels. Cohen earned praise from manager Alan Pardew when he became the youngest player to appear in West Ham's first team since Billy Williams in 1922 – making his debut as a sub 12 minutes from the end of the thrilling 3-2 home win over Sunderland in December 2003. Pardew said: "I really think Chris is going to be a player for the future. He's a terrific talent and I want him in the squad. I feel Chris has a fantastic chance of being a West Ham player for some time. He's got a good mentality, a lot of talent and Tony Carr's been really pleased with his progress." Also able to operate on the left side of midfield.

COLE, Joe
1999-2002

Born: Islington, London, 8.11.81
League apps: 126 (10 goals)
Cup apps: 18 (3 goals)

RARELY CAN THE departure of a home-grown talent from his first club have been accompanied by the kind of furore and the fury that surrounded Joe Cole's move to Chelsea in August 2003. Yet following Hammers' fall from the Premiership and Roman Abramovich's revolution in west London, which had claimed team-mate Glen Johnson for a similar £6 million-plus fee just weeks earlier, the move was an inevitable fact of Nationwide life for Hammers. Cole was a sublimely gifted central midfielder who had been hyped in the media from the age of 12. By 17 he was earning £6,000 a week at West Ham, had a lucrative boot deal with Adidas and his name registered as a trademark by the PFA – all before he had featured in a full first team fixture. Some, though, branded him a "show pony", convinced his bewildering array of tricks and at times mesmerising skills served only to disguise a lack of basics. Although in the fullness of time it might be Glen Johnson's departure the more discerning of Hammers fans regret the most, there is no doubt that Joe Cole will go down as one of the great performers in the history of West Ham. A schoolboy prodigy, his rise to fame was meteoric, especially as he didn't play in an organised game of football until the age of 12 with Sunday side Paddington – at centre-back! But it wasn't until the following year, 1994, that the budding starlet received any proper guidance and direction when he joined another local north London team, Chapel, who were managed by brothers John and Tony Field, former England Under-18s and the first major influences in his early days. A boarder at Lilleshall's prestigious FA School of Excellence, Joe rose steadily through the ranks from an England Schoolboy international right up to full international recognition when he made his debut in Sven Goran Eriksson's side as a substitute (along with team-mate Michael Carrick) against Mexico at Derby County's Pride Park in May 2001. Before then, he made his West Ham debut in the 1-1 Third Round FA Cup draw with Swansea City in January 1999, but manager Harry Redknapp used his talent sparingly after giving him his first Premiership start against Wimbledon at Selhurst Park later that month and just one more full start and six sub outings in 1998/99. It was a different story the following campaign however, when Redknapp played the then 18-year-old Young Hammer of the Year and FA Youth Cup Final medal winner in 31 League and Cup appearances. But he suffered a broken leg away to Derby County in April 2000 meaning he played no further part in that campaign and missed Euro 2000. He made 36 outings in all competitions in 2000/01 but failed to convince Sven Goran Eriksson to pick him. Before his shock departure, Redknapp also left Cole on the bench illustrating that even he, his greatest admirer, had nagging doubts about the player, not least over his lack of goals. In 2001/02, though, he returned to the England fold, making substitute appearances against Holland, Italy, Paraguay, South Korea, Sweden and a start versus Cameroon. Ironically, the season that saw West Ham relegated also witnessed Joe Cole finally coming of age to win over his detractors as he took on the captain's armband. In fact, so committed was Cole that he and team-mate Rufus Brevett almost played under the threat (not realised) of criminal charges from Greater Manchester police following a fracas in the tunnel after West Ham's Premiership defeat at Bolton Wanderers on April 19, 2003. Instead, the issue dragged on controversially until January 2004 when he served a two-match ban with his new employers Chelsea. Ironically, in his last season at Upton Park Joe seemed to have addressed his poor goal scoring record in the claret and blue and with a stunning 25-yard winner against

Serbia and Montenegro in his tenth and final appearance for his country as a Hammer after coming on as sub at Leicester City's Walker's Stadium in June 2003 to secure a 2-1 win. The West Ham board sold the club's most coveted piece of family silver on August 6, 2003. The Hammer of the Year explained the reasons for his departure: "It was a difficult decision but I feel now is the time to make a break. The club will always be an important part of my career and I still have great affection for the club and fans. More than 18 months ago I was asked by West Ham to sign an extension to my contract. The club had finished seventh in the Premiership, but I felt to further my international career I needed to move onto a club which was playing regularly in Europe. For all my belief in West Ham, I could not see them competing at that level. Now I wish the club and all its great supporters the very best for the future. I hope that they follow my career and appreciate the effort I have given to West Ham." Former captain, director and caretaker manager Trevor Brooking claimed the club had to sell Cole – along with Glen Johnson, Freddi Kanoute

and Trevor Sinclair – to avoid receivership. "Without the sales we would have run out of money halfway through (2003/04)... we wouldn't have been able to pay the wages." Brooking also said Cole decided to leave before the club was relegated and there was no option but to cash in on him. In the press conference held to herald his arrival at Stamford Bridge the player who grew up just minutes from Highbury claimed: "I used to come and watch Dennis Wise and before that Kerry Dixon from the Shed. I settled at West Ham because I felt comfortable there. I had an enjoyable time but my career has come full circle and I'm back at Chelsea. It's such a great club." It was a far cry from May 2001 when he told *Hammers News*: "I want to be loyal to this club and stay here for the rest of my career. I'm not just saying that, I truly mean it, all I want to do is win trophies and medals in a West Ham shirt." But the trophies have come with Chelsea, winning Carling Cup and Premiership winners' medals in 2004/05. Up to the end of the season Joe had made 96 appearances for Chelsea, scoring 19 goals.

Chris Cohen (see page 49)

COLLINS, Jimmy 1924-36

Born: Brentford, Middlesex, 1903
League apps: 311 (3 goals)
Cup apps: 25

AFFECTIONATELY REFERRED TO by the fans as "Lottie" after the famous music-hall artiste, Collins is one of the longest-serving players in the club's history. He first played at the Boleyn Ground in 1917 as captain of East Ham Boys and, the same year, was chosen to represent England against Scotland; but as the game was cancelled, he never received his School's cap. Modelling his game on his idol, Syd Puddefoot, he soon put that disappointment behind him, and after doing the rounds with Chelmsford, Clapton and Leyton, signed amateur forms for Hammers in 1921. Two years later, he was elevated to full professional status, and the following season made his First Division debut against Spurs at Upton Park on February 9, 1924. Owing to the abundance of forward talent at West Ham in those days, his baptism was to be one of his few appearances in the front line, and he converted to wing-half to win a regular place. He made the switch well enough to make 160 consecutive appearances until a cartilage injury ended the run. He was valued highly enough to be one of the few professionals retained after Irons' relegation season of 1931/32; going on to appear in the gallant FA Cup Semi-final defeat to Everton at Molineux the next season. When he finally retired from the game in 1936, he found plenty to occupy his time, following the example of Vic Watson before him by going into the horticulture trade. As well as being a keen motorist – he claimed in 1921 to be the first West Ham player to own a car! – he also trained greyhounds in his spare time, owning kennels along with his brother Ted, who was himself an England amateur international and won Amateur Cup Final medals with both Leyton and Walthamstow Avenue, as well as playing for Hammers as an amateur. The brothers' most famous canine was the aptly-named Golden Hammer, who finished second in the Greyhound Derby. Jim retained his allegiance to West Ham United throughout his life and, with his wife, was a season ticket holder at Upton Park until his death in May 1977, at the age of 74.

Career record

	League		FAC		LC		Europe		Total	
Played	App	Gls	App	Gls	App	Gls	App	Gls	App	Gls
1923-24	5	1	0	0	0	0	0	0	5	1
1924-25	2	0	1	0	0	0	0	0	3	0
1925-26	24	0	1	0	0	0	0	0	25	0
1926-27	42	1	3	0	0	0	0	0	45	1
1927-28	42	0	2	0	0	0	0	0	44	0
1928-29	39	1	5	0	0	0	0	0	44	1
1929-30	21	0	4	0	0	0	0	0	25	0
1930-31	38	0	1	0	0	0	0	0	39	0
1931-32	35	0	2	0	0	0	0	0	37	0
1932-33	33	0	6	0	0	0	0	0	39	0
1933-34	17	0	0	0	0	0	0	0	17	0
1934-35	12	0	0	0	0	0	0	0	12	0
1935-36	1	0	0	0	0	0	0	0	1	0
TOTAL	**311**	**3**	**25**	**0**	**0**	**0**	**0**	**0**	**336**	**3**

COLEMAN, Keith 1973-77

Born: Washington, County Durham, 24.5.51
League apps: 101
Cup apps: 16

A SOLID, COMPETENT full-back signed from Sunderland for £20,000 after a period on loan. Made his League debut against Burnley at Upton Park on October 6, 1973, but had to be content to share the full-back berths with McDowall and Lampard, often deputising when either were injured. Won a European Cup Winners' Cup runners-up medal in 1976, and played his last game in the 1-1 draw at Leeds (April 26, 1977). He then signed for KV Mechelen of the Belgian Second Division and later had a spell at Darlington. After taking his FA Coaching badge in 1980 and coaching at schools in the Forest Gate area, he worked at a sports centre in Brentwood, Essex for several years. Kept in touch with the professional game, until 2003, as a part-time scout for Sheffield Wednesday under their chief scout and former Hammers team-mate Bill Green. Keith has since emigrated to Pafos, Cyprus.

CONNOLLY, David 2003-04

Born: Willesden, London, 6.6.77
PL apps: 42 (10 goals)
Cup apps: 6 (4 goals)

FEW PLAYERS CAN have enjoyed as varied a career and controversial a start to their time as a Hammer than diminutive Republic of Ireland international striker David Connolly. Having signed for Glenn Roeder, and featuring in his pre-season preparations he was promptly left on the bench for the opening game of 2003/04 (at Preston North End) as the manager preferred to play a new loan signing, Liverpool's Neil Mellor, who'd only met with the team the night before the game. Connolly was so aggrieved he considered making an immediate transfer request. As he claimed post-match: "It was a mind boggling, terrible decision, a real kick in the teeth. I was very disappointed with the manager and I told him so." Roeder replied with his now famous riposte: "David Connolly is an angry ant. I gave him his debut as a 16-year-old at Watford. That's what I want – competition." In his short time left at the helm he certainly got that from Connolly, as has his

successor Alan Pardew. A wonderfully mobile player, who played Gaelic football and hurling as a youngster, his game is all about 100 per cent commitment, harrying, tracking back and of course, a hunger for goals. London born to Irish parents, David signed pro forms for Watford in November 1994 and scored eight times in his first 13 First Division games for the Hornets, six after coming off the bench to earn a "super-sub" tag. Altogether he hit 14 goals in 33 League and Cup games during his time at Vicarage Road. He scored three times in 11 minutes for the Republic of Ireland in a 5-0 victory over Liechtenstein in Dublin in May 1997 and that summer he became one of the first players to take advantage of the newly invoked Bosman ruling to join Dutch giants Feyenoord on a free transfer. He scored his first goal in the Netherlands in a 5-1 home hammering of Vitesse Arnhem in September 1997, but with only two goals in ten appearances during his first season in Holland, he spent the entire 1998/99 season on loan to First Division Wolverhampton Wanderers. Returning to Holland he was again put out on loan to second division Excelsior then recalled to Feyenoord for 2000/01 after 29 goals in 32 matches. He returned to England to sign on a free transfer to First

Division Wimbledon in July 2001 and established an impressive partnership with Neil Shipperly, scoring 18 goals in his first season. With the Dons in financial trouble, Roeder swooped to sign him for a bargain £285,000. His move was the first of a mass exodus of Dons stars to Upton Park as he was joined by former team-mates Nigel Reo-Coker, Jobi McAnuff and Adam Nowland when the transfer window opened in January. David was surprisingly sold to Leicester City in 2004 and up to the end of the 2004/05 season had made 49 appearances scoring 13 goals for the Foxes. Joined Wigan in August 2005.

David Connolly

CONWAY, Herman — 1934-38

Born: Gainsborough, Lincolnshire, 11.10.1908
League apps: 121
Cup apps: 5

A SIX FOOT, dependable goalkeeper signed from Burnley, having previously made a name for himself with Midland League side Gainsborough Trinity. He was inspired as a boy by Sam Hardy of Aston Villa, Liverpool and England fame and joined Burnley on the recommendation of another ex-England keeper, Jerry Dawson, who spent 21 years between the sticks for the Clarets. With his safe handling inspiring confidence among his fellow defenders, Herman made 41 League appearances during 1934/35, the end of which saw the Irons just pipped for promotion to Division One by Bolton Wanderers on goal average. He lost his place to Harry Medhurst in December 1938, but was to have one last moment of glory as a member of the Hammers team that won the Football League War Cup at Wembley in 1940. Soon after, he began his wartime service and rose through the ranks to become commandant of a supply camp at Accrington as adjutant-quartermaster during the conflict. When his military commitments permitted he turned out for the losers of that 1940 final, Blackburn Rovers, and was invited to stay on at Ewood Park when the war ended. But he decided to return south to continue his building trade interests. Living at Chadwell Heath, Herman and his wife were regular matchday visitors to Upton Park until his death in April 1983.

CONWELL, Larry — 1935-37

Born: Aberdeen, Scotland, date unknown
League apps: 8 (1 goal)

A SCOTTISH OUTSIDE or inside-forward who had the unusual experience of representing the Irish League against the Football League in Belfast while on Portadown's books in 1935. He crossed the Irish Sea to join Hammers on October 12 of the same year and made his Second Division debut later that month, against Bradford City at the Boleyn. At the end of that campaign he was a member of the West Ham United party that embarked on a close-season tour of Switzerland, but the following season managed only two senior outings before his transfer to Coventry on March 17, 1937.

COOPER, Fred — 1956-57

Born: West Ham, London, 18.11.34
League apps: 4

REGULAR RESERVE TEAM skipper who had progressed through the junior ranks after signing from school (earning honours with West Ham, London and Essex Boys) to the groundstaff. He made his League debut against Fulham at Craven Cottage in August 1956. Fred played in the first schoolboy international ever staged at Wembley, between England and Scotland, conceding a penalty in the opening minutes when he saved a "cert" by catching the ball on the goal-line. (England won 8-2.) He retired from the professional ranks after playing two games in the promotion season of 1957/58 to become the full-time licensee of the Essex Arms, Stratford. Fred died aged just 38 in April 1972.

COPE, Billy — 1914-22

Born: Stoke-on-Trent, Staffordshire, 25.11.1884
League apps: 137
Cup apps: 10

AN EXCEPTIONALLY HARD tackling full-back, many reckoned the Hammers skipper to be a better

exponent of the offside trap than Newcastle United's famous Bill McCracken. Cope's first senior club was Burslem, Port Vale, joining them in 1904/05 and spending three seasons at the Athletic Ground before they resigned from the Football League Second Division. He then moved across the Potteries to join Stoke City for the 1907/08 season, playing 25 times before they also left the League. Bill next moved to Oldham Athletic (then beginning their second season as a League club), but failed to establish himself and signed for West Ham in 1914. Billy had a steadying influence on the West Ham rearguard during their first three seasons of League football following World War I and later continued his career with Wrexham. Known as a "hard man" even in those tougher days, he was regularly sent off. Died at Stoke on February 18, 1937.

CORBETT, David — 1936

Born: Camelon, Falkirk, Scotland, 1.2.10
SL apps: 4

LIKE HIS YOUNGER brother, Norman, Dave was a tough-tackling right-half. He made his debut in a 3-3 draw at Carrow Road against Norwich City (October 10, 1936), but after three further Second Division appearances before Christmas, did not play for West Ham again. He earlier played for Old Plean Amateurs, Linlithgow Rose, Hearts, Camelon Juniors, Ayr United and Dundee United in his native Scotland. After leaving Irons, he saw service at Southport, Dumbarton and St Mirren. He died in 1995.

CORBETT, Fred — 1899-1902

SL apps (TIW): 3
League apps (WHU): 33 (13 goals)
Cup apps: 2 (2 goals)

A LEADING LIGHT in the Irons' first season under the new banner of West Ham United FC in the Southern League, Fred scored the only goal of the game in his initial appearance before the Memorial Ground crowd against Swindon Town on October 6, 1900. He continued to be a source of goals afterwards, his best display coming in a game against Wellingborough Town on September 30, 1901. Hammers won 4-2, with Fred scoring a hat-trick. Described as "strong and determined", he went on to have successful spells with Bristol Rovers, Bristol City and Brentford.

CORBETT, Norman — 1937-50

Born: Camelon, Falkirk, Scotland 23.16.19
League apps: 166 (3 goals)

A LONG-THROW EXPERT and one of three brothers associated with the club. Had it not been for the war it was generally thought that "Norrie" would have emulated his brother Willie (who guested for Hammers during hostilities and won full Scottish international honours). Represented the Football Combination against Belgian opposition and won a Football League War Cup medal – even though he did not appear in the 1940 Final against Blackburn Rovers at Wembley; having already played in enough earlier rounds to qualify for the honour. While a youngster, he had skippered Falkirk when they won the Scottish Schools Trophy, and also played for Scotland Boys and Scotland Juniors (while at Musselburgh). He signed pro for Hearts at the age of 15, then joined Hammers in April 1937. His World War II service as TA volunteer with the Essex Regiment in 1939 ended with the rank of sergeant-major PTI. He appeared as a guest for Southampton during the war, and after 1950 continued playing in the reserves and became an FA coach, later joining Clapton. He died in 1990.

Norman Corbett

COSHALL, John — 1928-29

Born: London, date unknown
League apps: 2

AN ADVENTUROUS FULL-BACK who was signed on pro forms along with his Erith club-mate Arthur Smith after impressing during Hammers' practice matches prior to the 1928/29 campaign. He was destined never to appear in a senior match at Upton Park, however, his first two first team appearances both being away from home in defeats at Bolton (4-1) and Derby (6-0).

COSTELLO, Frank — 1908-09

Born: Birmingham, West Midlands, 1884
League apps: 12 (3 goals)

ALTHOUGH POSSIBLY NOT the most prolific of goalscorers, with a record of three goals in 12 appearances, West Ham never lost a match in which Frank found the net. Indeed, his efforts proved vital to the club in a season (1908/09) which saw Hammers struggle to finish 17th in the Southern League. Normally an inside-left, he played centre-forward against Millwall at Cold Blow Lane. Beginning his football life with Soho

COTTEE, Tony — 1983-88/1994-97

Born: West Ham, London, 11.7.65
League apps: 279 (115 goals)
Cup apps: 56 (30 goals)

THE MOST PROLIFIC West Ham striker since Geoff Hurst, Tony Cottee made Hammers history when he joined Everton in July 1988 for £2.5 million – a British record at the time and the most West Ham had ever received for a player. Tony was short but had an insatiable appetite for goals, catching the eye even in his schooldays for Barking, Havering, East London and Essex before signing apprentice for Hammers on May 11, 1981. He turned pro on August 31 the following year and on New Year's Day, 1983, aged 17, he scored in the 26th minute of his First Division debut against Tottenham at Upton Park – the first of five goals in eight appearances that season. In 1985/86 he established himself in the England Under-21 side and won PFA Young Player of the Year, Fiat Uno Young Player of the Year and Hammer of the Year awards. He was top scorer in four of his five full seasons with tallies of: 15, 17, 20, 22 and 13. His 20-goal haul in 1985/86 was bettered only by strike-partner Frank McAvennie, who hit 26 in a brilliant partnership that propelled West Ham to their best-ever First Division placing – third, behind only Liverpool and Everton. Soon after the start of the following season, he made his full England debut as a second-half sub in Stockholm, Sweden (September 10, 1986). He also appeared as a sub in the next game, against Northern Ireland at Wembley (October 15). His only other England appearance while with West Ham was again as sub, this time against Hungary in Budapest on April 27, 1988. But Tony's frustration at Hammers' failure to build on their success in 1986/87, and his belief that the club's ambitions did not match his own, led to unrest. He withdrew one transfer request but after the team narrowly avoided relegation at the end of 1987/88, Arsenal and Everton led the chase with Cottee choosing the latter. Tony's first season on Merseyside under Colin Harvey brought him three more England caps as sub, before his one full appearance against Scotland at Hampden on May 27, 1989. Although Tony maintained his formidable strike-rate at Everton, he was at times unsettled and found himself battling to prove his worth in a team struggling to recapture the glories of the mid-1980s. At West Ham, however, there was never any doubt about his value as a natural goalscorer; a poacher of half-chances who was lightning in the penalty box. It was these qualities that led Harry Redknapp to re-sign Cottee, in September 1994, in the swap deal that took David Burrows to Goodison Park. TC's return was typically explosive: he was sent off on his second debut, at Liverpool (September 10, 1994) and then scored the winner against Aston Villa on his Upton Park homecoming one week later! In that first season back it was as if he'd never been away as TC reached 100 League goals for West Ham when he hit the winner

in a 2-1 victory at Leicester City on February 4, 1995. But the 1995/96 campaign was less successful as he finished just one goal ahead of defender Julian Dicks with 12 goals in 39 League and Cup games. He signed for Malaysian side Salangor in October 1996 for £750,000, even though their season did not commence until January 1997. The move helped to balance the books at Upton Park and appeared very lucrative for the player – but it did not work out and he returned to England to play for Leicester City under manager Martin O'Neill in August 1997 for £500,000. O'Neill loaned him out to First Division Birmingham City early in 1997/98 but Cottee hit the 200th league goal of his career for Leicester in a 2-0 win at White Hart Lane. Having tasted defeat the previous year as the Foxes lost 1-0 to Spurs at Wembley, Tony was back at the famous old stadium for another League Cup Final in 2000 to win his first major trophy as City defeated Tranmere Rovers 2-1. With Peter Taylor taking over from O'Neill as manager Cottee found himself on the subs bench at the start of 2000/01. He was given a fitting finale when he was called into action at Upton Park for his last appearance in a Leicester shirt as an 81st-minute sub on August 23, 2000. He must have had mixed emotions as he bade farewell to the Premiership on a ground he'd first graced more than two decades earlier with West Ham's youth team. He accepted a free transfer to First Division Norwich City in September before returning to London to take up the position of player-manager at Third Division Barnet. Although he was scoring on a regular basis, the team began to drop down the table and he was replaced by former boss John Still in March 2001. Cottee moved on to Second Division Millwall to complete an amazing

record of appearing for four different clubs in four different divisions in the same season. But just two substitute appearances at the New Den convinced Tony to bring the curtain down on an illustrious career in the summer of 2001. He is now a respected commentator and match summariser for Sky Sports and often filled the role of master of ceremonies in the hospitality lounges on Upton Park match days until he was banned for his involvement in a takeover bid.

Career record

Played	League App	League Gls	FAC App	FAC Gls	LC App	LC Gls	Europe App	Europe Gls	Total App	Total Gls
1982-83	8	5	1	0	0	0	0	0	9	5
1983-84	39	15	4	0	4	4	0	0	47	19
1984-85	41	17	5	4	4	3	0	0	50	24
1985-86	42	20	7	4	3	2	0	0	52	26
1986-87	42	22	5	1	6	5	0	0	53	28
1987-88	40	13	2	2	2	0	0	0	44	15
1994-95	31	13	2	1	3	1	0	0	36	15
1995-96	33	10	3	0	3	2	0	0	39	12
1996-97	3	0	0	0	2	1	0	0	5	1
TOTAL	**279**	**115**	**29**	**12**	**27**	**18**	**0**	**0**	**335**	**145**

Villa, Frank (sometimes also known as Frederick) joined West Bromwich Albion as an amateur in September 1904 before a brief spell with Halesowen prior to signing up with Southampton in May 1907. He made a total of 48 appearances for the Saints, in which he scored 13 goals, before joining Irons in March 1909, as a straight exchange for Jack Foster. He left the Boleyn for Bolton Wanderers in June 1909 and later turned out with Nelson, Merthyr Town and Salisbury City. He returned to Hampshire to settle in the Southampton area but was killed in action in France serving his country at the beginning of World War I.

COTTON, Charles   1903-06

Born: Plymouth, Devon, 1882
SL apps: 18
Cup apps: 1

A GOALKEEPER SIGNED from Reading along with Ernest Watts and Tommy Allison, Charlie began the 1903/04 season as first choice, but lost his place after only eight matches to the more experienced Welsh international, Fred Griffiths. Later an understudy to Matt Kingsley and George Kitchen, he was allowed to seek pastures new in the close season of 1906. After West Ham, he joined Liverpool, but was not long at Anfield, transferring to Southend United on that club's formation in 1906, after a brief return to West Ham. Also played for Sheppey United and Reading before retiring in November 1909. He contracted Bright's disease and died in January 1910.

COURTOIS, Laurent   2001-02

Born: Lyon, France, 11.9.78
League apps: 7
Cup apps: 1

THIS STYLISH LEFT-SIDED midfielder began his career with French first division club Olympique Lyonnais where he was a team-mate of Freddi Kanoute but failed to break into the senior side. A brief loan spell with Ajaccio was followed by a permanent move to Toulouse FC in 1999 and, after a season in the reserves, he made 23 appearances in 2001/02 but couldn't prevent his side being relegated to Division Two. When the club were subsequently found guilty of financial irregularities and further demoted to Division Three, Laurent jumped at the chance of a trial at Hammers (on the recommendation of Kanoute) and duly joined.

Saved from the impending obscurity of the French Third Division, the 22-year-old Courtois debuted on the 2001/02 Premiership's opening day 2-1 defeat against Liverpool at Anfield before starting the 3-0 demolition of Newcastle United a month later. In direct competition to Joe Cole, first team appearances were destined to be few and far between and so he returned to France to join second division FC Istres in January 2003.

COWELL, Herbert   1921

League apps: 1

HERBERT MADE HIS one and only League appearance in the inside-right berth against Rotherham County at Upton Park on April 9, 1921 when a Dick Leafe goal won the spoils for West Ham.

COWIE, George   1982-83

Born: Buckie, Scotland, 6.5.51
League apps: 8
Cup apps: 1

WHEN GEORGE WAS appointed captain of the Scottish Youth XI in 1978, Hammers had the unique distinction of having the skippers of Scotland and England among their apprentice ranks – Paul Allen winning the equivalent honour for the latter. After gaining honours in schools football with North of Scotland, the young defender joined his local side Buckie Rovers from where he signed for West Ham United in July 1977. Made a full pro just over a year later, he had his First Division debut against Ipswich Town at Portman Road on April 13, 1982. Despite proving himself a valuable squad member, George was allowed to transfer to Hearts in 1983, where he was later joined by another former Hammer in striker Sandy Clark. Although hampered by injuries at Tynecastle, Georgie scored twice in 68 games for the Jambos. After a brief loan stint with Greenock Morton in 1986/87 he transferred to Dunfermline Athletic in 1987/88 and made 14 appearances for the Pars. He then returned to Morton and made 24 appearances between 1989-91. He spent a year coaching reserve and youth teams at East End Park before being appointed manager of Highland League club Forres, where he spent six seasons. Once he earned his SFA coaching badge, he emigrated to Australia where he coached Wynnum to Queensland Cup success in his first season. He was then appointed head coach of the Sunshine Coast area. In April 2003, he was national coach of the Solomon Islands.

COWPER, Peter   1924

Born: Tyldesley, Lancashire, 1.9.1902
League apps: 2

RIGHT-WINGER SIGNED FROM Rossendale after spells at Burns Celtic, Parkside Rangers, Atherton, Bolton Wanderers and Wigan Borough. His first XI opportunities at West Ham were limited by the fine form of rival flankmen Tommy Yews and Bill Edwards so he made just two First Division outings – against Bury at Upton Park (October 11, 1924) and Nottingham Forest at the City Ground the following Saturday. He joined Grimsby on leaving Hammers and later played for Lancaster Town, New Brighton, Southampton, Southport, Carlisle United, Wigan Athletic, Altrincham and, finally, Prescot Cables in 1936. Died September 26, 1962.

COX, Chas William   1927-32

Born: West Ham, London, 31.7.1905
League apps: 88

A WING-HALF WHO came as understudy to Albert Cadwell in 1927 from Ilford in the Isthmian League. Bill

Laurent Courtois

made the first team grade fairly quickly (playing 26 times in his first season), but was granted a free transfer at the end of 1931/32 and joined Southend United. Bill died in 1978 aged 73. (Note: Another half-back named Tom Cox signed for Hammers in 1928. There appears to have been some confusion regarding the two Coxes, but there is no record of Tom Cox playing in the first team.)

COYNE, Chris
1999

Born: Brisbane, Australia, 20.12.78
League apps: 1

A CENTRAL DEFENDER signed for £150,000 from Perth SC on New Year's Day 1996 who was subsequently a member of the Hammers youth team that won the South East Counties League and reached the Final of the FA Youth Cup in 1996. Coyne was loaned out to Brentford in August 1998, and later Southend United in March 1999 before being recalled to Upton Park as cover for the injured Rio Ferdinand. But Chris got just one Premiership opportunity at Upton Park when he came off the bench during the 5-1 home defeat to Leeds United (when Hammers had three players sent off) on May 1, 1999. After failing to break into the first team in 1999/2000 he joined Irano Bonetti's Dundee on a free transfer in March 2000. After Chris gained Inter-Toto Cup experience and played over 20 matches for the Dens Park club, the canny Scots sold him for a £50,000 profit to Third Division Luton Town in September 2001. He is a fixture at the heart of the Hatters' defence and was voted Player of the Year in their 2003/04 promotion campaign.

CRAIG, Charles
1899-1902

Born: Dundee, 1863
SL apps (TIW): 17
SL apps (WHU): 53
Cup apps: 7

CHARLIE LEFT HIS hometown club Dundee to join Thames Ironworks and enter the ranks of professionalism in 1899. A member of the last Thames Ironworks side and the first under the West Ham United title at the turn of the century, he tried a number of positions before settling his six-foot-one-inch, 13-stone frame at left-back. One of the last links with the old Ironworks club was severed when Charles joined Nottingham Forest in the Football League. By a strange twist of fate, he passed away on the same day in 1933 as his former full-back partner and Hammers manager, Syd King. Described by a contemporary scribe as being a "genial, good natured giant", Charles was also a keen athlete and won a host of medals for his achievements on the track. He left Forest for Bradford Park Avenue, then moved on to Norwich City in 1908, but returned to Bradford PA at the end of 1908/09. Originally came south to work as a mechanic at Tate Sugar Refinery at Silvertown and then Thames Ironworks.

CRAWFORD, Ian
1961-63

Born: Edinburgh, Scotland, 14.7.34
League apps: 24 (5 goals)
Cup apps: 2 (2 goals)

A SCOTLAND UNDER-23 international winger signed from Hearts for £7,000 in July 1961 after he had won every possible club honour north of the border. At home on either flank, Ian was unlucky not to have been given an extended run in the First Division, and surprisingly transferred to the then Second Division Scunthorpe United. Afterwards joined Peterborough United. He became player-manager of Stamford in the Midland League towards the end of 1969/70 and later had youth coaching posts at Everton and Arsenal. He also managed Norwegian Division One club Hamkan in the early 1980s.

Chris Coyne

CRIPPS, Harry   1957-59

Born: East Dereham, Norfolk, 29.4.41

SIGNED FROM THE groundstaff in 1956. Although he never played for the first team, this colourful character became something of a legend after leaving Hammers for Millwall and deserves a mention. A product of West Ham's youth policy, he was a member of the FA Youth Cup Final side narrowly defeated by Blackburn Rovers in 1959. Managed Barking after ending his League career at Charlton Athletic and later became assistant to Bobby Moore at Southend. He was manager of London side Crown & Manor after leaving Roots Hall and was more recently coach to East Ham United. He worked as a broker for Royal London Assurance before his untimely death in 1992.

CROSS, David   1977-82

Born: Heywood, Lancashire, 8.12.50
League apps: 179 (77 goals)
Cup apps: 44 (20 goals)

SIGNED FROM WEST Bromwich Albion for a then record club fee of £180,000 on December 9, 1977, he made his League debut for Hammers a week later – against his old club! West Ham had tried, unsuccessfully, to sign David when he left Coventry City a year earlier, but he was well worth the wait. Nicknamed "Psycho" by the fans, this tall, lean, though very tough, striker was fearless and won most aerial battles. He was the ideal target man alongside first Bryan Robson and then Paul Goddard, playing a prominent part in the entertaining and successful side that romped to the Second Division championship in 1981. Bearded David's touch improved in his time under John Lyall and no one worked harder in the 1980 FA Cup Final triumph over Arsenal than the uncompromising number 9, who was asked to play as the lone striker on that sweltering afternoon. Formerly with Rochdale, Norwich City and Coventry City before going to The Hawthorns, he proved to be one of West Ham's best-ever buys, scoring regularly in the First and Second Divisions. Although his nine goals in 21 League games failed to keep Hammers

David Cross

Roger Cross

CROSS, Roger   1968-69

Born: East Ham, London, 20.10.48
League apps: 7 (1 goal)
Cup apps: 1

in Division One in May 1978, he notched 18 goals in his first full season, 12 the next and 22 in the title-winning season, in which he also gained European experience and a League Cup Final runners-up medal. When Hammers made it back into the First Division for 1981/82, David top-scored for the second consecutive season with 16 League goals – including the only one in his farewell game against Wolves at Molineux (May 15, 1982). He twice scored four in one game – at Grimsby (April 11, 1981) and at Spurs (September 2, 1981 – Ray Clemence's home debut!). After leaving West Ham, Dave had spells with Manchester City and Oldham and was back with WBA in 1984/85 before joining Bolton Wanderers for the 1985/86 season. He ended his career on loan to Bury at the end of that campaign. On retiring from the game David sold life and pension policies for Allied Dunbar Insurance for nine years, then began working part-time for Oldham Athletic in 1990. After coaching youngsters and scouting for the Latics, he was appointed youth team manager in 1997. He stepped up to become first team manager Iain Dowie's assistant in 2002 and was on duty at Upton Park in November of that year when the Lancastrians defeated Hammers 1-0 in the Worthington Cup. Later a victim of cost-cutting at Boundary Park.

SIGNED TO THE club as an apprentice in July 1964, this underrated striker was the reserve team's top scorer for two consecutive seasons. But Cross was forced to drop into the lower echelons of the League with Brentford to find regular first team soccer. He was at one time taken on loan by Leyton Orient before making the move to Griffin Park for the sum of £12,000. He later went on a merry-go-round of the London clubs, signing with Fulham (£30,000), Brentford again and Millwall (£8,000). He travelled across the pond to play in the United States with Seattle in 1977, and was appointed youth team manager at Millwall in 1979. He was later made a coach at Queen's Park Rangers and Spurs where he became assistant manager to Gerry Francis. Assuming the role of reserve team coach during the summer of 2001 at Upton Park, Roger has successfully survived the tenures of four different managers during his second career with the club! Although West Ham born and bred, Roger made most of his Football League appearances with Brentford and Fulham, scoring 79 goals in 228 Football League and Cup appearances in two spells with the Bees and ten goals in 46 Football League and Cup appearances for the Cottagers. Roger's hobby is breeding dogs and exhibiting them at Crufts.

CROSSLEY, Charlie — 1922-23

Born: Hednesford, Staffordshire, 1892
League apps: 15 (1 goal)
Cup apps: 1

AN EXPERIENCED INSIDE-RIGHT signed from Everton (55 apps, 21 goals). Chas, as he was better known, made his first appearance for Hammers in a 2-1 defeat to Bradford City at Upton Park on the opening day of the eventful 1922/23 season. He was also in at the start of the dramatic FA Cup run that campaign, when he played in the 3-2 First Round victory over Hull City at Boothferry Park. He later left Upton Park to join Swindon Town and from there joined Ebbw Vale as player-manager in September 1925. During World War I he guested for Clapton Orient, Huddersfield Town and Spurs – while on leave from serving as a stoker on a destroyer. When the conflict was over he returned to Sunderland whom he had joined from Walsall in February 1914. Played for the North versus England in an international trial game in February 1920. He began his career with local side Hednesford Town in 1909 before moving to Walsall in 1913. In February 1914, he joined Sunderland, where he provided cover for the great Charlie Buchan. He died in his native Black Country on April 29, 1965.

CROWTHER, George — 1920

Born: Bishop Middleham, County Durham, 1892
League apps: 3

AN INSIDE-LEFT WHO made his Second Division debut in a 1-0 victory over Wolves at Upton Park (September 6, 1920). He made just two more League appearances – at home and away against Fulham. Later played for Hartlepool and Tranmere Rovers. George had earlier served Manchester United (1911), Huddersfield Town (1912), Rotherham Town (1912) and Bradford Park Avenue (1920).

CUMMING, James — 1919-20

Born: Alexandria, Scotland, 1890
League apps: 20

AN OUTSIDE-RIGHT SIGNED from Manchester City who totalled 15 Second Division appearances during Hammers' first League season and a further five the following campaign without getting on the scoresheet. He began his career with Clydebank Juniors.

CURBISHLEY, Alan — 1975-79

Born: Forest Gate, London, 8.11.54
League apps: 85 (5 goals)
Cup apps: 11

A SCHOOLBOY PRODIGY signed as an apprentice in July 1974 who was reluctantly allowed to join Birmingham City for a huge fee in 1979 after a dispute over his role in the side. Curbishley was a stylish midfield play-maker who looked confident on the ball, and made his first team debut against Coventry City at Upton Park (April 19, 1975), aged 21. Alan, though, found himself in the shadow of Trevor Brooking and with another creative midfielder, Alan Devonshire, emerging in the late 1970s, he was squeezed out of the first team too often for his liking. He made his last appearance for Hammers as a sub against Leicester City at Upton Park on March 26, 1979. In addition to

John Cushley

starring at schoolboy level he also won six caps for England Youth and was a member of the Hammers side that reached the FA Youth Cup Final in 1975. Finished his playing career at Charlton Athletic after a spell with Aston Villa and over the past decade Alan has established himself as one of the most resourceful managers in the country – at Charlton, where former Hammers keeper Mervyn Day is his assistant. West Ham's first choice to replace Harry Redknapp, Curbishley decided to stay on the other side of the water and consolidate the Valliants' Premiership status and drive for a place in Europe.

CURTIS, Frank — 1909-11

League apps: 6 (4 goals)

A CENTRE-FORWARD WHO made his debut as deputy to Albert Scales in a 1-0 defeat at New Brompton on April 2, 1909. He scored in both his other two outings that season – a 3-3 draw at Queens Park Rangers and a 2-1 reverse at home to Luton Town. His goals ratio was the same the following campaign thanks to a brace in the 3-0 Boleyn win over QPR on October 1, 1910, in his penultimate Hammers appearance.

CUSHLEY, John — 1967-70

Born: Blantyre, Scotland, 21.1.43
League apps: 38
Cup apps: 8

A CENTRE-HALF SIGNED from Glasgow Celtic for £25,000. This likable Scot (nicknamed "Wilbur") was

Alan Curbishley

given the unenviable task of filling the number 5 shirt vacated by Ken Brown. The Scot made his debut in the opening game of the 1967/68 season, against Sheffield Wednesday. After a run of 27 games alongside Bobby Moore, manager Ron Greenwood replaced him with Alan Stephenson from Crystal Palace and John made only 11 more first team appearances – as cover for injured team-mates. His last game was a 0-0 draw with Ipswich Town at Upton Park on March 14, 1970. He then returned north of the border with Dunfermline Athletic and from there to Dumbarton where he played part-time while beginning a new career as a teacher at Motherwell College. Hanging up his boots in 1976, John remained in teaching until 2003 but stayed involved in the game throughout that time, fulfilling various roles at Dumbarton and Clyde before doing some scouting for West Ham between 1993 and 1995 when he took up a similar post with Celtic. Later, he became involved with the youth set-up at Parkhead before giving up teaching to take up his current post as the club's education and welfare officer in July 2003.

D

DAILLY, Christian
DANI
DARE, Billy
DAVENPORT, Calum
DAVIDSON, William
DAWKINS, Trevor
DAWSON, C
DAWSON, Harold
DAY, Mervyn
DEACON, Richard "Dickie"
DEANE, Brian
DEAR, Brian
DEATH, Stephen
DEFOE, Jermain

DELL, Fred
DENYER, Albert
DENYER, Frank
DEVONSHIRE, Alan
DEVLIN, Ernie
DI CANIO, Paolo
DIAWARA, Kaba
DICK, George
DICK, Johnny
DICKENS, Alan
DICKIE, Alan
DICKS, Julian
DIXON, Robert
DIXON, Tommy

DOLAN, Eamonn
DONALD, Warren
DOW, James
DOWEN, John Stewart
DOWIE, Iain
DOWSEY, John
DUMITRESCU, Ilie
DUNMORE, Dave
DUNN, Richard
DUNN, Thomas
DURRELL, Joe
DWYER, Noel
DYER, James

Paolo Di Canio

DAILLY, Christian   2001-

Born: Dundee, Scotland, 23.10.73
League apps: 126 (3 goals)
Cup apps: 15 (2 goals)

IT'S EASY TO draw parallels between Christian Dailly's career and another Scottish Hammer from an earlier era, Ray Stewart. Both share the distinction of being feisty defenders who began their careers with Dundee United and went on to play for Scotland. Despite being maligned by large sections of the Upton Park support since his £1.75 million transfer from Blackburn Rovers in January 2001, many more think he has been unfairly treated and made the scapegoat for the shortcomings of others. Something of a prodigy at Tannadice, young Christian made his debut for the Terrors at just 16 in 1990/91 and a year later made his bow in the Scottish Under-21s against Romania for the first of his record breaking 34 caps at that level. After making 175 outings and scoring 19 goals for United, he transferred to Premiership Derby County for £1 million in August 1996. He began his time at Pride Park in a defensive midfield role but then switched into the back four after an injury to Igor Stimac. His performances there impressed Scotland manager Craig Brown sufficiently for him to hand him his first full cap versus Wales in May 1997 and a week later he was on the scoresheet in his second full international appearance in a 3-2 victory against Malta in Valetta. One of the few Scotland stars to emerge with any credit from the 1998 World Cup finals in France, his performances persuaded Blackburn Rovers manager Roy Hodgson to part with £5.3 million. (Dailly also starred in Scotland's famous 1-0 victory over England at Wembley in the Euro 2000 Play-off.) Having been a fixture at the centre of Derby's defence where he chipped in with four goals in 78 games, it was assumed he would take over from the departed Colin Hendry to fill a similar role at Ewood Park but instead was given his Rovers debut in midfield and then moved to right-back where he failed to impress. Although he again weighed in with four goals in 82 games for the Lancastrians, Christian fell out of favour with manager Graeme Souness and, after weeks of protracted on-off transfer negotiations, he became Harry Redknapp's last cash buy in a cut-price deal. Initially forming a formidable partnership with Tomas Repka at the heart of Hammers' defence, the pair's performances made a major contribution to the seventh place finish in 2001/02, but then failed to command the same consistency the following campaign as Hammers' all-star side fell out of the Premiership. Despite the downturn of his club form and Nationwide Division One football, his

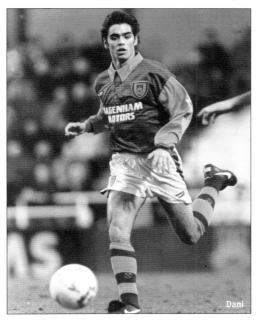
Dani

Christian Dailly

name was still first on Scotland manager Bertie Vogts's team-sheets – indeed, the experienced German had no hesitation in giving him the captain's armband as his caps total rose over the half century mark by April 2004. During 2003/04, Glenn Roeder, Trevor Brooking and Alan Pardew all showed faith in the under-fire Scot's ability by picking him week in, week out in a remarkable show of solidarity. Pardew walked onto the Upton Park pitch to shake his captain's hand after he had been vilified by sections of the crowd during the 2-1 home victory over Gillingham in the aftermath of the humiliating 4-1 defeat at Millwall in March 2004 when the defender was unfortunate to concede an own goal. The 2004/05 season turned into a nightmare for Christian when he was injured after only three Championship matches and didn't return to the first team due to the seriousness of the injury until Hammers' deja-vu meeting with the Tractor Boys in the 2005 Semi-final Play-offs! Christian was then given an even greater boost when he was recalled to the Scotland side by new manager Walter Smith for the World Cup qualifying match against Moldova at Hampden Park in June 2005 when he scored the vital opening goal in a morale boosting 2-0 win.

DANI   1996

Born: Lisbon, Portugal, 2.11.76
League apps: 9 (2 goals)

DANIEL DA CRUZ Carvalho arrived at Upton Park amid a blaze of publicity on a £130,000 loan deal from Sporting Lisbon in early February 1996 and the 19-year-old Portuguese international striker immediately lived up to his high-profile status with a stunning header against Spurs at White Hart Lane to secure a 1-0 win for the Hammers in his first full start in the Premiership. Five days later it was from a pin-point corner from Dani that Julian Dicks headed Hammers' equaliser in a 2-1 victory over Chelsea at Stamford Bridge to cap an exciting week for the youngster with the film-star looks and an array of female fans. Having come to prominence when he scored the two goals that eliminated England from the 1996 European Under-21 championships in the qualifying stages, Dani made his full debut for Portugal in the 1-1 draw with Terry Venables's England side at Wembley in December 1998. Despite his undoubted skills, Dani started just three games for Hammers and played just one match in its entirety. With six of his nine appearances coming from the subs bench, it was almost as if manager Harry Redknapp didn't want to get too dependent on a

player he knew he couldn't afford to sign on as Sporting Lisbon wanted over £2 million for his full transfer. He left Upton Park fans with just one more goal to remember – against Manchester City – when he seemed to have the ball on a piece of string as he strolled through the Mancunian defence to nonchalantly slot home. After his final appearance against Aston Villa at Villa Park, Dani found himself playing against Hammers for Sporting Lisbon at Upton Park in the club's Centenary match barely a week later. Many in the sparse crowd were unaware that Dani had gone back to Portugal until they saw him listed in the Sporting line-up in the match programme! But it was to be his last game for the Lisbon club too, which, suffering severe financial problems, finally found a club willing to match their asking price – Dutch giants Ajax. Surrounded at the Amsterdam Arena by a galaxy of international stars (including Marc Overmars, Patrick Kluivert and Mario Melchiot) big occasion player Dani immediately felt at home and was regarded as one of the few successes of the 1996/97 campaign – scoring four goals in 17 League Championship appearances and three more in four Champions League outings. In 1997/98 Ajax won a domestic League and Cup double to which the now midfielder contributed three goals in 18 League appearances, but come the following season Dani was used mainly as a substitute and he returned home to Portugal to join Lisbon giants Benfica for 2000/01, but moved on loan to Atletico Madrid after just five starts. He made just one start and seven sub appearances there and has since embarked on a new career as a night club promoter, while Atletico still hold his registration.

DARE, Billy   1955-59

Born: Willesden, London, 14.2.27
League apps: 111 (44 goals)
Cup apps: 8 (5 goals)

THIS POPULAR FORWARD made a major contribution to Hammers' Second Division triumph of 1958. Signed from Brentford for £5,000, he made a perfect foil for his more robust scoring partners, Johnny Dick and Vic Keeble. Unfortunately he was in the veteran stage of his career when the club re-entered the First Division, and made only two appearances at the higher level. He later joined Southern League Yiewsley where he came under the managership of Bill Dodgin (Snr) and later the great Jackie Milburn. Bill died in April 1994.

DAVENPORT, Calum   2004

Born: Bedford, Bedfordshire, 1.1.83
League apps: 10

THE THREE-MONTH LOAN of this talented England Under-21 defender from Tottenham Hotspur to West Ham, just weeks after the north Londoners had signed the player for £3 million from Coventry City, is one of the most controversial transfer transactions the club have ever entered into. The move angered the Sky Blues, who were looking to secure first refusal on his services, if Spurs opted to farm him out on loan. Instead, much to City's chagrin, Spurs allowed the 21-year-old to join Coventry's Coca Cola Championship rivals, Hammers. Manager Alan Pardew, desperate to bolster Hammers' defence in the wake of the long-term injury to captain Christian Dailly, played down the controversy saying: "I wanted him before Spurs came in. We had been tracking him for a while, but obviously Spurs were able to sign him. He is a great talent – very composed and great in the air. He will be a big player for us and we have done Spurs a few favours in the past." The following day, Friday September 10, 2004, the Hammers boss rubbed salt into City's wounds when he signed Norwich City's Scottish international centre-back Malky Mackay after his proposed move to Coventry broke down! The two new signings duly made their debuts the next day in the

2-1 defeat of Sheffield United at Bramall Lane. Davenport, whose last appearance for Coventry had been in the 2-1 win over Hammers ten days earlier, looked cool and composed as he helped to fill the gap left by Anton Ferdinand – who'd suffered a leg break scare playing alongside his replacement earlier the same week in England Under-21s' fine 3-1 victory over Poland. A product of the Coventry youth scheme, centre-back Calum was voted Player of the Season at Highfield Road in 2003/04 and had made 77 League and Cup appearances for the Sky Blues up to the start of the 2004/05 season. Calum was recalled by Spurs in November 2004. He started 2004/05 with Southampton.

DAVIDSON, William   1902-03

Born: Beith, Scotland, 1879
SL apps: 9 (2 goals)

A CENTRE-FORWARD PREVIOUSLY with Third Lanark, Glossop, Manchester City and Reading – from where he joined the Irons in 1902 – Davidson was described as "a fearless player but rather erratic". Bill was given just nine first team opportunities to make a name for himself at The Memorial Grounds. After his debut in the 2-1 home defeat by Southampton on Christmas Day 1902, he had to wait until his fourth game to open his account, when he scored in the 3-0 victory over Wellingborough Town (January 10, 1903). He scored again in a 3-2 win against Northampton Town but it proved to be his last for the club. He moved to Luton Town, then on to Fulham for 1903/04.

DAWKINS, Trevor   1964-66

Born: Rochford, Essex, 7.10.45
League apps: 6

GREAT THINGS WERE expected of this highly talented and creative wing-half who his manager and mentor, Ron Greenwood, signed as an apprentice in October 1962. But Dawkins failed to win a regular place in the first team and was transferred to Crystal Palace, where he met up with fellow ex-Hammers Dave Bickles and Eddie Presland. He ended his League career at Brentford.

DAWSON, C   1908-10

Born: Barking, Essex, 1888
League apps: 6

A GOALKEEPER WHO made one third of his appearances for the early century Irons against arch rivals Millwall. The first was one of four outings in 1908/09 in a 3-0 defeat at The Den in Cold Blow Lane, the inhospitable former home of The Lions. The second came the following season, at the same ground, but with happier consequences as he kept a clean sheet in a 0-0 stalemate. His first team chances were, however, impeded by the consistency of regular keeper, George Kitchen.

DAWSON, Harold   1911-13

Born: Bolton, Lancashire, date unknown
SL apps: 22 (3 goals)

AN OUTSIDE-LEFT WHO made his debut against Luton Town at Kenilworth Road (March 16, 1912) in a 2-1 defeat. He had better luck and scored on his Boleyn bow the following week in the 6-2 thrashing of Bristol Rovers, his only goal in ten outings that campaign. He scored again against Exeter City on the opening day of 1912/13 as Hammers romped home 4-0. His final goal for Hammers made it a hat-trick

DAY, Mervyn   1973-79

Born: Chelmsford, Essex, 26.6.55
League apps: 194
Cup apps: 39

SUCH WAS THE impact this brilliant England Youth international goalkeeper, signed as an apprentice in July 1971, made on breaking into the first team that he prompted the normally reticent Ron Greenwood to declare: "This is the West Ham goalkeeper for the next ten years." Alas, Mervyn never quite lived up to that expectation and his departure from Upton Park was not helped by media exposure, which seemed to blow up any little mistake out of all proportion. He made his first team debut, aged 18, as Bobby Ferguson's replacement in a 3-3 draw with Ipswich Town on a rainy east London night (August 27, 1973). But during a period in the club's history when survival in the First Division was no mean achievement in itself, Mervyn was pleased to win an FA Cup medal in the 2-0 victory over Fulham at Wembley in 1975. More seasons of struggle followed as Day shared the number 1 shirt with Ferguson in 1977/78 and 1978/79, before their respective Hammers' careers were ended by the arrival, in February 1979, of Phil Parkes from QPR. Mervyn's final appearance at Upton Park resulted in another 3-3 draw (against Sunderland on February 10,1979). He rebuilt his shattered confidence at Leyton Orient, who paid £100,000 for him in the summer of 1979 and even made him club captain in 1982. Day was chosen as the England B sub goalkeeper against New Zealand at Leyton in October 1979 and also won four England Under-23 caps. In 1985 he signed for Second Division Leeds United (after a spell in the First Division with Aston Villa). A European Cup Winners' Cup runner-up with West Ham in 1976, he was also the recipient of the PFA Young Player of the Year award in 1975. After a career of over 700 League and Cup matches, Mervyn became player-coach at Carlisle United and is currently assistant to Charlton Athletic manager Alan Curbishley, his former West Ham team-mate in the 1970s.

against West Country opposition when Plymouth Argyle were defeated 3-1 at Upton Park. Harold signed from Croydon Common during 1911/12 and returned there in the summer of 1913.

DEACON, Richard "Dickie"   1932-33

Born: Glasgow, Scotland, 26.6.11
League apps: 3

SIGNED FROM WOLVERHAMPTON Wanderers where he had made a fine left-wing partnership with Barraclough, Dickie played his first game for Hammers at Upton Park against Bradford City at inside-left on August 29, 1932. He was later tried at inside-right and centre-forward to complete a trio of first team appearances before moving to Chelsea. He failed to make a single League appearance at Stamford Bridge, but had spells with Glentoran, Northampton Town and Lincoln City, where he made 113 Third Division North appearances between 1936 and 1939.

DEANE, Brian   2003-04

Born: Leeds, Yorkshire, 7.2.68
League apps: 29 (6 goals)
Cup apps: 3 (1 goal)

Brian Deane

A VASTLY EXPERIENCED, much travelled striker whose arrival on a free transfer from Leicester City in November 2003 gave Alan Pardew's men some much needed cover in the goalscoring department as his team battled through to the Division One Play-offs. "Deano" experienced mixed emotions on his debut versus West Bromwich Albion at Upton Park when he scored twice to contribute towards a 3-0 lead against the Baggies but scored a third in his own net that sparked an amazing comeback that saw Hammers lose 4-3! But to many Upton Park patrons it was the big striker's passing that most impressed – slide-rule accuracy straight to feet. Brian played exclusively for Yorkshire clubs for the first 13 years of his senior career: Doncaster Rovers, Sheffield United (with whom he won three senior and three England B caps) and, after a phenomenal 105 goals in 239 League and Cup appearances in four seasons, Leeds United to whom he was signed by Howard Wilkinson for £2.9 million in September 1993. After four seasons at Elland Road, he returned to Sheffield United for £1.5 million in September 1997, moving for £1 million to Benfica in January 1998 and Middlesbrough for £3 million in October 1998. After three seasons with Boro he joined Leicester City for £150,000 in November 2001. Two years later, his goalscoring ability was required at the Boleyn where he was tantalisingly close to a career total of 200 goals – a target still ahead of him when he rejoined Leeds after their relegation in August 2004, but he'd added another six to his total until an injury cut short his season in February 2005. At the end of 2004/05 he was assisting Sunderland's charge back to the Premiership. Joined Perth Glory in October 2005.

DEAR, Brian   1962-69/1970

Born: West Ham, London, 18.9.43
League apps: 69 (33 goals)
Cup apps: 16 (6 goals)

THIS RUMBUSTIOUS STRIKER, who joined the club at the age of 15, is one of the few ex-Hammers who've enjoyed a second spell at Upton Park. A member of the victorious European Cup Winners' Cup side of 1965, Brian holds the national record for the quickest-ever five goals in one match, achieving the feat in an incredible 20-minute spell – either side of half-time – against West Bromwich Albion at Upton Park (April 16, 1965). He also distinguished himself by scoring five times in seven matches while on loan to Brighton & Hove Albion, but decided against a permanent move to the South Coast club. "Stag" transferred to Fulham for £20,000 in 1969, but rejoined his former colleagues after a short spell at Millwall in October 1970, only adding a further four appearances to his previous total before being given a free transfer at the end of that campaign. His last game in claret and blue was in the number 9 shirt at Chelsea (December 19, 1970), shortly before the much-publicised Blackpool nightclub affair – also involving players Moore, Greaves and Best and physio Rob Jenkins – that so concerned manager Ron Greenwood at the time. Brian later played for Woodford Town and, after a succession of jobs as a publican in Essex, he has held the post of catering manager at Southend United for the past ten years.

DEATH, Stephen   1969

Born: Elmswell, Suffolk, 19.9.49
League apps: 1

ALTHOUGH THIS FINE goalkeeper made only one full appearance for West Ham in a 1-1 draw against Manchester City in the final match of the 1968/69 season at Maine Road, he went on to enjoy an outstanding career in the lower divisions with Reading. A product of Suffolk Boys, Steve was one of the smallest goalkeepers in the League at only five foot seven inches and it may have been his lack of height that restricted his progress at the Boleyn. After winning a London Challenge Cup winners' medal against Spurs in 1969, Steve was loaned out to Fourth Division Reading for 1969/70 and his performances for the Royals prompted the Berkshire club to splash out their then record fee of

Brian Dear scoring one of his five goals against WBA

£20,000 to secure his signature. It proved to be the best twenty grand they'd ever spent as Steve went on to achieve legendary status at Elm Park with a remarkable 537 appearances in all competitions between 1969 and 1982. As would befit a professional who shared England schools duties with the great Peter Shilton, Death went on to set a Football League record that still stands today – 11 games and 1,103 minutes without conceding a goal. From the moment he let in a shot from Rochdale's Bobby Hoy in the sixth minute of the Reading versus Dale Fourth Division clash on March 24, 1979, to when he conceded an own goal from his own full-back Stewart Henderson in the 29th minute against Division Three Brentford on August 18, Death remained defiant, setting a record that only Dino Zoff of Inter Milan and Chris Woods of Glasgow Rangers have bettered in the world game. Steve was in two promotion sides with the Royals and an ever-present in the Fourth Division Championship winning team of 1978/79. He was voted Reading's Player of the Year on four occasions and was awarded a deserved testimonial season in 1979/80, when over 7,000 watched his benefit match against a young England XI managed by his former boss at West Ham, Ron Greenwood. Steve sadly died of cancer in November 2003.

DEFOE, Jermain   2001-04

Born: Beckton, London, 7.10.82
League apps: 93 (29 goals)
Cup apps: 12 (12 goals)

JERMAIN DEFOE JOINED West Ham amid a storm of controversy and left in the same circumstances when Hammers accepted £6.7 million and Bobby Zamora from Spurs for him, just before the transfer window closed on February 2, 2004. Poached from London rivals Charlton Athletic in 1999, the Addicks were left resentful over the £400,000 fee they initially received under the terms of the transfer tribunal and a further £1 million in appearance-related fees. Even an extra windfall of £1 million in their cut of the Spurs money failed to ease their bitterness over a player they'd nurtured from a schoolboy. But if the Charlton fans were aggrieved, West Ham's loyal supporters were even more upset as they witnessed their former hero slap in a transfer request before the tears of relegation had dried. Prior to the prodigious star's transfer, West Ham's chairman Terry

Brown had inflamed matters by claiming that the player's "head wasn't right", prompting the 21-year-old to hit back by saying: "I accept I was wrong to hand in the transfer request when I did, but I never withdrew it. I think my transfer request could have been handled differently. It was a mistake, but I would like to thank the West Ham fans who gave me great support since I joined the club as a 17-year-old. I really appreciated that. At the same time his [Brown's] comments were a shock and hurt me." In retrospect, the chairman seemed to have got something right regarding a player whose mind did indeed seem to be somewhere else during his final months at Upton Park and his performances, commitment and disciplinary record left much to be desired as he missed no less than 12 matches due to needless suspensions and bans. Certainly, Defoe's petulant attitude did not endear him to the West Ham fans, leaving the manager with no option but to move him out. Sadly, he became a liability to the side and lost any remaining goodwill from the supporters. But what of the other Jermain Defoe? The Jermain Defoe who was so sought after that West Ham were prepared to sacrifice the proud ethics and principles of the renowned Academy to steal him from Charlton to obtain the signature of a player who drew comparisons with the great Pele at the same stage of his development. Excelling in the Hammers Under-19 team that won the FA Academy Play-offs in 1999/2000, Defoe underlined his obvious potential when he scored the only goal of the game just three minutes after coming off the bench in the Second Round Worthington Cup win at Walsall on his first team debut in September 2000. Rather than risk over-exposing the young player, then manager Glenn Roeder put him out on loan to Second Division Bournemouth for the rest of the season. Scoring on his debut at Stoke, he went on to break a Football League record by scoring in 11 consecutive matches! In 30 League and Cup appearances, Jermain hit 19 goals for the Cherries before returning to Upton Park to make his Premiership bow as a sub in the 2-1 defeat at Middlesbrough in the last game of the season. Just days before the start of the 2001/02 campaign the young east Londoner gave notice of his intentions for the coming season when he scored twice for the England Under-21s against Holland – the first in record-quick time of just three seconds! Having made his Under-21 debut against Mexico the previous season, he went on to gain 19 caps at that level and it seemed only a matter of time before he received full recognition. Despite being used mainly as a substitute in 2001/02, the young hitman finished the season as Hammers' top scorer with 14 goals in all competitions, including a golden strike in the 1-0 Premiership win over Manchester United at Old Trafford. But during the ill-fated 2002/03 season the first doubts began to be raised regarding the player's goalscoring pedigree at the top level as, despite appearing in every senior fixture, he only managed 11 goals. Although it was a total that again enabled him to claim Hammers' top scorer crown, in reality it represented a paltry return for both the player and the club in what was a miserable season. Many wondered if the superstar lifestyle had distracted him as even his great admirer, Sir Alex Ferguson, lost interest in signing him, switching his attentions briefly towards the sublime talents of his ultra-professional team-mate Paolo Di Canio, who had scored the same number of Premiership goals (nine) in far fewer games. To say Defoe's heart wasn't in it for West Ham's reluctant return to the First Division would be a major understatement and, as chairman Brown so perceptively observed, neither was his head. Nevertheless, his move to Spurs still came as a major disappointment to the Upton Park faithful. Indeed, had it not been for some timely strikes by the Spurs new boy, the north Londoner's could have found themselves joining Hammers in the First Division wilderness as they nearly dropped through the relegation trap door to leave a young man from Beckton wondering where it had all gone wrong.

DEVONSHIRE, Alan   1976-90

Born: Park Royal, London, 13.4.56
League apps: 358 (29 goals)
Cup apps: 88 (3 goals)

ARGUABLY WEST HAM'S best-ever buy, Eddie Baily and Charlie Faulkner spotted "Dev" playing for non-League Southall in the Isthmian League, and manager Ron Greenwood signed him in September 1976 for just £5,000. That was after Crystal Palace (where his father, Les, used to play on the left-wing) told Alan he was "too small" at the age of 14. He returned to Selhurst Park two years later but, after a handful of youth games, he was among a number of youngsters released by the manager, former West Ham star Malcolm Allison. Reading, Wimbledon, Southampton and another of his father's old clubs, Brentford, also showed interest, but could not tempt him away from Southall. Their loss was definitely Hammers' gain, as Dev – who starred for Ealing and Middlesex Schools as a kid – emerged from non-League obscurity (and his full-time job as a fork-lift truck driver at the Hoover factory!) to become one of the biggest favourites and most skilful players in the club's history. A down-to-earth character, Dev was a first team star at Upton Park while still travelling to home matches by tube train from his west London home! It was a rather frail-looking Dev, sporting his familiar dark moustache, who made his West Ham debut in a 2-0 League Cup defeat by QPR at Upton Park (October 27, 1976). His League debut came three days later in a 3-0 defeat at West Bromwich Albion. Dev made 28 appearances in his first season, showing plenty of promise on the left side of midfield. Although Hammers just managed to avoid relegation from Division One in May 1977, they could not repeat their escape act a year later. But in the next three seasons, Alan enjoyed an almost telepathic understanding with fellow midfielder Trevor Brooking that formed the cornerstone of West Ham's successful return to the top flight as record-breaking Division Two champions in 1981. A year earlier, Alan had played an outstanding part in Hammers' FA Cup success. In the Semi-final replay at Elland Road, he scored a brilliant individual goal against Everton and it was Alan's cross, following a typical shimmy and surging run to the by-line, that led to Brooking's headed winner against Arsenal in the final. Frank Lampard, at left-back, completed an irresistible left-sided trio that tore opposing defences to shreds, created so many goals and scoring chances and enthralled fans everywhere. A few days after the 1-0 victory over Arsenal, Dev was back at Wembley to gain the first of his eight full England caps in a 1-1 draw with Northern Ireland (May 20, 1980). The 1980/81 season brought him European experience and another Wembley visit – in the League Cup Final against Liverpool. The first match was drawn 1-1 before the Reds came from behind to win the Villa Park replay 2-1. By then, however, Hammers were going flat out for the Second Division title and achieved it, losing only four matches. Dev was unlucky not to be included in Ron Greenwood's squad for the 1982 World Cup Finals but the disappointment he felt then was nothing compared to the heartbreak he suffered in a Third Round FA Cup tie at home to Wigan Athletic (January 7, 1984). Dev snapped three ligaments in his right knee and, apart from making an abortive comeback bid in two FA Cup clashes with Wimbledon in March 1985, it was 19 months before he was fit enough to resume for the first team. The long rehabilitation was a test of mental, as well as physical, strength and Alan passed it with flying colours. Although he lost a yard or two of pace, his return to the top flight heralded some of the most stylish and effective football of his career. As creator and provider, Dev set up a large proportion of the goals scored by Cottee and McAvennie in Hammers' best-ever 1985/86 campaign, during which he made his 300th League appearance against Spurs (March 31, 1986). Dev's first serious injury would have finished lesser men, yet he fought back from another serious blow. The first game of the 1987/88 term was just 15 minutes old when Alan snapped his Achilles tendon and faced another year on the sidelines. It was no happy return either, because Hammers were relegated at the end of 1988/89, with Dev playing in only 20 First Division matches. His appearances were more infrequent under Lou Macari, who picked him to start only two matches and used him as sub on 12 other occasions. Alan certainly won't recall his last game for the club with any relish – the 6-0 Littlewoods (League) Cup Semi-final slaughter at Oldham Athletic (February 14, 1990) that preceded Macari's departure the following weekend. Alan was given a free transfer by Billy Bonds in May 1990, but his Football League career was still not quite finished. He moved on to Second Division Watford, where former West Ham director Jack Petchey had taken over the chairmanship from Elton John. But after playing 24 League games in 1990/91, the classy midfielder was restricted to just one more sub appearance the following season before fading from the Vicarage Road scene. Dev cut his teeth in football management with Osterly in the Middlesex League and, after leading them to two Cup Finals, he was appointed boss of Maidenhead United in the Icis First Division in 1997. Steering the little Kent club to the Ryman League Premier Division, he became the first manager of the club to be voted Manager of the Month in December 2002. As diverse a manager as he was a player, he coached Brentford ladies and helped out training youngsters at local junior schools in west London, commenting: "The development of our youngsters doesn't seem to be at the top of any agenda. I hope things improve one day." Having quit as manager of Maidenhead, Dev hopes to have a stab at League management, but as he says: "It's not what you know but who you know, to get in on this game." A loyal club

Career record

Played	League		FAC		LC		Europe		Total	
	App	Gls	App	Gls	App	Gls	App	Gls	App	Gls
1976-77	28	0	0	0	1	0	0	0	29	0
1977-78	34	3	3	0	1	0	0	0	38	3
1978-79	41	5	1	0	1	0	0	0	43	5
1979-80	34	5	8	1	7	0	0	0	19	6
1980-81	39	6	3	0	9	0	4	0	55	6
1981-82	35	1	1	0	5	0	0	0	41	1
1982-83	39	3	1	0	6	0	0	0	46	3
1983-84	22	1	1	0	4	2	0	0	27	3
1984-85	0	0	2	0	0	0	0	0	2	0
1985-86	38	3	6	0	3	0	0	0	47	3
1986-87	20	2	3	0	4	0	0	0	27	2
1987-88	1	0	0	0	0	0	0	0	1	0
1988-89	20	0	7	0	4	0	0	0	31	0
1989-90	7	0	0	0	3	0	0	0	10	0
TOTAL	358	29	36	1	48	2	4	0	446	32

nothing by manager Syd King, Albert finished third top scorer behind big names Danny Shea and George "Gatling-gun" Hilsdon with a respectable tally of 12 goals in 33 League and Cup appearances in 1912/13. Initially a centre-forward with Hammers, his form plummeted the following season when he played in several forward positions in an effort to rectify the situation. His strike rate was down to five from 17 Southern League showings. East End born and bred, Albert was the better-known of the two Denyer brothers and represented West Ham Boys in the final of the English Schools Shield in May 1907 at Sunderland. The Wearsiders won 2-0 before 25,000 fans. A pupil of Balham St School, he and Frank were the first brothers to appear in the same team for Irons. He moved to Swindon Town in 1914 and had a long career with the Wiltshire club, which extended into the 1920s. Albert holds the distinction of being the first London Schoolboy to be capped for England.

DENYER, Frank   1913-14

League apps: 2

DEFENDER FRANK JOINED his more illustrious brother for Irons' away clashes at Cardiff and Southend at the tail-end of 1913/14. He played at right-back in the 2-0 defeat at Ninian Park on Good Friday and turned out in the right-half position at Roots Hall on Easter Saturday. Like his more famous brother, Frank also began his career with Ilford.

DEVLIN, Ernie   1946-52

Born: Gateshead, Tyne & Wear, 6.3.20
League apps: 70
Cup apps: 2

AFFECTIONATELY NICKNAMED "JOE" by the Upton Park faithful, this full-back was immensely popular with the fans thanks to his never-say-die attitude. Making his League debut with the long-defunct Gateshead in his native north-east, he was transferred to Hammers in 1946, and had to wait a further two years before gaining a regular place in the senior side. A bad knee injury hampered his career and he ended his time at the Boleyn captaining the combination team before moving to Darlington in 1953/54. He died in 1976, aged 56.

servant, only 13 players in Hammers' history have made more League appearances than Alan Devonshire. Not bad for a skinny lad who cost a mere £5,000!

England caps: 1980 vs Northern Ireland, Australia (sub); 1982 vs Holland, Iceland, West Germany; 1983 vs Wales, Greece, Luxembourg (8).

Fred Dell

DELL, Fred   1936-38

Born: Dartford, Kent, 10.12.15
League apps: 4

A TOWERING SIX-FOOTER, signed by Hammers from non-League Dartford in 1935, Fred made his initial Second Division appearance in a 2-0 defeat against Sheffield United at Bramall Lane in September 1936. Making one more first team outing that season and a further two in 1937/38, he was transferred to Doncaster Rovers – where he met up with former Hammers, Albert Walker and Jackie Kirkaldie. Fred died in 1973.

DENYER, Albert   1912-14

SL apps: 46 (16 goals)
Cup apps: 4 (1 goal)

AN AMATEUR SIGNED from Ilford for next-to-

DI CANIO, Paolo   1998-2003

Born: Rome, Italy, 9.7.68
League apps: 118 (47 goals)
Cup apps: 12 (2 goals)

A MANAGER'S DREAM or a manager's nightmare? Di Canio was certainly the former for Harry Redknapp and the latter for his successor, Glenn Roeder. So take your pick: a maestro, a genius, an enigma. All these superlatives and more were attributed to the gifted Italian who could make or take goals in equal measure, but who will go down in the history books as a striker supreme, due to the quality and quantity of his goals. Considered by some as "the world's best trainer" and others as a disruptive influence in the dressing room and on the practice pitch, even neutral observers thought that Redknapp had taken a massive gamble in signing the fiery Roman for £1.7 million from Sheffield Wednesday in January 1999, after he'd served an 11-match ban following his infamous push on referee Paul Alcock. The red tops certainly thought it was a case of a madman signing a lunatic. But Harry's shrewd swoop turned out to be a masterstroke as Di Canio, recognising that "H" had offered him a Premiership lifeline, responded with a showcase of brilliant performances in the second half of the 1998/99 season. Making his debut in a 0-0 draw with Wimbledon at Selhurst Park (January 30, 1999), the born-again striker went on to notch three goals in 13 appearances as Hammers finished a creditable fifth in the Premiership and qualified for a stab at Europe via the much maligned Intertoto Cup. It was against the Dons at Upton Park the following season that the "Roman Emperor" conjured up one of his most famous goals in a West Ham shirt with a stunning "cushion" volley in front of live TV cameras that ended the Goal of the Season contest there and then. In that eventful 1999/2000 season, Di Canio finished top scorer with 17 goals in 44 League and Cup games, and won the Hammer of the Year trophy. But there was still no silverware to show for his sublime talents – a situation that did not go unnoticed by Sir Alex Ferguson at Old Trafford, who'd long been an admirer of the fiery Italian. Criticised for throwing a "sickie" when West Ham faced a journey the wrong side of Watford, he made his detractors eat their words with a coolly taken winner in the Fourth Round of the FA Cup against Manchester United in the Theatre of Dreams as United's keeper Fabien Barthez appealed vainly for offside, and then turned in an impressive display in the next round as Hammers disposed of Sunderland 1-0 at the Stadium of Light! In the Premiership, Paolo turned from sinner to saint in the eyes of the football authorities when, with Everton goalkeeper Paul Gerrard lying injured on the Goodison Park turf he chose to catch the ball rather than take an easy scoring chance. His sportsmanship won praise from FIFA president Sepp Blatter and a Fair Play award. Eleven goals in 37 League and Cup appearances saw him finish second-top scorer behind Freddi Kanoute in what was an eventful 2000/01 season for the self-confessed former football hooligan, but Redknapp, his great ally, was gone. Scoring only nine times in 26 Premiership starts in 2001/02, showman Paolo still mesmerised the Upton Park patrons and opponents alike with his bewildering array of skills, arrogance and talent. Who else would have the audacity to chip a penalty (at Liverpool) and then repeat the riskiest ruse in football again at Leicester? Despite some terrible results, Hammers had somehow managed to finish seventh in the Premiership but on the eve of the fateful 2002/03 season, many wondered how long it would take the temperamental Italian to fall out with the inexperienced new boss Glenn Roeder. After all, he'd actually come to blows with three previous bosses – Giovanni Trapattoni at Juventus, Fabio Capello at AC Milan and Ron Atkinson at Sheffield Wednesday. The answer came in a tense relegation battle at West Bromwich Albion in late February 2003, when number 10 flashed up on the subs

board just once too often for the hot-headed Italian's liking. After an angry exchange, Paolo was never picked by Roeder again, only regaining his place when Trevor Brooking took over as caretaker boss from the stricken Glenn with three matches of the season left to play. Inevitably it was Di Canio who almost saved the day, scoring the crucial goal in a 1-0 Boleyn win over Chelsea in the penultimate fixture and then the equaliser in the 2-2 draw against Birmingham at St Andrews. But it was to no avail; the 1-0 defeat at Bolton remained decisive and Paolo's goal against Brum seemed destined to be the club's last in the Premiership for some time to come. In the close season, team captain Paolo became one of 16 players either released or sold as Hammers held a fire sale following relegation. In September 2003, Paolo was offered another Premiership lifeline by ex-Hammer Alan Curbishley at Charlton Athletic and he duly joined the Addicks

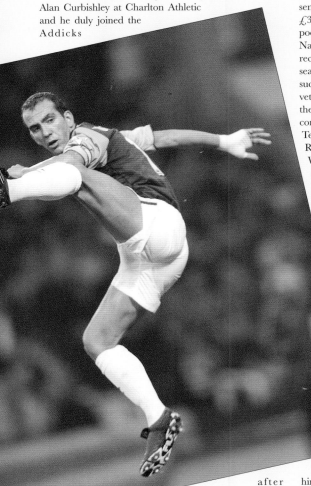

after taking a big pay cut on the £35,000 a week he was earning at Upton Park. Hammers' chiefs had claimed they could not afford to pay his wages in Division One but Paolo hit back saying: "Everyone knows I would have stayed for a lot less. Now look... Trevor Sinclair, Glen Johnson, Joe Cole and Freddi Kanoute have all been sold. The club is falling apart." Even though he'd taken a substantial pay cut to stay in the Premiership, the volatile Italian's wage at the Valley was a thousand times higher that the pittance he'd received when he joined Ternana in Serie C2, Italy's version of the Fourth Division, from Lazio's youth team in 1986. His salary was set, after much negotiating by his father, at 750,000 lire a month, but he didn't receive any pay for seven months as the club's owner went bankrupt. The young Di Canio made 27 League appearances for Ternana in 1986/87 and scored twice, only surviving on cash handouts from his father – who was determined to help his son become a professional footballer. Returning to Lazio, he didn't make his Serie A debut until October 1988 in a 0-0 draw at Cesena and went on to appear 30 times that season,

scoring one goal. Another 24 outings (and three goals) followed in 1989/90, but Paolo had done enough to persuade Juventus to sign him for close to £5 million – not bad money for a kid from the poor Quarticciolo district of Rome! From 1990-93 Di Canio made 73 Serie A appearances (six goals) for Juve and capped his three seasons in Turin with a UEFA Cup winners' medal following a 6-1 aggregate win over Borussia Dortmund. Yet, even in that moment of success, cracks were beginning to appear in his relationship with coach Giovanni Trapattoni, who was increasingly using his Roman recruit as a late second-half substitute. After the pair's bust-up, Di Canio was loaned out to Serie A rivals Napoli and was voted into the Serie A team of the season for his efforts. Perhaps mindful that they'd had to put their Championship celebrations on ice due to Di Canio's sensational winner against them, AC Milan splashed out £3 million in a cash-plus-player deal to take the "party pooper" to the San Siro, despite the fact that 15,000 Napoli fans signed a petition to keep him in Naples. The recipient of a Serie A Championship medal in his second season wearing the famous red and black stripes, the success tasted even sweeter as the now talismanic young veteran was forced to miss almost the whole first half of the 1994/95 season due to illness. Even so, he still contributed 15 appearances (one goal) that campaign. Teaming up again with his former Juve team-mate Roberto Baggio and others of George Weah, Franco Baresi and Marcel Desailly, the following season Paolo made himself at home in their company and scored five times in 22 appearances, even though 18 were as sub, as Milan stormed to their fourth Serie A title in five years. But it all ended in tears after a bout of fisticuffs with coach Fabio Capello and Di Canio soon found himself on a plane to sign for Glasgow giants Celtic for a knockdown £800,000. Paolo's stay at Celtic Park was short but eventful as he scored 15 goals in 32 Scottish Premier League and Cup appearances, became the darling of the Celtic support and was voted Player of the Year by the SPFA. Scoring in the 2-0 Scottish Cup Quarter-final victory over Rangers further endeared him to the fans but a falling out with the then Celtic chairman Angus McCann over a contract dispute saw the Hoops cash in by selling the player to Sheffield Wednesday for £3 million in August 1997. Once again, the temperamental star became a firm fans' favourite at Hillsborough and, after top scoring with 14 goals in 40 League and Cup appearances in his first season in Yorkshire, they showed their appreciation by voting him Player of the Season. The following season he went from cult hero to zero after his fall from grace, making just eight League and Cup appearances before leaving the Owls under a cloud. By May 1999, he'd fallen so low in the Wednesday fans' esteem that the club's London Owls supporters club threatened to sue their former idol for the return of their £85 Player of the Year trophy. Subsequently the Wednesday fans laid the blame for their proud club's fall through the divisions firmly at the doors of Di Canio and his fellow countryman Benny Carbone, accusing them both of a lack of loyalty. Certainly the West Ham fans never doubted his commitment to the cause during his four years at Upton Park. He remains very much a hero, fondly remembered for his schoolboy enthusiasm, his theatrical tantrums and as the inspiration behind a thousand renditions of Guiseppe Verdi's *La Donna e Mobile*, especially adapted in his honour by the Boleyn Ground Choir! Despite signing a new one-year deal at Charlton, Di Canio returned to his first love, Lazio, in August 2004. He was soon in trouble with the authorities for giving what appeared to be a fascist salute in the Rome derby – a gesture that cost him a £7,000 fine.

DIAWARA, Kaba   2000-01

Born: Toulon, France, 16.12.75
League apps: 11

THIS SWARTHY, WELL-BUILT striker scored on his debut for Girondins de Bordeaux in a 2-0 victory at Lille OSC on the last day of the 1995/96 season and hit a further seven goals in 29 French First Division appearances in 1996/97, 23 of which were off the subs bench. The following season his prospects as a top striker seemed to be over as he managed just one goal in an unlucky 13 appearances, but in the following campaign (1998/99) he was a member of the Bordeaux squad that won the French Championship by one point from Olympique Marseille. His contribution of five goals in 17 appearances was enough to persuade Arsene Wenger to splash out £2.5 million to take the French Under-21 international to Highbury. Homesick Kaba had a torrid time in north London, however, failing to score in 15 Premiership and Cup appearances and returned to France to sign for Marseille for £2 million in July 1999 after just five months in England. The hapless target man went another 15 games without scoring at the Velodrome before being sold on at a significant loss to Paris St Germain where he finished the 1999/2000 season on a miserable note with no goals in ten outings. Loaned out to First Division Blackburn Rovers in August 2000, he had little success in his six outings under Graeme Souness – his only goal coming in a Worthington Cup tie against Rochdale. Hammers manager Harry Redknapp stepped in to take over his contract and give the striker another unsuccessful move as the itinerant Frenchman failed to hit the net in 11 outings in the claret and blue. On the plus side, he was only on the losing side twice as a Hammer and featured in five Premiership victories out of six in one spell from October to November 2000. Returning to France, his career took on something of a renaissance when he joined newly promoted OGC Nice in the French Le Championnat and finished 2002/03 as their top scorer with 12 goals in 37 appearances. In December 2004 he moved to capital club Paris St Germain before moving on to play for El Quos in Qatar. He is now with Saudi Arabian side, Al Ittihad with former West Ham team-mate Titi Camara.

DICK, George   1948-49

Born: Torphichen, Scotland, 12.6.21
League apps: 14 (1 goal)
Cup apps: 1

NO RELATION TO his namesake in the next item, George was signed by Charlie Paynter from the then star-studded Blackpool in an attempt to solve a goalscoring problem. A member of the Tangerines' Cup Final side of 1948, he made his first appearance for Hammers against Luton Town at Upton Park in October the same year and went on to make 13 more that season, but the hoped for  goals didn't materialise. He later regained his scoring touch on his travels with Carlisle, Stockport and Workington, and also coached on the continent. George tragically died in a motor accident in Carlisle in 1960.

DICK, Johnny 1953-62

Born: Govan, Scotland, 19.3.30
League apps: 326 (153 goals)
Cup apps: 25 (13 goals)

THIS TALL, RANGY Scot was West Ham's major source of goals for nearly a decade. Indeed, he still holds joint third place in the club's all-time highest scorers' list behind Vic Watson (326), Geoff Hurst (248) and Jimmy Ruffell (166). Four of his 166 total came in the record-breaking 8-0 home win over Rotherham during the promotion year of 1958. John was transferred to Brentford for £17,500 in September 1962, and later returned to the club in the early 1970s to help run the junior side, after ending his playing career at Southern League Gravesend. John pursued full-time employment outside of football with the Inner London Education Authority in company with ex-Hammers Lawrie Leslie, Eddie Presland and Dave Bickles. After retiring, John still retained his infectious enthusiasm for the game he loved and managed his local boys' side Santos in the Essex Corinthian League

Johnny Dick in action for Scotland versus England in 1959

Career record

	League		FAC		LC		Europe		Total	
Played	App	Gls	App	Gls	App	Gls	App	Gls	App	Gls
1953-54	39	13	3	0	0	0	0	0	42	13
1954-55	39	26	2	0	0	0	0	0	41	26
1955-56	35	8	6	6	0	0	0	0	41	14
1956-57	36	8	2	1	0	0	0	0	38	9
1957-58	41	21	3	2	0	0	0	0	44	23
1958-59	41	27	1	0	0	0	0	0	42	27
1959-60	24	11	1	1	0	0	0	0	25	12
1960-61	34	16	2	1	2	2	0	0	38	19
1961-62	35	23	1	0	2	0	0	0	38	23
1962-63	2	0	0	0	0	0	0	0	2	0
TOTAL	**326**	**153**	**21**	**11**	**4**	**2**	**0**	**0**	**351**	**166**

right up to his untimely death in September 2000. Born just a street away from another footballing legend, Sir Alex Ferguson, in the austere pre-war days of the depression, he played his earliest football in the time honoured tradition of so many of his era with a sixpenny ball amid the bomb sites of that "no mean city" and dreamt of playing for his heroes, Glasgow Rangers. But West Ham manager Ted Fenton had other ideas and it was one of Ted's legendary swoops in the transfer market that ensured that Jackie, as he was better known, would don the claret and blue of Hammers rather than the famous light blue of the Gers. Ted was just in time as an hour later Spurs' boss was knocking on the sought-after marksman's door!

Scotland cap: 1959 vs England (1).

DICKENS, Alan 1983-89

Born: Plaistow, London, 3.9.64
League apps: 192 (23 goals)
Cup apps: 39 (6 goals)

THE TERM "LOCAL LAD" can genuinely be applied to Alan Dickens, who was born a corner kick away from Upton Park and has continued to live at nearby Barking even since leaving the club in June 1989, to try his luck across west London with Chelsea and then Brentford. "Dicko" first made his mark for Newham, Essex and London Schoolboys, signing apprentice for West Ham on July 14, 1981, after playing for Hammers' FA Youth Cup-winning side that beat Spurs (1981). He signed pro on August 2, 1982 and, at 18, made a memorable scoring League debut only four months later in a 2-1 win at Notts County (December 18, 1982). Having won four England Youth caps, Alan made the first of his two Under-21 international appearances as sub against Finland (October 16, 1984). A number of promising performances in central midfield earned Dicko rave reviews and when Trevor Brooking retired in May 1984, many regarded him as the player equipped to fill his number 10 shirt. It was an enormous burden for any youngster to bear and the Upton Park crowd were, unfortunately, never slow to voice their dissatisfaction with young Alan in the games when he didn't measure up to those high expectations. Yet Dicko was a player in the club's best traditions; stylish and a good passer who could unlock the tightest defences with a perfectly-weighted through-ball. Or, if there were no options available, he could score spectacular goals himself from long-range. For such a tall player (six foot one), Alan possessed unusually good ball skills and neat control as well as awareness. As he gained more experience, he learned to add more aggression to his game. A shy, unassuming man, Alan's confidence was affected as much as anyone's by relegation in May 1989 and within days of John Lyall's departure, and with West Ham still in turmoil, he made a £600,000 move to Chelsea. It seemed, at the time, like the ideal transfer to enable Alan to finally fulfil his undoubted potential in the top flight. But after playing 22 League games in his first season at Stamford Bridge under Bobby Campbell,

the classy midfielder made only a handful more appearances before being given a free by Ian Porterfield. A brief spell on loan to West Bromwich Albion, around Christmas 1992, was followed by a slightly longer stint at Brentford as the 1992/93 season closed. When David Webb – the next Chelsea manager, who was technically loaning Alan to the Bees – arrived at Griffin Park as the new boss in May 1993, it was Dicko's cue to move on again. This time he joined Colchester United's bid to re-establish themselves in the Third Division of the Football League. Alan scored three goals in 32 League appearances during his one season at Layer Road as the Essex club successfully avoided relegation, but it was to be his last port of call in the Football League as he decided to quit as a full-time pro. Instead, he took the drastic step of learning "The Knowledge" to become a black cab driver while playing part-time. It took Alan two years to qualify for his cab driver's badge and it must have been a huge culture shock for someone who 18 months earlier had been walking out at Highbury and Old Trafford, to be riding around London on a moped memorising routes. Continuing to play non-League with Chesham United, Alan got his badge claiming: "The Knowledge was the hardest thing I ever had to do and I admire anyone who does it." After spells with Collier Row, Billericay Town and Purfleet, Alan turned his back on the game completely in 1997. His disillusion happily didn't last and he now runs his son Luke's Sunday side Ascot, at Under-10 level. Dicko also earned himself another badge – of the coaching variety – through the Essex FA and hopes to progress further in that field.

DICKIE, Alan   1962-66

Born: Charlton, London, 30.1.44
League apps: 12
Cup apps: 3

A RELIABLE, COMPETENT keeper, Alan travelled as 12th man during the victorious European Cup Winners' Cup campaign of 1964/65, after making one appearance in the preliminary round against La Gantoise of Belgium. He transferred to Coventry City after impressing the Midland club in a friendly against them. He later played for Aldershot and is now in the police force.

DIXON, Robert   1928-33

Born: West Stanley, County Durham, 30.8.1904
League apps: 65
Cup apps: 3

MAINLY AN UNDERSTUDY to Ted Hufton during his first two seasons at Upton Park, this former Stoke City goalkeeper had a good run in the First Division side during 1930/31 and 1931/32, proving himself a capable net-minder. However, the arrival of George Watson and the emergence of Pat McMahon as his deputy on West Ham's return to Division Two the following season limited Bob to just three more senior outings.

DIXON, Tommy   1952-54

Born: Newcastle-upon-Tyne, 8.6.29
League apps: 39 (21 goals)
Cup apps: 3 (2 goals)

THE TOP SCORER for Hammers with 19 League and Cup goals in the 1953/54 season, this likable Geordie played only four times in the following campaign. Tommy was transferred to Third Division (South) Reading in March 1955, where he topped the Biscuitmen's scoring charts for two consecutive seasons. His success at Elm Park drew the attention of Brighton & Hove Albion, and he subsequently joined up with former team-mate Dave Sexton at the Goldstone Ground, before seeing out his playing career with Workington and finally Barrow.

DICKS, Julian   1988-93/1994-99

Born: Bristol, Avon, 8.8.68
League apps: 262 (50 goals)
Cup apps: 64 (15 goals)

ONE OF THE most popular players ever to wear the claret and blue, Julian Dicks was a cult hero to many modern-day Hammers fans. And it is a measure of his enormous popularity that on his first appearance back at Upton Park, following his transfer to Liverpool (September 16, 1993), he received a tremendous ovation. West Ham fans had been dreading the departure of the tough-tackling, no-nonsense left-back for some time. He was the club's biggest asset and with Hammers struggling near the bottom of the Premiership after seven matches of the 1993/94 campaign, there was an inevitability about his move to Anfield – in the £2.5 million valued swap deal that brought David Burrows and Mike Marsh in the opposite direction. It was a deal that suited both clubs, as well as Julian, at the time, although the man they call "The Terminator" did not find it easy to win over the Anfield fans. He spent a number of weeks sidelined by a knee injury that led to a cartilage operation. And when he got back in the side, manager Graeme Souness was about to resign. Unlike some fans on Merseyside, the West Ham crowd have been in no doubt about Julian's qualities since he was signed by John Lyall from Birmingham City for £300,000 (March 24, 1988) and made his debut at Sheffield Wednesday (April 2, 1988). Ferocious in the tackle, with a thunderbolt shot to match, deadly Dicks terrorised the opposition with his surging runs deep into opposition territory. Sometimes he tackled too recklessly, as in the 1992/93 First Division promotion-winning season when he was sent off three times (the most by any player at West Ham in one season) and missed 13 games due to suspension. So disillusioned was he by his disciplinary problems and the "Bad Boy" reputation he was getting among referees, Julian said once during a moment of deep despair that he thought seriously about quitting the game. But his ample collection of yellow and red cards should not overshadow the natural talent he possesses. For all his hard man image, as a rebellious character who wears his hair short and rides a Harley Davidson for fun, there is another, more subtle, side to the man who dotes on his young twin daughters. Julian has a sweet left foot and is comfortable on the ball. His biggest strengths are turning defence into attack, winning aerial battles, striking dead balls and spraying accurate passes with a subtlety not usually associated with many modern-day defenders. It's easy to see that he began his career playing left-midfield for Birmingham under Gary Pendrey and Ron Saunders, before settling at full-back. His direct, pinpoint passing from one side of the field to the other, with almost effortless ease, changed the dimension of many attacks. And although a large proportion of his 36 goals were from the penalty spot, Julian contributed more than his fair share of others (often spectacularly) from varying range. Julian's fighting qualities were demonstrated most vividly when he snapped the cruciate ligament in his left knee in October 1990. He missed most of that promotion-winning season and it was 14 months before he resumed in the first team, in December 1992, in the midst of the First Division relegation struggle. Julian regained the captaincy from Ian Bishop and there was another big boost around the corner when he was called up by England manager Graham Taylor for the "B" internationals against Czechoslovakia and the CIS in Eastern Europe. After returning from his long lay-off Julian scored in his comeback game versus Sheffield United (December 21, 1991) – no one did more than Dicksy to try and save Hammers from the drop in May 1992. His valiant efforts were rewarded with a new four-year contract in February 1992 and the fans' vote as Hammer of the Year (even though he played only half that season!) three months later. In their heart of hearts, though, few at Upton Park expected Julian to see out his new contract. Despite his indiscretions on the field during the early part of 1992/93, Julian still contributed 11 vital goals in 34 League appearances as Hammers bounced straight back into the top flight. But once he learned of Liverpool's interest, and with Hammers languishing near the foot of the Premiership, a parting of the ways was inevitable. The "second coming" of Julian Dicks on his return from Liverpool for £1 million just 399 days after leaving for Merseyside really was like the return of the prodigal son – such was the welcome he received from the Upton Park faithful. Truly a sight to behold as he charged upfield to support or set up an attack. Julian finished his first season back with five goals in 33 League and Cup games among which were a spectacular free-kick at Nottingham Forest and two match-winning penalties in home victories over Wimbledon and Leicester City. In 1995/96 Jules did even better in the goalscoring stakes by finishing joint top scorer on ten League goals with Tony Cottee, but still fell foul of referees on a regular basis – most notably when seeing red for the fifth time during his Hammers career at Arsenal. Dicksey was then found guilty of bringing the game into disrepute following an alleged stamping incident involving Chelsea's John Spencer. Despite a bad press, England manager Terry Venables looked long and hard at the uncompromising defender in the run-up to Euro 96, but eventually passed him over despite the fact that the bristling Bristolian was playing the best football of his career to claim the Hammer of the Year award for the third time. He effectively gave up all hope of gaining full international recognition when he claimed he'd rather build dog kennels for his Bull Terriers than pull on an England shirt after all the rebuffs he'd had to endure. Many at Upton Park and the more discerning of neutral observers thought his continued absence was England's loss entirely. So Hammers' captain courageous carried on at club level in the only fashion he knew, giving 100 per cent week in, week out. It was largely down to his fighting qualities and his new-found ability to clean up his disciplinary record that Hammers avoided relegation in 1996/97 when he again found himself the club's joint top scorer with eight goals and Hammer of the Year for the fourth time. Disaster struck in the close season however, when his troublesome left knee was found to be severely damaged and he was forced to miss the whole of the 1997/98 campaign after going under the knife on a career-threatening ligaments injury. The many who wrote him off failed to reckon on his incredible fighting resolve and in a miraculous recovery, The Terminator made his comeback in a Worthington Cup tie against Northampton Town eight games into season 1998/99. Voted Man of the Match versus

the Cobblers, Jules was given the same accolade in a 1-0 win over Southampton and rescued his team in the home FA Cup tie with Swansea City when scoring the equaliser in a ragged 1-1 draw. But after 12 games Hammers' "Iron Man" eventually had to accept that the wear and tear on his knee was simply too much to bear and unless he retired he would end up in a wheelchair. So ended the first class career of the most popular player ever to don the claret and blue. After 11 years and 315 competitive games during which he scored an incredible 61 goals, Julian was awarded a richly deserved testimonial match. A brief comeback with Canvey Island was followed by an injury aborted attempt to become a golf professional and now Julian contents himself by running The Shepherd and Dog public house at Langham near Colchester, Essex.

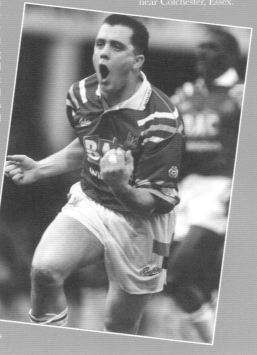

Johnny Dick and Tommy Dixon (see previous page)

DOLAN, Eamonn   1987-91

Born: Romford, Essex, 20.9.67
League apps: 15 (3 goals)
Cup apps: 4

NICKNAMED "THE PROFESSOR" for gaining 12 "O" levels and one "A" level at school in Chelmsford, Essex, the likable Eamonn may consider that he deserved more than nine starts and six sub outings to prove his first team worth at Upton Park. Born in Romford of Irish parents, he was a product of Hammers' youth team and scored a hat-trick for the Republic of Ireland Under-17s against Northern Ireland in January 1985 – three months before turning pro. Capped at Under-21 level while still 19, Eamonn made his senior Hammers debut as sub against Manchester City (May 9, 1987) on the final day of the 1986/87 season. After a Simod Cup start against Millwall (November 10, 1987), he started his first League match against Charlton Athletic at Selhurst Park (March 12, 1988). He scored his first senior goal after coming on as sub against West Bromwich Albion (September 30, 1989), but his most memorable match was against Sunderland (October 18, 1989), when he netted twice in a 5-0 victory. The tall striker's best run in the side was a nine-game stint under Lou Macari in 1989/90. In February 1989 he went on loan to Bristol City (three matches), but West Ham manager John Lyall denied Eamonn the chance of playing for City in the League Cup Semi-final against Nottingham Forest because Hammers were in the other semi, against Luton Town, and he would have been cup-tied if required for the final. Eamonn was set to sign for Birmingham City in the summer of 1990 but the initial deal fell through when he dislocated his shoulder in pre-season training. The move did eventually go ahead, but Eamonn made just 12 League appearances – most of them under Macari, who returned to football as Blues' boss following his shock resignation at West Ham – before moving on to Exeter City shortly after the start of 1991/92. After spending all of his career trying to establish a first team place, Eamonn faced his biggest battle in 1993 when he underwent treatment for cancer. Eamonn's twin brother, Patrick, played centre-half for Walsall. Eamonn became one of the many ex-Hammers to enter management when he was appointed boss at Third Division Exeter City in the summer of 2003, but then had the task of steering the Grecians out of the Nationwide Conference. Early in the 2004/05 season, Eamonn was appointed Youth Academy coach at Reading.

DONALD, Warren 1983-84

Born: Hillingdon, Middlesex, 7.10.64
League apps: 2

A BATTLING MIDFIELD play-maker who made his initial senior appearance in the 1982/83 friendly clash with Scottish champions Dundee United, Warren had to wait until Boxing Day 1983 for his League baptism against Southampton at Upton Park, coming on as sub for the injured Frank Lampard in a 1-0 defeat. His only other senior game was the final match of that season (May 14, 1984) against Everton in Trevor Brooking's farewell. Despite his limited first team opportunities at Upton Park, this former Berkshire and England schoolboy star looked set for a bright future in the game. "Wozzer" joined Fourth Division Northampton Town for a fee of £11,000 in October 1985 and linked up with another ex-Hammer, Mark Schiavi, at the County Ground.

DOW, James 1902-03

Born: Dundee, Scotland, 1873
SL apps: 13
Cup apps: 1

THIS WELL-BUILT DEFENDER, who could perform equally well at either right or left-back, signed from Middlesbrough in time for the start of the 1902/03 season. He made his debut in the opening match against Reading at the Memorial Grounds, but by the end of the season he couldn't get past unlucky 13 in Southern League appearances and he was released. Before Middlesbrough, Dow had seen service with Newton Heath and Glossop North End. At the start of 1904/05 he was captain at Luton Town.

DOWEN, John Stewart 1936

Born: Wolverhampton, West Midlands, 1914
League apps: 1

PROMINENT IN JUNIOR football with Walsall Schools and Courtaulds, this left-back went on to win schooboy caps against Scotland and Wales in 1929, and also represented the Birmingham FA against Scotland in 1934. He was signed from Wolves and made one Second Division appearance for West Ham (May 2, 1936) in a 4-2 defeat against Sheffield United at Bramall Lane before returning to Molineux. Unable to win a regular spot in the Wolves side, his fortunes changed on his move to Hull City, where he struck up a fine partnership with the redoubtable Cliff Woodhead at Anlaby Road and chalked up 39 appearances in 1938/39.

John Dowen

DOWIE, Iain 1991/1995-98

Born: Hatfield, Hertfordshire, 9.1.65
League apps: 80 (12 goals)
Cup apps: 15 (3 goals)

IAIN FULFILLED A lifetime's ambition when Billy Bonds signed him from Luton Town in March 1991 for £480,000 as cover for the injured Trevor Morley. But his dream move (he supported Hammers as a kid and stood on the North Bank) turned sour five months later when he

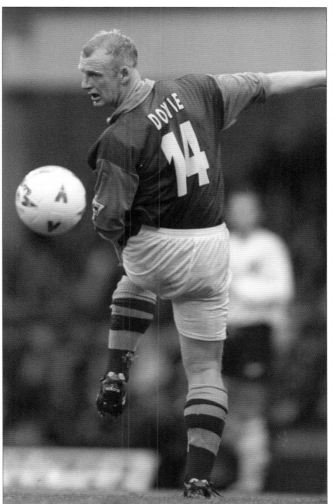

was sold to Southampton in a shock £500,000 move, having played only 12 matches in the 1990/91 Second Division promotion campaign. A striker in the old-fashioned centre-forward mould, he had little time to win over the fans and show that he could settle into Hammers' style of play. Even so, Iain still contributed four important goals (including one on each of his first three outings at Upton Park) and proved a particular threat in the air. He made his West Ham debut at Hull City (March 23, 1991), having made his Football League bow for Luton against Spurs (March 28, 1989). Ironically, Southampton initially signed Iain as an associate schoolboy, but let him go because he was "too small". Determined to prove Saints wrong, he made his mark in non-League circles for Cheshunt, St Albans, Bishop's Stortford and Hendon. This also gave him the time to gain a Masters degree in mechanical engineering and he became a development engineer for British Aerospace. He was signed by Luton for £30,000 in late 1988 and impressed by scoring 15 First Division goals in 53 starts. The thick-set striker enjoyed some of the most successful football of his career with the South Coast outfit, scoring 32 times in 144 outings in all competitions for the Saints, before a £400,000 move took him back to London and Crystal Palace in January 1995. Some outstanding performances at Selhurst Park, most notably in an FA Cup Semi-final

against Man Utd, persuaded Hammers boss Harry Redknapp to part with £500,000 to bring the target man back to the Boleyn for a second spell in August the same year. The transfer elicited an unsolicited prediction from Dowie's former boss at the Dell, Alan Ball, who claimed that "buying Dowie will ultimately cost Redknapp his job". Undeterred and seemingly intent on proving Ball wrong, Iain's first season back (1995/96) was relatively successful as he notched eight goals in 33 Premiership appearances and was voted runner-up behind Julian Dicks in the prestigious Hammer of the Year awards. But there were barren times ahead as the big hitman endured a heart-breaking run of 38 Premiership matches without a goal, lasting 22 months between what proved to be his last Premiership goal against Manchester City in March 1996 and his departure to QPR in January 1998, with Iain and fellow Northern Ireland International Keith Rowland used as makeweights in the deal that brought Trevor Sinclair to Hammers. The only bright spots during that torrid time, when the hapless striker also scored a disastrous own goal in a nightmare Coca Cola Cup defeat at Second Division Stockport County, were two memorable strikes in an earlier round in a 4-1 win over Nottingham Forest under the Boleyn bulbs and marking his appointment as captain of his country by scoring both goals in a 2-0 win versus Albania at Windsor Park in December 1996. Although disappointed to be leaving his boyhood heroes for a second time, Iain's move to QPR turned out to be a blessing in disguise. It gave the ambitious veteran his first opportunity in management when he was appointed reserve team boss at Loftus Road in 1999, while continuing to play for the Hoops and his country as he chased Northern Ireland's all-time goalscoring record of 14, but remaining frustratingly on unlucky 13 as he took his full caps haul to an impressive total of 59. After scoring twice in 33 League and Cup outings for the west Londoners, Iain took over as caretaker manager at Shepherd's Bush between Ray Harford's resignation and the arrival of Gerry Francis and was subsequently appointed player-coach of the reserves at centre-half. Moving north to take up his first proper management post with Oldham Athletic in 2002, Iain lost no time in appointing former Hammers striker and youth team boss David Cross as his assistant at Boundary Park, and the pair were in charge when the Lancastrians dumped Hammers out of the Worthington Cup with a shock 1-0 Third Round win at Upton Park in November 2002. Dowie went on to lead the unfashionable, cash strapped Second Division outfit to the Play-offs in May 2003 where they lost at the Semi-final stage to his old club QPR. But his achievements on a shoe-string hadn't gone unnoticed in the world of football, and when Oldham couldn't afford to offer their ambitious young manager a contract, Crystal Palace swooped to offer him one at Selhurst Park with the brief of avoiding relegation from the First Division. The West Ham academy graduate had another idea, however, and an amazing points haul of 45 from 21 games saw the high flying Eagles soar into the Play-off Final at Cardiff, where Dowie once again found himself famously pitting his wits against the team he had supported as a boy. Despite the importance of his success that day, Iain was never less than magnanimous in his unexpected triumph and fully deserved the victory, which meant that Palace not West Ham would return to the Premiership.

DOWSEY, John   1926

Born: Gateshead, Tyne & Wear, 1905
League apps: 1

A WINGER-CUM-INSIDE-FORWARD WHO started his career with Hunswick Villa, John was secured from Newcastle United after scoring 54 goals for the Magpies' second-string during two seasons in the North Eastern League. He found success hard to come by at Upton Park, making only one First Division appearance against Sheffield Wednesday at Hillsborough in September 1926. John joined Carlisle when he left West Ham in August 1927. He moved on to Sunderland in 1928, Notts County in 1929 and was with Northampton between 1931 and 1934. John made three appearances for the Magpies, 11 for Sunderland (one goal), 98 for Notts County (four goals) and 86 for Northampton (five goals). He died in 1942.

DUMITRESCU, Ilie   1996

Born: Bucharest, Romania, 6.1.69
League apps: 10
Cup apps: 3

AN EXTREMELY GIFTED attacking midfielder who won over 60 caps and scored 20 goals for Romania, Ilie signed for Spurs in a club record-breaking £2.6 million deal from Steaua Bucharest by Ossie Ardiles after his two dramatic goals had dumped the latter's countrymen Argentina out of the 1994 World Cup Finals in the USA. A three time League and domestic Cup winner with Steaua, Dumi made an impressive start to his Spurs career at the beginning of 1994/95, but his dream move to the Premiership turned into a nightmare when Ardiles was sacked and his successor Gerry Francis abruptly dropped him from the side and put him out on loan with Spaniards Sevilla FC. His Spanish stay was highlighted by the partnership with Davor Suker during the second half of the 1994/95 Spanish Primera Liga campaign, during which he matched the 13 Premiership appearances (four goals) he'd made before his fall out with Francis, but only managed to score once, in the 2-0 win at Athletic Bilbao. Back at Spurs for 1995/96, the disillusioned star made just six appearances (one goal) before Harry Redknapp threw him a Premiership lifeline with a £1.5 million move to Upton Park in February 1996. The player's nightmare continued when it took two months cutting through red tape to renew his work permit and then when the situation was finally resolved, the unlucky Romanian pulled a hamstring in the 4-2 home win over Manchester City after just three games in a West Ham shirt and was subsequently ruled out of his country's Euro 96 campaign in England. The 1996/97 season didn't bode much better and after just ten Premiership and Cup games, despite playing a "blinder" in a 2-2 Upton Park draw against Premier League champions Manchester United in early December, Redknapp decided to cut his losses and sell the player he'd pinned his hopes on so doggedly for £1 million to the Mexican club Futbol America. His international career continued, however, and he was on duty to pick up his 62nd cap against Tunisia at the 1998 World Cup Finals in France, while playing for another Mexican side, Atlante. The following campaign (1998/99) found him back at Steaua where he'd begun his career in 1988/89 following a season's loan at FC Olt (32 appearances, one goal). Seven appearances and one goal enabled him to finish with a impressive record of 71 goals in 160 First Division appearances for the Bucharest club.

DUNMORE, Dave   1960-61

Born: Whitehaven, Cumberland, 8.2.34
League apps: 36 (16 goals)
Cup apps: 3 (2 goals)

Ilie Dumitrescu

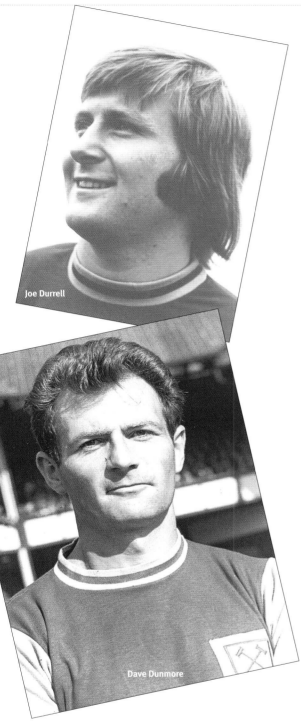

Joe Durrell

Dave Dunmore

DUNN, Richard — 1937-47

Born: Easington, County Durham, 23.12.19
League apps: 11 (2 goals)

AN INSIDE-FORWARD WHO joined the club in 1937 from Ferryhill Athletic, Richard was one of many players who had their careers decimated by World War II, in which he served for over six years in the Essex Regiment and the Royal Artillery. During the conflict he made one guest appearance for Spurs at Reading (September 9, 1944), when Spurs arrived for the match with only four men! Fortunately Dunn was at the game as a spectator and was able to turn out at the last minute at inside-left. He also played for Hartlepool United, Preston North End and York City during the war. He managed ten Second Division appearances with the resumption of normal League activities in 1946/47, before transferring to Hartlepool. He passed away in December 1985 at the age of 65.

DUNN, Thomas — 1899-1900

Born: Falkirk, Scotland, 1872
SL apps (TIW): 35
Cup apps: 7

THAMES IRONWORKS SIGNED Tom from Chatham and he made his first appearance in a 4-1 win at Wycombe (January 14, 1899). A member of the Wolves team that were defeated 2-1 in the 1896 FA Cup Final by the Wednesday at Crystal Palace, he was equally at home in either of the full-back berths and appeared in the final 13 matches of 1898/99. On duty for the opening match of the following season in a 1-0 defeat at Reading, he missed only six Southern League games that season and was also an ever-present in Irons' extended FA Cup run, which ended in a 2-1 defeat by Millwall at the Memorial Grounds, after disposing of Royal Engineers (6-0), Grays (4-0), Sheppey (4-2), Dartford (7-0) and New Brompton (2-0). Tom had left the club before it made the momentous decision to become West Ham United FC and fully embrace professionalism.

DURRELL, Joe — 1971-72

Born: Stepney, London, 15.3.53
League apps: 6

A DIMINUTIVE, NIPPY winger, Joe always showed up well on his rare first team appearances. Replacing Johnny Ayris, he made his debut in the 2-1 home win over Stoke City (September 25, 1971) and his remaining four full and one sub appearances all came in that 1971/72 season. His last outing came in the final match against Southampton (May 1, 1972). Competition for places led to his transfer to Bristol City and he later played for Cardiff City and Gillingham.

DWYER, Noel — 1956-60

Born: Dublin, Republic of Ireland, 30.10.34
League apps: 36
Cup apps: 2

COURAGEOUS IRISH INTERNATIONAL goalkeeper Noel signed from Wolverhampton Wanderers in December 1958. He could be brilliant one match and infuriating the next, and it was this inconsistency that prompted his transfer to Swansea Town. He returned to Upton Park with the Swans for an FA Cup Fourth Round tie in March 1963 and put in an impressive display to limit Hammers to a 1-0 passage into the following round. He was not always as competent, however, and much of the blame for a 5-3 home defeat by Newcastle United (February 20, 1960) was attributed to him. Indeed, there were newspaper reports suggesting that the result of the match had been "rigged", following the unusual amount of money being taken by bookmakers on the outcome of the game. One West Ham director was said to have walked out of the match in disgust at the result. But the rumours were never proven to be true and the scandal blew over. Noel Dwyer never played for Hammers again, however, joining the Swans for a fee of £3,000. Capped 24 times by his country, he later had spells with Plymouth Argyle and Charlton Athletic. He sadly died in 1992.
Republic of Ireland caps: 1959 vs Sweden; 1960 vs Chile, West Germany, Sweden (4).

DYER, James — 1908-09

Born: birthplace unknown, 1884
SL apps: 3

JAMES THREW IN his lot with Hammers at the beginning of the same season that his former Manchester United colleagues brought the FA Cup back to their Bank Street headquarters. Making his debut in a 2-0 win over Queens Park Rangers at the Boleyn Ground, in the season's opening fixture, it proved to be the inside-forward's last taste of success as a Hammer. His other two appearances, against Brighton and Brentford respectively, ending in defeat.

AN EXPERIENCED CENTRE-FORWARD, Dave arrived at Upton Park in an exchange deal that took Johnny Smith to Spurs. He acquitted himself well during his two years in the claret and blue, scoring some useful goals and beefing-up the forward line at a time when Hammers were struggling to consolidate their First Division status. He found himself involved in another exchange, this time with neighbours Leyton Orient, in a transfer that resulted in Alan Sealey joining the club. Dave top-scored for O's in their 1961/62 Second Division promotion season with 22 goals from 39 appearances and scored 58 times in 168 League and Cup matches during five seasons at Brisbane Road. He later returned to the team where he started his career – York City – and in another two seasons there he scored 13 goals in a further 63 outings, but could not prevent the Yorkshiremen from finishing bottom of Division Three in 1965/66 and third from bottom in the Fourth the following year. After scoring 132 goals in a total of 369 League games, Dave went into non-League soccer in 1967 with Wellington. He is now a sheet metal worker in his native York.

Noel Dwyer

E

EADIE, Doug
EARL, Alfred
EARL, Arthur "Mick"
EARLE, Stanley
EASTMAN, George
EASTWOOD, H
ECCLES, George
EDWARDS, Bill
ENGLAND, Ernest
EPHRAIM, Hogan
ETHERINGTON, Matthew
ETTE, Clifford
EUSTACE, Peter
EVANS, Arthur "Albert"
EVANS, Roger

Matthew Etherington

EADIE, Doug — 1966-68

Born: Edinburgh, Scotland, 22.9.46
League apps: 2

A FLYING, SCOTTISH winger, Doug's first team outings were extremely limited. In fact, he made only two League appearances, making his debut against Spurs at Upton Park in May 1967 and his final showing four days later against Manchester City in the last match of that campaign. He later went on loan to Leyton Orient where he had the same number of matches. In 1970/71 Doug was at Bournemouth under the management of John Bond and Ken Brown with ex-Hammers Tony Scott, Trevor Hartley and Keith Miller, but couldn't break into the first team. It was reported that he returned to Scotland to play for Greenock Morton, but there is no record of him playing for the first team. He turned up to watch Hammers on a pre-season tour of Scotland at the beginning of the 1992/93 campaign.

EARL, Alfred — 1925-33

Born: Earlsfield, London, 19.3.1903
League apps: 181
Cup apps: 15

A TALL, CONSTRUCTIVE defender who held the right-back position during his eight seasons at Upton Park, Alfred made close to 200 senior appearances in the process. Signed from Summerstown in 1925, he is remembered not only as a cool, thoughtful player but also for having collapsed on the field one Good Friday, having eaten four hot cross buns before a match! A contender, if ever there was one, for the current fans' song "Who ate all the pies?" He went on to play for Streatham Town and French team Souchaux, in Paris. Alfred died on August 17, 1951.

EARL, Arthur "Mick" — 1903

Born: Loughborough, Leicestershire, 1878
SL apps: 1

AN OUTSIDE-LEFT, MICK made just one appearance for Irons versus Bristol Rovers in a 4-1 Memorial Ground defeat (October 17, 1903). He had deputised for Charlie Satterthwaite at outside-left but failed to do anything to grab the headlines and thus ensure a more lasting testimony. In 1904/05 while at Spurs he was a South Eastern Football League champion and London Football League Premier Division runner-up, making 24 appearances in these two reserve team competitions and being on the losing side only twice. Mick started his career at Coalville Albion in October 1897 before being picked up by Loughborough Town in July 1899 where he made five appearances, debuting against Newton Heath – now Manchester United – on September 16, 1899. He then moved to Chesterfield Town (via Coalville Albion again) where he made 14 appearances, scoring three goals in 1900/01. In 1901/02 he made a further 31 League appearances and one FA Cup appearance for the Spireites before playing the 1902/03 season for Walsall and then moving to West Ham. After his brief spell with Hammers, Arthur went back to Chesterfield Town in January 1904 (16 apps, three goals) where he made his final League appearances versus Barnsley (April 30, 1904) scoring the only goal of the game. He then saw out his

EARLE, Stanley — 1924-32

Born: Stratford, London, 6.9.1897
League apps: 258 (56 goals)
Cup apps: 15 (2 goals)

A SUPERBLY CREATIVE six foot-plus inside-right who followed his former Clapton FC colleague Vivian Gibbins in signing for Irons. He had played Division One football for Arsenal before coming to Upton Park. Stan won an FA Amateur Cup winners' medal with Clapton in 1924 and was honoured with a full cap versus Ireland in Belfast in 1927. Initially reluctant to relinquish his amateur status, he became a leading light in Hammers' attack and struck up a fine understanding with Vic Watson. Often getting among the goalscorers, it was his ability to take as well as create chances that made him such a valued member of West Ham's team in the 1920s and early 1930s. He ended his career with Clapton Orient. Honours include: England Amateur caps versus Ireland 1922/23 and 1923/24; France 1923/24. Essex cap. London cap. Represented FA XI versus Army 1922/23 and 1923/24; also represented the Isthmian League. Later had spells as Walthamstow Avenue coach and Leyton manager. The son of Harry Earle, an 1890s centre-half with Clapton, Millwall and Nottingham Forest. Stan passed away in September 1971 at Colchester after a long illness.
England cap: 1927 vs Ireland (1).

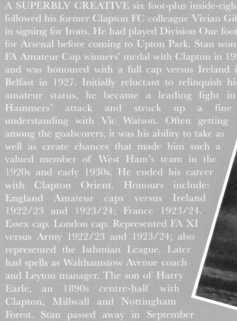

Career record

Played	League		FAC		LC		Europe		Total	
	App	Gls	App	Gls	App	Gls	App	Gls	App	Gls
1924-25	18	6	0	0	0	0	0	0	18	6
1925-26	37	9	1	0	0	0	0	0	38	9
1926-27	42	13	3	0	0	0	0	0	45	13
1927-28	31	11	1	0	0	0	0	0	32	11
1928-29	41	6	5	2	0	0	0	0	46	8
1929-30	36	3	4	0	0	0	0	0	40	3
1930-31	36	8	1	0	0	0	0	0	37	8
1931-32	17	0	0	0	0	0	0	0	17	0
TOTAL	**258**	**56**	**15**	**2**	**0**	**0**	**0**	**0**	**273**	**58**

career in the lower divisions and reserve competitions, signing for first Grassmoor Red Rose (September 1904), then Tottenham Hotspur (November 1904 to April 1905), Chesterfield Town again (December 1906), Moores Athletic and finally Shirebrook Athletic. Described in *Lucky Whites and Spireites* as: "A lively, unpredictable presence on the wing, apparently adept at drawing defenders out of position before slipping accurate passes into the space he created. He was highly popular with the fans."

EASTMAN, George — 1925-26

Born: Leyton, London, 7.4.1903
League apps: 2

A REMARKABLE FEATURE of George's two First Division outings for Hammers was that they were both against Everton in direct confrontation with the legendary Dixie Dean. He proved himself a more than capable understudy to George Kay and, later, Jim Barrett in the two Upton Park clashes with the Toffeemen, which, incidentally, took place almost a year to the day of one another, with West Ham victorious on both occasions. The first (April 18, 1925) ended 4-1 in favour of Irons, and the second (April 17, 1926), 1-0. George was, somewhat surprisingly, overlooked after that. He later joined Clapton Orient. The brother of a well-known Essex cricketer he was no slouch with the bat and ball, playing 48 matches for Essex as a wicketkeeper between 1926 and 1929, taking 29 catches and making 21 stumpings. He played 18 times for the O's after joining them from Chatham in 1928, scoring one goal. George died at his Eastbourne home on March 16, 1991.

EASTWOOD, H — 1908-09

League apps: 6

THIS RIGHT-WINGER MADE his Southern League debut against Portsmouth at the Boleyn (October 10, 1908), when centre-forward Jack Foster scored a hat-trick in the 3-1 win. It was the start of a five-match run in the first team, which culminated in a 1-0 victory over Millwall at The Den with Foster again doing the goalscoring honours. His Christmas Day appearance, however, in the 1-0 Upton Park win over Southampton proved to be his last for Hammers.

ECCLES, George — 1902-04

Born: Newcastle-under-Lyme, Staffordshire, 1874
SL apps: 59
Cup apps: 5

GEORGE WAS A sturdy defender, equally at home in either of the full-back berths. The former Everton man (60 apps) made consistency his byword during his two seasons at the Memorial Grounds, missing only five Southern League outings in that time and being an ever-present in the 1903/04 campaign. But even that proud record could not save him from the ruthless purge of the playing staff that saw only five players retained and a major influx of new faces to coincide with the move to Upton Park. However, when one door closes another opens, and George joined Bolton Wanderers, against doctors' advice that the Lancastrian climate would not agree with his health. He married the trainer's daughter and stayed at Burnden Park for 40 years as assistant and then trainer. Bolton's directors had a special medal struck for George in 1930 to commemorate his handling of three successful Wanderers' FA Cup Final XIs, including the 1923 Final against West Ham. Described as "a grand tackler and an untiring worker", George Eccles died just before Christmas, 1945. George played for four

local clubs – Wolstanton Brotherhood FC, Stoke Peters, Titbury Town and Middleport – before Burslem Port Vale in June 1893. It was at Vale in 1895 that Eccles misread the timetable and selected a non-existent train that only ran on Bank Holidays, thus missing a game at Notts County. He then had spells at Wolverhampton Wanderers and Preston North End before his stint at Everton.

EDWARDS, Bill — 1923-26

Born: Aston, Birmingham, 1896
League apps: 37 (3 goals)
Cup apps: 2

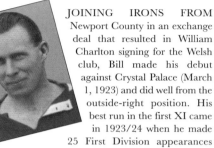

JOINING IRONS FROM Newport County in an exchange deal that resulted in William Charlton signing for the Welsh club, Bill made his debut against Crystal Palace (March 1, 1923) and did well from the outside-right position. His best run in the first XI came in 1923/24 when he made 25 First Division appearances and two in the FA Cup. He later went back to Newport after spells with Shrewsbury Town and Llanelly, and on retiring from soccer became a licensee at Hereford. A very good bowls player, he was a leading light in the Hereford Bowls Club and a member of their team that won the English Bowling Association's triples championship in 1950. Bill died on June 4, 1952. He also played for Brentford, Watford, Fulham and Hereford United.

ENGLAND, Ernest — 1930-31

Born: Shirebrook, Derbyshire, 3.2.1901
League apps: 5

ERNIE WAS A long-serving left-back with Sunderland when they were a force in the land, boasting such illustrious figures as England international keeper Albert McInroy and a trio of Scottish internationals: Billy Clunas, Tommy McInally and Adam McLean. The experienced defender made his Hammers debut in the amazing 5-5 home draw with Aston Villa (January 3, 1931) and later proved invaluable in passing on his wealth of knowledge to younger players before joining Mansfield Town. Ernie died at Radcliffe-on-Trent on February 22, 1982.

EPHRAIM, Hogan — 2005-

Born: Islington, London, 31.3.88
Cup apps: 1

HOGAN JOINED THE club in 1999 and has represented England at Under 16 and Under 17 levels. He has scored several important goals for his country in his role as striker where he prefers to play. A star in West Ham's FA Youth Cup run in 2004/05, he played in the UEFA European Championships for England in Italy in May 2005, scoring twice in three games. He made his senior bow in the Carling Cup tie against Sheffield Wednesday at Hillsborough on September 20, 2005 when he came on as a substitute with his youth team colleague Tony Stokes in the 87th minute of the 4-2 victory over the Owls.

ETHERINGTON, Matthew — 2003-

Born: Truro, Cornwall, 14.8.81
League apps: 80 (10 goals)
Cup apps: 9

AN EXCITING LEFT-SIDED midfielder, Matt joined the Hammers as part of the deal that took Freddi Kanoute to Spurs in August 2003. With a price tag of £1 million, Hammers have had value for money out of the English Under-21 international who won the coveted Player of the Year award in his first season. He came up through the ranks with Third Division Peterborough to become the Posh's third-youngest ever player, making his debut for them as a 15-year-old in the last match of the 1996/97 season against Brentford while still an associate schoolboy. After scoring six times in 58 League and Cup outings for the London Road club, he was prised away by Tottenham Hotspur with his Posh youth team-mate Simon Davies in a £1.2 million double deal in January 2000. Brentford were again the opposition when the highly rated youngster made his Spurs bow in a satisfactory first season in north London. But regular first team action evaded him in 2001/02 and he was loaned out to First Division Bradford City in October 2001,

Left and below: Matthew Etherington

Ernest England

where he was voted Man of the Match on no less than six of his 13 senior outings, and where he scored on his debut against Watford. Recalled to White Hart Lane, he made 15 Premiership starts under Glenn Hoddle in 2002/03, but the opportunity for regular first team action with Hammers in 2003/04 swayed him to drop down a division to join his new team's quest for promotion. That sadly ended in Play-off Final defeat against Crystal Palace in May 2004, and during the uncertain times that followed, West Ham began their second fire sale of players. When David Connolly and Michael Carrick were both sold, Matthew Etherington seemed to be one of the few saleable assets the club had left. His departure really would be more than Hammers' long-suffering fans could bear, after a series of events that might never see the club recover completely. Certainly Matt's displays were one of the few bright spots in a hugely disappointing 2003/04 season, with a superb hat-trick against Wimbledon in March a particular breath of fresh air in what proved to

be an otherwise claustrophobic campaign. Matt's form was again a revelation as Hammers put in a late run at the end of 2004/05 to clinch a return to the top table of English football. It was largely due to his ability to beat defenders to get to the byline and release pin-point centres into the six-yard box that saw Hammers overcome Ipswich Town in the Play-off Semi-finals for the second successive season to reach the Final at the Millennium Stadium in Cardiff. It was from the winger's crosses that Bobby Zamora and Marlon Harewood scored Irons' goals in the first leg 2-2 draw with Town at Upton Park and, of course, it was another run and centre from the tricky flankman that provided the only goal of the game for Zamora that defeated Preston North End at Cardiff and returned the team to the Premiership after a two year absence. If Matty can continue the same form in the Premiership, one wonders how long it will be before he is considered for England recognition. Certainly it would be no less than the player deserves. Matty was quick off the mark in Hammers' first match back in the top flight when he scored his tenth League goal for the club with the final tally in the 3-1 victory over Blackburn Rovers on the opening day of the 2005/06 season at Upton Park, via a pass from Yossi Benayoun. Matthew, by his own admission, took a little time to readjust to life in the Premiership saying: "The tempo is much faster than it was in the Championship, but I think we did very well against Rovers. Obviously it is a massive step up, but we will thrive on that. I think we play better on the big occasions as we proved last season."

ETTE, Clifford — 1934

League app: 1 (1 goal)

INSIDE-RIGHT CLIFF SCORED on his West Ham debut in the Second Division clash at Deepdale against Preston North End (February 3, 1934). Hammers lost 3-1 and, mysteriously, he never appeared for the first team again. Cliff began his career with Northampton Nomads and signed amateur forms for Hammers after being asked personally, in a letter by West Ham manager Charlie Paynter, to turn out in the match against PNE. He later captained the London League side Park Royal, which dumped Swindon out of the 1935/36 FA Cup, before losing 3-1 at Cardiff in the Third Round. He represented the London League against Paris League and scored a goal in his side's 3-1 victory at the famous Parc des Princes Stadium in the French capital. His team-mate in that match was Dick Walker, who also played for Royals. A bad knee injury ended his career and brought about the onset of arthritis, which partially disabled Cliff in later life. In 1989 he was awarded the Arthritis and Rheumatism Council's Running Man trophy for his service to sport in collecting thousands of postage stamps to raise funds for ARC's cause over the years.

EUSTACE, Peter — 1970-72

Born: Stocksbridge, Yorkshire, 31.7.44
League apps: 44 (6 goals)
Cup apps: 5 (1 goal)

BOUGHT FROM SHEFFIELD Wednesday for a then Hammers record fee of £90,000 to replace Martin Peters, Peter never quite succeeded in doing so. A creative wing-half on the verge of full international honours with Wednesday, he could not reproduce the same form under Ron Greenwood at West Ham and was allowed to rejoin the Hillsborough club at a reduced fee after only two years at Upton Park (part of which he spent on loan to Rotherham United and his former club). Peter was manager of Sheffield Wednesday in the later 1980s after being assistant to Howard Wilkinson prior to the latter's appointment as boss of Leeds United. He was the youth team boss at Charlton before becoming assistant to Frank Clark at Leyton Orient, and took charge at Brisbane Road in 1991, where he stayed until April 1994. In 2000, Harry Redknapp appointed Peter the club's "northern scout", although the title was something of a misnomer as his brief instructed him to travel all over the world assessing players.

EVANS, Arthur "Albert" — 1930

Born: Barking, Essex, 1906
League apps: 1

EVANS JOINED BARKING Town in 1921. He spent four seasons in the Athenian League club's reserves before making the outside-right position his own. Described by the distinguished football reporter Norman Ackland as: "Tremendously fast, at ball control he has few masters. He centres splendidly, anticipates the run of play like a veteran, and converges in on goal from the outside-left." From the mid-1920s onwards, honours were bestowed thick and fast on this lead-burner by trade, including an FA Amateur Cup Final medal, London Senior cap and badge and an Athenian League cap and badge. After an impressive display in a trial for England against The Rest, Arthur became the first Barking Town player to be capped for England when he was selected for the match against Wales at Brighton February 16, 1928. However, by May 1933 Arthur had retired and was working for the Gas Light and Coke Co. In a newspaper article of that time he said: "Professional football is a full-time job if you have the ambition to progress and become a star player. My choice went to my job because I was married, but I had some great times touring the Continent and Europe with Middlesex Wanderers – as an amateur."

EVANS, Roger — 1902-03

SL apps: 1

Peter Eustace

A CENTRE-FORWARD, ROGER played in the penultimate Southern League fixture of the 1902/03 season; the 4-0 defeat by Luton Town at Dunstable Road. He failed to get on the scoresheet and consequently to make any more appearances in the claret and blue. An amateur with Clapton, where he was a club-mate of W Miecznikowski, Roger also appeared for Ilford, Queens Park Rangers and London Welsh.

F

Anton Ferdinand

FAIR, Aubrey — 1901-07

SL apps: 31 (1 goal)
Cup apps: 2

NORMALLY A LEFT-BACK, although he sometimes switched to the right and on one occasion played at centre-forward (scoring at Brighton), Aubrey was sufficiently well thought of to survive a purge on the playing staff in the close season of 1904, which saw himself, Tom Allison, Billy Bridgeman, Charles Cotton and Len Jarvis the only survivors of the previous season's squad. Making his debut in an FA Cup tie at Leyton in November 1901 – in his solitary appearance that season – he was by no means a first team regular and failed to appear during the entire 1905/06 season. His last outing was against Queen's Park Rangers when Hammers won 2-1 at Upton Park (February 25, 1907).

FAIRMAN, Robert — 1909-12

Born: Southampton, Hampshire, 1885
SL apps: 90
Cup apps: 12

SIGNED FROM BIRMINGHAM in the close season of 1909/10, this left-back made his Southern League bow in the 2-1 home win over Exeter City on the opening day of the season, in which Danny Shea scored both goals. It was the first of 90 first team outings – quite a run in those days – and he showed his versatility by switching to right-back when the need arose in his final season of 1911/12. Robert played in the Football League with the Birmingham side relegated from Division One at the end of 1907/08. He stayed at St Andrews for one season of Second Division football, during which he scored one goal in 19 games, before moving south to Irons. He moved back to Brum in 1912, but was unable to command a regular place in the first XI, appearing only 16 times (in Division Two) in 1912/13 and 1913/14. He seems to have dropped out of senior soccer after this, as he was not registered with any League club for 1914/15. The *Athletic News* described him as a "cool, calculating defender".

FARRELL, John — 1902-03

Born: birthplace unknown, 1874
SL apps: 20 (3 goals)
Cup apps: 1

"JACK" FARRELL MADE his name with Southampton when the Saints won the Southern League Championship for the third year running in 1899 and was also on duty when the south coast club lost 4-0 to Bury in the 1900 FA Cup Final at Crystal Palace. The following year, the hard-hitting centre-forward came under the guidance of the future legend Herbert Chapman – then making his way as player-manager of little Northampton Town – who, with Jack's help, found success in only his second season by winning the Southern League. It was considered a major coup on West Ham's part when, as a relatively new club, they managed to sign such a well-known player for the start of the 1902/03 season. Duly making his Hammers debut in the season's opening fixture against Reading at the Memorial Grounds, he went on to make 20 Southern League appearances and, although slightly past his best, proved that he could still hold the line together. He began his top-class career with Stoke City in October 1894 when the Potters signed him from Dresden United for £40 – a great deal of money back then. Prior to his move to Northampton, Jack spent a year with New Brighton Tower from June 1901 and actually had two spells with Stoke, returning there from Saints in the close season of 1898. He joined Southampton again for the 1899/1900 season and in his two spells at The Dell scored 54 goals in 97 Southern League and Cup games. He retired after his one season at

the Memorial Grounds and became a publican in his home town of Tunstall. He died on February 22, 1947.

FASHANU, Justin — 1989

Born: Hackney, London, 19.2.61
League apps: 2
Cup apps: 1

A CONTROVERSIAL STRIKER, Justin spent just one month (November 1989) on loan; in which he started two Second Division matches and one League Cup tie under Lou Macari's management. The former Dr Barnardo's boy was struggling to re-establish himself in Britain at the time, having battled to overcome a serious knee injury that threatened his colourful career. He made his debut as a 76th minute sub against Wimbledon in the Littlewoods Cup at Upton Park (November 22, 1989), and also played the full 90 minutes at Blackburn Rovers and at home against Stoke City. An expensive £1 million signing by Nottingham Forest from Norwich City in August 1981, "Fash" – the elder brother of Wimbledon striker John – also had brief spells with Southampton, Notts County, Brighton & Hove Albion, Manchester City, Leyton Orient, Torquay United and, in Scotland, for Hearts and Airdrionians. Tragically, he committed suicide in Shoreditch, London, on May 2, 1998.

Benny Fenton

FEATHERSTONE, Arthur — 1905-08

Born: Barking, Essex, date unknown
SL apps: 24 (1 goal)
Cup apps: 1

A RIGHT-WINGER WHOSE forte was making, rather than scoring, goals, Arthur did score one during his two dozen outings in the claret and blue. It came during a 3-0 Upton Park win over Queens Park Rangers on Boxing Day, 1907. He made only five Southern League appearances that season and his last for the club came in the penultimate fixture of the season, when Rangers got their revenge with a 4-0 victory at the Park Royal

PROMINENT FOOTBALLERS.

A. FEATHERSTONE. WEST HAM UNITED.

Ground. He won a number of medals as a youngster with the national school side, including a Glenny Shield award, and was a member of Barking St Andrews, the winners of the East Suburban League. He also won medals with Barking Victoria (London Junior Shield), Newportians (South Essex League) and Barking (London Junior Cup and South Essex League). A keen athlete of some repute, he won the 100-yard sprint event at the Barking Athletics meeting seven times out of eight. Affectionately known as "Moppy".

FENN, George — 1958

Born: West Ham, London, date unknown

ALTHOUGH THIS FORMER schoolboy prodigy never made a League appearance while at West Ham, he did play against Reading in a Southern Floodlight Cup match: a competition virtually regarded as a first team tournament in those days (borne out by an attendance of over 13,000 at Elm Park) when floodlights were still a novelty. Equally at home at centre-forward or on the wing, George transferred to Southern League Bedford Town in the close season of 1959. A far cry from the days when, in Ted Fenton's words: "George Fenn is the most exciting prospect in the country", and was expected to be the "cream of the crop" of a batch of starlets being nurtured by Malcolm Allison. When asked who he wanted to keep, Big Mal said: "I'll have the boy Scott, the boy Cartwright and the boy Moore." "But what about Fenn?" asked Fenton, "every club in the country is after him." Mal replied prophetically: "I don't think he'll make it." But George, who was once offered a turkey by Spurs as an incentive to move to White Hart Lane, didn't bear any ill-feeling towards Big Mal and even named his daughter after the man who was his idol.

FENTON, Benny — 1937-39

Born: West Ham, London, 28.10.18
League apps: 21 (9 goals)
Cup apps: 1

BROTHER OF THE famous former West Ham player and manager Ted Fenton, Ben followed in Ted's footsteps as a West Ham, Essex and London schoolboy representative player, and joined him in West Ham United's League side before World War II. Ben served in the same Territorial Army unit as his Hammers colleagues, but had not been retained by the claret and blues at the end of the 1938/39 season. Mainly playing at outside-left with Hammers, Ben converted to wing-half when football resumed in 1946 and served Millwall, Charlton and Colchester (where he played on loan before World War II) as a defender. He later managed all three clubs in turn, as well as Leyton Orient. Ben guested for Norwich City, Manchester City, Charlton Athletic, Crystal Palace and West Ham and was also an Essex County lawn bowler and a keen cricketer.

FENTON, Frederick — 1900-01

Born: Gainsborough, Lincolnshire, date unknown
SL apps: 14 (2 goals)
Cup apps: 1 (1 goal)

A PRODUCT OF Midlands football, Freddie was signed from a club later to become a sort of unofficial nursery for Hammers – Gainsborough Trinity. An extremely modest man, he filled the outside-left position with verve and flair in the opening 13 fixtures of the club's initial season, but managed only one further Southern League appearance before transferring to Swindon Town. He also played for West Bromwich Albion. Although the Fenton name is more remembered in the annals of West Ham history for the exploits of Fred's more illustrious namesake, Ted Fenton and, to a lesser extent, the latter's brother Benny, our subject does have the honour of scoring the club's first FA Cup goal under the banner of West Ham United (against Olympic November 3, 1900).

FENTON, Ted   1933-46

Born: Forest Gate, London, 7.11.14
League apps: 163 (27 goals)
Cup apps: 13

ALTHOUGH HE HAD already left Upton Park to become player-manager of little Colchester United when full League football was resumed for the 1946/47 season, Ted did in fact play for Hammers in their four FA Cup ties, regarded as official, in the previous year's campaign. He guided the Essex minnows to the Fifth Round of the FA Cup in 1947/48, and it soon became apparent that their success was not solely due to the players thriving on the local specialty – oysters! Inundated with management offers from elsewhere, Ted plumped to return to his former club and was officially appointed manager in August 1950 – taking over from the legendary Charlie Paynter. A schoolboy international as a forward, he made his League debut for Hammers in 1934 at centre-half. But it was at wing-half that he really made his mark, winning a Football League War Cup medal in 1940 and playing five times for England. His greatest achievement as manager was undoubtedly returning the team to the First Division in 1958, after an absence of 26 years. He later managed Southend United before going into the pub trade when he retired from the game. After that he opened a sports shop in Brentwood, Essex, passing on the business to his son Alan (who played for Hammers' "A" team in the 1950s) upon his retirement. Ted died tragically in July 1992, aged 77, following a car crash near Peterborough.

FENWICK, Alfred   1914-19

Born: Hamsterley, County Durham, 26.3.1891
SL apps: 19 (1 goal)
League apps: 2

DESPITE A TENDENCY to neglect his defensive duties for frequent forays upfield, Alf was a fine utility player who filled all the rearguard positions (with the exception of goalkeeper) for Hammers, as well as the two inside-forward positions in wartime matches. Beginning his career with Cragheart United in County Durham, he progressed to Football League status with Hull City, making 16 appearances for the Tigers and scoring seven times in the centre-forward role, following the transfer of Hull's regular number 9, Tom Browell, to Everton. Joining Hammers in the close season of 1914, he made his Southern League debut against Gillingham in the opening game of the season at Upton Park in the right-half berth. The combative north-easterner totalled 19 appearances in the uncertain times of the initial war-time season, managing to get himself sent-off in one of them. But by 1918/19 he was guesting for Hartlepool United. Returning to Upton Park to make two appearances in the club's first Football League season, Alf was transferred to Coventry City in December 1919 and had 53 games for the Bantams before returning "home" to join Blyth Spartans in 1921.

FERDINAND, Les   2003

Born: Acton, London, 8.12.66
League apps: 14 (2 goals)

FOR YEARS WEST Ham fans wondered why their Spurs counterparts called centre-forward Les Ferdinand "Sir Les". But after witnessing the peerless performances of the England international at first hand nearly all were of the opinion that his unofficial title was fully merited. Signed for a bargain £200,000 from Spurs in the January transfer window his contribution to the team was immense, despite only scoring twice in his 14 Premiership games for Hammers, as he held the ball up, supported fellow-strikers Kanoute and Defoe and tracked back to marshal the defence at set pieces. Born in the year that England won the World Cup, his first big break came when he was spotted playing in the Vauxhall Opel League with Hayes by QPR, who signed the 21-year-old for £15,000 in March 1987 and gave him his first team debut against Coventry the following month. He was loaned out to Brentford, where he made three appearances, and Turkish club Besiktas, where he scored 21 times in 33 games and became a hero when he scored the winning goal in the Turkish Cup Final against Fenerbahce. A much improved player upon his return to London, he went on to score 90 goals in 183 League and Cup games for the Hoops before a massive £8 million move to Newcastle United in June 1995. On Tyneside he hit 49 goals in 83 games in all competitions to help the Magpies' fans forget a previous hero – Andy Cole. Awarded the prestigious PFA Player of the Year award in 1996, Les left St James's Park to return to London and join Spurs for £6 million in August 1997. Although not such a prolific scorer at White Hart Lane (39 goals in 148 games in all competitions), he was still a huge crowd favourite. It was ironic that the player scored his first goal for Hammers in the 2-0 Upton Park victory over Spurs in March 2003 as the side staged a late, but valiant, fight against relegation. The holder of 17 caps for England (five goals), Les scored in the 2-2 draw against Birmingham City at St Andrew's, which, despite the point gained, sealed Hammers' relegation and made it financially unviable to offer the popular striker a new contract. Instead he moved on to Leicester City to face another ultimately unsuccessful battle against the dreaded drop from the Premiership in 2003/04. Even at the age of 37 he continued to show his worth as a top-class striker with 13 goals in 31 League and FA Cup games for the Foxes, where he became the first player to score for six Premiership sides. A spell with Bolton was followed by a lucrative move to Championship side Reading, who in early 2005 tempted Les with a package reportedly worth £18,000 a week. Up to the end of 2004/05 Les had scored one goal in 14 appearances for Reading. On September 15, 2005 the striker joined Watford on a non-contract basis.

Ted Fenton

FERDINAND, Anton   2003-

Born: Peckham, London, 18.2.85
League apps: 52 (1 goal)
Cup apps: 10

ALTHOUGH NAMED AS a substitute by then West Ham manager Glen Roeder for the Premiership visit to Manchester United in December 2002, where he would have faced his older brother Rio had he been called into action, this confident right-back or central defender was still considered to be a season or so away from a regular spot in Hammers' rearguard. That view changed rapidly following relegation however and, ready or not, the England Under-18 international was promptly plunged into the first team for the Division One fixture at Preston North End in August 2003. That the young man from Peckham finished the campaign with 26 senior appearances gives some indication of progress made. Brother of Rio, distant cousin of Les, Anton has tough acts to follow, but remains unfazed. "My aim this season is to be a first team regular, from that I can gain more confidence," the player stated at the start of 2004/05. That ambition seemed quite a modest aim a week later when England Under-21 manager Peter Taylor selected him for the friendly international with the Ukraine at Middlesbrough's Riverside Stadium and played the youngster for the full 90 minutes of the 3-1 win, in which he was joined by his team-mate Nigel Reo-Coker. Thought by some observers to be almost over-confident and too casual on occasions, a bright future seems to beckon if he can remedy these aspects of his play as he'd already shown signs of doing as the 2004/05 season progressed. Anton was voted Young Hammer of the Year by the fans for his performances in 2003/04.

FERDINAND, Rio   1996-2000

Born: Peckham, London, 7.11.78
League apps: 127 (2 goals)
Cup apps: 33 (1 goal)

"OUR ENGLAND UNDER-18 captain from Peckham is a very fine central-defender. He has got great height, strength and will get stronger. Rio has got good ability with the ball and looks an excellent prospect." So wrote West Ham's youth team manager Tony Carr when introducing 17-year-old Rio Ferdinand in the programme notes on the eve of the second leg of the 1996 FA Youth Cup Final at Upton Park, between his young Hammers side and Liverpool's counterparts, who included Jamie Carragher and Michael Owen. One wonders if master coach Tony ever thought that one day his young pupil would realise a world-record transfer fee for a defender just five years later? His meteoric rise was even more remarkable given his somewhat slow progress after signing schoolboy forms in January 1994, when he found himself almost continually on the bench during the youth team's South East Counties League programme in 1994/95, playing just eight matches compared to team-mate Frank Lampard's 24 outings. But a young Rio went from bit part player to taste the big time when he featured in a youth team League Cup Final against Chelsea at the end of that same season. Trailing 5-2 from the first leg of the tie at Upton Park, the young Irons went to Stamford Bridge and won the trophy against all the odds with a 4-1 victory and successful penalty shoot-out. It was a youth team classic witnessed by Harry Redknapp's father, also named Harry, and Redknapp senior wasted little time informing his son of Rio's potential. "That was the game when I realised I was going to be a footballer. I scored a goal and we won on penalties." Rio recalled when he'd made the grade. Consequently, Rio came on as sub for Lee Boylan in the reserves' last match of the season, and after those uncertain beginnings his rise was rapid. Less than a year later, he made his Premiership debut, coming on as sub in the 1-1 draw with Sheffield Wednesday in the last 22 minutes of the final match of the season at Upton Park, just five days after featuring in the losing FA Youth Cup Final against Liverpool. By this time Carr had switched his young starlet into defence from midfield and it turned out to be an inspired move. Scoring his first Premiership goal for Hammers at Blackburn in February 1997, having come on as a substitute forward, he showed his versatility by operating at the centre of defence, midfield and left-back when covering for the injured Julian Dicks during the closing weeks of the season, during which he was capped by England at Under-21 level. Earlier in the campaign he'd been loaned out to Second Division Bournemouth, where he played 11 times for his manager Redknapp's old club. Obviously destined for great things, the young man from Peckham's tough Friary Estate in south-east London began to reap the rewards the strict discipline imposed by his parents had helped him achieve. Ever mindful of the fate that befell some of his old school mates who got in with "the wrong crowd", he grasped his opportunity with both hands and impressed the West Ham fans, who voted him Young Hammer of the Year. In September 1997, however, it did seem that the impressionable young star had indeed taken "the wrong road" when, after being selected for England's squad for the World Cup qualifier against Moldova in September 1997, he was sent home by manager Glenn Hoddle following a drink-driving charge. Given a reprieve, he duly made his England debut in the 2-0 win over Cameroon in November 1998, after making the 22 for France 98, but staying on the bench throughout. The writer of these notes first realised the player's immense potential in a

mundane midweek 1-1 draw between Wimbledon and West Ham at Selhurst Park in March 1997 when, as a mere 17-year-old, he drove forward from defence with all the confidence and class of a Bobby Moore or Franz Beckenbauer, to lift and illuminate a drab south London night with his rare talent. His superlative performances, which belied his tender years, had Hammers fans in raptures, neutral observers awestruck and his manager drooling over his "Rolls Royce of a player". Unsurprisingly, others coveted his sublime skills. Not least, Manchester United supremo Alex Ferguson, who would eventually lure him to Old Trafford. Before that move, however, and his fleeting stint at Leeds, he was West Ham's to savour. Certainly the player's four-year Upton Park tenure between 1996 and 2000 was in direct correlation with the club's most successful times in recent history as the team finished 17th, 8th, 5th and 9th in the Premiership and also qualified for Europe for the first time since 1981. More important was the quality of football and entertainment and, as the names on the team-sheet tripped off the tongue like fine vintage claret, descent to the Nationwide/Coca Cola Championship (call it what you like, it's still the Second Division) seemed inconceivable. During those halcyon days, when the academy classes of 1996 and 1999 were joined by a host of domestic and foreign stars, Rio reigned supreme. Desperately disappointed at being overlooked for Euro 2000 by Kevin Keegan, Hammers' hottest property attracted a £16 million bid from Barcelona after the finals. It was turned down, as was a £15 million offer from Leeds in August 2000. After some outstanding performances for Hammers, Rio won back his England place in the 1-0 friendly defeat by Italy in November but was still the centre of transfer speculation and, after playing a blinder in a 1-0 victory at Elland Road, Leeds finally went for broke with their £18 million bid, which was too good for West Ham United plc to refuse. Yet, just 24 hours before he learnt of the world-record bid and totally unaware of the events that were about to engulf him, Rio told *Hammers News* magazine: "I've said all along that I don't want to leave and the only way I would go is if West Ham said they wanted to sell me. We are capable of achieving success here and if we can get into Europe by winning one of the cups, that will provide the funds to improve the squad even more." After the deal was sealed he added: "West Ham accepting the bid came as a big shock to me. It was a big wrench to leave. It is well documented that I love West Ham. All the coaches have got me to where I am now and I can't thank them enough." Given the captain's armband in his first season at Leeds, he recovered from a shaky start to become a mainstay in defence and also showed his prowess in attack by scoring headers in the Champions League against Deportivo La Coruna and in a 2-1 win at Liverpool. But if Leeds thought they'd found the answer to their prayers they were to be rudely awakened when, despite a successful 2001/02 season for the Yorkshire men, when he was voted into the PFA's Premiership team for the season and featured in his country's World Cup quest in Japan and South Korea, Leeds found themselves in the same position West Ham had been in 17 months earlier when Manchester United tabled a massive £30 million offer in the summer of 2002. Again, Rio took time to find his feet at United, a situation not helped by sustaining an ankle injury in pre-season, which restricted him to just nine starts between August and November. But after overcoming another injury he was the lynchpin of a United defence that boasted the best goals against record of the season as the Red Devils went on to take the Premiership title. Having scored his first goal for England in a 3-0 victory against Denmark in the 2002 World Cup Finals, and making a major contribution to the team's progress to the Quarter-finals, Rio was the first name on Sven

Goran Eriksson's team sheet and seemed destined to be key to the Swede's selection plans for the foreseeable future. That was until the fateful day of Tuesday, September 23, 2003. Only Rio knows why he left United's Carrington training ground without taking a mandatory random drugs test, but his decision not to do so – claiming later that he'd simply forgot – had disastrous ramifications that left his season in tatters and his hopes of representing his country for the 2004 European Championships in Portugal in ruins. Although he eventually passed a rearranged test

48 hours later, the FA were not placated and the events became public knowledge when they omitted Ferdinand from the England squad for a vital qualifying game in Turkey. The player was charged with "the failure or refusal to submit to drugs testing". An eight-month ban and £50,000 fine followed on December 19, 2003 and Rio began his suspension four days later having announced his intention to appeal. The appeal was dismissed on March 18, 2004, however, and the only crumb of comfort for the 25-year-old superstar was that the panel – chaired by

Ian Hill QC – also rejected a request from the FA to have the ban increased to a year. The FA's intention to increase the player's punishment seemed harsh in the extreme, especially in light of revelations of the shenanigans going on in their own organisation. Rio's suspension was lifted on September 20, 2004, leaving him with a lot of catching up to do and a lot to prove. Following indifferent displays in the 4-1 friendly defeat against Denmark in Copenhagen in August 2005, the slender 1-0 World Cup qualifying victory over Wales – courtesy of Joe Cole's goal – at the Millennium

Stadium the following September and the near-catastrophic 1-0 defeat to Northern Ireland in the World Cup qualifier at Windsor Park that same month, Rio was unceremoniously dropped for the vital qualifying clash with Austria at Old Trafford in favour of Arsenal's Sol Campbell on October 10, 2005. Rio showed his true mettle, however, when called upon as a second-half substitute for his ham-strung replacement to give an immaculate performance marshalling ten-man England to a 1-0 win over the Austrians and into the World Cup finals in Germany, 2006.

FERGUSON, Bobby — 1967-80

Born: Ardrossan, Scotland, 1.3.45
League apps: 240
Cup apps: 36

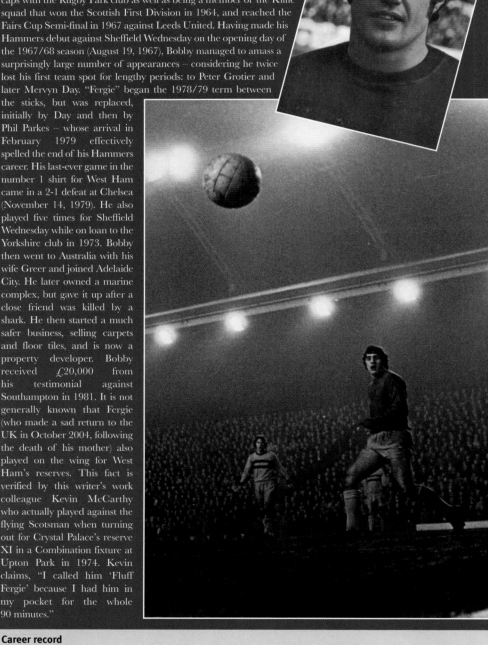

BOBBY WAS SIGNED for the then record British fee for a goalkeeper of £65,000 from Kilmarnock, after winning a string of international caps with the Rugby Park club as well as being a member of the Killie squad that won the Scottish First Division in 1964, and reached the Fairs Cup Semi-final in 1967 against Leeds United. Having made his Hammers debut against Sheffield Wednesday on the opening day of the 1967/68 season (August 19, 1967), Bobby managed to amass a surprisingly large number of appearances – considering he twice lost his first team spot for lengthy periods: to Peter Grotier and later Mervyn Day. "Fergie" began the 1978/79 term between the sticks, but was replaced, initially by Day and then by Phil Parkes – whose arrival in February 1979 effectively spelled the end of his Hammers career. His last-ever game in the number 1 shirt for West Ham came in a 2-1 defeat at Chelsea (November 14, 1979). He also played five times for Sheffield Wednesday while on loan to the Yorkshire club in 1973. Bobby then went to Australia with his wife Greer and joined Adelaide City. He later owned a marine complex, but gave it up after a close friend was killed by a shark. He then started a much safer business, selling carpets and floor tiles, and is now a property developer. Bobby received £20,000 from his testimonial against Southampton in 1981. It is not generally known that Fergie (who made a sad return to the UK in October 2004, following the death of his mother) also played on the wing for West Ham's reserves. This fact is verified by this writer's work colleague Kevin McCarthy who actually played against the flying Scotsman when turning out for Crystal Palace's reserve XI in a Combination fixture at Upton Park in 1974. Kevin claims, "I called him 'Fluff Fergie' because I had him in my pocket for the whole 90 minutes."

Career record

Played	League App	Gls	FAC App	Gls	LC App	Gls	Europe App	Gls	Total App	Gls
1967-68	39	0	3	0	2	0	0	0	44	0
1968-69	39	0	3	0	3	0	0	0	45	0
1969-70	30	0	1	0	2	0	0	0	33	0
1970-71	23	0	1	0	0	0	0	0	24	0
1971-72	36	0	4	0	10	0	0	0	50	0
1972-73	31	0	2	0	0	0	0	0	33	0
1973-74	9	0	0	0	0	0	0	0	9	0
1974-75	0	0	0	0	0	0	0	0	0	0
1975-76	1	0	0	0	0	0	0	0	1	0
1976-77	0	0	0	0	0	0	0	0	0	0
1977-78	19	0	3	0	0	0	0	0	22	0
1978-79	11	0	0	0	1	0	0	0	12	0
1979-80	2	0	0	0	1	0	0	0	3	0
TOTAL	**240**	**0**	**17**	**0**	**19**	**0**	**0**	**0**	**276**	**0**

FEUER, Ian — 1994/2000

Born: Las Vegas, USA, 20.5.71
League apps: 3

ORIGINALLY SIGNED IN May 1994 for £70,000 from Los Angeles Salsa as cover for Ludek Miklosko, Ian had two spells at the Boleyn, but failed to make the first team first time round. Six foot six inches in height, Ian had previously spent five years in Belgium with FC Bruges as a reserve, but had a 35-match spell with RWD Molenbeek before returning home to join Salsa. He represented the States at the Barcelona Olympics and just failed to make the USA's 1994 World Cup squad. Ian was loaned to Second Division Peterborough United in February 1995 and made ten League appearances at London Road before returning to Upton Park to take part in the club's Centenary Tour to Australia that summer. Hammers made a cool £500,000-plus profit on the big American when they sold him to First Division Luton Town in September 1995 where he made 115 League and Cup appearances for the Hatters and was voted Player of the Year in 1997. Allowed to leave Kenilworth Road on a free transfer to the New England Revolution of the US Pro League in March 1998, he moved on to Colorado Rapids the following season. Another free took him back to the UK in January 2000, but he was only at Cardiff City for six weeks when he embarked on his second spell at Hammers on another free transfer. It was the unlikely scenario of an American taking over from a Canadian between Hammers' goalposts that saw big Ian finally make his first team debut – six years after first signing for the club! Drafted in to replace injured Canadian international Craig Forrest in the 2-1 win at Derby, the man from Nevada (whose former brother-in-law was film star Mickey Rourke and whose father played keyboards with Elvis Presley) kept his place for the following two matches, conceding just two goals in the three games in April 2000 before being replaced by Stephen Bywater for the last three matches of 1999/2000. Taking another free transfer to First Division Wimbledon in June 2000, the wandering star made seven League and Cup outings for Dons before a loan move to Derby saw him make a return to Premiership action on two occasions with the Rams before yet another free transfer saw him move on to Second Division Tranmere Rovers in August 2002. Fittingly, after making two appearances at Prenton Park, he appears to have ended his wanderings at Wolverhampton Wanderers where he moved the following month!

FINN, Neil — 1997

Born: Rainham, Essex, 29.12.78
League apps: 1

A PRODUCT OF the West Ham Youth Academy, goalkeeper Neil will probably never forget New Year's Day, 1997. Just three days after his 17th birthday and following injuries to both first-choice Ludek Miklosko and standby Les Sealey, he became the then youngest player ever to appear in a Premiership match. His eleventh hour selection in a 2-1 defeat to Manchester City at Maine Road was sprung on the young rookie after he'd appeared in just three reserve team fixtures, making his accomplished performance all the more remarkable. Able to call on the experience of not only the great, late Les "The Cat" Sealey and Ludo, but also Peter Shilton, Neil made a major contribution towards the youth team's progress to the 1996 FA Youth Cup Final in which he gained a runners-up medal with Frank Lampard and Rio Ferdinand. But the future held no England caps or Champions League Football for Finn as the 2004/05 season found him practising the noble art of goalkeeping for Romford in the Essex Senior League. Yet, he was still earning rave reviews at that level, as a

Romford Recorder report of Boro's 4-0 FA Cup qualifying round defeat at Brook House bore testimony: "It was hard not to feel sympathy for visiting keeper Neil Finn. The former West Ham youngster had produced a series of astounding saves to keep his side in contention for a replay."

FLETCHER, Albert — 1923-24

Born: Wolverhampton, West Midlands, date unknown
League apps: 8 (1 goal)

A REGULAR MEMBER of Hammers' London Combination XI who could operate effectively in either of the inside-forward positions. Chosen to represent the London League on three occasions, Albert made his League debut during the exciting 1922/23 season, in a 2-0 win over Fulham at Craven Cottage. He was previously with Brentford and went back to Griffin Park in 1927, where he made 23 Third Division South appearances and scored one goal.

FLETCHER, Carl — 2004

Born: Camberley, Surrey, 7.4.80
League apps: 33 (2 goals)
Cup apps: 3

WELSH INTERNATIONAL CENTRAL-DEFENDER and midfield man Carl arrived at West Ham with glowing references from his manager at AFC Bournemouth, Sean O'Driscoll – the mentor who guided him through the Cherries youth scheme and made him club captain at Dean Court in 2002. "The biggest compliment I can pay Carl," he said, "is that as his transfer saga evolved, a fee was agreed on Sunday afternoon. Carl spoke with West Ham that evening to settle personal terms. Yet despite the deal being 'done and dusted', he still insisted that he would play in our August Bank Holiday game at Luton. To West Ham's credit, they allowed Carl to play and, with only 11 members of our squad fit, we were delighted to include Carl in the starting line-up. His performance, attitude, and commitment, despite his imminent move to West Ham, and the fact that any injury could have proved disastrous to his future career, are part of the reason he was made captain and why he will be impossible to replace." His former coach at Bournemouth and now number two to Alan Pardew, Peter Grant, was also upbeat about the new signing's prospects: "It speaks volumes for Carl that he was in the Second Division and got picked for Wales, when you look at the quality they've got in their team now. He's a good leader and likes the big occasion, as he proved in the play-offs for Bournemouth at the Millennium Stadium, when he scored two goals as a defender." Welsh coach Mark Hughes gave the 23-year-old his international debut in the 4-0 thrashing of Scotland in February 2004 and has since capped him against Holland, Norway and Canada. After signing for Hammers for a fee of £270,000 on August 31, 2004, Fletcher (who'd made 225 appearances in seven years at Bournemouth) had to dash off to join the Welsh squad ahead of their World Cup qualifying matches against Azerbaijan and Northern Ireland, returning to make his Hammers debut in the 2-1 win against Sheffield United at Bramall Lane (November 11, 2004). Carl experienced all the highs and lows of football in one rollercoaster week in February 2005: on Sunday the 6th, he scored the only goal of the game against Cardiff City at Upton Park; on the Wednesday, he made a major contribution to Wales' 2-0 win against Hungary at the Millennium Stadium; and on the following Sunday, missed the decisive spot-kick in the FA Cup Fourth Round replay against Sheffield United! Carl must have been disappointed to have been limited to a solitary Play-off substitute appearance in the Semi-final against Ipswich at Portman Road, thus missing another opportunity to shine at the Millennium Stadium. September 2005 saw Carl agree a one-month loan signing with Championship outfit Watford.

Carl Fletcher

FLETCHER, Jack — 1904-05

SL apps: 25 (7 goals)
Cup apps: 1

JACK WAS AN inside-right who also played at inside-left in his 25 appearances during Hammers' first season at the Boleyn Ground. He scored the first of his seven goals against arch-rivals Millwall in a 1-1 draw at The Den (September 17,1904). Signed from Reading in 1904, he joined Queens Park Rangers for 1905/06 and then transferred to Fulham.

FLYNN, Jack — 1904-05

Born: birthplace unknown, 1875
SL apps: 20 (3 goals)
Cup apps: 1 (1 goal)

JACK FLYNN IS officially credited with scoring one of Hammers' goals when they defeated Millwall 3-0 in the first match at the Boleyn (September 1, 1904). Some historians have listed Billy Bridgeman as netting all three – a fact unsubstantiated by the newspaper reports of the day. Jack served Bristol City in the Second Division of the Football League in 1901/02 and joined Reading in the close season of 1902. Hammers signed him from the Biscuitmen in 1904.

FOAN, Albert — 1950-56

Born: Rotherhithe, London, 30.10.23
League apps: 53 (6 goals)
Cup apps: 7 (3 goals)

A LONDONER WHO escaped the attention of the capital's clubs until Hammers signed him from Norwich City, Albert was equally at home on the wing or at inside-forward. His finest hour at Upton Park came during the great Cup run of 1955/56, when he scored a hat-trick against Preston North End. Albert joined up with former Hammer Almer Hall at Kent League Margate when he left the club. He later enjoyed four seasons with Lowestoft, where his former Hammers' team-mate Mike Grice was on the opposite wing, and for whom the pair were in action against Leyton Orient in an FA Cup First Round tie in November 1966 at Brisbane Road.

FOE Marc-Vivien — 1999-2000

Born: Nkolo, Cameroon, 1.5.75
League apps: 38 (1 goal)
Cup apps: 10 (1 goal)

THE SHOCKING DEATH of Cameroon international Marc-Vivien Foe during his country's Confederations Cup Semi-final against Columbia in Lyon, France on June 26, 2003 stunned the football world and all who'd come in contact with the genial "gentle giant". He'd become West Ham's record signing when he arrived at Upton Park from French First Division side Lens in January 1999 for a fee of £4.2 million. The player's wife, Marie-Louise, was in the Gerland Stadium – the home of Marco's club Olympique Lyonnais – when the tragedy unfolded and watched in horror as her husband collapsed on the pitch and was pronounced dead 45 minutes later without regaining consciousness. Soccer's ruling body FIFA confirmed the player had suffered from diarrhoea before the game, but Cameroon team doctor Olivier Assamba said the player had recovered from the stomach upset. Of a death that seemed to present more questions than answers, Assamba said: "We definitely think there is no cause-and-effect link between this problem and what happened." FIFA issued a statement backing up his view, which read: "The results confirmed that there was no infection. Treatment was infusion of NaCl (sodium chloride) and Imodium. On the evening of June 25, the player felt well." Cameroon team captain Rigobert Song, was moved to say: "It's terrible, yesterday at half-time, his last words were 'Boys, even if it means dying on the pitch, we must win this Semi-final', and he was the victim." Although an aneurysm in the brain was initially suspected of being a possible cause of death, Hammers manager Harry Redknapp revealed he had failed a medical before joining West Ham because of an enlarged heart. The then Hammers chief explained: "At first it seemed his enlarged heart may be a problem. But when we sent him to a heart specialist we were told this was perfectly normal in African players and that we could go ahead with the signing." At his post mortem the cause of death was "natural causes" and ruled out the possibility of any stimulants in Foe's body, but determined that his death was of cardiac origin. The season before his death Marc had been on loan to Manchester City where he'd become a firm favourite with the City fans and, in his final and 35th Premiership game for the Sky Blues, had the eternal honour of scoring the last ever goal at Maine Road. His tally of nine goals for the Mancunians was the most he'd scored in ten seasons in Europe, where he'd built his reputation more as a maker, rather than a taker, of goals. He'd managed one less than that total in 64 internationals for Cameroon. His one Premiership goal for Hammers came in a thrilling 4-3 home win over Sheffield Wednesday in November 1999. Frank Lampard Snr, who was assistant manager during Foe's spell with the club, recalled: "He was a coach's dream in that he was always early into training and always got on with his work. I can't emphasise that enough. He was very fit and you could never fault his attitude. To come and play in England and adapt so well was incredible, but he was always so conscious of his family back home. He never left West Ham because we wanted him to; it was purely financial circumstances at that time." Club physio John Green recalled just how fit he was: "Everyone remembers the time Marc came back pre-season, after having malaria and, in his first running session, smashed his best time. He was a tremendous athlete and, for me, he would have made a fantastic captain of this club – he was very vocal when he wanted to be. He also did a lot of work for needy people back home in Cameroon and I remember him buying £20,000 worth of crutches to ship back there on one occasion." Another who remembers Marc fondly is club lensman Steve Bacon, who recalled: "One day Marc asked me to print up some photographs to send back home to his family. When I gave him the prints a few days later he was delighted, saying, 'thank you, these are for my father, he will be so proud'. Then putting his hand across his chest he added, 'thank you, thank you from my heart'. They were just a few pictures but they obviously meant so much to him. It was a real shock to hear of his death at such a young age, he really was a gentleman." A benefit match was staged between Cameroon and a Friendship XI at the Stade Gerland, where he died in October 2003, and was attended by Kevin Keegan and his City team-mates Sylvain Distin and Antoine Sibierski. Foe left Upton Park in a £6 million switch to Olympique Lyonnais in the summer of 2000, but left behind many friends at West Ham.

FORD, William   1905-06

Born: Scotland, 1881
SL apps: 7 (1 goal)

BILL FORD MADE seven Southern League appearances during West Ham's second year at the Boleyn Ground in 1905/06. His initial outing came in the opening fixture against Swindon Town at inside-right but he played his remaining matches at outside-right, the final one in the penultimate game of the campaign – a 3-1 defeat at Brentford. Bill began his career in earnest with Scottish junior side The Rovers before signing for the then Scottish Northern League club Arbroath. He later played for Hearts and Motherwell before moving south to join Portsmouth from where he transferred to Irons at the end of 1904/05.

FORDE, Steven   1937-51

Born: South Kirkby, Yorkshire, 29.8.14
League apps: 170 (1 goal)
Cup apps: 6

S. FORDE (Full-back)

YET ANOTHER WHO had his playing career badly disrupted by World War II, Steve saw service with Sheffield Wednesday, Wolves and Rotherham United before arriving at the Boleyn Ground in 1937. Making his debut against Tottenham in April 1938, he looked set for a long run in the first XI, but circumstances decreed otherwise. He did, however, play in the victorious War Cup Semi-final against Fulham that saw Hammers through to Wembley. It was after demobilisation that the tough Yorkshireman showed his true worth, turning in some sterling performances and being ever-present in 1947/48. One of the finest full-backs to appear for the club in the immediate post-war period, Steve retired from League soccer in 1951 and later managed Penzance in the Western League.

FOREMAN, Alec George   1939-46

Born: West Ham, London, 1.3.14
League apps: 6 (1 goal)
Cup apps: 3 (1 goal)

NOT TO BE confused with the other pre-war Hammer of the same surname, this former England and Walthamstow amateur was shaping up well at centre-forward when World War II broke out. The highlight of his fragmented time with the club must surely have been the Football League War Cup Final at Wembley in 1940. It was from a shot by George, which the Blackburn keeper fisted out, that Sam Small scored the

only goal to take the cup to Upton Park. George's wartime playing record was second to none. He scored a staggering 154 goals in 156 Football League South and London League appearances and netted a further 34-goal haul in 46 various Cup competitions. Transferred to Spurs, where he scored 15 goals in 37 matches in 1946/47. George died in June 1969.

FOREMAN, John   1934-36

Born: Tanfield, Newcastle-upon-Tyne, 1914
League apps: 49 (7 goals)
Cup apps: 2

A DURHAM SCHOOLBOY, previously with Sunderland, John made his first appearance for West Ham on the right-wing against Plymouth Argyle at Upton Park (September 29, 1934). He went on to make 21 Second Division outings that season and only one less the following campaign before being superseded by Stan Foxall in 1936/37. In order to obtain regular first team football the speedy flankman transferred to Bury (November 3, 1937).

FORREST, Craig   1997-2003

Born: Vancouver, Canada, 20.9.67
League apps: 30
Cups apps: 7

SIGNED FROM IPSWICH Town for £500,000 in July 1997, this giant six foot four inch goalkeeper became Hammers' first Canadian-born player since amateur Mickey Newman, who featured in the 1957/58 promotion season. A product of the Suffolk club's successful youth policy, Craig made 304 senior appearances for the Tractor Boys after a brief 11-match spell on loan to neighbours Colchester United in 1988. In 1994/95 his consistency was rewarded by the Ipswich fans, who voted him their Player of the Year as he put his huge frame to good use on his team's behalf and kept opposing forwards at bay with his ability to stand up until the last possible moment. Put out on loan to Chelsea after losing his place in the Town side following an injury, he made three Premiership outings for the Blues at the end of the 1996/1997 campaign before joining Hammers at the close of the season. Beginning his Upton Park career as understudy to the great Ludek Miklosko, Craig kept a clean sheet on his Boleyn bow, taking over from the injured Ludo in the 3-1 win over Bolton Wanderers in October 1997 and went on to claim the number 1 spot in 20 of the next 23 matches in what was his best spell at the club. During his tenure between the posts, Hammers lost just four of their 13 Premiership games and progressed to the Quarter-finals of both the Coca-Cola Cup and the FA Cup, where they lost out in both competitions in three titanic matches with Arsenal. Indeed, it was the penalty shoot-out heroics of Forrest that got his side through a nail-biting Fifth Round FA Cup replay at Blackburn Rovers to earn another crack at the Gunners. With the tie all square at 1-1 after extra time at Ewood, Craig saved Ian Hendry's spot-kick and then watched as Steve Lomas connected to put Irons through 5-4 on penalties. "Penalty shoot-outs are a bit like tossing a coin to see who wins, and when Hendry stepped up I was beginning to run out of

Alec George Foreman

ideas, but you have to stay sharp and I managed to keep his shot out with my foot." Unfortunately there was a price to pay for his valiant display and an injury sustained against Rovers sidelined him for the rest of the season. With Shaka Hislop taking over from Forrest's original replacement Bernard Lama at the beginning of the 1998/1999 season, the

unlucky custodian made only one start that season having to wait for the last game of the campaign to do so in the 4-0 trouncing of Middlesbrough at Upton Park that enabled the club to reach fifth in the Premiership. He was still rated number one by Canada, however, and they rewarded his loyalty with the captaincy against Northern Ireland in April 1999. Despite sustaining a broken finger and only managing nine Premiership appearances in 1999/2000, Craig continued to represent the Maple Leafs and was selected for both the World Cup qualifiers and the Confederation Cup tournament by his country, garnering a total of 56 caps. The 2000/01 season provided even fewer opportunities for the popular Canadian as he made just four Premiership appearances and five for the reserves, but dark days were looming for Craig that would put life into perspective. Diagnosed with testicular cancer, Craig fought his greatest battle with the disease and, like Bobby Moore in 1965, overcame it. Although he bravely played in two reserve fixtures in 2001/02, Craig took the advice of his doctors who instructed him to retire from the game. Reluctantly hanging up his boots to pursue his media work, having had a successful spell commentating on the 2002 World Cup for Canadian TV, Craig left a message before leaving the Boleyn: "I would like to thank a lot of people at the club for their support. Glenn (Roeder), the medical staff, the board, the staff at the club and not least the fans who sent me letters of encouragement. I would like to go on the record to thank the club for the sensitive way they handled my situation and although it is difficult to face up to my career coming to an end, the main thing is I've come through my illness."

FORSTER, Harry   1912-14

SL apps: 40
Cup apps: 4

THIS LEFT-BACK WAS signed from Sunderland and made his Boleyn bow in the 4-0 win over Exeter City on the opening match of the 1912/13 season. He played in 25 Southern League games in that campaign, in addition to four FA Cup ties, but lost his place to George Irvine after appearing in a 1-0 home defeat to Southend United (December 6, 1914).

FOSTER, Colin   1989-94

Born: Chislehurst, Kent, 16.7.64
League apps: 93 (4 goals)
Cup apps: 14 (2 goals)

COLIN WAS LOU Macari's second signing when he moved from Nottingham Forest back to east London in a £750,000 deal in September 1989. At six foot four inches, "Fozzie" was one of the tallest central defenders in the country and made his debut at Upton Park against Watford (September 23, 1989) – the club he finally left Hammers for in March 1994. Colin, who made his League debut for Leyton Orient at Grimsby (January 9, 1982) while still an apprentice, played 174 League matches for the O's before his £50,000 transfer to Forest (May 1987). He made a further 72 League appearances under Brian Clough at the City Ground. Although Colin was Macari's most expensive signing, he failed to earn a regular first team place in his first season. He was, however, a regular during the 1990/91 Second Division promotion campaign, but a succession of injuries limited his contribution in the next three seasons when he struggled to win a first team place. A projected £400,000 transfer back to Forest fell through when Colin failed to agree personal terms at the start of the 1992/93 season and he remained with Hammers on a weekly contract from then until his eventual move. Notts County looked likely to end his spell in the wilderness of the Combination League when they took him on loan for two months from January 1994, but West Ham finally cut their losses and accepted £100,000 for Colin from First Division Watford, just prior to the March 1994 transfer deadline.

The undoubted highlight of Fozzie's time at Upton Park was his volleyed goal in the 1991 FA Cup Quarter-final victory against Everton that set up the Semi-final showdown with his former club, Forest. Colin went on to play 86 League and Cup games for the Hornets before leaving on a free transfer to join Third Division Cambridge United in March 1997 where he made a further 38 League and Cup appearances before being released in the summer of 1999.

FOSTER, Jack — 1908-09

Born: birthplace unknown, 1883
SL apps: 15 (9 goals)

SIGNED FROM SUNDERLAND, centre-forward Jack made a scoring start in the first game of the season against Queens Park Rangers at Upton Park. His scoring rate was a match for any, as he rifled home nine goals in 15 Southern League appearances, including a hat-trick in a 3-1 victory over Portsmouth at the Boleyn. But Jack's exploits had caught the attention of Southampton, and he was soon back in red and white stripes again, this time down on the south coast in exchange for Saints' Frank Costello. After only one goal in six appearances at the Dell, Jack transferred back to his native Yorkshire with Huddersfield Town in May 1909. He joined Castleford Town in 1910.

FOXALL, Joseph Stanley — 1934-39

Born: Crowle, Lincolnshire, 8.10.14
League apps: 106 (37 goals)
Cup apps: 7 (5 goals)

STAN (OR JOE) was another import from Gainsborough Trinity. Partnering Johnny Morton in the latter's first game for the Midland League club against local rivals Lincoln St Andrews, he had three seasons in Lincolnshire. Sometimes known as the "Mystery Man", because his unorthodox methods were baffling to opponents (and occasionally to his team-mates), he was nevertheless a fine player who could operate anywhere in the forward line. He started for London Combination against Central League in November 1936, he was also a member of the West Ham team that won the Football League War Cup in 1940. In the season leading up to World War II, Stan was encouraged to adopt a more direct approach by manager Charlie Paynter, who switched him into the near-centre of attack. With Sam Small moving out to the wing, the results were devastating. In the 1938/39 season his name became a byword for concern to rivals Spurs when, in four meetings, beginning with a League match at White Hart Lane on October 29, he hit a nap-hand of goals. "He was in his own half when he received the ball," *The Times* reported, "but a combination of swerve and speed took him right through the defenders until he had only Hooper to beat and he equalised." West Ham lost 2-1, but it was a different story when the two sides met there in the Fourth Round of the FA Cup. *The Times* again: "On a pitch that was so generously covered in sand as to suggest spades and donkey rides rather than football, not only did Foxall score two brilliant goals but his mere presence in the centre – after a somewhat unprofitable time on the right wing until West Ham were two down – seemed to revitalise the team. Almost immediately he scored a magnificent goal after a long dribble, and when he did very much the same sort of thing again ten minutes from the end, West Ham drew level." In the Upton Park replay, Foxall and Small again switched roles. After Archie Macaulay had missed a penalty, Spurs went in front on 29 minutes, but four minutes later Foxall equalised for the third time in three matches. In the second replay in front of a 50,000 crowd at Highbury, Spurs led again, but after 55 minutes the "Fox" struck again. He latched on to a long clearance, held off the challenges of two defenders and beat Hooper with a stinging, low shot from outside the area. A crucial goal that led the way for Macaulay to hit the winner. Stan scored 63 goals in 156 League and Cup matches during World War

II, but suffered a knee injury against Queens Park Rangers in September 1944, which effectively ended his career. Stan died at the age of 76 on August 12, 1991.

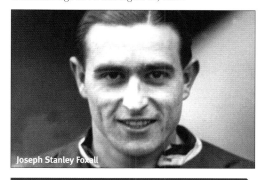
Joseph Stanley Foxall

FOXE, Hayden — 2000-02

Born: Sydney, Australia, 23.6.77
League apps: 11
Cup apps: 1

HARRY REDKNAPP OBVIOUSLY thought highly of this gritty, Aussie defender, having tracked him for some time before signing him from J-League side Sanfrecce Hiroshima. Before his spell in Japan, Foxe had made one senior appearance for German side Arminia Bielefeld and had been at Dutch giants Ajax at the same time as Hammers star Dani, but had failed to make any impact. Trouble with a work permit delayed his debut an incredible eight months and by the time he had made his Premiership bow at the end of March 2001, his manager's tenure was nearly over at Upton Park. After a miserable season under Glenn Roeder, during which he made only six Premiership outings and one in the 3-0 FA Cup win at Macclesfield Town, the player rejoined his old mentor at Portsmouth for a fee of £400,000 and played 32 times (one goal) in Pompey's charge to the First Division Championship. A further ten appearances were curtailed by a foot injury that kept him out of action for the rest of 2003/04.

FREEMAN, Thomas — 1895-96 TIW

Born: Northfleet, Kent, c. 1869

PLAYED MAINLY IN the Irons' reserve team but won a Cup winners' medal in the West Ham Charity Cup final of 1895/96 and played in the club's first ever FA Cup match against Chatham.

FROST, A — 1910-12

Born: birthplace unknown, 1888
SL apps: 4

THIS CENTRE-FORWARD-CUM-INSIDE-FORWARD made his first team baptism in the 2-0 Upton Park win over Luton Town (February 18, 1911) from the inside-right berth after joining Irons from Southend United. He was on duty again on the 18th of the following month, again at the Boleyn, in a 4-1 thrashing of Exeter City. His final game was in the last match of the 1911/12 season at Coventry.

FROST, James — 1907-08

Born: Wolverton, Buckinghamshire, 1880
SL apps: 20 (4 goals)
Cup apps: 5

JIM MADE HIS first Hammers bow on the right-wing in the 1-0 home win over Luton Town (January 25, 1908). It was the start of an uninterrupted 13-match run in the Southern League side that saw him get on the scoresheet against Portsmouth, Watford and Norwich City. His last appearance for the club was also against Luton, but this time the scores were reversed, with the Hatters winning

1-0 at Kenilworth Road (January 20, 1909). Previously with Northampton Town and Chelsea, he transferred with colleague Bill Yenson to play for Croydon Common in that club's first season in the First Division of the Southern League in 1909/10. He played for his local Wolverton team as a 16-year-old and played against TIW in the Second Division of the Southern League in January 1899.

FRYATT, William — 1931-32

Born: Matlock, Derbyshire, date unknown
League apps: 3

BILL WAS A reserve left-back who made his League debut in a 1-0 defeat by Derby County at Upton Park (March 28, 1931). He failed to make any First Division appearances the following season, but had two more outings on Hammers' return to Division Two in 1932/33 in successive defeats against Bury and Lincoln City. Bill had a novel experience when, with team-mates Bill Johnson and Jimmy Ruffell, he played in the first FA official floodlight match in England (January 4, 1933). The experimental game was staged at the White City Stadium using players picked from London's League clubs and with the ball being dipped frequently in a bucket of whitewash before a crowd of 12,000 curious onlookers!

FURNELL, David — 1897-98 TIW

Born: West Ham, London, June 1874

PREVIOUSLY WITH THE Old Castle Swifts club, this keeper played in all three of Thames Ironworks' FA Cup ties in 1897/98 and was a regular in the London League side. He moved to Hammersmith Athletic in 1898/99.

FUTRE, Paulo — 1996

Born: Montijo, Portugal, 28.2.66
League apps: 9

THOUGH THIS PORTUGUESE legend was signed in the same week that Hammers recruited four other international stars, including Romanian club record signing Florin Raducioiu, in a frantic three-day spending spree in July 1996, it was the free transfer capture of 31-year-old Paulo from AC Milan under the Bosman ruling that caught the public's imagination and made the biggest headlines. Having cost his six previous employers almost £20 million there could be no doubting the pedigree of a player whose sublime skills had graced the arenas of FC Porto (where he helped win the Portuguese Championships in 1985 and 1986), Atletico Madrid (Spanish Cup winners in 1991/92), Benfica (Portuguese Cup winners in 1993), Marseille and Milan. His fitness, however, was another matter as the injury-plagued star had suffered a knee tendon problem that ruled him out of all but one game in his year at the San Siro. Signed on a two-year contract with a one-year option, the player was so determined to allay West Ham's fears over his fitness that he took the unusual step of signing a clause in his contract stating that if, for any reason, he had a problem with his knee, West Ham would have the option to tear up the agreement. The importance of that stipulation soon became apparent when, despite some mouth-watering glimpses of his talent, it became obvious that Paulo was only a shadow of the player who had terrorised Europe and represented Portugal 41 times at international level. Having set himself a personal target of 12 goals for the season and winning back his international place, a hamstring injury after just five outings saw him sidelined once again, as the Hammers management no doubt thought about invoking the contract clause. After returning for a run of four further matches in 1996, Futre's bad knee played up again and by mutual agreement he retired, regretting that the West Ham fans hadn't seen the best of him. Futre is now director of football at Atletico Madrid.

G

GALE, Tony
GALL, Herbert
GALLAGHER, Joe
GAMBLE, Frederick
GARCIA, Richard
GARDNER, David
GATLAND, Bill
GAULT, James
GAZZARD, Gerry
GEGGUS, John
GIBBINS, Vivian
GILMORE, Henry
GLOVER, Horace
GODDARD, J
GODDARD, Paul
GOODACRE, Reg
GORDON, Dale

GORE, Reg
GOULD, Bobby
GOULDEN, Len
GRASSAM, William
GREAVES, Jimmy
GREEN, Bill
GREEN, Tommy
GREEN, Tommy
GREGORY, Ernie
GREGORY, John
GRESHAM, George
GRICE, Mike
GRIFFITHS, Frederick
GROTIER, Peter
GUEST, Billy
GUNNING, Harry
GURKIN, John

Jimmy Greaves

GALE, Tony   1984-94

Born: Westminster, London, 19.12.59
League apps: 300 (5 goals)
Cup apps: 59 (2 goals)

ONE OF THE most stylish and accomplished central defenders in Hammers' history, Tony proved a real bargain when John Lyall signed him from Fulham for £200,000 – the fee decided by tribunal – in the summer of 1984. It is perhaps unfortunate that, despite giving Hammers sterling service in 359 League and Cup games over a ten-year period, the one match fans will remember most is that fateful 1991 FA Cup Semi-final when "Galey" was controversially sent off 26 minutes into the game against Nottingham Forest. Sheffield referee Keith Hackett must have been the only person inside Villa Park that afternoon who thought the West Ham number 4 deserved a red card for an alleged professional foul, after clashing with Forest winger Gary Crosby. West Ham supporters – who saw their side tumble to a 4-0 defeat after Tony's dismissal – have never forgiven Hackett, who did not officiate again at Upton Park between that black day (April 14, 1991) and his retirement from the League list in May 1994. Ironically, it was in this same month that Tony's long and distinguished West Ham career also ended. He was given a free transfer on the day of his testimonial game (against a Republic of Ireland XI, on May 8, 1994), 24 hours after making his 300th, and final, League appearance for Hammers against Southampton. That sending-off – the only blemish in a career spanning 577 League appearances for two clubs – will haunt Tony forever, but it should not overshadow his immense contribution and loyalty to the club. He first caught the eye with London and Middlesex Schools and signed as an apprentice for Fulham in 1977. Tony made the first of 277 League appearances for the Cottagers against Charlton Athletic at Craven Cottage (August 20, 1977), although his first team debut came at Leyton Orient (Anglo-Italian Cup, August 11, 1976) while he was still only 16 years old. Tony was given the huge responsibility of trying to replace Bobby Moore, who had moved there from West Ham in 1973 and was nearing the end of his illustrious career. Although disappointed to play only one match alongside the legendary Moore – a reserve team game against Bristol City – Tony was, however, privileged to be a team-mate of another football superstar, George Best (seven times) as well as acting as boot boy for Rodney Marsh during the most colourful era in the club's history. Manager Bobby Campbell appointed Gale captain of Fulham's first team at the age of 18 (a role he occasionally fulfilled at Upton Park in the absence of others) and, under Malcolm MacDonald in 1982, he led the team to promotion to Division Two. When Billy Bonds seemed set to retire at the end of the 1983/84 season, Hammers boss John Lyall turned to Tony for his replacement. Having followed in Moore's footsteps at Craven Cottage, this was another huge burden for the west Londoner. "Bonzo" subsequently

made several remarkable comebacks before finally retiring as a player in May 1988, but he did not prevent Galey from firmly establishing himself at the heart of West Ham's defence. In his second season in east London, Tony formed a formidable partnership with Alvin Martin that served Hammers so well, as they achieved their highest-ever First Division placing – third – in 1985/86. Tony saw it all in his time at Upton Park – two relegation and two promotion seasons – but he never compromised his own high standards. No one has ever seen Tony Gale aimlessly boot the ball into touch. He has always been comfortable on the ball – a talent underlined by the fact that he occasionally pushed forward into midfield. A classy player who epitomised the best traditions of West Ham United, Tony was a perceptive reader of the game who used the ball well. His effective execution of free-kicks was illustrated when he curled home the fourth goal in a memorable 4-1 1988 League Cup victory over Liverpool. His scoring efforts were few and far between, but Tony helped create a number of goals with his near-post flicks from corners and, although not a naturally aggressive defender, he added another dimension to his game in his last two

seasons at Upton Park, when he had to assume a more dominant role in the air, alongside his shorter partner, Steve Potts. A dressing room comic who was dubiously nicknamed "Reggie" (after notorious East End gangland boss Reggie Kray!) for his wicked sense of humour, Tony Gale was a true character and quality footballer who served the club with distinction. In a sensational turnaround of his fortunes, Tony was called upon by Blackburn Rovers on the eve of the 1994/95 season to play in a prestige friendly against Celtic at Hampden Park and impressed Kenny Dalglish and his assistant Ray Harford sufficiently to earn a three-month contract and a Charity Shield appearance at Wembley – his first at the famous venue in 17 years as a pro! Tony was given an extension on his contract at Ewood and famously went on to win a Champions medal with Rovers in the twilight of his career. Galey, who had been training with Third Division Barnet when he got the call from Rover's manager Kenny Dalglish, must have had to pinch himself as he fulfilled a dream ending to his first-class career, and the most amazing "swansong" in Premiership history! Tony spent the 1995/96 season back in London with Crystal Palace, but was plagued by an ankle-tendon injury, which saw him restricted to just two First Division outings and one in the FA Cup. After playing under three managers in that campaign – Steve Coppell, Ray Lewington and Dave Bassett – and a season as player-coach with his old mate Alan Devonshire at Maidenhead United, he wisely decided to announce his retirement and go into the media, forming a seven-year association with Capital Gold and working alongside Jonathan Pearce as a summariser. He soon earned the tag of "the people's pundit" at the station. Having partnered "Pearcey" almost as long as he had Alvin Martin, Galey switched seamlessly from radio to television as a summariser on Sky TV and also pens a weekly column for the *Sun* newspaper.

GALL, Herbert   1935

Born: Glasgow, Scotland, date unknown
League apps: 1

A TRICKY OUTSIDE-LEFT, Herbert made his only first team appearance in the 3-0 defeat against Newcastle United at St James's Park (February 23, 1935). Signed from Aberdeen prior to the 1934/35 season, he returned north of the border the following summer to join St Mirren.

GALLAGHER, Joe   1983

Born: Liverpool, Merseyside, 11.1.55
League apps: 9
Cup apps: 2

JOE WAS AN emergency signing from Wolves, where he was at loggerheads with the Molineux management over a difference of opinion. Drafted into the side following the suspension of Alvin Martin during the 1982/83 season, he proved a capable deputy. An experienced professional, he was with Birmingham City before joining Wolves. He teamed up with former Hammer John Bond's multi-million pound Burnley squad in the summer of 1984. Joe was forced to retire in 1987, and gained coaching qualifications but failed to break into management and, after a short spell with Birmingham City in their community departments, he took a job with Land Rover, where he still works. He is a matchday host at St Andrews.

GAMBLE, Frederick   1931

Born: Charing Cross, London, 29.5.1905
League apps: 2 (2 goals)

FREDDIE WAS A magnificently built centre-forward whose six-foot frame was capable of unsettling the

Career record

	League		FAC		LC		Europe		Total	
Played	App	Gls	App	Gls	App	Gls	App	Gls	App	Gls
1984-85	37	0	0	0	3	0	0	0	40	0
1985-86	42	0	7	0	3	0	0	0	52	0
1986-87	32	2	4	1	4	0	0	0	40	3
1987-88	18	0	2	0	0	0	0	0	20	0
1988-89	31	0	5	0	6	1	0	0	42	1
1989-90	36	1	1	0	7	0	0	0	44	1
1990-91	24	1	7	0	1	0	0	0	32	1
1991-92	25	0	2	0	4	0	0	0	31	0
1992-93	23	1	0	0	0	0	0	0	23	1
1993-94	32	0	1	0	2	0	0	0	35	0
TOTAL	**300**	**5**	**29**	**1**	**30**	**1**	**0**	**0**	**359**	**7**

strongest of defences. At Upton Park, however, Fred had stiff competition for the first team places in the form of Vivian Gibbins and Victor Watson; and although he scored in both his First Division appearances, at Bolton and Leicester respectively, he was never given the opportunity to show the Boleyn fans his undoubted talent at the highest level. Starting his career with Southall, as did former Hammers favourite Alan Devonshire, he signed professional forms for Brentford before joining West Ham in 1931. He later returned to Griffin Park. Fred died on May 15, 1965.

GARCIA, Richard — 2001-04

Born: Perth, Australia, 9.4.81
League apps: 16
Cup apps: 6

THE LONGEST-SURVIVING MEMBER of Hammers' Australian Youth Academy graduates, Richard joined fellow Aussies Chris Coyne, Steve Laurie and Michael Ferrante in seeking his future away from Upton Park when he transferred to Second Division Colchester United in early September 2004. After making his 22nd and final appearance in the claret and blue in the 2-1 defeat against Coventry City at Highfield Road, Richard joined the U's in a deal arranged during the summer. Richard spent his formative years in the Western Australian State League with Kingsway Olympic and left for the UK at the age of 15 in July 1997, signing apprentice forms for Hammers in September of the same year. The 1998/99 season was a productive one for the young Aussie as he scored in every round of the Hammers youth team's success in winning the FA Youth Cup, represented Australia in the Youth World Cup and signed pro for West Ham. From 2000/01 Garcia was loaned out in time-honoured tradition to Third Division neighbours Leyton Orient and caught the eye with some impressive displays at Brisbane Road. He made his O's debut in a 1-0 win at Plymouth Argyle and two weeks later hit a brace against Blackpool at Bloomfield Road, the second a spectacular overhead kick to secure a point in a 2-2 draw. Set to sign a year's extension on the loan agreement in November 2000, disaster struck at Cheltenham Town when he was injured in a tackle with another Hammers loanee, Grant McCann. The result was snapped cruciate ligaments, which put paid to his Orient career after he'd scored four times in 21 League and Cup games. Recovered after specialist treatment in Australia, Richie signed a new one-year deal with Hammers in May 2000 and made his senior debut against Reading in the Worthington Cup in a Second Round clash that saw his side go down 5-4 on penalties after a 1-1 draw after extra time. The following February he made his Premiership debut in a 1-0 defeat at Bolton. Hoping to establish himself more than last term, his early season form was encouraging until he suffered ligament damage in September. Returning to action, he was picked to play for the Australian Under-23 team in Olympic trials in January 2004, but unfortunately twisted a cartilage and was ruled out for the rest of the season. Of Garcia's switch, manager Alan Pardew said: "The move was perfect for Richard and I think he'll do well for Colchester. He's a terrific lad and he needs to play. But I felt if I kept him here it would only have been as a squad player."

GARDNER, David — 1904-07

Born: Glasgow, Scotland, 31.3.1873
SL apps: 77
Cup apps: 3

DAVID BEGAN HIS career with his local club Third Lanark as an amateur before turning pro in 1896. Transferring to Newcastle United in May 1899, he made his Football League debut for the Magpies in his usual left-

Gerry Gazzard

back berth against West Bromwich Albion at Stoney Lane (September 2, 1899). In all he made 80 appearances in the famous black and white stripes before his next move, to Grimsby Town for a reported fee of £250 in May 1902. A healthy 51 appearances were added to his growing record following his debut for the Mariners in August 1902, and he was soon appointed captain of the team; an honour bestowed on him by every club he served. His move to West Ham coincided with the club's switch to the Boleyn Ground, and he was on duty there for the first Southern League match with Millwall (September 1, 1904). An ever-present for the 1905/06 season, he was described variously as: "A thoughtful player, as fast as most forwards and possessor of an excellent kick. A great favourite with the spectators, an intelligent and elegant player, a perfect gentleman, too." Dave possessed a crowd-pleasing trick of back-heeling the ball to fool his opponent. He assisted Croydon Common when he left Hammers in 1907, and was Leicester City's trainer from 1919 until his death in 1931, which occurred while he was indulging his second greatest sporting passion – golf. David won one cap for Scotland against Wales in 1887.

GATLAND, Bill — 1921

SL apps: 1

A RIGHT-WINGER, BILL made a solitary Second Division appearance in Hammers' penultimate fixture of 1920/21 – a 2-1 win over South Shields at Upton Park.

GAULT, James — 1907-09

Born: Aberdeen, Scotland, date unknown
SL apps: 49
Cup apps: 2

A RIGHT-BACK OF average height and weight, James joined Hammers from Aberdeen and made his first Southern League appearance in a 1-1 draw at Swindon (September 14, 1907), when West Ham fielded a club-record six Scots. Absent on only two occasions up to the end of that season, his appearances were greatly reduced in the following campaign when he faced rivalry for the number 2 spot from Fred Shreeve, who eventually won the battle, the Aberdonian's fate being settled after taking part in a 6-0 defeat at Northampton Town (February 27, 1909). Syd King had earlier acclaimed him: "The best full-back

in Scotland." James spent his formative years with Victoria Thistle and Abergeldie, north of the border.

GAZZARD, Gerry — 1949-54

Born: Cinderford, Gloucestershire, 15.3.25
League apps: 119 (29 goals)
Cup apps: 7 (3 goals)

THE ORIGINAL "PIRATE OF PENZANCE", this likeable West Countryman was discovered playing as an inside-forward for Penzance, but had turned out 20 times as an orthodox winger for the County of Cornwall XI. Signing pro for Hammers in May 1949, he made his first team bow against Luton Town on the opening day of the following season. He had 37 appearances in 1949/50, and was one game short of being an ever-present the next campaign. Troubled by a cartilage injury, he moved to Brentford after losing his place to John Dick, and played out the rest of his career back at Penzance as a reinstated amateur with the Magpies. Gerry's grandson, Carl Gazzard, is wicketkeeper of Somerset CC.

GEGGUS, John — 1909-12

League apps: 31

JACK, AS HE was better known, made his Hammers debut between the posts in a 2-2 Southern League draw against New Brompton at Upton Park, but things didn't always go smoothly for the former Custom House custodian. In a match at Leyton in April 1912, Jack walked off the field with the hump after being on the receiving end of some disparaging remarks by his team's fans. He was coaxed back onto the pitch and Hammers lost 3-1. Significantly, he was not on duty for the next match when his place was taken by Joe Hughes. He played only one more game in the first team – a 2-0 defeat at Coventry on the last day of the 1911/12 season. He later joined Gravesend.

GIBBINS, Vivian — 1923-32

Born: Forest Gate, London, 10.8.1901
League apps: 129 (58 goals)
Cup: 9 (5 goals)

AS AN AMATEUR, he appeared in the line-up as "VWT Gibbins", to distinguish him from the pros – who were not then given Christian names in programme details. A pupil of Godwin Road School, like that other great West Ham United and England amateur international before him, Harry Stapley, Viv became a schoolmaster by profession and also a centre-forward for club and country. The last of the great amateurs imbued with the Corinthian spirit to serve the club, he became the first player from the non-paid ranks since World War I to head a League club's scoring lists with 18 goals for Hammers in 1930/31. Making his debut against Aston Villa on Boxing Day 1923, Viv found the pace of First Division soccer somewhat faster than that which he'd experienced previously with local amateurs Clapton, but nevertheless laid on the only goal of the match for Billy Moore. His pen-picture in a 1925/26 club handbook gives some idea of the esteem in which he was held at the Boleyn: "The name of Gibbins is a household word in London football, and it is our great regret that he cannot assist us regularly, for we would always find a place for him." The writer of those notes must have been happy when Vivian decided to play permanently for West Ham United in 1927/28 while still retaining his amateur status, but not so pleased when he transferred to Brentford (February 19, 1932). Retiring from his post as headmaster at Harold Road School in the early 1970s, he kept his interest in the game alive by watching local schools' football and with occasional visits to Upton Park. One of the last amateurs to gain full England recognition when he was capped while with

Clapton against France in 1924 and 1925, he left an impression on the French by scoring three times in the two matches. He also won FA Amateur Cup winners' medals with Clapton in the same two years, and was a losing finalist with Leyton in 1934, whom he had joined following spells with Bristol Rovers and Southampton, after leaving Brentford in the close season of 1932. He joined his last club, Catford Wanderers, in 1934, retiring in 1939. Viv died in Herne Bay, Kent on November 21, 1979.

Vivian Gibbins

GILMORE, Henry
1899-1900 TIW

Born: Berwick, Northumbria, 1877
SL apps: 5

JOINED THAMES IRONWORKS from Woolwich Arsenal in 1899, he could play either wing-half or left-wing. In 1898/99 he played just one game in the Southern League Second Division, scoring against Southall. He made four Southern League appearances the following season before joining South West Ham, where he played until 1903.

GLOVER, Horace
1911-12

Born: Ashford, Kent, 1883
SL apps: 29
Cup apps: 5

A STURDY LEFT-BACK signed from Southampton, Horace made his first appearance for his new team in the fourth match of the 1911/12 season against Reading at Upton Park; the 5-0 win providing a perfect start. He held on to the number 3 shirt for most of the season in the Southern League matches and was an ever-present in Hammers' five-match FA Cup run that campaign. His dubious claim to fame while a Hammer came against the team that ended that run – Swindon – when he conceded two own goals in the replayed cup-tie at the County Ground, which was lost 4-0. An architect's assistant during his early career as an amateur with Ashford, Hastings and St Leonards, he went to Saints on the recommendation of former player Jimmy Yates. He went straight into Southampton's Southern League side and made 174 League and Cup appearances and scored four goals from 1906-11. He was made team captain at The Dell in 1909 and played for Boscombe after leaving Irons in 1912. He lived within earshot of The Dell in later years and died at Winchester on January 28, 1967.

GODDARD, J
1913-14

SL apps: 1

A LEFT-BACK WHO played his solitary game in Hammers' Southern League side in the 4-1 defeat at Swindon (December 27, 1913), when Syd Puddefoot scored West Ham's goal. His place was taken the following match by Frank "Bronco" Burton, who held the position to the end of the season.

GODDARD, Paul
1980-86

Born: Harlington, Middlesex, 12.10.59
League apps: 170 (54 goals)
Cup apps: 43 (17 goals)

A STOCKY STRIKER, Paul created a slice of history on his one and only full England international appearance against Iceland (June 2, 1982). He ran on to Glenn Hoddle's pass to net the 69th-minute equaliser on a frozen pitch in the 1-1 draw in Reykjavik, becoming the first England player to score having played less than a full match (he subbed for the injured Cyrille Regis). Paul was signed by John Lyall for a club record £800,000 from Queens Park Rangers in August 1980. He had impressed the previous season by scoring 16 goals alongside Clive Allen, having made his First Division debut for Rangers as sub against Arsenal in April 1978 (Phil Parkes was in goal for QPR that day). He made his Hammers debut against Liverpool in the Charity Shield at Wembley and went on to prove a valuable asset. In his first season with Hammers "Sarge" – as he was known to his team-mates, after his Boys' Brigade days – netted 17 goals in a formidable partnership with David Cross that proved the cutting edge to West Ham's record-breaking Second Division championship term. He also played a key role in the 1980/81 League Cup campaign, scoring in the Semi-final second leg against Coventry City at Upton Park and in the Final replay against Liverpool at Villa Park, which Hammers lost 2-1. The following season the powerful, diminutive striker finished just one goal behind Cross, on 15, although he top-scored in 1982/83 with ten. It was midway through that season when Tony Cottee burst upon the scene, and his sensational pairing with Frank McAvennie – who arrived in the summer of 1985 – severely restricted Sarge's first team chances. Injuries also took their toll and it was after dislocating his shoulder at Birmingham City in the opening game of the 1985/86 season that Paul lost his place to McAvennie. After his 31 minutes at St Andrews, he did not start another League match all season, and made just five appearances as sub. His only goal came in a memorable 8-1 demolition of Newcastle United at Upton Park. Paul added just one more goal to his tally, at Norwich City (October 18, 1986), before his final appearance, against Everton at Upton Park (November 2, 1986). Paul then became West Ham's double record-transfer breaker when, frustrated at the lack of chances, he moved to Newcastle United (November 7, 1986) in a £415,000 deal – Hammers' biggest transfer receipt at that time. Sarge spent only 15 months in the north east before another big-money move to Derby County for £425,000. However, just a season-and-a-half later, Paul was back in London with Millwall, who paid Derby £800,000 for his services in December 1989. It was an expensive buy for the Lions, who released him on a free transfer to Ipswich Town a little over two years later, having played only 20 League matches. John Lyall, who was criticised in some quarters at West Ham for allowing Paul to leave, was delighted to be reunited with him at Portman Road. And Sarge responded by helping Ipswich win promotion to the Premier League in his second season in Suffolk. In the summer of 1994, he and another experienced pro, John Wark, were appointed by general manager Lyall as the new first team coaches at Ipswich. Paul took over as manager at Ipswich for a short time before continuing in charge of the youth set-up at Portman Road, but jumped at the chance to return to Upton Park as Glenn Roeder's assistant in 2001. A former team-mate of Glenn's at both QPR and Newcastle, Paul was a tower of

strength during his manager's enforced absence in 2002/03 and a great help to Trevor Brooking. He left Upton Park following Alan Pardew's arrival, but he too commended Paul's "professionalism".
England cap: 1982 vs Iceland (sub) (1).

GOODACRE, Reg
1931-33

Born: Boston, Lincolnshire, 24.7.08
League apps: 20

A LINCOLNSHIRE LAD, Reg had three seasons at Upton Park after signing from non-League Boston United. Usually employed in the right-back position, Reg was the cousin of a more famous pro, Eric Houghton, the Aston Villa left-winger and England international. Making his debut against Manchester United at Old Trafford in February 1931, Reg proved an invaluable deputy for Hammers' more experienced backs and gave the club good service until his move to Mansfield Town, where he scored a solitary goal in 18 appearances. After leaving Field Mill, he had spells at Peterborough United and Gainsborough Trinity. Reg had begun his career with local sides Sleaford GS, Lincoln City and Billingborough before joining Boston United.

GORDON, Dale
1993-96

Born: Great Yarmouth, Norfolk, 9.1.67
League apps: 9 (1 goal)
Cup apps: 1

A MAJOR £750,000 signing by Billy Bonds in the summer of 1993, Dale suffered a dismal first year ravaged by injury. He scored Hammers' first-ever FA Carling Premiership goal in the 1-1 draw at Coventry City (August 21, 1993) but was plagued by persistent knee problems and made only nine first team appearances. Dale, nicknamed "Flash" for his flamboyant dress sense and ball trickery, made his name as a dazzling right-winger with his local club, Norwich City, and went on to represent England at Schoolboy, Youth, Under-21 and "B" level. He was Player of the Year in the Canaries' successful 1988/89 campaign (fourth in Division One), but after 206 League (31 goals) and 40 Cup (nine goals) appearances, he moved to Glasgow Rangers for £1.2 million in November 1992. He celebrated his debut there by scoring twice at Dunfermline Athletic (November 9, 1991) and was a first team regular (28 games, five goals) as Rangers romped to the Premier League title. But in a large Ibrox squad of proven internationals and big-name stars, Dale found it difficult to hold down a regular first team spot in his second season in Scotland. A recurrence of a shoulder injury, sustained during his Carrow Road days, didn't help his cause, limiting him to 22 League games in 1992/93 (one goal) as the championship was retained in style. He jumped at the chance of moving back to England, making his West Ham debut in the opening game of 1993/94 against Wimbledon (August 14, 1993). Dale was loaned out to Second Division Peterborough United in March 1995 (during his injury-plagued time at West Ham) scoring one goal in six games. He was loaned out again, to First Division Millwall, in March the following year, playing six games there. Given a free transfer to AFC Bournemouth in the Second Division in August 1996, he scored one goal in 19 League and Cup games for the Dean Court side before having to retire from the game through injury in January 1997.

GORE, Reg — 1938-39

Born: Henthorne, Lancashire, 1.8.13
League apps: 5 (1 goal)

SCORING ON HIS debut against Bradford at Park Avenue, this useful left-winger won the right to keep his place for the remaining four fixtures of the 1938/39 season on the strength of that display. Big for a winger, he joined West Ham from his local works side, Frickley Colliery. Having previously played with Southport 16 times and scored two goals in the Third Division North in 1934, he moved on to St Mirren and Cowdenbeath when he left West Ham. He is also listed as having played for Hepthorne Lane Primitives (1931),

Dale Gordon

Chesterfield (1932) and Birmingham (1933) but not for the first teams of the latter two clubs.

GOULD, Bobby — 1973-75

Born: Coventry, West Midlands, 12.6.46
League apps: 51 (15 goals)
Cup apps: 7 (4 goals)

A GREAT-HEARTED COMPETITOR, Bobby's signing from Bristol City coincided with a big uplift of team spirit at Upton Park, culminating in the 1975 FA Cup Final triumph. A much-travelled striker, his list of clubs includes: Coventry City, Arsenal, Wolves, West Bromwich Albion, Bristol City, Hammers, Wolves again, Bristol Rovers, Hereford United, Chelsea, Wimbledon

and Aldershot. He then managed Coventry City and took charge of Bristol Rovers before managing Wimbledon to their shock 1988 FA Cup Final success over Liverpool. After working as a TV pundit, Bobby was appointed manager of Wales but resigned after a 4-0 thrashing by Italy in 1999. In January 2003 he was appointed manager of Third Division Cheltenham Town, but parted company with the Robins in October the same year. In January 2004, Bobby was lending his experience to Hartpury College Football Academy, devising training programmes and coaching the college teams. He was also put in charge of Hellenic League Gloucester United, whose players are mainly students and lecturers from Hartpury, in an attempt to save them from relegation. He then had a short spell with Peterborough United.

GOULDEN, Len — 1933-39

Born: Hackney, London, 16.7.12
League apps: 239 (54 goals)
Cup apps: 14 (1 goal)

ALTHOUGH IT IS not necessarily the intention in this work to determine Hammers' all-time greats, the name of Len Goulden would inevitably figure highly on any list of that nature. Born in Hackney, he moved a few miles nearer to the scene of his eventual triumphs when his family relocated to Plaistow three years later. One of the most revered of all manager Charlie Paynter's discoveries, he graduated through his school side to West Ham Boys and then to England Schoolboys, playing against Wales and Scotland in 1926. Len signed amateur forms for Hammers in 1931, but as there was no youth team in those days he was farmed out to Chelmsford, and later Leyton, to gain experience. During the summer months in this period Len worked on the redevelopment of Highbury Stadium, which was being transformed into the finest football arena in the country at the time. As Len laboured, concreting the terraces, he was openly envious of the Arsenal players as they trained on the pitch. Little could he have realised then that his own son, Roy, would one day play for the famous Gunners, and later Southend. But back to dad. Returning to Upton Park towards the end of 1932/33 he went straight into the League side, after signing pro, against Charlton Athletic at The Valley to commence a much-talked about partnership with the legendary Jimmy Ruffell from the inside-left berth. He became an automatic choice and despite the fact that Hammers were in the Second Division, his impressive displays drew the attention of the England selectors, culminating in the first of his 20 appearances for his country (against Ireland in 1937). His ability to take as well as create chances was much in evidence during his outings for England in overseas internationals, getting him on the scoresheet in the 6-0 victory against Norway in Oslo in 1937; against Germany in Berlin in 1938 – when the England team were duped into giving the Nazi salute before the match; and also against Romania, during the longest tour undertaken by England at that time. The nearest he got to a major

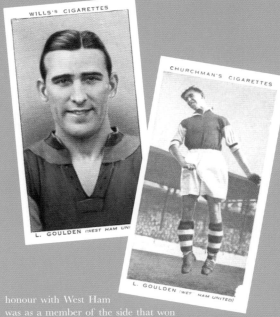

honour with West Ham
was as a member of the side that won
the Football League War Cup with a 1-0 victory over Blackburn Rovers at Wembley in 1940. During the conflict he joined the police force and continued to play for Irons and his country in those matches that could be arranged. He also made guest appearances for Chelsea (winning a Football League South Cup winners' medal in 1945), which paved the way for his eventual transfer to Stamford Bridge after World War II. Although Hammers' management of that time were reluctant to part with their biggest star, they did not want to stand in the way of one who had served them so well. So Len stepped up to the First Division stage with the Pensioners for a reported fee of £5,000. He joined the Blues in time to appear against the legendary Moscow Dynamos in 1945, and had five happy years with them as a player in the top flight, without, alas, winning any medals. He played 111 League and Cup matches, in which he scored 19 times. The nearest he came to appearing at Wembley again was when Chelsea were pipped by Arsenal in an FA Cup Semi-final replay at White Hart Lane in 1950 – a situation that was repeated

Career record

	League		FAC		LC		Europe		Total	
Played	App	Gls	App	Gls	App	Gls	App	Gls	App	Gls
1932-33	7	1	0	0	0	0	0	0	7	1
1933-34	40	7	2	1	0	0	0	0	42	8
1934-35	40	3	2	0	0	0	0	0	42	3
1935-36	38	15	2	0	0	0	0	0	40	15
1936-37	42	15	2	0	0	0	0	0	44	15
1937-38	35	9	1	0	0	0	0	0	36	9
1938-39	37	4	5	0	0	0	0	0	42	4
TOTAL	**239**	**54**	**14**	**1**	**0**	**0**	**0**	**0**	**253**	**55**

GRASSAM, William   1900-10

Born: Larbert, Scotland, 20.11.1880
SL apps: 169 (65 goals)
Cup apps: 10 (3 goals)

BILLY BEGAN HIS career in Glasgow junior soccer with Redcliffe Thistle before joining Maryhill in 1897, where his early enthusiasm for the game was rewarded with a medal for "regular training". After playing in county matches and an international trial for Scotland, he came south to join Burslem Port Vale in 1899, staying a year in the Potteries before signing for the newly-formed West Ham United at the turn of the century. A goalscoring inside-right, Bill scored four goals in a Southern League match against

W. GRASSAM.
WEST HAM UNITED.

Gravesend on his debut (September 1, 1900), thus becoming the first Hammer to score a hat-trick. He was also the first Hammer to score three goals in an FA Cup tie, a feat he achieved against Clapton in December 1900. After three seasons at the Memorial Grounds he signed for Manchester United but by 1905/06 was back in east London after spells at Glasgow Celtic and Leyton. Living in East Ham while with West Ham, Bill captained the side following MacEacrane's departure to Woolwich Arsenal in 1902.

GREAVES, Jimmy   1970-71

Born: East Ham, London, 20.2.40
League apps: 38 (13 goals)
Cup apps: 2

ALREADY A LIVING legend when he arrived at Upton Park as a £54,000 makeweight in the deal that took Martin Peters to Tottenham, Jimmy was, quite simply, the greatest goalscorer in the world. The fact that he had performed his finest feats, and was past his best, when he came to West Ham didn't really matter; it was almost enough for many fans just to see him in a claret and blue shirt. He characteristically kept up his record of scoring on every debut by giving Manchester City a double dose of the old "Greavesie" magic with his first appearance for Hammers at Maine Road in March 1970. West Ham won 5-1 that day, typical of the effect Jimmy had on new team-mates. Although his performances the next season fell short of the very high standard he had set earlier with Chelsea, AC Milan and Spurs, one can't help feeling, with the benefit of hindsight, that he retired too soon. An England youth international, Jimmy made his League debut for Chelsea at the age of 17. He scored in the first match of the season, a 1-1 draw against Tottenham – the first of 357 goals he scored in the Football League, all of them in the First Division. His 41 in 1960/61 still stands as the Blues' League record. Capped 11 times at England Under-23 level, Jimmy earned his first full cap in Peru (May 17, 1959). He stayed with Chelsea until June 1961 when he joined AC Milan. Despite the notoriously tough Italian defences, Jimmy still netted on his debut and went on to score nine goals in 14 matches. But this effervescent cockney character soon tired of the strict disciplines of Italian football life and he was delighted to make a rapid return to England in December 1961, when he joined Spurs for £99,999 (Bill Nicholson denying him the distinction of becoming the first £100,000 British footballer!). The north London club (Jimmy's favourite team as a boy) certainly got their money's worth from the naturally gifted marksman. Greavesie celebrated his debut with a hat-trick and quickly turned the talented Tottenham double side into one of the most exciting in Europe. A member of Spurs' FA Cup-winning teams of 1962 (scoring the first goal) and 1967, he also scored twice in the European Cup Winners' Cup triumph of 1963. His 37 League goals in 1962/63 still remains a Spurs club record, as do his totals of 220 League and 32 FA Cup goals. When he topped the First Division scoring chart in 1964/65, Jimmy became the first player to do so in three consecutive seasons. He also holds the record of top-scoring in the First Division on six occasions. In his time at White Hart Lane, Jimmy gained 42 full England caps (28 goals) but, unfortunately, hepatitis caused him to miss England's greatest victory. He played in the early stages of the 1966 World Cup Finals but had not fully recovered from illness and Geoff Hurst replaced him for the later stages. In March 1970, Jimmy and Geoff became team-mates at Upton Park, as Greavesie moved back to east London. But despite scoring twice on his debut for

Hammers at Manchester City, and netting another 11 in 38 games, he retired at the end of the 1970/71 season at the age of only 31. It is a measure of Jimmy Greaves's greatness that a crowd of 45,799 turned out to pay tribute at his testimonial game against Feyenoord at White Hart Lane in October 1972. Jimmy found it difficult to cope soon after his playing days were finished, but he successfully beat the threat of alcoholism and now football fans everywhere know Jimmy as the cheeky soccer pundit who has established a successful career for himself as a TV personality and after-dinner speaker.

Jimmy Greaves

GREEN, Bill   1976-78

Born: Newcastle-upon-Tyne, Tyne & Wear, 22.12.50
League apps: 35 (1 goal)
Cup apps: 5

A £100,000 SIGNING from Carlisle United, Bill's promising First Division career was badly disrupted by injuries. A giant centre-half, he joined the Brunton Park club from unfashionable Hartlepool and played a major role in the Cumbrians' promotion to Division One in 1974. The unlucky Geordie was sold to Peterborough United for £90,000 in 1978 and later played for Chesterfield. He then joined Doncaster Rovers in June 1983. He was appointed manager of non-League Buxton in October 1994.

GREEN, Tommy   1936-39

Born: Droitwich, Worcestershire, 1913
League apps: 40 (6 goals)
Cup apps: 4

A SCHEMING INSIDE-FORWARD, Tommy made his Hammers debut against Bradford City (December 5, 1936) in the shadow of the Main Stand at Valley Parade (which burnt down with such tragic consequences in 1985). Signed from West Bromwich Albion, he returned to Bradford on Christmas Day to do battle with the City's other footballing denizens – the now defunct Park Avenue – scoring his first goal for West Ham in a 2-1 defeat. Providing invaluable cover for both the inside-forward berths, Tom remained at Upton Park until 1938, when he joined Coventry. He began his career with Droitwich Spa and then Droitwich Comrades before joining WBA, whom he also guested for during World War II. Tommy won junior international honours in 1932.

GREEN, Tommy   1919

Born: Liverpool, Merseyside, 25.11.1893
League apps: 3

A LEFT-WINGER SIGNED by manager Syd King from Southport Central, Tom was an unfortunate

two years later, with Len in a non-playing role as coach to the west Londoners. In the summer of 1952 he took up the manager's job with Watford, remaining in that capacity until 1956. There then followed a period of seven years out of full-time football when he worked as a postmaster, but the lure of the game proved too strong and Hammers' former star subsequently took off to North Africa for two years to fulfil a coaching commitment. When he returned to England he was appointed manager to little Banbury Town for a similar period, and then coached Oxford United reserves until 1969. He still retained his allegiance to Hammers, however, watching his old team whenever he could when they played in the Midlands. It must have been strange for Len when he moved to Cornwall to retire – a county without a single Football League club. In his heyday he played with the outstanding players of London football; men of the calibre of Vic Watson, Jimmy Ruffell, Jackie Morton and Archie Macaulay at Upton Park, and at Chelsea with the two Tommies – Walker and Lawton. With his midfield mastery and ability to change the point of attack with devastatingly accurate crossfield passes to the opposite flank, he was well at home in such esteemed company. Still living just a short distance from the Upton Park ground until his death in 1995, you could safely say Len Goulden was one of the "Greats".

England caps: 1937 vs Sweden, Norway, Wales, Northern Ireland, Czechoslovakia; 1938 vs Germany, Switzerland, France, Wales, Rest of Europe; 1939 vs Italy, Scotland, Romania, Yugoslavia (14).

GREGORY, Ernie · 1946-60

Born: Stratford, London, 10.11.21
League apps: 382
Cup apps: 24

THE LONGEST-SERVING MEMBER on the Upton Park staff, Ernie actually joined the groundstaff in 1936 – one year before that other great club servant, Eddie Chapman. Catching the attention of Charlie Paynter when he appeared for the West Ham Boys team, which met Preston in the English Trophy Final at the Boleyn Ground (the Northerners had Tom Finney as 12th man!), it proved to be the beginning of an association that lasted a record breaking 50 years. Winner of an Isthmian League Championship medal as an amateur with Leytonstone, this great goalkeeper first appeared for Hammers in their midweek League team in 1938. It was another eight years before he made his League debut against Plymouth Argyle at Upton Park in December 1946, due to serving in the Essex Regiment and the RAF during World War II. A regular member of the 1958 promotion side, he received the Football League long-service statuette when he retired. He then became coach to the reserves and later to the first team, specialising in the art of goalkeeping. Ernie also helped with general coaching and team administration, and received a special award for 50 years' service. He could have transferred to Arsenal in the mid-1950s and would surely have added full international recognition to his solitary England "B" cap, against France in 1952, in the higher profile of the First Division, but he decided to remain loyal to Hammers. Making his final West Ham appearance against Leeds United at the Boleyn in September 1959, he was awarded a fully deserved testimonial match the following year, against the LDA club of Costa Rica. Ernie officially "retired" in May 1987, after completing 51 years' exceptional service to his one and only club and is still a regular visitor to Upton Park. Not so many years ago, he was often to be seen at the training ground putting the club's young keepers through their paces!

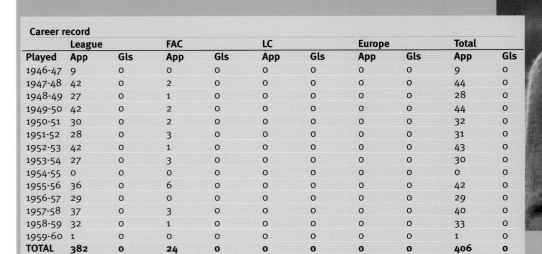

Career record

Played	League App	Gls	FAC App	Gls	LC App	Gls	Europe App	Gls	Total App	Gls
1946-47	9	0	0	0	0	0	0	0	9	0
1947-48	42	0	2	0	0	0	0	0	44	0
1948-49	27	0	1	0	0	0	0	0	28	0
1949-50	42	0	2	0	0	0	0	0	44	0
1950-51	30	0	2	0	0	0	0	0	32	0
1951-52	28	0	3	0	0	0	0	0	31	0
1952-53	42	0	1	0	0	0	0	0	43	0
1953-54	27	0	3	0	0	0	0	0	30	0
1954-55	0	0	0	0	0	0	0	0	0	0
1955-56	36	0	6	0	0	0	0	0	42	0
1956-57	29	0	0	0	0	0	0	0	29	0
1957-58	37	0	3	0	0	0	0	0	40	0
1958-59	32	0	1	0	0	0	0	0	33	0
1959-60	1	0	0	0	0	0	0	0	1	0
TOTAL	**382**	**0**	**24**	**0**	**0**	**0**	**0**	**0**	**406**	**0**

debutant in the record 7-0 hammering at Barnsley (1.9.19), but switched to inside-left for his other two Second Division outings, at Rotherham County and against Stoke City at Upton Park. He returned to Southport Central, and later had spells with South Liverpool, Accrington Stanley (30 apps, 23 goals) in 1921, Stockport County (31 apps, 16 goals), Clapton Orient (24 apps, ten goals) in 1923 before heading over the border for stints with Hearts (1924) and Third Lanark (1925). During World War I, he guested for Liverpool and Stockport, and won a Lancashire Cup during his second spell at Southport. In September 1923, when he was with the O's, he scored a hat-trick against Nelson. Tom passed away in Liverpool in October 1975, aged 81.

GREGORY, John · 1951-53

Born: Shoreditch, London, 24.9.26
League apps: 24 (6 goals)
Cup apps: 1

A FORMER ENGLAND amateur international, John played his early soccer with Hackney and Middlesex Boys before progressing to senior amateur status with Bromley and, later, Hayes. He remained an amateur when he joined the Boleyn club for the 1950/51 season, but signed as a full pro the following campaign when he made the first of 24 League appearances. He transferred to Scunthorpe United, where he scored a lot of goals for the other Irons before moving on to Aldershot. He later became player-coach to St Neots Town.

GRESHAM, George · 1895-98 TIW

Born: Gainsborough, Lincolnshire, 1874
SL apps: 15

AN INSIDE-FORWARD, GEORGE was the first of many players to join Thames Ironworks/West Ham United from Gainsborough Trinity. In addition to appearing at least 15 times in the Ironworks' first season, he also turned out in three FA Cup ties in 1897/98. He scored twice against Arsenal XI in a friendly on April 16, 1896.

GRICE, Mike · 1955-61

Born: Woking, Surrey, 3.11.31
League apps: 142 (17 goals)
Cup apps: 8 (1 goal)

ANOTHER MEMBER OF the 1958 promotion-winning side, this blond-haired, flying winger made a big contribution to that success. A maker, rather than a taker, of goals, he provided the perfect complement to his opposite flankman, Mal Musgrove. Signed from Colchester United for £10,000, he moved to Coventry City for the 1961/62 season where he scored six goals in 38 Third Division games before falling out with Jimmy Hill and returning to Layer Road the following year to end his League days with the Essex club. Mike was still scoring regularly for Lowestoft in the Eastern Counties League in 1966, where he had fellow ex-Hammer Albert Foan on the opposite flank.

GRIFFITHS, Frederick · 1902-04

Born: Presteigne, South Wales, 1876
SL apps: 48
Cup apps: 4

THE SON OF a Presteigne coal merchant, Fred commenced his career in Welsh junior football but began at senior level with South Shore in 1894, moving to Clitheroe in 1896. He returned to South Shore in

1897 and was with them when they amalgamated with Blackpool in 1899. In an age when big goalkeepers were fashionable, Fred's towering six-foot-two-inch frame and 15-stone bulk must have provided a daunting sight for opposing forwards. Capped at full international level by Wales in 1900 he represented his country on three occasions against England and Scotland (twice) while with Blackpool. He was the first Blackpool player to win an international cap, an honour he held for 20 years, and also served Stalybridge, Millwall, Preston North End and Tottenham before

Mike Grice

Billy Guest

joining Hammers. Managing only nine Southern League appearances with Spurs in 1901/02, Fred fared far better upon his arrival at the Memorial Grounds. After taking over from William Biggar following a disastrous 5-1 reverse at Wellingborough Town, he made the first team spot more or less his own for the next two seasons before moving on to New Brompton in the close season of 1904 and Middlesex in 1906. Fred later worked as a coalminer at Shirebrook where he trained the Central Alliance team. He fell in France on October 30, 1917 fighting for his country in the Great War while serving with Sherwood Foresters.

GROTIER, Peter   1969-74

Born: Stratford, London, 18.10.50
League apps: 50
Cup apps: 4

SO GREAT WAS the impression this capable goalkeeper made when transferred on loan to Lincoln City that the Imps' fans whipped round to raise the £16,666 necessary for his permanent transfer. Always a useful contender for Bobby Ferguson's first team place at Hammers, he had earlier been loaned to Cardiff City before moving to Sincil Bank. As reserve-team coach at Grimsby, he made a sensational return between the posts when he turned out for the Mariners' home FA Cup tie against Watford in 1985 – at the age of 36.

GUEST, Billy   1936-37

Born: Denaby, Yorkshire, 8.2.13
League apps: 3 (1 goal)

A COLLIER WHO played part-time for Denaby United, Bill joined Hammers as a left-winger from the Yorkshire club in March 1936. In an era when the club had such luminaries as Jimmy Ruffell, Stan Foxall and Johnny Morton available as flank players, he found it difficult to hold down a regular Second Division place and had only a brief sojourn at Upton Park before transferring to Birmingham FC. He joined Blackburn Rovers in 1938 and was on duty for Rovers against Hammers in the 1940 League War Cup Final at Wembley. After World War II he saw service with Blackburn and Walsall. Bill passed away in November 1973, aged 60. Not to be confused with the player of the same name who also played for Brum and Warwickshire CC.

GUNNING, Harry   1952-53

Born: Leigh-on-Sea, Essex, 8.2.32
League apps: 1

THIS OUTSIDE-LEFT MADE only one appearance in the first team, away to Lincoln City in May 1953. Signed from Gravesend, he later made 62 League outings for Crystal Palace, whom he joined from Hammers. He had one season with Reading before signing for Guildford City in the Southern League.

GURKIN, John   1921

Born: Murton, County Durham, 9.9.1895
League apps: 1

SIGNED FROM SOUTH Hetton Rovers, this centre-half was given only one first team outing – a 2-0 reverse at the Victoria Ground against Stoke City – before transferring to Norwich City. In 1923 he transferred to Stalybridge Celtic and the following season joined Durham City. In August 1928 he rejoined Stalybridge. From May 1929 to September 1932 he was with Jarrow and he ended his playing days with his hometown team, Murton.

Peter Grotier (right)

H

HALES, Derek	HARWOOD, Alfred	HITCH, Alf	HOWE, Bobby
HALL, Almeric George	HAWKINS, Bert	HITCHENS, J	HUBBARD, Cliff
HALL, Richard	HAY, Sam	HODGES, Harry	HUFTON, Edward
HALLAS, Geoff	HAYNES, Vincent	HODGES, Lee	HUGHES, Joe
HAMILTON, John	HEATH, Robert	HODGSON, Tommy	HUGHES, Michael
HAMMOND, Syd	HEBDEN, Jack	HODSON, James	HUGHTON, Chris
HAMPSON, Tommy	HEFFER, Paul	HOLLIGAN, Gavin	HUGO, Roger
HAREWOOD, Marlon	HENDERSON, R	HOLLAND, Pat	HULL, Archie
HARKES, John	HENDERSON, William	HOLMES, Jim	HUNT, Fergus
HARLEY, John	HILSDON, George	HOLMES, Matthew	HURST, Sir Geoff MBE
HARRIS, Jimmy	HILSDON, Jack	HOOPER, Harry	HURST, Joseph
HARRISON, Fred	HILTON, Paul	HORLER, George	HUTCHISON, Don
HART, Joseph	HINDLE, Harry	HORLOCK, Kevin	HUTTON, EG
HARTLEY, Trevor	HIRD, Henry	HORN, George	
HARTSON, John	HISLOP, Shaka	HOUGHTON, Ray	

Sir Geoff Hurst MBE

HALES, Derek — 1977-78

Born: Lower Halstow, Kent, 15.12.51
League apps: 24 (10 goals)
Cup apps: 3

A STRIKER WITH an insatiable appetite for scoring goals, Derek was snapped up by Charlton Athletic from Luton Town for a bargain fee and later transferred to Derby County for £300,000 – the highest ever paid for a Second Division player at that time. Hammers got him for a third of that price, but the player found it hard to settle at the Boleyn and returned to The Valley the following year. He then moved to Gillingham (he is in fact the son of former Gills centre-forward William Hales).

HALL, Almeric George — 1946-49

Born: Hove, Sussex, 12.11.12
League apps: 50 (11 goals)
Cup apps: 6 (3 goals)

A CLEVER INSIDE-FORWARD, Almer had seen service with Brighton, Spurs, Southend and Bradford City before the war. Formerly a prodigy with Southwick and England Schools, he signed for West Ham in December 1945. He made his official Hammers debut at Plymouth Argyle on August 31, 1946 – the day that normal service resumed in League soccer. He also appeared in 44 wartime League and Cup matches, scoring 25 goals. He scored twice on his Spurs debut against Grimsby Town on Boxing Day, 1934, but the win was Spurs' last before a fateful run of 16 matches without another victory that saw Hall dropped and the north Londoners relegated at the end of the season. He played just four matches the next campaign, but remained at White Hart Lane until April 1937, when he moved to Southend United after scoring eight times in 24 League and Cup games for Spurs. He hit ten goals in 41 League Division South and Cup games for the Shrimpers.

HALL, Richard — 1996-99

Born: Ipswich, Suffolk, 14.3.72
League apps: 7

WEST HAM TOOK a big gamble when splashing out a whopping £1.9 million for a player who had been dogged by injuries in his last season at Southampton. Discarded as a 16-year-old by his hometown club Ipswich, the disappointed youngster was considering a career with British Telecom before Fourth Division Scunthorpe United gave him a bell to offer him an unlikely lifeline at Glanford Park. After 34 League and Cup appearances with those other Irons, Hall found himself on his way to First Division Saints for £200,000 in a remarkable reversal of fortunes. The young centre-back was a revelation at the Dell and within two years the rising star had won England Under-21 recognition with a string of caps at that level, the last of which he skippered in a win over France in 1993. A big, physical player who was dangerous coming forward for set pieces and who scored several goals for the Saints, he was out of contract at the end of 1995/96. Despite an injury-stricken end to the season, Hammers duly signed the 24-year-old, who'd made 156 appearances and scored 15 goals in all competitions during his time on the South Coast, in July 1996. But disaster struck before he could kick a ball in earnest when he picked up a foot injury in a meaningless pre-season friendly at Carshalton that kept him out of action for all but the final seven fixtures of 1996/97. His delayed debut in the 0-0 home draw with Middlesbrough in April 1997 and the six remaining matches of the season were

Marlon Harewood

destined to represent the whole sum of his Upton Park career, but not before he'd fought a two-year battle against the toe injury that forced his retirement in May 1999. As club physiotherapist John Green echoed at the time: "The biggest disappointment of all this season was Richard Hall's decision to retire. It was a blow for Richard and for everyone involved over the last three years striving to get him fit after two operations in Seattle, USA on his injured foot. Eventually Richard recovered sufficiently to play, but the soreness and stiffness suffered afterwards was too much for him to bear." As Richard's football dream ended at Manchester United's "Theatre of Dreams" in his last appearance for Hammers in the final Premiership match of 1997, his replacement, Rio Ferdinand, was in the same team – and perhaps mindful of the many pitfalls that lay ahead on his own journey to Old Trafford.

HALLAS, Geoff — 1954-55

Born: Lydgate, Lancashire, 8.12.30
League apps: 4

A PROMISING YOUNG full-back, Geoff had his career tragically terminated when he developed eye trouble. Signed from Warminster in March 1954, he was granted a joint testimonial by the club along with Brian Moore, who suffered a similar fate.

HAMILTON, John — 1904-05

Born: Glasgow, Scotland, 1880
League apps: 5

THIS RIGHT-WINGER WAS one of two forward-line changes imposed by manager Syd King in an abortive attempt to halt a mid-season slump. Coming into the side against Portsmouth at Fratton Park, along

with centre-forward John Blackwood, on Boxing Day 1904, Hammers presented Pompey with a post-Christmas gift in the form of a 4-1 scoreline, although his co-debutant did score Hammers' goal. He was in for the next three matches, all 1-0 defeats, but his brief West Ham career ended on a happier note in a 3-0 victory over Watford at Vicarage Road. John was also with London rivals Millwall (1902/03) and Queen's Park Rangers (1903/04).

HAMMOND, Syd — 1904-08

Born: Woolwich, London, date unknown
League apps: 32
Cup apps: 2

RIGHT OR LEFT-BACK, Syd made his 34 first team appearances thinly spread over four seasons – quite a long stint considering the fact that the club was operating a "revolving door" policy at the time. A debutant in the 1-0 defeat at Tottenham (January 21, 1905), his final appearance came in another away defeat, 3-0 at manager Syd King's former club, New Brompton (April 7, 1908). A commercial clerk by profession, Syd joined Irons as an amateur after learning the game with Leyton National School, Leyton Ashville, Leyton Rovers, Leyton and Woodford. Occasionally playing at centre-forward in his early career, he played for Woodford against Clapton in the final of the West Ham Charity Cup in 1902.

HAMPSON, Tommy — 1920-25

Born: Bury, Lancashire, 20.5.1898
League apps: 70
Cup apps: 9

SIGNED FROM SOUTH Shields to understudy Ted Hufton, Tommy proved to be a shrewd capture and an able deputy when the great man suffered a serious knee injury during the 1923/24 season. Showing form far superior to his performances in the reserves, Tommy grabbed his chance, literally, with both hands, with the result that Ted was hardly missed. He later joined Blackburn Rovers.

HAREWOOD, Marlon — 2003-

Born: Hampstead, London, 25.8.79
League apps: 79 (31 goals)
Cup apps: 10 (5 goals)

SIGNED FOR A bargain £500,000 from cash-strapped Nottingham Forest in November 2003, "Marvellous Marlon" was an immediate hit with Hammers fans after scoring twice on his debut against Wigan Athletic and went on to be the club's top goalscorer, having already bagged 11 at the City ground. A product of Forest's youth scheme, this big striker in the Emile Heskey mould had made his League debut as far back as 1997/98. Following a spell on loan to Finnish side FC Haka during that summer, he made his Premiership bow for Forest in a 0-0 draw with West Ham in Nottingham. Taking time to win a regular place at Forest, he was loaned out briefly to Ipswich Town in January 1999, but came good for Forest in 2001/02 when he was second-top scorer with 11 goals and almost doubled that total the next campaign. Showing the same kind of form in the first quarter of 2003/04 and making public his decision not to sign a new contract at the season's end led West Ham to swoop for a striker who could not only score goals but could hold the ball up and lay-off unselfishly for colleagues and also play out wide. As the 2004/05 push for promotion began to show momentum, Marlon was showing all of those attributes and ended the victorious campaign as top goalscorer with 22 goals in all competitions as Hammers booked their place back to the Premiership.

HARKES, John — 1995-96

Born: New Jersey, USA, 8.3.67
League apps: 11
Cup apps: 2

THEY SAY THERE'S nothing new in football and Calum Davenport's unorthodox recent signing had a precedent nine years ago when the US Soccer Federation paid £500,000 to Derby County for American John Harkes in October 1995 and then loaned him to West Ham until March 1996! A versatile midfielder who could also operate at right-back, the 28-year-old had made over 70 appearances for the US national side and had gained extensive First Division and Premiership experience with Sheffield Wednesday (120 League appearances, 11 goals) and the Rams (85 League and Cup appearances, three goals) before arriving in east London to join Harry Redknapp's rapidly expanding foreign legion. John made his Hammers debut at Hillsborough against the side who'd brought him to the UK for a £70,000 fee from North Carolina University in 1990, contributing in the final 20 minutes of a 1-0 away win over the Owls. He remained something of an unknown quantity during his six-month stay. Now head of youth development at Major League Soccer club Washington DC United.

John Harley

HARLEY, John — 2004

Born: Maidstone, Kent, 26.9.79
League apps: 15 (1 goal)
Cup apps: 1

ANOTHER YOUNG ENGLISH player pushed out of Chelsea by the relentless influx of foreign imports, this stylish left-sided midfielder was loaned out to First Division Wimbledon in October 2000 after scoring two goals in 42 League and Cup appearances with the Blues. After eight games for the Dons, he was recalled to Stamford Bridge only to be sold for a weighty £3.5 million to west London rivals Fulham on the eve of the 2001/02 season. He was unable to oust Rufus Brevett from the left-back position, however, and hardly figured for the Cottagers after making his debut in the opening day fixture against Manchester

United at Old Trafford. Farmed out to First Division Sheffield United in January 2002, John regained his form at Bramall Lane and returned to Loftus Road a new man, winning back his place from the suspended Brevett to keep it when the latter was transferred to West Ham. The glut of left-sided players at Fulham saw the England youth and Under-21 international overlooked at the start of 2002/03 and he returned to Sheffield United again on loan in September 2002. Something of a crowd favourite with the Yorkshiremen, he returned to London after adding another five League appearances to the 11 League and Cup outings he'd made on his previous spell there, and in January 2004 tested the Blades fans' loyalties to the full when he returned to Bramall Lane with his new loan side West Ham to score a spectacular goal in a televised 3-3 thriller. Despite his fine displays, John was not offered a permanent move to Upton Park and continued instead his love affair with Sheffield United when he was finally transferred to the Blades for 2004/05. He joined Burnley in 2005.

HARRIS, Jimmy — 1930-32

Born: Tunbridge Wells, Kent, 1907
League apps: 7 (1 goal)

NORMALLY A LEFT-WINGER, Jimmy made his West Ham debut in the inside-left position in a 4-3 victory over Portsmouth on Christmas Day, 1930 at Upton Park. Signed from Kent League Folkestone, he made a further four First Division appearances that season and two more the next before moving on to Southampton in July 1932, for whom he made his debut at Millwall (August 27, 1932). He only made one more first team appearance and, after playing 44 Combination games and scoring eight goals, he was given a free transfer.

HARRISON, Fred — 1910-13

Born: Winchester, Hampshire, 2.7.1880
SL apps: 54 (19 goals)
Cup apps: 8 (4 goals)

SIGNED FROM FULHAM with team-mate George Redwood, Fred got off to a flying start in Hammers' colours by scoring on his debut on Good Friday, 1911 against one of his former clubs, Southampton, in a 4-1 win at the Boleyn. He also played several games at centre-half for Hammers, notably the 1913 FA Cup tie versus Aston Villa. Discovered by a famous Saints player, Joe Turner, when he spotted Fred playing on Southampton Common, "Buzzy", as he was known by his adoring Dell public, was soon knocking in the goals. A product of local Hampshire clubs Fitzhugh Rovers and Bitterne Guild, Fred scored five goals in consecutive Southern League games against Wellingborough Town and Northampton Town at the Dell in 1902/03 and ended the season with 17 goals from just 13 matches. The following campaign he netted 27 times in 32 games as Saints clinched the Southern League Championship and he earned an England trial. Altogether he scored 88 goals in 166 Southern League and Cup appearances for Saints. In 1907, Fulham offered the huge sum of £1,000 to take him and a team-mate to Craven Cottage, which was duly accepted. He had two-and-a-half seasons at Hammers before transferring to Bristol City in August 1913. After being gassed during action in World War I, he set up a master plasterers business in Southampton. He died in 1969, aged 89.

HART, Joseph — 1921

Born: Bulwell, Nottinghamshire, date unknown
League apps: 1

THIS RIGHT-BACK MADE only one League appearance – in a 1-1 draw against Port Vale at the Boleyn during Hammers' second season as a Football League club in 1921. Later with Millwall.

HARTLEY, Trevor — 1966-68

Born: Doncaster, Yorkshire, 16.3.47
League apps: 5

JOINED FROM HOLLOWAY School on July 1, 1964. A speedy, fair-haired winger who made a handful of First Division appearances, Trevor was granted a move to Bournemouth for a small fee to enable him to pursue regular first team soccer. A brother-in-law, incidentally, of fellow former Hammer Bobby Howe. Trevor later managed the Cherries for a short time in 1974 (when he took over from John Bond) and, at the age of 27, was the youngest manager in the Football League until his departure after a year at Dean Court. After a spell as coach at Sunderland in the mid-1990s, Trevor got the travel bug and embraced overseas experience in Singapore, Malaysia (where he was national coach), the USA and Canada. In his third spell at Luton Town, Trevor was head scout until June 2003, when the club were taken over and he was made redundant. More recently scouting part-time for Lennie Lawrence at Cardiff City and reporting on their future opponents, Trevor is itching to get back to coaching as he says: "I'm happier on the training field."

HARTSON, John — 1997-99

Born: Swansea, Wales, 5.4.75
League apps: 60 (24 goals)
Cup apps: 13 (9 goals)

MORE THAN A few eyebrows were raised when Hammers manager Harry Redknapp swooped sensationally to sign this big, raw 21-year-old Welsh international striker from north London giant Arsenal for a club record of £3.2 million in February 1997. Along with those from the other inspired signing Paul Kitson, John's goals saved Irons from relegation at the end of 1996/97. The red-haired hitman began his career with First Division Luton Town and scored on his debut at Kenilworth Road, a feat he was to better twice over on his debut for Wales Under-21s versus Cyprus. Thirteen goals in 63 senior outings with the Hatters didn't seem a massive return but it was enough to persuade Gunners boss Arsene Wenger to break the British record transfer fee for a teenager when he splashed out £2.5 million to bring him to Highbury in January 1995. It soon proved to be a wise investment as the by now full Welsh international proved to be an able deputy for Alan Smith as he added his own qualities to Arsenal's attack, most notably his power in the air, ability to hold off defenders and a surprisingly deft first-touch for such a big man. Indeed he reminded many of the Gunners' older fans of a sort of hybrid of Ray Kennedy and John Radford. Between his signing and the end of the 1994/95 campaign the new boy cracked seven goals in 15 matches, including the Gunners' solitary goal in the disappointing European Cup Winner's Cup Final defeat to Real Zaragoza in Paris. The following season, Hammers witnessed the young Welshman's prowess as a goalscorer first-hand when, in a rare first team opportunity, he scored the only goal of the match at Upton Park at the end of February. With the frustrated striker unable to displace either Dennis Bergkamp or Ian Wright on a regular basis at Highbury, it might have been the memory of that goal that spurred Redknapp to offer Hartson the guarantee of regular Premiership football at the Boleyn. So, after 17 goals in 71 first team appearances at Arsenal and almost as many yellow cards to go with them, the angry young man from Neath duly joined Hammers. So too did his poor disciplinary record as he quickly picked up a yellow card 15 minutes into his debut at Derby County to earn a third suspension of the year. All was forgiven the following week though, when he got on the scoresheet in his Upton Park introduction in the thrilling 4-3 victory over Spurs. Although five goals in 11 Premiership starts was a fair return and he finished the season with his first goal for Wales against Scotland, he really showed his worth in the first half of 1997/98 and looked like he might develop into one of the all-time great West Ham strikers. But after a whirlwind start to the season when he'd scored 19 times before Christmas, he fell away badly in the New Year and missed two vital penalties in the Sixth Round of both major Cup competitions against Arsenal, which seemed to affect his confidence for the rest of the campaign of which he missed six matches through needless suspensions. In direct contrast to his performances of a year earlier, the player's form declined to such an extent that he'd notched just three League goals before Christmas 1998. An abysmal defeat in the FA Cup Third Round to his hometown team Swansea City in a replay at the Vetch, followed by a 4-1 defeat to Manchester United at Old Trafford seemed to convince Redknapp that the time was right to cash in on his record signing and he did so – accepting a massive, almost mind-blowing £7.5 million bid from Cinderella club Wimbledon. It seemed great business for West Ham to double their money on a player whose form was obviously on the wane and had attacked team-mate Eyal Berkovic in an unsavoury training ground incident some months before. Following his move to Selhurst Park, Hartson found himself up against his former club on his Dons debut almost before the ink had dried on his contract and he was subsequently shocked and hurt by the verbal abuse directed at him by many of the huge contingent of Hammers fans there that day as he admitted in an interview with the West Ham retro magazine *Ex* in August 2004: "I was disappointed at the reception I got off the West Ham fans at Wimbledon. I got slaughtered and I thought it was a bit unfair considering I'd scored goals which kept them up. But then again I went back to West Ham for the first time about two years after that with Coventry on a Monday night and got a great reception." Perhaps the point John missed was the reason behind the fans turning on him during that dire 0-0 draw at Selhurst Park. They knew he had the ability to have become one of the Hammers all-time greats but had thrown away the opportunity by not keeping fit and, on his own admission, not applying himself properly. It was a lesson learned because the big striker did indeed get his act together and resurrected his career with Wimbledon (21 goals in 57 apps) Coventry (six goals in 12 League apps) and most famously Glasgow Celtic (91 goals in 159 League and Cup apps) where he has achieved the true greatness he was always capable of at domestic, European and international level as his cache of Scottish Premier and Cup medals, Champions League

appearances and 42 full caps (12 goals) for Wales bear ample testimony. What a shame he didn't achieve those triumphs with West Ham. Hartson capped his season by winning the Scottish Football Writers' Footballer of the Year award and shared the SPFA's Player of the Year prize and then made it a unique hat-trick by winning the *Four Four Two* SPL Player of the Season vote.

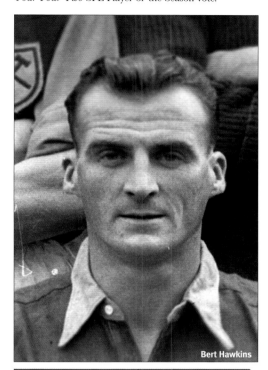

Bert Hawkins

HARWOOD, Alfred   1907-09

Born: Bishop Auckland, County Durham, 16.5.1881
SL apps: 12

ALF WAS A centre-forward with Fulham, where he scored only two goals in 28 appearances, before transferring to Leeds City, the forerunners of Leeds United, in May 1906. He stayed at the Old Peacock Ground (now Elland Road) for just one season before joining Hammers in 1907. With only one Second Division appearance, albeit a scoring one, to show for his time in Yorkshire (although he had scored over 40 times for City's reserves), he fared better at Upton Park after being converted to left-back and making his debut in that position in a 1-0 victory at Reading (November 23, 1907). Alf began his career with famous amateurs Crook Town, winning an FA Amateur Cup winners' medal in 1900/01. He then moved to Bishop Auckland with whom he gained a losers' medal in the same competition in 1901/02. He represented the Northern League, Southern League (Division Two) and won two London League and a West Yorkshire Cup medal. Alf was one of several Hammers players affected by a wholesale clear out of playing staff in 1909. He then moved on to Spennymore United in August 1909 before joining Bishop Auckland in 1913.

PROMINENT FOOTBALLERS.

A. HARWOOD,
WEST HAM UNITED.

HAWKINS, Bert   1951-53

Born: Bristol, Gloucestershire, 29.9.23
League apps: 34 (16 goals)
Cup apps: 3

ENJOYED A BRIEF, but spectacular, stay at Upton Park following his transfer from Southern League Bath City, where he was on loan from Bristol City. He scored on his debut for Hammers in a 1-1 draw versus Hull City at Boothferry Park, and went on to net 15 goals in 32 Second Division appearances during that 1951/52 campaign. Not bad for a player plucked from the obscurity of non-League football. He sustained an injury in a pre-season practice match, however, and failed to regain a regular place, moving on instead to London rivals QPR where he met with further success.

HAY, Sam   1895-99 TIW

Born: Renfrewshire, Scotland, date unknown

A STRONGLY-BUILT INSIDE-RIGHT. Played in the Ironworks' first season at Hermit Road in 1895/96 when he was a regular choice after joining from Victoria.

HAYNES, Vincent   1909-10

Born: birthplace unknown, 1887
League apps: 15 (5 goals)

A SIX-FOOT CENTRE-FORWARD signed from Crewe Alexander, Vince scored in his second match for Hammers in a 3-1 win at Norwich in September 1909. His five goals in 15 Southern League outings were a fair return, but he had George Webb to contend with as a rival for the number 9 shirt. He subsequently lost the battle and after making his last appearance in a 5-0 defeat at Swindon on the final Saturday of the 1909/10 season, he transferred to West Bromwich Albion.

HEATH, Robert   1897-98 TIW

Born: Deptford, London, March 1874

A GOALKEEPER SIGNED from West Ham Garfield after assisting that club in winning the West Ham Charity Cup against TIW in April 1897.

HEBDEN, Jack   1921-27

Born: Castleford, Yorkshire, 12.11.1900
League apps: 110
Cup apps: 6

THIS STRONG-TACKLING FULL-BACK joined Hammers from Bradford City, following spells with Rochdale and Castleford Town, in May 1921 in time to make his debut against South Shields as partner to Billy Cope on the last day of the season. After recovering from a bad injury sustained during the following campaign, Jack settled down to figure consistently in the First Division side during the mid-1920s and was appointed skipper in 1926/27. Leaving West Ham for Fulham in 1928, along with fellow full-back George Horler, for a combined fee of £850, he later captained Thames FC, who played at the old West Ham stadium in Prince Regent Lane. Disbanded in 1933 because of crippling debts, Thames's problems were evident as early as December 6, 1930, when they sent out the smallest cheque ever received as a share of an away gate to Luton Town. The attendance for the Third Division South fixture was 469 and Luton's cheque was for 1s 8d. But back to Jack. The demise of the Thames club saw him continue his League career with Hereford United, Clapton Orient, Halifax Town, Chesterfield and Sheffield United. He continued to play in local soccer as a permit player with Dorman Long and found employment at the Electricity Works in Nelson Street, East Ham. He lived at 210 Central Park Road and later in Hatherley Gardens, East Ham. Jack was a good friend of George Robson (who later joined Hammers' coaching staff).

HEFFER, Paul · 1967-69

Born: Upton Park, London, 21.12.47
League apps: 15
Cup apps: 2

BORN WITHIN EARSHOT of the "Upton Park Roar", this tall, commanding centre-half had his promising career cut short by injury. Paul, signed as a pro in August 1965, made his senior debut against Nottingham Forest in March 1967 and was given a testimonial by the club when it became clear he had to give up the game. His son, Steve, played for West Ham youth before moving on to Southend United. Paul returned to West Ham in 1994 to help Tony Carr train the youngsters after holding the post of youth team manager under the late Bobby Moore at Southend United and also assisted David Webb with the promotions at Roots Hall. He is now the Youth Academy assistant manager.

HENDERSON, R · 1899 TIW

A TALENTED FORWARD who became the first Irons player to score four goals in a competitive match, versus Uxbridge. He went on to make 15 appearances, scoring ten goals in all competitions before leaving to join Gravesend United for the 1899/1900 season.

HENDERSON, William · 1922-28

Born: Whitburn, County Durham, 5.1.1900
League apps: 162
Cup apps: 21 (1 goal)

LIKE HIS FULL-BACK partner Jack Young, Billy was a native of Whitburn; sadly the comparison between the two players does not end there, as Billy, too, was affected by poor health and died of tuberculosis at a tragically early age in 1930. Joining Hammers from Welsh club Aberdare (then in the Second Division of the Football League) to replace the injured Jack Hebden in January 1922, the well-built defender went on to win a place in the first Wembley Cup Final the following season, playing in every match leading to that famous confrontation with Bolton Wanderers. An ever-present in 1923/24, and only one short the next campaign, he was selected for the FA versus The Army and for the Professionals versus Amateurs during those seasons. On the verge of international honours until a bad knee injury forced him to miss half the 1925/26 season and the whole of the next, he was given the following tribute in a club history published in 1947: "Willie was a stylist and recognised as the greatest right-back the Hammers ever had." An amazing coincidence surrounded Bill's only goal in 183 first team appearances for West Ham United. It was scored in an FA Cup tie against his former club, Aberdare! He had actually begun his career with Whitburn and Brighton & Hove Albion before joining the Welshmen.

HILSDON, George · 1904-05/1912-15

Born: Bromley-by-Bow, London, August 1885
SL apps: 85 (31 goals)
Cup apps: 7 (4 goals)

"GATLING GUN" GEORGE'S early career was unusual in that he was transferred from West Ham to London rivals Chelsea even though he was obviously a great prospect and had scored seven times in 16 Southern League appearances. A pupil of Marner St School with Billy Bridgeman, who later became his colleague at West Ham and Chelsea, the Hilsdon family moved to East Ham where George switched to Plashet Lane School and captained East Ham Boys to victory in the 1900/01 Corinthian Shield. Played as an amateur for Clapton Orient and Luton Town in 1902 before Hammers, after learning his trade with South West Ham and Castle Swifts. Spotted by Irons manager Syd King playing in a Sunday League match on the eve of the 1904/05 season, the club duly signed the slimly-built 18-year-old who promptly scored four goals against Bristol Rovers in a Western League fixture. After suffering a foot injury, he was seen playing for Hammers' second string by the shrewd Chelsea player-manager, John Tait Robertson, who had turned up to watch another player. In his official report on his mission the canny Scot enthused at the time: "I never even set eyes on the player I went specially to see. They were glued all the time to the inside-left; a cockney lad, 19 years of age." Added to this was an amazingly accurate prophesy: "If I get him he'll be our first team centre-forward next season." And so he was. In his initial appearance for his new club, against Glossop in a Second Division fixture at Stamford Bridge, George made a sensational start by scoring five of Chelsea's nine goals. His old colleagues at West Ham showed their delight at his success when the whole team turned out to see the young sharpshooter play for the South versus the North in a trial for the England team. Within six weeks he was selected to lead the Football League attack versus Irish League, scoring a hat-trick. His 26 goals for Chelsea that campaign made a major contribution to their promotion to the First Division in only their second League season. But after winning eight full England caps and once bagging six of the Pensioners' nine goals in a 1908 FA Cup romp over Worksop, George almost inevitably suffered a loss of form. His plight at this stage of his career is best summed up in an extract from Reg Groves's *Official History of West Ham United* in the Famous Football Clubs series, published in 1947: "After several great seasons with Chelsea, 'Gatling Gun' George had fallen on bad times. He had been too sociable, too careless with his strength and vitality and had lost his place in the Chelsea first team during season 1911/12. A sad falling off, but West Ham found a place for their former player, re-signing him for season 1912/13." It proved a good move: George, who was only 26, brought a skill and experience in first-class football that proved invaluable to many up-and-coming youngsters – and his lively, jesting and good-natured humour helped a lot to keep a good team spirit. It seems there were temptations to distract top footballers from their profession even in those austere days. But if Chelsea thought George was finished, they had made a big mistake... as their former star was to prove when he returned to neutral Stamford Bridge in January 1913 to do battle for Hammers versus First Division West Bromwich Albion in an FA Cup First Round play-off. Southern League Irons thrashed the Thistles 3-1, with George scoring twice on his old stamping ground to give Chelsea a timely reminder that they may have been too hasty in letting him go. As well as proving he was far from finished on the playing field, he was also spending more and more time developing the skills of the club's younger players. One he particularly helped was later to become a West Ham legend... Sydney Puddefoot. Charlie Paynter once recalled: "Yes, you could say George Hilsdon was the making of Syd." Even after the Great War (in which George was badly affected by mustard gas poisoning) the two former England centre-forwards remained close friends, Syd often popping in to the Hilsdon family home in Westbury Road (off Green Street) when he, too, returned to Upton Park in 1932. So, one way or another, George Hilsdon was responsible for the making of quite a few legends in his lifetime. He ended his career with Gillingham, and Kent League Chatham in 1919. In 1924 George went into another brand of entertainment when he joined Fred Karno's Troup, a famous vaudeville act. George died in September, 1941.

HILSDON, Jack · 1903-04

League apps: 1

THE BROTHER OF George, he made a solitary appearance in an uninspiring 0-0 Memorial Ground stalemate with Luton Town (September 24, 1903) at inside-right. Earlier in his career his scoring exploits had rivalled those of his brother, as he scored both goals in Clapton Orient's first London League match versus Barnet in September 1898. He won a West Ham Charity Cup winners' medal with O's in April 1902 when Clapton were defeated 1-0 at the Spotted Dog Ground. A month later he was in the O's side that defeated Ealing 1-0 to annex the Middlesex Charity Cup. It set the seal on a successful last season with O's for Jack, as he joined Luton after scoring 50-plus goals for Hammers' near neighbours, including a 26-goal haul in 1901/02.

HILTON, Paul · 1983-89

Born: Oldham, Lancashire, 8.10.59
League apps: 60 (7 goals)
Cup apps: 5

IT WAS A case of "If you can't beat 'em, join 'em!" for this tall central defender. On the receiving end of Hammers' record 10-0 League Cup thrashing of Bury in 1984, Paul made the transition from Fourth to First Division with relative ease. A former England Schoolboy international in the centre-forward position ("Hilts" once scored 70 goals in a season at schoolboy level), he was snapped up by Bury after scoring a first-half hat-trick in a trial game versus Newcastle United in 1977, having earlier been rejected by Lancashire rivals Blackpool. He made his League debut at Wrexham (August 12, 1978) and went on to make 136 League appearances for the Shakers. Transferred to West Ham in February 1984 for £100,000 and made his debut versus Watford (February 21, 1984) at Upton Park. His debut was delayed due to a freak training injury when, two days after signing, he twisted his knee and lost a tooth! Initially, Paul played in midfield to ease Hammers' injury problems, but centre-back was his more familiar role. Although he was used mainly as cover for first team regulars Alvin Martin and Tony Gale, Hilts still had plenty of senior outings, including a crucial end-of-season clash with Chelsea at Upton Park in 1987/88. His goal in the 4-1 victory proved vital in avoiding relegation. Unfortunately, Hammers could not avoid the drop a year later when big Paul's career ended. A series of cartilage and knee injuries had taken their toll and after months of battling for fitness, he received the sad news in October 1989 that he would have to quit playing at the age of 31. The heartbreak was eased, however, when he was appointed youth team coach by Billy Bonds, after Bonzo stepped up from that position to first team boss in February 1990, and in May 1991 he was awarded a testimonial by the club. After two seasons managing the youngsters, Hilts took charge of the reserves in 1992/93. Paul joined up with former team-mate Paul Goddard, who was coaching Ipswich Town's U-19s, with Hilts doing a similar job with the U-15s at Portman Road in 2001. Now living at Great Dunmow, Essex, Paul still coaches at the town's youth academy.

HINDLE, Harry · 1905-06

Born: Blackburn, Lancashire, 1882
SL apps: 3

HAROLD HAD NOT made the first team in two seasons with Blackburn Rovers, but fared slightly better at the Boleyn, playing in the opening two matches of the 1905/06 season, against Swindon and away to Millwall, at right-half. But he played only once more, at centre-half against Reading in a 3-2 defeat at Elm Park (October 28, 1905). A mill worker by trade, he had spent his pre-professional years with a Blackburn junior side, St James Road FC. He then progressed to the Lancashire Combination with Oswaldwistle Rovers, and from there on to Ewood Park, where he teamed up with Fred Blackburn and his left-wing partner Lionel Watson, who both joined him at the Boleyn and played with him in the aforementioned opening games of 1905/06. Harry actually joined Hammers from Lancashire Combination team Nelson, where he had gone after failing to break into Rovers' First Division side. He was also approached to join Second Division Grimsby Town, but Blackburn demanded a £75 transfer fee and the deal fell through. He was able to join Irons on a "free" because their Southern League status put them outside the jurisdiction of the Football League.

HIRD, Henry — 1897-1900 TIW

Born: West Hartlepool, County Durham, 1874

A FAST, TRICKY right-winger who crossed the ball extremely well, Henry helped Irons win the London League Championship in 1897/98, netting five times and providing many more for team-mates. He made 19 League appearances the following season, scoring three goals. He has the dubious honour of being the first recorded Irons player to be sent off when he was dismissed against Leyton in October 1897, during a London League match.

HISLOP, Shaka — 1998-2002/2005-

Born: Hackney, London, 22.2.69
League apps: 105
Cup apps: 27

IN COMMON WITH John Harkes, Shaka began his career with an American college side, Howard University, from where Second Division Reading signed him in September 1992. The giant goalkeeper was an instant hit at Elm Park and after making ten League appearances in 1992/93, he was an ever-present in the Royals' Second Division Championship-winning side of 1993/94 and again in 1994/95 when they finished runners-up in the old First Division in the transitional season in which only one team (Middlesbrough) was promoted to the Premiership. Voted Player of the Year and selected PFA's First Division top goalkeeper, the big shot-stopper was soon Premiership bound when Reading accepted a £1.5 million British record offer for a goalkeeper from Newcastle United after he'd made 126 League and Cup appearances for the Berkshire club and contributed hugely to their improved status. Responding enthusiastically to his new brief to stop goals for Newcastle, Shaka conceded just 20 goals in his first 28 games on Tyneside and kept 11 clean sheets. Facing stiff competition from Shay Given and Pavel Svnicek, he nevertheless got the call to join up with the full England squad for the game against Chile, but had to be content with an Under-21 cap against Switzerland in March 1998. Out of contract during the summer of 1998, Harry Redknapp finally swooped after a will-he-won't-he transfer saga to take the sought after keeper to Upton Park free of charge under the Bosman

ruling after the player had made 71 appearances in three years at St James's Park and served under Kevin Keegan and Kenny Dalglish. Having put his decision of whether or not to take up the option to represent Trinidad and Tobago on hold while he weighed up his chances of playing for England, Shaka found himself in the unusual position of winning caps with two countries when he made his debut in a friendly for Trinidad and Tobago against Jamaica after joining Hammers. Voted Hammer of the Year in his first season at the Boleyn when he missed just one game and kept 17 clean sheets, the 31-year-old suffered a serious setback in 1999/2000 when he sustained a broken leg in an innocuous challenge with Bradford City's Dean Saunders at Upton Park in February 2000 that kept him out of the rest of the campaign. Back in the first team for the start of 2000/01, he wasn't quite the force he'd been the previous campaign, but it was only an injury in the game with Sunderland at Upton Park that caused him to lose his place briefly to Craig Forrest and then Stephen Bywater, after which he went on to total 42 League and Cup appearances and keep ten clean sheets. Following the signing of England international David James by new manager Glenn Roeder, the popular Shaka thankfully decided to stay and fight for his place and when James was injured on England duty on the eve of the 2001/02 season, Hislop stepped in to fill the breach. By now having difficulty taking goal kicks, he was on the end of a couple of heavy defeats at Everton (5-0) and Blackburn (7-1) and the 4-4 draw at Charlton in November 2001 proved to be his last for Hammers as James returned from injury. Newly installed as manager of First Division Portsmouth, Shaka's shrewd old boss Harry Redknapp swooped to sign him on a free transfer for a second time and rescue the still capable keeper from the wilderness of West Ham's reserves. Just how capable he still was couldn't have been illustrated better than by Pompey's promotion to the Premiership in 2002/03 as they passed Hammers on the way down. An ever-present with 16 clean sheets in Portsmouth's rise, Shaka was back to his best and was deservedly selected for the PFA Division One team of the season. Successfully retaining his number one spot as the south coast club did likewise with their hard won Premiership status in their first season in the top flight since 1958, the 35-year-old was still first choice at Fratton Park as the 2004/05 season got under way. To keep him company, Shaka had four ex-Hammers in the Portsmouth first team squad: Eyal Berkovic, Svetoslav Todorov, Hayden Foxe and David Unsworth! After making 100 appearances for Pompey Shaka returned to Hammers in August 2005.

HITCH, Alf — 1898 TIW

Born: Walsall, West Midlands, March 1877
League apps: 5
Cup apps: 1

JOINED THAMES IRONWORKS from Walsall FC. Made six appearances, including an FA Cup tie, wearing the number 5 shirt before moving to QPR.

HITCHENS, J — 1877

League apps: 1
Cup apps: 1

FORMERLY WITH OLD St Lukes, this inside-left played one Southern League and one FA Cup tie in Hammers' colours. His first outing was in a 0-0 stalemate at Watford (October 19, 1901) and the second came in a 1-0 FA Cup victory at Leyton the following month.

HODGES, Harry — 1923-24

Born: Dagenham, Essex, 1897
League apps: 2 (1 goal)

MADE AN AUSPICIOUS First Division scoring debut

against Arsenal at Highbury (September 10, 1923) in the centre-forward berth, but spent most of his time as understudy to the great Vic Watson. Made only one more first XI appearance, versus Spurs at Upton Park, the same season. Harry joined Hammers from the same Essex club that provided fellow striker Les Robinson — Stirling Athletic. His brother, John, played for Hammers as an amateur and was nicknamed "Digger". Played for Lincoln for a time after leaving West Ham. An enthusiastic member of the former Old Players' Association, Harry died in December, 1966 at the age of 69.

HODGES, Lee — 1998

Born: Plaistow, London, 2.3.78
League apps: 3
Cup apps: 3

ANOTHER PRODUCT OF the much vaunted West Ham United Youth Academy, left-midfielder Lee played in the Hammers youth team that won through to the two-leg 1996 FA Youth Cup Final against Liverpool, which also featured Frank Lampard and Rio Ferdinand. Like the rest of that talented team, Lee failed to reach the dizzy heights of his two world famous team-mates but has enjoyed the most successful career of the remainder who lost on aggregate to that Michael Owen-inspired Liverpool side in the spring of 1996. Something of an individualist, the young eastender was loaned out to Third Division Exeter City in December 1996 and made 17 League appearances for the Grecians before embarking on another loan spell with neighbours Leyton Orient in February 1997. The diminutive former England schoolboy international made his second Division Three debut against London rivals Barnet in early March but was recalled to Upton Park early after making just two more shows with O's when he sustained a knee injury. The following season (1997/98) saw him heading west again for another loan spell with Second Division Plymouth Argyle where he made another ten appearances before being recalled to Hammers to strengthen a squad battling to fulfil fixtures in both the FA and Coca Cola Cup competitions as well as its Premiership commitments. Lee finally made his senior bow for Irons in the 1-0 defeat against Spurs at White Hart Lane in January 1998 and was also called off the bench again for the following week's 2-2 Upton Park draw with Everton as all the experience gained on loan began to pay dividends. He was then pitched in to the FA Cup Fifth Round clash with Blackburn Rovers at the Boleyn, which ended 2-2. Hodges went close to winning the tie with a late header, but at Ewood Park Hammers won the replay on penalties. The Sixth Round tie against Arsenal at Highbury also saw Lee involved as Hammers drew 1-1, with Lee coming off the bench. He did so again in the replay, which Hammers lost on penalties following a 1-1 draw after extra time. Unfazed by the capacity crowd and electric atmosphere, he caused the north London giants a lot of problems down the left flank. But it was his last outing at senior level for the club. In November 1998 he was loaned out to First Division Ipswich Town where he made four League appearances and in March 1999 he was on his travels again with another loan spell at Third Division Southend United, where a scintillating performance in a 3-0 win at Leyton Orient helped to ease the Shrimpers' relegation fears. In all, he made 11 appearances at Roots Hall. In June 1999, Lee at last found a club of his own when he was transferred to those other less famous Irons, Scunthorpe United, for an initial fee of £50,000 set to rise after 25 appearances and eventually realise West Ham £130,000. Although they were relegated to the Third Division in Lee's first season at Glanford Park he remained their most talented player and in 2000/01 he was honoured by winning a place in the PFA's Third Division Team of the Season for the second successive year. After eight goals, Lee was surprisingly released by Scunny in the summer of 2002 to make eight appearances with Rochdale before signing for Bristol Rovers. He made a good start to 2003/04 when he came off the bench to score against his old club Scunthorpe and Kidderminster but sustained another knee injury which required an operation and kept him out for four months. Given a free transfer by Rovers last summer, Lee signed for Nationwide Conference South side Thurrock FC, where he is a team-mate of Hammers youth coach Paul Heffer's son, Steve Heffer, and ex-Hammers striker Danny Shipp.

HODGSON, Tommy 1922-29

Born: Hetton, County Durham, 19.1.1903
League apps: 87 (1 goal)
Cup apps: 5

A FORMER COAL miner, this rugged full-back served West Ham United throughout the 1920s and would have totalled many more first team appearances had illness and injury not interrupted his career. Signed from Hetton Colliery in 1921, he made his Hammers debut against Blackpool at Bloomfield Road in the final match of the 1921/22 season. He became one of the renowned Hammers' "5-H" quintet of defenders: Hufton, Hebden, Henderson, Hodgson and Horler. Tommy transferred to Third Division South Luton Town in 1930, teaming up with his old Hammers colleague George Kay, who was then manager at Kenilworth Road. After making 67 League appearances, injury ended his career. Tommy went on to create a unique record with the Bedfordshire club by becoming the only man in soccer to be player, captain, director, managing director, chairman and president of one Football League club. He also had the honour of leading out the Hatters at Wembley for the 1959 FA Cup Final against Nottingham Forest, when Town were without a manager. Tommy, who also played for Luton Postal after retiring from League soccer, passed away in 1989.

HODSON, James 1916-18

Born: Horwich, Lancashire, date unknown
League apps: 49

ALL HODSON'S 49 games for West Ham took place during the 1914-18 war, in a good many of which he partnered his former Oldham Athletic colleague Bill Cope. He was with Oldham when they won the Lancashire Combination in 1906/07. Oldham joined the League for 1907/08 and between then and 1914/15 Hodson played in 252 League matches including 32 in Division Two (1909/10) when Latics finished runners-up and won promotion. He also won a First Division runners-up medal in 1914/15 with the Lancastrians. After the Armistice, he joined Brentford in the Southern League for 1919/20 and was with the Bees for their first season in the League. Hodson made 68 appearances with Brentford in the first two peacetime seasons of 1919/20 and 1920/21. He joined new Southern League club Guildford United for 1921/22. Jimmy's first team was St Helens Recreation, from whom he joined Bury. After West Ham, he had a stint with Belfast Celtic. He selected Upton Park as the venue for his benefit match in September 1922 when he was manager of Guildford. In June 1923, he took up a post with Bereham Sports Club in Antwerp, Belgium. He died in Holland in February 1938.

HOLLIGAN, Gavin 1999

Born: Lambeth, London, 13.6.80
League apps: 1

THEY SAY EVERYONE gets 15 minutes of fame and

HOLLAND, Pat 1969-81

Born: Poplar, London, 13.9.50
League apps: 245 (23 goals)
Cup apps: 51 (9 goals)

ONE OF THE unsung heroes of Upton Park who, nevertheless, played his part in the side that beat Fulham in the 1975 FA Cup Final and lost to Anderlecht in the European Cup Winners' Cup Final a year later. Indeed, Patsy scored in the 4-2 defeat in front of 58,000 fans in Belgium's Heysel Stadium. A 90-minute grafter who never gave less than 100 per cent effort and to whom fate was not particularly kind, Patsy sustained the knee injury that ended his career in typical fashion – going in where it hurts and scoring a vital promotion goal in the process. That happened at Notts County (January 17, 1981) and although he made a comeback in the reserves, he couldn't win back his first team place. Curly-haired Pat, who played mostly on the right wing, had been plagued with knee problems for some time and it was this that cruelly forced him to miss the 1980 FA Cup Final versus Arsenal – the team he supported as a boy! Pat remained at Upton Park for a while in a coaching capacity before being given a free transfer in 1984. He joined up with near-neighbours Orient as player-coach and enjoyed a fond farewell to Upton Park during his testimonial match with Spurs. Pat was later appointed reserve team coach at Queens Park Rangers and youth team coach at Orient. In 1988 he joined Spurs to coach their youth and reserve teams. Ironically, Tottenham wanted to sign Pat way back in 1965, but Hammers' chief scout Wally St Pier got in before Bill Nicholson to snap up the East London Schools star who was then on his way to the English Schools Final. Pat combined his duties at White Hart Lane with the running of his wine bar, Hollands, at Shenfield, Essex.

Career record

Played	League App	Gls	FAC App	Gls	LC App	Gls	Europe App	Gls	Total App	Gls
1968-69	1	0	0	0	0	0	0	0	1	0
1969-70	8	1	0	0	0	0	0	0	8	1
1970-71	3	0	0	0	0	0	0	0	3	0
1971-72	4	0	0	0	0	0	0	0	4	0
1972-73	32	1	2	1	2	0	0	0	36	2
1973-74	23	2	2	1	2	0	0	0	27	3
1974-75	22	4	7	2	2	0	0	0	31	6
1975-76	35	2	1	0	5	0	7	2	48	4
1976-77	6	0	0	0	1	2	0	0	7	2
1977-78	21	3	1	0	0	0	0	0	22	3
1978-79	39	3	0	0	1	0	0	0	40	3
1979-80	26	4	1	0	8	1	0	0	35	5
1980-81	25	3	2	0	4	0	3	0	34	3
TOTAL	**245**	**23**	**16**	**4**	**25**	**3**	**10**	**2**	**296**	**32**

Gavin Holligan got his stab at the big time on February 20, 1999. A shock inclusion on the subs bench for West Ham's visit to Liverpool, the promising 18-year-old had been bought from non-League Kingstonian just the month before for £100,000. In the 77th minute of the second half, he was brought on in front of a 44,511 crowd at Anfield as a substitute for cramp victim Joe Cole. Within seconds of coming on, Holligan found himself in a one-on-one situation with David James and the chance to end West Ham's 36-year sequence without a win at Anfield, but the ball cannoned off James's legs and the chance was lost. Then, with the game still at 2-2, Eyal Berkovic's 83rd minute through ball split the Reds' defence, sending Trevor Sinclair clean through, with Holligan alongside. Ignoring the new boy, Sinclair curled his shot over the bar. Holligan, who scored 12 goals in his first five weeks as a Hammer reserve and Under-19 player, never got another chance to make an impression at West Ham. The youngster began his career with Walton and Hersham in August 1997 and, after his brief first team outing at West Ham, was loaned out to Leyton Orient in August 1999. Again, after just one Third Division appearance against Torquay United, plus a further game in the Worthington Cup against Grimsby Town, Gavin returned to Upton Park. Another loan spell at Exeter City followed. In March 2001, he went back on loan to his old club Kingstonian, but could not prevent his old team being relegated. He was given a free transfer to Second Division Wycombe Wanderers in May 2001 and scored ten times in 50 first team outings for the Adams Park outfit before being given a free transfer by manager Tony Adams at the end of 2003/04. Having had loan spells with non-League Crawley and

Hornchurch earlier in the season he signed a permanent deal with Conference South side Havant and Waterlooville where he teamed up with ace striker Dean Holdsworth for 2004/05. A far cry from Anfield.

HOLMES, Jim 1936

Born: Skelmersdale, Lancashire, 27.12.08
League apps: 2

A POWERFUL PIVOT signed from Sheffield United, both his Second Division appearances took place in away matches against Blackpool, in a 1-0 reverse (September 5, 1936), and in a 5-3 defeat at Newcastle four days later. He began with Sutton Schools as a right-winger, then Sutton Commercial and Sutton Parish. He joined Liverpool as an amateur, Wigan Borough, Prescot Cables and Chesterfield before joining the Blades. Found himself on the "not retained" list at the end of the season and joined Reading. He made 73 appearances and scored five goals for the Biscuitmen before the outbreak of World War II, to add to the 26 League outings he made for Chesterfield and the 135 he made for Sheffield United. He died in 1971.

HOLMES, Matthew 1992-95

Born: Luton, Bedfordshire, 1.8.69
League apps: 76 (4 goals)
Cup apps: 13 (1 goal)

THE FIRST OF several ex-Bournemouth players assistant manager Harry Redknapp brought with him to Upton Park. Matt cost Hammers an initial fee of

£40,000 in August 1992, with a further £60,000 due to the south coast club after his 60th League appearance for Hammers. This diminutive, shy midfielder made an eventful debut at Newcastle (August 29, 1992), where he suffered a broken nose after just 20 minutes! Mattie, who has a sweet left foot, close control and excellent ball skills, was unlucky to start only six League matches in the 1992/93 Second Division promotion campaign, although he did feature 12 times as sub. But, despite dislocating his finger in the opening game of the 1993/94 Premiership season against Wimbledon, he held down a regular place on the left side of midfield with a number of promising performances. His efforts did not go unnoticed by the fans, who voted him runner-up (to Trevor Morley) in their

Matthew Holmes

Hammer of the Year poll. He supported Luton Town as a kid but was rejected by Hatters who told him he was too small to make the grade. Likeable Matt finally proved himself on the south coast, but it was during a loan period with Cardiff City that he made his League debut as sub versus Aldershot (March 25, 1989). Matt's brother, Danny, plays for non-League Farnborough Town. After a stunning televised display against Liverpool at Upton Park, Matty's profile soared and he couldn't resist a £1.2 million transfer to Premiership champions Blackburn Rovers in August 1995. It proved a fateful decision, however, as Matty's time at Ewood Park was highlighted by injuries and he made a mere 12 appearances (one goal) for Rovers before the Lancastrians cut their losses and transferred him to Charlton Athletic for £250,000 in July 1997. His first class career was virtually ended in the Addicks' FA Cup Fourth Round replay clash against Wolves in February 1998 following a dreadful foul tackle by Kevin Muscat. Backed by video evidence and several witnesses, Matt took legal action but accepted a £250,000 out-of-court settlement plus costs that were running at £500,000. So after just 19 League and Cup appearances (one goal) Matty was forced to give up top class football and join up with non-League Dorchester Town, whom he helped gain promotion to the Conference South before finally hanging up his boots in May 2005. He then set up a coaching school for local youngsters.

HOOPER, Harry — 1950-56

Born: Pittingdon, County Durham, 14.6.33
League apps: 119 (39 goals)
Cup apps: 11 (5 goals)

THE SON OF Hammers trainer, Harry Hooper Snr, this dashing, goal-scoring winger from Hylton Colliery, was the star attraction at the Boleyn during his reign. While with Hammers he represented the Football League versus Irish League (1954) and the Scottish League (1955). When Wolves came dangling an open cheque book, there was little the club could do to stop their England Under-23 international from joining the then most famous club in the land for £25,000. However, the game turned sour on him at Molineux and after scoring 19 times in 39 matches, he moved on to Birmingham City. In 105 League games with Brum he plundered another 34 goals but in September 1960 he moved to his home-town club, Sunderland, where he ended his career with 65 games and another 16 goals. One wonders, in retrospect, whether he would have been better off staying with the "Homely Hammers".

H. HOOPER (West Ham United)

HORLER, George — 1922-27

Born: Frome, Somerset, 1895
League apps: 45
Cup apps: 5

HIS FULL-BACK PARTNERSHIP with Jack Hebden in the old London Combination was reckoned to be the finest in the Reserve League, and led to the pair being chosen to represent the competition before progressing to the first XI. Signed from Reading, he had several seasons with the Biscuitmen before donning the claret and blue, and continued to reside in Berkshire while a Hammer. George was also an accomplished singer and often formed a duet with pianist Tommy Yews to entertain at social gatherings, both at home and on tour. He joined Fulham on leaving the club in September 1927, and also had a spell at Aldershot.

HORLOCK, Kevin — 2003-04

Born: Erith, Kent, 1.11.72
League apps: 27 (1 goal)
Cup apps: 2

IT TOOK COMBATIVE midfielder Kevin Horlock 15 years to realise his dream to play for West Ham's first team, but just a season to be shown the door for the second time by the club he has supported all his life. Kevin finally achieved his cherished ambition after signing for a £300,000 fee in August 2003, making his long-awaited debut in the 0-0 home draw against Sheffield United later that month. Three months later he actually scored a goal for his beloved Hammers in the 4-0 victory over Wigan Athletic. Before all that, though, Kevin first joined his boyhood heroes as a starry eyed trainee in 1989 and was a member of the Hammers youth squad that included Matt Holland, Steve Heffer, Paul Marquis, Michael Macari and Danny Williamson, the only player from those ranks to really make the big time at the Boleyn. With only reserve games on his CV, Kevin was glad of the offer of a free transfer to First Division Swindon Town in August 1992. The Robins made it to the Premiership via the play-offs in 1993/94. Equally at home in the midfield or at left-back, his versatility won him the first of 32 full caps for Northern Ireland in April 1995 versus Latvia. After making one short of 200 League and Cup appearances and scoring 26 times during five years at the County Ground, Kevin really arrived when Manchester City manager Joe Royle weighed out a cool £1.25 million to take him to Maine Road to join City's quest to return to the Premiership. That goal was eventually achieved in 2000, but not before the Citizens had slipped down a division and relied on Kevin's stubborn resolution to recover lost ground. Amassing 233 League and Cup appearances with the Blues and scoring 42 times, Kevin was in no hurry to leave the new City of Manchester Stadium, but explained his reason for leaving in emotional terms before returning to Upton Park with his new club Ipswich Town in September 2004: "I had a great time at Manchester City. I was there seven years and still had two years on my contract. But when West Ham showed interest I thought it was probably the only chance I will get to pull on the claret and blue shirt." The 32-year-old was released on a free transfer in the summer after losing favour with manager Alan Pardew and missing the play-offs. On the eve of his return with the Tractor Boys he continued: "It's not personal but I would love to go back there and win and have a great game. I'm not bitter though. Alan Pardew was honest and told me I would not be playing regularly, which I appreciate. I see it as a massive boost that Joe [Royle] took me on again, having been at Man City when he was manager there. But I'm still a West Ham supporter and always will be."

HORN, George — 1906-08

SL apps: 8
Cup apps: 1

BETTER KNOWN AS "Johnny", he'd played for the Army and Navy (Anchor FC) and joined Hammers from Tunbridge Wells in 1906. Said to be "a terror for his size", half-back George transferred to Chelsea in 1909.

Kevin Horlock

HOUGHTON, Ray — 1984

Born: Glasgow, Scotland, 9.1.62
League apps: 1

DUE TO INTENSE competition for midfield places (Trevor Brooking and Alan Devonshire played the starring roles then), John Lyall allowed this talented young Scot to join Fulham in 1982. He held the unique record for the least amount of playing time for West Ham's first team – coming on as sub (for fellow Scot George Cowie) for the last half-hour against Arsenal at Highbury (May 1, 1982). That sole appearance puts him some way behind Billy Bonds in the record books, but he made the First Division grade with Oxford United following a £147,000 transfer from the west Londoners in September 1985. He then moved on to Liverpool in 1987 for £825,000 and, after winning two championship and one FA Cup winners' medal, he moved to Aston Villa in July 1992 for £900,000. The dynamic little midfielder helped them to a shock League Cup Final victory, which denied Manchester United the treble, in March 1994. Three months later he was the toast of the Republic of Ireland as he scored the winning goal in their opening World Cup game against Italy at USA 94. Although born in Glasgow, he was first capped for the Republic of Ireland in 1986, through family qualification. Ray transferred to Crystal Palace for £300,000 in March 1995 and helped them return to the Premiership in 1997 via the play-offs. He moved on to Reading in August 1997 and saw out his illustrious career with the Royals having amassed more than 700 League appearances with 94 goals, plus 73 caps for his country.

HOWE, Bobby   1966-71

Born: Chadwell St Mary, Essex, 22.12.45
League apps: 75 (4 goals)
Cup apps: 7

A MODEL PROFESSIONAL and fine wing-half, Bobby served the club well during his five years in first team contention. A former Essex Schools star, he signed professional in December 1962 and was a member of the club's Youth Cup-winning side the following year. After ending his playing career at Dean Court, Bobby and his old pal Harry Redknapp went out to the States together as assistant coaches to Seattle Sounders, a grounding that led to Bobby staying in America to manage the USA Under-18 side in the early 1990s. Then another ex-Hammer, the late Clive Charles, recommended Bobby for the position as head coach of Portland Timbers, a club from the state of Oregon who play in the Pro A League. "It's difficult to compare standards," explained Bobby on a recent visit back to the UK, "but I think we could give English Third Division teams a good run for their money. We average 6,000 crowds and we are one level down from the Major League Soccer, which is the top division in the US." Before taking up his post with Portland, Bobby was director of coaching to the US Soccer Federation and is now happily settled at a place called Lake Oswego, seven miles outside Portland.

HUBBARD, Cliff   1939

Born: Worksop, Nottinghamshire, 1911
League apps: 1 (1 goal)

PREVIOUSLY WITH SCUNTHORPE United (1932-33), after spending his formative years with Worksop Schools, Notts Schools and Manton Colliery, this centre-forward was signed from Hull City towards the end of the 1938/39 season for £3,000 after scoring 62 goals in 182 League appearances for the Tigers. He emulated the feat of Dick Bell before him by scoring on his solitary Second Division appearance for the Hammers. He earned his one-game, one-goal distinction with a brilliant display against Manchester City at Upton Park in the final match of 1938/39. An extremely versatile player who had appeared in every position (including goal for Hull), he was strongly tipped for a regular place in the first team when League Football was suspended in September 1939. After World War II he played for Ransom and Marles (Newark), Goole Town and Worksop Town, where he was trainer-coach from 1960 until his death in November 1962.

BOBBY HOWE   West Ham United

HUFTON, Edward   1919-32

Born: Southwell, Nottinghamshire, 25.11.1892
League apps: 370
Cup apps: 31

TED RIVALS ERNIE Gregory, Phil Parkes and Ludo Miklosko for the title of West Ham's greatest-ever goalkeeper. The meteoric rise of his early career with Sheffield United was almost matched by the suddenness of its temporary decline, following a bizarre chain of events in his first season with the Yorkshiremen. Signed by the Blades from local works side Atlas and Norfolk in 1913, Ted soon seized the first team spot and acquitted himself well enough to prompt United to transfer their regular goalkeeper. However, they did obtain the services of another young keeper as cover, one Harold Gough from Castleford, and when Hammers' hero-to-be broke his nose in a practice match, the situation reversed itself; Gough going on to play for Blades in the 1915 FA Cup Final and later gain England honours. Ted, meanwhile, joined the Coldstream Guards and was swept up in the horrors of World War I and wounded in action in France. If fate had been unkind to Ted Hufton, it certainly wasn't the case as far as West Ham United were concerned. Having recovered from his shrapnel wounds, he made the first of 64 wartime guest appearances for the club, paving the way for his eventual transfer when hostilities ceased. Once again it was a fellow goalkeeper who had a big hand in Ted's future fate – best illustrated in a story traditionally handed down over the years at Upton Park. Legend has it that during that last wartime season, Joe Hughes, then Hammers' regular keeper, saw the young Ted Hufton keeping goal in a practice match. After a while, Joe turned to manager Syd King and asked to be put on the transfer list. "Why?" came the reply, as Joe was a fine player himself. "He's my governor – let me go," Joe reportedly answered. "He's a better goalie than I'll ever be." And so it was. Joe Hughes transferred to Bolton Wanderers, later joining Chelsea; and Ted joined Hammers for £350! Irons' first season in the newly-formed Second Division was a memorable one for Ted, and it was around this time that he acquired the nickname "Penalty King" by saving 11 out of 18 spot-kicks against him in two seasons. During the 1920/21 season he had two former Sheffield United men for company in the first team: Dick Leafe (who was later appointed the club's assistant secretary) and another forward, Jimmy Simmons (who had scored for the Blades in the aforementioned FA Cup Final of 1915). Jim, incidentally, has often been confused with another

Gallaher's Cigarettes.

ARTHUR E. HUFTON
WEST HAM UNITED

ex-Hammer of the same surname, "Chippy" Simmons, who was signed from West Bromwich Albion in 1904 and was with the club for four seasons. The 1920/21 campaign also saw Ted scale new heights of excellence when he received the notable record of not conceding more than two goals in any of the 38 League matches he played – the best goals-against record in the country that year. International recognition followed the Cup Final and promotion year of 1923, but Ted had to decline joining fellow West Ham team-mates Jack Tresadern and Billy Moore in action for England versus Sweden in Stockholm due to injury. So his debut was delayed to the following year, when he won the first of his six caps against Belgium – and he remained the only goalkeeper to play for England while with West Ham until David James assumed the jersey against Holland in 2002. He played against the immortal Scottish "Wembley Wizards" in 1928, when Alex James and co ran amok, but even in defeat Ted was magnificent. The case was the same when Hammers lost a vital League match against Everton at Goodison Park towards the end of the club's relegation season in 1931/32. The Toffeemen ran out 6-1 victors, virtually assuring themselves of the League championship with the help of a hat-trick from the legendary Dixie Dean. A subsequent match report in an Everton programme of that period exonerated Hammers' keeper for the reverse. "The display against the Londoners was brimful of interest, and though there was but a narrow margin at the interval, there could be no mistaking our superiority during the second portion. Dunn was the star artist in the forward-line, though not among the scorers because of the brilliance of the West Ham goalkeeper Hufton, but for whom a double score might have been established." West Ham's return to the Second Division saw the veteran keeper lose his place to George Watson, and he was granted a free transfer at the end of the 1932/33 season, joining Watford for a brief spell. After World War II, he returned to Upton Park to take up the position of press-room steward on match days. Beset by ill health in later life, Ted moved to Swansea to convalesce. On February 2, 1967 a great Englishman died in Wales, and left behind a lasting legend.
England caps: 1923 vs Belgium; 1927 vs Northern Ireland; 1928 vs Scotland; 1929 vs France, Belgium, Spain (6).

Career record										
	League		**FAC**		**LC**		**Europe**		**Total**	
Played	**App**	**Gls**	**App**	**Gls**	**App**	**Gls**	**App**	**Gls**	**App**	**Gls**
1919-20	38	0	4	0	0	0	0	0	42	0
1920-21	38	0	1	0	0	0	0	0	39	0
1921-22	33	0	3	0	0	0	0	0	36	0
1922-23	39	0	9	0	0	0	0	0	48	0
1923-24	15	0	0	0	0	0	0	0	15	0
1924-25	7	0	0	0	0	0	0	0	7	0
1925-26	38	0	1	0	0	0	0	0	39	0
1926-27	40	0	3	0	0	0	0	0	43	0
1927-28	25	0	2	0	0	0	0	0	27	0
1928-29	31	0	4	0	0	0	0	0	35	0
1929-30	30	0	4	0	0	0	0	0	34	0
1930-31	14	0	0	0	0	0	0	0	14	0
1931-32	22	0	0	0	0	0	0	0	22	0
TOTAL	**370**	**0**	**31**	**0**	**0**	**0**	**0**	**0**	**401**	**0**

HUGHES, Joe 1911-15

Born: London, 1892
League apps: 90
Cup apps: 15

A WHOLE SUCCESSION of rival goalkeepers laid claim to Joe Hughes' jealously guarded position as the last line of Hammers' defence. The able custodian saw them all off with the exception of Ted Hufton, as is told in the previous entry. Joe was transferred to Chelsea, who he played for in World War I, but later transferred to Bolton and played over 50 matches for the Trotters until the famous Dick Pym took over between the posts for the Lancastrians. He then returned to London to join fellow former Hammers Bailey, Burton and Lane at Charlton Athletic, who were about to embark on their first season (1921/22) as a League club. Hughes (and Bailey) were at Clapton Orient at the start of 1923/24, but neither made a League showing. He began with Tufnell Park and then South Weald, from where Hammers signed him in 1911.

HUGHES, Michael 1994-97

Born: Larne, Northern Ireland, 2.8.71
League apps: 73 (5 goals)
Cup apps: 14 (1 goal)

ALTHOUGH HE'D ALREADY become part of the furniture at Upton Park, following a successful 18-month loan spell from Racing Club de Strasbourg, this fast, tricky flankman finally took full advantage of the Bosman ruling to make a permanent move from the French First Division side on a free transfer in July 1996. Beginning his career with Carrick Rangers in his native Northern Ireland in 1986, Michael joined Manchester City as a trainee in 1987 and signed pro in August 1988, making his City debut in a Second Division fixture at Plymouth Argyle in October that year. After scoring one goal in 33 League and Cup games at Maine Road he was transferred to Strasbourg for £450,000 in the summer of 1992, and promptly proceeded to set the French Le Championnat alight with his frenetic, industrious displays. With team-mates of the calibre of Olivier Dacourt, Frank Leboeuf and Hammer-to-be Marc Keller, the young Irishman made an impressive 36 appearances in his first season at the Stade de la Meinau and got himself on the scoresheet in the 2-1 victory over St Etienne and the 4-2 defeat at home to FC Nantes. The 1993/94 season was even more successful when he scored seven times in 34 outings. After the player had made a further 13 appearances at the start of 1994/95, a chance remark by Keith Rowland led to Harry Redknapp securing his services on a loan basis for the remainder of the season, which was then extended further until his contract ran out and he became a free agent to become the first British player to sign under the Bosman ruling. "Hughsie" made his Premiership debut in the 2-1 defeat at QPR in early December 1994 then his home bow just before Christmas in the 3-0 demolition of Manchester City and immediately endeared himself to the Hammers fans with his fully committed, unselfish wing play. Already an established international with Northern Ireland, Michael scored his first goal for Hammers in the 3-1 home win over Nottingham Forest on the last day of 1994 and his second in the final game of the season against Manchester United at Upton Park to prevent the Reds taking the title. Starting the 1996/97 season in fine fettle, the little winger with the rare ability to play on either flank scored three times in his first eight appearances as he claimed another campaign as a regular first-teamer. Discipline remained a problem, and but for seven bookings and a sending-off at Leeds, Michael would have been an ever-present. Just seven games into the 1996/97 season, Hammers fans were

dumbfounded at the news that the popular Hughsie had been sold to London rivals Wimbledon for £1.6 million. In five years with the Dons, Hughes scored 17 times in 130 League and Cup appearances, but after a three-match loan spell with Birmingham City a contractual problem caused him to miss the whole of the 2002/03 season. He returned to haunt Hammers, however, with Crystal Palace in the Division One Play-off Final at the Millennium Stadium in Cardiff. Michael was sent off playing in his 70th international for his country in the 2-2 World Cup qualifier with Wales in September 2004.

HUGHTON, Chris 1990-92

Born: Forest Gate, London, 11.12.58
League apps: 33
Cup apps: 7

RETURNED TO EAST London as cover for injured left-back Julian Dicks in November 1990, this popular Republic of Ireland international proved a solid, dependable member of the 1990/91 Second Division promotion-winning side. Made his debut at Notts County (November 3, 1990) and following a two-month loan spell, Billy Bonds signed him from Tottenham on a free transfer in December 1990. Played in every game, including the ill-fated FA Cup Semi-final defeat by Nottingham Forest, as Hammers returned to the top flight. An articulate pro, Chris brought a wealth of experience to the back four, having previously made 297 League appearances for Spurs and gained 53 full Irish caps. The arrival, in August 1992, of his former White Hart Lane team-mate Mitchell Thomas left Chris out in the cold at Upton Park. He made only one appearance that season, which turned out to be his last for the club – and that sub appearance at home to Notts County meant

Michael Hughes

he'd made his first and final appearance for Hammers against the same club. At that stage of his career Chris wanted first team football and, after a spell on the transfer list, joined Brentford on a free for the last 13 games of the 1992/93 term. A recurrence of a knee injury midway through the following season forced the likable Chris into retirement at the age of 34. At Spurs, Chris won UEFA Cup, FA Cup and League Cup winners' medals, and in the summer of 1993 he returned to White Hart Lane as coach to their Under-21 team. Appointed manager of the reserves in July 1994.
Republic of Ireland caps: 1991 vs Chile; 1992 vs Turkey (2).

HUGO, Roger 1964

Born: Woking, Surrey, 6.9.42
League apps: 3 (2 goals)

A FINE INSIDE-FORWARD whose opportunities were restricted by a surplus of candidates for the inside berths during his time with the club. Scored in two of his first three First Division appearances in 1963/64 – all away from home, against Leicester City, Stoke City and WBA respectively – so he was unable to show the Upton Park crowd his undoubted skill at senior level. Transferred to Watford in the summer of 1965. Roger later emigrated to South Africa, playing for Port Elizabeth. He is now a successful businessman in Johannesburg, running a string of video shops.

HULL, Archie 1928

Born: East Ham, London, 8.8.1902
League apps: 2

RATED THE BEST amateur centre-half in London when his club side Ilford were sweeping all before them in the late 1920s, he was unable to assist West Ham on a regular basis due to his commitment to the Isthmian League outfit. A team-mate of a later West Ham centre-half at Ilford, Wally St Pier, Archie made his debut against WBA (February 19, 1927) and had one more First Division outing with Hammers in a 4-0 defeat against Huddersfield Town (December 22, 1928). A chemist in private life, he was well known as a fine singer at concerts and banquets in the east London and Essex area, and later joined Clapton Orient with whom he made one appearance, in 1931. Archie died on March 6, 1978.

HUNT, Fergus 1900-02

Born: Masborough, South Yorkshire, 1875
SL apps: 42 (9 goals)
Cup apps: 6 (1 goal)

"FERGIE" HUNT WAS a fast-raiding outside-right who came from Woolwich Arsenal on the back of 34 goals in 77 appearances, which made him top scorer from 1897 to 1899. He missed only one match in the club's first season as West Ham United. He began his career with Mexborough in Yorkshire and later played for Middlesbrough Ironopolis and Darwen, with whom he scored 27 times in 58 games after switching to centre-forward, gaining a reputation for scoring late, match-winning goals. Returned to Woolwich for 1902/03, where he made three appearances in 1903/04 and was with Fulham, where he scored four goals in 30 appearances. In 1905/06 he joined Burton United. In September 1907 he joined Shildon.

HURST, Joseph 1895-96 TIW

Born: West Ham, London, c. 1875

A TOUGH-TACKLING FULL-BACK who played in Irons' first ever season and the first three games of the next before moving to St Luke's.

HURST, Sir Geoff MBE   1960-72

Born: Ashton-under-Lyne, Lancashire, 8.12.41
League apps: 411 (180 goals)
Cup apps: 91 (68 goals)

NO MORE THAN a competent wing-half who by sheer determination and hard work became one of the most feared and revered strikers in world football. Of course, he had some help on the way to achieving that goal. Notably from his father, former professional with Oldham, Bristol Rovers and Rochdale, Charles Hurst, who came south to play for Chelmsford City; from family friend Jack Redfern, who recommended Geoff to Hammers; and, most of all, from Ron Greenwood, who converted him to striker. Geoff made his first senior appearance against Fulham in a Floodlight Cup tie in December 1958, signed pro forms four months later and had his First Division baptism at Nottingham Forest (February 27, 1960). After that, his goalscoring exploits became legend. His World Cup Final hat-trick against West Germany at Wembley in 1966 and six goals against Sunderland (October 19, 1968) two years later, have been woven into the fabric of football folklore. Geoff is still the only player to score three goals in a World Cup Final, while his six-of-the-best for Hammers is a club record he shares with Vic Watson, who first managed the feat nearly 40 years earlier. The second-highest Hammers marksman of all time, behind Watson, with 180 League goals, (but easily the best Cup goalscorer with 68); holder of 49 full England caps (24 goals); winner of FA Cup (1964), and European Cup Winners' Cup (1965) medals; World Cup winners' medal and Football League Cup runners-up medal (1966). These are the landmarks the fans remember most. Geoff's first-ever senior goal for West Ham came in a 4-2 win over Wolves at Upton Park (December 18, 1961) – he was wearing the unfamiliar number 4 shirt that day. Despite the challenge from the young Bobby Moore, Eddie Bovington, Bill Lansdowne and Malcolm Pike, Geoff was delighted to start the 1962/63 season at wing-half. But he was dropped for the next match and played the following five games in the reserves. When Greenwood summoned him to his office, Geoff expected a rocket for his poor form. Instead, Greenwood was looking for "someone big and strong and not afraid to work", to play inside-left for him at home to Liverpool. Geoff agreed, Hammers won 1-0 and the rest is history. His first season as a regular first-teamer was 1963/64, which netted him 26 League and Cup goals including West Ham's second in the 3-2 FA Cup Final triumph over Preston North End. By then he had made the number 10 shirt his own and truly arrived as a first class striker, developing alongside the more naturally gifted Johnny Byrne. In his book, *The World Game*, Geoff wrote: "The coming of 'Budgie' Byrne was a great thing in my career. He and I worked up a great partnership, and as the team began winning I was perfectly happy to be the bread-and-butter part of the partnership. I rate Budgie as the best player I have ever played alongside." Geoff totalled 40 goals in the season before he became England's World Cup-winning hero, which meant he was the First Division's leading scorer. But his best-ever haul was the 41 he amassed in 1966/67. Only four goals by Southampton's Ron Davies on the last day of that season prevented Geoff from repeating the feat. Along with West Ham and England team-mates Bobby Moore and Martin Peters, Geoff enjoyed worldwide fame. But Geoff was most respected by his fellow pros for his unselfish running. He perfected the near-post run that produced so many great goals under Greenwood and his strength in the penalty area was renowned. He took a lot of punishment from close-marking opponents, but remained brave and strong, shielding the ball and laying off passes with the use of his chest. That memorable sunny afternoon at Wembley in July 1966 provided a clear illustration of

Geoff's all-round qualities. His first goal in the 4-2 victory over the Germans came from his head; the second with his right foot; and the third with his left foot. The powerful hat-trick-clinching strike into the roof of the net, just seconds from the end of extra-time, prompted those immortal words from BBC

commentator, Ken Wolstenholme: "Some people are on the pitch, they think it's all over . . . IT IS NOW!" It was an incredible end to a tournament that began with Geoff on the subs' bench and Jimmy Greaves leading the England attack. Moore admitted his surprise that Hurst had successfully switched from wing-half to striker: "Ron (Greenwood) turned Geoff from a bit of a cart-horse at wing-half into a truly great forward. None of us thought Geoff was going to make the switch. It took him years of hard work and patience. He was so willing he ran himself into the ground. He ran and ran and ran and was always just short of everything. I don't know how he put up with the abuse but it was worth it because in the mid-sixties he became, for a few seasons, a genuine world-class player." Indeed, Geoff's life has been full of turning points. Even before he made his name with West Ham, he might have emerged as a useful county cricketer. He played in the same Essex Schools XI as Bobby Moore, turned out for Essex Seconds for three summers and appeared in one championship match for the county – against Lancashire at Liverpool in 1962, although without scoring in either innings! Geoff's final season for West Ham earned him 16 League and Cup goals and only the great Gordon Banks denied him a 17th. The epic League Cup Semi-final clashes with Stoke City produced many memorable moments spanning the first two legs and both replays, but they still talk now of the great save Banks made to block Geoff's thunderbolt penalty in extra-time of the second leg at Upton Park. Ironically, after his final Hammers' appearance, against Liverpool (April 15, 1972), Geoff joined Stoke City the following season in an

Hurst forces the ball past Fulham opponent (and England colleague) George Cohen at Craven Cottage

Career record

Played	League		FAC		LC		Europe		Total	
	App	Gls	App	Gls	App	Gls	App	Gls	App	Gls
1959-60	3	0	0	0	0	0	0	0	3	0
1960-61	6	0	0	0	0	0	0	0	6	0
1961-62	24	1	1	0	2	0	0	0	27	1
1962-63	27	13	0	0	2	2	0	0	29	15
1963-64	37	14	7	7	6	5	0	0	50	26
1964-65	42	17	1	2	1	0	9	0	53	19
1965-66	39	23	4	4	10	11	6	2	59	40
1966-67	41	29	2	3	6	9	0	0	49	41
1967-68	38	19	3	1	3	5	0	0	44	25
1968-69	42	25	3	2	3	4	0	0	48	31
1969-70	39	16	1	0	2	2	0	0	42	18
1970-71	39	15	0	0	2	1	0	0	41	16
1971-72	34	8	4	4	10	4	0	0	48	16
TOTAL	**411**	**180**	**26**	**23**	**47**	**43**	**15**	**2**	**499**	**248**

£80,000 deal. He made over 100 appearances for the Potters (30 goals) in three years before moving on to end his League career at West Bromwich Albion, where he played ten games and scored two more goals, before spending a season in the USA with Seattle Sounders. He then became player-manager of non-League Telford before moving into full League management with Chelsea. He later assisted Ron Greenwood in the running of the England side. He joined forces with former team-mate Peters as director of a motor insurance company, but in recent years has become increasingly involved in promotions work, notably with former club sponsors BAC and as host to the 66 Club in the Bobby Moore Stand at Upton Park. A footballing legend in his own right, Geoff Hurst lies ninth in the list of Hammers' all-time League appearance-makers. Perhaps only the inimitable Moore enjoyed more worldwide fame and acclaim than this golden great. Geoff was chosen as an official England ambassador for the 2006 World Cup and was further recognised when a statue was erected in his and his 1966 World Cup colleagues Bobby Moore, Martin Peters, and Ramon Wilson's honour in the summer of 2003 on the Barking Road. More humble recognition was forthcoming when Unibond Division One club Hyde United invited Sir Geoff to become their Senior Vice-President in September 2004. West Ham's first knight chivalrously accepted, saying: "I wouldn't normally agree to fulfil a request such as this, but as my father Charles was an ex-player of Hyde United I feel I have a connection with the club." Hyde hope to welcome Sir Geoff to Ewan Fields in the near future.

England caps: 1966 vs West Germany (twice), Scotland, Yugoslavia, Finland, Denmark, Argentina, Portugal, Northern Ireland, Czechoslovakia, Wales; 1967 vs Scotland, Spain, Austria, Wales, Northern Ireland, Russia; 1968 vs Scotland, Sweden (sub), West Germany, USSR, Romania, Bulgaria; 1969 vs Romania, France, Northern Ireland, Scotland, Mexico, Uruguay, Brazil, Holland; 1970 vs Holland (sub), Belgium, Wales, Northern Ireland, Scotland, Colombia, Ecuador, Romania, Brazil, West Germany, East Germany; 1971 vs Greece (twice), Wales, Scotland, Switzerland (twice); 1972 vs West Germany (49).

Hurst scores against WBA at Upton Park

Hurst, Moore and Peters

HUTCHISON, Don   1994-96/2001-05

Born: Gateshead, County Durham, 9.5.71
League apps: 99 (16 goals)
Cup apps: 11 (2 goals)

AN ATTACKING MIDFIELDER who became the club's record signing when he moved from Liverpool soon after the start of the 1994/95 season for a £1.5 million fee. "Hutch" scored on his debut at Upton Park against Newcastle United (August 31, 1994) – the club he supported as a boy. Don first caught the eye while playing for Paul Gascoigne's former club, Redheugh Boys, but he made the breakthrough to League status for Hartlepool United. The gangling Hutch was used either as a striker or central defender before settling into his now familiar attacking midfield role. But struggling Pool were eager to cash in on their promising youngster and attempted to sell their prized asset by sending a video of him in action to all First and Second Division clubs. It was as a result of this unusual marketing ploy that Liverpool boss Kenny Dalglish signed Don for £300,000 in November 1990, after he had made just 24 League appearances for the north-east minnows. At Anfield, where he scored seven goals in 45 League outings, Hutch more than justified that fee. And, despite some controversial off-the-field antics that earned him a somewhat dubious reputation, it was with great reluctance that Roy Evans finally agreed to make him Harry Redknapp's first signing as manager at Upton Park. Although the player's immense skill was in little doubt, question marks over his temperament remained and the two conflicting characteristics of his game were graphically illustrated in the explosive 1-0 home win over Leicester City on November 5, 1994. Making only his eighth Premiership start for Hammers against the Foxes, Hutchison drew gasps of disbelief from the Upton Park crowd as he hit an inch-perfect 50-yard pass from the south-west corner of the pitch to team-mate Ian Bishop, who was positioned over by the Chicken Run in the Leicester half – even though his back was to Bish as he struck the ball. Moments later "Deadly Don" was yellow carded for a wild lunge at Leicester's Lee Philpott and as the ink was still drying, a red card followed for a second reckless tackle on the same player. Hutchison, who had previously scored four times in 11 Premiership and Coca Cola Cup games, had to sit out a four-match ban with two red and four yellow cards already against him and then another seven through injury until returning for the 2-1 win over Leicester at Filbert Street in February 1995. But that was Hutch; inspiring, infuriating, irrational – in short, an enigma. Despite starting 1995/96 as a first team regular, the arrival of the more dependable Iain Dowie saw Don gradually pushed out of the picture and in January 1996 he was transferred to First Division Sheffield United, who had shelled out a club record of £800,000 to take the future Scotland international to Bramall Lane. But he'd be back. His disciplinary problems followed him north and after incurring persistent bookings he accumulated 45 penalty points during his second season with the Blades in 1996/97. Not expected to figure in United's early 1997/98 games due to the shoulder injury he'd sustained during the Yorkshiremen's unsuccessful Play-off Final showdown with Crystal Palace at Wembley, he shook it off to turn in some outstanding displays, which took his total League and Cup appearances for the red half of Sheffield to 90 (six goals) before returning to the Premiership in a £1 million move to Everton in February 1998. It proved to be an inspired switch as he excelled playing in his preferred role in central midfield; he was voted Player of the Season by the club's fans, appointed team captain by manager Walter Smith, and called into the Scottish international squad by Craig Brown! He then proceeded to celebrate his full Scotland debut against European champions Germany with the winning goal against them

in Bremen! Now playing the best football of his career with club and country, Don got on the scoresheet in all three of the Scots' European Cup Qualifier victories against Bosnia, Lithuania and, most famously, England in the 1-0 play off win at Wembley. Despite the honour of scoring Scotland's last ever goal at the famous old stadium, it wasn't enough to win a passport to Holland and Belgium for the Euro 2000 finals. Just when it seemed the former fork-lift truck driver had found a permanent parking bay with 11 goals in 89 League and Cup appearances for Everton, Don was on the move again to join former Everton great Peter Reid at Sunderland for £2.5 million. After a slow start the goals again began to flow freely (including a free kick against Hammers) and Hutch was voted Player of the Season by yet another set of admirers. Yet, after just 39 League and Cup appearances (ten goals) on Wearside, "Budweiser" was on his way back to east London to conduct the Bobby Moore lower choir! On his return, Don was dealt a cruel blow when he sustained an injury that players dread even more than a broken leg – a cruciate knee ligament injury in the 1-0 Premiership home win over Middlesbrough in February 2002. Manager Glenn Roeder's club record £5.5 million signing looked even more of a gamble, but the durable Geordie fought his way back to fitness and into Hammers' doomed relegation fight in 2002/03 albeit mostly off the bench. Rumoured to be on his way again in the fire sale summer of 2003, he stayed to assist in the battle for promotion and scored some vital goals, most notably the winner at Derby and a late equaliser at home to Burnley. Despite featuring in the pre-season build-up and mini tour to Sweden, Hutch was given the shock news from manager Alan Pardew that he didn't feature in his plans for 2004/05 as he was too good for the Coca Cola Division One Championship and should look for a Premiership club. That move never materialised, and he was back in the side against QPR. He added a further six appearances by the end of November, when he again found himself back in the reserves. Don joined Millwall on a trial basis in July 2005 and signed a six-month contract on August 5, 2005.

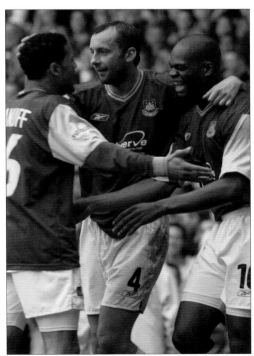

HUTTON, EG   1896-98 TIW

AN INSIDE-RIGHT SIGNED from Reading in August 1896, he played in a disastrous 8-0 first qualifying round FA Cup defeat at Sheppey United (October 10, 1896) and also three further FA Cup ties the following season. Played in an unspecified number of League fixtures over the same period.

I-J

LIC, Sasa
MPEY, Andy
NCE, Paul
NGHAM, William
NNS, Tommy
RVINE, George

ACKMAN, Derek
ACKSON, James
ACKSON, Tom
ACKSON , William
AMES, David
AMES, Wilf
AMES, William
ARVIS, Len
ENKINSON, William
ENNINGS, Billy
ENNINGS, Samuel
OHNS, Stan
OHNSON, Glen
OHNSON, W Joseph
OHNSON, William
OHNSON, William
OHNSTONE, Robert Gordon
ONES, Rob
ONES, Steve
ONES, William
OYCE, Bill

David James

ILIC, Sasa — 2000

Born: Melbourne, Australia, 18.7.72
League apps: 1

YUGOSLAVIAN INTERNATIONAL KEEPER Sasa Ilic made his West Ham debut against Everton at Upton Park in February 2000 after being signed from Charlton Athletic two days earlier to avert a goalkeeping crisis after first-choice Shaka Hislop had broken a leg, Craig Forrest was away on international duty with Canada and a young Stephen Bywater was still reeling from the previous week's 5-4 cliffhanger with Bradford City at the Boleyn. But Everton minus contract rebel Don Hutchison hit four without reply to ensure that Sasa's debut was his first and last appearance in a Hammers jersey. Sasa returned to the country of his father's origin and kept goal for Yugoslav giants Partizan Belgrade playing four times in 1993/94 and twice the season after. After a spell with another Yugoslav side – Radnicki – he returned to Australia to feature for a clutch of clubs down under including Daewoo Royals, St Leonards, Stamcroft and Ringwood. He made 59 appearances at the Valley between October 1997 and September 2001 before moving on to join Portsmouth on loan where he played seven First Division games in 2001/02 under Harry Redknapp who obviously hadn't held that 4-0 defeat to Everton against him! Indeed Harry signed Sasa again on a free transfer in February 2002 from Hungarian First Division side Zalaegerszegi Te for whom the nomadic goalie made four appearances in 2002/03. He continued his travels to join Barnsley in August 2003 and made 33 appearances at Oakwell before making the short trip to team up with Sheffield United on another free transfer in February 2004. He continued to move around Yorkshire when he joined up with Leeds in April 2005, following youngster Scott Carson's move from Elland Road to Anfield.

IMPEY, Andy — 1997-98

Born: Hammersmith, London, 30.9.71
League apps: 27
Cup apps: 7

THE FIRST MEMORY most Hammers fans have of Andy Impey was when, playing for QPR, he ran the length of West Ham's half and crashed an unstoppable shot past Ludek Miklosko to seal a 1-0 win that put the Hammers out of the FA Cup in the Fourth Round at Loftus Road in January 1995. The right-sided player joined Rangers for £35,000 in June, 1990 and scored 18 goals in 228 League and Cup appearances for the Hoops before transferring to West Ham for £1.3 million in September 1997. Unfortunately, the stocky west Londoner couldn't reproduce that sort of magic in his 30-plus matches at Upton Park. He did make a decent fist of his job as wing-back though, to such an extent that manager Harry Redknapp was apoplectic with rage when the club sold him to Leicester City without telling him! In fact, Harry had already included the player in his squad to fulfil a Premiership fixture at Filbert Street on November 14, 1998, and wasn't informed until the morning of the match that the player was to be transferred to the Foxes for £1.6 million "to balance the books". Even a 3-2 away win failed to quell Harry's anger as he criticised the West Ham board on live TV after the game "for selling a player behind my back". Unused to being the centre of controversy, mild-mannered Andy duly signed for City ten days later, but the England Under-21 international took time to bed down, only improving when moved to his favoured wing-back role. In 2000, he won a Worthington Cup winners' medal alongside ex-Hammer Tony Cottee when Leicester defeated Tranmere Rovers 2-1 in the last Final to be staged at Wembley, making up for missing the Foxes visit to the famous Twin Towers for the previous year's Final versus Spurs when he was Cup-tied. After 178 League

and Cup appearances with City, Andy was loaned to First Division Nottingham Forest in February 2004 and made 16 appearances and scored one goal (equalling his total during his whole time at Leicester!) at the City Ground, where he has now moved permanently.

INCE, Paul — 1986-89

Born: Ilford, Essex, 21.10.67
League apps: 72 (7 goals)
Cup apps: 19 (1 goal)

DESPITE WHATEVER HIS many Upton Park critics say, Paul is one of the most talented young players ever produced by West Ham and at his peak worth more than any other on the transfer market. Midfielder Paul established himself as a firm favourite at Manchester United, where, after a subdued start (he even found himself filling in at full-back for a while), he developed into a leading Premiership star and England regular. In five hugely successful seasons at Old Trafford, "Incey" collected two Premiership championships (1993, when he was voted Player of the Year, and 1994), two FA Cups (1990 and 1994) and one League Cup (1992). Paul also became the first black player to captain England, during the US Cup matches under Graham Taylor in the summer of 1993. Not many unforgiving West Ham fans would have shared in his pride that day, as the circumstances surrounding Paul's controversial transfer to United in September 1989 provoked a stormy reaction from supporters. They were understandably incensed by Paul's somewhat naive appearance in a national newspaper wearing a Man Utd shirt – three months before he left Upton Park! And when the player hit back in print after receiving a hostile reception from the terraces in the opening game of the 1989/90 season at Stoke City, it was obvious that Ince and West Ham would soon part company. New manager Lou Macari was looking to cash in on Paul's undisputed talent but the big transfer deal almost fell through when Paul failed his Old Trafford medical. An old hernia injury

Paul Ince

showed up on X-rays and Alex Ferguson only agreed to sign Paul for £800,000 with the balance payable in instalments. In a unique pay-as-you-play deal, West Ham collected £5,000 for each first team appearance Paul made, up to a total of £1.5 million. United certainly got good value for a player who first showed promise for Essex Schoolboys. He joined Hammers on the YTS scheme in July 1984 and made such rapid progress, he turned pro a year later. But for manager John Lyall – who was like a father figure to Paul – the precocious Ince might never have made it in football. In trouble at school, Paul was taken under the wing of the West Ham manager who never doubted his ability with a football, but kept a watchful eye on his young prodigy. Lyall gave Paul his first team debut in a nondescript Full Members' Cup tie versus Chelsea at Upton Park (November 25, 1986) and he made his League debut five days later in a live TV game at Newcastle (November 30, 1986) in which Hammers were crushed 4-0. Showing good awareness with the ability to spray long and short passes with accuracy, Paul displayed maturity in his football. After missing an opening game defeat by QPR in 1987/88, he was recalled to the side in the role of sweeper. He could also fill in at full-back, although his best position was as a hard-running midfielder who liked the ball at his feet. Yet it was only in his third, and last, season at Upton Park that he retained a regular first team place. The 1988/89 season was a miserable one in general, culminating in relegation, but one amazing night will forever remain in the memory of West Ham fans, and Paul Ince in particular. Mighty Liverpool were crushed 4-1 in the Littlewoods Cup (November 30, 1988) – Reds' biggest Cup defeat since 1939 – and Paul emerged from nowhere to score the two sensational first half goals and project him into the football limelight. United, and the rest of the big guns, were suddenly alerted to his talent and it was not long before Paul was on his way. His desire for fame and glory only increased with the departure in July 1989 of his long-time mentor, Lyall. Four-and-a-half years had passed when Paul returned to Upton Park with title-chasing Man Utd in February 1994. This time Ince denied Hammers a memorable victory with the last-gasp equaliser in a 2-2 classic, but the main media talking point surrounded the torrent of abuse he received from large sections of the crowd. For all his undoubted ability, the fans in claret and blue made it abundantly clear that they will never forgive or forget. You could fill a book on Paul Ince's career since the last *Who's Who of West Ham United* was published in November 1994, but this one might not sell if we did! However, it would be churlish if we didn't exercise the same attention to detail as we have with everyone else. Those so inclined could draw satisfaction as their favourites denied Manchester United the 1994/95 Premiership title with a heroic last day of the season display that earned a 1-1 draw and ensured the Championship was destined for Blackburn Rovers, not Old Trafford. Weeks later, Ince's misery was completed by a 1-0 defeat to Everton in the FA Cup Final at Wembley. After 273 games for the Red Devils, he then embarked on his Italian adventure with Inter Milan, having cost the Milanese giants £8 million. But Ince almost quit immediately after suffering racist abuse from Cremonese supporters. He soldiered on at the San Siro, but never really cut it in Milan and returned to England a better player technically but with no honours to show for 54 Serie A games, with nine goals, for Inter. A £4.2 million transfer took him to Liverpool, but there would be no silverware there either as the Anfield trophy cabinet remained bare during his two-season stay on Merseyside. So, after adding another 95 League and Cup appearances to his career total and scoring 17 times for the Reds, he changed his club but not the colour of his shirt when moving to Middlesbrough in August 1999. A tower of strength in Boro's midfield in three seasons at the Riverside, Paul clocked up exactly 100 League appearances on Teesside plus another 13 Cup appearances, scoring nine goals, before moving down a division to join Wolves for 2002/03. At Molineux, he was the driving force behind the return to the top flight of the wearers of the famous old gold after two decades in the wilderness. He couldn't prevent his former club West Ham inflicting a grievous 3-1 defeat in the Fourth Round of the FA Cup at Molineux, however, although he did gain a modicum of revenge with the third goal in a 4-2 Championship win over the Hammers in January 2005. Having made nearly 100 League and Cup appearances and scoring another six times for Wolves as the 2004/05 season drew to a close, Paul can look back on a tremendous club and 53-cap international career that demonstrates that he really was the guv'nor.

INGHAM, William — 1903-04

Born: birthplace unknown, 1882
SL apps: 2

IN AN AGE when goals were the demanded prerequisite of centre-forwards, Billy's failure to get on the scoresheet in the two opportunities afforded to him makes his demise self-explanatory. Making his first appearance on the season's opening day at Millwall, he was given another chance to shine in a 1-1 home draw with Reading in September 1904, which proved to be his last Southern League outing with Hammers. He was signed from Aberdare Athletic, who were finalists in that season's Welsh Cup, and again in 1905. He played for Bristol City in Division Two of the League in 1905/06 and moved further west to join Plymouth Argyle for 1908/09. The following season saw him at Accrington Stanley.

INNS, Tommy — 1933-34

Born: Plaistow, London, 30.1.11
League apps: 4

A TOUGH-TACKLING FULL-BACK signed from local amateurs Clapton, Tom made his first appearance in West Ham's colours against Swansea Town at Vetch Field on Boxing Day, 1933. Making three more Second

Division outings that season, Tom remained a reserve thereafter and transferred to London rivals Millwall in the summer of 1936, along with team-mate Dave Mangnall, where he built up a fine reputation as an accomplished defender and formed a successful partnership with his fellow full-back Ted Smith. Played 36 matches when Millwall won the Third Division South Championship in 1938 and became the first Third Division side to reach the Semi-finals of the FA Cup. Represented Essex County and West Ham Schoolboys in addition to being an Essex Senior Cup finalist with Clapton, the famous London amateur side. A commercial artist by profession, he designed the front cover of the Millwall Supporters' Club publication, *Focus on the Lions*. A relative, L Inns, also played for Clapton.

IRVINE, George — 1912-14

Born: birthplace unknown, 1882
SL apps: 2

THIS TOUGH DEFENDER could perform equally well at either right or left-back and made his debut alongside another new signing, left-back Harry Forster, in the 4-0 win over Exeter City on the opening day of the 1912/13 season. Signed from Barrow, he made his last appearance in the 6-0 defeat at Watford (April 1, 1914).

James Jackson

JACKMAN, Derek — 1948-50

Born: Colchester, Essex, 20.8.27
League apps: 8

YET ANOTHER PLAYER with Hammers/Palace connections, having played for the Glaziers before the war. An uncompromising wing-half, Derek's League appearances were sparsely spread over three seasons, making his first outing in a 2-1 win over Blackburn at Upton Park in the number 10 shirt. His last was in a 2-1 home defeat against Brentford (September 2, 1950).

JACKSON, James — 1905-06

Born: Cambuslang, Scotland, 15.9.1875
SL apps: 24

JAMES WAS A major capture for West Ham when they signed him following his resignation as player-manager to Leyton. A big name with Woolwich Arsenal, whom he captained for four of the five seasons he was with them and played 204 times, he was a strong, forceful defender who formed a fabled full-back partnership with another Scot, Dave Gardner, at Upton Park. His family had emigrated to Australia when he was just two years old, leaving young "Jemmy" to the mercy of Australian Association (a mixture of soccer and rugby) and Australian rules football. He nevertheless proved capable enough to play at centre-half for Scottish side Newton Thistle when he returned to his native country in 1898. A strict teetotaller, his displays soon drew the attentions of Glasgow Rangers and he duly signed for the Ibrox club the same year. At the end of his first season with the Light Blues, Jackson came south to join Newcastle United, who he helped to promotion to the First Division of the League in his first season with the Magpies. After scoring 37 times in 68 League and Cup appearances for the Geordies, his fame spread further south culminating in his move to the Woolwich Arsenal "Reds". "Rambler", of the *East Ham Echo*, drafted an interesting report following his move to Hammers, part of which read: "While with Arsenal, Jackson was regarded as one of the finest backs in the south, and it was with great regret that the Woolwich club's supporters learned that the skipper was leaving to take up the position of player-manager to Leyton. A few days ago, the sporting public were greatly surprised to read in the London papers that Jackson had tendered his resignation, which had been accepted by the Leyton directorate. This was indeed a sensation, and was quickly followed by the startling, but welcome, news that he had been signed on for West Ham. True, the news appeared in the London press a day before the signature had really been obtained, but, nevertheless, no great harm was done by that, for Jackson is now the wearer of the red, white and blue colours." In addition to participating in North versus South and Anglo-Scots versus The Scots representative matches, it is also recorded that the footloose Scot also played for Newton Heath and Cambuslang before he joined Newcastle, although the exact dates are a bit hazy. Having begun his career with Hamilton Accies and then Elmtown Rosebuds in Australia, he returned to Rangers in 1906 before moving to Greenock Morton in 1911. After leaving the game, Jackson became a blacksmith in Greenock. His two sons played football as well; one was a past skipper of Liverpool, the distinguished Rev James Jackson, while Archie appeared for Tranmere. James's nephew was Australian Test cricketer Archibald Jackson.

JACKSON, Tom — 1921-22

Born: Sunderland, Tyne and Wear, date unknown
League apps: 3 (1 goal)

AT HOME IN either of the inside-forward positions, Tom made a scoring debut in a 3-0 victory over Stoke City at

Upton Park (October 3, 1921) and went on to make a further two Second Division outings that campaign.

JACKSON, William 1927

Born: Farnworth, Greater Manchester, 15.7.1902
League apps: 2

SECURED FROM LEEDS United, where he had made 40 League appearances, Bill came into the West Ham side for the Christmas holiday matches against Sheffield United, making his debut in a 6-2 defeat at Bramall Lane on Boxing Day, and playing against the Yorkshiremen again the following day in the return fixture at Upton Park that ended 1-1. Signed as an understudy to Jimmy Ruffell, they were his only League appearances with Hammers and he subsequently moved to Chelsea. He made 26 appearances at Stamford Bridge, scoring six times between 1927 and 1930, but he was a real rolling stone and moved on to Leicester City in 1931. Having helped Chelsea to win promotion the previous year, he himself found First Division outings hard to come by with his new club, and after just four appearances and a loan spell with Ashford, he found himself on the move again in 1932 – this time west to Third Division South Bristol Rovers where he scored twice on his debut against Crystal Palace in August 1932. Teaming up with ex-Hammer Vivian Gibbins at Eastville, he scored 14 times in 37 games for the Pirates over two seasons, but moved on again to Cardiff City in May 1934. After a dozen games for the Bluebirds, he moved on again in January 1935 to Watford where he ended his League career with one goal in four matches. In the close season of 1935 he signed for Chorley and in September 1936 Netherfield. Having already served Leyland (1922), Altrincham (1923), Darwen (1923) and Sunderland (1924) prior to joining Leeds, altogether Billy had served 14 clubs in a nomadic career during which he was always striving to find a regular first team place, but never quite succeeding. Bill died in Blackpool in November 1974.

JAMES, David 2001-04

Born: Welwyn Garden City, Hertfordshire, 1.8.70
League apps: 91
Cup apps: 11

DESPITE ASSURANCES FROM Sven Goran Eriksson that his selection for England wouldn't be put in jeopardy by West Ham's fall from the Premiership, this shot-stopper supreme still opted to join Manchester City for a £2 million fee in January 2004. Recommended to City boss Kevin Keegan by the legendary figure he succeeded between England's posts, David Seaman, James also found himself taking over from the retiring Seaman at the City of Manchester Stadium. Strangely, the Mancunians also played a part in James's rise to prominence in 1990 when he was in the shadow of Tony Coton at Second Division Watford and the latter left for Maine Road to leave the way clear for the promising keeper to make the first team spot his own at Vicarage Road. His headline-grabbing displays with the Hornets soon won him international recognition at Under-21 level and with it a £1 million move to Liverpool after 98 League and Cup appearances with his local team. On Merseyside the first doubts were cast on his ability to deal with crosses and high balls into his area, as he lost his place three times in his first season and the first references to "Calamity James" began to appear in the headlines. But despite occasional well-publicised lapses, he overcame these difficulties to become an ever-present at Anfield for two successive seasons in the mid-1990s and kept enough clean sheets to win his first full cap for England in the 2-0 defeat of Mexico in 1997. During the following two seasons, however, his international career was on hold as his Jekyll and Hyde performances enthralled and infuriated the Kopites in equal measure

and eventually led to his leaving Liverpool after 277 League and Cup appearances via a £1.7 million move to Aston Villa. Although he resurrected his England career there, his stay at Villa Park was destined to be a short one and after making 85 League and Cup appearances for the Villians, James became new West Ham manager Glenn Roeder's first signing when he moved to Upton Park for £3.5 million in July, 2001. His Hammers debut was delayed when he was accidentally kicked on a knee by his own team-mate Martin Keown keeping goal for England versus Holland, but when he did eventually take his place in the West Ham goal he seemed to have left his "enigma" tag behind him forever as he kept nine clean sheets out of 26 games to the end of 2001/02 as Hammers finished a lofty seventh in the Premiership. Although he didn't make an appearance for England during the 2002 World Cup

Finals in Japan and South Korea, David established himself as England's number one despite Hammers' battle against relegation for the whole of 2002/03, when he earned rave reviews for his inspired performances against Liechtenstein and Turkey in the Euro 2004 qualifiers. Another ten clean sheets for Hammers in 31 League and Cup appearances up to January 10, 2004 hadn't done his hopes for a plane ticket to Portugal any harm either, but the giant goalkeeper decided his future would be better assured elsewhere and it was as a Man City player that his ambition to figure in Euro 2004 was achieved. Unfortunately, the "Calamity James" headlines and worse were back following a nightmare performance in the 2-2 World Cup 2006 qualifier with Austria in September 2004, and David subsequently lost his place for the next qualifier against Poland in Katowice, five days later, when it was left to his former Hammers team-mate Jermaine Defoe to grab the glory with England's first goal in a 2-1 victory. James was a patient of a sports psychologist during his time at West Ham and in his private life revealed his hobbies of portrait painting, yoga and collecting vintage Raleigh Chopper pushbikes. The complex character has also expressed an interest in becoming a criminal psychologist when he retires. One of football's mavericks, who bizarrely blames his moments of madness on his love of PC games, he should do well in that field as he's witnessed enough criminal defending in his time! David was pitched into attack in the final minutes in City's vital last match of 2004/05 versus Middlesbrough by boss Stuart Pearce in a vain attempt to qualify for the UEFA Cup. Up to the end of 2004/05, James had made 56 League and Cup appearances for City.

JAMES, Wilf — 1930-32

Born: Cross Keys, Monmouthshire, Wales, 19.2.07
SL apps: 40 (7 goals)
Cup apps: 1

WILF WAS A fine inside-left and a great character who had a deep affection for his bowler hat. In fact, it was the first article of clothing he would put on when he changed after a match, often standing stark naked in the dressing room wearing only his titfer! Wilf began his career with Cross Keys School just after World War I and graduated to local Welsh sides Abercarn Welfare and Ynysddu Crusaders before signing for Newport County in 1925, where he had a reputation for "good distributive work" and scored eight goals in 20 League appearances between 1925 and 1927. He went to Yorkshire works team Thorne Colliery before moving on to Owston Park Rangers for 1927/28. He re-entered League football with Notts County in October 1928, where he scored six goals in 16 appearances up to his transfer to Hammers in May 1930. Transferring to Charlton Athletic for £600 in February 1932, he scored three times in 28 League games at the Valley but decided to move to Workington in the 1933 close season where he found it hard to hold down a first team place. Carlisle offered him a trial period in September 1935 and he signed on six weeks later. Wilf played most of his football for the Cumbrians with the reserves in the North Eastern League but at the end of the 1936/37 season he was given a free transfer.
Wales caps: 1931 vs Northern Ireland; 1932 vs Northern Ireland (2).

JAMES, William — 1920-22

Born: Stockton, North Yorkshire, 1882
League apps: 54 (7 goals)
Cup apps: 3

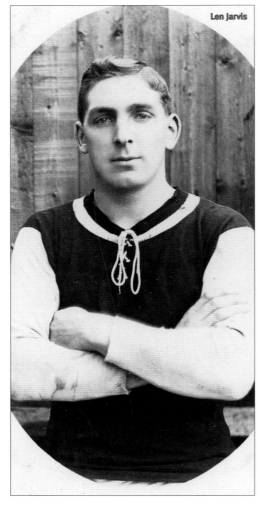

Len Jarvis

BILL CAME FROM Portsmouth (where he had scored three goals in 22 games during 1919/20) for the 1920/21 season, making 18 League appearances, and played in 36 matches the following campaign before leaving the club. An inside or outside-right, he was succeeded by Jimmy Ruffell. He played 24 matches as far back as 1910-12 for Middlesbrough, scoring eight times for his local club.

JARVIS, Len — 1903-09

Born: Grays, Essex, 1884
SL apps: 133 (5 goals)
Cup apps: 7

WITH HIS NEVER say die attitude to the game, Dick – as he was popularly known – was one of Irons' most consistent performers in the transitional years following the move from the Memorial Grounds at Canning Town to the Boleyn. His spirit was typified in a match against Brighton when he was kicked in the face and sustained a deep cut that required several stitches. He was soon back in the fray, however, heavily bandaged but making light of his injuries, a la Billy Bonds. Employed at a Grays cement works, Dick was spotted by a Hammers director playing in local Essex soccer and brought to the Memorial Grounds. His wholehearted approach sometimes got him in trouble with referees and he was suspended for 14 days in late 1906, arising from an incident in a Western League game against Millwall at Upton Park (September 17, 1906). Equally at home in any of the half-back positions, he

eventually made the number 6 shirt his own. Dick made his last appearance for Irons in a Southern League fixture at Reading on the final day of the 1908/09 season, playing at centre-half. Transferring to First Division Bury, he played 22 League matches in 1909/10, 13 in 1910/11 and 20 in 1911/12 when the Shakers were relegated.

JENKINSON, William — 1901-02

Born: Chesterfield, Derbyshire, 1877
SL apps: 19 (2 goals)

BILL DID NOT get off to the best of starts with Hammers, as he was tried in three different positions in three consecutive defeats. Formerly with Burnley, where he spent four years and scored 11 goals in 33 games, he eventually settled down at inside-left as the side finished the season on a brighter note by going the last 11 matches unbeaten. Later on he returned to Burnley, where he played another 17 matches, scoring one goal.

JENNINGS, Billy — 1974-79

Born: Hackney, London, 20.2.52
League apps: 99 (34 goals)
Cup apps: 25 (5 goals)

A QUICKSILVER STRIKER whose £110,000 arrival from Watford coincided with a distinct revival of fortunes for Hammers, culminating in the 1975 Cup Final win over Fulham. That victory put Hammers back in Europe, and after a disastrous start to the Quarter-final of the Cup Winners' Cup versus Den Haag of Holland, when they trailed 4-0, Billy's two second-half goals kept his team in with a chance for the return leg at Upton Park. A serious Achilles tendon injury threatened to end Billy's career in

1977 and he struggled to hold a regular place from then on. A former England Youth international, Billy played just short of 100 League games and scored many vital goals before taking the well-worn transfer trail between Upton Park and Brisbane Road in 1979 where he made 78 senior appearances (26 goals) for O's before leaving for Luton. He made only two sub appearances in the Second Division (scoring once) for the Hatters, however, before deciding to retire in 1981. Bill spent three years running the Fleet Street wine bar and was later the proprietor of a Brentwood brasserie. In between, he had made an ill-fated comeback with non-League Dagenham and then had brief spells with Bishop's Stortford and Heybridge Swifts. In 1993 Bill had a spell working for former club sponsors BAC, then ran a restaurant in the City. For the last ten years Bill has been a successful football agent, running Premier Management International, which has Hammers star Hayden Mullins on its books.

JENNINGS, Samuel — 1924-25

Born: Cinderhill, Nottingham, 18.12.1898
League apps: 9 (3 goals)

A FINE CENTRE-FORWARD who joined West Ham from Reading (110 apps, 45 goals), he was also on Middlesbrough's books at one time. With Victor Watson in such good fettle in the middle of Hammers' attack, Sam played his first League game at inside-left – scoring the only goal of the game against Preston North End on the opening day of the 1924/25 season at Upton Park. On other occasions he switched to inside-right with equal effect.  He left Hammers for Brighton and Hove Albion where he hit 61 goals in 110 appearances between 1924 and 1927. In 1928 he joined his home-town club Nottingham Forest, where he further distinguished himself with 15 strikes in 27 appearances in 1927/28. Next stop was Port Vale (1929-31) where he scored another 42 times in 63 games to help Vale win the Third Division North Championship (1929/30) and consolidate their position in the Second Division of the League the following season. Two short spells with Stockport County (14 apps, six goals) and Burnley (six apps, two goals) in 1931/32 brought the curtain down on his League career as a player for whom Middlesbrough paid out the enormous sum of £2,500 to sign him from Norwich City in 1919. He managed only two goals in ten games for Boro before commencing on his happy wanderings to hit 172 goals in 349 League games. But it was by no means the end of the tall centre or inside-forward's extraordinary career in football, which had seen him beginning his career at such diverse locations as Highbury Vale Methodists, Basford United, The Coldstream Guards, Basford National Ordnance Factory and (as a guest player in World War I) both Notts County and Tottenham Hotspur. In 1932, Sam was appointed coach of non-League Wisbech Town from where he took the road to the Continent to join Olympic de Marseilles in a similar capacity. He returned to manage Scarborough in September 1934, but went back to the Continent in 1935 to work as a player-coach in Switzerland. There he met the internationally recognised coach Jimmy Hogan and became greatly influenced by the man who, in his partnership with the equally renowned Hugo Meisl, reshaped the game in Europe to the extent that it became tactically superior to the British game. Armed with new ideas he crossed the Irish Sea to coach Glentoran (1936/37) and then returned to England to manage little Rochdale in October 1937. However, the inhospitable playing grounds of the Third Division North proved no place to implement the techniques and tactics that would revolutionise football in

Europe and Sam quit less than a year later in September 1938 due to ill-health. The brother of William Jennings, who played for Luton Town and Northampton Town, Sam passed away at Battle, Sussex on August 26, 1944.

JOHNS, Stan   1950-51

Born: Liverpool, Merseyside, 28.6.24
League apps: 6 (2 goals)

SIGNED FROM UNDER the noses of Liverpool and Everton in August 1950 from those well-known providers of football talent, South Liverpool. Stan's career at Upton Park was short and sweet – the striker making half-a-dozen Second Division appearances in 1950/51.

JOHNSON, Glen   2002

Born: Greenwich, London, 23.8.84
League apps: 15
Cup apps: 1

AHEAD EVEN OF the late, great Bobby Moore and Rio Ferdinand at the same stage of their development, the departure of the awesomely talented England Under-21 defender caused more resentment and fury among West Ham fans than the exits of the dozen or so stars who eventually followed him out of Upton Park after the club's relegation in 2003 put together. The youngster, who made an impassioned plea in the press urging his team-mates not to "desert the sinking ship" after the final day draw at Birmingham City sealed Hammers' fate, was ironically the first to go in a £6 million move to Chelsea in July 2003. As feelings ran deep, fans wrote in to the local *Recorder* newspaper in anger: "I've followed the Hammers for 25 years and have never felt as betrayed as I was when Johnson's sale was announced. So West Ham and I parted company…"

Andrew Williams. "I could not believe it when I heard that the club had sold Glen Johnson. Have they lost the plot or what? He is the last player in the whole squad I would have sold." David Pitchford. "The Hammers are doing it again, shooting themselves in the foot. I've seen all the great defenders at the club in the last 54 seasons and Glen Johnson was up there with them all." Brian Mason. It was difficult not to agree with the letter writers as the furore surrounding the club's most controversial outgoing transfer since Harry Hooper was sold to Wolves in 1956 raged on. Having attended matches at Upton Park since April 1961 I can't recall seeing a prospect as exciting as Glen Johnson in a West Ham shirt. England manager Sven Goran Eriksson obviously felt the same because it was shortly after his infamous clandestine meeting with new Chelsea owner Roman Abramovich that Glen was earmarked for the Chelsea Village Plc. When Abramovich asked the shrewd Swede who the best young players in the country were he named Joe Cole and Glen Johnson at the top of his list and in doing so virtually rubber stamped their transfers to join in the "Russian Revolution" at Stamford Bridge. Eriksson, a virtual season ticket-holder at Upton Park – but conspicuous by his absence after the asset-strippers had been in – was a big devotee of Johnson and duly capped him in November 2003 in the 3-2 defeat against Denmark at Old Trafford. Yet the "Theatre of Dreams" must have seemed just that to the young prodigy as he was loaned out to First Division Millwall in October 2002, when Hammers should have introduced him to their own leaky defence instead. Equally effective at full-back or centre of defence, the young south Londoner immediately made his presence felt at the New Den and showed a maturity beyond his years in eight fine performances for the Lions before being recalled to Upton Park in December 2002, where he was selected for England Under-20s against Switzerland at the Boleyn ground. The following month he made his first team debut when he came on as a substitute in the 6-0 FA Cup

Glen Johnson

Billy Jennings

Fourth Round defeat against Manchester United at Old Trafford and then his Premiership bow, again as sub, in the 4-2 defeat against Charlton Athletic at the Valley, 11 days later. It was probably no coincidence that West Ham eventually won their first home match when Glen Johnson made his full Premiership debut in the 2-1 win over Blackburn Rovers on January 29, 2003. Together with the introduction of Rufus Brevett at right-back, Johnson's inclusion led to a major tightening up of a defence that he'd personally witnessed conceding ten goals in two games in his first taste of top-class senior football as a substitute. That he survived that baptism of fire with his confidence intact spoke volumes for his character as he came through unscathed to remain an ever-present to the end of that ultimately heartbreaking campaign. Not even the great Moore or Ferdinand retained their places after making their debuts as young, both having to go back to the reserves to await further opportunities. People unaware of Johnson's rare talent even claimed that Chelsea had taken a gamble to spend £6 million on a young player who'd only made 15 Premiership appearances, but those 15 consecutive outings in the toughest division in the world was what proved his worth. The fact that he stayed in the team and kept his place on merit, proved his true value. Which, in different circumstances, would have been a lot more than £6 million. A statement issued by the West Ham supporters trust in the wake of the 18-year-old's shock transfer to the west Londoners on July 16, 2003 seemed to sum up the mood of the rank and file West Ham fans. "The sale of Glen Johnson has been met by the fans with massive anger and disappointment. Subsequent to recent statements by the club on their own website, issued by Tony Gale and Trevor Brooking, it is apparent that the club are aware of the absolute need to maintain and build upon the core of young players that have come through the youth system and many fans have expressed misgivings regarding the cynical sale of Glen Johnson, hard on the heels of season ticket renewals. The transfer has taken everyone by surprise and, given our defensive frailties during the first two thirds of last season, a particularly poor footballing decision." There's no doubt that it was a bitter pill for the West Ham fans to swallow, seeing their brightest young star, who had just been voted Young Player of the Year for the second year running and newly capped at Under-21 level, sold from under their noses to bitter rivals Chelsea so soon after the heartbreak of relegation. Yet few would begrudge him the success he initially enjoyed during his first season at Chelsea under Italian coach Claudio Ranieri. A whirlwind first three months with the Blues saw Glen figure in seven of Chelsea's first nine League fixtures, score his first goals at senior level against Newcastle and MSK Zilina in the Champions League and win his aforementioned first cap for England. Less than a year after his loan spell at Millwall he was mixing it with Europe's best and had displaced one of the most dependable right-backs in the country in Mario Melchiot. Injury curtailed his progress but he was back to fire a last gasp special at Blackburn to earn a 3-2 win and keep his side in touch with leaders Arsenal, but was again sidelined before coming back to score again in a 4-0 rout of Southampton at the Bridge on May Day. In all he featured in 19 League, two Carling Cup, one FA Cup and nine Champions League games for his new club in 2003/04 – a total he would have been more than happy to achieve in 2004/05 under new boss Jose Mourinho for whom he had still to start a match at the end of September 2004. In a special cost-per-match breakdown of the Chelsea stars in the *Daily Mail* based on last season's games, Glen came out favourably with a cost per match of £3068. He was somewhat better value that Juan Veron at £19,133 cpm and the next most expensive Hernam Crespo who was £11,700 cpm. The cost per match was worked out by dividing the players' time on the pitch with their weekly wage and transfer cost. It was all a far cry from Glen's wages as a young professional at

Hammers just a year earlier! But on the eve of the England versus Wales World Cup qualifier at Old Trafford in October 2004, as he was preparing for the Under-21s' clash with the Welsh at Ewood Park, he must have wondered whether he had made the right decision in joining Chelsea apart from the financial benefits, when his Under-21 coach Peter Taylor expressed doubts. With Johnson out of favour with new coach Jose Mourinho and having failed to make a single first team outing up to early October 2004, a worried Taylor said: "Maybe Glen needs to go on loan. There is an opportunity if the Chelsea manager lets him." Since then Mourinho appears to have realised Johnson's true worth to the team as he began to include him on a regular basis, culminating in the youngster picking up his first major honour in the 3-2 Carling Cup Final victory over Liverpool at the Millennium Stadium, Cardiff in late February 2005. Having become a regular in the side Glen proudly picked up a Premiership winners' medal as Chelsea won the League with a record 95 points, having conceded only 15 goals in 38 matches. Up to the end of 2004/05 Glen had made 60 League and Cup appearances for Chelsea, scoring four goals.

JOHNSON, W Joseph · 1927

Born: Wednesbury, Staffordshire, 23.6.1898
League apps: 15 (7 goals)

A SHARP-SHOOTING INSIDE-FORWARD who achieved the obligatory goal-every-other-game for strikers of those days during his 15 First Division appearances in the 1926/27 season. Born in the Black Country, Joe's first professional club was Talbot Stead in the Birmingham Combination, whom he joined from Bradley United in 1920/21. From then on it was very much a case of "have goals, will travel", with Cannock Town his next port of call. Then he joined Crystal Palace (29 apps, six goals) for his first taste of League football, moved on to Barnsley (17 apps, two goals) and transferred to Hammers from the Yorkshire club in 1927. Joe made a scoring debut against Huddersfield Town at Upton Park (February 5, 1927). Switching to the outside-left position on occasions, he held his place to the end of the season. Despite his promising beginning at the Boleyn, Joe made only one first XI appearance the following season before moving on to Walsall (no apps), then Wigan Borough in 1930 (29 apps, nine goals), Halifax Town in 1931 (26 apps, seven goals) and finally Accrington Stanley in 1932 (26 apps, seven goals).

JOHNSON, William · 1919

Born: Aberdeen, Scotland, date unknown
League apps: 2

A SCOTSMAN FROM Aberdeen, Bill made his first appearance in Hammers' colours in a cracking 4-1 win against Lincoln City at Sincil Bank (September 6, 1919), and was on duty at right-half again two days later against Barnsley at the Boleyn – when the Yorkshiremen spoiled his second, and what was to prove to be his last, League outing by winning 2-0.

JOHNSON, William · 1932

Born: Leigh-on-Sea, Essex, date unknown
League apps: 5

BILL MADE THE first of his handful of Second Division appearances at centre-half for Hammers in the 5-2 victory over Oldham at Upton Park (October 15, 1932). After coming to prominence in the Southend Schools XI and later Leigh Amateurs, the tall defender followed the natural progression by signing for his local League club – Southend United – then playing at the Kursaal Ground, for whom he made 45 appearances in

the Third Division South. A public-spirited individual who was a member of Southend Fire Brigade and also drove the police ambulance, he found his first team opportunities limited after his transfer to Hammers due to the fine form of Jim Barrett and Wally St Pier.

JOHNSTONE, Robert Gordon · 1956-57

Born: Edinburgh, Scotland, 19.11.34
League apps: 2

A FINE WING-HALF in the best Scottish tradition, Gordon played his early soccer with Edinburgh Schoolboys and East of Scotland Select while with junior side Ormiston Primrose. Came to the Boleyn for a trial, and impressed sufficiently to sign pro forms in April 1953. National Service commitments interrupted his soccer career – delaying his initial senior appearance until November 1956, when he played at Doncaster Rovers. He made only one more Second Division showing before being transferred to Ipswich Town. He served the Suffolk club well, scoring four times in 35 appearances, until 1959, when he gave up the game to embark on a professional singing career in Canada.

JONES, Rob · 1999

Born: Wrexham, Wales, 5.11.71
Cup apps: 1

ONE OF THE few Welsh-born players to play for England, this accomplished right-back made just one appearance for Hammers in the 1-1 draw against FC Jokerit in the Intertoto Cup in Finland. Rob began his career under the legendary Dario Gradi at Crewe and after 92 League and Cup appearances at Gresty Road, signed for Liverpool in October 1991. Picked eight times for England while at Liverpool, his career was blighted by a botched knee operation and, after winning an FA Cup winners' medal in 1992, a League Cup medal in 1998 and playing over 243 League and Cup games for the Merseysiders, he accepted Harry Redknapp's offer of a trial to prove his fitness in the summer of 1999. Sadly, though, it didn't work out and Rob was forced to retire.

JONES, Steve · 1992-94/1996-97

Born: Cambridge, Cambridgeshire, 17.3.70
League apps: 22 (4 goals)
Cup apps: 8 (1 goal)

A TALL, PACY striker who lived in a caravan and was made redundant from the Yardley soap factory at Basildon shortly before he joined Hammers from non-League Billericay Town in November 1992 for £22,500. Steve made his debut for the club in the reserves versus Southampton (November 17, 1992) but his senior bow came in the Anglo-Italian Cup at Cosenza (December 8, 1992). On a waterlogged pitch, Steve set up Clive Allen's winning goal but he had to wait until the visit of Barnsley for his full First Division debut (February 6, 1993), having played only the last two minutes as sub in the previous match at Leicester. Replacing the injured Clive Allen, Stevie was only ten minutes into his full debut when he scored his first goal for the club. He then followed it by netting in the next game against Peterborough United. But Steve, who began his non-League career with Basildon United before becoming Billericay's goal machine in the Diadora League, was still striving to prove himself at Upton Park. Although very popular with the fans, who appreciated his wholehearted endeavour, "Jonah" was described as "raw" by the management, who gave him just three starts in the 1993/94 Premiership. In October 1994, Steve was put out on loan to Harry Redknapp's old club, Bournemouth and joined the Cherries for a fee of £150,000 that month. Steve was Bournemouth's top scorer for two

Steve Jones

consecutive seasons before he rejoined Hammers after scoring 28 times in 84 League and Cup games for the south coast outfit, with Mark Watson moving to Dean Court plus a cash adjustment. Steve's second spell at Upton Park was goalless however, and after a further 11 League and Cup appearances he moved on to Charlton Athletic for £400,000 in February 1997. He enjoyed mixed fortunes at the Valley despite scoring some valuable goals for the south Londoners, notably a spectacular effort against Liverpool, which earned the Addicks a 3-3 draw at Anfield. But after scoring eight times in 58 League and Cup games he was transferred to Bristol City for £425,000 in September 1999 having scored five times in six matches while on loan at Bournemouth. Things didn't go well at Ashton Gate, though, and after just two goals in 19 games he was loaned out in quick succession to Brentford (ten apps), Southend (nine apps, two goals) and Wycombe Wanderers (six apps). Despite some scintillating performances for the Bristolians, they allowed the big striker to drift into the non-League scene as he returned to his Essex roots as player-coach with ambitious Hornchurch in June 2002. Steve now runs a sports memorabilia business in Shaftesbury Avenue, London.

JONES, William   1901-02

Born: Penrhiwceiber, Wales, date unknown
SL apps: 15

BILL JONES BECAME the first West Ham player to be capped for his country when he played for Wales versus England and Scotland in 1902, adding to the two caps already won with Aberdare against the same countries the previous year. Although a bit on the slow side, Bill was a sound tackler adept at supplying his wingers from the half-back berth. Captain of Aberdare, it was a great loss to the Welsh club when he embarked on a disastrous move to Southern League Kettering Town in September 1901. Unable to settle with the Poppies, his fortunes improved considerably when he was transferred – in a straight swap for West Ham's Peter Kyle – in December 1901, as he went on to complete 15 Southern League appearances at centre-half before returning to the valleys at the season's end to join Aberamen, whom he helped steer to the Final of the Welsh Cup in 1903. They lost 8-0 to Wrexham, but became the first club from South Wales to reach the Final. He left Aberamen to join a club named Rogerstone in 1904 and stayed until 1906. Bill is believed to have been killed in action in Serbia in May 1918 while serving with the Royal Welsh Fusiliers.
Wales caps: 1902 vs England, Scotland (2).

JOYCE, Bill   1899-1900

Born: Prestonpans, Scotland, 8.4.1877
SL apps (TIW): 28 (11 goals)

BILL JOINED THAMES Ironworks for their last season of existence from Spurs after scoring 26 goals in 38 matches for the north Londoners. A centre-forward typical of the Victorian era, he achieved a more modest total with Hammers, although there were some vital strikes among them, none more so than his celebrated hat-trick on his return to neutral Tottenham – along with fellow-former Tottenham man Ken McKay – in Ironworks' 5-1 Test match victory against London rivals Fulham, which preserved their jealously guarded senior status. At the turn of the century Bill left Irons to join Portsmouth as replacement for Sandy Brown, who had ironically joined Spurs. A year later, he moved to Burton United where he played for another two seasons and appeared in 29 matches. He had begun his career with Greenock Morton in his native Scotland before transferring to Bolton Wanderers in the close season of 1894, where he sustained a broken leg in 1896.

K

KAINE, William
KANE, Alex
KANOUTE, Frederic
KAY, George
KAYE, Albert
KEARNS, Fred
KEEBLE, Vic
KEEN, Kevin
KELLER, Marc
KELLY, David
KELLY, Paul
KELLY, William
KEMP, Fred
KENNEDY, William
KILGALLON, Matthew
KING, Syd
KINGSLEY, Matthew
KINSELL, Thomas Harry
KIRBY, William
KIRKALDIE, Jack
KIRKUP, Joe
KITCHEN, George
KITCHENER, Bill
KITSON, Paul
KYLE, Peter

Freddi Kanoute

KAINE, William   1924-25

Born: East Ham, London, 27.6.1900
League apps: 7

A MEMBER OF the Hammers' reserve team that carried off the London Combination championship in the big goalkeeper's first season at Upton Park. Bill followed that success by being selected to represent London Combination versus London League. After touring Germany with Hammers in the summer of 1924, the popular cockney returned to England to share the task of deputising for the injured Ted Hufton in the League side with Tommy Hampson. He moved across London to join Spurs in 1925 (playing 11 times in the League and one Cup game) and later went to Luton Town and moved on to Bradford City in March 1928. Bill joined Hammers from the Stirling Athletic club of Dagenham. He died on January 3, 1968.

KANOUTE, Frederic   2000-03

Born: Sainte Foy les Lyon, France, 2.9.77
League apps: 84 (29 goals)
Cup apps: 8 (4 goals)

A FORMER FRENCH Under-21 international, Freddi was signed from Olympique Lyonnais after impressing during a three-month loan spell at the start of which he scored the winning goal in his debut against Wimbledon at Upton Park. West Ham were able to afford Lyon's £3.75 million asking price for the sought after centre-forward by sending Marc-Vivien Foe in the opposite direction for a considerably larger fee of £6 million in a typical piece of wheeling and dealing by Harry Redknapp! He was at loggerheads with his coach at Lyon, who failed to give the lanky striker a single start in 1999/2000. It seemed inconceivable that he could be kept out of any side given his tremendous pace, power and tactical awareness as he took the Premiership by storm. Forging a mouth-watering partnership with the maestro Paulo Di Canio, the six-foot-three-inch hit man immediately set about paying back Redknapp for rescuing him from his French Le Championnat wilderness and struck a vein of irresistible form that saw him score five goals in four games around Christmas and New Year 2000/01. Top scorer for the season with 14, Freddi was again impressive in 2001/02 forming a three-man strike force with Jermain Defoe and Di Canio and again hit a "purple patch" when scoring four times in consecutive victories against Southampton, Chelsea and Ipswich Town. Showing his unselfish side, he helped to create chances for Defoe and was content to finish the campaign as second top scorer with 12 goals behind his diminutive new team-mate's total of 14. The only cloud on the horizon was his susceptibility to niggling injuries, which sidelined him on numerous occasions and would be a continuing problem throughout his career. Certainly it was a weakness that would cost West Ham dear in the fateful 2002/03 season when, because of a persistent groin injury, the big striker missed over half of Hammers' League fixtures and by the time he returned in late March 2003, after treatment in Canada, Hammers were in deep relegation trouble. Although his return sparked a revival that saw him score vital goals against Sunderland, Aston Villa and the winner at Manchester City, it was too little, too late as Hammers crashed out of the Premiership. It was obvious that the club would have to cash in on the fit again striker given their circumstances, but his £3.5 million move to north London rivals Spurs in August 2003 proved a bitter pill to swallow. After surviving a pre-season injury scare, Kanoute scored on his Spurs debut against Leeds at White Hart Lane – just one of six goals in his first eight games – but after another strike versus Wolves on December 6 he failed to register a goal in the Premiership for the rest of 2003/04. He did add another five in the Cups to bring his season's total to 12, but by then he had his former Hammers team-mate Defoe to share the goalscoring burden. During a crucial period in January and February, when Spurs were embroiled in a relegation fight, the new signing infuriated his paymasters at White Hart Lane by taking up his option of representing Mali in the African Nations Cup, missing several League matches in the process. But under new rules confirmed by FIFA concerning his father's birthright, the player was perfectly entitled to play and scored twice on his debut in the tournament in a 3-1 win over Kenya. New Spurs boss Jacques Santini breathed a sigh of relief when the player resisted his "new country's" overtures to play for them in the Olympic Games in Athens as it would have meant he would have been unavailable for the first four Premiership matches of 2004/05. In March 2005, despite the loyalty Freddi had shown his adopted country, Mali, he was forced to flee the ground in Bamako after angry fans invaded the pitch following the 2-1 World Cup qualifying defeat by Togo. The unsavoury incident led to Kanoute reconsidering his international future at the time. Up to the end of 2004/05 Freddi had scored 21 goals in 72 appearances for Spurs. In August 2005, Kanoute transferred to Seville for £4.4 million.

KANE, Alex — 1926-27

Born: Aberdeen, Scotland, 22.1.1900
League apps: 2

OFTEN CONFUSED WITH fellow goalkeeper William Kaine and vice versa, Alex played just two First Division matches for Hammers – at home, against Liverpool (January 16, 1926) and Derby County on New Year's Day, 1927, both of which ended in 2-1 defeats. Alex began his career with Hearts before moving south to join Reading in 1922 (42 apps) and then Portsmouth in 1923 (96 apps) before joining Irons.

KAYE, Albert — 1900-01

Born: Stavely, Derbyshire, 1875
SL apps: 14 (2 goals)
Cup apps: 6 (3 goals)

BERT'S FOOTBALL EDUCATION began when his school days ended with his local village side, Stavely. Spotted by a Sheffield Wednesday scout, he subsequently spent four years with the Yorkshire club before coming south to join Chatham. West Ham United signed him in time for their first season, during which he made the majority of his senior appearances at inside-left, although he did appear once at centre-forward and on two occasions the left-wing. He later crossed the Irish Sea to play for a club in Belfast in company with Walter Tranter, a former TIW player.

KEARNS, Fred — 1949-54

Born: Dublin, Republic of Ireland, 8.11.27
League apps: 43 (14 goals)
Cup apps: 2 (1 goal)

THIS LIKABLE IRISHMAN enjoyed a chequered career at Upton Park. Signed from Shamrock Rovers as a full-back, he found brief fame and international recognition when switched to the centre-forward berth! He was transferred to Norwich City in the summer of 1954, where he scored ten goals in 28 appearances in 1954/55, shortly after winning his first international cap.
Republic of Ireland cap: 1954 vs Luxembourg (1).

KEEBLE, Vic — 1957-59

Born: Colchester, Essex, 25.6.30
League apps: 76 (45 goals)
Cup apps: 4 (4 goals)

HAMMERS HAD GAINED a mere 12 points from the same number of games when this great centre-forward joined them from Newcastle United in October 1957 for £10,000. At the end of that campaign West Ham were back in the First Division, and Vic had grabbed 19 precious goals and much of the credit for getting them there. Originally signed for Colchester United by Ted Fenton when he was manager there in 1950, he moved to Tyneside for £15,000 and played for the Geordies in the 1955 Cup Final at Wembley. Ted remembered his protégé and brought him to Upton Park just in the nick of time! Vic's career was brought to a sadly premature conclusion at the age of 29, due to worsening injury problems. He later worked as a football reporter and became general manager of Southern League Chelmsford City where he is now club secretary. The Essex club gave him a testimonial match in 1985/86 for which Hammers provided some players in the opposing team. Vic scored 23 times in 46 appearances for Colchester and 56 in 104 outings for Newcastle. Vic scored one of the Geordies' goals when they beat Manchester City 3-1 in the 1955

KAY, George — 1919-26

Born: Manchester, 21.9.1891
League apps: 237 (15 goals)
Cup apps: 22 (2 goals)

THIS FINE CENTRE-HALF was one of the first former West Ham players to make a mark in football management and could justifiably lay claim to being the pioneer behind the famous West Ham managerial "Academy". Formerly with Bolton, George recorded another first when he became the only Englishman ever to captain an Irish League team during his spell with Belfast Celtic. He served with the Royal Garrison Artillery in the Great War and signed for Hammers in 1919, making his debut against Barnsley in September of that year. Taking over the team captaincy from Billy Cope for the 1922/23 season, he led Irons to Wembley and promotion to the First Division during his initial campaign as skipper. One of the few members of Hammers' Cup Final side not to win an international cap, he nevertheless became the first Hammer to play more than 200 League games for the club. He picked up the managerial reins with Southampton when he retired from playing, after a spell with Stockport, and did sufficiently well during his five years with the Saints to attract an offer from Liverpool to fill the manager's job at Anfield. Appointed in 1936, he had to wait until after the war for his first success with the Liverpudlians. Under his guidance the Reds won the first post-war First Division championship in 1946/47, and were narrowly defeated by Burnley in a replayed FA Cup Semi-final at Maine Road. George was affected by ill health in the late 1940s, and was a sick man when the Pool reached their first Wembley Final against Arsenal in 1950. Although confined to his sick bed during the two days prior to the game, he still proudly led his players on to the Wembley turf for presentation to His Majesty The King. George retired from football in February 1951 on medical advice, and sadly passed away in April 1954.

Played	League		FAC		LC		Europe		Total	
	App	Gls	App	Gls	App	Gls	App	Gls	App	Gls
1919-20	27	3	4	0	0	0	0	0	31	3
1920-21	36	1	1	0	0	0	0	0	37	1
1921-22	39	5	3	0	0	0	0	0	42	5
1922-23	36	0	5	0	0	0	0	0	41	0
1923-24	40	3	3	1	0	0	0	0	43	4
1924-25	41	2	6	1	0	0	0	0	47	3
1925-26	18	1	0	0	0	0	0	0	18	1
TOTAL	**237**	**15**	**22**	**2**	**0**	**0**	**0**	**0**	**259**	**17**

FA Cup Final and in an interview in the *Sun* in March, 2005 was anxious to clear up some confusion surrounding that triumph: "Probably 99 per cent believe Jackie Milburn wore number 9 that day. But it was me," he said proudly.

KEEN, Kevin — 1986-93

Born: Amersham, Buckinghamshire, 25.2.67
League apps: 219 (21 goals)
Cup apps: 44 (6 goals)

ANOTHER HOME-GROWN PRODUCT who made it through the youth ranks to become a first team regular. Kevin battled hard over several seasons to establish himself in the side, often appearing as sub under John Lyall. But Billy Bonds used him regularly and Kevin repaid that faith by playing a key role in the promotion-winning campaigns of 1990/91 and 1992/93. Ironically, many believed that Kevin's last season – in which he was ever-present, scored seven goals and made countless others for team-mates – was his best at the club. Yet, within weeks of reaching the Premiership with Hammers, "Keenie" was on the move to free-spending Wolves in a £600,000 deal that suited all parties. Although Wanderers were still only mid-table in Division One, the ambitious Midlands club were keen to spend on new players and made Kevin an offer he could not refuse. The transfer ended his ten year association with West Ham, which began when he signed as an apprentice on July 1, 1983, after playing three games for Wycombe Wanderers in 1982/83. Turned pro March 6, 1984 and six months later he made his League debut at Upton Park against Liverpool (September 6, 1986) in a 5-2 defeat. Capped 15 times by England at Youth level and eight times as a Schoolboy, Kevin scored his first senior goal against Leyton Orient in the FA Cup (January 31, 1987) – his only goal in that competition. Scoring goals was never Kevin's main strength, although he still managed one or two spectacular efforts. He was essentially a very hard-working winger or midfielder, who chased up and down either the right or left flank to support the attack and, when required, assisted his full-back. His pace and willingness to run at defenders unsettled the opposition, even though he was somewhat lightweight. Kevin set up many goal chances for team-mates, but never forgot his defensive duties and was a good team man, appreciated by fellow players. Ironically, it was not until he showed consistently brilliant form in 1992/93 that Kevin, a shy, unassuming lad, finally won over the majority of the Upton Park crowd, who had, at times, treated him harshly in the past. His father, Mike, won a League Cup winners' medal with QPR in the first final to be played at Wembley, in 1967, and also played for Luton Town and Watford in the 1960s. An intelligent man who once said it was his ambition to become a schoolteacher when he gives up the game, Kevin was not only missed on the field by his team-mates when he left for Molineux. For it was invariably Keenie who supplied the board games that kept everybody entertained on the long coach trips to away games! In 1994 Kevin joined former West Ham manager Lou Macari at Stoke City for a fee of £300,000. After scoring nine goals in 54 games for Wolves, Kevin proved to be a valuable acquisition for the Potteries club and he cut swathes through the First Division and then Second Division rearguards when they were relegated in 1997/98. After scoring ten times in 175 games for City he was released in the summer of 1999 but was soon snapped up by Macclesfield Town who had just dropped into the Third Division. Although nearing the veteran stage, Kevin enjoyed something of an Indian summer at the Moss Rose Ground and made over 70 appearances as a Macclesfield lad as well as gaining his UEFA "A" coaching certificate while with the Cheshire club. It was a qualification that stood him in good stead when he returned to the Boleyn in the summer of 2003 to take over as youth team manager following the retirement of Peter Brabrook. Still registered as a player, Kevin proved there's life in him yet when he turned out for the reserves in an emergency!

Kevin Keen

KELLER, Marc — 1998-2000

Born: Colmar, France, 14.1.68
League apps: 44 (5 goals)
Cup: 13 (1 goal)

THIS FRENCH INTERNATIONAL winger or wing-back was a star of the German Bundesliga when the artful Harry Redknapp signed him on a free transfer from Karlsruhe in July 1998. Able to operate on either flank, this tidy performer with a penchant for scoring occasional, spectacular goals began his career with his home town club Colmar before moving up a rung in the French League system to join Mulhouse where he made 88 League appearances and scored 11 goals in three seasons between 1987 and 1990. Catching the eye of top French side RC Strasbourg in the French Le Championnat, Marc took two years to break into the first team at Stade de la Meinau but when he did get his chance in 1992/93 he quickly became a regular and scored 24 goals in 125 appearances over the next four seasons, by which time he'd earned full international recognition. He did his profile no harm when scoring the only goal of the match for France versus England in the Tournoi de France at Montpellier in June 1997, after a successful season with his new club Karlsruhe for whom he hit the net nine times in 33 Bundesliga outings – and his team won every one of the eight games he scored in! He lost his lucky charm status the next season, however, when Karlsruhe lost all but one of the four fixtures he scored in – the exception being the 3-3 draw at VFL Bochum. His four goals in 28 appearances were good enough for Redknapp who needed cover for Andy Impey and Stan Lazaridis, but the Frenchman soon staked his claim and quickly established himself in the Hammers starting line-up with his quick, incisive passing and explosive shooting. Indeed he was a contender for Goal of the Season for his 20-yard scorcher that flew into the top corner of Derby County's net to seal a 2-0 away win. Although not a

Premiership regular in 1999/2000, he was extensively used in Hammers' ill-fated run to the Fifth Round of the Worthington Cup and scored another gem against Bournemouth in the Third Round 2-0 victory with a stunning angled drive from the edge of the penalty area. It was also in the League Cup that Marc made his final and only appearance for Hammers in 2000/01 in the first leg Second Round 1-0 win over Walsall in the Bescott Stadium in September. Loaned to Portsmouth the following month, he made three First Division appearances for Pompey before joining Blackburn on a free transfer in January 2001. He only made five League and Cup appearances at Ewood Park before rejoining RC Strasbourg as director of football. Marc led Strasbourg into the UEFA Cup in 2005/06 after his side had won the French League Cup.

KELLY, David — 1988-90

Born: Birmingham, West Midlands, 25.11.65
League apps: 41 (7 goals)
Cup apps: 20 (5 goals)

SNAPPED UP BY John Lyall for £600,000 in the summer of 1988 despite competition from Tottenham, Paris St Germain and Bayern Munich, who were all impressed by his scoring record for Walsall, where he netted 70 goals in two seasons. But "Ned" found the transition from Third to First Division quite difficult and, in a side that was struggling badly at the time, he (and Allen McKnight) quickly came under fire from supporters who expected much more from Tony Cottee's replacement. David's ordeal began on his debut when Hammers were crushed 4-0 at Southampton on the opening day of the season (August 27, 1988). He managed six goals in his first 21 League outings but his partnership with Leroy Rosenior was floundering and David found himself replaced by Stuart Slater early in 1989. Hammers could not avoid relegation that season and David's misery continued under new manager Lou Macari, who started him in only eight Second Division games. Playing for his third manager in ten months, David managed to score in Billy Bonds' third match in charge, but his next game (versus Portsmouth, March 10, 1990) was his last for the club. The recent arrival of Trevor Morley and Jimmy Quinn again left him out in the

David Kelly

cold and shortly before the end of the 1989/90 season David was on his way to Leicester City for £300,000, making a swift return to Upton Park for their visit on May 2, 1990. He made 75 appearances for the Foxes (25 goals) before joining promotion-chasing Newcastle United in December 1991 for £250,000. He helped the Magpies win the First Division (at Hammers' expense) in May 1993 and scored 39 goals in 83 appearances for the Geordies before joining Kevin Keen at Wolves in a £750,000 transfer a month later. So the striker who struggled at Upton Park had been involved in almost £2 million pounds worth of transfer deals. A regular member of the Republic of Ireland squad, David scored a hat-trick on his full debut against Israel (November 10, 1987) and appeared as sub against Norway in the 1994 World Cup Finals in America. After forming a successful partnership with Steve Bull at Wolves and scoring 36 times in 111 appearances in the old gold, Dave moved on to Sunderland for a £1 million fee in September 1995, but was plagued by injuries on Wearside. Having scored just two goals in 34 League and six Cup games for the Black Cats they cut their losses just two years later by selling him to First Division Tranmere Rovers for a knock down £350,000, whereupon the veteran striker found a new lease of life with the famous cup fighters of Birkenhead. Seen as his obvious successor by Rovers manager John Aldridge, Ned, as he was affectionately known, was appointed club captain, topped the club's scoring charts and resurrected his international career in his first season at Prenton Park. Although hampered by injuries in his second season on the Wirral, David seemed to save his best performances for cup ties and, often playing when not fully fit, he scored an incredible 13 goals in 17 League Cup ties in his three seasons with Rovers, including the Merseysider's only goal in the last League Cup Final to be played at Wembley when going down valiantly 2-1 to a Tony Cottee inspired Leicester City in February 2000. Having scored a handsome 37 times in 117 appearances for the least fashionable of the Merseyside triumvirate, Kelly was given a free transfer to Sheffield United and there, too, he continued to display his goalscoring prowess with six goals in 35 First Division appearances and, of course, two in four League Cup ties in a productive year at Bramall Lane. Next stop was Scottish Premier club Motherwell on a free transfer and it didn't take the wandering star long to christen the Scottish League Cup with a goal in his only outing of the tournament! Six goals in 19 League appearances was a fair return, but Ned returned to England to sign on another free for Third Division Mansfield Town, where he ended his career with another four goals in 17 appearances for the Stags. David is now assistant manager of Preston North End.

Republic of Ireland cap: 1989 vs Tunisia (sub) (1).

KELLY, Paul   1990

Born: Bexley, Kent, 12.10.69
League apps: 1

PAUL STARRED FOR England at Schoolboy and Youth level and spent two years at the FA's National School of Excellence before returning to Hammers' apprentice ranks in 1986. This diminutive midfielder/right-back was a reserve team regular, but featured in only one League game – as second-half sub for Steve Potts against Hull City at Upton Park (January 20, 1990). Paul's only full outing at senior level came in a 5-1 Zenith Data Systems Cup defeat at Luton (December 19, 1990). He was given a free transfer by West Ham in May 1991.

KELLY, William   1900-03

SL apps: 33
Cup apps: 4

THIS SCOTTISH JUNIOR international was signed from Everton at the beginning of the century and played in the club's first three seasons under the new banner of West Ham United. A centre-half, he made his debut in a 2-0 defeat at Bristol Rovers (November 24, 1900). Transferred to Notts County in 1903, he was with Brighton for 1904/05.

KEMP, Fred   1906-07

Born: Tottenham, London, 1887
SL apps: 11

FRED PLAYED FOR his school team in north London

before his family moved to Barking and he took up with Ethelburgas and Barking St Andrews. He spent one season with Newportonians before moving on to the Barking Victoria Club. Kemp made the big time with Woolwich Arsenal playing at inside-left. He made his initial appearance in Irons' Southern League side in a 3-1 Boleyn Victory over Brentford (October 6, 1906) in the outside-left position. He later reverted to the left-wing berth where he made his last appearance at Bristol Rovers (November 9, 1907).

KENNEDY, William   1910-12

Born: Grays, Essex, date unknown
SL apps: 21 (10 goals)
Cup apps: 2

BILL CAME TO West Ham from the club that was later to become known as Spurs' "nursery" – Northfleet – and had also played for Grays. A schoolteacher by profession, he marked his debut in the 3-1 Guy Fawkes Day demolition of Brighton at Upton Park with a goal, and completed ten Southern League appearances with four goals to his credit in that 1910/11 season. Looking likely to greatly overhaul those totals in the following campaign, all was well until he sustained a knee injury in a Third Round FA Cup replay with Middlesbrough, which effectively ended his first-class football career. Although not considered fit enough for the rigours of pro soccer, he was, however, given the all-clear to participate in the greatest conflict ever known to man – World War I – and subsequently lost his life serving the London Scottish Regiment in France.

KILGALLON, Matthew   2003

Born: York, Yorkshire, 8.1.84
League apps: 3
Cup apps: 1

THIS YOUNG CENTRAL defender made his Hammers debut at left-back in a 2-1 win at Ipswich Town in August 2003 after being signed on a three-month loan period from Leeds United following the long-term injury sustained by Rufus Brevett. The youngster had played against Hammers for Leeds at Elland Road in 2002/03 as an 18-year-old and impressed sufficiently to be brought in to help fill the breach at Upton Park. Having impressed many with his performance in the 1-0 Carling Cup defeat at Spurs in October 2003, he returned to Leeds after his loan period expired and enjoyed a short run in the Premiership and scored his first goal against Southampton. He also gained his first international recognition when he came on as a substitute for England Under-21s against Sweden in Kristinsund in March 2004 in a 2-2 draw.

KING, Syd   1899-1903

Born: Chatham, Kent, 1873
SL apps (TIW): 16
SL apps (WHU): 59
Cup apps: 7

ANYTHING THAT ES (Syd) King achieved in his playing career was destined to be eclipsed by his success as the first manager of West Ham United FC. Beginning his career as a full-back with Northfleet, grammar school-educated Syd once claimed to have conceded a hat-trick of own goals for that club against Swindon Town. Transferring to New Brompton (now Gillingham) in 1897, he spent two seasons with the Kent club before joining TIW in the close season of 1899. King was considered to be the best full-back in the Southern League and, as if to underline the fact, TIW immediately received an application for his transfer from Derby County before he had kicked a ball for the Irons. He suffered a bad ankle injury in a match

Syd King (right) and Charlie Paynter

against Spurs at the Memorial Grounds (March 10, 1899), however, which ruled him out for the rest of the term and although he recovered sufficiently to continue playing for the new West Ham United club the following season, he was never quite the same player. He still managed to form a formidable full-back pairing with Scotsman Charlie Craig, but the fact that he was appointed club secretary in 1902, while still continuing to play, suggested that he saw his future in administration. Syd made his last Southern League appearance in Irons' 1-1 draw at Kettering (April 15, 1903) and, although he still played the occasional match in the London or Western League, his retirement heralded a new era that saw him successfully oversee the club's embracement of professionalism, the move to the Boleyn Grounds and the eventual elevation to Football League membership in 1919. The latter was achieved by skilful manipulation of the media over many years, King having long since realised the power of the press. Ably assisted by Charlie Paynter, Syd gradually improved the team's performances in their first three League seasons, until 1922/23 when he really hit the jackpot, leading the team to the first-ever FA Cup Final at Wembley and out of the Second Division wilderness. After nine long and hard seasons in the First Division, West Ham were relegated at the end of 1931/32 and Syd King's world fell apart. Despite West Ham's fall back to Division Two, his position was not under threat because of it. However, during a board meeting (November 7, 1932), when team matters were being discussed, King was drunk and insubordinate and insulted at least one director. At an emergency board meeting the following night (only the third in the history of the club) it was decided that "Mr ES King be suspended for three calendar months from November 9, 1932, without salary and further stipulate that he shall not visit the ground during this period". The terse statement sounded the death knell for the man who had done so much for West Ham, but was now strictly persona non grata. The board had also expressed concern about King's honesty in the day-to-day business of running the club and in a further meeting (January 3, 1933), concluded that it could not re-engage him in any capacity. The new secretary, Alan Searles (himself sacked for defalcation in 1940), advised King of the decision and informed him of the board's offer of an ex-gratia payment of £3 per week. But King saved them their money by taking an alcoholic drink laced with a corrosive liquid and committing suicide less than a month after his dismissal.

KINGSLEY, Matthew   1904-05

Born: Turton, Lancashire, 1879
SL apps: 29
Cup apps: 1

ALREADY ESTABLISHED AS one of the country's top goalkeepers when he joined Hammers at the age of 29 from Newcastle United in the summer of 1904, Matt was on duty between the posts in the inaugural Southern League match against Millwall at Upton Park on September 1, that year. Starting his career amid humble surroundings with his village side Turton, and then Darwen, he signed for Newcastle in 1898. He made his Magpies debut in the club's first-ever First Division fixture against Wolves (September 3, 1898) at St James's Park and, three years later, experienced the thrill of keeping goal for England against Wales at the same venue, thus becoming Newcastle's first bona fide English international. Also awarded three League caps, Matt was a feisty character who had a habit of fisting the ball away instead of catching it, to avoid being bundled into the back of the net as was the practice in those days. He also had the habit of swinging his arms wildly as he waited for action. After making 189 Football League appearances for the Tynesiders, his Hammers career began promisingly enough, but was destined for a premature end following a fracas with former West Ham player Herbert Lyon in a Southern League clash with Brighton in March 1905. After Kingsley kicked Lyon, the crowd invaded the pitch and ugly scenes ensued before Kingsley was sent off and Lyon was carried off to the dressing room for treatment. It was to be Kingsley's last game in the claret and blue and, after his suspension, he joined London rivals Queens Park Rangers in the close season. One season and 20 Southern League appearances with Rangers was followed by a year out of football before he made a comeback with Rochdale and then Barrow, whom he played for until retiring to settle in the Blackburn area.

KINSELL, Thomas Harry   1951-56

Born: Cannock, Staffordshire, 3.5.21
League apps: 101 (2 goals)
Cup apps: 4

HARRY WAS ALREADY an experienced England international defender when he arrived at the Boleyn from Reading for £5,250. He had also seen service with West Bromich Albion (whom he helped to promotion to Division One in 1949) and Bolton Wanderers, as well as guesting during wartime with Grimsby Town, Middlesbrough and Blackpool (where he had won Football League and North Cup medals). His signing was another shrewd venture into the transfer market by manager Ted Fenton, who had been a colleague in the England team. He gave Hammers five seasons' yeoman service, often captaining the side, before being given a free transfer to Southern League Bedford Town. Although more renowned for stopping his opponents from scoring, Harry did manage to get on the scoresheet twice as a Hammer, on both occassions against men in blue, when scoring in the 2-1 Upton Park reverse against Birmingham City (April 28, 1951) and also in the 3-3 draw against Everton, also at the Boleyn (November 24, 1951). He was mine host of the Alma Arms public house at Stratford in 1981, and later took over at an off-licence. Harry had returned to his roots and was living in the heart of the Black Country, at Brierley Hill, in 1990. Harry sadly died in September 2000.

KIRBY, William   1903-04

Born: Preston, Lancashire, 1882
SL apps: 33 (10 goals)
Cup apps: 3 (1 goal)

AN OUTSIDE-RIGHT WHO liked a crack at goal, Bill was given a spell at centre-forward in an attempt to further encourage his goalscoring inclinations, but only one goal resulted from his three appearances in the number 9 shirt, although he still continued to deliver the goods when returned to his natural position. Formerly with Swindon Town, he scored on his opening-day-of-the-season debut against Millwall, and missed only one match throughout the campaign – funnily enough, the last fixture of the season against Swindon at the Memorial Grounds. Nicknamed "Sunny Jim" by colleagues and fans alike, Bill returned to Swindon for 1904/05 and then commenced (1905) a seven-year stay at Portsmouth. His wanderings were far from over, however, the 1912/13 season seeing him with his home town club, Preston North End. He then had spells with Merthyr Tydfil and Exeter City up to the outbreak of World War I, during which he assisted Croydon Common and Brentford. He joined the Royal Engineers early in the war but was invalided out of the service. He then worked in munitions at the Woolwich Arsenal but found the confined conditions did not agree with him and re-enlisted with his old regiment in 1917.

Harry Kinsell

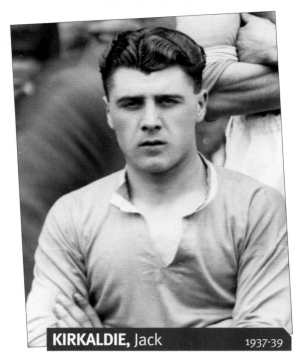

KIRKALDIE, Jack   1937-39

Born: Coventry, West Midlands, 2.8.17
League apps: 11 (1 goal)
Cup apps: 1

A FORMER RUGBY player, Jack was discovered in Warwickshire junior football by Southend United scout Syd Gibson after converting to soccer. When Syd joined the Upton Park groundstaff he subsequently recommended the speedy winger to Hammers, who in turn promptly signed him from the Shrimpers. Although facing stiff opposition from Johnny Morton and Stan Foxall, he made his Second Division baptism at the Boleyn in the 4-0 victory over Southampton (March 27, 1937). His solitary goal during his Hammers' career came against those other distinguished wearers of the claret and blue, Aston Villa, at Villa Park the following month. Only six first team appearances in 1937/38 and a paltry two the next campaign made him unsettled, with the result that he transferred to Doncaster Rovers in April 1939, after his 18 goals for Irons' reserves had alerted the Yorkshire club to his potential. Alas, after participating in the false start of the truncated 1939/40 season, Jack found himself playing wartime football along with fellow ex-Hammers Albert Walker and Fred Dell at Belle Vue. He returned to Rovers with the resumption of normal football in 1946, and made his mark with 16 goals in 51 appearances during the immediate post-war period.

KIRKUP, Joe   1958-66

Born: Hexham, Northumberland, 17.12.39
League apps: 165 (6 goals)
Cup apps: 22

A CONSTRUCTIVE, RESOURCEFUL full-back, the popular north-easterner was a product of the club's groundstaff and signed pro when he was 17, making his First Division debut against Manchester City at Maine Road in December 1958. His highlight with Hammers must have been playing at Wembley in the 1965 European Cup Winners' Cup Final versus TSV Munich, after gaining Youth and Under-23 honours. Hammers made a killing when they sold Joe for £27,000 to London rivals Chelsea in March 1966, but although Joe played 53 First Division games for the Blues, just as he had missed the 1964 Cup Final versus PNE, he was again unlucky when passed over for Chelsea's 1967 Wembley meeting with Spurs. It was in that year another sizeable fee took him to his last port of call as a player, Southampton. He amassed a further 169 First Division appearances with the Saints, which, added to his 165 Division One games for Hammers, made a grand total of 387 League appearances – and not one of them outside the First Division. In 1975 he emigrated with his family to become player-manager at Durban City in South Africa, taking over the post vacated by his old Hammers team-mate Budgie Byrne. But it was a shorter stay for Joe who couldn't settle there, especially when the club chairman began meddling in team affairs. So he returned to England during that scorching summer of 1976 and left football for good when he joined Byfleet Machine & Tool Co Ltd as a progress manager, in the employ of his old MD at Chelsea, George Thomson. After three years as a "trouble-shooter" Joe fancied another change and dispensed hospitality as mine host of the Rose & Crown at Upper Farringdon in Hampshire. With his children Tony and Nick growing up Joe decided to leave the pub trade so he could spend more time with his sons and wife Jill and went back to engineering. As Hammers were winning the Cup in 1980, Joe made another career change when he took over a sports shop in Cranleigh, near Guildford. After running a newsagents in Ewell Village, Surrey for many years, Joe has retired to live in France.

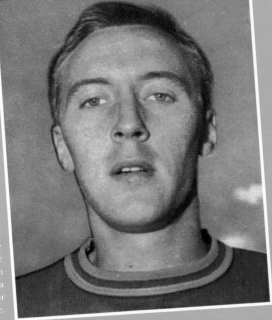

Joe in action scoring against Leeds

KITCHEN, George
1905-11

Born: Fairfield, Derbyshire, 1876
SL apps: 184 (5 goals)
Cup apps: 21 (1 goal)

MANY PLAYERS HAVE marked their debut for West Ham by scoring one goal or more, but to George Kitchen goes the distinction of being the only goalkeeper to do so! The unique event in Hammers' history occurred when George fired the ball past his opposite number in the Swindon Town goal from the penalty-spot in the opening fixture of the 1905/06 season at Upton Park. By the end of that winter his successful conversions had become a major talking-point among fans up and down the country, as had his equally successful efforts in keeping his own goal intact. Considered one of the finest uncapped keepers in the country when with Everton, George had begun his career with Buxton and then Stockport County in the Lancashire League in 1897, and won a Manchester Cup Winners' medal with them. Awarded a benefit at Goodison, his services were similarly recognised at the Boleyn Ground when he was given joint-share of the receipts for a match with Coventry, along with Fred Blackburn. Seriously injured in a Cup match at Newcastle in February 1908, he bounced back to earn his cash reward and founder

membership of Hammers' goalkeeping Hall of Fame. Signed to replace the equally high profile Matt Kingsley, who had transferred to QPR, George was a first-class golfer and became a professional at the age of 14. He made a good living at that sport but eventually decided to concentrate on soccer. He was also a fine cricketer and acted as coach to the Dulwich College team. Asked for his views on the new ruling in 1905, that stipulated that goalkeepers must remain under their crossbar when facing penalty kicks, Kitchen laughingly observed: "It won't make it easier for the goalkeeper; I should say that there will not be many penalty kicks stopped." It was a rule that both helped and hindered him in his almost unique role of penalty-stopper and taker! Transferred to Southampton in 1912, he served Saints for two years and made 39 Southern League and Cup appearances (but no goals!) before retiring from football to become a golf pro. George was "still alive and kicking" and working as a doorman at Lee Green Working Man's Club in 1969.

KITCHENER, Bill
1966-67

Born: Arlesey, Bedfordshire, 3.11.46
League apps: 11

A TALL, SKILFUL full-back who signed pro forms in November 1963, after playing in the Youth Cup-winning team of that year. Returned from a six-month loan period at Torquay United (where he played under ex-Hammer Frank O'Farrell) to make his initial First Division appearance against Nottingham Forest at the City Ground in March 1967. He won an extended run in the first team, being a member of the Hammers side that gained maximum points from their three Easter engagements that year. Permanently transferred to Torquay in December 1967, he later moved along the coast to end his League days at Bournemouth, before joining the Devon and Cornwall Constabulary. He was

later stationed in Bournemouth and then at Burley in the New Forest, Hampshire.

KITSON, Paul
1997-2002

Born: Murton, County Durham, 9.1.71
League apps: 63 (18 goals)
Cup: 18 (4 goals)

THERE CAN BE little doubt that West Ham United owe a big debt to Paul Kitson. For, until his signing from Newcastle United for a £2.3 million fee in February 1997, shot-shy Hammers were looking at almost certain relegation from the Premiership. In two short months, the goals scored by Kitson and his strike partner John Hartson had turned the season around and ensured Hammers' safety from the dreaded drop. The fact that Paul and John with eight and five goals respectively ended the season as first and second top scorers only underlined the extent of the goal famine at Upton Park that 1996/97 season. The former England Under-21 international's hat-trick in the 5-1 win over Sheffield Wednesday at the Boleyn in the last but two match of the season effectively banished the fears of relegation and made the razor sharp striker an overnight hero in London's East End. But life hadn't always been sweet for the laid-back Geordie who was frozen out at St James's Park following the big money buys of Alan Shearer and Les Ferdinand on Tyneside. Kitson, who started his professional career at Leicester City (63 apps, 11 goals) and moved on to Derby County for £1.3 million in March 1992 (132 apps, 49 goals) – whom he left acrimoniously in September 1994 to join the Magpies for £2.25 million – had begun to experience injury problems at St James's Park and his bad luck continued at Upton Park in that respect as he managed just an unlucky 13 League appearances in his second season of 1997/98. Faring better in 1998/99 with 17 League appearances, his three-goal tally was disappointing though, even if two came in separate Upton Park victories over two of his previous clubs, Leicester and Newcastle, and the third was the only goal of the game against Chelsea at Stamford Bridge. Struggling even more against injuries in 1999/2000, when he made just ten League appearances with no goals to show for them, his only tallies came in the cups with a goal apiece in victories against FC Jokerit (Intertoto), Osijek (UEFA) and little Bournemouth in the Worthington Cup. He was loaned to Charlton Athletic and Crystal Palace with only meagre success as he failed to feature in any of West Ham's fixtures in 2000/01 to become the forgotten man of Upton Park, as his relationship with Harry Redknapp sank to an all time low. But new manager Glenn Roeder gave the near veteran striker one more chance of glory when starting him in the Premiership clash with Charlton Athletic at the Valley. Showing opportunism unseen from a West Ham player since the days of Pop Robson, Kitson took the Valiants' defence apart with a textbook display of finishing. His three stunning goals set the Valley alight and catapulted him back into the headlines again as a strike by Jermain Defoe added to the drama of a see-saw 4-4 thriller and saw the born again striker leave the Valley happy with the match ball. They were to be his last goals for West Ham, but what a way to sign off! Given a free transfer to Brighton and Hove Albion he hit two goals in ten Division Two games for the Seagulls before changing clubs again when joining Rushden and Diamonds on another free in September 2003. Contracted on a month-to-month basis at Nene Park, his first goal for the Diamonds was a gem that won the game at Blackpool's Bloomfield Road and he followed that sparkling display with two goals against Wrexham! Despite at last proving his fitness by featuring in 30 matches for the Northamptonshire club and scoring five times, Paul was released at the end of 2003/04 following the club's relegation to the new Football League Two – or the good old Fourth Division to you and me.

KYLE, Peter
1901-02

Born: Glasgow, Scotland, September 1880
League apps: 1
Cup apps: 2

A LARGER THAN life character who learnt his football with Glasgow and District schools and his first club Glasgow Parkhead, Peter was rejected after trial periods with Clyde, Hearts and Hammers. A state of affairs that led to the player returning to Scotland briefly to play for junior club Larkhall Thistle. The trepidation of his earlier potential employers proved to be well-founded when the extrovert centre-forward was suspended, and then sacked, by Spurs after scoring 19 goals in 41 appearances for the north London club in the spring of 1905, for "a breach of the club's training rules" along with team-mate Chris Carrick, who also played for West Ham. It seemed there was little doubt over his footballing ability but a big question mark over his temperament. His sole appearance for Irons came in an unremarkable 2-1 defeat at Queens Park Rangers (November 9, 1901), after which he was involved in a straight swap for Welsh international full-back Bill Jones from Kettering Town. A month after falling foul of the Spurs' management, Kyle was transferred to Woolwich Arsenal, in April 1906, who then played at Manor Road. He scored 22 goals in 60 senior outings for Arsenal, and joined the last club he played against for Gunners – Aston Villa – in March 1908. By October the wayward star was on the move again, to Sheffield United, but once again his old failing came to the fore when he failed to train properly with the Blades and returned to Scotland to join Royal Albert FC. He did return to Southern League football with Watford in November 1909, but soon returned home again north of the border. A sad decline for a player who had taken part in a trial match for his country in 1907.

Paul Kitson

L

LABANT, Vladimir
LAMA, Bernard
LAMPARD, Frank Snr
LAMPARD, Frank Jnr
LANDELLS, Jack
LANE, Harry
LANSDOWNE, Bill Snr
LANSDOWNE, Billy Jnr
LA RONDE, Everald
LAVERY, William
LAZARIDIS, Stan
LEAFE, A Richard
LEE, James Alf
LEE, Robert
LEE, Thomas
LEONARD, Patrick
LESLIE, Lawrie

LEWIS, Eddie
LEWIS, Harry
LILL, Mickey
LINDSAY, David
LINDSAY, James "Jamie"
LINDSAY, Jimmy
LINWARD, William
LIVETT, Simon
LLEWELLYN, David
LLOYD, David
LOCK, Kevin
LOMAS, Steve
LONSDALE, Thomas
LOUGHLIN, James
LUTTON, Bertie
LYALL, John
LYON, Herbert

Lawrie Leslie

LABANT, Vladimir 2002

Born: Zilina, Slovakia, 8.6.74
League apps: 12
Cup apps: 1

A VASTLY EXPERIENCED Slovakian international full-back, with a left foot to die for, who surprisingly failed to cut the mustard during his short stay at the Boleyn after a £900,000 move from crack Czechs Sparta Prague in January 2002. Beginning his career with Slovakians Dukla Banska Bystrica (28 apps, three goals) in 1996/97, he moved to Slavia Prague for 1997/98 and 1998/99 (49 apps, one goal) before crossing the soccer-mad city to join local rivals Sparta, where he made 52 appearances and scored four goals between 1999/2000 and 2001/02 and then joined Premiership Hammers. However, things didn't work out at Upton Park for the six-foot Slovakian who was signed by Glenn Roeder as a long-term replacement for veteran defender Nigel Winterburn, and a disastrous performance by Labant in a 1-1 draw with Spurs at White Hart Lane in April 2002 led to Winterburn being given a one-year extension on his contract and the crestfallen Vladimir returning to Sparta on loan, never to return.

LAMA, Bernard 1998

Born: St Symphorien, France, 7.4.63
League apps: 12
Cup apps: 2

THIS EXPERIENCED, 35-TIMES French international goalkeeper arrived on loan from Paris St Germain hoping to resurrect his dreams of representing his country in the 1998 World Cup Finals after falling foul of the French football authorities. A flamboyant, complex character with a high opinion of himself, Lama eventually got the chance he craved in the Premiership when Craig Forrest was injured. A clean sheet in a 0-0 Upton Park draw with Arsenal wasn't a bad start and the big keeper was soon facing the Gunners again in the FA Cup Sixth Round 1-1 draw at Highbury. In the replay back at the Boleyn, Hammers lost agonisingly on penalties and although Lama was not at fault in conceding any of the Gunners spot kicks in the epic tie, the situation gave him the chance to be a hero and make his claims for an international recall by France impossible to ignore. But it was not to be, Arsenal went through and although he performed well in the next seven League fixtures, of which only one was lost, a catastrophic lapse in concentration saw the West Ham defence leak 15 goals in their last four matches to end any chance of a UEFA Cup spot and seemingly dash Lama's own hopes. However, in a surprise move he was selected for France's 22-man World Cup squad, then bizarrely not called upon. There was another shock when he signed another contract with Paris St Germain after seemingly "burning his bridges" with the Paris giants. Having played in two European Cup Winner's Cup Finals and amassed almost 500 French League and Cup appearances in a 12-year career that embraced spells with Lille, Metz, Brest Lens and Paris St Germain, major player Lama suffered something of a culture shock when selected for West Ham reserves at Oxford United's sparse Manor Ground when first arriving at Hammers. But the experience probably left him something to reflect upon in his retirement after he'd continued his amazing career in French football with another two full seasons in Le Championnat with Paris St Germain in 1998/99 and 1999/2000 (65 apps) and then moved on to Stade Rennais FC for 2000/01 where he clocked up another 32 appearances to complete a glorious "swan song" in the top flight of French football.

LAMPARD, Frank Snr 1967-85

Born: East Ham, London, 20.9.48
League apps: 551 (18 goals)
Cup apps: 112 (4 goals)

WHEN FRANK'S OUTSTANDING career as a West Ham full-back finally came to an end, he went down in the history books as one of the greats of the post-war era. Signing apprentice forms in 1964 and full professional a year later, he twice fought off serious injury to continue his advancement. He made his League debut against Manchester City at Upton Park (November 18, 1967) – six months and 19 senior outings later he suffered his first setback, breaking a leg against Sheffield United at Bramall Lane. Slowly, and with a great deal of sweat and toil, Frank recovered to regain his confidence and with it his first team place. International recognition followed with four Under-23 appearances and then the first of his two senior England caps against Yugoslavia (October 11, 1972). Alf Ramsey also gave Wembley debuts that night to Mick Mills, Jeff Blockley and Mick Channon, but England – led by Bobby Moore – were fortunate to salvage a 1-1 draw and Frank had to wait another eight years for his other cap. This time the man who brought him to West Ham - Frank played in the 2-1 victory over Australia in Sydney (May 31, 1980 – Alan Devonshire made a substitute appearance), although he can consider himself very unlucky not to have been selected more often. But the sweet and sour intermingled in 1972/73, with Hammers' heartbreaking knock-out in the League Cup Semi-final marathon by Stoke City. Frank duly got to Wembley in 1975, however, picking up a winners' medal in the 2-0 victory over Fulham. Frank experienced the thrill of European competition the following season and contributed a vital goal in the 3-1 Quarter-final home win over Den Haag, after Hammers had lost the first leg in Holland 4-2. But, typical of Frank's roller-coaster career, the European Cup Winners' Cup Final in Brussels against Anderlecht brought about the biggest disappointment of his soccer life. A goal ahead with only minutes to go to half-time, Hammers were playing like world-beaters and seemed to be cruising to victory, when Frank went to play a ball that, 99 times out of 100, he would have got safely back to keeper Mervyn Day. But on this occasion his studs caught in the turf, causing him to sustain an excruciating stomach injury. To make matters worse the Belgians scored from the incident and went on to win 4-2. Frank was flown home immediately after the game for an emergency operation. Once again he fought back to fitness, although at one time there was talk of a transfer to Norwich City. It must have been particularly gratifying for him when he scored the Semi-final winner against Everton in the epic replay at Elland Road to take Hammers to Wembley for the victorious FA Cup Final against Arsenal in 1980. Frank's celebratory dance of delight around the Leeds corner-flag will be remembered probably as much as his timely headed winner! Frank was now at the peak of his illustrious career and in the season after gaining his second full cap he won League Cup runners-up and Second Division Championship medals (1980/81). In September the following year he joined the exclusive band of West Ham players who have played 500 or more League games for the club. Frank was awarded a free transfer after playing in the final fixture of 1984/85 against Liverpool (May 20, 1985). He joined Southend United, pairing up with his old mate Bobby Moore who was managing the Shrimpers. It was like a Hammers mini reunion, with central defender Kevin Lock in the side and Harry Cripps on the coaching staff. But after 38 League and Cup appearances for Southend in Division Three, Frank hung up his boots at the same time Moore resigned as manager. Then a new Lampard emerged on the Upton Park scene, his son, Frank junior, a star in the youth team. Young Frank had a very tough act to follow, but has since become as big a star as the "old man". His dad, quietly spoken off the field, was as hard as nails on it. But he played with brains as well as brawn. His fierce tackles visibly shook many opponents, but Frank was much more than a solid full-back. Comfortable in possession, he made himself available to receive passes from fellow defender Moore and would begin many attacks himself from deep within his own half. His triangular link up with those two other gifted left-sided players, Trevor Brooking and Alan Devonshire, proved the cornerstone of so many victories over a period of six years. At times in the 1980/81 Second Division promotion-winning campaign, they were unstoppable. Frank also packed a ferocious shot and claimed his fair share of spectacular goals from long-range. And only Billy Bonds made more League appearances for West Ham United than fearless Frank. Despite pursuing a number of business ventures outside the game, West Ham has remained close to Frank's heart. He regularly worked for the club in a part-time scouting and coaching capacity before being appointed assistant to his brother-in-law, Harry Redknapp, when "H" stepped up to take over from Billy Bonds in August 1994. He left West Ham along with Redknapp in May 2001 and has yet to return to the game, preferring to follow his son's progress proudly from the stands.

England caps: 1972 vs Yugoslavia; 1980 vs Australia (2).

Career record

Played	League		FAC		LC		Europe		Total	
	App	Gls	App	Gls	App	Gls	App	Gls	App	Gls
1967-68	19	0	3	0	0	0	0	0	22	0
1968-69	1	0	0	0	0	0	0	0	1	0
1969-70	30	0	1	0	2	1	0	0	33	1
1970-71	41	1	1	0	2	0	0	0	44	1
1971-72	39	1	4	0	10	0	0	0	53	1
1972-73	38	0	2	0	2	0	0	0	42	0
1973-74	42	2	2	0	2	0	0	0	46	2
1974-75	40	4	8	1	3	0	0	0	51	5
1975-76	37	3	1	0	4	0	9	1	51	4
1976-77	36	1	2	0	1	0	0	0	39	1
1977-78	40	0	3	0	1	0	0	0	44	0
1978-79	29	3	1	0	1	0	0	0	31	3
1979-80	36	0	7	1	6	0	0	0	49	1
1980-81	39	1	2	0	8	0	6	0	55	1
1981-82	28	0	2	0	5	0	0	0	35	0
1982-83	37	2	1	0	4	0	0	0	42	2
1983-84	18	0	3	0	3	0	0	0	24	0
1984-85	1	0	0	0	0	0	0	0	1	0
TOTAL	551	18	43	2	54	1	15	1	663	22

LAMPARD, Frank Jnr   1996-2001

Born: Romford, Essex, 21.6.78
League apps: 147 (23 goals)
Cup apps: 38 (14 goals)

IT SEEMED A straightforward, fortuitous situation when West Ham legend Frank Lampard senior decided to set his talented son along the same path he'd trodden so gloriously three decades earlier and put his promising future in the safe hands of the much vaunted West Ham United Youth Academy. As there had already been a famous precedent at Upton Park when trainer Harry Hooper did the same thing with his equally gifted son, Harry Hooper junior in the 1950s, Frank senior was probably only too aware that young Frank would have extra pressure to bear in addition to all the usual pitfalls of making it as a pro, when with human nature being as it is, cries of nepotism would be sure to arise. But young Frank was made of stern stuff and claims that he was getting preferential treatment because of his background were rightly dismissed and treated with the contempt they deserved. A pupil of the same "class of 96" West Ham youth team that contested the 1996 FA Youth Cup Final over two legs with Liverpool and also produced that other prodigious talent, Rio Ferdinand, Frank soon discovered that having a famous father as assistant manager at the club could be more of a hindrance than a help, especially when the "green-eyed monster" emerged in people, yet he didn't let it delay his inexorable progress. Indeed, he'd already made his Football League debut (on loan at Second Division Swansea City), his Premiership debut (as a sub against Coventry City and Sheffield Wednesday) and been called up to the England Under-18s before facing Liverpool, Michael Owen et al, in that 1996 YCF. Benefiting from West Ham's tradition of putting young players out on loan to gain first team experience, albeit at a lower level, Frank junior definitely matured quicker due to his spell at the Vetch where he scored once in 11 outings and was described in the Swan's programme as "tough tackling and ferocious". Ferocious or not, Frank continued making good progress in 1996/97, making his full League debut in the 2-0 opening day defeat at Arsenal, two more starts and 11 sub appearances before, in an uncanny echo of his father's early career, disaster struck when he broke a leg at Aston Villa in March 1997. A big blow at 19 years of age. Frank senior had sustained a similar leg break in April 1968 at Sheffield United at the age of 19. Like his dad, Frank junior overcame what was a serious setback and came on as sub in the first game of the 1997/98 campaign at newly promoted Barnsley to make a dream comeback by scoring the winner against the Tykes with only his second touch! It was a great start to what was destined to be a big season for the young man with a lot to live up to. He certainly proved that his manager Harry Redknapp's prediction that he would "reach the very top of his profession" was on course when he made remarkable progress in establishing himself as a first team regular with Hammers, made his debuts for both the England B team and Under-21s and hit his first hat-trick against Walsall in the Coca Cola Cup! Apart from his obvious attributes of building attacks from deep, fetching and carrying and being general dogsbody, his ten goals from midfield were particularly welcome – being the first of any significance from that department since the departure of Martin Allen. Now the engine room of the team and boasting the best football bloodline in the Premiership with dad Frank senior, Harry Redknapp his uncle and Jamie Redknapp his first cousin, Frank set about ramming the false criticisms of his detractors down their throats with an impressive ever-present season in 1998/99 during which he was appointed captain of England's Under-21s – for whom he scored against Poland and Luxembourg – and got the call from Kevin Keegan to join the full squad to play Hungary. Maybe conscious that his progress was running slightly behind that of his team-mate and great pal Rio Ferdinand who, despite being slightly younger had already broken into the full England team, the young contender began the 1999/2000 season in magnificent form and was duly handed his first full England cap in the 2-1 win against Belgium at Sunderland's Stadium of Light in October 1999. Despite signing an extension to his contract that tied him to Upton Park until 2005, Liverpool, Aston Villa and Spurs all made attempts to prise him away from his East End roots, which was hardly surprising given his 13 goals in 48 appearances in all competitions during 1999/2000, a season that nevertheless had ended in disappointment in the League table and exits from the UEFA, Worthington (following the Villa fiasco) and FA Cups. But young Frank's future was decided for him by West Ham, who inexplicably decided to sack his uncle Harry Redknapp and his father at the end of another frustrating season in May 2001. From a personal perspective, 2000/01 had been another successful season for the young man from Romford who had to miss the last three games due to a groin operation. Having weighed in with another nine goals in 37 appearances to ensure Hammers were safe from relegation, Lamps had also been awarded his second cap against Spain when he set up two goals in the 3-0 win at Villa Park. But now his position at West Ham was untenable. With the enthralling excitement of the great FA Cup run that took the team to a home Sixth Round tie with Spurs, after they had toppled the mighty Manchester United and Sunderland on their way, just a distant memory, Frank Lampard junior's £11 million move to bitter London rivals Chelsea was as inevitable as it was infuriating to his fans who, in the wake of Rio's £18 million transfer to Leeds earlier in the season, were forced to witness the departure of another irreplaceable home grown talent. First under Claudio Ranieri and then Jose Mourinho, Lampard's career has gone from strength to strength and now participation in the early rounds of the Football League Cup are a thing of the past, replaced by the glamour of the Champions League for the Essex boy who once dreamt of getting there with West Ham. Now with almost 170 games and 30 goals behind him as a fully paid member of Roman Abramovich's "Blue Revolution" at Stamford Bridge and a fixture in Sven Goran Eriksson's England team, Lamps has proved that there is life after West Ham – but not as we know it! Season 2004/05 for Chelsea has been Frank's most successful yet, with a Carling Cup winners' medal and a Premiership winners' medal to his name as well as being voted the Football Writers' Association Footballer of the Year. Up to the end of 2004/05 Frank had scored 49 goals in 217 League and Cup appearances for Chelsea.

LANDELLS, Jack   1933-34

Born: Gateshead, Tyneside, 11.11.1904
League apps: 12 (3 goals)
Cup apps: 1

ALTHOUGH HE WAS born in the north-east, Jack played all his football in the south after his family moved to Essex. He spent his formative years in that county and gained experience with local sides Thames Board Mills, Jurgens, Grays Athletic and Grays Thurrock. He then joined Millwall (176 apps, 69 goals) and had eight years at The Den, winning FA honours. Signing for Irons in the summer of 1932, he made his Second Division bow against Bolton Wanderers on the opening day of the 1933/34 season at Upton Park. The inside-forward transferred to Bristol City (30 apps, four goals) in 1934. In June 1935, he moved on to Carlisle United (33 apps, six goals) and the following summer joined Walsall (20 apps, one goal). He was back in London with Clapton Orient in June 1937 (two apps). He was selected for a Test match appearance against South Africa in July 1929 and also represented The Rest versus England in March of the same year. He and Millwall colleague John Page were known as the "Grays Twins", a reference to their earlier association with the Essex club. John was responsible for 33 of Lions' 127-goal haul when they won the Championship of the Third Division South in 1929. A former clerk, he went into the motor trade after hanging up his boots. Also acted as midlands scout for Arsenal. His brother, George Landells, was a player with Tunbridge Wells Rangers in 1933. Ending his career with Chelmsford City in 1938, Jack died in 1960.

LANE, Harry   1919-21

Born: Hinckley, Leicestershire, 23.10.1894
League apps: 19

A SCHOOLMASTER SIGNED from Sutton, Harry made his Second Division bow as a right-half and later showed his versatility by switching to the centre-forward position and then right-back. He transferred to London rivals Charlton Athletic in 1921 and joined QPR in July 1922. Harry began his career with Hinckley United, then had spells with Nottingham Forest and Notts County in 1913 and 1914 before joining Sutton Town. An amateur all his career due to his teaching commitments, he was mainly a reserve at his numerous clubs and served with distinction in World War I with both the Army and the RAF.

LANSDOWNE, Bill Snr   1956-62

Born: Shoreditch, London, 9.11.35
League apps: 57 (5 goals)
Cup apps: 3

SIGNING PRO AFTER his demobilisation from the RAF in April 1956, this consistent wing-half made his League debut later the same month against Lincoln City at Upton Park and was a frequent member of the Second Division championship side in 1958. Appointed coach to the juniors in 1965, he left a year later to become manager of Eastbourne United (where Ron Greenwood served his managerial apprenticeship) after qualifying for his FA coaching badge. Bill returned in 1967, however, to take charge of Hammers' youth squad, later coaching the reserves. He then became connected with Dagenham FC.

LANSDOWNE, Billy Jnr   1978-81

Born: Epping, Essex, 28.4.59
League apps: 9 (1 goal)
Cup apps: 5 (3 goals)

A LIVE WIRE young striker who was well schooled by his above-mentioned father. Scored a celebrated hat-trick

to end the League Cup marathon with Southend United in 1979 and made his League debut when he came on as sub against Wrexham the previous season. Bill transferred to Charlton Athletic in 1981, and later had a spell in Sweden but returned home to feature in Dagenham's great FA Cup run in 1984/85.

LA RONDE, Everald   1982-83

Born: Forest Gate, London, 24.1.63
League apps: 7

A PROMISING YOUNG defender who appeared to have a bright future at Upton Park. Captained the 1981 Youth Cup-winning side and showed up well when drafted into the senior side, making his League debut versus Coventry City in April 1982. Then joined up with former Hammer Harry Redknapp at Bournemouth, but after a spell he returned to local junior soccer.

LAVERY, William   1909-11

Born: Fleetwood, Lancashire, 1887
SL apps: 17
Cup apps: 2

Bill Lansdowne

Billy Lansdowne

A RIGHT-BACK WHO made his Southern League debut for Irons in a 4-2 defeat at Luton (December 11, 1909). Bill next appeared at left-back in a 0-0 draw at Brentford (January 22, 1910) – his last outing that season. The second game of the following season, at Coventry, saw him embark on an uninterrupted 14-match sequence back at his favourite right-back position in the Southern League side. He was to make just one more appearance, however, in a 6-0 win at Southend (December 31, 1910). Transferred from PNE in 1909 where he had appeared in 14 First Division matches in 1906/07 and eight in 1908/09. Mostly a reserve at the Boleyn Ground due to the fine displays of Fairman and Shreeve, he later played in Ireland.

LAZARIDIS, Stan   1995-99

Born: Perth, Australia, 16.8.72
League apps: 69 (3 goals)
Cup apps: 17

THIS FLEET-FOOTED WINGER came to West Ham's notice when he played a "blinder" for Western Australia in a 2-2 draw against Hammers during the club's Centenary Tour in May 1995. Although forced to limp out of the action prematurely, assistant manager Frank Lampard had seen enough to fly the wing wizard from Oz to London for a trial and was sufficiently impressed to pay £300,000 to his club West Adelaide for his services. Stan had made more than 80 appearances for the Sharks in the NSL, but was sidelined with a broken leg sustained in a freak fall in the FA Cup tie against Grimsby Town in February 1996, having made his Premiership debut against Chelsea in September 1995. Already an established Australian international, "Skippy" as he was inevitably known at Upton Park, spent the summer of 1997 with Terry Venables on World Cup qualifying duty for his country, which ended in a heartbreaking defeat in the play-offs to Iran. Fast and a great crosser of the ball, Stan proved he was capable of scoring, too, with a late equaliser in a 1-1 draw against Wimbledon at Selhurst Park in March 1997 and a 35-yarder for the only goal of the game at Newcastle the following February. At his best when taking on defenders before whipping in a cross at breakneck pace, lively Laz began to attract interest from other clubs and the wily old fox Harry Redknapp just couldn't resist making a massive profit when First Division Birmingham City offered £1.6 million to take the son of a Greek railway worker on the fast track to St Andrews. It proved to be an ultimately great move for Laz as, after winning a Worthington Cup runners-up medal with the Blues in 2001, he found himself back in the Premiership after Brum defeated Norwich City in the 2002 Play-off Final at the Millennium Stadium. Stan signed a new two-year contract with City in May 2003 and, having scored eight goals in 180 League and Cup appearances for Brum up to the end of 2003/04 and played 53 times at full international level for his country, Laz richly deserved his new deal.

LEAFE, A Richard   1913-22

Born: Boston, Lincolnshire, 1891
SL apps: 63 (33 goals)
Cup apps: 6 (4 goals)

DICK LEAFE BEGAN his career with Boston Town and, along with his elder brother Tom, a wing-half, signed amateur forms for Grimsby Town in May 1909. He made one appearance for the Mariners before returning to his home town club in 1910, but then signed for Sheffield United in November 1910. Dick joined Hammers from the Blades in

1913 during the club's Southern League days and quickly made his impact as a goalscoring forward, ending up leading marksman in 1914/15. Making only a handful of appearances in wartime competitions, he returned to the first team following the election of the club to Division Two of the Football League in 1919, his versatility proving an asset in the higher grade. Appointed assistant secretary when he retired from playing in 1922, he held the post up to the outbreak of World War II, when the management was forced to reduce the staff. Also had an interest in a pre-war bookmaker's business.

LEE, James Alf   1919-21

Born: Rotherham, Yorkshire, 1892
League apps: 26

BEGAN HIS CAREER with Rotherham County. Transferred from Grimsby Town in time to participate in Hammers' first-ever Football League match against Lincoln City on the opening day of the 1919/20 season, he understudied regular full-backs Billy Cope and Frank "Bronco" Burton. Moved on to Newport County in 1921. Described as: "A deceptive player in that he might give an impression of lacking concentration and then be found difficult to outwit. His speciality, a clean kick. Could also play half-back."

LEE, Robert   2003-04

Born: Plaistow, London, 1.2.66
League apps: 16
Cup apps: 3

LIKE KEVIN HORLOCK, Bobby Zamora and more recently, Teddy Sheringham, England international Rob Lee realised a lifetime's ambition to play for the team he supported as a boy when he finally signed for Hammers in August 2003. Making his long-awaited West Ham debut in the opening day 2-1 victory over Preston North End at Deepdale, his experience was of immediate benefit to youngsters like Anton Ferdinand and Richard Garcia as he steadied the midfield while his new team-mates came to grips with the rough and tumble of life in the Nationwide First Division. Having previously won promotion with Charlton and Newcastle he had, in fact, warned his colleagues what to expect on the eve of the season saying: "Some of the games are not pretty, in fact they're bloody ugly, you need grit and determination as well as skill and talent. The opposition will try to bully you, but you have to stand up and be counted." As Hammers found out to their eventual cost, Lee's advice was spot on and Hammers missed his tireless toil in the middle of the park when he picked up a knee injury in the 1-1 draw at Coventry City in November 2003 and played no further part in the League programme. The former England star was at West Ham for a brief spell as a schoolboy, but left to go to Charlton via Hornchurch. He had almost ten happy years at the Valley and scored 65 goals in 345 League and Cup games before a £700,000 deal took him to Newcastle in September 1992. He scored another 56 goals in 402 appearances in all competitions on Tyneside where he was the engine room of Kevin Keegan, Kenny Dalglish and Sir Bobby Robson's Geordie teams. In February 2002, Rob switched to Derby County for £250,000 but couldn't prevent the Ram's relegation from the Premiership at the end of 2001/02. He left Pride Park on a free transfer after adding another two goals and 50 League appearances to his impressive CV in the summer of 2003 and then realised his dream of playing for his beloved Hammers before hanging up his boots for good. "I just want to pull on that claret and blue shirt and go out at Upton Park and play for my team," he enthused at the time, adding: "I've always been a West

Ham supporter and it's always been my ambition to play for this club. I've got close on a few occasions, but had come to the conclusion the chance had passed me by when Glenn Roeder, who had been trying to sign me in the last couple of years, gave me my opportunity at long last."

LEE, Thomas   1907-08

SL apps: 6

TOMMY SHOWED HIS versatility when he played in three different positions in his first three games for West Ham, at outside-right, inside-right and inside-left. Previously with Woolwich Arsenal, he made six Southern League appearances that season, his final outing coming in the last fixture of the campaign at Plymouth. Transferred to Coventry City, Lee played in the same side as E (Patsy) Hendren, the well-known England and Middlesex cricketer, but only had six outings with the Bantams.

LEONARD, Patrick   1898-99

Born: Scotland, 1877
SL apps (TIW): 12 (8 goals)

THIS FORMER MANCHESTER City winger caused a sensation when he scored a hat-trick in his first outing for Irons in a friendly against Upton Park. He also scored twice on his second Southern League showing in a 4-3 win at Wolverton which was just one of a run of 16 consecutive victories in the Southern League Second Division. He hit four in the 10-0 win over Maidenhead in the last match of the season at the Memorial Grounds and also scored in the 3-1 championship decider at Millwall against Isle of Wight team Cowes, who had won a low-profile six-club section of the Southern League representing the South-West. But they were not pleased with the choice of venue which was 100 miles from the Solent and only three from the Memorial Grounds. By the following season he had returned to Manchester City after only five months at Canning Town.

LESLIE, Lawrie   1961-63

Born: Edinburgh, Scotland, 17.3.35
League apps: 57
Cup apps: 4

ONE OF THE most popular goalkeepers ever to appear for West Ham, Lawrie played his first competitive football with Hawkhill Amateurs from where he graduated to Newton Grange Star and part-time pro status in the early 1950s. Joining the Army in 1956, Lawrie was stationed at Oswestry in the Artillery and played for the Regimental side, progressing to a command trial with the great Duncan Edwards and Bobby Charlton of Manchester United. Midway through his service he met one of the Hibs players, Jock Buchan, who persuaded him to write to Easter Road for a trial. After a test for the reserves he duly signed pro forms and in 1958 he was in the Hibs side that lost to Clyde in the Scottish FA Cup Final. He transferred to Airdrie in November 1959 for £4,475

and was appointed captain at Broomfield Park where he also won five international caps for Scotland. Courageous almost to a fault, this daring Scot had broken almost every bone in his body before arriving at Upton Park, from Airdrie, for £14,000. He was run over by a truck as a small boy and told he would be lucky to walk again, but confounded the doctors to reach the pinnacle of his profession. His worst playing injury occurred at the Boleyn Ground (November 3, 1962) when he sustained a broken leg while repelling a Bolton Wanderers' attack. Although he made a remarkable recovery to regain his place in the first XI for the final four matches of the season, he was passed over for the start of 1963/64 and asked for a transfer. He did not have to wait long for Stoke City to offer him a regular First Division spot and a move to the Victoria Ground for a fee of £15,000. After three successful seasons with the Potters, Lawrie returned to the East End with Millwall and earned great respect at The Den as a trainer-coach after he had ended his playing career at Southend United. Lawrie represented the Scottish League on three occasions. After finishing his playing days at Southend, he then sought a career outside the game and began working on a part-time basis for the council in north London and had a dual role of head of centre at the Cardinal Pole School in Homerton and youth centre organiser for Hackney Borough Council. Now he has retired, he likes a round of golf at Bexley Heath Golf Club, where he celebrated his 70th birthday with family, friends and former playing colleagues on April 2, 2005.

LEWIS, Eddie   1956-58

Born: Manchester, Greater Manchester, 3.1.35
League apps: 31 (12 goals)
Cup apps: 5 (3 goals)

A FORMER "BUSBY BABE", Eddie joined Hammers from Preston North End in an exchange deal that resulted in Frank O'Farrell going to Deepdale. Originally a centre-forward, he was successfully converted to the full-back berth when he joined Leyton Orient. He had previously turned in some useful performances during Hammers' promotion season and later did the same for the O's when they too were elevated to the First Division in 1962.

Lawrie Leslie

He later played for Folkestone Town and went on to manage Ford Sports in the Greater London League. Eddie emigrated to South Africa in the late 1960s and has become a well-known figure in the South Africa game, making up a quartet of former Hammers living there – Johnny Byrne, Johnny Sissons, Andy Malcolm and Ed. Now 70, Eddie works as an analyst for the Supersport TV channel covering the English and other European Leagues with expats Terry Paine (Southampton) and Gary Bailey (Manchester United). He was also involved with the South Africa Football technical team at the World Cup in France 1998 and the CAF Cups in Burkina Faso 1998 and Nigeria/Ghana in 2000.

Lawrie Leslie dives forward to punch clear

Simon Livett

Jimmy Lindsay

LEWIS, Harry — 1935-36

Born: Abergavenny, Wales, 25.10.10
League apps: 4 (4 goals)

A WELSH SCHOOLBOY international, Harry joined Arsenal after a spell with Rochdale (62 apps, 16 goals), and then played for Southend United (18 apps, six goals) and Notts County (32 apps, seven goals) making his Hammers debut in a 3-0 drubbing at the hands of Bury at Gigg Lane (September 28, 1935). He had ample revenge in the return fixture at Upton Park the following February, when he blasted a hat-trick in a 6-0 win against the Shakers. It was the highlight of the versatile Welshman's contribution to a season that saw West Ham narrowly miss promotion back to the First Division. Moving back to his native Wales, Harry joined Swansea Town (45 apps, 13 goals) in 1936 and spent two years at the Vetch before moving north to join Queen of the South who finished sixth in the Scottish First Division in 1938/39.

LILL, Mickey — 1954

Born: Romford, Essex, 3.8.36

A BRILLIANT YOUTH team winger who was lured away to Wolves in 1954 before he had a chance to play for Hammers' League side. Sold to Everton six years later for a big fee, he had the satisfaction of scoring a goal against his former Hammers' team-mates at Goodison Park in September 1960. An England Youth international, he played his early football with Storey Athletic, and later had spells with Plymouth Argyle and Portsmouth after he left the Merseysiders. He then went out of the League to play for Guildford City, later coaching in South Africa. In total, Mickey scored 38 goals in 121 League appearances in England before emigrating to South Africa where he hit 13 goals in 13 matches for Germiston Callies to help them avoid relegation. He was also a PE teacher at a state school just outside Johannesburg.

LINDSAY, David — 1906-08

SL apps: 50 (4 goals)
Cup apps: 2

CAME TO HAMMERS from Heart of Midlothian in the close season of 1906. Formerly with St Mirren, he was capped for Scotland versus Ireland in 1903. Dave missed only one match on the right-wing in 1906/07 and his accurate crosses led to many goals for his inside men, Stapley, Grassam and Watson.

PROMINENT FOOTBALLERS.
D. LINDSAY,
WEST HAM UNITED.

LINDSAY, James "Jamie" — 1894-95 TIW

Born: Scotland, c. 1870

AN INSIDE OR centre-forward from the Old Castle Swifts club who played in a number of early games for the Irons and probably in the very first fixture against Royal Ordnance (September 7, 1895).

LINDSAY, Jimmy — 1968-70

Born: Hamilton, Scotland, 12.7.49
League apps: 39 (2 goals)
Cup apps: 6

A SCHEMING MIDFIELD motivator plucked from Scottish junior football where he had gained considerable respect playing for Glasgow Boys. Signing pro forms in the summer of 1966, he won a Scottish Youth cap the following year and made his initial First Division appearance as sub against Burnley in October 1968. Transferred to Watford (65 apps, 12 goals) in 1971, later playing for Colchester United (45 apps, six goals), Hereford United (79 apps, six goals) and Shrewsbury Town (86 apps).

LINWARD, William — 1901-02

Born: birthplace unknown, 1878
SL apps: 40 (3 goals)
Cup apps: 2 (1 goal)

BILL'S PHOTOGRAPH IN a 1902 club handbook portrays a fine example of fashionable Edwardian manhood, resplendent in a polkadot cravat and stiff-starched collar, setting off his moustachioed features just right for the times. He was no slouch on the field either, appearing in 40 consecutive Southern League fixtures following his transfer from Doncaster Rovers. An ever-present in 1901/02, he made all his appearances at outside-left. Billy joined London rivals Woolwich Arsenal in December 1902 and moved on to Norwich City for 1905/06.

LIVETT, Simon — 1990-91

Born: Plaistow, London, 8.1.69
League apps: 1
Cup apps : 1

A CREATIVE MIDFIELDER whose patience was finally rewarded when he was given his League debut against Wolves at Upton Park (September 15, 1990). Wore the number 9 shirt as a replacement for the injured Stuart Slater but, unfortunately, Simon was also struck by the injury jinx and forced out of the 1-1 draw at half-time due to a knee problem. His only other competitive senior appearance was as half-time sub for Colin Foster against Aldershot in the FA Cup Third Round tie at Upton Park (January 5, 1991). Also played the full Zenith Data Systems Cup game at Luton (December 19, 1990) and appeared in other first team friendlies. A mainstay of Hammers' reserves from 1985 until he left on a free transfer to neighbours Leyton Orient in 1992/93. Unable to command a regular place at Brisbane Road, Simon had a short spell on loan to Cambridge United and joined them on a full transfer for 1993/94. Spent the latter part of that season on loan to his local GM Vauxhall Conference League club Dagenham & Redbridge where he scored four goals in 12 Vauxhall Conference appearances for the Daggers. After making 18 League and Cup appearances for Second Division Cambridge, Simon was given a free transfer to Dagenham & Redbridge in the summer of 1995. In July 1998 Livvy was given the chance to resurrect his League career when Third Division Southend United signed him on a free transfer from nearby Grays Athletic and he went on to score one goal in 27 League and Cup appearances for the Shrimpers before drifting back into non-League football with spells in the Conference with

Dover Athletic and Boston United. In 2001, after a short spell playing in the USA, he signed for Ford United and helped the Motormen win the Ryman Division One title.

LLEWELLYN, David — 1969-71

Born: Cardiff, Wales, 9.8.49
League apps: 6

FORMER CARDIFF BOYS star who attracted the attention of the Welsh Under-23 selectors with his prolific goalscoring exploits in Hammers' reserve side. Despite this success he was unable to win a regular place in the first team pool and was reluctantly allowed to join ex-Hammer Noel Cantwell at Peterborough United (then manager at London Road). Won a Welsh Under-23 cap against Scotland (1972). Dave made 13 League appearances for Posh and scored three goals before being loaned out to Mansfield Town where he played eight times – his last in the League.

LLOYD, David — 1898-99

Born: Hackney, London, June 1872
SL apps (TIW): 13 (14 goals)
Cup apps: 3

STANDING AT SIX foot four inches, David must have been an imposing sight for opponents. Signed from the Third Grenadier Guards, he played his first two TIW matches as full-back, but caused a sensation when he scored three times on his debut at centre-forward against St Albans. He scored 14 goals in 11 matches as a forward, including a vital opening goal in a Southern League championship decider in a 3-1 victory over Cowes (Isle of Wight) at neutral Millwall. He also scored Irons' goal in a Test match against Sheppey United, who had finished 12th out of 13 clubs in the First Division of the Southern League, enabling them to draw 1-1 at Chatham. In the end it was all academic, as the senior division was enlarged for 1899/1900 so the four Test match combatants, plus QPR and Bristol Rovers from outside the League, were admitted. Irons were in the Southern League First Division, but Lloyd had moved on before they played the first match at Reading.

LOCK, Kevin — 1972-78

Born: Plaistow, London, 27.12.53
League apps: 132 (2 goals)
Cup apps: 29

A FIRST-CLASS DEFENDER, given the unenviable task of filling Bobby Moore's number 6 shirt after Hammers' skipper had taken the road to Craven Cottage. He did well. Indeed, Kevin took the opportunity to show how well he had learned from the old maestro in the unique 1975 Cup Final confrontation, making a major contribution to West Ham's 2-0 victory. Hammers then made a £60,000 profit when Kevin joined the Cottagers, having paid out no more than the statutory signing-on fee in 1969. Kevin won three England Under-23 caps in 1973. Ironically, his link with Moore was rekindled in 1985 when he moved to Southend United on a free transfer and played ten League games under the management of his former mentor, as well as alongside another ex-Hammer, Frank Lampard. Fair-haired Kevin, a tall, lean central defender, stayed at Roots Hall in a

coaching capacity after his playing days were over. Kevin is now a licensee near Brentwood in Essex.

LOMAS, Steve — 1997-2005

Born: Hanover, Germany, 18.1.74
League apps: 189 (10 goals)
Cup apps: 26 (3 goals)

Steve Lomas

THIS COMBATIVE CLUB-MAN was a great stalwart for West Ham. The son of an engineer in the armed forces, Steve returned to Coleraine as a youngster and, after signing schoolboy forms for his local side, soon found himself playing first team football at the Showgrounds. Spotted by the same scout who originally bought City team-mate Michael Hughes to Maine Road, the red-haired midfielder duly crossed the Irish Sea to sign YTS forms for the Mancunians. Making his Premiership debut for the Citizens against Sheffield United at Bramall Lane as a 19-year-old, Steve had to overcome the twin demons of disciplinary problems and many injuries in his Maine Road days. He won his first cap for Northern Ireland in the 2-0 win against Romania at Windsor Park in March 1994. His early progress was halted in a horrific incident in a Premiership clash versus Crystal Palace when Steve fractured a shin bone and swallowed his tongue at the same time. Unfortunately,

Steve's injury jinx followed him south after he'd joined Hammers for £1.6 million just before the transfer deadline in March 1997, exactly a year after he'd been sent off in City's 4-2 defeat at Upton Park – a result which was instrumental in their ultimate relegation from the Premiership at the end of 1995/96. Steve's transfer after scoring 11 times in 137 League appearances for City was actually confirmed by fax from Northern Ireland's Belfast training HQ ahead of his country's 0-0 draw with Portugal at Windsor Park. With his all-action box-to-box foraging and aggressive style, Steve was the obvious choice for the captain's armband in the absence of long-term injury victim Julian Dicks. Certainly, manager Harry Redknapp had no qualms about giving his new signing the responsibility he already held with his country and he relished the role. In his first full season in 1997/98, Steve marked a quick return to Maine Road with the winner against City in an FA Cup Fourth Round tie and then became the hero of the hour when dispatching the decisive shot in a nail-biting penalty shoot out victory in a Fifth Round replay at Blackburn Rovers. Out of action for almost the whole of 2001 following a bad knee injury, enforced absences because of injury were an inevitable by-product of the player's 100 per cent ball-winning, foot-in style and a sad price to pay for never giving less than his all. In between the injury lay offs and suspensions, his appearances for Northern Ireland continued to pile up and he was also on duty with Hammers team-mates Michael Hughes, Iain Dowie and Keith Rowland on numerous occasions wearing the green of his country. But Steve's ambitions suffered a blow when he was told by Northern Ireland manager Lawrie Sanchez that his international days were over. Long-throw expert Steve was still a major part of manager Alan Pardew's promotion plans for 2004/05, but after eight years as a Hammer, he joined QPR on a free transfer on August 31, 2005.

LONSDALE, Thomas — 1913-14

Born: Bishop Auckland, County Durham, 21.9.1882
SL apps: 21

AFTER MAKING HIS way with north-eastern amateur clubs West Auckland and the more famous Bishop Auckland, Tom entered League football with Grimsby Town in 1908. A safe, reliable goalkeeper, he made his Mariners debut on December 5, 1908, and went on to make 87 Second Division appearances for the Humberside club and won a Midland League Championship medal with them in 1910/11, before joining Hammers in October 1913. Taking over the first team spot from Joe Hughes, he made his first appearance against Crystal Palace at Upton Park (October 2, 1913) and all was well until January 14, 1914, when Tommy was reported at a board meeting for being "absent without leave". The board's reaction was to fine the player a week's wages and demote him to the reserve team. With the senior side in the middle of a seven-match winning run it was some weeks before he regained his place, which he retained until the end of the season, after which he transferred to Southend United and played 28 games in 1914/15. He saw service with Stalybridge Celtic (in Division Three North) and Port Vale after World War I, and in the early 1970s proved there was no lingering animosity between himself and West Ham over the 1914 incident when he sent a nice letter to club press officer Jack Helliar. In it he gave details of both himself and Hammers' 1923 Cup Final inside-right, Billy Brown, who lived near him at Fence Houses, Houghton-le-Spring, County Durham. An extract from Doug Lamming's *Who's Who of Grimsby Town* gives a further insight into the former Hammer's playing style: "Singularly elusive once he had gathered the ball, in the days when keepers could be bundled over the line. One writer couldn't remember Tommy ever being so treated. Thoroughly capable in other respects, too, not least in the divining of opponents' intentions. Sold to West Ham to finance Willis Rippon's transfer." Originally a centre-half. He died on March 17, 1973.

LOUGHLIN, James   1927-28

Born: Darlington, County Durham, 9.10.1905
League apps: 10 (4 goals)

A GOAL-SCORING CENTRE or inside-forward signed from Newcastle United to supplement the fire power of Vic Watson and Vivian Gibbins. A prolific marksman with the Magpies, he scored in his first appearance in Hammers' colours against Huddersfield Town. After a pleasant introduction on West Ham's tour of Scandinavia during the close season, he found it difficult to hold down a regular place in the first team once League action got underway. So the former blacksmith made only ten First Division outings before moving on to join Coventry City (January 2, 1929), where he scored 39 goals in 65 games for the Bantams. Joined the Magpies from Darlington Railway Athletic. Transferred from Coventry (61 apps, 32 goals) to Northwich Victoria in the close season of 1931. James joined his home town club, Darlington, in 1933. Before joining Vics, James had short spells with Dolphin, Bray Unknowns and Worcester City.

LUTTON, Bertie   1973-74

Born: Banbridge, Northern Ireland, 13.7.50
League apps: 12 (1 goal)
Cup apps: 1

DESPITE HIS BRIEF sojourn at Upton Park, this midfield man holds the distinction of being the first West Ham player to be capped at full international level by Northern Ireland. Signed from Brighton & Hove Albion (29 apps, four goals) after proving his ability on a month's loan from the Seasiders, Bertie made his Hammers debut against Norwich City at Carrow Road in February 1973. He began his career with Wolves (25 apps, one goal), where he won the first two of his six appearances for his country against England and Scotland.
Northern Ireland caps: 1973 vs Cyprus (sub), Scotland (sub), Wales (sub), Portugal (4).

LYON, Herbert   1903-04

Born: birthplace unknown, 1877
SL apps: 29 (4 goals)
Cup apps: 4 (5 goals)

PREVIOUSLY WITH LEICESTER Fosse (1898-1900), Nelson (1900/01), and Watford (1901/02), Herbert was one of four players signed from fellow Southern League side Reading, mostly recognised as an inside-right, but was also tried at number 9 during Hammers' last season at the Memorial Grounds. Indeed, he scored two goals against Kettering Town in his first appearance at centre-forward in the second fixture of the 1903/04 campaign, an event that may have persuaded the management to persevere with him in that position until seven goalless outings saw him revert to the number 8 shirt. A victim of the major clear-out of players at the season's end, Herbert transferred to Brighton & Hove Albion in the close season of 1904 and, in a match against Hammers at the Goldstone Ground in March 1905, was involved in an unsavoury incident with goalkeeper Matt Kingsley, which led to the custodian being sent-off and suspended. Herbert later served Swindon Town, Carlisle United, Swindon Town again and Blackpool before World War I.

LYALL, John   1960-63

Born: Ilford, Essex, 24.2.40
League apps: 30
Cup apps: 4

AS PLAYER, OFFICE assistant, first-team coach and ultimately manager, John Lyall features prominently in Hammers' history having served the club in various capacities for 33 years. A solid, capable full-back who had won England Youth honours, John had an unusual beginning to a playing career beset with injury problems. Like secretary Eddie Chapman before him, the young Hammer doubled as office-boy-cum-apprentice professional. It was a grounding that would stand him in good stead in the years ahead. A member of the team that reached the Final of the FA Youth Cup in 1957, he made his League debut against Chelsea in February 1960. Then followed a three-year fight against persistent injuries, during which time he first showed the qualities of character now so well known. Finally succumbing to defeat, he was given a testimonial match on the eve of the 1964 FA Cup Final, and then began his long haul up the managerial ladder where his record with West Ham remains second to none. Taking over as team manager from his mentor Ron Greenwood in 1974, the FA Cup was on the Upton Park sideboard by the following year. His 1976 team is still the last to represent West Ham in a major European Final (the Cup Winners' Cup), and although he couldn't prevent a fall from grace in 1978, with relegation from the First Division, the winning of the Cup against Arsenal in 1980 and the Second Division Championship and League Cup Final season of 1980/81, amply compensated. Under his management West Ham became one of the most feared cup-fighting teams in the country, twice reaching the Sixth Round of the FA Cup and Semi-finals of the League Cup in 1989. In 1985/86 he guided the team to their highest-ever position in the First Division, when they finished third (behind champions Liverpool, and Everton) and kept hopes of a first-ever First Division championship alive up until the final Saturday of the season. Relegation at the end of 1988/89 led to his controversial dismissal but John was not short of job offers. After assisting Spurs and Bobby Robson's England on a part-time basis, he was appointed manager of Ipswich Town whom he quickly elevated back to the top flight. John then "moved upstairs" at Portman Road as board member and general manager. A man of honesty and integrity, John learned much about the game from his mentor, Greenwood, and he did as much as anyone to establish West Ham's reputation for attempting to play open, attractive football, even in the face of adversity. Now happily retired in his Suffolk farmhouse.

JOHN LYALL
WEST HAM UNITED Manager

M

McALISTER, Tom
McANUFF, Jobi
McATEER, T
McAVENNIE, Frank
McCANN, Grant
McCARTNEY, Alex
McCARTNEY, William
McCLENAHAN, Trent
McCRAE, James
McDONALD, Alex
McDONALD, Terry
McDOWELL, John
McEACHRANE, Roderick
McGEORGE, Robert
McGIVEN, Mick
McGOWAN, Danny
McKAY, Ken
McKNIGHT, Allen
McMAHON, Patrick
McMANUS, Peter
McPHERSON, Keith
McQUEEN, Tommy
MACAULAY, Archibald
MACDOUGALL, Ted
MACKAY, Malcolm
MACKESY, Jack

MACKIE, Charles
MACKLEWORTH, Colin
MALCOLM, Andy
MANGNALL, David
MAPLEY, Percy
MARGAS, Javier
MARJORAM, Arthur
MARQUIS, Paul
MARSH, Mike
MARSHALL, Dr James
MARTIN, Alvin
MARTIN, Dean
MARTIN, Tudor James
MASSEY, Frederick
MAUTONE, Steve
MEAN, Scott
MEDHURST, Harry
MELLOR, Neil
MELVILLE, Andy
MERCER, Frederick
MIECZNIKOWSKI, WL
MIELLEAR, Joe
MIKLOSKO, Ludek
MILLER, Keith
MILLER, Walter
MILLS, Hugh

MILNE, Ralph
MILNES, Frederick
MINTO, Scott
MITCHELL, Paul
MONCUR, John
MONTEITH, Hugh
MOORE, Bobby OBE
MOORE, Brian
MOORE, Ian
MOORE, Tommy
MOORE, William "Billy"
MORGAN, Nicky
MORLEY, Trevor
MORONEY, Tommy
MORRIS, Robert
MORRISON, J
MORRISON, John
MORTON, John
MORTON, William
MOYES, James
MULLINS, Hayden
MURRAY, Frank
MUSGRAVE, Joe
MUSGROVE, Malcolm

Bobby Moore OBE

McALISTER, Tom   1981-89

Born: Clydebank, Scotland, 10.12.52
League apps: 85
Cup apps: 14

A ONCE UNDERRATED keeper who was on the verge of breaking into the Scottish squad to go to Munich for the 1974 World Cup Finals, when he had to cry off with a broken leg. Disaster struck once more when he tried to come back too soon and broke the leg again. All this happened with Sheffield United in their First Division days. He then moved to Rotherham (January 1976) and Blackpool (July 1979). Tom signed for Hammers on a free transfer in May 1981 from Bristol Rovers, where he was on loan from Swindon Town. The experienced Scot was understudy to Phil Parkes and made his senior debut at Birmingham City (October 3, 1981). But it was not until 1984/85 that he had a reasonable run in the side, playing 32 League matches before suffering a broken rib and punctured lung at QPR at the end of that season. The stocky Scot was helping out at Chadwell Heath, training goalkeepers in 1993. He has since become a cabbie.

McANUFF, Jobi   2004-05

Born: Edmonton, London, 9.11.81
League apps: 14 (1 goal)

A JAMAICAN INTERNATIONAL midfielder/winger, Jobi signed for Hammers for a fee of £300,000 from Milton Keynes Dons in February 2004 and joined fellow ex-Dons stars David Connolly, Nigel Reo-Coker and Adam Nowland at Upton Park. Although he signed a three-and-a-half-year contract, his stay in east London was destined to last just six months however when, after starting just four First Division fixtures for Irons, he made a surprise £250,000 switch to link up with promotion rivals Cardiff City at the start of 2004/05. McAnuff, who scored 15 times in 104 senior outings for the Dons, had been courted by the Bluebirds before and, although he didn't want to leave his London roots, decided his best opportunity for regular first team football lay in South Wales. Many at the Boleyn were sorry to see him go, recalling in particular a memorable strike against Crewe when, leaving a trail of defenders in his wake, he completed his run with a cool finish into the bottom corner of the net. Up to the end of 2004/05, Jobi had scored three goals in 48 appearances for Cardiff. In June 2005, Jobi transferred to Championship side Crystal Palace for a £600,000 fee.

McATEER, T   1902-03

SL apps: 13

IN COMMON WITH team-mate James Dow, this centre-half's Southern League appearances for Hammers got stuck on the number least liked by the superstitious – 13 – and stayed there. The former Bolton man made one of his outings at outside-right, but with little apparent success as the team crashed 6-0 at Southampton. "A big, strapping fellow who brought a big reputation from Burnden Park, but it never materialised at the Memorial Grounds." He joined Brighton for 1903/04.

McCANN, Grant   2000-03

Born: Belfast, Northern Ireland, 14.4.80
League apps: 4
Cup apps: 1

THIS TOUGH, LEFT-FOOTED midfielder scored an unfortunate own goal in one of his rare Premiership outings at Blackburn. Previously loaned to Notts County to get some first team experience, Grant was already a

McAVENNIE, Frank   1985-87/1989-92

Born: Glasgow, Scotland, 22.11.60
League apps: 153 (49 goals)
Cup apps: 33 (8 goals)

A HUGELY POPULAR striker and charismatic character who is fondly remembered by his many fans at Upton Park. Frank was relatively unknown when he signed from Scottish League St Mirren (135 apps, 50 goals) for £340,000 in the close season of 1985, having first made his mark for St Johnstone Boys' Club in the early 1980s. But he made an immediate impact in the English First Division. After making his debut in midfield at Birmingham City (August 17, 1985), injury to Paul Goddard meant John Lyall pushed Frank up front to partner Tony Cottee on his home debut, against QPR, three days later and he scored twice in a 3-1 victory. "Super Mac" had arrived and there was no stopping the new goal-scoring sensation with the bleached-blond hair and dazzling skills to match. A remarkable spell of 12 goals in 11 matches earned him his first full Scottish cap, in Australia. Frank's goal in the return World Cup qualifying clash with the Aussies at Hampden Park helped the Scots to clinch their place in the 1986 Finals in Mexico. Frank became the idol of east London football and his celebrity status brought him a number of TV appearances as people clamoured for a look at the new West Ham star (no matches were screened this season due to a dispute between ITV and the Football League). Pictured regularly attending West End nightspots with Page Three beauties on his arm, Frank was enjoying himself to the full. His partnership with Cottee was among the most formidable in the country. It was a strong team, but their goals (Frank scored 26 in the League – bettered only by Everton's Gary Lineker – while Tony netted an impressive 20) stole the limelight and ensured Hammers enjoyed their highest-ever placing in Division One – third behind champions Liverpool, and Everton. It seemed everything Frank touched turned to gold, although he worked hard for his rewards. He was an unselfish striker who chased for 90 minutes in the team's cause. He would regularly feature in the build-up to goals that he himself finished off. Indeed, Frank has always

maintained that he is not a natural striker, more an attacking midfielder. After the disappointment of missing out on the title, there was a big feeling of anti-climax around Upton Park in 1986/87. Although Cottee maintained his high standards with 22 goals in the League, Frank's contribution slipped to seven. And he had not found the net once in the first eight League matches of

1987/88 when Celtic – the team he supported as a boy – came in with a £750,000 offer that neither he nor Lyall could refuse. Frank soon recaptured his scoring touch in his home city, spearheading Celtic to the Scottish League and Cup double in his first season, but before the end of the following season he was back in London to try and save Hammers from relegation. Lyall, coming under increasing pressure, splashed out a club record £1.25 million to re-sign Frank, who turned down the chance to join Arsenal after scoring 27 goals in 55 League games for the Celts. The return of the Scottish favourite lifted everyone associated with West Ham, but an injury – Frank broke his arm at Celtic shortly before returning south – limited the number 8 to just eight games as Hammers bowed out of Division One in May 1989. There was another disaster awaiting Frank three months later when, on the opening day of the season at Stoke, he broke his leg in a tackle by Chris Kamara. By the time Frank declared himself fit again, Lou Macari had been replaced by Billy Bonds, who gave him four sub outings in the closing weeks of 1989/90. The good times returned to Upton Park in 1990/91, but Frank had difficulty winning a regular first team place in the face of competition from Morley, Quinn and Rosenior. His frustration boiled over in a home game against Bristol City – a sending off that cost him a place in the FA Cup Semi-final against Nottingham Forest. Yet he still managed ten vital goals despite starting only 24 matches in the promotion campaign. Forest were not immune to Frank's deadly touch in front of goal, though. After managing just three goals in 15 First Division starts in 1991/92, Frank doubled his tally with a sensational hat-trick in his farewell game against Brian Clough's boys. His army of Upton Park admirers were in full cry. "There's only one McAVEN-E-E-E-E!" reverberated around the ground as Frank appeared from the subs bench and proceeded to take Des Walker (playing his last game before his big money move to Sampdoria) and the rest of the Nottingham defence apart with a performance that was straight from the script of *Roy of the Rovers*. Frank McAvennie left Upton Park as he arrived – with a bang. At 31, he was given a free transfer. A month on trial with Aston Villa at the start of 1992/93 came to nothing when they signed Dean Saunders instead. A spell in Hong Kong with South China FC was followed by another stint with Celtic (30 apps, ten goals) and then, in 1993/94, he was given another run in the Premiership with struggling Swindon Town (seven apps). Frank returned to Scotland for 1994/95 to join ex-Hammer Tony Parks at Premier League Falkirk (three apps, two goals). His career turned full circle when he returned to his first club St Mirren for whom he made his second debut at Love Street in a 1-0 defeat against Airdrie (October 15, 1994) and made seven appearances without scoring. Frank likes nothing better than visiting Upton Park occasionally where he is always given a hero's welcome. He also plays for the West Ham Vets in the Carling Masters. In 2003, Frank launched his life story, *Scoring – An Expert's Guide*, at Stringfellows, where else!

Scotland caps: 1985 vs Australia; 1986 vs Australia, Denmark (sub), West Germany (sub) (4).

Northern Ireland youth international and went on to represent his country at Under-21 and full international level after he'd joined Cheltenham Town following a short loan spell with the Third Division club. Grant found it difficult to make the cut at Upton Park, but since his move to Gloucestershire he has really established himself. Indeed, he was the Robins' top scorer with 12 goals in all competitions in 2003/04 and also cemented his place in the Northern Ireland team. Grant had endeared himself to the Cheltenham fans soon after joining the Whaddon Road outfit for a club record fee of £50,000 in January 2003 when he scored twice in a thrilling 3-3 draw at Huddersfield Town. He had previously had two loan spells at Cheltenham in 2000 and 2002 and up to the end of 2003/04 had scored 22 goals in 124 League and Cup appearances. He'd earlier had brief loan spells with Livingston (four apps) and Notts County (three apps) in 1999 and 2000.

McCARTNEY, Alex   1905-06

Born: Belfast, Northern Ireland, 1882
League apps: 6

SIGNED FROM EVERTON, right-back Alex made his first appearance in a West Ham shirt in the opening fixture of 1905/06 in a 1-0 win over Swindon Town at Boleyn Castle. His last outing was in a 3-1 reverse at Watford (November 4, 1905). Alex played in the Irish League with Belfast Celtic in 1907/08. Capped six times for Ireland, against Scotland (3), Wales (2) and England. He also played for the Rosetta National School in Ireland and later for Ferndale, a team that competed in the North Belfast Alliance League. On leaving that team he played for Hatfield, who won the Woodville Alliance Cup. He progressed to Distillery, Ulster and then Linfield. Joined Hammers with George Kitchen from Everton.

McCARTNEY, William   1904-05

League apps: 28 (3 goals)
Cup apps: 1

BILL MISSED ONLY six matches during 1904/05 on the right-wing for Irons after spending the previous campaign with Manchester United who he'd joined from Edinburgh Hibs. Two of his three goals were scored in home and away fixtures with Southampton, the other coming in a 5-1 Boleyn thrashing of Northampton Town (April 15, 1905).

McCLENAHAN, Trent   2004-

Born: Australia, 4.2.85
League apps: 2
Cup apps: 1

THIS TOUGH-TACKLING AUSSIE defender emulated his fellow countrymen Chris Coyne and Richard Garcia by making his First Division debut when coming on as a sub in the 3-2 victory against Crewe Alexandra at Grestry Road in August 2004. A regular in the reserves in 2003/04 he also featured prominently in Youth Academy manager Tony Carr's Under-19 side where he was equally at home at full-back or central defence. Trent made his first full start in the 2-0 Carling Cup victory over Southend United in August 2005. After joining MK Dons, where he made eight appearances, Trent's season ended on a high when he captained Australia in their preparations for the World Under-20 Championships in June 2005.

McCRAE, James   1919-21

Born: Bridge of Weir, Scotland, 2.9.1894
League apps: 50
Cup apps: 4

HAMMERS SIGNED THIS stubborn Scottish defender from Clyde, and he settled down to claim a regular place during the 1919/20 season, totalling 35 League and four FA Cup outings in the club's first campaign as a Football League outfit. Usually employed at left-half, he made another 15 Second Division appearances the following season before moving on to Bury where he scored ten times in 84 games for the Shakers. He then signed for Wigan Borough in 1923 and scored six goals in 32 outings there before moving on to New Brighton the following year to make six appearances. He joined Manchester United in 1925 (nine apps) and then Watford (two apps) before embarking on his third spell with Clyde following a brief loan spell with Third Lanark in 1926. He'd originally begun his career with Clyde before joining Glasgow Rangers and then returning to Clyde in 1919.

McDONALD, Alex   1901-02

Born: Greenock, Scotland, 1878
League apps: 4 (2 goals)

A TOP-CLASS GOALSCORER, centre-forward Alex began his career with Jarrow before joining Everton in February 1900. He made an explosive start at his next port of call, Southampton, who he joined in May 1901, scoring five goals in five starts. Transferring to Hammers in December the same year, he was true to his nature on his debut against Bristol Rovers, scoring both goals in a 2-0 win. Curiously, he failed to score in his three other Southern League appearances and headed back to the more temperate climes of the south coast when he joined

McDOWELL, John   1969-79

Born: East Ham, London, 7.9.51
League apps: 249 (8 goals)
Cup apps: 47 (1 goal)

A VERSATILE, TALENTED defender who operated mainly at right-back after Billy Bonds moved into midfield. He made his League debut against Blackburn Rovers in October 1969, and was picked 12 times for the England Under-23 side after gaining a Youth cap. John had ten years as a first teamer, but missed the entire 1976/77 season through injury. Honours include an FA Cup Winners' medal (1975), and a European Cup Winners' Cup runners-up medal (1976). He transferred to Norwich City in 1979, where he joined up with ex-Hammers John Bond and Ken Brown, then bossing the City outfit. John later carved out a successful career as an advertising sales director. He is now awaiting knee-replacement surgery due to wear and tear sustained during his distinguished West Ham career.

John McDowell (right) on the receiving end of a rather unorthodox tackle from Norwich's Jimmy Bone

Portsmouth in March 1902. But he continued to move around; to Luton Town in 1905, Croydon Common in 1907 and back to Luton in 1910.

McDONALD, Terry   1957

Born: Plaistow, London, 12.11.38

A PRODUCT OF West Ham's youth policy, this fast, tricky winger was a member of the Hammers team that reached the 1957 FA Youth Cup Final against Manchester United. Although he played only one match for the first XI, against Sparta Prague of Czechoslovakia in a friendly game, he was obviously too good for reserve team soccer. He benefited from a move to Second Division Leyton Orient, scoring on his debut for O's and helping them into the top flight in 1961/62. He later moved to Reading and then out of the Football League with Wimbledon and Folkestone Town. In later years, he coached in the USA and back at his old club, Orient. Nowadays Terry is a frequent visitor to both West Ham and Orient where he alternates his Saturday afternoons with his son and *Hammers News* editor Tony McDonald. Terry recently celebrated the 65th birthdays of two of his former West Ham Youth team-mates, George Fenn and Clive Lewis, who played in that FA Youth Cup Final over two legs against Manchester United in 1957. In what turned out to be a right old East End sing-song at The Carpenter's Arms in Whitechapel, the trio were joined by a host of former boxers including West Ham's own Billy Walker.

Career record										
	League		FAC		LC		Europe		Total	
Played	App	Gls	App	Gls	App	Gls	App	Gls	App	Gls
1970-71	25	0	0	0	0	0	0	0	25	0
1971-72	40	0	4	0	10	0	0	0	54	0
1972-73	38	2	2	0	2	1	0	0	42	3
1973-74	33	2	1	0	2	0	0	0	36	2
1974-75	34	1	8	0	2	0	0	0	44	1
1975-76	37	0	0	0	5	0	7	0	49	0
1976-77	0	0	0	0	0	0	0	0	0	0
1977-78	14	1	3	0	0	0	0	0	17	1
1978-79	28	2	1	0	0	0	0	0	29	2
TOTAL	**249**	**8**	**19**	**0**	**21**	**1**	**7**	**0**	**296**	**9**

McEACHRANE, Roderick 1898-1902

Born: Inverness, Scotland, 3.2.1877
SL apps (TIW): 53 (1 goal)
SL apps (WHU): 53 (5 goals)
Cup apps: 7

RODDY MADE THE long journey from Inverness in northern Scotland to Orchard Yard, Blackwell, London to work at the Thames Ironworks and continue his football career with the works side. Having already earned a considerable reputation as a hard-tackling half-back with Inverness Thistle, he set about making a name for himself in the bigger spotlight of Southern League soccer and succeeded to the extent of being an ever-present in 1898/99 and 1899/1900. The metamorphosis from the old works team into the new West Ham United Football Club was also marked by his 100 per cent presence, and it was becoming obvious that future fame was beckoning, although not with Hammers. Another fine season in 1901/02 (in which he missed only five Southern League outings) followed and prompted Woolwich Arsenal to offer him the opportunity of Football League status. If his form with Hammers had been outstanding, it was even more so at Plumstead; being a major factor in the Gunners' promotion to the First Division in 1903/04. But, despite the merits of his transfer, major honours continued to elude Rod, his witty sense of humour probably helping him to overcome the disappointments, especially when the Gunners fell at the Semi-final stages of the FA Cup in 1906 and 1907. He made his last appearance for Arsenal in 1913/14, just after the move to Highbury and the dropping of the Woolwich prefix. His place in the team went to another Scot, Angus McKinnon, who, according to an extract from an Arsenal club history by Bernard Joy, "was bigger and more robust but lacking McEachrane's constructive ability". Roderick McEachrane passed away in 1952.

McGEORGE, Robert 1901-02

Cup apps: 2

A RIGHT-HALF WHO came from amateurs Leytonstone, Bob played in Irons' two FA Cup ties in 1901/02 but, strangely, no Southern League fixtures. His Cup outings were against Leyton (1-0) and Grays (2-1).

McGIVEN, Mick 1973-77

Born: Newcastle-on-Tyne, Tyne & Wear, 7.2.51
League apps: 48
Cup apps: 7

A GEORDIE WHO was burdened with the responsibility of trying to replace Bobby Moore in the number 6 shirt after the legend left for Fulham in 1973. Signed from Sunderland for £20,000 after a period on loan from the Wearsiders, with whom he had 107 League games. He had the toughest possible baptism against Liverpool at Anfield in December 1973, but came through with flying colours. He later joined the senior coaching staff at the club then followed John Lyall to Ipswich Town and succeeded him as manager at Portman Road. He then became Football Development Officer with the East Anglians. Mick is now a major figure on the coaching staff at Chelsea. Affectionately nicknamed "Cappa" at Upton Park after a well-known TV character.

McGOWAN, Danny 1948-54

Born: Dublin, Republic of Ireland, 8.11.24
League apps: 81 (8 goals)
Cup apps: 2 (1 goal)

A SKILFUL REPUBLIC of Ireland international inside-forward, who converted to wing-half when competition for the inside-berths increased. Signed from League of Ireland club Shelbourne, after being recommended by their manager and pre-war Hammer, Charlie Turner. Danny arrived at Upton Park at the same time as two of his fellow countrymen, John Carroll and Fred Kearns. He completed six seasons at the Boleyn until his transfer to Southern League Chelmsford City in 1954. A year later, he joined Folkestone Town in the Kent League before retiring from football and embarking on a 22-year career with the London Electricity Board. Danny sadly died in March 1994 after a long fight against Parkinson's Disease. West Ham sent a floral tribute to Dan's funeral at St Margaret's Church, Canning Town, which was attended by his former team-mate, Scottish International John Dick.
Republic of Ireland caps: 1949 vs Portugal, Sweden, Spain (3).

McKAY, Ken 1899-1900

Born: Wishaw, Scotland, 1876
SL apps: 27 (8 goals)
Cup apps: 10 (1 goal)

INSIDE-FORWARD KENNY WON a First Division Championship medal in his one season with Sheffield United – 1897/98. The subject of a surprise transfer to Spurs for the following season, he made a scoring debut for the north Londoners against TIW on September 3, 1898, in common with Tom Bradshaw who joined him at the Memorial Grounds along with fellow former Spur Bill Joyce the following season. Joyce benefited greatly from McKay's presence at both Northumberland Park and Irons, the latter laying on many scoring opportunities for the centre-forward, most of which he gratefully accepted. McKay scored eight Southern League goals in 28 appearances himself in 1899/1900 for Irons as well as five in seven FA Cup ties. Ken moved on to Scottish club Wishaw United in September 1900 and then joined Fulham after TIW changed to West Ham United FC in July 1900, helping the Cottagers to win the Second Division of the Southern League in 1901/02. Ken scored in his first matches of three different competitions for Spurs, but had to wait until his second outing for Irons before scoring twice in a 4-0 Southern League victory over Chatham on September 18, 1900 at the Memorial Grounds. Having begun his career with Hamilton Academical, Ken returned north of the border to play for Royal Albert in October 1902.

McKNIGHT, Allen 1988-90

Born: Antrim, Northern Ireland, 27.1.64
League apps: 23
Cup apps: 10

A NORTHERN IRELAND international goalkeeper signed from Celtic in the summer of 1988 for £250,000. Allen kept a clean sheet on his League debut at Wimbledon (September 10, 1988) in the third game of 1988/89, after taking over from Tom McAlister. But he endured an alarming spell (described in big tabloid headlines as a "McKnightmare!") in which Hammers lost 12 of their next 20 League games. After 33 consecutive matches, which culminated with a dismal 3-0 home defeat in the first leg of the Littlewoods (League) Cup Semi-final against Luton Town in February 1989, he was finally dropped by John Lyall, who turned again to the veteran Phil Parkes to try and save Hammers' First Division bacon. His confidence shattered by bad publicity and sustained abuse from the Upton Park terraces, Allen was recalled for the last two games of the season. The last of his 23 senior League appearances came on that emotional night at Anfield (May 23, 1989) when Hammers lost their fight for survival in a 5-1 defeat by Liverpool. Lyall's successor Lou Macari did not give Allen even a single League outing after taking over for season 1989/90 and his brief, though eventful, Hammers career ended ignominiously with a 5-1 thrashing at Luton in the Zenith Data Systems Cup and a diabolical 11-0 crushing by Crystal Palace Reserves. Allen started his career with Distillery before crossing the Irish Sea to sign for Glasgow Celtic. He spent a year on loan to Albion Rovers in the Second Division before making 12 appearances for Celtic in their Championship-winning campaign of 1987/88. He also won a Scottish Cup winners' medal. After short spells with Stockport County, Rotherham United and Walsall, following fruitless trials at Falkirk and Airdrie, Allen returned to play, with little success, for Exeter City late in the 1993/94 season. But he was turning out in the Diadora League Division Three, for Collier Row, at the start of the next season. Allen also had a spell in Hong Kong playing for South China. He is now in the timber business.
Northern Ireland caps: 1989 vs Republic of Ireland, Hungary, Spain (twice) (4).

McMAHON, Patrick 1933

Born: Glasgow, Scotland, 26.10.08
League apps: 16
Cup apps: 1

HIS SENSATIONAL DEBUT between the posts against Birmingham in the FA Cup Sixth Round at Upton Park in March 1933 played a major part in Hammers' progress to that year's Semi-finals. With regular goalkeeper George Watson sidelined by injuries received in a car crash, young Pat stepped in and kept a clean sheet as West Ham thrashed their First Division opponents 4-0. Although he lost his place against Everton in the next round at neutral Molineux, he went on to total 13 Second Division outings that season. After leaving school in his native Scotland, the capable keeper had joined his local junior club Pollokshaws Hibernians – and from there went to those famous star-finders, St Anthony's. In addition to providing Hammers with Pat McMahon, the Saints later supplied Hughie Mills and Arthur Tonner to the Upton Park payroll. Pat eventually returned to Scotland to join St Mirren and then moved to Wrexham during the end of the 1934/35 season. He made 113 appearances in TDN between 1934 and 1938 before joining Stoke City, where he appeared three times in 1939 as war clouds gathered.

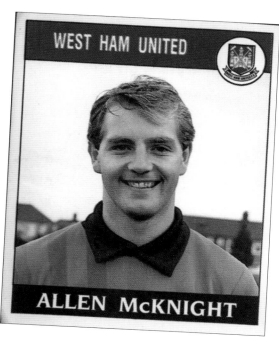

ALLEN McKNIGHT

McMANUS, Peter — 1899-1900

Born: Wynchburgh, Scotland, 1873
SL apps (TIW): 10
Cup apps: 5

SOMEWHAT SHORT FOR a centre-half, standing just five foot seven inches in height, Pete made his name with Edinburgh St Bernards who he helped to annex the Scottish FA Cup in 1895, when they defeated the redoubtable Renton team at Ibrox Park. Previously with West Bromwich Albion, the stocky defender joined Irons from Bristol side Warmley in 1899 and was said to "play a cautious and waiting game". He was on the winning side in his first five games for Irons, beginning with his debut in a 1-0 win against St Albans and culminating in a club record 10-0 Memorial Ground rout of Maidenhead in the last Southern League match of the season.

McPHERSON, Keith — 1985-86

Born: Greenwich, London, 11.9.63
League apps: 1

THIS YOUNG DEFENDER was thrown in at the deep end, along with Football Combination colleague George Parris, in Hammers' last fixture of 1984/85 against League Champions Liverpool at Upton Park, and did enough to justify his selection. Joining West Ham as an apprentice in the summer of 1980 after representing Blackheath and Inner London at schools level, Keith was a member of the team that won the FA Youth Cup in 1981. A regular member of the reserves, he had spells on loan to Cambridge United (11 apps, one goal) and Northampton Town before signing for the Cobblers for a reputed fee of £10,000. He made 216 League and Cup appearances (nine goals) before joining Reading in August, 1990. With the Royals Keith scored another nine goals in 224 League and Cup showings before moving to Brighton and Hove Albion where he made ten appearances in 1998/99. In 2000/01 Macca was shoring up Slough Town's defence in the Ryman League and he became a big favourite with the Rebels fans.

McQUEEN, Tommy — 1987-90

Born: Bellshill, Scotland, 1.4.63
League apps: 30
Cup apps: 6

A MILD-MANNERED LEFT-BACK signed by John Lyall in March 1987 to help solve an injury crisis. He cost £150,000 from Aberdeen, where he made 44 appearances and won a Scottish Premier League Championship (1985) and Scottish Cup winners' medal (1986). Tommy began his career with Clyde in 1981 and was ever-present in their Second Division title-winning side in his first season. The slightly-built McQueen made his Hammers debut against Watford at Upton Park (March 28, 1987) but his hopes of establishing himself as a first team regular disappeared a year later when Julian Dicks arrived from Birmingham. After being released by Hammers, McQueen returned to Scotland to join Falkirk. At Brockville, Tommy scored seven goals in 117 Scottish League games for the Bairns between 1990/91 and 1994/95 of which only 26 were out of the top flight. He dropped down a division to join Dundee in 1995/96 and made 37 appearances at Dens Park before retiring in May 1997. Having previously made 113 Scottish League appearances for Clyde and a further 53 for Aberdeen before coming south, he reached a career total of 320 Scottish League appearances altogether.

MACAULAY, Archibald — 1937-46

Born: Falkirk, Scotland, 30.7.15
League apps: 83 (29 goals)
Cup apps: 7 (2 goals)

CHARLIE PAYNTER SIGNED this volatile red-haired Scot from Glasgow Rangers where he won a Scottish League Championship medal in 1934/35, and he soon made his presence felt at the Boleyn Ground. Like so many other players of this period, Archie had his career interrupted by the war, although he did win a Football League War Cup medal in 1940. After he had seen service with the Essex Regiment Territorials and hostilities had ceased, the former Sergeant-Major PTI found it difficult to settle and was transferred to the then more glamorous Brentford (26 apps, two goals) in the First Division. He then moved on to Arsenal, winning a League Championship medal in his first season and a string of Scottish caps, and played for Great Britain versus the Rest of the World in 1947. After making 103 First Division appearances for Gunners, Archie finished his playing days with Fulham, where he scored four goals in 49 games, later going into management, first with Guildford and then guiding Norwich City to the FA Cup Semi-finals when they were still a Third Division club in 1959. He was one of the first managers to implement the 4-3-3 system and generally regarded as being tactically ahead of his time. After leaving the Canaries, he joined Scottish First Division club Dundee in an administrative capacity and was connected with Liverpool in 1970. He retired from the game after taking charge of West Bromwich Albion and Brighton & Hove Albion, respectively. He was working as a traffic warden in Chelsea in the 1970s. At the start of his career he'd played for a plethora of Scottish Junior teams – Comely Park FC, Lauriston Villa, Camelon Juniors and Sawyer. He was also trainer-coach at Dundee between December 1955 and April 1957.

MACDOUGAL, Ted — 1973

Born: Inverness, Scotland, 8.1.47
League apps: 24 (5 goals)
Cup apps: 1 (1 goal)

A BIG-MONEY SIGNING, who never settled at Upton Park. Signed from Manchester United to cure a goalscoring problem, he had previously seen service with Liverpool, York City and Bournemouth (where he had been under the managership of ex-Hammer John Bond). Re-joined his former boss at Norwich City, for a £140,000 fee, after being a West Ham player for just ten months, and then went on to Southampton, Bournemouth and Blackpool where he was player-coach and assistant manager from March 1980 to October the same year, before concentrating on his south coast sports shop. He later became a licensee, coming out of retirement to occasionally play for Salisbury, Poole Town and Gosport Borough. Ted won seven Scotland caps and can lay claim to being the 15th post-war player to score 250 League goals. Once scored a record nine goals for Bournemouth versus Margate in an FA Cup tie.

MACKAY, Malcolm — 2004

Born: Bellshill, Scotland, 19.2.72
League apps: 18 (2 goals)
Cup apps: 4

THE £300,000 SIGNING of this big, strong Scottish international central defender from Norwich City represented a major coup for Hammers manager Alan Pardew and his assistant Peter Grant who played with Mackay both with Norwich and his previous club, Glasgow Celtic. The West Ham management pair see his signing as a major step towards the club regaining its Premiership status and a timely replacement for long-term injury victim and fellow Scottish international Christian Dailly. Ironically, big Malky had to pull out of Berti Vogts's Scotland squad to face Norway and Moldova for their World Cup qualifying match in early October 2004 because of a calf strain which, with Don Hutchison recovering from injury, left Hammers with no representative on duty for the Scots. Having scored a remarkable 16 times in 231 League and Cup appearances for the Canaries, Mackay made a major contribution to the Carrow Road club's First Division Championship triumph in 2003/04 and ended the season being voted into the PFA Division One Team of the season and also winning his first cap for Scotland in a friendly against Denmark. Born in the tough Bellshill area of Glasgow, Malky began his career with the famous Glasgow club Queens Park and, after scoring six times in 75 games for the Spiders, moved across the city to join Glasgow Celtic in August 1993. At Parkhead he found it difficult to break into the team on a regular basis, but continued his penchant for scoring goals despite his defensive duties, managing five in 53 appearances in all competitions for the Bhoys. He moved to Norwich for £350,000 in September 1998 and endeared himself to the City fans by scoring four times against their East Anglian rivals Ipswich Town. When he joined Hammers he continued the trend, scoring on only his second Upton Park appearance against the Tractor Boys in a hard-fought 1-1 draw after making his debut as sub in the 2-1 win at Sheffield United. In August 2005, Malky moved to Watford on a two-year deal.

MACKESY, Jack — 1910-23

Born: Deptford, London, 1890
SL apps: 10 (2 goals)
League apps: 10

AN EVERGREEN STALWART who gave the Hammers unstinting service from the old Southern League days right through to the club's entry into

Archibald Macaulay (left) watches as West Ham's Len Golden scores for England versus Scotland in 1944 at Wembley

League football. He scored ten goals in 33 wartime appearances. Originally an inside-forward, Jack dropped back to half-back in later years, captaining the reserves in the London Combination. Always hungry for the ball, he was awarded two benefits during his 13 seasons at Upton Park.

MACKIE, Charles — 1905-06

Born: Peterhead, Scotland, 1882
SL apps: 10 (3 goals)

AN INSIDE-RIGHT OR centre-forward, Chas, as he was better known, joined Manchester United from Aberdeen in the close season of 1904, but had only one season with the Reds, playing in five Second Division and two Cup (four goals) matches, before joining Irons in the close season of 1905. He made his West Ham debut in the first match of 1905/06 in a 1-0 win against Swindon Town at Upton Park, but had to wait until his fifth match before opening his goalscoring account in a 2-1 home win against Plymouth Argyle. He scored again in a 2-0 Boleyn victory against Brighton and also in the following match, a 2-1 defeat at Northampton (November 18, 1905) – his last for the club. In December 1905, Charlie returned to Aberdeen and the following year he joined Lochgelly United.

MACKLEWORTH, Colin — 1966-67

Born: Bow, London, 24.3.47
League apps: 3

SERVED HAMMERS WELL after signing apprentice professional in 1962 and full pro two years later. Winner of a Youth Cup Final medal in 1963, he had to wait until 1966 to make the first of only three senior appearances (against Blackpool). Transferred to Leicester City in November 1967, where he provided cover for Peter Shilton and made six First Division appearances before joining Southern League Kettering Town in 1970. Entered the police force when he packed in playing and was stationed at Bow, often being on duty at Upton Park.

MANGNALL, David — 1935-36

Born: Wigan, Lancashire, 21.9.1905
League apps: 35 (28 goals)
Cup apps: 2 (1 goal)

A FORMER COAL-MINER at Maltby Colliery. After service with Leeds United (1927-30), Huddersfield Town (1930) and Birmingham (1934-35), this bustling centre-forward was signed as a replacement for Vic Watson. Dave set the Second Division alight in his second season at Upton Park when he scored 22 goals in 25 outings and numbered two hat-tricks among his harvest of net-finding efforts. Somewhat surprisingly transferred to Millwall the following season, the lad from Wigan Pier territory continued his happy goalscoring trend with Lions and later Queens Park Rangers whom he managed after the war. The highlight of his career came with Millwall in 1937, when he led the Third Division side's attack in the FA Cup Semi-final against Sunderland at Leeds Road. Re-signed by the Lions after a spell running a Sutton Coldfield cafe and grocery business, he joined Queens Park Rangers in May 1939, where he was manager from 1944 to 1952 – taking the R's into Division Two for the first time in 1948. A guest player for Southend, Fulham and Millwall in World War II, winning a Division III (South) Championship medal in 1938 with the latter, when he scored 18 goals in 25 League games. Once scored ten goals for Leeds against Stockport County in a Northern Midweek League match. He began his career with Maltby New Church, Maltby Colliery and had trials with Rotherham United, Huddersfield Town and Doncaster Rovers

MALCOLM, Andy — 1953-62

Born: Upton Park, London, 4.5.33
League apps: 283 (4 goals)
Cup apps: 23

FEARED BY THE leading inside-forwards of his day because of his ability to close-mark and block his opponents out of the game, Jimmy Greaves, Johnny Haynes and Denis Law all gave testimony to Andy's prowess. A tough-tackling, unassuming character, he must rank as one of the finest wing-halves the club ever employed. There was to be no room for Malcolm's uncompromising style of play at Ron Greenwood's West Ham, however. And although he was only one season away from qualifying for a testimonial match, Andy left Hammers for London rivals Chelsea in November 1962 in return for £10,000 and centre-forward Ron Tindall in part-exchange. It was good business for West Ham to receive a player plus cash for someone who'd cost them only a £10 signing on fee in 1950. Especially as they had a ready-made replacement in Eddie Bovington, ironically a very similar type of player. Tindall was later sold to Reading for £12,000 so the deal eventually realised £22,000 profit for the club. Although he was on better money at Chelsea, Andy couldn't see eye to eye with boss Tommy Docherty and it turned out to be a bad move for him. Not only were Chelsea relegated at the end of that 1961/62 season, Andy was on the move again – to Third Division Queens Park Rangers for another £10,000 fee. Managed by Alec Stock, Rangers had just finalised negotiations for moving to the plush White City Stadium and were looking for players worthy of their new surroundings. Football became fun again under the genial Stock until an eye injury threatened to end Andy's career. But, characteristically, he fought back to fitness to end the 1964/65 season as strongly as ever and complete a total of 84 Division Three appearances for Rangers before emigrating with his family to South Africa to join Greek Port Elizabeth side Apollen FC, and later Port Elizabeth. He had two enjoyable seasons in South Africa before returning to the UK for the 1967/68 season, and joined up with Southern League Brentwood Town. When he retired from playing at the end of the 1960s, he joined Lyons, the ice cream people, and he worked for them until 1977 when he took over the Ship & Anchor public house in Maldon, Essex. Later he had another pub, The Lion at Latchendon, but in 1986 decided to give it another go in South Africa where he still lives at Port Elizabeth. Although he was West Ham's first-ever England Youth international, Andy never won a full cap for his country, having to content himself with his selection (along with team-mate John Bond) for the Football League versus Scottish League in 1959, as his sole senior representative honour. But if honours were awarded for wholehearted endeavour and 100 per cent commitment, Andy Malcolm would have had few peers.

Career record

Played	League		FAC		LC		Europe		Total	
	App	Gls	App	Gls	App	Gls	App	Gls	App	Gls
1953-54	14	0	3	0	0	0	0	0	17	0
1954-55	38	0	2	0	0	0	0	0	40	0
1955-56	22	0	6	0	0	0	0	0	28	0
1956-57	37	0	2	0	0	0	0	0	39	0
1957-58	42	3	3	0	0	0	0	0	45	3
1958-59	42	0	1	0	0	0	0	0	43	0
1959-60	40	0	2	0	0	0	0	0	42	0
1960-61	40	1	2	0	2	0	0	0	44	1
1961-62	8	0	0	0	0	0	0	0	8	0
TOTAL	**283**	**4**	**21**	**0**	**2**	**0**	**0**	**0**	**306**	**4**

before making the grade at Elland Road. Dave died at Penzance, Cornwall, in April 1962. Altogether he scored 142 League goals in 213 games for his various clubs.

MAPLEY, Percy — 1903-04

Born: birthplace unknown, 24.11.1882
SL apps: 13
Cup apps: 4

IT WAS A case of unlucky 13 in Southern League matches for left-back Percy who also managed four FA Cup appearances in his season at the Memorial Grounds. Making his debut in a 0-0 home stalemate against Luton Town on September 24, 1903, he missed the next match and then had a straight run of 12 matches, the last being in the 4-1 win over

Wellingborough Town in east London. Transferred to Spurs in February 1904, he made his bow for them in a London League match the same month. He spent most of his time at White Hart Lane in the reserves, but he did manage ten senior appearances for the Lillywhites before being put on the not retained list at the season's end.

MARGAS, Javier — 1998-2000

Born: Santiago, Chile, 10.5.69
League apps: 21 (1 goal)
Cup apps: 5

EXPECTATIONS RAN HIGH when West Ham opened up a new avenue of the transfer market and splashed out £2.7 million to sign this rugged, 55-times capped Chilean international from Deportivo

Universidad Catolica de Chile in August 1998. Described in a France 98 preview book as: "very much from the old school of South American defending – ruthless to the point of cynical – but he is also a very composed ball player and the man who holds the back line together." That "style" had seen him win four League titles and Copa Libertadores with Colo Colo and Universidad and also scoop Chile's Player of the Year award on five occasions. West Ham were first linked to Margas after he'd had an outstanding game in Chile's 2-0 victory over England at Wembley in February 1998 when the home forwards hardly got a kick due to the close attentions of the authoritative central defender. So his credentials seemed impeccable, especially after his impressive displays at France 98. But Margas, who'd also had a spell with Mexican side America, was never able to reproduce even a semblance of his previous form and achievements in a nightmare stay at Upton Park. The fact that he fulfilled only six months of his four-year contract at Hammers gives some indication of how far the player fell short of the high hopes held for him. Making a satisfactory debut in a 0-0 draw at Coventry City where he was introduced to the niceties of the Premiership with an elbow in the face, which necessitated four stitches, Javier was found to be sadly wanting in Hammers' next match at home to Wimbledon when, after being 3-0 up, the defence collapsed to hand the Dons a shock 4-3 win. Clearly caught out by the pace of the Premiership, it would be three long months before he would return to first team action after struggling with a groin injury in another four-goal drubbing at Leeds after which he returned to Chile to receive treatment on a badly injured knee and missed the rest of the 1998/99 season completely! Quoting from the club handbook, which was published in August 1999, the player's entry began: "Chilean international whose Upton Park future is still clouded in confusion with the player having made no contact with the club since the end of last season. With rumours circulating that his family were unsettled in London, the club are no longer paying his wages but still hold his registration and are hoping to find a buyer for him soon. However, his appearance this summer for Chile against Brazil in the Copa America has fuelled speculation that he may return with Harry Redknapp admitting he is in desperate need of defensive cover." The player did indeed return, sporting a claret and blue coloured hairstyle in an attempt to prove his loyalty to West Ham's rightly peeved fans. To be fair, 1999/2000 did see him make a better fist of things as he appeared more regularly in the first team, but his expensive purchase will go down as one of the most bizarre transfer sagas in the club's history. Retired in 2000.

MARJORAM, Arthur — 1898-99

Born: birthplace unknown, 1877
SL apps (TIW): 8

A FORMER ASTON Villa amateur, Arthur joined Irons from Swanscombe and played at left-back in the first TIW pro XI against Sheppey United (September 1, 1898) and the inaugural Southern League fixture (Division Two) nine days later against Shepherds Bush.

MARQUIS, Paul — 1994

Born: Enfield, Middlesex, 29.8.72
League apps: 1

A CENTRAL DEFENDER who played just 60 seconds of League football for West Ham – as a 90th minute sub for Mike Marsh at Manchester City (February 12, 1994). But tall Paul did at least manage a touch as Hammers cleared a corner in the goalless draw! His only other senior experience came in the Ray Stewart testimonial versus Ipswich Town (May 6, 1992). Joined Hammers'

Mike Marsh

youth ranks after a spell with Cheshunt in the close season of 1989 and showed plenty of promise as he graduated to the reserves. A Combination League regular, Paul's hopes of making the breakthrough in 1993/94 suffered a setback when he dislocated his shoulder in a pre-season friendly. Later joined GM Vauxhall League Dagenham & Redbridge on loan. He was given a free transfer by West Ham in March 1994 and signed for Doncaster Rovers. Paul made over 30 League appearances for Doncaster before spells with St Albans City, Gateshead, Gainsborough Trinity and Bradford Park Avenue. In August 2002, Paul joined Unibond Premier side Frickley Athletic.

MARSH, Mike — 1993-94

Born: Liverpool, Merseyside, 21.7.69
League apps: 49 (1 goal)
Cup apps: 12 (1 goal)

A TRUE SCOUSER who suddenly found himself miles from home when Liverpool swapped him and David Burrows for Julian Dicks in a shock £2.5 million deal in September 1993. Mike joined the Reds from local non-League side Kirby Town on a free transfer in 1987 and impressed with his creative midfield flair. He played well at right-back for Liverpool in the goalless draw at Upton Park in November 1991 and Billy Bonds had long been an admirer of "Marshie" before he made his Hammers debut – along with Burrows and Lee Chapman – in the number 34 shirt at Blackburn Rovers (September 18, 1993). Mike showed all his clever, deft touches and good passing skills that afternoon in the 2-0 victory that transformed Hammers' Premiership season. He struck up an excellent understanding with midfield partner Ian Bishop and played an influential role in many matches, although his talent seemed rather wasted when asked to play wide on the right. Marshie's first goal for West Ham was a late FA Cup Third Round match-winner against Watford (January 8, 1994), while his only League goal of his first season capped a brilliant 4-1 victory at Tottenham (April 4, 1994). Unfortunately, within days of the 1993/94 season ending, it was revealed that his family were unsettled and wanted to move back to Merseyside, where Mike's five sisters and a brother all live. He was placed on the transfer list at his own request but was still a Hammer when the 1994/95 season began. Transferred to Coventry City for £450,000 in December 1994, Mike only made 19 League and Cup appearances (two goals) at Highfield Road before mysteriously losing his aversion of travelling too far from his Liverpool roots to join Graeme Souness in Turkey in a £500,000 move to Galatasaray! But his stay there was even shorter when he returned home after only three matches for the Turks

MARTIN, Alvin 1978-96

Born: Walton, Liverpool, Merseyside, 29.7.58
League apps: 469 (27 goals)
Cup apps: 117 (5 goals)

ONE OF WEST HAM UNITED'S all-time greats who rose to seventh place in the club's list of League appearance-makers early on in the 1994/95 season and to fifth place with League and Cup appearances combined. Capped 17 times by England at full international level, Alvin became one of the most outstanding central defenders in Britain. Not only strong in the air, but a very classy performer equally comfortable in possession of the ball. Alvin arrived at Upton Park as a schoolboy in the close season of 1974, the year after Bobby Moore left for Fulham. He had impressed for Bootle and Lancashire Schoolboys but after being turned down by his local club, Everton, Alvin made his mark at West Ham. Played in the side that reached the FA Youth Cup Final in 1975 and signed pro July 29, 1976. His first team debut came in a 4-1 defeat at Aston Villa (March 18, 1978) but despite scoring in his first full game, at Leeds (April 8, 1978), and starting all of the last five matches, West Ham could not avoid relegation that season. Not that Second Division football hampered young Alvin's development. On the contrary, he took over Tommy Taylor's number 5 shirt in February of the following season and went on to establish himself as regular partner to Billy Bonds in the centre of the back four. In May 1980, Alvin won an FA Cup winners' medal. A year later he missed just one League game as Hammers romped to the Second Division title and returned to Wembley to face Liverpool in the League Cup Final. It was Alvin's header – handled on the line by Terry McDermott – that led to Ray Stewart's dramatic penalty equaliser. Six European Cup Winners' Cup ties provided further education for Alvin, who was heading for international recognition. He made his full England debut against Brazil at Wembley (May 12, 1981) and emerged with credit from a tough baptism against Reinaldo and Zico, who netted the 12th minute winner. England manager Ron Greenwood (who signed Alvin as a kid at Upton Park) recalled him as sub against Scotland in the next game at Wembley and Alvin was back in the starting line up – alongside Phil Thompson – the following November when England beat Hungary 1-0 to book their ticket to the 1982 World Cup Finals. Unfortunately, Alvin's long and distinguished career has been punctuated by injuries, which is why he did not go to Spain with the England World Cup party in 1982. However, Alvin was back to full fitness in 1982/83 and, as well as helping Hammers to a creditable eighth place in Division One, he soon gained the recognition of Greenwood's successor, Bobby Robson, who included Alvin in most of his squads over the next few seasons. When Billy Bonds indicated that he would be retiring at the end of 1983/84, Alvin took over the club captaincy and formed a new formidable partnership with Tony Gale. As a central defensive pairing, they were probably the most accomplished in the First Division – rarely can a club have paired such footballing centre-backs together in the same side. It was a formula that was to provide the backbone to West Ham's most successful ever season, 1985/86, when they challenged Liverpool and Everton for the title before having to settle for third spot. Alvin missed only two of the 50 senior matches that season and was also involved in one of the most bizarre matches ever seen at Upton Park, against Newcastle United (April 21, 1986). It was that night when Alvin scored a hat-trick against *three* different keepers – Thomas, Hedworth and Peter Beardsley – in an 8-1 thrashing of the Magpies! Alvin was playing at his peak and the highlight of his international career came in the 1986 World Cup tournament in Mexico. England had begun the finals none too impressively but Alvin got his chance in the Second Round match against Paraguay in Mexico City

(June 18, 1986) and played his part in a 3-0 victory. To this day, Alvin finds it difficult to understand why Robson inexplicably dropped him for the Quarter-final against Argentina and brought in Terry Fenwick to face Diego Maradona and that "Hand of God" in the match that ended England's hopes. Significantly, Alvin was recalled for the first international of the following season (against Sweden, when Tony Cottee made his debut as sub), but that was to prove his last game for his country before injuries took their toll. Problems with his instep resulted in a series of operations and further setbacks that have restricted Alvin's appearances since the winter of 1986. The 42 games he managed following Lou Macari's appointment in 1989 represented his best run in the side for four seasons. Alvin was still playing some of the best football of his career when an Achilles injury, in December 1990, ruled him out midway through that promotion term. Missing from the first team for 16 months, and given a free transfer by Billy Bonds, many had written off Alvin… until he re-emerged to play in the last seven games of 1991/92 in a brave, though vain, attempt to save the club from relegation. His heroics earned him a new one-year contract. Alvin started 1992/93 at the heart of defence but a serious Achilles tendon injury, sustained in February 1993, resulted in another long lay-off. Once again, though, he confounded the sceptics who said he was finished. Almost ten months after bowing out at Derby, the big Scouser was back in the top flight, boosting Hammers' Premiership challenge. He made 11 first team appearances and was warmly welcomed back by the fans, who chanted: "Alvin, Alvin Martin… he's got no hair, but we don't care!" Nor did Billy Bonds and Harry Redknapp, who decided Alvin had done enough to earn yet another Premiership contract, at the age of 36. So Alvin played on in 1994/95 and with an authority and excellence that got his younger team-mates out of jail on many occasions. Opponents felt the full weight of his experience, most notably Stan Collymore who he shut out completely in a memorable 3-1 Boleyn victory over Nottingham Forest on the last day of 1994. Sidelined by a hamstring injury sustained at Coventry in February 1995 that kept him out for the rest of the campaign, Alvin astounded seasoned observers by continuing his Premiership career the following season. Called in to bolster the defence after a bad start to 1995/96, his ten games alongside Marc Rieper witnessed just one defeat during that spell. Granted a poignant last appearance in the final match of that season against Sheffield Wednesday at his beloved Boleyn Ground, "Sir" Alvin was given a standing ovation at the end of the 1-1 draw and his last as a Hammer. After a West Ham career that is unlikely ever to be matched in the modern game, Alvin still wasn't ready to hang up his boots and joined

Third Division Leyton Orient on a free transfer. Calling on his vast experience of 20 seasons standing, Alvin marshalled the young O's defence so well that with fellow former Hammers goalkeeper Les Sealey adding his own wealth of knowledge the team kept five clean sheets in the first ten matches. Immediately installed as club captain at Brisbane Road (who else could they pick?) everything was hunky dory until the sacking of ex-Hammer Pat Holland as manager and his replacement with another former Academy member – the centre-half Alvin had ousted from the West Ham team 20 years earlier – Tommy Taylor. His arrival and increasing injury problems finally hastened the end of the boy from Bootle's illustrious career, but not before he'd added another 19 League and Cup appearances to push his impressive career total to 605 not out! Appointed manager of Southend United in July 1997, like the late, great Bobby Moore and Ted Fenton before him, Alvin found the Roots Hall "hot seat" a difficult proposition for ex-Hammers. Despite initially having his ex-West Ham team-mates Jerome Boere and Mike Marsh with him at Roots Hall on the playing side, Alvin couldn't halt the trend, which saw the Shrimpers relegated for the second season running and resigned at the end of March 1999. Since then, Alvin has continued to run his own successful office furniture business with his wife Maggie while acting as a presenter for Talk Sport and a host of other TV and radio programmes.

England caps: 1981 vs Brazil, Scotland (sub), Hungary; 1982 vs Finland, Greece, Luxembourg (twice); 1983 vs Wales, Greece, Hungary (twice); 1984 vs Wales; 1985 v Northern Ireland; 1986 vs Israel, Canada, Paraguay, Sweden (17).

Career record										
	League		FAC		LC		Europe		Total	
Played	App	Gls	App	Gls	App	Gls	App	Gls	App	Gls
1977-78	7	1	0	0	0	0	0	0	7	1
1978-79	22	1	1	0	0	0	0	0	23	1
1979-80	40	2	7	0	8	1	0	0	55	3
1980-81	41	1	3	0	9	1	6	0	59	2
1981-82	28	4	2	0	5	0	0	0	35	4
1982-83	38	3	0	0	7	0	0	0	45	3
1983-84	29	3	1	0	5	1	0	0	35	4
1984-85	40	1	5	0	4	0	0	0	49	1
1985-86	40	4	7	0	3	0	0	0	50	4
1986-87	16	2	1	0	3	0	0	0	20	2
1987-88	15	0	0	0	2	0	0	0	17	0
1988-89	27	1	5	0	5	2	0	0	37	3
1989-90	31	0	10	0	1	0	0	0	42	0
1990-91	20	1	0	0	3	0	0	0	23	1
1991-92	7	0	0	0	0	0	0	0	7	0
1992-93	23	1	1	0	2	0	0	0	26	1
1993-94	7	2	3	0	1	0	0	0	11	2
1994-95	24	0	2	0	2	0	0	0	28	0
1995-96	14	0	1	0	2	0	0	0	17	0
TOTAL	**469**	**27**	**49**	**0**	**62**	**5**	**6**	**0**	**586**	**33**

to join First Division Southend United for another £500,000 in September 1995. Mike scored 13 goals in 112 League and Cup games for the Shrimpers before graciously retiring from League football due to a persistent knee injury that had dogged his whole time at Roots Hall in October 1997. He then joined Unibond League side Barrow and continued his non-League travels with Southport, Kidderminster (where he won a Conference medal in 2000), Boston United in 2001/02 and Acrington Stanley where he helped the famous old club into the Conference in 2003. Mike was managing little Unibond Premier outfit Burscough FC with fellow scouser and West Ham team-mate Ian Bishop as his assistant at the start of 2003/04 but resigned in October 2003. He signed as a player again for Skelmersdale in November 2003.

MARSHALL, Dr James — 1935-37

Born: Avonbridge, Stirlingshire, 3.1.1908
League apps: 57 (14 goals)
Cup apps: 2

THE CAREER OF this famous thrice-capped Scottish international inside-forward followed a remarkably similar path to another wearer of the claret and blue, Archie Macaulay. The latter was understudy to Doctor Jim at Glasgow Rangers in the early 1930s, and didn't win a regular place at Ibrox until Jimmy (a medical practitioner) transferred in July 1934 to Arsenal, with whom Archie also played later in his career. Joining the Gers in 1925 from junior side Shettleston, "Doc" Marshall, as he was mostly known, won six Scottish League Championship medals (1927, 29, 30, 31, 33 and 34) and three Scottish Cup winners' medals (1930, 32 and 34) with the Light Blues. His three appearances for Scotland were all against England, and he also represented the Scottish League. Hammers signed Jimmy from the Gunners in March 1936 and he played in the Second Division side at the inside-right position fairly regularly up to the commencement of 1937/38, when he was once again succeeded by Archie who had been purchased from Glasgow Rangers for a reported fee of £3,500. Later an employee of Bermondsey Borough Council, James passed away in December 1977.

MARTIN, Dean — 1991-92

Born: Islington, London, 31.8.72
League apps: 2
Cup apps: 1

A DIMINUTIVE, BLOND striker who quit his job installing air conditioning units to join Hammers from non-League Fisher Athletic for £25,000 in May 1991. His first senior outing was versus Panathinaikos (Greece) in the Makita Tournament at Highbury in August 1991. He came on as sub in the FA Cup at Wrexham (February 4, 1992) and was booked within seconds of making his League debut at Coventry (April 25, 1992). Played his only full game in the final match of 1991/92 versus Nottingham Forest at Upton Park (May 2, 1992). Dean went on loan to GM Vauxhall Conference League side Kettering Town in December 1992 and later joined Colchester United on a free transfer.

MARTIN, Tudor James — 1936-37

Born: Caerau, Wales, 20.4.1904
League apps: 11 (7 goals)

A FORMER COAL miner, Tudor had the amazing experience of scoring a hat-trick on his debut for Hammers at St James's Park versus Newcastle United (September 9, 1936) and ending up on the losing side, Magpies winning the encounter 5-3. At home in the centre-forward position or at inside-left, Hammers signed the goalscoring Welshman from Swansea Town, where he had scored 45 goals in 116 League outings and rarely has a West Ham player made such a sensational start. Goalscorers then were not at the premium they are today and, on February 16, 1937, Tudor was allowed to join Southend United. Beginning his career with Bridgend Town, he made a giant leap to join West Bromwich Albion in 1926. He won his solitary Welsh cap versus Ireland in 1930 during his year with Newport County when he scored 34 goals in 27 Third Division South matches and drew the attention of Wolves manager Major Frank Buckley. He signed for the Midlanders and scored nine times in 15 First Division appearances between 1930 and 1932. He also scored a mammoth 60 times for Wolves reserves when they won the Central League Championship in 1932. Tudor died at Newport on September 6, 1979.

MASSEY, Frederick — 1909-12

Born: East Ham, London, 2.11.1883

ORIGINALLY WITH LEYTON, Fred played one Southern League game for Tottenham in 1909 before transferring to West Ham where he was successfully converted to wing-half. Making his Hammers debut at left-half in a 2-2 Upton Park draw with Swindon Town on December 18, 1909, he eventually went on to fill all three half-back positions and gave three seasons' sterling service. He'd played two seasons at the then professional Leyton club before his move to Spurs in the summer of 1907. He spent a similar period with Tottenham, but made only five senior outings, three in the secondary Western League, one in a friendly and that solitary Southern League appearance. Fred died at Watford, Hertfordshire, on January 26, 1953.

MAUTONE, Steve — 1996

Born: Myrtlford, Australia, 10.8.70
League apps: 3

STEVE MUST BE one of the unluckiest goalkeepers ever to play for West Ham. Another by-product of the club's 1995 Centenary Tour of Australia, Stefano, as his Italian heritage demands he be known, was given the seal of approval by no less a school of authority that messrs Miklosko, Shilton and Sealey. But despite never finishing on the losing side and only conceding one goal during his three senior outings for Hammers, he was largely overlooked at Upton Park. A member of the Australian 1992 Olympic Games team and international room-mate of fellow Hammer Stan Lazaridis, the young goalkeeper had gained extensive experience Down Under with Aussie sides Parramatta Eagles, Morwell Falcons and Canberra Cosmos before signing for West Ham for a £30,000 fee in March 1996. Having previously tried his hand in Italian football as a rookie keeper, Steve shared the West Ham reserve goalkeeper jersey with his aforementioned tutors and youth team custodian Neil Finn in his first months in east London. His breakthrough came in September 1996 when, deputising for Miklosko, he made three consecutive first team appearances in seven days when featuring in the 1-1 Coca Cola Cup draw against Barnet at Underhill, the 2-0 Premiership win at Nottingham Forest and the 1-0 return leg victory over the B's at Upton Park. Not a bad week's work for the raw-boned youngster. Loan duty

at Crewe witnessed the plucky Antipodean achieving a similar success rate in three games for the Gresty Road outfit, the young Aussie with an Italian passport seemed to have a bright future at the Boleyn, but he was soon shipped out on loan again, this time to First Division Reading where he saved two penalties to impress the Royals enough to make the move permanent for a fee of £250,000 in February 1997. However, a freak injury sustained warming up for a game at Port Vale led him to being replaced before kick-off and despite extensive treatment and physiotherapy at Lilleshall, Steve never added to the 34 League and Cup appearances he'd made for the Berkshire club. Once linked to a £1 million move to Coventry City when at his peak with the Royals, he was forced to lower his sights and, after brief spells at Wolves, Crystal Palace and Gillingham, where he made one emergency appearance – after regular keeper Vince Bartram was stuck on the M25 due to a road accident – and helped the Gills to an important 2-1 win over Wigan, he played for Barry Town in the European Cup qualifying rounds, in July 1999. Soon after the former Australian Under-21 international signed for Slough Town and was so popular the Rebels fans voted him their player of the season despite being relegated from the Ryman League Premier Division in 1999/2000.

MEAN, Scott — 1998

Born: Crawley, Sussex, 13.12.73
League apps: 3

THIS PROMISING YOUNG central midfielder had his career decimated by persistent injury problems. Signed for £100,000 from Harry Redknapp's old club Bournemouth, Scott had scored eight goals in 89 League and Cup appearances for the Cherries, but only managed three sub appearances for Hammers in three years at Upton Park. Loaned out to First Division Port Vale, his injury hoodoo continued at Burslem when he limped out of his debut versus West Bromich Albion with a bad cruciate ligament injury in his first start for three years. Released by West Ham in the summer of 1999, Scott was a skilful performer when fit, but was destined to go down as one of the game's unlucky ones.

MEDHURST, Harry — 1938-46

Born: Byfleet, Surrey, 5.2.16
League apps: 24
Cup apps: 9

ALTHOUGH HE BECAME a Hammers pro in 1936, this capable custodian had to wait a further two years before making his League debut versus Fulham in December 1938. He finished that season with 21 League games under his cap and started the next as first choice keeper, only for war to interrupt his promising start. Harry reached the rank of Sergeant PTI, having served with the Essex and Royal Artillery from 1939 to 1946. When things had returned to normal and full League soccer resumed at Upton Park in 1946, the club found itself with a glut of goalkeepers, so Harry was transferred to Chelsea in exchange for "Ten-Goal" Joe Payne, after making a further three Second Division appearances. Harry enjoyed great success at Stamford Bridge and, after making 102 League and Cup appearances, returned there after his playing days as trainer and, eventually, head coach to the first team. He was also a capable batsman, playing at county level for Surrey. Harry died in April 1984.

MELLOR, Neil — 2003-04

Born: Sheffield, Yorkshire, 4.11.82
League apps: 16 (2 goals)
Cup apps: 5

LOOKING UNCANNILY LIKE a young Geoff Hurst, Neil's loan signing from Liverpool was considered something of a coup and he was put straight into the side ahead of David Connolly for Hammers' opening day fixture at Preston despite having hardly met his new team-mates. It's doubtful manager Glenn Roeder's decision to elevate the young Yorkshire lad so quickly helped his cause, but he eventually settled in to prove a useful acquisition. Having already scored his first goal in half a dozen games for the Reds and been an integral part of Gerard Houllier's pre-season build up, Hammers probably expected a few more goals than the two the big striker plundered in the 3-0 win over Crystal Palace at Upton Park and when an ankle injury hindered his progress he was sent back to Liverpool where he ended 2003/04 with ten goals in four games for the Anfielder's reserves. Since returning to the Liverpool fold in the summer of 2004, the long-term injury to record signing Djibril Cisse has afforded Neil Mellor first team opportunities he might not have expected and at times he has produced; especially in front of the Kop where he scored a brace against Middlesbrough in the Carling Cup, finished Arsenal off with a glorious last-minute winner in the Premiership and netted the timely second goal in a stunning comeback against Olympiakos, which ultimately sent the Reds through to the next phase of the Champions League. The arrival of Fernando Morientes from Real Madrid, however, and continuing doubts about Mellor's ability to perform at the highest level, cast doubts about his Anfield future. Neil was sidelined by injury up to early October 2005.

MELVILLE, Andy — 2004-

Born: Swansea, Wales, 29.11.68
League apps: 20
Cup apps: 1

THIS VASTLY EXPERIENCED central defender who is commanding in the air and confident on the ground had made almost 800 League and Cup appearances and played 60 times for Wales before arriving at West Ham in January 2004 as makeweight in the deal that saw Ian Pearce go in the opposite direction. Andy was in the Swansea City first team at the age of 16 and won his first cap for the Principality against West Germany in Cologne in November 1989. After scoring 29 goals in 223 appearances for the Swans the ambitious young Welshman moved up a division when he joined Second Division Oxford United in July 1990 for £275,000 and he kept up his very respectable goal ratio for a defender by hitting another 15 goals in 159 appearances during his three-year stay at the Manor Ground. Moving onwards and upwards again with a £750,000 move to First Division Sunderland in August 1993, Andy finally realised his dream of playing in the Premiership when he was a member of the Sunderland team that won the First Division Championship in 1996. After making 236 senior appearances on Wearside and chipping in 14 goals, Andy turned down the offer of a further year at the Stadium of Light to team up again with former Black Cats assistant boss Paul Bracewell, who'd been newly appointed manager of Fulham. Having already had a short spell on loan at Bradford City (six apps, one goal) the now very experienced defender decided to take up his Bosman option with a free transfer to Craven Cottage in July 1999 where he became part of a three-man central defence with fellow Welsh internationals Kit Symons and Chris Coleman. In 2000/01 Melville had another First Division Championship gong to add to the one he'd won

at Sunderland as Fulham ran away with the division with a points total of 101, and also another chance in the Premiership. After making 193 appearances (four goals) in all competitions for the west Londoners, all east London eyes were on Andy in the hope that he could achieve a personal hat-trick and help Hammers back to the Premiership before bringing the curtain down on an amazing career. But, after 21 League and Cup appearances for Hammers Andy made a move to Nottingham Forest on loan in January 2004 and made 15 League and Cup appearances for the club up until the end of the 2004/05 season.

MERCER, Frederick — 1903-04

SL apps: 8 (1 goal)

FRED MADE HIS Irons debut in the volatile atmosphere of a West Ham/Millwall London derby meeting at the Memorial Grounds on January 2, 1904. Lions won 1-0, and left-winger Mercer went back to the reserves. He was back in the team for another 1-0 defeat at Luton, however, on March 26, 1904, which signalled the start of a seven-match run in the first team. His solitary goal came in a 3-1 win at Northampton on April 7, 1904.

MIECZNIKOWSKI, WL — 1902-03

Born: Paddington, London, 1877
SL apps: 3

A PROMINENT EAST End amateur with Pemberton and Clapton, who had played for and against West Ham at intervals. Also played for Portsmouth, but still retained his amateur status. He won innumerable county honours. In December 1899 the *Morning Reader* announced that due to so many wrong spellings of this player's name it would in future refer to him simply as "Kowski". A winger of east European descent, he was happy on either flank.

MIELLEAR, Joe — 1910-12

SL apps: 3
Cup apps: 1

AN OUTSIDE-RIGHT SIGNED from leading amateur club Bromley prior to the start of the 1910/11 season, he was listed under the heading of "Promising youngster" in that year's handbook. He made his debut in a 2-1 reverse versus Northampton Town at Upton Park on March 4, 1911 – his only appearance that campaign. He trebled his Southern League outings the next season, being involved in fine wins at New Brompton and at home to Exeter City in February 1912, but he was also in the side that crashed out of that season's FA Cup following a 4-0 Third Round replay defeat at Swindon, never to be heard of again at senior level.

MILLER, Keith — 1968-70

Born: Lewisham, London, 26.1.48
League apps: 3

A TOUGH-TACKLING WING-HALF signed from Walthamstow Avenue, his first team opportunities were extremely limited. First appeared in the senior side when coming on as a sub versus Ipswich Town at Portman Road in November 1968. It was not until his move to Fourth Division Bournemouth that he was guaranteed regular League football and with whom he won promotion to Division Three under the management duo of John Bond and Ken Brown, in the company of ex-Hammers Tony Scott, Pat Holland (on loan) and Trevor Hartley, in 1970/71.

MILLER, Walter — 1908-09

Born: birthplace unknown, 1885
SL apps: 11 (5 goals)
Cup apps: 6 (1 goal)

WALTER JOINED HAMMERS as a 23-year-old centre-forward from Sheffield Wednesday in the 1908/09 close season and scored in his second Southern League appearance at New Brompton. His best performance came in a 4-1 Upton Park victory over Exeter City, to which he contributed two goals, and he was also an ever-present in Hammers' fine FA Cup run that season, which ended with a Third Round replay defeat at Newcastle. Left to join Blackpool for the 1909/10 season and scored 14 goals in 31 outings for the Seasiders.

MILLS, Hugh — 1932-35

Born: Dumbarton, Scotland, 9.3.1909
SL apps: 21 (15 goals)
Cup apps: 2 (1 goal)

ALERTED BY HIS prolific goalscoring feats in Scottish junior football for St Anthony's and Bridgetown Waverley of the Scottish Central League, Hammers brought the sharp-shooting centre-forward south along with his brother George during the summer of 1932. An athlete of some renown in his native Scotland, his ability to run 100 yards in 11 seconds made him a difficult proposition for opposing centre-halves, and stood him in good stead in the scoring stakes. Netted on his debut on the opening day of the 1932/33 season against Bradford City at the Boleyn, he managed an amazing goal-a-game scoring ratio in 12 first XI appearances in 1934/35, scoring in ten successive games. Hughie was transferred to Celtic in June 1935. Nicknamed "Bunty", Hugh made just one appearance for Celts in a 1-0 defeat at Dunfermline Athletic on December 14, 1935. As a juvenile with Vale Oakville he had formed the inside-forward trio at centre with brother George at inside-right and brother Willie (who later played for Aberdeen and Scotland) at inside-left. Having also played with distinction for Renton Thistle and St Roch's early in his career, Hugh left Celtic to join Luton Town in March 1936 (after a spell on loan to French side Cannes) but played just twice for the Hatters before moving on to Carlisle United in March 1937, where he scored 28 goals in 56 appearances. He joined Clyde on loan in 1941.

MILNE, Ralph — 1990

Born: Dundee, Scotland, 13.5.61
Cup apps: 1

A FORMER DUNDEE United, Bristol City and Manchester United midfielder who made just one brief appearance for Hammers while on loan – as sub in the goalless League Cup Fifth Round replay at Derby County (January 24, 1990).

MILNES, Frederick — 1904-06

Born: Wortley, South Yorkshire, January 1878
SL apps: 2
Cup apps: 2

ONE OF THE most famous amateurs of his day, full-back Fred resisted the overtures of a host of top clubs who wanted him to turn pro. He steadfastly refused to relinquish his jealously-guarded amateur status, preferring instead to keep his allegiance to his first love, Sheffield FC, the oldest football club in the world and with whom he won an FA Amateur Cup winners' medal in 1904. As an amateur he was free to play for any club he wished, but chose not to sign for any of them.

MIKLOSKO, Ludek 1990-98

Born: Protesov, Ostrava, Czechoslovakia, 9.12.61
League apps: 315
Cup apps: 50

AFFECTIONATELY KNOWN AS "Ludo", the giant six foot four inch Czech goalkeeper will probably go down as Lou Macari's most telling contribution during his brief seven-month stay as manager. Macari gave Ludo trials in December 1989, although it was some two months later before he received work permit clearance to play in Britain, having made his name back home for First Division Banik Ostrava. Ludo spent 12 years with the club from northern Czechoslovakia and helped them win the Czech title before joining Hammers in 1989. Yet, ironically, Macari suddenly quit Hammers just hours before Miklosko made his debut in the Second Division at Swindon Town (February 18, 1990)! Thankfully for West Ham, Ludo stayed much longer than the man who signed him. His outstanding performances in England earned him a recall to the Czech national side in 1990 and he was in the World Cup for Italia 90 without getting a game. In his first full season, under Billy Bonds, he kept 22 clean sheets – equalling the club record set by Phil Parkes – and his popularity was underlined as he was voted Hammer of the Year by the fans on the day Hammers clinched promotion. Ludo's consistent contribution in 1990/91 was crucial because as many as 16 League matches were won by a single goal margin, while the club also enjoyed an FA Cup run all the way to the Semi-finals. When Hammers were relegated a year later, Ludo missed six matches – and four of them were lost. Significantly, he was ever-present again the following season when Hammers bounced back to the top flight at the first attempt. Ludo retired from the international scene in December 1992 – his 40th, and last, full cap came against England at Wembley (April 25, 1990). Happily settled in Essex with his wife and son, Ludo underlined his long-term intention to live in England by adopting British citizenship in 1995. It was a far cry from that winter when Macari's "Mystery Czech" bounced into Upton Park, speaking barely any words of English and facing an agonising wait for a work permit. At a transfer fee of just £266,430, Ludek Miklosko proved a tremendous bargain. An ever-present in 1994/95, his marathon run of 162 consecutive appearances was only halted by a suspension following a red card at Everton in December 1995. Declining a surprise recall to the Czech Republic's Euro 96 squad in England, Ludo made a sensational U-turn and returned to the international arena as emergency cover against Yugoslavia in 1997, but unfortunately his cameo appearance was not repeated. Having successfully fought off all contenders for his number one spot for the best part of a decade, chinks eventually began to show in his armour and he lost his place in the West Ham first team to Craig Forrest during the 1997/98 season. It must be said his departure from Hammers to QPR in October 1998 left something of a bad taste in the mouth as, with the west Londoners cash-strapped and unable to stump up all of the £50,000 fee required for his services, Ludo paid out £30,000 of his own money so the deal could go through! Later forming an enclave of ex-Hammers in Shepherds Bush in company with Keith Rowland, Tim Breacker and Iain Dowie, Ludo went on to make 65 League and Cup outings for the First Division strugglers before, maybe mindful of the rather shabby nature of his departure, West Ham manager Glenn Roeder offered the grateful Czech his dream job in the summer of 2001 to be goalkeeper coach at Upton Park. Now the excellence of his skills can be seen in the ever improving displays of Stephen Bywater and James Walker.
Czechoslovakian caps: 1990 vs Spain, England; 1991 vs Albania (twice), Iceland, France; 1992 vs England (7).

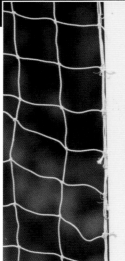

Career record

	League		FAC		LC		Europe		Total	
Played	App	Gls	App	Gls	App	Gls	App	Gls	App	Gls
1989-90	18	0	0	0	1	0	0	0	19	0
1990-91	46	0	7	0	3	0	0	0	56	0
1991-92	36	0	3	0	4	0	0	0	43	0
1992-93	46	0	2	0	2	0	0	0	50	0
1993-94	42	0	6	0	3	0	0	0	51	0
1994-95	42	0	2	0	4	0	0	0	48	0
1995-96	36	0	3	0	3	0	0	0	42	0
1996-97	36	0	2	0	3	0	0	0	41	0
1997-98	13	0	0	0	2	0	0	0	15	0
TOTAL	315	0	25	0	25	0	0	0	365	0

Beginning his career with Sheffield Wycliffe before the turn of the century, he graduated to Sheffield FC and by 1902 had turned out for three Steel City teams by virtue of his appearances for First Division Sheffield United. Fred played two Southern League matches for West Ham United in the right-back position in 1904/5 versus Wellingborough Town (4-0) and Southampton (2-2) at The Dell. In September 1905, he was a member of the Pilgrims, virtually footballing missionaries selected from England's best amateur players, who voyaged to North America for a tour that was one of the first efforts to popularise the game over there. On returning, Fred signed Southern League forms for Spurs on the recommendation of that other great amateur, Vivian Woodward, but played only two Western League games for Spurs. In March 1906, he joined Manchester United and in 1907 had spells with Leicester Fosse, Reading and Ilford. He also played for Norwich City in 1908. He eventually emigrated to the USA and was reportedly still playing out there in 1912.

MINTO, Scott 1999-2003

Born: Heswall, Cheshire, 6.8.71
League apps: 51
Cup apps: 11

ORIGINALLY BROUGHT TO Upton Park in a £1 million deal from Portuguese giants Benfica in January 1999 as a replacement for the retiring Hammers legend Julian Dicks; although Scott was an experienced and skilful defender, he was always going to be struggling to fill such a daunting brief. His debut in the humiliating 4-0 home defeat to Sheffield Wednesday in the same month of his signing seemed to set the tone for his torrid start at the club, which also saw him succumb to injuries that ruled him out for almost the whole of the 2000/01 season. Destined to feature only as a bit-part player thereafter, he did however show considerable skill and commitment when chosen. Having begun his career across the Thames with Charlton Athletic in 1989, Scott went on to make 205 League appearances (ten goals) for the Addicks before transferring to Chelsea for £775,000 in May 1994 to make 72 League appearances at the Bridge (five goals) and cement a burgeoning reputation as a skilful, constructive defender with good distribution. Benfica didn't have to pay a penny when they signed him under the Bosman ruling and took him to the original Stadium of Light in June 1997. In his first season in Lisbon, Scott made 21 First Division appearances as the Eagles finished runners up to FC Porto, but the following campaign his outings were restricted to ten when he was a team-mate of ex-Hammer Hugo Porfirio and Hammer-to-be Gary Charles. Now plying his trade at Rotherham United's humble Millmoor home, Scott made 35 League and Cup appearances for Ronnie Moore's perennial relegation fighters in 2003/04 and has twice been back to Upton Park on duty for the Millers, most recently for the 1-0 defeat to Hammers in September 2004. Up to the end of 2004/05, Scott had made 51 appearances for Rotherham.

MITCHELL, Paul 1993-96

Born: Bournemouth, Dorset, 20.10.71
League apps: 1

JOINED HAMMERS FOR just £40,000 in August 1993 in the deal that also saw Keith Rowland switch from Bournemouth, where they had both previously played under Harry Redknapp. Paul made just 12 first team appearances for the Cherries, having made his League bow at Chester in Division Two (September 7, 1991). Played either full-back or midfield. Paul was hampered by injury soon after arriving in east London, although he was non-playing sub at Oldham and soon afterwards managed to make his Premiership debut as sub – six minutes from time – in the home game versus Blackburn Rovers (April 27, 1994). He was given a free transfer back to his home-town club Bournemouth in 1996, adding just four appearances to the 14 he'd made first time round at Dean Court. Paul was given another free to Torquay United in August 1996. He scored one goal in 45 appearances at Plainmoor before joining Barry Town in 1999.

MONCUR, John 1994-2002

Born: Mile End, London, 22.9.66
League apps: 175 (6 goals)
Cup apps: 28 (3 goals)

IT WAS JUST like coming home for East Ender John when he moved from relegated Swindon Town to West Ham for £1 million in the summer of 1994. This talented midfield creator first impressed for Harlow, South-West Essex and London Schools before joining Tottenham as an apprentice in April 1983, turning pro a year later. John trained with Arsenal, Orient and Hammers as a youngster but was no doubt influenced by his father, John senior, who was Spurs' youth development officer. "Moncs" made his debut at Everton (May 11, 1987), in what was virtually a reserve side, five days before the 1987 FA Cup Final. He already had some League experience, though, having played four times while on loan to Doncaster Rovers in September 1986. John made his League debut versus York City (September 27, 1986) but his spell there ended when he

John Moncur

broke a leg. With talented, flair players like Paul Gascoigne and Vinny Samways at Tottenham, John was always on the fringe of the first team but unable to command a regular place. He spent much of his time on loan and as well as Doncaster, he also had spells with Cambridge United, Portsmouth, Brentford, Ipswich Town and Nottingham Forest. He did play 21 senior games, scoring one goal, before his £75,000 transfer to Swindon in March 1992. Under the management of former Spurs favourite Glenn Hoddle, the blond Moncur emerged as a vital member of the Robins side that earned promotion to the top flight at the end of his first full season with the club. In fact, he scored in the crucial Play-off Semi-final at Tranmere that helped Swindon towards an epic 4-3 victory over Leicester City at Wembley in May 1993. Although the West Country club finished bottom of the Premiership a year later, John had impressed a number of people and, indeed, Hoddle was keen to re-sign him after he took over at Chelsea. But John, who played 58 League matches for Swindon, chose Hammers instead. Classy and composed in possession with good vision, he was naturally left-footed although could perform well with both feet and had the knack of losing opponents with a rapid change of direction. Missed the start of the 1994/95 season due to an ankle injury but soon established himself as a favourite after making his debut at Norwich City (August 27, 1994). Ironically his first, match-winning, goal for West Ham came at… Chelsea! (October 2, 1994). John made 35 League and Cup appearances and scored three goals in that initial season at Upton Park in what was a tantalising foretaste of the enthusiasm, commitment and 100 per cent effort

to come from a man with a big heart. But there would be disappointments along the way, as in 1995/96 when, after playing in the first 12 League games, the demons of injuries and suspensions reared their familiar heads to restrict Moncs to just nine matches that term. The following season saw him back to his best and virtually running the midfield. In 32 outings he showed his true worth to the team, harassing, haranguing and hassling the opposition at every opportunity, while chipping in with the vital strikes in 1-0 home and away victories over Leicester City. By now a great crowd favourite, he was also building a reputation as the joker in the West Ham pack and the chief instigator of a number of hilarious practical jokes and pranks. No dressing-room was quiet when Moncs was about! Although the original chirpy cockney character who always had a gag at the ready, John must have felt the opposite at times when he seemed to be spending more time on the bench than off it, but typically he never let the team down when called upon and remained ever popular with the fans who'd accorded him cult status with his own song to boot: "He's here, he's there, he's every f@*&!ng where, John Moncur, John Moncur." And how he loved conducting his orchestra! Joker he may have been, but no one was more serious about the game and the West Ham cause than John Moncur. He could easily be one of the traditional West Ham characters Tony Gale laments the passing of in his thought-provoking foreword to this book and one of the last to clock up over 200 appearances and almost ten years' service to West Ham United FC. John has confounded many of his fans, friends and former team-mates by shedding his "bad boy" image to become a committed born-again Christian.

MOORE, Bobby OBE   1958-73

Born: Barking, London, 12.4.41
League apps: 544 (24 goals)
Cup apps: 98 (3 goals)

WITHOUT QUESTION, THE greatest Hammer of all time and, at his peak, the finest defender in the world. No British footballer was more revered or loved by the nation than the legendary Bobby Moore. As captain, he led Hammers to FA Cup victory in 1964 and, their biggest triumph, the European Cup Winners' Cup a year later. But on a hot summer's day in 1966, Bobby was back at Wembley – an arena he graced with such distinction so many times – for his finest achievement… leading England to their first, and only, World Cup Final victory over West Germany. It was a measure of the great man's immense stature, not only in football but in life itself, that his tragic and untimely death in February 1993, aged only 51, was mourned by millions all over the world. Quite simply, Moore, capped 108 times by his country, was a sporting hero, a player of incomparable style and grace both on and off the pitch. Yet he achieved every major honour – apart from a League Championship medal – despite not being particularly naturally gifted. He reached the pinnacle and earned the respect and admiration of the people through sheer hard work and dedication. Robert Frederick Chelsea Moore was born at 43 Waverley Gardens, Barking, on April 12, 1941, the only child of Robert Edward and Doris. He attended nearby Westbury School and began to play for a local Saturday morning side, South Park Boys, in the Ilford League. Rather short and a little on the tubby side, young Bobby did well enough in his centre-half role without, at that stage, showing signs of greatness. His first notable honour was winning the Crisp Shield as captain of Barking Primary Schools and he went on to represent Leyton Schools, while a pupil at Leyton's Tom Hood High School, and Essex. Bobby, typically, was usually successful at whatever he attempted, and he might have gone on to become a top cricketer rather than develop in football. Although Ted Fenton was manager at the time and Wally St Pier chief scout, it is understood that a local scout, Jack Turner (who would later become involved in some of Moore's earliest business dealings), filed the first report on the blond youngster after being alerted by sports master, Tom Russell. It went something like: "He looks fairly useful but won't set the world alight." He was duly invited along to West Ham who had founded a new youth policy to challenge the likes of Chelsea and Spurs. Under the watchful eye of influential senior pro Malcolm Allison, Moore attended coaching sessions at Upton Park on Tuesday and Thursday evenings. He was not the most outstanding kid around. But Moore, a quiet, modest boy, listened and learned under Mal. His thirst for greater knowledge of the game impressed the senior pros. He might have lacked pace but even at that young age, Bobby perfected the art of reading the game, positioning himself so that any weaknesses he had were rarely exposed. His awareness of team-mates and opponents alike was uncanny, even then. It was easy to see why Bobby had such great respect for that other footballing visionary, Fulham's Johnny Haynes. Bobby made his debut for England Youth against Holland in Amsterdam (October 2, 1957) while continuing to develop in Hammers' Metropolitan League side. West Ham had created its own highly acclaimed Youth Academy and Moore was rapidly becoming head boy. Ironically, his big chance came at the expense of his mentor, Allison, who, in November 1957, was diagnosed as having tuberculosis. West Ham went on to win promotion to Division One at the end of that season and the big time beckoned for

Moore. With Allison still struggling to find a way back via the reserves, and fellow half-backs Bill Lansdowne and Andy Nelson both injured, Bobby was thrust into the spotlight for the first time when Manchester United visited Upton Park on the night of Monday, September 8, 1958. Noel Cantwell, the senior member of the team, was consulted by manager Fenton about who to pick at left-half to face United. The choice was between the vastly experienced, but still not fully fit, Allison, or the up-and-coming Moore. Cantwell jeopardised his long-time close friendship with Allison by recommending the kid. At the age of 17, Bobby had arrived on the big stage, playing his part in a 3-2 win in front of 35,672 fans. He wore the number 6 shirt, the one he later made famous, on just four more occasions that season, as first Nelson and then Johnny Smith reclaimed it. Bobby had to wait until the 13th League match of 1959/60 before being called upon and only 12 more appearances followed that term. But after Smith was transferred to Tottenham, Bobby started the 1960/61 campaign and never looked back. When Ron Greenwood arrived in 1961 to take over from Fenton, it was the

start of the most golden era in West Ham's history. Greenwood wanted to build his side around Moore and did so to great effect in the mid-1960s. Although never in serious contention for the Championship, West Ham won many new friends away from east London with their exciting brand of attacking football. They beat Preston North End 3-2 in the Final of the 1964 FA Cup, although it was perhaps the 3-1 Semi-final victory over Manchester United, on a rain-soaked Hillsborough pitch, that really signalled West Ham's emergence as a major force that decade. Moore played at his immaculate best to outwit a star-studded United side boasting superstars such as Charlton, Law and Best. The victory over Preston, although not a vintage Hammers' performance, put the seal on a remarkable season for Bobby who, 48 hours before the Final, was named Footballer of the Year. At 23, he was the youngest-ever recipient of the annual football writers' award. A year later, and he was back at Wembley to lead West Ham to a glorious 2-0 win over TSV Munich 1860 in the European Cup Winners' Cup Final. That performance against the Germans is ranked by many as West Ham's finest ever, and they became only the second English club (after Tottenham in 1963) to lift the coveted trophy. Greenwood also helped Moore progress along the international ladder in his early years, as coach of England Youth and Under-23 teams. Bobby earned a surprise late call-up to England's World Cup squad for the 1962 tournament in Chile. It was in the last friendly game in the build up to the finals, in Lima, Peru on Sunday, May 20, that manager Walter Winterbottom gave the 21-year-old West Ham defender his full international debut, in a half-back line that also included another debutant, Maurice Norman, and Ron Flowers. Despite his inexperience, Moore gave his customary assured performance in a fine 4-0 victory in which his old mate Jimmy Greaves scored a hat-trick after Flowers had

given England the lead from the penalty spot. It was the launch of a glittering international career for Bobby, who played in all four of England's World Cup matches in 1962. Winterbottom gave Moore his first taste of top-class international football, but it was obviously Alf Ramsey – appointed in February 1963 – who reaped the richest reward of having such a quality defender and leader at his disposal. Bobby, who had married Tina by this time, flourished under Ramsey – two men, both calm and sometimes detached from the pack, who came from neighbouring towns, Barking and Dagenham. Together, they would conquer the world. Ramsey immediately identified Moore's leadership qualities and when Jimmy Armfield was injured, he had no qualms about handing him England's World Cup captaincy. He played every game of the 1966 tournament against a background of unrest at West Ham, where his future was far from settled. In his authorised biography, *Bobby Moore, The Life and Times of a Sporting Hero*, by Jeff Powell, Bobby revealed that he was at loggerheads with Greenwood over his contract and refused to sign a new one. So, for seven days between June 30 and the start of the World Cup Finals on July 7, he was unregistered to an English club! As Powell put it: "Legally, he did not exist as a player in the eyes of the Football Association, whose team he was about to lead into the World Cup Finals." Moore actually signed a temporary one-month agreement so that he was eligible to play in soccer's showpiece event. More importantly for Hammers, Greenwood refused to sanction a possible move to Spurs, who were keen to sign him. But the professional manner in which he coped with the distraction of his contract dispute in 1966 was nothing compared to the personal crisis that threatened

Clockwise from below: Hurst, left, and Moore, centre background, hail Peters' goal, which put England 2-1 up in the World Cup Final versus West Germany at Wembley in 1966; Bobby Moore and Uwe Seeler watch the toss up; Moore helps to thwart a West Germany attack

his preparations for the 1970 Finals in Mexico. Bobby was falsely accused of stealing a bracelet while in Bogota, Colombia with the England party and was held under house arrest, just days before the tournament began. Once cleared of all charges, Bobby proceeded to produce one of his classic defensive performances against the brilliant Brazilians, who went on to win the final after Ramsey's title defence had ended at the hands of West Germany in the Quarter-finals. The only other time Moore came close to leaving Upton Park, before his eventual departure to Fulham in 1974, was a year earlier than that. Controversial Derby County manager Brian Clough tabled a bid for Moore and Trevor Brooking, but a mooted £400,000 deal was again blocked by Greenwood – much to Moore's dismay at the time. Many people inside the game were surprised that he spent so long with Hammers who, after losing the 1966 European Cup Winners' Cup Semi-final, slid into decline and a long period of under-achievement. They possessed England's famous World Cup trio but, for all their flair and entertaining football, were often regarded as a soft touch by opponents and failed to mount a serious bid for the First Division Championship. Moore was the supreme individual during a golden era for English football – he became an overnight superstar, rubbing shoulders with famous film stars, politicians and other big name celebrities. Yet the club he captained were never in contention for the title, and the highest they finished under him was sixth, in season 1972/73. Ironically, it was "Mooro's" last full season in the claret and blue number 6 shirt. He was ever-present, but the team was in a period of transition. Many of the old favourites had already gone – Peters to Spurs and Hurst to Stoke City, who had prevented West Ham from reaching the League Cup Final in 1972. That dramatic Semi-final marathon with the Potters was memorable for Hurst's penalty miss (or rather, a stunning Gordon Banks save) and Moore's decision to take over the goalkeeper's shirt after Bobby Ferguson was injured in the third game at Old Trafford. He even managed to push out Mike Bernard's penalty, who luckily hit home the rebound! Yet Hammers followed their promising 1972/73 campaign with a more typical battle against relegation the following season. Bobby played in 22 League and two Cup matches in 1973/74 but his career at West Ham and for England was drawing to a close. His errors were so rare

that the mistake that proved costly in Poland, in the World Cup qualifier of 1973, was magnified and he was dropped for the first time by Ramsey for the decisive return clash at Wembley later that year. Then, ironically, it was a blunder by Bobby's replacement, Norman Hunter, which finally ended England's bid to reach the 1974 finals in Germany. Ramsey first awarded the captaincy to Moore for the game against Czechoslovakia in Bratislava on May 20, 1963. It was only his 12th senior international but he was well equipped for the task of leading his country. He always did so with immense pride and dignity. The notable victory over the 1962 losing World Cup Finalists was England's first under the Ramsey regime – and note the scoreline… 4-2. A similar result, on July 30, 1966, would catapult Moore and Ramsey to legendary status in world football. For that was the afternoon on which England defeated West Germany in extra-time of the 1966 World Cup Final. Moore set up the first and third goals for his West Ham team-mate Geoff Hurst, who claimed a unique hat-trick, while the other goal was netted by the third member of Hammers' heroic trio, Martin Peters. Moore led the red-shirted England team up the steps to collect the Jules Rimet trophy from Her Majesty the Queen. And typical of the gentleman of football, after all the drama of the occasion, he still had the presence of mind to wipe mud from his hands before accepting football's ultimate prize! But then Moore was always unflappable. Bobby's 108th – and last – England cap was a friendly versus Italy at Wembley (November 14, 1973). It was a record haul – and still is for an outfield player – and was bettered only by goalkeeper Peter Shilton's 125. Bobby's last-ever first team appearance for West Ham was against little Hereford United in the FA Cup Third Round at Upton Park on Saturday, January 5, 1974. Bobby sustained the worst injury of his illustrious career in that game – twisted knee ligaments that forced him out of the reckoning for eight weeks. The relatively unknown Mick McGiven eventually took over the celebrated number 6

shirt and a series of good performances by the Geordie helped Hammers to avoid the drop. Bobby's dispute with Greenwood over his chance to join Cloughie at Derby dragged on into the early weeks of 1974, a period when Ron decided to take more of a back seat and hand first team responsibilities to John Lyall. Moore had no problem with Lyall but he knew that his days were numbered at West Ham. He was "angered" by the Board's refusal to grant him a free transfer at the end of the season and to seek a fee of £25,000 instead. There was no shortage of interest in Bobby from the Second Division, including Norwich City, who were then managed by former West Ham team-mate John Bond, and Portsmouth. Bobby hoped that Crystal Palace, managed by his old mentor Malcolm Allison, would come in for him, but it was Fulham boss Alec Stock who eventually signed the Upton Park colossus on the March 14 transfer deadline day. After 16 years and a remarkable record of 642 first team games, 544 in the top flight, and 98 in various cups, Moore's final game for the club was a nondescript reserve fixture against Plymouth Argyle at Upton Park. Bobby's first appearance for Fulham doubled the Craven Cottage crowd to 18,000 for the visit of Middlesbrough (March 19, 1974). A disastrous debut (4-0 home defeat) was soon forgotten, though, as the following season Moore and another vastly experienced former England international, Alan Mullery, inspired revitalised Fulham to their first FA Cup Final appearance. Their Wembley opponents on Saturday, May 3, 1975? Who else but West Ham! Fulham won the support of the neutrals with their flair and ambition, but the dream was ruined by Hammers' two-goal hero Alan Taylor. Moore could cope with the disappointment probably better than any other player in white. After all, Wembley was his second home and he had been there often enough and done it more often than the rest. They were happy days at Craven Cottage, enjoying the twilight of his playing career alongside Mullery and, later, two of the game's great entertainers, George Best and Rodney Marsh. The last of Bobby's 124 League and 26 Cup appearances for the west London club, over a four-season period, came at Blackburn Rovers (May 14, 1977). It was his 668th in the Football League and, including England, West Ham and Fulham appearances, his 1000th in all competitions. Incidentally, Bobby was only once used by Hammers in the role of substitute – when he replaced Bobby Howe in a home game versus Derby County (February 6, 1971). Bobby knew his own value to West Ham and fought hard for what he believed he was worth, even during his younger days after Hammers lifted the FA Cup in 1964 when he held out for improved contract terms for the first time. He was estimated to be earning about £60 per week at that time, although he was among the country's most highly paid players at an estimated £200 per week by 1972. He tried to lay the foundations for his future by pursuing a number of wide-ranging business interests, including ownership of a sports shop opposite the Boleyn Ground in the 1960s. Commercially, he was a very attractive commodity and, with the help of trusted agent Jack Turner, he earned as much from advertising and product endorsement, newspaper and magazine columns, as he did playing football for club and country. Not all of his business ventures were a success, though, and after some costly investments turned sour, he reverted again to football for a fresh challenge. In the summer of 1976, aged 35, Bobby joined other greats, such as Pele, in the rich North American Soccer League. He spent one season with Texas-based San Antonio Thunder and then, in 1978, a spell with Seattle Sounders. In between, he returned to England for one more season with Fulham. When his playing days were finally ended at the age of 36, Moore wanted desperately to stay in football. But, for all his incredible talent and experience, Bobby received few offers. He had to settle for a brief managerial stint in tandem with former West Ham team-mate Harry Redknapp at non-League Oxford City between 1979 and 1981. With nothing on offer at home, Mooro went to Hong Kong for six months in 1983 to coach Eastern Athletic. Between June 1984 and April 1986 he tried in vain to make a go of management at Southend United, but presided over relegation in his first year and 20th position in the Fourth Division in his second, although a boardroom battle did nothing to help matters. Despite having the backing of the directors, and with two years of his contract still to run, he decided to resign three games from the end of 1985/86 and turn instead to promotions work as well as reporting for the controversial new *Sunday Sport* newspaper. His Roots Hall connections were not entirely severed, though, because he agreed to serve on the board and was still club president right up until his death. Divorced from Tina early in 1986, Bobby found true love again with the new lady in his life, air stewardess Stephanie Parlane-Moore, whom he had met several years earlier on a flight to South Africa. Bobby's football interests were rekindled in 1990 when he joined London radio station Capital Gold as their match analyst for the World Cup Finals in Italy. Bobby was back but his career behind the microphone would be cruelly cut short. In the spring of 1991 came the news that he was suffering cancer of the colon, which had spread to his liver. It was terminal. But Bobby Moore had never resisted a battle and he wouldn't this time either. He kept the tragic news a secret from all but his closest family, daughter Roberta

and son Dean, and friends. He continued to cope with chemotherapy and radiotherapy, enjoy a round of golf, swim and live as normally as possible. He didn't want pity, only as much enjoyment of life as possible in the short time he knew he had left. In December 1991, Bobby married Stephanie at a private ceremony at Chelsea Register Office. On February 15, 1993 came the first public announcement of his illness. Two days later he attended Wembley Stadium for the last time, commentating for Capital Gold on England's 6-0 World Cup qualifying victory over San Marino. Exactly a week later, early on Wednesday, February 24, 1993, Bobby died peacefully, surrounded by his family, at home in Battersea. A private funeral service was held at Putney Vale Crematorium on March 2, but a much bigger memorial was happening in east London and right across the globe. West Ham supporters had lost their favourite son and the tributes came flooding in. Upton Park, its main gates covered in scarves, hats, mascots, mementoes and flowers, became a shrine. Some kept a vigil at the main entrance, where men, women and children wept in memory and respect for the greatest player the club had ever seen. Many made the pilgrimage to Sunderland for Hammers' next match, and West Ham's next home game against Wolves (March 6, 1993) became a tearful occasion. Fans came on to the pitch to lay flowers on the centre-spot, while Greenwood, Hurst and Peters carried a giant wreath designed in the form of the number 6 shirt, which was not worn by a West Ham player that day. The West Ham directors, criticised in some quarters for ignoring Moore's immense contribution to the club after he left 20 years earlier, were eager to make amends. They announced that the new South Stand would be named after him and prior to the home game versus Chelsea (October 2, 1993), Stephanie Moore sealed a time capsule, containing items of memorabilia relating to her husband's career, in the foundations of the new two-tier, all-seater stand. And Hammers turned back the clock again (March 7, 1994) when the stand's official opening ceremony was performed by Bobby's team-mates from the Cup-winning sides of 1964 and 1965, prior to the Memorial Match between West Ham and a Premier League XI. Ten years after his tragically premature and untimely death from cancer at the age of 51 in February 1993, former West Ham United and England captain Bobby Moore OBE was still making headlines. On March 7, 2003 the *Daily Mirror* informed its readership of something that many of them had known for 33 years… Bobby Moore was innocent! That's how long it had taken Whitehall to release secret files held in the Public Records office to officially clear his name of having anything to do with the disappearance of a £600 gold bracelet in Bogota, Columbia prior to the 1970 World Cup Finals in May 1970. England's preparations

for the Finals in Mexico were severely disrupted by their skipper's subsequent arrest, but the documents released by the Foreign Office revealed that the police quickly established that Bobby had no part in the crime and knew the identity of the prime suspect – a woman who was hawking the trinket around her underworld contacts trying to sell it. On June 11, 1970 – after Bobby had been released from four days house arrest to rejoin his team-mates – a British embassy official wrote to the Foreign Office: "The police have traced the bracelet, which has been hawked around the underworld during the last week. They have also established the identity of the thief, a woman, and hope to make an arrest soon. The antecedents of the jeweller and his witnesses have been thoroughly scrutinised and some suspicious circumstances established." The official also had assurances that the discredited witnesses would be pursued and it transpired that not even the head of Columbia's police believed Moore was guilty. Moore's lawyer, Dr Vicente Laverde, believed police had "very strong" evidence for perjury charges against some of Bobby's accusers. Released after the personal intervention of Prime Minister Harold Wilson in time to participate in England's opening fixture against Romania, Bobby hoped he'd heard the last of the matter, but the investigation dragged on to long after the World Cup Finals were over and there were fears that the case could be bogged down by the country's notoriously slow legal system. In an entirely unsatisfactory sequel on August 21, 1970, an embassy official wrote: "It is not the opinion of judges but public opinion which largely decides whether an individual is innocent or not. Dr Laverde feels the publication of recent police evidence has convinced public opinion in Columbia that Moore is innocent." In what amounted to a damming indictment of Columbia's judicial system it seemed Moore's worldwide popularity had played in his favour. But it was two and a half years before a Columbian judge said Moore had no case to answer. Ironically, Bobby's name was in the headlines again 11 years and one month to the day of his sad passing when the famous number 6 shirt he wore against Brazil in that never-to-be-forgotten group game in Mexico came under the hammer at Christie's auction house in South Kensington. Yes, *the* shirt that our hero swapped for Pele's after the epic confrontation at Guadalajara. The specifically designed white airtex number 6 shirt, complete with mud and sweat stains from the game was snapped up by former dental surgeon turned collector Steve Gilbert for a cool £60,000. Thankfully, going by his comments after the sale, Steve realised the intrinsic value of what he'd bought: "I am very pleased. It is the connection that Bobby Moore, the captain of England, had exchanged this shirt with Pele – the greatest of all players. That

Career record										
	League		**FAC**		**LC**		**Europe**		**Total**	
Played	**App**	**Gls**	**App**	**Gls**	**App**	**Gls**	**App**	**Gls**	**App**	**Gls**
1958-59	5	0	0	0	0	0	0	0	5	0
1959-60	13	0	0	0	0	0	0	0	13	0
1960-61	38	1	2	0	2	1	0	0	42	2
1961-62	41	3	1	0	2	0	0	0	44	3
1962-63	41	3	5	0	1	0	0	0	47	3
1963-64	37	2	7	0	6	0	0	0	50	2
1964-65	28	1	0	0	0	0	7	0	35	1
1965-66	37	0	4	0	9	2	6	0	56	2
1966-67	40	2	2	0	6	0	0	0	48	2
1967-68	40	4	3	0	3	0	0	0	46	4
1968-69	41	2	3	0	3	0	0	0	47	2
1969-70	40	0	1	0	2	0	0	0	43	0
1970-71	39	2	1	0	2	0	0	0	42	2
1971-72	40	1	4	0	10	0	0	0	54	1
1972-73	42	3	2	0	2	0	0	0	46	3
1973-74	22	0	1	0	1	0	0	0	24	0
TOTAL	**544**	**24**	**36**	**0**	**49**	**3**	**13**	**0**	**642**	**27**

particular embrace is one of the greatest images of football. It is probably the second important shirt there is." The most prized sporting possession, he maintains, is Moore's famous red 1966 World Cup winning shirt. In 1999, a shirt made for the England captain's 1966 Final was auctioned for £44,000, the actual one Bobby wore remains elsewhere. In a strange coincidence the same Christie's sale also boasted the "Jason Leonard Rugby World Cup 2003 Shirt Collection" for auction to the highest bidder. Which leads us to ask the question: What is it about Barking? Bobby Moore OBE, England's most honoured outfield player with 108 caps; Sir Trevor Brooking MBE with 47 caps for his country; and Jason Leonard MBE, a Rugby World Cup winner and proud record-holder of the most international caps of any player in the world... all hail from the little Essex town now hopelessly swallowed up by London's great urban sprawl. From the outside it hardly looks like a hotbed of sport with its grim tower blocks and mean side streets, but its output of world-renowned sporting heroes is second to none, which brings us to 43 Waverly Gardens. The most famous building in Barking, the house where Bobby Moore was born, was sold in 2003 for the relatively modest sum of £157,000. The fully modernised three-bedroom end of terrace had been home for the previous six years to Mark Concannon and family, but they left London and sold the property to a relation for three times the amount they paid for it. "When we moved in I jokingly thought of selling the lawn for £5 per square foot. Not being a football fan I thought there might be others who would appreciate the hallowed ground where Bobby took his first kicks more than me. My brother-in-law, who bought the property, is seriously considering contacting the Football Association to try and get a plaque installed at the house." A great idea but given the FA's scandalous lack of recognition towards Bobby after he quit football, the chances of Barking acquiring its first Blue Plaque are probably slim to say the least. Nearby, in East Ham, residents adjacent to Flanders Road playing field were thrilled to hear that a £300,000 grant had been awarded from the lottery cash distributor Sport England to reinstate Flanders Field to its former glory, as would befit a ground where West Ham scouts first discovered Bobby Moore. A community sports development officer, Peter Laing has been appointed, who hopes to raise funds to rebuild the changing rooms that were burnt down. He said: "This is a great opportunity to bring Flanders Field back to the community and perhaps discover some more

stars like Bobby!" Bobby's widow, Stephanie Moore OBE, has toiled tirelessly since his death raising funds for the charity off-shoot she instigated, the Bobby Moore fund for Cancer Research UK and it's good to see lottery money being put to good use and perpetuating the legacy of Flanders Field. Since the tenth anniversary of his death, Bobby has had the honour of having a statue depicting himself, Martin Peters, Geoff Hurst, and Ramon Wilson celebrating England's 1966 World Cup victory unveiled by none less a personage than HRH the Duke of York, a national newspaper campaign for the new Wembley Stadium to be named in his honour and been elected England's greatest ever footballer in an FA internet poll to earn a place in the UEFA Hall of Fame. Long may his legend continue.

England caps: 1962 vs Peru, Hungary, Argentina, Bulgaria, Brazil, France, Northern Ireland, Wales; 1963 vs France, Scotland, Brazil, Czechoslovakia, East Germany, Switzerland, Wales, Rest of the World, Northern Ireland; 1964 vs Scotland, Uruguay, Portugal (twice), Republic of Ireland, Brazil, Argentina, Northern Ireland, Belgium; 1965 vs Scotland, Hungary, Yugoslavia, West Germany, Sweden, Wales, Austria, Northern Ireland, Spain; 1966 vs Poland (twice), West Germany (twice), Scotland, Norway, Denmark, Uruguay, Mexico, France, Argentina, Portugal, Northern Ireland, Czechoslovakia, Wales; 1967 vs Scotland, Spain, Austria, Wales, Northern Ireland, USSR; 1968 vs Scotland, Spain (twice), Sweden, West Germany, Yugoslavia, USSR, Romania, Bulgaria; 1969 vs France, Northern Ireland, Wales, Scotland, Mexico, Uruguay, Brazil, Holland, Portugal; 1970 vs Belgium, Wales, Northern Ireland, Scotland, Colombia, Ecuador, Romania, Brazil, Czechoslovakia, West Germany, East Germany; 1971 vs Greece (twice), Malta, Northern Ireland, Scotland, Switzerland (twice); 1972 vs West Germany (twice), Wales (twice), Scotland, Yugoslavia; 1973 vs Northern Ireland, Wales (twice), Scotland (twice), Czechoslovakia, Poland, USSR, Italy (twice) (108).

Left to right: Alan Sealey, Bobby Moore, Peter Brabrook and Jackie Burkett in training at West Ham Stadium prior to the 1964 FA Cup Final

MONTEITH, Hugh
1900-02

Born: New Cumnock, Ayrshire, Scotland, 1875
SL apps: 53
Cup apps: 7

HUGHIE BEGAN HIS career with one of Glasgow Celtic's nursery sides, Parkhead Juniors, and subsequently joined the famous Glasgow club. Staying at Celtic Park for just one season, he then moved south to join Loughboro Corinthians, and from there transferred to Bristol City for their first season as professionals, where he was regarded as one of the finest net-minders in the country. It was from the West Country club that the able custodian joined Hammers in the dawn of the Edwardian era, and at the very beginning of their existence under the banner of West Ham United FC. The goals against column totalled a miserly 28 in the club's first season, seven of which were conceded during Hugh's five absences that campaign. The following season saw the well-built Scotsman miss only one match, and again the debit account stayed on 28. A fine record, and one that Football League clubs were quick to notice. His growing reputation led to his transfer to Bury – then a force to be reckoned with – and his appearance for the Shakers in the 1903 FA Cup Final at Crystal Palace versus Derby County. The 6-0 scoreline in favour of the Lancastrians remains as a record margin of victory in a Final.

See pages 142-146 for Bobby Moore

MOORE, Brian
1954-55

Born: Belfast, Northern Ireland, 29.12.33
League apps: 9 (1 goal)

A BALL-PLAYING NORTHERN Irish inside-forward, who had his promising career tragically terminated by injury. Signed from Glentoran in February 1955, he was granted a joint testimonial along with team-mate Geoff Hallas, who suffered a similar fate.

MOORE, Ian
1977

Born: Birkenhead, Merseyside, 26.8.76
League apps: 1

THE SON OF former Tranmere Rovers coach and now Rotherham United manager Ronnie Moore, Ian began his career at Tranmere (76 apps, 13 goals) in 1994 but was signed by acting Nottingham Forest manager and later Hammer Stuart Pearce, after a short loan spell with Bradford City, for £1 million in March 1997. Unable to oust twin strikers Pierre Van Hooijdonk and Kevin Campbell from Forest's first team he was loaned to West Ham at the end of September 1997, but made just one appearance from the bench in the 2-1 defeat at Leicester City the following month before returning to the City ground. He has since proved himself to be a very able striker, though sometimes playing deep or out wide. Since serving Hammers for that solitary subs outing he has enjoyed a successful career with Stockport County whom he joined for £800,000 in July 1998 and scored 23 goals in 104 appearances, and Burnley whom he joined for £1 million in November 2000 and had scored 44 times in 175 appearances up to the end of 2003/04. He has been particularly successful in the FA Cup for the Clarets, scoring ten times in 13 ties.

MOORE, Tommy
1898-1901

Born: Stoke, Staffordshire, 1877
SL apps (TIW): 48
SL apps (WHU): 4
Cup apps: 10

A SORT OF Bruce Grobbelaar character of his day, Tom was nicknamed the "Dancing Dervish" because of his unorthodox methods in evading challenging forwards. Despite having his critics, he managed to attain a fair level of consistency during Hammers' last two seasons as Thames Ironworks, missing only two Southern League matches in that time. Although called up for the second match of the 1900/01 season against his former club Millwall, a 3-1 mauling from the Lions did little to help him wrest the first team spot away from the more experienced Hughie Monteith, and a 4-1 home defeat, inflicted by London rivals Spurs on February 16, 1901, signalled the end of his tenure at the Memorial Grounds. Dispatched to little Essex side Grays, Tommy seemed destined for obscurity, but football, and the FA Cup in particular, has a habit of throwing up opportunities to prove past masters wrong. Tom got, and took, his chance the very next season, when his inspired display of goalkeeping was largely responsible for the Essex village team's shock 2-1 Second Qualifying Round win over West Ham, on a foggy November afternoon at the Memorial Grounds.

MOORE, William "Billy"
1922-29

Born: Newcastle-upon-Tyne, Tyne & Wear, 6.10.1894
League apps: 181 (42 goals)
Cup apps: 21 (6 goals)

ANOTHER FAMOUS MOORE from an earlier era, Billy joined Hammers from Sunderland in 1922, where he'd struck up a renowned left-wing partnership with England international H Martin after joining from Seaton Dalaval. His arrival at Upton Park heralded the beginning of an even more famous liaison with the immortal Jimmy Ruffell and, in an age when exceptional inside-forwards were commonplace, Billy shone as brightly as any of his contemporaries. After winning amateur caps against Belgium, Denmark and Sweden, he gained full England international honours versus the latter country, scoring twice, shortly after appearing in the first Wembley Cup Final in 1923, and further distinguished himself as an ever-present in West Ham's promotion side in his eventful first season at the Boleyn. Although recognised as a maker rather than taker of goals during his eight seasons as a West Ham player, Billy was not one to pass up scoring opportunities when they arose, as amply confirmed by his near half-century of goals while in the claret and blue. Appointed assistant trainer when he retired from playing in 1929, he was promoted to trainer-in-chief in 1932 and remained in that capacity until his full retirement in 1960. Two years earlier, he'd realised his greatest personal ambition in seeing Hammers return to the First Division after an absence of 25 years. Living in nearby Plashet Road, Billy and his wife were regular visitors to Upton Park throughout the 1960s and, indeed, journeyed on many away trips, on which Bill often acted as unofficial courier, making sure everyone was accounted for on the coach that carried club officials and guests.

It was a sad day for West Ham United, and the game of football in general, when Billy died on September 26, 1968 at the age of 73.

England cap: 1923 vs Sweden (1).

MORGAN, Nicky
1979-83

Born: Eltham, London, 30.10.59
League apps: 21 (2 goals)
Cup apps: 4

A USEFUL STRIKER who was unable to win a regular place in the first team. He signed apprentice professional in July 1976, full pro in October 1977. Nicky made his League bow against Luton Town in April 1979 and gained invaluable experience on the Continent when loaned out to Hammers' 1976 Cup Winners' Cup opponents – Den Haag – during 1981/82, scoring seven goals in 16 appearances for the Dutch club. He returned to England to play for Portsmouth where he scored 32 times in 95 games between 1982 and 1986 before transferring to Stoke City where he made 88 appearances and scored 20 goals. He joined Bristol City in 1989 and continued his strike rate in the West Country, where he appeared in well over 100 League matches and teamed up with ex-Hammer Leroy Rosenior. It was four vital strikes by Morgan that were largely responsible for City's second place finish behind bitter rivals Bristol Rovers in the Third Division in 1989/90 to secure promotion to the Second Division. His goals against Preston North End, Fulham, Huddersfield Town and Walsall enabled City to grab the runners-up spot just two points behind the Pirates' tally of 93. The following season Nicky scored against Hammers in the 1-1 draw at Ashton Gate and finished the season as the Robins' top scorer with 17 goals.

MORLEY, Trevor   1989-95

Born: Nottingham, Nottinghamshire, 20.3.61
League apps: 178 (57 goals)
Cup apps: 37 (13 goals)

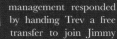

A HARD-WORKING, BUSTLING striker who proved a shrewd signing by Lou Macari when he swapped Mark Ward for Manchester City's Morley and Ian Bishop in December 1989. Apart from 1991/92, when he was often out of favour and started only 13 matches of the First Division relegation campaign, Morley has registered double figures each season and was leading scorer in 1990/91, 1992/93 and 1993/94 with 12, 20 and 13 goals respectively. A target man who relished a physical battle, Morley's unstinting efforts were recognised by the fans who voted him Hammer of the Year for 1993/94. The son of a former Nottingham Forest player, Trevor was rejected by Derby County as a youngster and forced to prove himself in non-League circles with Corby Town and Nuneaton Borough (where he won a Southern League championship medal in 1982), while also running a fruit and veg market stall. He gained League status initially with Northampton Town, who signed him for £20,000 in the summer of 1985. Trevor made his debut at Burnley (August 17, 1985) and helped Cobblers to win the Fourth Division championship in 1986/87 – the second of his three seasons with the Midlands club. After scoring 39 League goals in 107 appearances for Northampton, Morley was signed by Manchester City manager Mel Machin for £175,000 in January 1988, and he contributed 12 vital goals in just 15 games to boost City's promotion from Division Two that season. He scored a dozen League goals in the top flight and added two more in the opening 17 games of 1989/90 before he was involved in the shock swap deal. Machin became one of chairman Peter Swales's many managerial casualties and his replacement at Maine Road, Howard Kendall, saw no place for either Morley or Bishop in his new set-up. West Ham should be pleased that he didn't, because both of the former City crowd favourites were a big success. Morley and Bishop both made their Hammers debut at Leicester City (December 30, 1989), although they were ineligible for the Littlewoods Cup run that was ended agonisingly at the Semi-final stage by Oldham Athletic. Morley's goals played a large part in the promotion campaigns of 1990/91 and 1992/93 and it is a measure of his resilience that he won his place back despite the subsequent arrival of fellow strikers Iain Dowie, Mike Small and Clive Allen. It seemed at one stage that Morley would be leaving to join Watford in a £100,000 deal, but he stayed at Upton Park, reclaimed a regular first team place and went on to make a mockery of that proposed fee by leading the scorechart on West Ham's return to the top flight in 1993/94. Indeed, it was a big blow when he had to undergo a cartilage operation soon after the start of the 1994/95 Premiership season. Strong and ever willing to work hard for the team cause, Morley was a striker whose goals were scored from all angles and varying distances. His ability to "hold the ball up", often under extreme pressure from close-marking defenders, led Billy Bonds and Harry Redknapp to play Morley in a lone striker's role on numerous occasions. Married to a Norwegian girl, Morley had previously spent the English close season playing in Norway for Brann. But the 1993/94 season was destined to be a high watermark for Morley's West Ham career as he went from hero to zero during an injury-plagued 1994/95 campaign when he failed to score a single goal in 16 League and Cup appearances. The Hammers management responded by handing Trev a free transfer to join Jimmy Quinn at First Division Reading where the ex-Hammers striker was combining the jobs of joint manager and top scorer. He welcomed the support he got from his new strike partner though and West Ham fans were wondering if the cunning old fox Harry Redknapp had made a rare error in letting Morley go as tales of his human battering-ram attempts to score goals for the Royals filtered back to Upton Park on the football grapevine. Scoring on his debut with a bullet-header in a 3-2 win against Derby County, the unlucky but plucky striker suffered a fractured skull in only his third match against Portsmouth at Fratton Park and subsequently had to have a steel plate inserted in his head. It was an injury that would have had lesser men reaching for their insurance policy, but after a long lay-off he bravely returned to score five goals in seven games at the turn of the year. In 1996/97, Trevor was back to his best with 23 goals including a hat-trick against the eventual champions Bolton Wanderers, which probably clinched him the Player of the Season award from the grateful Elm Park fans. Forced to miss the start of 1997/98, due to an injury against Barnsley in the last game of the previous campaign, the now veteran centre-forward still returned a creditable nine goals from 27 games, saving his best efforts for the cup-ties and most notably two in the shock 3-2 Coca Cola Cup win against Leeds United at Elland Road. This writer remembers thinking that Hammers would have been better off keeping Morley on hearing of his goalscoring exploits against Leeds, especially as the striker bought to replace him at Upton Park – Iain Dowie – was experiencing one of the longest goal droughts in football at the time! But the Trevor Morley show was nearly over, on these shores at least, as at the end of the season he announced his decision to move to the country of his wife's origin – Norway. At home among the fjords he completed another summer season playing for Brann and a short stint with Sognal before retiring in 1998. He then went into the property business, but with football still very much in his blood, accepted an offer from Arsenal to be the Gunners scout in Norway. In 2000, he became manager of Norwegian Fifth Division club Brann Sparta, and guided them to promotion in his first season in charge! Now the proud holder of his first coaching badge, Trevor hopes to continue in management, so watch this space! Ooh Morley, Morley!

MORONEY, Tommy   1947-53

Born: Cork, Republic of Ireland, 10.11.23
League apps: 148 (8 goals)
Cup apps: 3

ANOTHER MEMBER OF the considerable Irish contingent assembled at Upton Park in the immediate post-World War II period, Tommy was signed by manager Charlie Paynter from Cork United while still an amateur. Although an established wing-half, he also occasionally played in the forward-line before injury problems began to erode his first team outings. He moved back to Ireland with Evergreen United, later becoming manager of the other major club of his native city – Cork Hibs.
Republic of Ireland caps: 1948 vs Spain; 1949 vs Portugal, Sweden, Spain, Finland (twice), England; 1950 vs Belgium, Norway; 1951 vs Norway; 1952 vs West Germany; 1953 vs France (12).

MORRIS, Robert   1919-29

Born: Coppull, Lancashire, 1900
League apps: 3

AFTER MAKING HIS debut in Hammers' first-ever League match versus Lincoln City at Upton Park on August 30, 1919, he made two more appearances that season – in a 7-0 thrashing at Barnsley and a 1-0 defeat against Bury at Gigg Lane (where George Kay was given his marching orders). He originally joined West Ham from Preston North End, whom he had joined in turn from Crosland (Chorley). Bob left West Ham for Fleetwood, then in 1920 moved back into the Football League with Barnsley, scoring three goals in 13 appearances for the Tykes. He then had spells with Accrington Stanley (17 apps, four goals) and Lancaster Town.

MORRISON, J   1911-12

SL apps: 15 (1 goal)

THIS LEFT-WINGER PLAYED his first match for West Ham in a 0-0 draw at Plymouth (September 16, 1911). His only goal in the claret and blue came against

Tommy Moroney with Ken Wright, behind, and, in background, Almer Hall

Northampton (December 2, 1911) in a 3-2 defeat at the County Ground.

MORRISON, John — 1896-98

SL apps (TIW): 27 (6 goals)

JOINING IRONS FROM South West Ham, this forward played in all competitions in 1896/97 but made only three appearances the following season.

MORTON, William — 1895-98 TIW

Born: Walthamstow, London, March 1875

THIS TOUGH-TACKLING MIDFIELDER played a large part in the Irons' first two seasons. Morton became the first Irons player to gain representative honours when he was picked to play for Essex against Suffolk.

MOYES, James — 1919

Born: Fife, Scotland, date unknown
League apps: 2 (1 goal)

EARNED HIMSELF AN eternal place in Hammers' history when he scored the club's first-ever League goal on his debut against Lincoln City in the opening game of the 1919/20 season at Upton Park. Signed from Dundee, he made only one other League appearance, also at the Boleyn, against Rotherham County in a match West Ham won 2-1 (and had Jack Tresadern sent off). An inside-right who began his career with the Scots Guards, Jimmy returned north of the border to join Clackmannan.

MULLINS, Hayden — 2003

Born: Reading, Berkshire, 27.3.79
League apps: 69 (1 goal)
Cup apps: 9 (1 goal)

ALTHOUGH STILL ONLY 25 when Alan Pardew made him his first signing for West Ham in October 2003, this abrasive England Under-21 international midfielder had amassed 246 League and Cup appearances (20 goals) for Crystal Palace up to the end of the 2002/03 season. Almost an ever-present that campaign, Hayden was appointed club captain and voted Player of the Year at Selhurst Park before switching to east London for a fee thought to be in the region of £600,000. Pardew was quick to praise his new signing saying: "He's quick, good in the tackle, comfortable in possession and he'll bring a calmness and sureness to the side. You know you're going to get seven or eight out of ten from Hayden every game and I feel sure he'll be a good player at West Ham for a number of years." Many would argue the experienced Mullens would have been better off staying the other side of the water, given the reversal of fortunes at Palace since Iain Dowie took over. But the player remained positive after the Hammers Play-off defeat against his old club at Cardiff in May 2004 and returned to the Millennium Stadium in May 2005 to banish that bitter memory as Hammers defeated PNE to win their passport back to the Premiership.

MORTON, John — 1931-39

Born: Sheffield, Yorkshire, 26.2.14
League apps: 258 (54 goals)
Cup apps: 17 (3 goals)

THE FIRST OF Hammers' many successful signings from Midland League Gainsborough Trinity, for £600, he became a pro at the age of 17, having learned the ropes with Woodburn Council School and Woodhouse Alliance before joining Trinity. Jackie went on to win international recognition when he partnered club-mate Len Goulden on England's left-wing against Czechoslovakia at White Hart Lane in 1937. The scorer of one of his country's goals in a thrilling 5-4 victory (Stanley Matthews contributed a hat-trick from the opposite flank), Johnny would have surely won more caps but for an untimely injury that resulted in Arsenal's Cliff Bastin taking his place. Although only a handful of his total appearances were in the First Division – during the ill-fated 1931/32 season – the speedy Yorkshireman became an automatic choice throughout the 1930s up to the outbreak of World War II, during which he served in the RAF. In 1935, John had the honour of being chosen for the Anglo-Scots XI in that year's Jubilee match, but overall could count himself unlucky not to have won more recognition. "Frail-looking winger. Fast, possessed a multitude of tricks and a good shot." He later worked in a bookmaker's business and died in March 1986, at the age of 72.

England cap: 1937 vs Czechoslovakia (1).

Career record

	League		FAC		LC		Europe		Total	
Played	App	Gls	App	Gls	App	Gls	App	Gls	App	Gls
1931-32	5	1	0	0	0	0	0	0	5	1
1932-33	36	11	6	2	0	0	0	0	42	13
1933-34	42	6	2	0	0	0	0	0	44	6
1934-35	40	7	2	0	0	0	0	0	42	7
1935-36	26	5	0	0	0	0	0	0	26	5
1936-37	39	14	2	0	0	0	0	0	41	14
1937-38	39	3	1	0	0	0	0	0	40	3
1938-39	31	7	4	1	0	0	0	0	35	8
TOTAL	**258**	**54**	**17**	**3**	**0**	**0**	**0**	**0**	**275**	**57**

Hayden Mullins

MURRAY, Frank — 1919

Born: Dundee, Scotland, date unknown
League apps: 2

SHARED IN THE delight of Hammers' first-ever League victory, against Lincoln City at Sincil Bank on September 6, 1919. He turned out again in the inside-left position two days later in a match that saw Barnsley triumph 2-0 at Upton Park. Frank played for Dundee FC prior to joining West Ham United.

MUSGRAVE, Joe — 1931-36

Born: Durham, County Durham, 1912
League apps: 29
Cup apps: 4 (1 goal)

FORMERLY WITH NON-LEAGUERS Spennymoor United, Joe made his Hammers debut in a 1-1 home draw with mighty Arsenal on March 26, 1932. Two days later, he was again in the side at left-half in a disastrous 6-1 defeat at Sheffield Wednesday. Although mainly a reserve, Joe nevertheless managed a fair total of appearances during his six seasons at the Boleyn – despite having no League games in 1934/35 and 1936/37. On January 27, 1937 he joined Swindon Town. "A hard worker with a good sense of position." After three goals in 23 appearances for Town, Joe moved back to his native North East in 1938 and scored another three times for Hartlepool United in 20 games before moving on to Spennymoor United the same year.

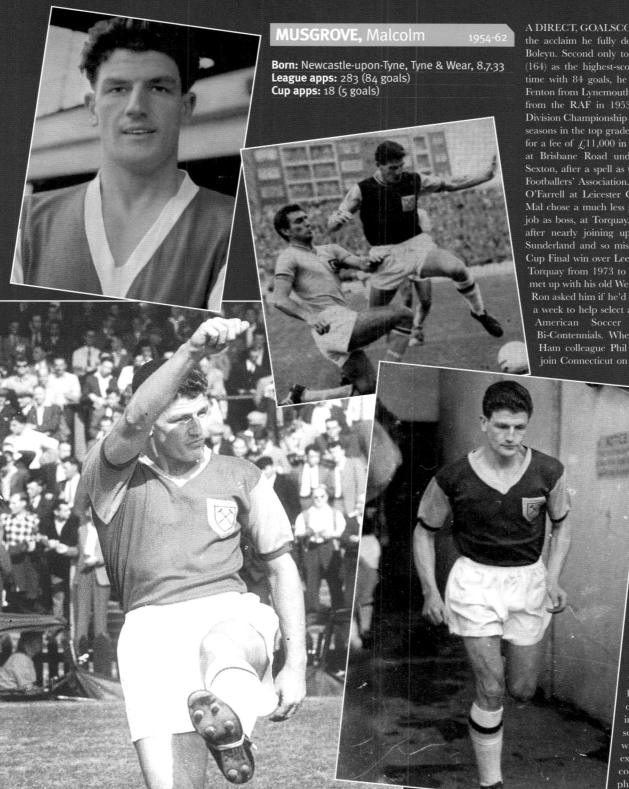

MUSGROVE, Malcolm 1954-62

Born: Newcastle-upon-Tyne, Tyne & Wear, 8.7.33
League apps: 283 (84 goals)
Cup apps: 18 (5 goals)

A DIRECT, GOALSCORING winger who didn't win the acclaim he fully deserved in ten seasons at the Boleyn. Second only to the legendary Jimmy Ruffell (164) as the highest-scoring Hammers winger of all time with 84 goals, he was signed by manager Ted Fenton from Lynemouth Colliery following his demob from the RAF in 1953. A member of the Second Division Championship team of 1958, he enjoyed four seasons in the top grade before joining Leyton Orient for a fee of £11,000 in 1962. He later became coach at Brisbane Road under fellow ex-Hammer Dave Sexton, after a spell as Chairman of the Professional Footballers' Association. Afterwards he assisted Frank O'Farrell at Leicester City and Manchester United. Mal chose a much less glamorous United for his first job as boss, at Torquay. He took the Plainmoor post after nearly joining up again with Bob Stokoe at Sunderland and so missed the Wearsiders' 1973 FA Cup Final win over Leeds. Malcolm held the helm at Torquay from 1973 to 1976 when, between jobs, he met up with his old West Ham boss Ron Greenwood. Ron asked him if he'd like to go over to the States for a week to help select a team franchise in the North American Soccer League for Connecticut Bi-Contennials. When he got there his old West Ham colleague Phil Woosnam persuaded him to join Connecticut on a pre-season tour to Portugal where they met Benfica and Sporting Lisbon. He helped manager Bobby Thomson, the former Wolves full-back, with training and the whole trip turned into a marvellous adventure. On his return he was offered a coaching post with Chicago Stings who had a really cosmopolitan playing staff including Americans, Scots, a Yugoslav, Germans, two Haitians and a young Dutchman named Dick Advocaat, whose tremendous training and tactical techniques led Holland to the 1994 World Cup Finals in the States. The one-week invite turned into a two-year stay in the USA. When he returned to the UK, he had one of his rare spells out of the game selling insurance but one day, while selling policies at Exeter City, was asked by Grecians manager, ex-Villa star Brian Godfrey, to come back into the game as physiotherapist at St James's Park. He spent three happy years there before being made redundant. Then he was off on his travels again, accepting a physiotherapist post in oil-rich Qatar in the Gulf. He accompanied the national side to the Asian games and the Under-16s to the Junior World Cup in China. Returning from the Gulf in 1984, he was lucky enough to land a job under Dave Smith at Plymouth Argyle as reserve team manager, coach and physio. Then his West Ham buddie Ken Brown took over the reins and Mal had five wonderful years at Home Park. After a long spell as physio at Shrewsbury Town and a lifetime in football, Mal is now living in retirement with his wife Jean at Torquay in Devon.

Career record

Played	League App	Gls	FAC App	Gls	LC App	Gls	Europe App	Gls	Total App	Gls
1953-54	4	0	0	0	0	0	0	0	4	0
1954-55	21	8	1	0	0	0	0	0	22	8
1955-56	8	0	1	0	0	0	0	0	9	0
1956-57	39	8	2	1	0	0	0	0	41	9
1957-58	39	9	3	0	0	0	0	0	42	9
1958-59	40	7	1	0	0	0	0	0	41	7
1959-60	41	15	2	1	0	0	0	0	43	16
1960-61	40	17	2	0	2	1	0	0	44	18
1961-62	36	13	1	0	1	1	0	0	38	14
1962-63	15	7	0	0	2	1	0	0	17	8
TOTAL	**283**	**84**	**13**	**2**	**5**	**3**	**0**	**0**	**301**	**89**

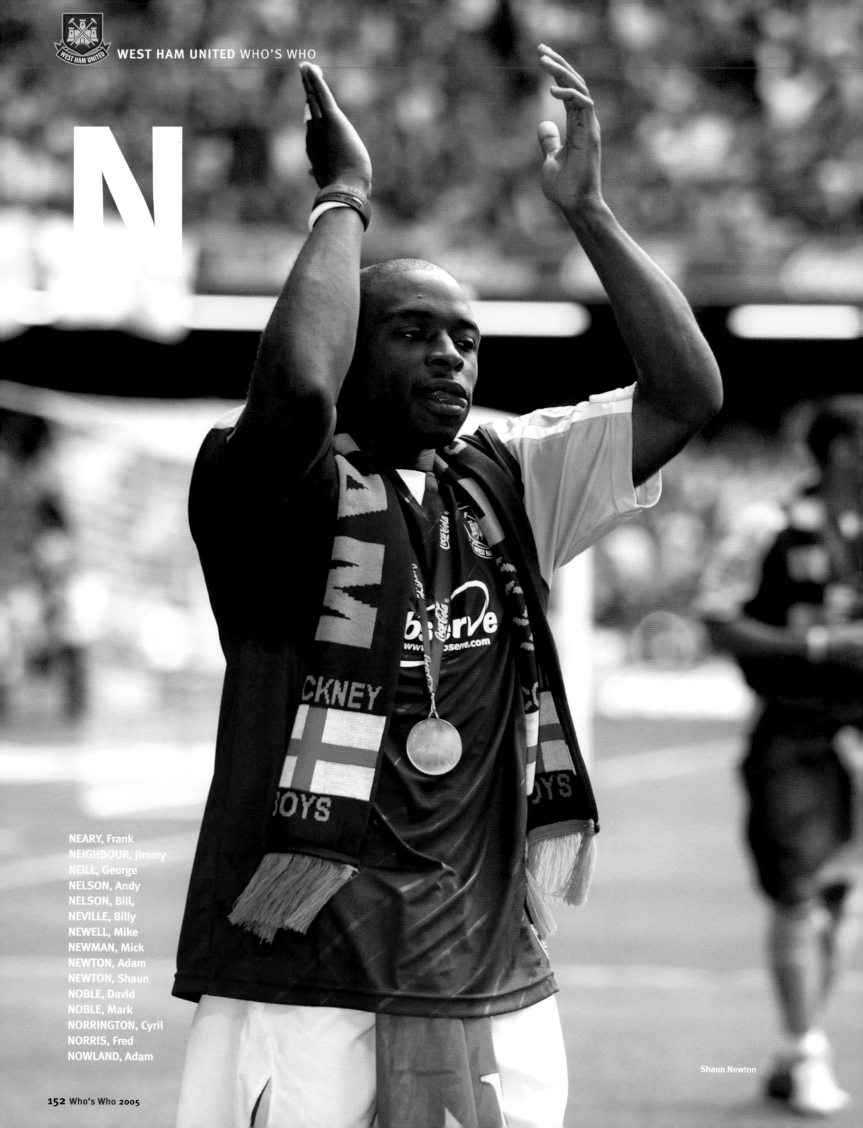

N

Shaun Newton

NEARY, Frank — 1946-47

Born: Aldershot, Hampshire, 6.3.21
League apps: 17 (15 goals)

SIGNED FROM QUEENS Park Rangers to replace Joe Payne, Frank scored 15 times in only 14 Second Division appearances in 1946/47. Possessor of a fearsome shot, he went on a tour of the London clubs after playing only three times for Hammers the following season, moving to Leyton Orient, QPR (again) and finally Millwall. He began his career with Finchley and was nicknamed "The Brown Bomber". The reason for Frank's sudden departure from West Ham to O's after his amazing goals per game ratio in 1946/47 has always been shrouded in mystery and as that doyen among football reporters and veteran scribe on all matters West Ham, Trevor Smith of *Recorder Sport* recalled in May 2003, the then legendary manager Charlie Paynter always refused to be drawn on the subject of big Frank's sudden fall from grace. But new light was shed on the affair when a reader contacted the paper shortly after Frank's death at the age of 82 in the spring of 2003. Ken Naylor of Chadwell Heath, whose cousin was married to Neary, explained: "The story was that Frank was being hacked and punched by a particularly nasty centre-half during a game and wasn't getting any help from the referee. Eventually he lost his temper and whacked the guy and, bearing in mind that Frank had been a PT instructor during the war, caught him pretty hard. The referee didn't see it, but the West Ham chairman WJ Cearns did. He said to Charlie (Paynter) 'I don't think he should be playing for West Ham anymore'. And, as a result, he didn't. That was the reason and Frank often told me the story." So in keeping up certain standards West Ham lost a proven goalscorer, but it would be difficult to envisage a similar outcome in more recent history as the Hartson-Berkovic incident proved. Certainly, Orient didn't have any qualms about buying the "bad boy" for £2,000 – half the fee Hammers had paid QPR – especially as the new signing's arrival coincided with more paying customers at the turnstiles! Disgruntled West Ham fans perhaps? At Brisbane Road, playing in the Third Division South, Frank started from where he'd left off and was O's top scorer in 1947/48 and 1948/49, breaking Ted Crawford's 13-year club scoring record by two goals when he finished with 25 from 29 League appearances in that latter campaign. Said to possess the hardest shot in the game at that time, his shooting was so powerful that he once knocked Torquay United's goalkeeper Archie McFeat unconscious with a thunderbolt drive and Bristol Rover's former West Ham custodian Jack Weare found himself in the back of the net with the ball in trying to stop a Neary penalty kick! Cash strapped O's allowed the player to return to QPR for a £7,000 fee in October 1949, after he'd scored 44 goals in 81 games, yet he made only 19 senior outings and scored five times during his second spell at Shepherd's Bush in the Second Division before moving across the metropolis again to join the Lions of Millwall for £6,000 in August 1950. Signed by the former Leyton Orient boss Charles Hewitt, Neary netted 50 goals in 123 Third Division South games and another nine in 19 Cup appearances while at the Den, but Millwall just failed to win promotion during Frank's stay at New Cross. After scoring 118 goals in 245 League appearances the ex-PT instructor, who'd begun his playing career in Northern Ireland while stationed there in World War II and also played for Fulham in wartime, moved into Southern League football when he signed for Gravesend and Northfleet for the 1954/55 season. A team-mate of the great ex-Arsenal forward Jimmy Logie at Stonebridge Park, Frank plundered 17 goals in 17 games for Fleet that campaign, including four in a 5-0 thrashing of Chelmsford, before retiring from the game.

Frank Neary

NEIGHBOUR, Jimmy — 1979-83

Born: Chingford, Essex, 15.11.50
League apps: 79 (5 goals)
Cup: 23 (1 goal)

ANOTHER WINGER NOT always given the credit he deserved. An experienced professional, he had seen service with Spurs (190 apps, 15 goals) and Norwich City (106 apps, five goals) before joining Hammers from the Norfolk club in 1979. Scorer of the goal that clinched a League Cup Final appearance for the club in 1981, he made his League debut versus Sunderland in September 1979. Jim had spent several years as youth development officer with Hammers, but resigned in May 1994 and joined Doncaster Rovers as first team coach in October of the same year. In 1996, he took over as boss of St Albans until, in 1998, his career turned full circle when he was appointed part-time coach at White Hart Lane assisting Hammers hero Patsy Holland. Having begun his coaching career at Enfield (for whom he also played five games) shortly after leaving Hammers for the first time and spent a short spell on loan at Bournemouth in 1983, Jimmy claimed in a recent interview: "Even though I supported Spurs as a boy and work there now, West Ham will always hold a special place in my heart."

NEILL, George — 1897-99

Born: Poplar, London, December 1874
SL apps (TIW): 2
SL apps (WHU) (1900): 1

A WING-HALF OR full-back, George probably played more than the three appearances credited to him above, but records were very sketchy at the time of his arrival from West Norwood in 1897. It is known that he first appeared in a TIW XI in October 1897 versus Leyton in the London League and played regularly until the club turned pro in 1898.

NELSON, Andy — 1956-59

Born: Custom House, London, 5.7.35
League apps: 15 (1 goal)
Cup apps: 2

CENTRE-HALF ANDY NELSON followed his older brother Bill to Upton Park from Custom House youth club in 1953. He had to wait until the spring of 1956 before making his first senior appearance in the 3-1 victory over Reading in the Semi-final of the Southern Floodlight Cup at Elm Park. Andy picked up a winners' medal in the 2-1 victory over Third Division Aldershot at Upton Park to add to the Football Combination and Cup medals he'd won in 1953/54. Making his League debut in the Second Division Championship-winning season of 1957/58 in the 2-1 victory over Doncaster Rovers at Belle View in March 1958, it seemed that rookie Andy was a lucky man as Hammers won their last two away games of the season at Cardiff City (3-0) and Middlesbrough (3-1) to clinch the title with Andy standing as tall as Nelson's column in both games! It was at left-half that he made his First Division and home debut in the 4-2 win over Chelsea in September 1958. "Ted [Fenton] told me to mark Jimmy Greaves very closely and although

Mark Noble

I did OK, he still scored both their goals!" Andy recalled in November 2002 in an interview with *Ex*, the West Ham retro magazine. It was the start of a 12-match run in the Hammers side, during which he scored the only goal of the match against Burnley at Upton Park, but someone else was watching his progress – Ipswich Town manager Alf Ramsey, who knew a good player when he saw one. Alf got his man for an £8,000 fee but had to give his new recruit a rise to the maximum wage of £20 and a £1,000 signing-on fee – a very unusual occurrence in those days for a relatively unknown player. But the shrewd Ramsey had spent his money wisely and as he proved later with Bobby Moore, he knew how to pick a captain. Skippering Town to back-to-back Second and First Division Championship successes in 1961 and 1962 – which paved the way for his boss's appointment as England manager in 1963 – Andy made 193 League appearances for the Suffolk club before returning to east London in September 1964 to join Second Division Leyton Orient, managed by Benny Fenton, brother of Andy's first boss Ted. Appointed captain at Brisbane Road, he stayed at O's for just 13 months, during which time he made 46 League and Cup appearances before moving on to Plymouth Argyle (93 League apps, one goal) for £4,000 in October 1965. Embarking on his first non-playing role in football at Millwall in the summer of 1969 under Benny Fenton at the Den, he was appointed manager of Gillingham FC in June 1971 and guided the Medway men to promotion in the runners-up spot in Division Four in 1973/74, before leaving to repeat the feat with Charlton Athletic from the Third to Second Division the following campaign. He was manager at the Valley from 1974 to 1980 and sold striker Derek Hales to West Ham for £100,000 in 1977 – a move that made him unpopular with the fans. He spent two years as commercial manager (1980-82) before deciding to retire and emigrate to Spain. Living at Javia, between Alicante and Valencia, he and his wife Margaret are only about 20 miles from where his brother Bill lives at Gandia. Bill (who played nine times for QPR after leaving Hammers in 1955) and Andy were the first brothers to appear for West Ham's first team since the war. Andy, in addition to being a captain under Sir Alf Ramsey, also shares another distinction with the great Bobby Moore – he has also had the honour of being presented with a major trophy by Her Majesty the Queen. His appointment with royalty came when he received the Forces Cup on behalf of the Army in 1958!

NELSON, Bill   1954-55

Born: Silvertown, London, 20.9.29
League apps: 2

ALTHOUGH HE MADE only two Second Division appearances for Hammers, one of them was as a member of the team that recorded a rare victory versus Liverpool in their Anfield fortress in September 1954. Transferred to London rivals Queens Park Rangers in 1955, he later moved to Southern League Guildford. Brother of Andy Nelson.

NEVILLE, Billy   1957

Born: Cork, Republic of Ireland, 15.5.35
League apps: 3

A CENTRE-FORWARD WHO played for Wembley Town before graduating through the reserve ranks to first team contention in 1957/58, when he played three Second Division matches in the promotion year. Making his initial senior appearance versus Sheffield United in September 1957, Bill was forced to give up the game on doctor's advice following continued illness.

Andy Nelson

NEWELL, Mike   1996-97

Born: Liverpool, Merseyside, 21.1.65
League apps: 7

IT WAS A case of "have goals will travel" for this footballing journeyman who had a seven-match stint on loan from Birmingham City at the turn of the year in 1996/97. Alas, it seemed Mike had left his shooting boots behind during his short stay with Irons when he failed to hit the onion bag in any of his six starts and one sub appearance at Upton Park. Making his debut in the 3-1 defeat against Chelsea at Stamford Bridge in December 1996, he did bring a touch of amusement to the proceedings when, being abused by a spectator in the West Stand lower at the Boleyn, he turned on his startled detractor and shouted: "Who's wearing the f@*&!ng shirt?" In a 17-year career in which he served Leicester City, Wigan Athletic, Luton Town, Crewe Alexander, Everton, Blackburn Rovers (where he won a Premiership winners' medal in 1995), Birmingham City, Bradford City, Aberdeen, Crewe again and Blackpool, Mike scored 165 goals in 674 League and Cup games and commanded almost £4 million in transfer fees. He has since become a successful manager with Hartlepool United and Luton Town, who he steerd to the Championship for 2005/06 after his side won the Coca-Cola League One in 2004/05.

NEWMAN, Mick   1957-58

Born: Canada, 2.4.32
League apps: 7 (2 goals)

THE LAST AMATEUR player to appear in Hammers' first XI. He made his Second Division debut versus Doncaster Rovers at Upton Park in March 1957, going on to total four appearances that campaign. Scored two goals during his three outings in the promotion season, he had previously been well known in local amateur soccer with Dagenham, Romford, Leytonstone and Rainham. Joined Dartford from Hammers. Now runs a business in Dagenham, Essex.

NEWTON, Adam   1999-2000

Born: Grays, Essex, 4.12.80
League apps: 2
Cup apps: 1

OF ALL THE players on duty for West Ham on the night the young Hammers completed a 9-0 aggregate rout of Coventry City in the second leg of the 1999 Youth Cup Final, televised live on Sky at Upton Park, wing-back Adam Newton left the biggest impression on the 24,000 crowd and the many more who saw the non-stop action from their armchairs. But, as is so often the case with those whose star burns brightest at youth level, Adam has so far failed to fulfil his full potential in the game and much less emulate the achievements of two of his team-mates that night, Joe Cole and Michael Carrick. In the time honoured tradition of the Academy, the budding star was put out on loan as part of his "apprenticeship" to First Division Portsmouth in July 1999 and, after one start and two sub appearances, he returned to Upton Park. Then, in a whirlwind week, the young man from Grays was thrust into the first team spotlight almost as fast as he could gallop down the wing when called off the bench in the 1-0 defeat at Coventry on September 25, 1999 and, five days later, he was on a plane to Croatia for the second leg of Hammers' UEFA Cup First Round clash with NK Osijek! With West Ham up 4-0 on aggregate, wily Harry Redknapp took Trevor Sinclair off at half time and replaced him with Newton as Hammers cruised home 6-1 winners over the two legs. To cap an amazing seven days, the stunned 18-year-old was then called up to the England Under-21 squad. Life couldn't have been much sweeter for the former Berkshire schools star with electrifying pace and ball skills to match. But that's about as good as it got for Newton at the Boleyn and after just one more Premiership outing as sub in the 5-0 Upton Park mauling of Coventry (again!), the player's Upton Park career degenerated into a succession of loan deals with lower League clubs Notts County (22 apps, one goal) and Leyton Orient (ten apps, one goal), before being given a free transfer to Second Division Peterborough United in July 2002. It seemed that Newton's natural inclination to attack and take defenders on with his pace and trickery were difficult to harness in the Premiership where defenders are encouraged to adopt a more cautious approach with so much at stake

Mick Newman

on a game-to-game basis. Young Adam found no such inhibitions with Barry Fry's Posh, however, and, operating on the right-hand side of midfield, scored on his debut in the 3-2 win at Luton Town for the London Road outfit and quickly added another tally at Wigan. Having tailored his game to the requirements of the Coca Cola League One, and now deployed in a more defensive role with Peterborough, Adam is approaching the 100 mark of appearances at London Road. But it's a travesty that such an exciting talent is plying his trade at least two levels below where he should be. A more fitting stage was provided by Concacaf country St Kitts and Nevis, who called up Adam and two of his Posh team-mates for their World Cup qualifying matches in the summer of 2004!

NEWTON, Shaun · 2005-

Born: Camberwell, London, 20.8.75
League apps: 16

THIS VERY EXPERIENCED right-sided midfielder was signed on loan from fellow Championship club Wolves in March 2005 to add weight to Hammers' promotion bid. The three-times capped England Under-21 international certainly helped the cause with his all-action foraging from box to box, and was particularly effective during the two-leg Play-off Semi-final victory over Ipswich Town. Having scored 25 times in 277 League and Cup appearances for Charlton Athletic and another 12 times in 123 League and Cup outings for Wolves, where he shared the midfield duties with Paul Ince, Shaun had still to open his scoring account with Hammers prior to the Play-off Final showdown with Preston North End at the Millennium Stadium in Cardiff. But Shaun turned in some impressive displays in his quest to earn a permanent move back to his native London.

NOBLE, David · 2003

Born: Hitchin, Hertfordshire, 2.2.82
League apps: 3
Cup apps: 1

A FORMER PUPIL at the National Centre for Excellence at the same time as Joe Cole and Jermain Defoe, David is a former graduate of the Arsenal youth team who arrived at West Ham on the last day of the transfer window on January 31, 2003. Unable to break into the first team at Highbury, the former England Youth international was put out on loan by the Gunners to First Division Watford in July 2001 to get some much needed senior experience and scored one goal in 18 League and Cup outings at Vicarage Road before being given a free transfer to Irons. The 21-year-old fired a bitter parting shot after agreeing terms with relegated West Ham, slamming the Gunners for failing to give young talent a chance saying: "It was frustrating at Arsenal and there was no opportunity for home-grown players. They have no money and are now thinking about playing a few of them, but I've no regrets." Making his first start in the 3-1 Carling Cup First Round clash with minnows Rushden and Diamonds at Upton Park, David soon found himself up against the same problems he'd experienced with the north London giants as he only ever made three substitute appearances before being given a free transfer to Boston United in February 2004. In fact, he made almost as many appearances for Scotland Under-21s during his time at the Boleyn, coming on as sub versus Austria (2003) and Norway (2004). He still has youth on his side, however, and perhaps one day the six foot midfielder will return to haunt Hammers, and Arsenal!

NOBLE, Mark · 2004-

Born: Canning Town, London, 8.5.87
League apps: 16
Cup apps: 5

MAYBE THE REASON for West Ham letting his namesake David go lies with this young man, another supremely gifted England Youth international midfielder who caused quite a stir when he made his first senior appearance in the somewhat fortuitous 2-0 First Round Carling Cup win over Southend United at Upton Park in August 2004. As one who likes to play right in the middle of the park, Mark first played in Hammers' reserves as a 15-year-old schoolboy, making him the youngest player ever to appear for the second-string. Working with Alan Pardew's first team squad on a regular basis in 2003/04, he impressed with his strength and phenomenal workrate in midfield, as well as his exceptional skill with the ball. This former captain of England's Under-16s is definitely a name to watch out for in the future. Indeed, he earned rave reviews for his performances in midfield as Hammers finally won promotion back to the Premiership in May 2005.

NORRINGTON, Cyril · 1927-29

Born: Kensal Rise, London, 3.6.1896
League apps: 27

WEST HAM BEAT Leicester City to the signature of this stylish left-half or left-back, who settled down in the latter position for Hammers to prove a useful acquisition. Previously with Leytonstone and Barking Town as an amateur, Cyril was also an accomplished billiards player, representing West Ham United in the *Evening News* Cup Competition. He made his First Division debut in the 2-0 victory over FA Cup winners Cardiff City at Upton Park (November 12, 1927). Joined Coventry City when he left Upton Park and then Peterborough and Fletton United.

NORRIS, Fred · 1928-33

Born: Aston, Birmingham, 14.8.1903
League apps: 65 (6 goals)

A MAN OF many parts, Fred occupied all the outfield positions for Hammers, with the exception of inside and outside-left, with equal success. Initially making his mark as an inside-right with Adelaide in the Birmingham Victorian League, his next move was to sign professional forms for Halesowen. He transferred to Midland giants Aston Villa in 1925 and, after three seasons at Villa Park, changed his club (but not his colours) when he joined Irons. Despite his versatility, West Ham considered right-half to be Fred's best position, although his appearances there were restricted by the presence of the great Jimmy Collins. Not to be denied, Fred scored a celebrated hat-trick while playing in the forward line versus Oldham Athletic at Upton Park in October 1932, and later continued his career with Crystal Palace. He also played in France.

NOWLAND, Adam · 2004-

Born: Preston, Lancashire, 6.7.81
League apps: 15 (1 goal)
Cup apps: 2

ADAM FOUND HIMSELF very much in the same boat as Jobi McAnuff when he first arrived at Upton Park from Milton Keynes Dons as far as regular First Division football was concerned. But unlike his former team-mate, Adam decided to tough it out hoping to be rewarded by his persistence. Signed for a bargain £75,000 fee from Dons while they were in administration, Adam is a product of Blackpool's youth system and scored seven goals in 80 first team appearances at Bloomfield Road, of which a  staggering 60 were off the bench. Moving to Selhurst Park in June 2001, he hit another seven goals in 61 League and Cup appearances with Dons where he continued his penchant for scoring in cup-ties to bring his career total to four in 15 Cup games – totally disproportionate to his goals per game ratio in League matches! Taking on a new lease of life after being converted from front-runner to central midfield at Selhurst, Adam proved he hasn't lost his scoring touch when hitting a stunning winner in Hammers' 1-0 victory over Burnley in August 2004 when he revelled in the rare luxury of a full 90 minutes! Handed the captain's armband by reserve team manager Roger Cross at the start of the season, the well-built midfielder revealed: "Some of the lads have been having a bit of a joke calling me 'skipper' since then. But if I can help some of the younger lads in reserve games and be a good influence for them, then that's something I'm happy to do. At the same time, it's not a job that anyone wants to hold on to for long. We've got some good midfielders in the first team, but I know I have to keep working hard and make sure that when opportunities do arise, I do enough to stay in the team." Early in October 2004, however, Hammers put Adam out on loan for a month to fellow Championship rivals Gillingham under the stipulation that he couldn't play against them later that month! Adam eventually signed for Nottingham Forest in November 2004 for £250,000 and up to the end of 2004/05 he had made five appearances. He began 2005/06 on loan at Preston North End.

O

OAKES, William
OBENEY, Harry
O'FARRELL, Frank
OMOYINMI, Manny
ORHAN, Yilmaz
ORR, Neil
OTULAKOWSKI, Anton

Neil Orr

OAKES, William — 1903-04

SL apps: 14

A LEFT-BACK WITH the Leyton club, Bill made his first appearance for Irons in a 2-0 win over Northampton Town at the Memorial Grounds (February 27, 1904). It was the start of a 14-match run in the Southern League side that ended on the final day of the campaign versus Swindon. He transferred to Second Division Leicester Fosse (now City) for 1904/05. Died September 8, 1927.

OBENEY, Harry — 1959-61

Born: Bethnal Green, London, 9.3.38
League apps: 25 (12 goals)
Cup apps: 2

ORIGINALLY A HALF-BACK, this whole-hearted player was converted to centre-forward when Hammers were looking for a replacement for Vic Keeble. He met with a measure of success in his new role, having waited some three years for senior recognition since signing full pro in May 1956 after playing for Briggs Sports. Harry was allowed to join Millwall after receiving a benefit from the club in 1961, making 75 League appearances for the Lions before a brief spell with Colchester. He later had a season at Southern League Dover, before settling down with Romford, for whom he made over 400 first team appearances. Later joined Essex side Aveley.

OMOYINMI, Manny — 1996-98

Born: Lagos, Nigeria, 28.12.77
League apps: 9 (2 goals)
Cup apps: 3

RARELY CAN A West Ham player have been pilloried, ostracised and sent into virtual exile as in the unfortunate case of Manny Omoyinmi. Yet life at Upton Park had started so brightly for the England schoolboy international who was a graduate of the club's Youth Academy, a member of the young Hammers side that won the South East Counties League title in 1995/96, and was also in the team that reached the two-leg Final of the FA Youth Cup in the company of Rio Ferdinand and Frank Lampard the same season. Although his progress was slower than his two more illustrious team-mates, wing-back Manny duly made his Premiership debut against Leeds United in March 1997 and over a year later, in May 1998, he scored two sensational match-saving goals in the 3-3 draw against already relegated Crystal Palace at Selhurst Park. But the young Nigerian still found first team opportunities few and far between and he had already been the subject of a number of loan deals to AFC Bournemouth in September 1996 (seven League apps) and Dundee United in February 1998 (four apps). In March/April 1999 he scored one goal in four appearances while on loan to near-neighbours Leyton Orient, but it was on his next loan assignment at Gillingham between September and November, 1999 that fate played its cruel hand. Although Manny scored on his debut for Gills against Oldham Athletic and cracked home a stunning winner versus Oxford United, it was to be his two outings against Bolton Wanderers in the Second Round of the Worthington League Cup that would be remembered when all else was forgotten and would ultimately cause far reaching ramifications on a scale far exceeding the so-called "Mickey Mouse" profile of the competition. Returning to West Ham, Manny was inexplicably

1904-2004

WEST HAM UNITED WHO'S WHO
The Boleyn Ground

O'FARRELL, Frank — 1950-56

Born: Cork, Republic of Ireland, 9.10.27
League apps: 197 (6 goals)
Cup apps: 13 (1 goal)

FRANK REPLACED TOMMY Moroney in the Cork United side when the latter joined Hammers in 1947, and later followed him to Upton Park. He became a regular in the senior side after playing over 50 reserve matches and won full international recognition for his country. One of the founder members of the famous West Ham managerial Academy, in company with Malcolm Allison, Dave Sexton, John Bond, Noel Cantwell, Ken Brown and Malcolm Musgrove, it was Hammers' longest-serving manager, Charlie Paynter, who gave Frank his first team debut in a Second Division match at Notts County in December 1950. Transferred to Preston North End in a straight exchange deal for Eddie Lewis in 1956, he went on to make 118 First Division appearances at Deepdale. Frank went into football management when he hung up his boots, serving Torquay United, Leicester City (whom he took to the 1969 FA Cup Final and Second Division Championship), Manchester United and Cardiff City after starting off with Southern League Weymouth. He vacated the Cardiff post to go to Iran. Frank earned seven Republic of Ireland caps between 1952 and 1956, then won two more while with Preston. He has now retired from the game after assisting Everton and Bolton Wanderers in a scouting capacity in 1993. Frank now lives in Torquay, Devon with his wife Ann, not far from his old West Ham team-mate and management partner Mal "Mussy" Musgrove and enjoys "the odd pint, a round of golf and keeping up with the news on Hammers", as he told West Ham retro magazine *Ex* in August 2003. He says: "I always look for the results of the teams I was associated with and, obviously, it was sad to see West Ham relegated. It was a nice club and I am very proud to say I played there."
Republic of Ireland caps: 1952 vs Austria (2), France; 1955 vs Holland, Norway, Yugoslavia; 1956 vs Holland (7).

included in the Hammers squad for the Worthington Cup Quarter-final clash with Aston Villa at Upton Park on December 15, 1999. Worse still, with the game deadlocked at 2-2, the little Nigerian was called into action off the subs bench in the 22nd minute of extra time to replace Paulo Wanchope to set in motion a chain of events that would – in Harry Redknapp's words – "haunt me forever". Although he made no real impact on the outcome of the match and only stood and watched as Shaka Hislop saved Gareth Southgate's penalty in the shoot-out to seemingly ensure Irons' progress to their first Cup Semi-final since 1991, within hours Villa lodged an appeal when they realised that the player had already appeared in the competition for Gillingham. The appeal was upheld and West Ham lost the replayed game. Amid rumours of threats of violence and hate-mail directed at the player, Redknapp wisely packed him off to Scunthorpe United while the furore subsided. But it never did and following another loan spell at Barnet, Manny was released on a free transfer to Oxford United in July 2000. Having mustered just one goal in six appearances at Scunny and none in another half dozen outings with the Underhill outfit, things could only get better at the Manor Ground for the man who rightly or wrongly was effectively regarded as an outcast in the game. But even with the U's the tricky winger couldn't call a first team spot his own and, although he scored nine times in 77 outings for the perennial strugglers who finished rock bottom of Division Two in 2000/01, by 2003/04 he again found himself left out in the cold and sent out on loan to non-League Margate and then Gravesend and Northfleet. In August 2005, he was playing for Conference outfit Canvey Island.

ORHAN, Yilmaz — 1976-77

Born: Nicosia, Cyprus, 13.3.55
League apps: 8
Cup apps: 1

DISCOVERED BY EX-HAMMER Terry Matthews at Aveley, who recommended him to his former club. Made his First Division debut versus Queens Park Rangers in January 1976, but failed to get on the scoresheet in nine senior outings. Left Hammers for Hawaii of the North American Soccer League in April 1977.

ORR, Neil — 1982-87

Born: Greenock, Scotland, 13.5.59
League apps: 146 (4 goals)
Cup apps: 29 (1 goal)

SON OF THE late Scottish international and Greenock Morton player, Tommy Orr, Neil followed his father to Cappielow Park from where Hammers signed him in January 1982 for £400,000 and made his debut at Manchester United (January 9, 1982). Recommended to the club by fellow team-mate Ray Stewart, Neil was capped seven times for Scotland Under-23s. One of the unsung heroes of Hammers' most successful League side, making 36 first team appearances in the 1985/86 campaign. A hard-running midfielder or defender, the versatile Neil went back north of the border to join Hibernian in 1987. Neil, who had made 196 League appearances during his first seven-year spell in Scottish football with his home town club Morton, soon settled in at Easter Road and scored three times in 167 Scottish Premier appearances during six seasons with the Hibees before dropping down a division to sign for St Mirren in 1995. Making 29 First Division appearances and scoring once in a year at Love Street, Neil ended the affair when moving on to see out the end of his career with Queen of the South, signing off with one more goal in seven Scottish Division Two appearances for the Doonhammers. Neil spent a year in the States coaching at summer camps after leaving Palmerston Park until returning to Scotland in 1996 to take control of Edinburgh University FC. After five years in the capital, during which he gained coaching badges and a degree in sports exercise and science, Neil was appointed as a youth development officer for the SFA based in Lothian in 2001. Now living at North Berwick, Neil's job description has changed recently and he has been given the major brief to restore the credibility of Scottish football, which has suffered from a severe lack of investment in recent years and a slowing down of home produced players. It could be a job that takes some time!

OTULAKOWSKI, Anton — 1976-78

Born: Dewsbury, West Yorkshire, 29.1.56
League apps: 17

SIGNED FROM BARNSLEY (42 League apps, two goals) on the strength of his performance against Hammers in a League Cup-tie in September 1976, the promising midfielder of Polish extraction didn't quite live up to expectations and was subsequently transferred to Southend United (163 League apps, eight goals) in April 1979. He then moved to Millwall (114 League apps, 13 goals) where he made a considerable impression, which led to his transfer to Crystal Palace in May 1986.

Harry Obeney

P

PADDON, Graham
PALMER, James
PARKER, Derek
PARKER, Reginald William
PARKES, Phil
PARKINSON, Harry
PARKS, Tony
PARKS, Walter
PARRIS, George
PARSONS, Eric
PAYNE, Joe
PAYNE, John
PEARCE, Ian
PEARCE, Stuart
PEARSON, Stuart
PETCHEY, George
PETERS, Martin MBE

PHILLIPS, Wilf
PHIPPS, Cecil
PIERCY, Frank
PIKE, Geoff
PINDER
POLLARD, Walter
PORFIRIO, Hugo
POTTS, Steve
POWELL, Chris
POWELL, Darren
PRESLAND, Eddie
PROCTOR, Norman
PROUDLOCK, George
PUDAN, AE "Dickie"
PUDDEFOOT, Sydney
PYKE, Malcolm

Martin Peters celebrates putting England 2-1 ahead in the 1966 World Cup Final versus West Germany at Wembley – as does Bobby Moore in the background

PADDON, Graham — 1973-76

Born: Manchester, Greater Manchester, 24.8.50
League apps: 115 (11 goals)
Cup apps: 35 (4 goals)

SIGNED FROM NORWICH City (for whom he made 290 League appearances and scored 25 goals in his two spells) as part of an exchange deal that resulted in Ted MacDougall going in the opposite direction, this fine midfielder was a great success at Upton Park. Originally bought from Coventry City (five League apps, one goal) for £25,000 by the Canaries, in October 1969, he was valued at £170,000 in the transaction that took him to Hammers. Blond, bearded Paddon formed a formidable midfield link with Billy Bonds and Trevor Brooking in the mid-1970s. He won an FA Cup winners' medal in 1975 and a European Cup Winners' Cup runners-up medal the following year, before returning to Carrow Road for £110,000 in November 1976. He had a spell with Tampa Bay Rowdies before returning to the UK for a brief spell at Millwall (five League apps, one goal). A member of the Norwich promotion side of 1972 and also a League Cup finalist in 1973. Later a licensee, running the South Walsham Country Club and squash courts. Returned to football as a member of the Portsmouth coaching staff in August 1985. In 1989, Graham moved to Stoke City as assistant manager to Alan Ball. He returned to Pompey in 1991, working under Jim Smith until the pair were fired in 1995. After that he worked in the Yemen and, more recently, scouted for Derby County. He was coaching locally in the Norfolk area in 2002. Looking back on his time at West Ham he said in an interview with *Hammers News* magazine: "To play with people like Billy Bonds, Frank Lampard and Trevor Brooking was the highlight of my career. Ron Greenwood and John Lyall were great too, and all the East End people were brilliant to me. The fans were top notch."

Graham Paddon

PALMER, James — 1919-20

League apps: 13 (1 goal)

THIS LEFT-WING FLIER made his Hammers debut in a 4-1 win at Lincoln (September 6, 1919) and went on to make a dozen Second Division appearances that season. Jim scored his only goal as a Hammer against Grimsby Town (October 18, 1919) to win the match. He had one more League outing the next season before transferring to Workington.

PARKER, Derek — 1946-57

Born: Colchester, Essex, 23.6.26
League apps: 199 (9 goals)
Cup apps: 8

THIS POPULAR player just failed to qualify for the exclusive "200 Club" with Hammers – his appearances adding up to 199 in the League. Joining Hammers from Grays Athletic in October 1944, he was originally an inside-forward but later converted to half-back. Also made over 250 Combination appearances for the reserves. He was chosen to tour Australia with an FA XI in 1951. Derek returned to his home town in March 1957 to play for Colchester United when Ben Fenton (then manager at Layer Road) persuaded his brother Ted to release him to assist in the Essex club's eventually unsuccessful promotion drive from the old Third Division South. Derek went on to make 130 League appearances at Layer Road.

Career record

Played	League App	Gls	FAC App	Gls	LC App	Gls	Europe App	Gls	Total App	Gls
1946-47	10	1	0	0	0	0	0	0	10	1
1947-48	2	0	0	0	0	0	0	0	2	0
1949-50	32	2	2	0	0	0	0	0	34	2
1950-51	38	1	2	0	0	0	0	0	40	1
1951-52	30	3	3	0	0	0	0	0	33	3
1952-53	39	0	1	0	0	0	0	0	40	0
1953-54	28	1	0	0	0	0	0	0	28	1
1954-55	7	0	0	0	0	0	0	0	7	0
1955-56	8	0	0	0	0	0	0	0	8	0
1956-57	5	1	0	0	0	0	0	0	5	1
TOTAL	**199**	**9**	**8**	**0**	**0**	**0**	**0**	**0**	**207**	**9**

PARKER, Reginald William — 1935

Born: Reading, Berkshire, 1913
League apps: 2

THIS TALL BERKSHIRE-BORN left-back tasted both the sweet and sour of victory and defeat in his two Second Division appearances for West Ham in September 1935. A member of the Hammers side that defeated Bradford Park Avenue 1-0 with a Len Goulden goal at Upton Park on the ninth of that month, he was also on duty when West Ham crashed 4-1 to Blackpool at Bloomfield Road five days later. Formerly with Bournemouth and Boscombe Athletic, for whom he had played 50 games between 1931 and 1934. He joined Torquay in 1936 and made 16 League appearances for the Gulls.

PARKES, Phil · 1978-90

Born: Sedgley, West Midlands, 8.8.50
League apps: 343
Cup apps: 93

PHIL PARKES

UNDOUBTEDLY THE FINEST GOALKEEPER in Hammers' history, this genuine giant of the game was the backbone of the club's success under John Lyall in the early 1980s and it was a measure of his stature and durability that he was still earning a first team place in Division One at the age of 39. A former carpenter by trade, "Parkesy" progressed from non-League Brierley Hill to make his League debut for another local club, Walsall, versus Mansfield Town (April 1, 1969), but after just 52 League matches he became a bargain £15,000 signing by Queens Park Rangers in 1970. In nine seasons at Loftus Road, Parkes established himself as one of the top keepers in the country. He helped the Super Hoops climb from the Second to the First Division and to within a point of the Division One Championship in 1975/76, only to be pipped at the post by Liverpool. At least that gave him UEFA Cup experience the following season. Ever-dependable Parkes was dominant in the air and had lightning reflexes on the six-yard line where he formed a human brick wall to defy the best attackers in the business. He kept the clean sheets while the flair players like Stan Bowles, Dave Thomas and skipper Gerry Francis did their stuff in an entertaining side. Phil was always on the verge of the England team, but unable to break the Peter Shilton/Ray Clemence monopoly under Alf Ramsey. His solitary senior international cap came under Don Revie, who named Parkes among six new caps for the visit to Lisbon to face Portugal on April 3, 1974 (Martin Peters and Trevor Brooking were also in the side that day). With the number 1 position being dominated by two great keepers, he was not bitter about his lack of opportunity and still savours the one cap they can't take away – a quiet, goalless debut, too! QPR had declined and were regularly involved in relegation struggles when, with a testimonial looming, he jumped at the chance to join West Ham in February 1979 for £565,000 – a then world record for a goalkeeper. Bobby Ferguson and Mervyn Day had shared the green jersey that season, but Lyall wanted to reconstruct his team from the back and Phil's signing proved a masterstroke. The fair-haired giant with the familiar moustache put his faith in Lyall and West Ham by dropping down a division and made his Hammers debut in a 3-0 home win versus Oldham Athletic (January 24, 1979). After finishing fifth at the end of that Second Division season, the quest for honours was really on. In May 1980, although missing out on promotion, Hammers defeated London rivals Arsenal 1-0 in the FA Cup Final, and Phil was back at Wembley the next March to face Liverpool in the League Cup Final. Reds eventually won the replay at Villa Park, but Hammers made amends by continuing their surge towards the Second Division title. Lyall's new boys, Alvin Martin, Ray Stewart, Paul Allen, Paul Goddard and Parkesy, had gelled well with the established stars like Bonds, Brooking and Alan Devonshire. Everyone played their part, none more so than Phil who set a club record by keeping 22 clean sheets in the victorious 1980/81 campaign. Regular supporters at the time believed that the team had never played better, in terms of results and entertainment value. They underlined their appreciation of his goalkeeping skills by voting him Hammer of the Year (1980/81). But Parkes was at the heart of another splendid West Ham side in 1985/86, when they challenged strongly for the championship before having to settle for a best-ever third, behind Liverpool and Everton. It was a season to remember for Phil, in particular, because, at the age of 36, he was again a first team regular after injury had forced him to miss all but the last two months of the previous campaign. It was not the last time he would come back to prove himself as he entered the final phase of his illustrious career. People sometimes joked about Phil's infamous "dodgy knees" but a career spanning more than 800 League and Cup games speaks for itself. Even after Hammers brought Allen McKnight down from Scotland as Phil's supposed replacement, after a serious elbow infection and the form of his long-time understudy Tom McAllister restricted him to just one senior game in 1987/88, Parkes rescued the club from their "McKnightmare". His recall in February 1989, aged 39, helped Hammers win an FA Cup Fifth Round tie versus Charlton Athletic… but came a week too late to spare them a bad League Cup Semi-final home defeat by Luton Town, when McKnight conceded three. Too late also to avoid relegation and manager John Lyall – axed in July 1989 – could only wonder what might have been had he recalled the "Old Man" sooner. While working in that capacity three days a week at Portman Road, Parkesy was approached by his former QPR team-mate Gerry Francis to fill a similar role at Loftus Road and, with John Lyall's permission, combined both jobs by working three days with the Tractor Boys and two at Shepherd's Bush! He stayed at Ipswich until the arrival of George Burley, then switched to Wycombe Wanderers under Martin O'Neill and Steve Walford. While doing occasional commentating work with Talk Sport Radio, Phil is also heavily involved with "The Boys of 86" who have formed a limited company. He is also current host and MC in the Premier Suite and Castle Lounge on match days at West Ham, but his main occupation is running his own building company in Wokingham where he still lives.

Career record	League		FAC		LC		Europe		Total	
Played	App	Gls	App	Gls	App	Gls	App	Gls	App	Gls
1978-79	18	0	0	0	0	0	0	0	18	0
1979-80	40	0	8	0	8	0	0	0	56	0
1980-81	42	0	3	0	9	0	6	0	60	0
1981-82	39	0	2	0	4	0	0	0	45	0
1982-83	41	0	2	0	7	0	0	0	50	0
1983-84	42	0	4	0	5	0	0	0	51	0
1984-85	10	0	0	0	0	0	0	0	10	0
1985-86	42	0	7	0	3	0	0	0	52	0
1986-87	33	0	5	0	6	0	0	0	44	0
1987-88	1	0	0	0	0	0	0	0	1	0
1988-89	13	0	3	0	1	0	0	0	17	0
1989-90	22	0	1	0	9	0	0	0	32	0
TOTAL	**343**	**0**	**35**	**0**	**52**	**0**	**6**	**0**	**436**	**0**

PARKINSON, Harry · 1902-03

SL apps: 2

HARRY MADE HIS first appearance for Irons in a 1-1 Southern League draw at Kettering Town (April 15, 1903) in the left-half position and his second and last showing in the 1-2 reverse at Millwall in the final match of the season playing at right-half.

PARKS, Tony · 1991-92

Born: Hackney, London, 28.1.63
League apps: 6
Cup apps: 3

A SMALLISH GOALKEEPER who was a big favourite with the fans on the handful of occasions that he came in as cover for regular first choice Ludek Miklosko. A chirpy cockney, Parks never fulfilled his early promise at Tottenham where, between 1981 and 1987, he played only 37 League games. There was one outstanding highlight though when, aged only 21, his dramatic penalty shoot-out saves earned Spurs victory over Anderlecht in the 1984 UEFA Cup Final at White Hart Lane. Tony admitted later that he let early success go to his head a little, although after spells on loan to Oxford United (five apps), Gillingham (two apps), Brentford (where he played 71 games) and Fulham (two apps), he appreciated being offered a fresh start at Upton Park. He never let Hammers down or lacked confidence in his nine appearances, screaming instructions to fellow defenders and generally fighting as hard as anyone in what was a traumatic relegation-haunted season, on and off the field. Disappointed to be offered only a new one-year contract by the club, Parks dropped out of the picture, although he did return to Chadwell Heath later to join in training sessions before moving from Essex to Scottish Premier League club Falkirk, where his team-mates included other ex-Hammers Tommy McQueen and Frank McAvennie. Tony's career enjoyed something of a renaissance at Brockville and although he experienced the disappointment of relegation in his first season with the Bairns in 1992/93, he played 41 times the following season when Falkirk were First Division Champions holding the best defensive record in the whole of Scotland, conceding a mere 32 goals. Back in the Scottish Premier, Tony continued to shine with 28 appearances in both 1994/95 and 1995/96 and won a B&Q Cup winners' medal when Bairns beat St Mirren 3-0 in the 1994 Final before he returned south to sign on a free transfer for Second Division Blackpool in September 1996. After spending a year in the reserves at Bloomfield Road, he made the short hop to sign for Burnley in August 1997, but made only two appearances for the Clarets before moving on again on a free transfer to Barrow in October 1998. Loaned to Doncaster Rovers in February 1999, he played six League games for Donny before signing for Scarborough where he made a further 15 Third Division appearances in 1998/99 in which he was unable to prevent the Seadogs finishing 92nd in the League. He then took a free transfer to Halifax Town and ended his League career at the Shay with nine League and Cup appearances in 1999/2000. In July 1999, Tony was appointed goalkeeping coach with the Shaymen.

Tony Parks

PARKS, Walter
1895-96 TIW

Born: Isle of Dogs, London, March 1872

WALTER PLAYED FOR both Old St Luke's and Castle Swifts. He appeared for Irons in the FA Cup tie with Chatham.

PARRIS, George
1985-93

Born: Ilford, Essex, 11.9.64
League apps: 239 (12 goals)
Cup apps: 51 (5 goals)

A SCHOOLBOY STAR with Redbridge, Essex, London and England, George joined Hammers as an apprentice professional in July 1981, and signed full pro the following year. He made his First Division debut in the last game of the 1984/85 season versus Liverpool at Upton Park (May 20, 1985) and was unlucky not to score. A regular member of the Football Combination side for two seasons, George made a considerable impact soon after the start of the 1985/86 campaign, and gained a regular first team spot at the expense of Steve Walford. Although not the most naturally gifted of players, George certainly worked hard to prove himself. The arrival of Julian Dicks in 1988 cost George the number 3 shirt, but this strong-running, powerful utility player went on to make his mark in a bustling midfield role. Solid in the tackle, he bounced back from breaking his leg in a home game versus Luton Town (January 2, 1988) and went on to re-establish himself as a regular as well as a crowd favourite. His best season for the club was probably the 1990/91 promotion-winning term, when he contributed eight goals – more than in all his previous seasons at Upton Park – and finished the campaign as runner-up to Ludo Miklosko in the Hammer of the Year poll. But Hammers' season-long struggle in the top flight the following season was an unhappy time for George personally. Knee ligament damage and then a mystery heart scare restricted his involvement. Even so, he still made 290 League and Cup appearances, scoring 17 goals in his West Ham career. Although he qualified for a testimonial after ten years at Upton Park, this honest pro accepted a surprise £100,000 move to First Division strugglers Birmingham City in March 1993 in the hope of regaining regular first team football. So, while Hammers were clinching promotion

to the top flight, wholehearted George was experiencing the blues on his way into Division Two with Barry Fry's beleaguered City side. In April 1995, he returned to Upton Park for a well deserved testimonial match against Ipswich Town who included ex-Hammer Stuart Slater in their line-up. George deserved every penny he got from his benefit game because West Ham certainly had the best out of him as a player. It's fair to say his career went into rapid decline after leaving Hammers. He was loaned out three times by Brum in 1994/95 to Brentford (seven apps, one goal), Bristol City (six apps) and Brighton (18 apps, two goals), so missed the Blues Second Division Championship triumph. George transferred to Brighton on a free transfer in September 1995, and went on to make 70 League and Cup appearances for the Seagulls. Signed on a non-contract basis by Southend United in August 1997, where Shrimpers manager and ex-Hammers team-mate Alvin Martin had the thankless task of telling his old pal it was time to call it a day after he'd made just one appearance for the Essex club. George played on in his inimitable fashion for St Leonard's FC for 1997/98, after which he finally hung up his boots. That was until he got the call to represent West Ham in the Masters seven-a-side tournament at London's Docklands in July 2001, along with a host of other "old boys" who duly defeated an Arsenal side that included Ian Wright and Liam Brady to claim the Southern Masters title! George is currently in collaboration with *Ex* magazine editor Tony McDonald to publish a book about his life, which should be available now.

Career record

	League		FAC		LC		Europe		Total	
Played	App	Gls	App	Gls	App	Gls	App	Gls	App	Gls
1984-85	1	0	0	0	0	0	0	0	1	0
1985-86	26	1	7	0	2	0	0	0	35	1
1986-87	36	2	5	1	6	0	0	0	47	3
1987-88	30	1	0	0	2	0	0	0	32	1
1988-89	27	1	1	0	3	0	0	0	31	1
1989-90	38	2	1	0	10	0	0	0	49	2
1990-91	44	5	7	3	3	0	0	0	54	8
1991-92	21	0	0	0	4	1	0	0	25	1
1992-93	16	0	0	0	0	0	0	0	16	0
TOTAL	**239**	**12**	**21**	**4**	**30**	**1**	**0**	**0**	**290**	**17**

PARSONS, Eric
1946-50

Born: Worthing, Sussex, 9.11.23
League apps: 146 (34 goals)
Cup apps: 6 (1 goal)

SIGNED AS A junior for Hammers after being spotted playing for Worthing Boys versus West Ham Boys at Upton Park. Given the affectionate nickname of "Rabbit" by the Upton Park patrons for the way he used to hare down the touchlines, this flying outside-right was sold to London rivals Chelsea in November 1950 for £23,000, a huge fee for those days. An ever-present member of the pensioners' 1955 First Division Championship-winning side and recipient of two England B caps, he later moved to Brentford where he pushed his total League appearances to over the 400 mark, despite sustaining a broken leg while at Griffin Park. He set up a successful signwriting business when he retired from playing.

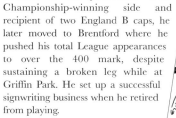

Eric Parson

PAYNE, Joe
1946

Born: Brimington Common, Derbyshire, 17.11.14
League apps: 10 (6 goals)
Cup apps: 1

A NAME INDELIBLY imprinted in the record books for his ten goals for Luton Town in his first appearance at centre-forward versus Bristol Rovers in the old Third Division South in April 1936. His 55 goals were largely instrumental in Luton winning the Third Division South title and at the end of that season he won his solitary cap for England, scoring twice in the 8-0 win over Finland. A former Derbyshire coalminer previously with Bolsover Colliery and Bigglesdale Town, he joined Chelsea in March 1938 and managed 36 League games for the Stamford Bridge club (21 goals) before war interrupted his career. Signed for Hammers in December 1946, but his brief spell at the Boleyn was beset with injury problems. He later ended his League days at Millwall but retired through injury without making a first team outing at the Den although he made a comeback with Southern League Worcester City in 1952. Also a good cricketer (he played for Bedfordshire in 1937) and snooker player. Joe was a Football League (South) Cup Finalist at Wembley with Chelsea (1944, winner 1945.)

PAYNE, John — 1926

Born: Southall, Middlesex, 3.1.1906
League apps: 4 (1 goal)

EFFECTIVE ON EITHER flank, this speedy winger progressed through junior amateur soccer with Botwell Mission and Lyons Athletic to senior amateur level with Southall. He remained on the Athenian club's books while he sampled First Division football with Hammers, scoring versus Manchester United at Upton Park in September 1928 and making two further appearances that season versus Portsmouth and Derby County respectively. He had earlier made one appearance for West Ham in 1926/27 and had been honoured by representing Middlesex County. Johnny transferred to Brentford (52 League apps, 18 goals) in 1928 and afterwards had the 1930/31 season with Manchester City (four League apps, one goal). He joined Brighton and Hove Albion (eight League apps, one goal) in August 1934; Millwall (six League apps) in July 1935 and Yeovil in May 1936.

PEARCE, Ian — 1997-2004

Born: Bury St Edmunds, Suffolk, 7.5.74
League apps: 142 (9 goals)
Cup apps: 21 (1 goal)

A TEAM-MATE OF Tony Gale in Blackburn Rovers' 1995 Premiership Championship side, this towering six-foot-three-inch defender overcame two of the worst injuries a player can get – a broken leg and cruciate ligament damage – to become once more the mainstay of the Hammers rearguard. During his early career at Chelsea and Rovers, Ian gained a reputation of being something of an all-rounder, being equally at home at full-back, midfield or as a striker if needed. After a handful of substitute appearances at Stamford Bridge, Ian moved to Ewood Park for a £300,000 fee in October 1993, but suffered more than his fair share of injuries with the Lancastrians, too. Even so, after the player had managed only 80 League and Cup appearances (three goals) in four seasons at Rovers, Hammers took a massive gamble when they laid out a hefty £1.6 million fee for the former England Youth and Under-21 international to bring him back south in September 1997. Ian soon put the club's management and fans minds at rest, however, with some

storming performances in his first season at the Boleyn when, aided by his steadying influence, Hammers fought through to the Quarter-finals of both domestic Cups and consolidated their position in the Premiership. 1998/99 was another successful campaign for the versatile defender who, surprisingly skilful for such a big man, was able to bring the ball out of defence at will and caused consternation in opposing penalty areas for crosses and corner kicks from which he scored two valuable goals. Unfortunately, the honour of being voted Hammer of the Year in recognition of his fine performances by the fans was tempered by disappointment when he had to accept the award on crutches after breaking a leg in the 2-1 win at Spurs four days before the season's end. As Harry Redknapp explained in his programme notes: "He fell heavily after defending a ball and received lengthy treatment on the pitch but continued playing to the final whistle, so we didn't think it was too bad. But when he turned up for training on Tuesday the knee had swollen and we sent him for a scan which revealed a fracture." Recovered in time to help Hammers to Semi-final victory over Dutch side Heerenveen in the Intertoto Cup, Ian was just 37 minutes into the opening Premiership clash of the season against Spurs at Upton Park when his injury jinx struck again. Torn cruciate knee ligaments in an accidental collision with team-mate and namesake Stuart Pearce led to a nightmare 14 months of gruelling rehabilitation work when it was feared the gutsy defender might never play again. But Ian was back for the 1-0 win over Newcastle United at the Boleyn at the end of October 2000 to complete a recovery of which Julian Dicks would have been proud. Although his first team appearances were punctuated by further spells of absence through other niggling injuries thereafter, it must have been a sweet moment when he scored a 25-yard equaliser in the last minute at White Hart Lane to enable Hammers to draw 1-1 in April 2002 and again he came up to head the winner in the last game of the season at Upton Park versus Bolton Wanderers to clinch a seventh-place finish in manager Glenn Roeder's first season in charge. Able to participate in pre-season training for the first time in five years in the pre-season of 2002/03, Ian continued to show his versatility as a makeshift striker as Hammers battled valiantly, but vainly, to stay in the Premiership. His battling qualities were even more crucial following Hammers' fall from grace, but hardly anyone could blame the veteran defender from accepting a dream move back to the Premiership with Fulham in January 2004 and the chance of one last big pay day as his slice of the £1 million move, which saw Andy Melville going in the opposite direction. But all parties must have been sweating on the results of his two medicals with Al Fayed's men before the deal could go through. Happily, Ian passed the most stringent of examinations of his fitness and was soon a firm favourite at Loftus Road and then Craven Cottage as the west Londoners returned to their spiritual home.

PEARCE, Stuart — 1999-2001

Born: Hammersmith, London, 24.4.62
League apps: 42 (2 goals)
Cup apps: 8 (1 goal)

ALREADY A LEGEND with England and Nottingham Forest when he arrived at Upton Park on a free transfer from Newcastle United in August 1999, where he was deemed surplus to requirements by Magpies manager Ruud Gullit. One man's loss as they say, and Harry Redknapp couldn't move quick enough to get the 76 times capped "Psycho" through the Upton Park gates after originally failing to sign him after he'd quit as player-manager of relegated Nottingham Forest in the summer of 1997. Finding it hard to conceal his excitement at bringing someone with the experience of over 600 League appearances and nearly 100 goals behind them to the table, he exclaimed: "I've finally got Stuart Pearce and he's gonna be tremendous for us!" And he certainly was! But no one could anticipate his recall to the England team for the Euro 2000 qualifiers against Luxembourg and Poland by Kevin Keegan, which left the player himself "as surprised as anyone". It proved to be an inspired selection as at the age of 37, Hammers' new England international once again showed the bulldog spirit so badly missed in the 6-0 Wembley rout over little Luxembourg. In the 0-0 draw with the Poles in Warsaw he was the only Englishman to walk tall and again outstanding. So, after only four games for Hammers, of which three had been won and the other drawn, Stuart had added another two for his country to bring his career total to 78. Then, in his first match back on Premiership duty against Watford at Upton Park, the fairytale ended when the old warhorse sustained a broken leg in a 50-50 tackle with Watford's Micah Hyde just before half-time in the 1-0 win. Typically courageous, Pearcey wanted to play on despite his injury, but an on-the-spot diagnosis provided by a new x-ray machine, brought in following Stuart's namesake Ian's injury the previous season, immediately revealed a fractured tibia to prevent any further damage being incurred. Never one to stay idle, Stuart used the time vacated by his enforced absence to swot up on his UEFA coaching badge and barely three weeks after his set-back against Watford he received the perfect boost when he was named England coach for the UEFA Under-18 Championship games against Spain, Cyprus and San Marino. With young Hammers Stephen Bywater, Michael Carrick, Joe Cole and Izzy Iriekpen in the squad, Stuart simply carried on the unofficial training sessions he'd already begun with the group at Upton Park, at national level, to highlight another advantage of having someone as dedicated as him on the payroll. Back in the West Ham first team at the end of February 2000, the unthinkable happened when, in an innocuous looking challenge with Southampton's Kevin Davies, Psycho again broke the same leg, ruling him out for the rest of the season and fuelling fresh speculation that this time his career really was finished. Those who thought it was all over failed to realise the indomitable spirit of the man and, against all odds, he was back pounding the beat in pre-season training in preparation for the 2000/01 campaign. Incredibly, only Shaka Hislop and Michael Carrick matched the lion-hearted defender's record of playing 34 Premiership matches and all eight Cup games that season, which saw Hammers famously dump Manchester United out of the FA Cup in a shock 1-0 win at Old Trafford and only succumb in a desperately close 3-2 defeat to Spurs at Upton Park in the Sixth Round, in which Pearcey kept Hammers' hopes alive with a superbly struck free-kick. With his champion Harry Redknapp gone before the season's end and uncertainty hanging over his Upton Park future, the "Iron Lion" couldn't resist one final Bosman move to rejoin his old pal Kevin Keegan at Manchester City. It proved to be another inspired move as, under his leadership, City ran away

with the First Division Championship with 99 points to return to the Premiership at the first attempt. Having made 38 appearances towards their triumph and scored three goals along the way, it was a perfect opportunity for this remarkable athlete to bring the curtain down on an illustrious career in which West ham United were honoured to feature. Stuart was appointed manager of City following the exit of Keegan in February 2005.

PEARSON, Stuart — 1979-82

Born: Hull, Yorkshire, 21.6.49
League apps: 34 (6 goals)
Cup apps: 16 (4 goals)

A GOALSCORING STRIKER of proven ability whose time at the club was dogged by injuries. Had already won 15 full international caps for England when he arrived at Upton Park from Manchester United for a big fee in August 1979. He first impressed Hammers when he played against them in an FA Cup tie for Hull City at Boothferry Park in January 1973; but the player spent the intervening years at Old Trafford, appearing in two Wembley Cup Finals for United – a feat he emulated with Hammers. Stuart had a brief spell in South Africa before opening a shop at Whitefield, near Manchester, which sells European tile imports. He was dismissed as assistant manger of Bradford City along with manager Frank Stapleton in April 1994. Before his spell with Bradford, "Pancho" spent five years as assistant manager at West Bromich Albion under Ron Atkinson, Brian Talbot and finally Bobby Gould, but didn't gel with Bobby. He still manages teams in the seven-a-side veterans tournaments and has kept in touch with former team-mate Paul Allen because of his links with the PFA. Stuart made 143 League and Cup appearances for Hull scoring 47 goals and in 179 League and Cup games for United was on the scoresheet 66 times. Although retired from football, Stuart played Rugby Union for Sale in 1985!

PETCHEY, George — 1952-53

Born: Whitechapel, London, 24.6.31
League apps: 2

GIVEN ONLY TWO Second Division outings during his time at Upton Park in the inside-right position, he went on to make over 250 appearances for Queens Park Rangers, who he joined in July 1953 as a wing-half. He transferred to Crystal Palace in May 1960, made a further 153 senior showings for the Glaziers, and was an ever-present as Palace won promotion to Division Three in 1961. George also helped them into the Second Division in 1964, before injury ended his career in 1965. He then won further fame as manager of Orient and Millwall, after cutting his teeth in management as Bert Head's assistant at Palace. In 1986 he was helping to run Brighton's junior teams and was then appointed Youth Development Officer at the Goldstone Ground. Later, George worked with Liam Brady when he took over at Brighton and then did some scouting and coaching with Newcastle United. He claims to have once had to discipline Orient's Glenn Roeder when manager at Brisbane Road – for spending too much time training his greyhounds!

Stuart Pearson

Stuart Pearce

PETERS, Martin MBE   1962-70

Born: Plaistow, London, 8.22.43
League apps: 302 (81 goals)
Cup apps: 62 (19 goals)

THE LEAST FAMOUS, but arguably the most complete footballer of the legendary West Ham/England triumvirate of Moore, Hurst and Peters, which did so much to win the World Cup for their country in 1966 and the European Cup Winners' Cup for their club a year earlier. A pupil of Fanshawe School, Dagenham, Peters' career charts a classic course rising from his school side to Dagenham Schools, London, Essex and England Schools and then England Youth after signing apprentice with West Ham in May 1959. Tagged "ten years ahead of his time" by England manager Sir Alf Ramsey in 1966, his career eventually exceeded that milestone and beyond with Hammers, Tottenham Hotspur, Norwich City and Sheffield United. Martin made the first of over 300 League appearances with the club on Good Friday, 1962 against Cardiff City at Upton Park and went on to play in every position – including goalkeeper! In fact, in only his third senior game – in the return at Ninian Park on Easter Monday – Peters found himself deputising for injured keeper Brian Rhodes, who had himself come into the side as cover for Lawrie Leslie, hurt versus Arsenal two days earlier! He played five times for England Under-23s and 67 times for the full England team after making his full international debut versus Yugoslavia at Wembley (May 4, 1966) in a 2-0 victory. Martin twice went close to marking his debut with a goal, but he had only to wait for the next game versus Finland in Helsinki (June 26, 1966) to open his scoring account for his country in a 3-0 win. His first 33 caps were achieved as a Hammer, the rest with Spurs in addition to representing the Football League on five occasions. Left out of the West Ham side that fought its way to Wembley for the 1964 Cup Final versus Preston North End in favour of "hard man" Eddie Bovington, he made up for the disappointment the following year by winning a European Cup Winners' Cup medal there after a faultless display against the German side TSV Munich 1860, returning again to the Twin Towers in 1966 to help his country lift the World Cup. Although he missed the opening game of the tournament versus Uruguay, Peters came in for the group victories over Mexico and France but it was the Quarter-final success over the ruthless Argentinians that really signalled his arrival on the world stage. It was from Peters' cross that Hurst headed in the winner – a goal that had "made in West Ham" written all over it. The understanding between Hurst and Peters was uncanny and proved so productive for the club and country over a long period. Of course, the 1966 final versus West Germany belonged to the Hammers' trio. Moore captained the side, Hurst netted a hat-trick and Peters scored the crucial second goal in an epic 4-2 victory. Peters flourished in Ramsey's new "wingless wonders" system from which the modern-day "midfielder" evolved. Three months before the Wembley highlight, Peters had received a League Cup runners-up medal with his club versus West Bromwich Albion – his goal in the second leg at The Hawthorns failing to prevent Hammers from losing 5-3 on aggregate. This was the last honour he was to gain as a West Ham player before his record £200,000 transfer to Spurs in March 1970. Spurs paid £150,000 plus Jimmy Greaves, but there was no doubt that Tottenham had the best of the deal. For Spurs, Peters – tall and lean – twice gained League Cup winners' medals versus Aston Villa in 1971 and Norwich City in 1973, both at Wembley. He also won a UEFA Cup winners' medal with Spurs in 1971 versus Wolves and a runners up medal in the same competition when Spurs lost to Feyenoord in 1974. He made 287 League and Cup appearances at White Hart Lane between 1970 and March 1975 and just over that total with his next club, Norwich City (£50,000) before being appointed player-manager of Sheffield United to end his

playing career at Bramall Lane in 1981 (although he did turn out as an amateur for Gorleston for a while.) He then worked for a motor insurance company (with Geoff Hurst) after a spell with a fruit machine company in East Anglia. He became involved in promotional work for Spurs as well as occasional TV appearances as a match analyst. One of the all-time greats at Upton Park, Peters was the complete midfielder – perceptive, an excellent passer with both feet, strong in the air and with a sharp eye for goal. He was so difficult for opponents to mark, often arriving in the box late on the blind-side, hence the title of his autobiography: *Goals from Nowhere*. Just look at his scoring record for Hammers – superb by any midfield player's standards and comparable to many strikers' goals ratio! His only hat-trick came versus West Bromwich Albion (August 31, 1968) – Harry Redknapp got the other in the 4-0 rout. Never one to seek the limelight, Martin Peters has retained his essentially shy and retiring nature while managing to hone his social skills to the level expected of someone who is constantly in demand as an after-dinner speaker at countless official functions and spends matchdays hosting hospitality alternately between White Hart Lane and Upton Park. That Martin carries

off his duties with such aplomb is more down to his amusingly dry sense of humour and almost "royal" demeanour, than any desire to court celebrity. Whether he is dispensing hospitality in the Billy Nicholson suite at Spurs or looking after guests in the White Horse suite at Upton Park, Martin is always the perfect host who loves to reminisce with fans about his playing career, of which he has razor-sharp recall. A successful businessman in his own right, who was a non-executive director at Tottenham until just recently, Martin loves to attend ex-players functions where he can relax in the company of ex-team-mates such as Brian "Stag" Dear and Eddie Bov, and perhaps raise a glass to Budgie, Sammy, Charlo, Dave Bickles and Mooro, the class of 1966, who are sadly no longer with us.

England Caps: 1966 vs Yugoslavia, Finland, Poland, Mexico, France, Argentina, Portugal, West Germany, Northern Ireland, Czechoslovakia, Wales; 1967 vs Scotland, Wales, Northern Ireland, USSR; 1968 vs Scotland, Spain (twice), Sweden, Yugoslavia, USSR, Romania, Bulgaria; 1969 vs France, Northern Ireland, Scotland, Mexico, Uruguay, Brazil, Holland, Portugal (sub); 1970 vs Holland, Belgium (33).

Career record

	League		FAC		LC		Europe		Total	
Played	App	Gls	App	Gls	App	Gls	App	Gls	App	Gls
1961-62	5	0	0	0	0	0	0	0	5	0
1962-63	36	8	1	0	2	1	0	0	39	9
1963-64	32	3	0	0	4	0	0	0	36	3
1964-65	35	5	2	0	1	0	9	1	47	6
1965-66	40	11	4	0	10	3	6	3	60	17
1966-67	41	14	2	0	6	2	0	0	49	16
1967-68	40	14	3	2	3	2	0	0	46	18
1968-69	42	19	3	3	3	2	0	0	48	24
1969-70	31	7	1	0	2	0	0	0	34	7
TOTAL	**302**	**81**	**16**	**5**	**31**	**10**	**15**	**4**	**364**	**100**

PHILLIPS, Wilf — 1931-32

Born: Brierley Hill, West Midlands, 9.8.1895
League apps: 21 (3 goals)
Cup apps: 2

A FAMOUS NAME from Millwall's Third Division South championship side of 1928 – which notched up a record 65 points and 127 goals in winning the title. "Peanuts Phillips" – as he was lovingly tagged by the Docker's fans – was one of the renowned inside-forward trio that contributed 83 goals towards that total: Wilf hit 26, former Huddersfield, Chelsea and England centre-forward Jack Cock added 25; and another Hammer-to-be, Jackie Landells, weighed in with 32. Switching his allegiance from the Lions to Irons, Wilf scored on his debut in a 4-2 victory at Ewood Park (November 28, 1931). It proved to be one of the few bright spots of a dismal season that saw Hammers relegated to the Second Division at its end and Wilf departed from the Upton Park scene to near-neighbours Clapton Orient. Before Millwall, Wilf scored goals regularly for Stoke City, Ebbw Vale, Darlaston, Bilston Unity and Bristol Rovers. He signed for Lions for a £500 fee in November 1925. Joined Thames in June 1930 from where he transferred to Irons for another £500 price tag in May 1931. After Clapton Orient he joined his last club, Stourbridge, in August 1933. A great practical joker, he was nicknamed "Winkie" by the fans. Altogether Wilf scored 58 League goals in 108 appearances for Millwall; three in 14 League appearances for Stoke; 35 in 90 League appearances for Bristol Rovers and four in 24 League appearances for Orient. He died in 1973 in Penzance, Cornwall aged 77.

PHIPPS, Cecil — 1919

League apps: 1

HIS ONLY LEAGUE appearance came against Stoke City at the Victoria Ground on September 27, 1919, when Hammers went down 2-1.

PIKE, Geoff — 1975-87

Born: Clapton, London, 28.9.56
League apps: 291 (32 goals)
Cup apps: 82 (10 goals)

THE WHOLEHEARTED ENDEAVOUR and perpetual motion of this key midfield man did much to cushion the blow of losing Patsy Holland through injury. A similar type of player to Pat and his predecessor Ronnie Boyce, Geoff made a major contribution to the club's promotion back into the top flight in 1981. Making his League debut as far back as March 1976 versus Birmingham City, he played much of his early soccer in the Thurrock district and later with Gidea Park Rangers, well-known providers of football talent. A member of Hammers' youth side that reached the FA Youth Cup Final in 1975 versus Ipswich Town. Diminutive Geoff had to wait a further five years for his first senior honour – an FA Cup Winners' medal in 1980. He followed it up with a League Cup runners-up medal and a Second Division Championship memento the next year, when he was ever-present, and runner-up in the Hammer of the Year poll. Transferring to Notts County for £35,000 in July 1987, he scored twice on his debut and went on to appear in 82 League games for the Magpies and score 17 goals, including the only hat-trick of his career versus Southend United. In September 1989 Geoff returned to east London to make 44 League appearances for Orient (one goal) and scored twice in 12 Cup appearances before taking charge of the youth team at Brisbane Road. Geoff then moved to non-League Hendon Town where he made 30 appearances for the famous former Amateur Cup winners while also acting as coach at Claremont Road. Geoff, who early in his West Ham career had the unusual and character building experience of spending

PIERCY, Frank — 1904-12

SL apps: 214 (7 goals)
Cup apps: 17

SIGNED FROM MIDDLESBROUGH during Hammer's initial season at the Boleyn in 1904, Frank was intimately involved in the affairs of West Ham United up to his untimely retirement through illness in 1931. He first took an active interest in the game as a 16-year-old with Southbank, a junior team competing in the Teesiders Minor League. He joined Boro in 1898, but retained his amateur status while continuing his trade as a blacksmith until the Teesiders left the Northern League to turn pro at the turn of the century and joined Division Two of the League. Frank captained the Reds for the four seasons leading up to his move south, during which time he won several Cleveland Cup medals. Nicknamed the "Old War Horse" at the Boleyn ground because of his robust style of defending, he often fell foul of referees and was suspended for one month following an incident in a match versus Swindon (September 1, 1907). The ban had little effect, however, as he got his marching orders again in a bruising encounter with arch-rivals Millwall (February 22, 1908). But the enforced absences didn't prevent him from amassing the third highest Southern League appearance record for the club, behind Herbert Ashton (224) and Fred Blackburn (217). A big crowd favourite, he was made skipper when Dave Gardner left for Croydon Common in 1907. A mainstay of the West Ham defence in the centre-half position during eight Southern League seasons until he packed up playing in 1912, after being awarded his first benefit by the club in 1910 when he kept the proceeds of the Brompton match. He was then appointed assistant trainer under Charlie Paynter. The end of World War I saw him in charge of one of West Ham's most successful reserve XIs in the London Combination during a period when he was often invited to be a "sponge man" for senior amateur representative sides including the Isthmian League XI. An all-round sportsman, Frank was prominent in local club cricket, won an Essex County Bowls Badge and held a golf handicap of two at his peak having received expert tuition from golf pro team-mate, George Kitchen, to whom he handed over the captain's armband when injuries began to take their toll. One of the club's finest ever servants, he was awarded a posthumous testimonial match following his death before the start of the 1931/32 season, when an Isthmian League XI provided the opposition to West Ham's First Division side on October 1, 1931 at Upton Park.

Career record

Played	League		FAC		LC		Europe		Total	
	App	Gls	App	Gls	App	Gls	App	Gls	App	Gls
1904-05	33	2	1	0	0	0	0	0	34	2
1905-06	24	0	2	0	0	0	0	0	26	0
1906-07	37	0	2	0	0	0	0	0	39	0
1907-08	23	0	2	0	0	0	0	0	25	0
1908-09	26	2	0	0	0	0	0	0	26	2
1909-10	29	0	5	0	0	0	0	0	34	0
1910-11	32	2	4	0	0	0	0	0	36	2
1911-12	10	1	1	0	0	0	0	0	11	1
TOTAL	**214**	**7**	**17**	**0**	**0**	**0**	**0**	**0**	**231**	**7**

Geoff Pike

Career record

Played	League		FAC		LC		Europe		Total	
	App	Gls	App	Gls	App	Gls	App	Gls	App	Gls
1975-76	3	0	0	0	0	0	0	0	3	0
1976-77	20	6	6	1	1	1	0	0	27	8
1977-78	28	2	1	0	1	0	0	0	30	2
1978-79	14	1	0	0	1	0	0	0	15	1
1979-80	31	5	8	1	6	1	0	0	45	7
1980-81	42	6	3	0	9	1	6	1	60	8
1981-82	34	2	2	0	5	0	0	0	41	2
1982-83	40	6	1	0	7	0	0	0	48	6
1983-84	28	2	2	1	5	1	0	0	35	4
1984-85	30	2	4	1	4	0	0	0	38	3
1985-86	10	0	5	1	0	0	0	0	15	1
1986-87	11	0	4	0	1	0	0	0	16	0
TOTAL	**291**	**32**	**36**	**5**	**40**	**4**	**6**	**1**	**373**	**42**

Geoff Pike

two summers in America playing for Hertford Bicentennials, took up a part-time post with the FA when he left Hendon in which he was employed to go around monitoring the football clubs to make sure things were being run within the FA rules and regulations – such as trialling boys for the correct length of time and ensuring that they received a certain standard of coaching. It was while he was on duty for the FA one day at Chadwell Heath that he noticed Hammers were flouting the rules by playing an Under-11 game against a local representative side that included youngsters from other clubs as an 11-a-side trial match. It was "completely against regulations and I ended up having a confrontation with Tony Carr and Jimmy Hampson on the sideline", Geoff revealed in a "clear the air" interview with Neale Harvey in *Hammers News* magazine in August 2001 and continued: "It was a difficult situation, because I'd been involved at West Ham for more than 20 years as a player and to have to say that what they were doing was illegal was very hard. The FA took West Ham to task over it. The club was hauled up to Lancaster Gate, fined and all their centres of excellence were closed down for a year." Not surprisingly, Pikey was portrayed as the villain of the piece and was consequently banned from Upton Park and Chadwell Heath by managing director Peter Storrie. But really Geoff was between a rock and a hard place and his position with the FA was compromised by his affection and loyalty to the club he loved. "Tony and Jimmy thought I was a major factor in closing their centres of excellence, and I'm sure a lot of fans out there thought the same, but that wasn't the case. The FA had a file on West Ham that was four or five inches thick and my piece was just one piece of A4 paper. I was just doing my job. I subsequently showed them both the contents of my report to the FA and we had a long meeting to discuss everything and I'm really pleased to say that they understood much more than they did before about how things happened. I just wanted the opportunity to put the record straight." Happily the situation was resolved amicably on all sides and Geoff has been welcomed back to the club he served so loyally with open arms in his role as a South Eastern representative of the PFA, a post he held for the past six years in which he helps youth players and senior pros gain coaching qualifications of their own. Geoff, who was granted a well deserved testimonial match by the club in 1988 against crack Yugoslavs Dinamo Zagreb concluded: "I had a tremendous career at West Ham and it disturbed me that what happened when I was at the FA could have tarnished my relationship with the club."

PINDER
1900-02

SL apps: 1
Cup apps: 1

THIS LEFT-BACK MADE just one League appearance, in a 2-0 Southern League win over Queens Park Rangers at Notting Hill.

POLLARD, Walter
1929-33

Born: Burnley, Lancashire, 26.9.1906
League apps: 37 (goals)
Cup apps: 6 (2 goals)

WALTER WAS SIGNED as a full professional by First Division Burnley at the age of 17 in September 1924, after impressing in the Burnley Sunday School League. He formed a memorable right-wing partnership with Clarets' famous England international Bob Kelly while at Turf Moor. Switching his allegiance (but not his colours) when he joined Hammers in 1929, he made his Upton Park debut later the following season against his former club. A member of the West Ham team that reached the FA Cup Semi-finals in 1933, he left the club to take up the appointment of player-coach of Soucaux in France during the 1933/34 season, but did not find the Gallic temperament of some players to his liking. Returning to England, he played out the remainder of his career with Fulham, Southampton (where he made 23 League appearances and scored three goals) and Brighton; the latter of whom he was serving when World War II called an abrupt halt to League Football. Finding

Walter Pollard

employment in the electricity department of Ilford Borough Council, he also coached their works side until he was struck down with a heart attack at the tragically early age of 38 in 1945.

PORFIRIO, Hugo   1997-98

Born: Lisbon, Portugal, 29.9.73
League apps: 21 (2 goals)
Cup apps: 4 (2 goals)

WHEN HE WAS asked why Portuguese giants Sporting Lisbon were allowing Hugo Porfirio to go on loan to West Ham in September 1997, Luis-Miguel Santos of Portugal's leading daily football newspaper *A Bola*, simply replied: "Because they are mad." It later transpired that they weren't mad but simply hard up and hoped to sell the Portuguese international to Hammers for £800,000 after he'd satisfactorily completed a six-month trial period at Upton Park. But after watching the little "Portugeezer" midfielder in successive matches against Liverpool and Everton, the West Ham management knew what Senor Santos meant, Hugo was a very skilful player indeed. But the questions still remained: why had Sporting constantly put one of their country's most promising young talents out on loan, first to FC Tirense where he made 19 First Division appearances as a 20-year-old in 1994/95, and then to Desportiva De Leiria with whom he scored eight times in 28 matches the following campaign and was voted their Player of the Year. Having previously only made two appearances for Sporting in 1992/93 and nine the next season, it was a bizarre state of affairs to say the least and it was next stop West Ham. Hammers had already run the rule over the player when he came on as a 44th minute sub in the club's special Centenary Match against Sporting, who also fielded Dani and Hammer to be Paulo Alves, so were aware of his pedigree, which included full international appearances against the Republic of Ireland in a friendly and a sub appearance against Turkey at Euro 96 that summer in England. The truth was, opportunities to display his undoubted talents had been denied him by a succession of frightened Sporting coaches who, living in a climate of fear over their jobs had been reluctant to give youth its fling. Living in the shadows of Benfica and Porto had seen 16 Sporting managers come and go in the previous 17 years, while in that time only one Cup had graced the trophy room at the superbly appointed Avalade Stadium. Having been recommended to Hammers by Paulo Futre, Hugo's prospects of earning a permanent move were not helped by that great player's career being ended by injury after such a short spell at the Boleyn, but Hugo gave a good enough account of himself in his 27 senior outings in 1997/98, most notably in the 4-1 Coca Cola Cup win over Nottingham Forest in October when he made two for a grateful Iain Dowie and scored one himself. For whatever reason, Porfirio never got his permanent move to east London and instead went back to Portugal to sign for Sporting's arch rivals Benfica. But as Greavsie says, football's a funny old game and after six months and just three sub appearances at the Eagles' famous Estadio da Luz, Hugo was back in England again on loan to Premiership strugglers Nottingham Forest, who'd obviously remembered his performance against them at the Boleyn. His silky skills couldn't save Forest from relegation, though, as he struggled with injury and scored one goal in nine games and returned to Benfica after four months at the City Ground. The previous season Porfirio had been a team-mate of Brian Deane, Scott Minto and Gary Charles in Lisbon, such was the village world of European football. By the following season they'd all moved on and so, soon, would Porfirio who, after only a meagre three outings for Benfica in 2000/01, was surely tired of travelling the world in search of regular first team football. Like another ex-Hammer before him – Alex Bunbury – Hugo's

Hugo Porfirio

wanderlust took him to the Portuguese island of Madeira to ply his trade with CS Maritimo where he continued the 2000/01 campaign and made a healthy 17 First Division appearances and scored one goal in the 1-1 draw at Vitoria Guimaraes. In 2001/02, Porfirio made another four substitute appearances for Benfica in the Portuguese Campeonato Nacional.

POTTS, Steve   1985-2002

Born: Hartford, Connecticut USA, 7.5.67
League apps: 398 (1 goal)
Cup apps: 95

STEADY STEVE MAY have been born in the United States, but he is an East Ender through-and-through having returned with his family to Dagenham, Essex at a very young age. Any hope of "Pottsy" earning a place in the host country squad for the 1994 World Cup Finals vanished when he appeared for England at Schoolboy and Youth levels. He starred for Barking, Essex and London Under-16s before joining Hammers straight from school in 1973. Steve captained the youth team to the South-East Counties Division One title in 1984/85. He made his first team debut in the First Division at Upton Park versus Queens Park Rangers on New Year's Day, 1985, as a replacement for Geoff Pike. It was his only senior outing of the season and he got only one sub outing in 1985/86, coming on for Steve Walford in a 1-0 win at Ipswich Town. But Steve continued to impress in the reserves and skippered the side to the Combination League Championship at the end of the most successful season, League-wise, in the club's history. His introduction to the first team was gradual, chances only usually presenting themselves when injury ruled out regular right-back Ray Stewart. More often than not, Pottsy found himself fulfilling a midfield slot as the team fought a series of relegation battles in the late 1980s. But he adapted well to playing in different positions – just as well too, because after establishing himself as first-choice right-back under Lou Macari in Division Two, Steve's place was under threat again when the next manager Billy Bonds made right-back Tim Breacker his first signing in October 1990. They shared the position for a while before Steve slotted back into midfield where his career took an unexpectedly welcome new turn. Long-term injuries to long-serving centre-backs Alvin Martin and Tony Gale caused Bonzo concern, but he found the answer in the versatile Potts. Gaining in confidence, this shy, unassuming man built a new reputation for himself as an accomplished central defender. He relied on Martin or Gale to win high balls, but made up for his lack of inches by reading dangerous situations in advance of the opposition's players. He brought much needed pace to the back four and quickly earned the respect of teammates and fans for his new-found qualities in the centre of defence. Steve's safety-first approach brought more solidarity to West Ham's defence – he preferred to leave the fancy stuff to others – if not goals at the other end. In more than 300 senior games for the club, Steve managed just one goal – a long range "bobbler" that crept under the Hull City keeper in a 7-1 Upton Park romp (October 6, 1990) en route to promotion from Division Two. But it would be impossible to count how many times the mild-mannered Potts has stopped goals going in at the other end with his clinically timed tackles. In the traumatic 1991/92 season, Potts was one of Hammers' few success stories. He ended that term voted runner-up (to Julian Dicks) in the Hammer of the Year poll. A year later, he not only became the fan's number one choice but also took over the captaincy at Dicks' expense and led the team back into the top flight. Steve remained consistent at the heart of Hammers defence in 1993/94 and was once again rewarded in the fans poll when voted runner-up with Mattie Holmes to winner Trevor Morley as Hammers finished a respectable 13th in their first season back in the Premiership. As the 1994 World Cup Finals in the USA

approached, Steve was even being tipped for a place in the Team USA squad. But further investigation revealed his Under-11 England Youth caps and ruled out his hopes of a call up. "I would have definitely gone to the States," he insisted at the time. "After all, I've got a US passport and I'm more entitled to play for America than a lot of people aren't I?" As a reward for playing consistently well during the 1994/95 season when he was an ever-present, Stevie won his second Hammer of the Year award as Hammers avoided relegation with a late flourish that saw them deprive Manchester United of the Premiership title in a 1-1 draw on the last day of the season at Upton Park. The following season was going well for skipper Pottsy too, until he picked up his first ever red card on a frenetic, rain-soaked March evening at Newcastle United for two bookings made inside a crazy 28-second spell trying to control the Geordie's French international David Ginola. After tugging his shirt, Steve claimed to have got the ball in the second bookable offence, but the ref thought otherwise and it was left to Les "the Cat" Sealey to spare Hammers' blushes by putting on a wonderful show to keep the score down to 3-0 in the match, broadcast live on Sky Sports. Suspended after missing one game in the previous 165 League matches, Steve suddenly found himself frozen out of the first team. He lost the captain's armband too, to Julian Dicks. The following 1996/97 season was also frustrating for the loyal defender, although he was brought back into the side for the last 11 games and made a major contribution to staving off relegation that year. Awarded a much deserved testimonial match against London rivals QPR in August 1997, when a 12,658 crowd did him proud, Steve was in the side on a more regular basis in 1997/98, making 23 League appearances against 20 the previous term; he also featured in the epic League Cup and FA Cup Quarter-final confrontations with Arsenal in the second half of what turned out to be an exciting season. Ever dependable, Steve was Harry Redknapp's rock in many a crisis and he played consistently well whenever called upon, most notably against Liverpool in 1998/99 when he helped to nullify the dual threat of Michael Owen and Robbie Fowler in the 2-1 win at the Boleyn. The following campaign he got his first taste of European football after a 16-year wait via the Intertoto Cup and UEFA Cup, but made an uncharacteristic error that cost a goal in the away leg against Steaua Bucharest. But his mistakes were few and far between and in 2000/01, Steve achieved a remarkable milestone when he made his 500th appearance in all competitions for Hammers to figure high among the club's all-time appearance record holders. When he eventually left the Upton Park scene at the end of 2001/02, Steve continued playing with his local conference side Dagenham and Redbridge and was involved in their exciting FA Cup run in 2002/03.

Steve Potts

Career record										
	League		**FAC**		**LC**		**Europe**		**Total**	
Played	**App**	**Gls**	**App**	**Gls**	**App**	**Gls**	**App**	**Gls**	**App**	**Gls**
1984-85	1	0	0	0	0	0	0	0	1	0
1985-86	1	0	0	0	0	0	0	0	1	0
1986-87	8	0	0	0	0	0	0	0	8	0
1987-88	8	0	3	0	1	0	0	0	12	0
1988-89	28	0	7	0	6	0	0	0	41	0
1989-90	32	0	1	0	7	0	0	0	40	0
1990-91	37	1	7	0	2	0	0	0	46	1
1991-92	34	0	5	0	3	0	0	0	42	0
1992-93	46	0	2	0	2	0	0	0	50	0
1993-94	40	0	6	0	3	0	0	0	49	0
1994-95	42	0	2	0	4	0	0	0	48	0
1995-96	34	0	3	0	3	0	0	0	40	0
1996-97	20	0	1	0	1	0	0	0	22	0
1997-98	23	0	5	0	4	0	0	0	32	0
1998-99	19	0	1	0	2	0	0	0	22	0
1999-00	17	0	1	0	1	0	9	0	28	0
2000-01	8	0	0	0	3	0	0	0	11	0
TOTAL	**398**	**1**	**44**	**0**	**42**	**0**	**9**	**0**	**493**	**1**

POWELL, Chris — 2004-

Born: Lambeth, London, 8.9.69
League apps: 39
Cup apps: 3

"EVERYTHING COMES TO those who wait" might be the motto of this no frills, no nonsense left wing-back who joined Alan Pardew's League One squad on a month's loan from Charlton Athletic in September 2004. After some impressive displays from the England international and some hurried consultations from the Addick's manager, ex-Hammer Alan Curbishley, his loan was quickly extended for another month as Hammers made no secret of their desire to sign the experienced defender on a permanent basis. Having failed to make the grade with his first club, Crystal Palace, where he made just a handful of senior appearances and was released on a free transfer to Southend United after making 11 League appearances on loan at Aldershot, Chris resurrected his career at Roots Hall and played 292 first team games for the Essex team before he got a dream £750,000 move to First Division Derby County on transfer deadline day in January 1996. It proved an inspired move on the part of the Rams manager Jim Smith as they won promotion to the Premiership, with Chris's thoughtful passing game proving a big asset. After 101 games and two goals in the black and white, Chris moved back down south to join Charlton Athletic in September 1998. Relegated in his first season, it didn't look a good switch at that stage, but the constructive, rather than destructive, full-back played a big part in getting the Addick's straight back up at the first attempt, and as First Division Champions to boot. Loving to get down the flanks and deliver crosses into the goalmouth, Chris scored a cracker against Spurs at White Hart Lane for his first Premiership goal. Maybe Sven Goran Eriksson was watching, because he was shortly afterwards called up for England duty and won a string of caps at an age when most players are thinking about retiring. His five caps for England represent the most ever won by a Charlton player and how Palace must have kicked themselves for letting him go! Certainly his performances for Hammers in the triumphant 2004/05 campaign proved his signing was Charlton's loss and Hammers' gain. Returned to Charlton in June 2005.

POWELL, Darren — 2004-05

Born: Hammersmith, London, 10.3.76
League apps: 5 (1 goal)

A POWERFUL DEFENDER signed on loan from Crystal Palace in time to make his Hammers debut in the fractious derby defeat at Millwall on November 21, 2004. He began his League career when he joined Third Division Brentford from Isthmian League Hampton for £15,000 in July 1998 and won a Division Three Championship medal in his first season at Griffin Park and was also voted the Bees' Player of the Season by the fans. The giant centre-half later went on to form a tremendous partnership with Icelandic international Ivar Ingimarsson at the heart of Brentford's defence and headed a crucial equaliser against Huddersfield Town in the 2001/02 Second Division Play-off Semi-final at the Millennium Stadium in Cardiff. Although they went down to the Potters, it was a feat he was to repeat when he joined Palace after scoring eight goals in 156 appearances for the west Londoners. Following his £700,000 move to Selhurst Park, Darren notched the vital last gasp goal in the 2004 Play-off Semi-final Second-leg versus Sunderland that forced the saga into extra time and a subsequent penalty shoot-out as the Eagles won their way back to the Premiership at Hammers' expense in the Play-off Final at Cardiff in May 2004.

PRESLAND, Eddie — 1965

Born: Loughton, Essex, 27.3.45
League apps: 6 (1 goal)

A TALL, ADVENTUROUS full-back who scored a goal on his League debut versus Liverpool at Upton Park in February, 1965. He signed professional forms in October 1960 after playing schoolboy soccer for East Ham, London and Essex, and as a junior for Hammers. Eddie was also a fine cricketer, being capped for England Boys and later joined Essex as a professional. Transferring to Crystal Palace in January 1967, he spent three seasons as a first team regular at Selhurst Park, playing 60 League matches before moving on to Colchester United where he played 69 games to conclude his League career. Eddie was encouraged to do work in East End schools by Ron Greenwood in the mid-1960s, along with fellow Hammers John Lyall, Billy Landsdowne, Harry Cripps and Dennis Burnett, so as not to waste their afternoons after their soccer commitments were completed for the day. In his capacity of PE and games teacher at Stepney Green School, Eddie reaped the benefits of that policy and was quick to give pupils a viewing of his most cherished possession — a copy of the BBC Match of the Day video for the Liverpool game! On leaving Layer Road, Eddie teamed up with former Busby Babe and ex-West Ham and Leyton Orient defender Eddie Lewis playing for Guild FC in South Africa. When he returned in the early 1970s he was appointed player-manager to Wealdstone, whom he led to the Southern League Championship. Similar posts followed at Dulwich Hamlet, Hendon, Gravesend and Northfleet, Dulwich again and then Dagenham. Initially coach at Victoria Road, Eddie was appointed manager in 1980 and led the Daggers to their last major trophy — a 2-1 Wembley win over Mossley in the FA Trophy Final. With West Ham

Chris Powell

winning the FA Cup the week before, the East End had rarely seen such celebration especially when John Lyall arranged for the two cups to be shown off in a dual display of solidarity. Daggers promptly rewarded him with the sack! After that kick in the teeth, Eddie understandably became disillusioned with the game for a while but later returned to the game to do scouting and opposition assessment for John Lyall, Paul Goddaard and Mick McGiven at Ipswich Town.

PROCTOR, Norman 1923-24

Born: Alnwick, Northumberland, 11.5.1896
League apps: 7 (1 goal)

EQUALLY EFFECTIVE IN either of the inside-forward positions, this midfield schemer made a name for himself when he represented Durham County as a schoolboy before being signed up by Rotherham County. Joining Hammers for their initial First Division campaign of 1923/24, he made his debut in a 1-1 draw versus Middlesbrough at Upton Park on September 22, and had a further six appearances that season to close his senior account. He joined Leicester City on leaving West Ham, but only made five Second Division appearances there before joining Tranmere Rovers in 1926 where he scored 13 goals in 56 Third Division North appearances. In 1927, he moved on to Halifax Town in the same division and in three seasons at the Shay he made 123 appearances and scored three times playing a deeper role. He then had spells at Workington and Newbiggin West End. Having begun his career with a trio of North East amateur clubs – Spen Black and Whites, Scotswood and Blyth Spartans – Norman retired from football in the early 1930s and died at the early age of 51 at Winlaton Mill, County Durham in February 1947.

PROUDLOCK, George 1946-47

Born: Stubswood, Northumberland, 19.9.19
League apps: 18 (5 goals)

ONE OF A multitude of professionals who had their League careers disrupted by World War II, in which he served in the Essex Regiment, and then the Royal Artillery in North Africa. George returned to Upton Park after hostilities had ceased and normal football activities resumed in 1946/47. Signed from Northumberland amateur side Amble in 1937, the clever inside-forward made a small but valuable contribution to West Ham's post-war fortunes before transferring to Workington.

PUDAN, AE "Dickie" 1900-03

Born: Canning Town, London, date unknown
SL apps: 7

DICKIE, AS HE was affectionately known by patrons at the Memorial Grounds, formed a notable, although short-lived, full-back partnership with Scotsman Charlie Craig during Irons' initial Southern League season in 1900/01. Formerly with amateurs Clapton for the first half of 1899/1900, he first appeared in Hammers colours at Bristol City (January 12, 1901). He made only two appearances that season and five in 1901/02 before transferring to the other Bristol club, Rovers, where he won a Southern League Championship medal in 1905. Now in demand, he moved to Newcastle United and appeared in the 1908 FA Cup Final, which the Magpies lost to Wolves. He left the Geordies in May 1909 for Leicester Fosse (now City), then playing in the Second Division of the Football League. He retired in 1910 to join Huddersfield Town as secretary-manager but returned to Leicester where he eventually became a director and a successful Midlands businessman. In his schooldays, Pudan captained the Canning Town XI. Dick played over 100 Southern League games for Bristol

Rovers, made 30 League and Cup appearances for the Geordies and then made a further 51 League and Cup appearances (seven goals) for Leicester Fosse.

PUDDEFOOT, Sydney 1913-22/1932-33

Born: Bow, London, 17.10.1894
SL apps: 55 (28 goals)
Cup apps: 6 (7 goals)
League apps: 125 (67 goals)
Cup apps: 8 (5 goals)

A GOALSCORING LEGEND whose sensational £5,000 transfer to Falkirk in 1922 became the most chronicled event involving an individual in the long history of West Ham United. A pupil at Park School, West Ham, which also produced England international Harold Halse and later Hammers legend "Big" Jim Barrett, Syd had come to prominence with Condor Athletic and Limehouse Town in local junior football before being discovered playing for London Juniors versus Surrey Juniors by manager Syd King. Young Syd was brought on by Charlie Paynter and George Hilsdon and came up quickly through the ranks to become a force in the Southern League side. How well he settled into the team can be ascertained from an extract of a newspaper report featuring Hammers' 4-1 win over Exeter City at Upton Park on January 21, 1915: "In every department the winners showed superiority, and from the beginning to the end they dominated the game. For a time the visitors maintained an excellent defence, their backs kicking and tackling finely, while Pym saved several shots in splendid style. Some 14 minutes elapsed before Puddefoot, who completely outshone every other forward on the field, opened the scoring for his side and ten minutes later he was again successful in finding the net." Syd scored a hat-trick in that match and shortly afterwards established an FA Cup goalscoring record for the club when he scored five times in an 8-1 victory over Chesterfield. Following the disbandment of the Southern League for the duration of World War I at the end of the 1914/15 season "Puddy", as he was affectionately known by the fans, made 126 appearances in the replacement wartime competition, the London Combination. As he was not recruited into the military until late in the conflict, Syd was able to pursue his footballing activities to the full and really excelled in wartime soccer as his near-100 goal haul and a sensational seven versus Crystal Palace in November 1918 (a London Combination record), bore ample testimony. When the Great War ended in 1918, he had his first taste of League football the following year when West Ham were elected to the enlarged Second Division. His 21 goals in 1919/20 led to his selection for two Victory Internationals for England versus Scotland and Wales. A further 29 tallies in 1920/21, and 19 more up to February 1922, prompted Falkirk (who Syd had guested for during the war) to make their impertinent transfer bid, which was duly accepted and included Syd's younger brother, Len, going north as part of the deal in February 1925. After three years in Scotland, during which he scored 45 goals in over 100 games for the Bairns, Syd moved to Blackburn Rovers for another big fee, and in addition to winning three more England caps in 1926 (versus Scotland at Old Trafford and Northern Ireland, twice) was a member of the Rovers' side that won the FA Cup with victory over Huddersfield Town at Wembley in 1928. Puddy was given his last representative honour when he was selected by the Football League versus the Irish League at Anfield in October 1925. Ten years after leaving Upton Park, 37-year-old Syd returned like a prodigal son to help in

Hammers' vain fight to stay in Division One at the end of the 1931/32 season. In 1933 Syd took the ambitious step of becoming coach to Turkish club Fenerbahce of Istanbul and began a volatile association with continental soccer. The following year he joined another Turkish club, Galatasaray, but it proved to be a bad move when he was badly manhandled while trying to calm down fighting players and spectators during a big game. Seventeen players were suspended and Puddy returned to England to take up a safer appointment as manager of Northampton Town in March 1937 and stayed up to the outbreak of World War II. On his return he was employed by the Blackpool Borough Police and later the Civil Service at the Ministry of Pensions but retired in 1963 to live at Southend. He was soon snapped up by Southend United who used his vast experience in a scouting capacity. Syd Puddefoot died in Rochford Hospital on October 2, 1972 after putting up a three-week fight against pneumonia, just before his 78th birthday. He had also been an accomplished cricketer playing for Essex on eight occasions.
England Caps: 1920 vs Wales, Scotland (2).

PYKE, Malcolm 1957-58

Born: Eltham, London, 6.3.38
League apps: 17

A STEADY, CONSTRUCTIVE defender who provided vital cover for the wing-half berths during the 1957/58 promotion season. Progressed through the junior ranks to make his initial Second Division appearance versus Bristol City at Upton park in April 1957. He won a Second Division Championship medal the following year, but didn't have any First Division outings when Hammers returned to the top flight in 1958/59. He subsequently transferred to Crystal Palace in the exchange deal that brought Ron Brett to the Boleyn. He played only two League games at Selhurst Park. Malcolm recently retired as licensee of the Papermakers Arms at Dartford, Kent.

QUINN, Jimmy   1989-91

Born: Belfast, Northern Ireland, 18.11.59
League apps: 47 (19 goals)
Cup apps: 9 (3 goals)

A TALL, PROLIFIC striker who proved excellent value for the £320,000 fee manager Lou Macari paid Bradford City for him in December 1989. The much-travelled, "old fashioned" centre-forward was a relatively late starter in the game. He was playing for non-League Oswestry Town when Swindon Town spotted him and signed him for £10,000. But he was already 22 years old by the time he made his debut for Robins in the Third Division versus Walsall (March 9, 1982). The Ulsterman scored ten goals in 49 League games before a £32,000 move to Blackburn Rovers in August 1984. It was during his spell at Ewood Park that Jimmy made his Northern Ireland debut versus Israel in Belfast (October 1984). He netted 17 goals in 71 League games for Rovers before Macari, then manager of Swindon, brought him back to the County Ground at a cost of £50,000 in December 1986. This time, Quinn found the target more regularly, notching 30 in 64 games. But after only 18 months into his second spell at Swindon, Jimmy was on his way again in 1988 – to Leicester City in a £210,000 deal. It was the unhappiest period in Quinn's career, though, as as he struggled to score six times in 31 Second Division appearances. He didn't hang around for long at Filbert Street and in December 1988 he joined Bradford, where he contributed 13 goals in 35 League appearances. Next stop Upton Park, where he made his debut in a 4-2 Second Division win versus Barnsley on New Year's Day, 1990. Although Jimmy was cup tied and could therefore take no part in Hammers' League Cup bid (which ended at the Semi-final stage), he proved himself in front of goal by hitting 13 in just 20 outings, including two as sub versus Brighton. But under Billy Bonds the following season, Quinn found himself replaced by the fit-again Frank McAvennie and confined to the subs bench. His hopes of a first team run were further hit by the signing of Iain Dowie. Jimmy started only 16 League games, but still weighed in with six goals in the 1990/91 promotion-winning campaign. His last appearance was in the number 12 shirt versus Charlton Athletic at Selhurst Park (May 4, 1991). His next port of call was Bournemouth, where Cherries manager Harry Redknapp showed his ability to spot a bargain by signing "Quinny" for just £40,000. It was money well spent as the Northern Ireland international scored 19 goals in 43 games in his only season at Dean Court. Yet this footballing nomad was on the move again in July 1992 when ambitious Reading signed him for £55,000. This, too, was a great investment because Quinn – who by that time had won more than 40 full caps – went on to amass 55 league goals in 88 matches over two seasons. His 35 in 1993/94 (plus five Cup goals) saw Royals romp to the Division Two Championship. In 1995/96, "Mighty Quinn" was top scorer for both Reading's first and second teams while continuing his role of joint manager with Mick Gooding with equal success. He even played half a match as stand-in goalkeeper against West Bromwich Albion and kept a clean sheet. He also retained his place in the Northern Ireland side with appearances against Latvia, Liechtenstein, Austria and Sweden. With his appearances scaled down in 1996/97, he resigned from his position at the end of the season after scoring a phenomenal 94 goals in 217 appearances for the Berkshire club. A model pro, Jimmy then continued his extraordinary career at Third Division Peterborough United on a free transfer in July 1997 and went on to score another 30 times in 62 appearances at London Road before being released by a grateful Barry Fry to take over as manager of Swindon Town in November 1998. Jimmy played 48 times for Northern Ireland. In February 2001, Jimmy was turning out for his 14th team, little Highworth Town in the Premier Division of the Hellenic League.
Northern Ireland caps: 1990 vs Norway; 1991 vs Yugoslavia (sub) (2).

QUINN, Wayne   2003-04

Born: Truro, Cornwall, 19.11.76
League apps: 22
Cup apps: 5

AN EXPERIENCED LEFT-BACK who could also operate in midfield, Wayne was signed on extended loan from Newcastle United to deputise for the injured Rufus Brevett in September 2003. An ever-present up to the turn of the year, Wayne lost his first team spot to John Harley. Quinny had scored six times in 169 appearances for his first club, Sheffield United, where his performances persuaded Newcastle to part with £750,000 for his services in June 2001. He found it hard to win a regular spot at St James's Park, however, and was loaned back to Blades in January 2003, where he made a further ten appearances for the Yorkshiremen in Division One. Wayne returned to St James's Park at the end of 2003/04.

QUINN, Jimmy
QUINN, Wayne

Jimmy Quinn

R

RADFORD, John
RADUCIOIU, Florin
RAISBECK, Lou
RANDALL, Tommy
RATCLIFFE, George
READ, Charles
REBROV, Sergei
REDKNAPP, Harry
REDWOOD, George
REID, George
REID, James
REID, Jimmy
REO-COKER, Nigel
REPKA, Tomas
REYNOLDS, Nigel
RHODES, Brian
RICHARDS, Dick
RICHARDSON, Frank
RIDGES, Victor
RIEPER, Marc
ROBERTS, Vivian
ROBERTSON
ROBINSON, Bill
ROBINSON, Leslie
ROBSON, Bryan
ROBSON, George
ROBSON, Keith
ROBSON, Mark
ROBSON, Stewart
ROBSON, William
ROSENIOR, Leroy
ROTHWELL, James
ROWLAND, Keith
RUDDOCK, Neil
RUFFELL, James
RUSH, Matthew
RUSSELL, John
RUTHERFORD, Jack

Harry Redknapp

RADFORD, John　　1976-78

Born: Pontefract, Yorkshire, 22.2.47
League apps: 28
Cup apps: 2

A FAMOUS NAME from Arsenal's 1970/71 double season, his two years in the claret and blue were dogged by the most unbelievable bad luck. In 30 senior outings he did everything but score. At times it seemed gremlins were at work to prevent him from doing so. As if by magic, his move to Blackburn Rovers in February 1978 saw him regain his scoring touch – including a goal on his debut! His 30 games for Hammers without a goal remained an unwanted record for a recognised West Ham striker until Iain Dowie experienced an even longer scoring drought in the 1990s. Became a successful manager with Bishop's Stortford whom he led to some exciting FA Cup exploits. Spoils include two England caps with Arsenal, FA Youth Cup Finalist 1965, Football League Cup Finalist 1968 and 1969, Fairs Cup winner's medal 1970, double winner 1971, FA Cup Finalist 1972. In direct contrast to his poor return with Hammers, Raddy scored 149 goals in 491 League and Cup appearances with Gunners between making his League debut in March 1964 versus West Ham and joining Hammers for £80,000 in December 1976. He also hit ten in 36 Second Division appearances in 1977/78 for Blackburn.

RADUCIOIU, Florin　　1996-97

Born: Bucharest, Romania, 17.3.70
League apps: 11 (2 goals)
Cup apps: 1 (1 goal)

THIS SUPREMELY GIFTED and talented striker had a European and international pedigree second to none when manager Harry Redknapp splashed out a then West Ham record fee to secure his services for £2.4 million from Spanish First Division club Espanol in July 1996. Having made his first team debut for his home town club Dinamo Bucharest at the age of just 16 in 1985/86, he went on to score 29 times in 76 League games for the crack Romanians and helped them to the League and Cup double in 1990. Florin then had an impressive 1990 World Cup representing his country in Italy, which enticed Bari to take him to Serie A. Just five goals in 30 matches at San Nicola persuaded Bari to put their expensive acquisition out on a series of loans in successive seasons to Verona in 1991/92 (30 apps, three goals), Brescia in 1992/93 (29 apps, 13 goals) and AC Milan in 1993/94 (seven apps, two goals) before selling him on to Espanol of the Spanish Primera Liga after the little striker impressed again in the World Cup Finals where he finished Romania's top scorer with five goals at USA 94. He immediately found life a lot tougher in England when he was on the receiving end of an opponent's elbow in a pre-season friendly at Torquay United and consequently found the physical nature of the English game (both in match situations and on the training pitch) difficult to come to terms with. With manager Redknapp quickly convinced he'd bought a "wrong un", the temperamental star was given short shrift by the Hammers boss whose patience was finally exhausted when the player famously went on a shopping trip in the West End when he should have been on duty for a fateful Fourth Round Coca Cola replay at Second Division Stockport County. Having scored the goal in the original 1-1 draw that had necessitated the replay at Edgeley Park, one would have thought the least he could have done was turn up. That counter and two more in Upton Park clashes with Manchester United (2-2) and Sunderland (2-0) were all he had to show for a dozen outings in the claret and blue, but before he'd alienated them with his no-show for the disastrous 2-1 defeat at Stockport, many Hammers fans liked the tricky little

Romanian and saw him as a means of lifting a gloomy season at the Boleyn. But the writing was on the wall and Radi was soon jetting back to sunny Spain to rejoin Espanol for a cut-price £1.7 million in mid-January 1997. He soon made an impact too! Both goals in the 2-0 win against Bobby Robson's Barcelona at Savria made him the returning hero as the Espanol fans celebrated a rare victory over their biggest rivals.

RAISBECK, Lou　　1900

League apps: 2

SOMETHING OF A utility player, Lou performed in any of the half-back positions and also as a forward when the occasion demanded. A product of Scottish junior soccer with Slamannan, he graduated to the professional ranks with Airdrieonians and from the Diamonds moved south to another team with a cutting edge, Sheffield United in Blades' FA Cup-winning year of 1899. A period spent back in his native Scotland with Third Lanark was followed by a further move to Middlesbrough. It was from Teeside that he moved to the Memorial Grounds in 1900, but his appearance in the number 5 shirt in the opening two matches of the season versus Gravesend and Millwall were to be his last with Hammers.

RANDALL, Tommy　　1906-15

Born: Barking, Essex, 1886
League apps: 189 (9 goals)
Cup apps: 16 (1 goal)

TOM BEGAN HIS Upton Park career as an amateur inside-forward and, although he scored on his debut in a 4-1 win over the already crowned Southern League Champions Fulham, the fans took an immediate dislike to his thoughtful, slow approach to the game (calling him "Old Mother Randall") and almost drove him out of football with their barracking. Then, at Charlie Paynter's benefit against Woolwich Arsenal (November 15, 1906), Hammers' trainer persuaded a disillusioned Randall to turn out at half-back as a personal favour. He was such a success in his new role that he was signed as a full pro for the princely sum of 30 shillings a week! Becoming a fixture in the Southern League at left-half, Tom was honoured with the captaincy of the Southern League Representative XI, playing against the English, Scottish and Irish Leagues in 1912, and the English and Irish again the following year. He was also selected for the Football Association XI. The transformation was so complete he was appointed captain and became one of the most popular players at the club. He spent his formative years in local junior soccer with Ethelburgers and Barking St Andrews, later graduating to Barking in the South-Essex League, with whom he was selected for a county match between Essex and Suffolk in which his performance for Essex earned him a trial at Upton Park. Succeeded in the first team by Jack Tresadern, Tommy passed away in 1946.

RATCLIFFE, George　　1900-02

Born: Hanley, Staffordshire, 1877
League apps: 41 (14 goals)
Cup apps: 2

SHARING HIS BIRTHPLACE with Hanley's most famous footballing son, Sir Stanley Matthews, George was also a winger although he preferred to operate on the left flank. His career began with the local Stone Town in the North Staffs League, preceding a series of moves that saw him take in spells at Crewe Alexandra, South Shore and Sheffield United before joining Grimsby Town in May 1898. His time with the Mariners was spent during the club's move from Abbey Park in 1898 to

Tommy Randall

Blundell Park the following year. But he proved to be equally at home on either pitch as he scored 18 times in 57 Football League appearances following his debut for the Humberside club (August 3, 1898). In 1900, George was involved in another exciting new development, transferring to West Ham United in their first year under that title. At the Memorial Grounds, George was moved into the middle of Hammers' attack. He eventually filled all the inside berths in turn. His goalscoring output remained steady, but not spectacular, and in 1902 he was transferred to Doncaster Rovers where he made 26 appearances in 1902/03.

READ, Charles　　1896-97 TIW

Born: Canning Town, London, 1870

CHARLES APPEARED AT full-back in a London Senior Cup defeat against Bromley in February 1897 and again the following week but then was moved to the forward line for the next five matches, including the West Ham Charity Cup Final, scoring three goals.

REBROV, Sergei　　2004-05

Born: Gorlovka, Ukraine, 5.6.74
League apps: 27 (1 goal)
Cup apps: 5 (1 goal)

ANOTHER PRODUCT OF the unlikely Tottenham Hotspur/West Ham United transfer pact, this experienced Ukraine international who Spurs paid a staggering £11 million for from Dynamo Kiev in June 2000, arrived at Upton Park on a free transfer in July 2004. Previously with Shaktar Donetsk for whom he scored 12 times in 26 appearances in the early 1990s, he went on to score 93 goals in 190 games for Dynamo spanning eight years. With Kiev, he won eight domestic Championships and four Cup winners' medals and was

voted Ukraine Player of the Year on two occasions in 1996 and again in 1998. Deemed a flop at White Hart Lane after an indifferent first season under manager George Graham, Rebrov was loaned to Turkish side Fenerbahce in January 2003 where he scored twice in 13 games in 2002/03. With the 2003/04 season almost over, the 65 times capped Sergei had still to prove himself at Upton Park after scoring just two goals. He was full of optimism on his arrival however, claiming: "I liked the way Alan Pardew spoke to me about the team and his determination to bring some success to the club. I am delighted to be here and I too have high expectations of helping the team back into the Premiership." Despite his optimism, Sergei still found it hard to win a regular first team place as Hammers blazed a glory trail back to the Premiership in May 2005. Sergei returned to Kiev in the close season of 2005.

REDKNAPP, Harry — 1965-72

Born: Poplar, London, 2.3.47
League apps: 149 (7 goals)
Cup apps: 26 (1 goal)

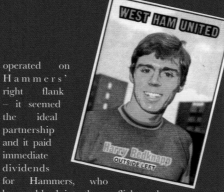

WEST HAM UNITED through-and-through, this cockney character joined the groundstaff straight from school, went on to become a first team favourite and then returned to Upton Park as manager. As a player, flame-haired Harry combined old-fashioned wing play with his own particular brand of artistry to win over the fans. Although not always a first team regular under Ron Greenwood, "Arry-boy" was a popular choice with the Upton Park faithful, particularly fans in the Chicken Run terrace. A former England Youth international, he was a member of the Hammers side that lifted the FA and London Youth Cups in 1963. Signing professional forms in March 1964, he made his senior debut in August the following year in a 1-1 draw versus Sunderland (August 23, 1965), replacing Peter Brabrook. But it was not until 1967/68 that Harry wore the number 7 shirt regularly. The next season was his most successful, when he appeared in 36 League games and created plenty of goals for the likes of Geoff Hurst and Martin Peters with his right-wing crosses. The nearest Harry came to winning a major honour was as a member of the Hammers team that featured in the League Cup Semi-final marathon with Stoke City in 1972, failing by a whisker to reach Wembley. In fact, it was Harry who was fouled by Gordon Banks for the penalty that England's keeper eventually saved from Hurst in the second leg at Upton Park. Transferred to AFC Bournemouth in August the same year, he had a short spell with Brentford before retiring from League football in 1976. He assisted Bobby Moore at Oxford City after trying his luck in America with Seattle Sounders. Then became manager-coach of Bournemouth, where he made a brief comeback as a player in the 1982/83 season for a League Cup tie against Manchester United at Old Trafford. Harry made quite a name for himself at the south coast club. In 1986/87 he led Cherries to the Third Division Championship with a record 97 points, taking the club into Division Two for the first time in its history. He earned a reputation as a managerial wheeler-dealer with a keen eye for a bargain. He could boast a number of shrewd signings early in his managerial career who went on to become stars in the Premier League, including Shaun Teale (Aston Villa) and Ian Bishop (Manchester City and West Ham) and of course his own son, talented midfielder Jamie, who was a big favourite at Liverpool and Spurs and a leading light for England. Harry had been linked with a number of bigger clubs, but after nine years with Bournemouth – during which time he opened his own Italian restaurant in the town and owned a couple of racehorses – he was delighted to return to West Ham in July 1992, as assistant to Billy Bonds. Big mates for many years – Harry was best man at Bill's wedding in 1967, when they both

operated on Hammers' right flank – it seemed the ideal partnership and it paid immediate dividends for Hammers, who bounced back into the top flight at the first attempt as runners-up to Newcastle United in Division One 1992/93. The following season they steered the club to a respectable 13th position in the Premiership before the summer upheaval that saw Bonzo quit the club after 27 years, just ten days before the start of the 1994/95 campaign. Harry was understandably most unhappy at the time about the circumstances surrounding his appointment as manager, but he agreed to step up into the hot seat and then appointed his brother-in-law, another former favourite, Frank Lampard as his new assistant. Harry's "streetwise" reputation and undoubted coaching ability stood him in good stead as he re-established West Ham in the senior division. With relatively little money to spend in comparison to the so-called elite clubs, his ability to strike a hard bargain in the transfer market was just what West Ham needed. Having said that, it was Harry who paid a club record £1.5 million to bring Don Hutchison from Liverpool in August 1994, to prove that he would spend big money on the right player. He also brought Tony Cottee and Julian Dicks back to the club in shrewd deals from Merseyside giants Everton and Liverpool. Unless you count the 1999 FA Youth Cup Final victory against Coventry City and the Intertoto Cup Final success over French side Metz the following year, Harry Redknapp failed to bring a major trophy to Upton Park in his seven seasons as manager. But what he undoubtedly did achieve in that relatively short space of time was to oversee the most successful youth policy in the club's recent history; bring back European football to the Boleyn ground for the first time since the early 1980s and raise the club's profile to its highest ever level by retaining Premiership status for the duration of his "never-a-dull-moment" tenure. The statistical records of his reign in east London are well documented elsewhere. His undeniable charisma, charm and good old cockney characteristics are more difficult to define. Unfashionable Portsmouth became the beneficiaries of his Midas touch and prolific wheeling and dealing in international transfer market which, it seems, was the very reason for his downfall at West Ham. In another major shock, Harry took over the reins at Pompey's bitter rivals Southampton in 2005!

REDWOOD, George — 1910-12

Born: Shoreditch, London, April 1885
SL apps: 10
Cup apps: 3

THIS VERSATILE DEFENDER was signed from Fulham (seven apps) along with West Ham team-mate Fred Harrison and made his West Ham debut at right-half in a 4-1 defeat at Swindon Town (March 25, 1911) – his sole appearance that season. He fared better during 1911/12, however, making 12 more team appearances, including a return to Swindon's County Ground in an FA Cup Third Round replay following a 1-1 draw at Upton Park. But it was another fruitless venture for George – he and his fellow defenders conceded four goals for no reply to go out of the competition after defeating Gainsborough Trinity and Middlesbrough in previous rounds. He also played at right-back and centre-half. George joined Hammers from London rivals Fulham, but we have no record of where he went after leaving the club. However, it is known that he learned his football at the Page Green Board School, served in the Fourth Battalion Royal Fusiliers Regiment and also played for Enfield Town.

REID, George — 1899

Born: Blackland Mill, Wiltshire, date unknown
SL apps (TIW): 6 (1 goal)

FOLLOWING THE DEMISE of the Warmley club in Bristol in February 1899, Francis Payne, the Ironworks secretary, signed three of the stricken organisation's leading players: Peter McManus, R Henderson and George (Geordie) Reid. Formerly with Reading, George was no relation to Jimmy Reid, who had also played for the Berkshire club at the same time as his namesake and by a strange twist of fate, was also on Ironworks' books and played in the same Irons team on several occasions. George was most at home at inside-left, but he did play one of his six games for Irons at centre-forward. He scored only one goal, versus Southall (March 25,1899). George played for Middlesbrough in the early 1900s and was in Scotland in 1906/07 with Johnstone (Renfrewshire) but returned south to Bradford Park Avenue in 1907/08.

REID, James — 1900-01

Born: Scotland, 1879
SL apps: 13 (5 goals)
Cup apps: 6

JIMMY SOON DISCOVERED his feet could make his fortune. Petershill (Glasgow) was his first club, followed by Hibernian. He then came south to Burslem Port Vale, without the Burslem prefix, from where Hammers also signed Billy Grassam. Very forthright and outgoing, he impressed the secretary of the newly-formed West Ham United assigned to negotiate his transfer by walking up to him on Sheffield Station and shaking hands as though he had know him all his life! He scored in six consecutive games for Watford in 1905/06, and another 16 times in 35 games, signing off with a couple versus Millwall. His career took in Hibs, Gainsborough, West Ham, Worksop Town, Notts County, Watford, Spurs (where he played for two seasons and scored 39 goals in 59 League and Cup games), New Brompton and Reading.

REID, Jimmy   1897-99

Born: Scotland, 1874
SL apps (TIW): 15 (9 goals)
Cup apps: 3 (1 goal)

ANOTHER REID FROM Reading, inside-forward Jimmy was the most prolific scorer of the trio; scoring ten times in his 18 confirmed League and Cup appearances, but he probably scored more as a member of the TIW side that won the London League by one point from Brentford and competed for the London Senior Cup in 1897/98, losing to Ilford 3-1.

REO-COKER, Nigel   2004-

Born: Southwark, London, 14.5.84
League apps: 60 (5 goals)
Cup apps: 5

INDUSTRIOUS MIDFIELDER NIGEL seems to be the ace in the pack of Alan Pardew's transfer raids on last year's crisis club, Wimbledon. An England Youth and Under-21 international, Reo-Coker became the youngest skipper in the First Division at Dons and, despite the club's troubles, his leadership qualities shone through. Having previously attracted the attentions of a host of other clubs including Spurs and Portsmouth, the player's agent Tony Finnigan said: "Once West Ham came in there was only one place he was going to go. The nice thing for Hammers fans is that he really wants to wear the shirt." Signed for a fee of about £575,000, the quick, combative Reo-Coker had scored half a dozen times in 64 games for Dons and was considered the debt-ridden club's prize asset. He certainly fitted the bill at Hammers scoring twice in 18 games during the latter part of 2003/04, although he blotted his copy book somewhat by being sent off in his first England Under-21 appearance as a Hammer in the 0-0 draw with Azerbaijan in Baku in October 2004. Also in Peter Taylor's side was loan star Calum Davenport who was replaced by another former Hammers loanee Matt Kilgallon in the 69th minute! And the skipper was a certain Glen Johnson. Of all Hammers signings over the past 18 months, Nigel Reo-Coker looks the best long-term prospect. Certainly this was borne out by some outstanding displays as Hammers won their passage back to the Premiership in May 2005.

REPKA, Tomas   2001-

Born: Slavicin Zlin, Czech Republic, 2.1.74
League apps: 151
Cup apps: 15

A GOOD, DEPENDABLE, old-fashioned style full-back, popular Tomas began his career with the same Czech club as current Hammers goalkeeping coach Ludek Miklosko – Banik Ostrava – where he made 77 appearances and scored three goals before signing for Sparta Prague in 1995. He enjoyed three seasons in the Czech capital and doubled his goal tally to six in 82 appearances there before transferring to Italian Serie A club Fiorentina in 1998, where he continued to add to his impressive total of full international caps for his country and made 88 Serie A appearances. A mainstay in the Czech Republic's defence when the unfancied outsiders reached the Final of the 1996 European Championships in England before losing to a golden goal extra-time winner by Germany. Tomas commanded a joint club record £5 million fee when Glenn Roeder signed him from Fiorentina in September 2001 to equal the sum paid for Don Hutchison a few days earlier. Fears about his temperament seemed well founded when he was sent off on his debut against Middlesbrough, but after receiving his marching orders for a second time less than a month later in the humiliating 7-1 defeat at Blackburn Rovers, Tomas at last settled down to form a formidable partnership with Christian Dailly at the heart of Hammers defence that made a major contribution to the side's seventh place Premiership finish. Tough in the tackle and good in the air, the wholehearted competitor soon became a firm favourite of the Upton Park fans and although not looking £5 million worth, he was a good man to have in the trenches with you. Sadly, Tom's disciplinary problems returned to haunt him during the ill-fated 2002/03 season as he was forced to sit out several games through suspensions after receiving one red and an unlucky 13 yellow cards during the course of the disappointing campaign. Another 16 yellow cards in 2003/04 showed that this is an aspect of his game he still needs to address, but the enduring memory of his performances for many remained his superbly timed goal-line clearance in the Play-off Final at the Millennium Stadium against Crystal Palace when he averted a certain goal. An ever-present in the first 14 games of the Coca Cola Championship in 2004/05, Tomas had shown signs of curbing his excesses on the card count. But it couldn't have been easy for him to achieve. After seeming set to leave Upton Park Tomas signed a new deal in the summer.

Tomas Repka

Nigel Reo-Coker

REYNOLDS, Nigel — 1898-99

SL apps (TIW): 12 (5 goals)

A TRICKY WINGER who was ahead of his time with use of "screw-shots" and "benders" to confuse opposing goalkeepers. Amazingly he was never on the losing side for Irons, being on the winning team in all but one (drawn) of his dozen Southern League matches in 1898/99. He was formerly with Leicester Fosse and Gravesend United.

RHODES, Brian — 1957-63

Born: Marylebone, London, 23.10.37
League apps: 61
Cup apps: 5

KNOWN AS "BRUEY" to his team-mates, this reliable, unspectacular goalkeeper made over 60 League appearances during his nine years at the Boleyn. A former Essex schoolboys player and reserve for England boys, he signed full pro forms in April 1954 after joining the staff in April 1952. As an amateur, he played for Essex Youth and made an appearance for the Rest versus London at Stamford Bridge. Brian won an honour in his first season as a pro in 1954/55, gaining a winners' medal in the London Mid-week League. Making his football debut versus Blackburn Rovers in September 1957, Brian made four further appearances in that Second Division Championship-winning season, but had to wait two years for his First Division baptism in the 3-2 Upton Park win over Wolves (November 21, 1959). He returned to first team action for the final 15 matches of the season, when he took over from Noel Dwyer. The following season he missed only six out of 42 League games, his best run in the team. Mainly a reserve, he always performed capably when called up for first team duty, and went to the States when the club competed for the International Soccer League and Challenge Cup in 1963. He rejoined his former manager Ted Fenton at Southend United the same year, but played only 11 times in their Third Division side before emigrating to Australia, where he became involved with Coaching the Australian Olympic squad. He later settled at Napier on New Zealand's North Island. Brian tragically lost a three-year fight against leukemia aged 55 in July 1993.

RICHARDS, Dick — 1922-24

Born: Chirk, Wales, 14.2.1890
League apps: 43 (5 goals)
Cup apps: 10 (1 goal)

JOINED HAMMERS AS an outside left from Wolverhampton Wanderers during the club's Cup Final season of 1922/23, switching to the opposite flank due to the brilliant form of Jimmy Ruffell. He'd been an automatic choice for Wales while at Wolves, winning five caps in 1920/22. Dick continued in that vein with West Ham, playing for the Principality when they won the Home International Championship in 1923/24, with victories over England, Scotland and Northern Ireland. His international appearances, all played from the inside-left position, further underlined his versatility. Transferring to Fulham (24 apps, two goals) in 1924, Dick found his brief stay at Craven Cottage beset with injury, although his fortunes did improve with his move to Mold in the Welsh League, gaining another cap in 1926. Dick played for a trio of non-League clubs before breaking into League football: Bronygarth, Chirk and Oswestry United. Either side of World War I he scored 22 goals in 86 League appearances for Wolves. He concluded his career with Colwyn Bay United in 1927/28. Dick took a job with an electricity company in Cheshire and it was while lifting electric light poles that he sustained the serious back injury from which he died at the age of 43 on January 29, 1934.

Wales Caps: 1924 vs England, Scotland, Northern Ireland (3).

RICHARDSON, Frank — 1923-24

Born: Barking, Essex, 29.1.1897
League apps: 10 (2 goals)

FRANK WAS A prolific goalscoring centre-forward and very much "one who got away" as far as West Ham were concerned. He began his career with local amateurs Barking Town, but then made the long journey west to play for Plymouth Argyle in the Third Division South. He was very likely a friend of another Barking Town player, Jack Leslie, who also joined Plymouth at that time and went on to score 131 goals in 383 matches at Home Park between 1921 and 1934. Jack, who was one of the few black players in the game at the time, worked in Hammers' "boot room" at Upton Park in the 1970s. Frank, however, only stayed with the Pilgrims for a couple of years, but still found time to score 37 times in 63 games between 1921 and 1922 to help Argyle to second place in the Third Division South table in 1921/22 – a position they would hold for the next five seasons before finishing third in 1927/28! Moving on to Stoke City for 1922/23, Frank scored three goals in 14 matches for the Potters before joining Hammers for 1923/24, as cover for the injured Vic Watson, and made his Hammers debut in a 2-0 win over Chelsea at Upton Park in October 1923. His first goal came in a 4-1 win against Birmingham a week later, also at the Boleyn, and his last goal was also against inhabitants of England's second city – in the 1-1 draw with Aston Villa at Villa Park on Christmas Day! The following year, Frank headed west again with all guns blazing as he scored a phenomenal 33 goals in 53 Third Division South outings for Swindon Town between 1924/25. He then transferred to Reading in the summer of 1925 and helped the Biscuitmen, as they were then nicknamed, to the Championship of the Third Division South just one point ahead of poor old Plymouth! Altogether he scored 44 goals in 91 games for the Elm Park club between 1925 and 1929 before returning to Swindon in 1930. He hit another dozen goals in 38 matches at the County Ground before moving on again to Mansfield Town, but there is no record of him making a senior showing at Field Mill. Frank died at the age of 90 in 1987, just a year before his Canning Town-born mate, Jack Leslie.

RIDGES, Victor — 1896-97 TIW

Born: Thirley, Hampshire, December 1871

THIS SWASHBUCKLING CENTRE-FORWARD began his career at South West Ham in 1893/94 and, after three successful seasons, joined Thames Ironworks where he made just one first team appearance in the 1896/97 season.

RIEPER, Marc — 1994-97

Born: Rodovre, Denmark, 5.6.68
League apps: 90 (5 goals)
Cup apps: 11

A GREAT DANE initially signed on loan from Danish First Division side Brondby IF in December 1994, Harry Redknapp had to move swiftly to sign him on a permanent basis after the man he dubbed "superman" turned in a string of impressive displays in the second half of the 1994/95 season. Warding off the attentions of Champions-elect Blackburn Rovers and big-spending Turks, Fenerbahce, Harry outwitted them both to sign the established Danish international defender just before the last day of the campaign for £1 million. The player then went out to start paying off his fee with an Upton Park performance that helped prevent Manchester United from winning the 1995 Premiership Championship that, by dint of the 1-1 draw, went to Blackburn! Rieper began his career by making 22 Danish First Division appearances with AGF Aarhus in 1990 and then another 18 in 1991/92 before switching his allegiance to Brondby to play 12 times for them in the same season, having scored against them earlier in the campaign! He went on to score three goals in 92 First Division appearances and win a domestic Cup winners' medal in 1994 with Brondby before moving to the Premiership with 42 caps for his country when he joined Hammers. Marc became the first West Ham player to be capped by Denmark when he was selected for the Euro 96 Finals in England. When the tournament was over, he'd created a new record for his country by winning 37 consecutive caps. It remained a standing joke among his international team-mates, however, that he'd yet to score for his country – he soon rectified the situation though by scoring in the Dane's 1998 World Cup qualifying win over Bosnia in the summer of 1997! He hadn't found scoring so difficult at Hammers, despite his role at the heart of defence, and got off the mark in his first season as a Hammer in the 2-0 win over Blackburn at Upton Park while nullifying the threat of Alan Shearer and Chris Sutton at the same time! But his favourite opponents were Coventry City against whom he managed to get on the scoresheet in three successive games – and just to even the balance he also scored an own goal against the Sky Blues in the 3-1 win at Highfield Road in March 1997! Having formed an impressive defensive partnership with an old foe from Euro 96, Croatia's Slaven Bilic, his future looked assured at the Boleyn Ground. But persistent speculation regarding a move to Scottish Premier giants Celtic failed to go away and Mark duly joined the Glasgow club for a £1.5 million fee in September 1997. It seemed a great move for the towering six-foot-three-inch defender who showed surprising skill for such a big man and a string of Viking-like displays soon had the Parkhead faithful singing his praises as the Bhoys won the Scottish League Cup and Scottish Premier title in his first season in Paradise. Having made 36 Scottish Premier and Cup appearances in that heady first season north of the border and getting on the scoresheet in the 2-1 win over Hearts at Tynecastle and the 1-0 victory against their Edinburgh rivals Hibs at Easter Road as well as scoring one of the goals in the 3-0 SLC Final win over Dundee United at Ibrox, Marc was looking forward to playing in the Champions League in 1998/99. But after just four appearances in that prestige tournament and one in its poor relation, the UEFA Cup, in addition to seven Scottish Premier appearances, the brave defender's career was cut short by a terrible injury which forced him to announce his retirement at the end of the season.

ROBERTS, Vivian — 1920

League apps: 1

NOT MUCH IS known of this goalkeeper, other than that he made his only League appearance in a 1-0 defeat versus Stockport County at Edgeley Park (April 26, 1920).

ROBERTSON — 1907-08

League apps: 1

MADE HIS SOLITARY Southern League appearance in a 0-0 stalemate against Southampton at the Dell (December 1, 1907) in the centre-forward berth.

ROBINSON, Bill — 1949-52

Born: Whitburn, Scotland, 4.4.19
League apps: 101 (60 goals)
Cup apps: 4 (1 goal)

HELD HAMMERS' POST-WAR scoring record with

Bill Robinson

26 goals in 40 League games in 1950/51, until John Dick surpassed him in 1957/58. A pre-war pro with Sunderland (with whom he once scored three goals in four minutes against Manchester United and scored 14 times in 27 League appearances), Bill came to Upton Park from Charlton Athletic (52 apps, 16 goals) in January 1949, after playing in a reserve match there the week before his transfer. Seven days later, he scored on his debut versus West Bromwich Albion at The Hawthorns. A member of Charlton's FA Cup-winning team of 1947 versus Burnley, Bill was appointed full-time organiser of the youth section when he retired from playing at the end of 1952/53. He was largely responsible for making it one of the finest in the country before being promoted to assistant manager in November 1957. Two years later, Bill became manager of Hartlepool. He passed away on October 7, 1992.

ROBINSON, Leslie — 1920-24

Born: Romford, Essex, 2.5.1898
League apps: 19 (2 goals)

OFTEN A TOP scorer in the reserves, this clever inside-right served the club well during the early League seasons, after arriving from Dagenham side Stirling Athletic, without being able to lay claim to a regular first team place. He had the honour of scoring their 100th goal in the London Combination in 1923/24. Les later joined Northampton (73 apps, 32 goals) and then Norwich City (31 apps, ten goals) in June 1927, Thames in September 1928 and, finally, Torquay United (23 apps, 16 goals) in July 1929. Chosen to represent the London League versus London Combination, Les also served in the Fourth Battalion Essex Regiment during World War I. Died in Barking, Essex in 1965.

ROBSON, George — 1928-31

Born: Newcastle-upon-Tyne, Tyne & Wear, 17.6.08
League apps: 17 (2 goals)
Cup apps: 1 (1 goal)

THE FIRST OF Hammers' trio of same-surname signings from Newcastle United, George actually made his West Ham debut versus the Magpies at St James's Park in the last fixture of the 1927/28 season. His first team opportunities at the Boleyn were limited by the availability of players of the calibre of Vic Watson, Viv Gibbins and Stan Earle, but he proved his worth

ROBSON, Bryan — 1971-74/1976-79

Born: Sunderland, County Durham, 11.11.45
League apps: 227 (94 goals)
Cup apps: 27 (10 goals)

BETTER KNOWN AS "Pop" to the fans, this prolific goalscorer was first signed from Newcastle United, where he had won a Fairs Cup winners' medal and a Second Division Championship medal, for a then club record fee of £120,000 in February 1971 and scored on his Hammers debut versus Nottingham Forest (February 24, 1971). Topped Hammers' scoring charts in 1972/73 with 28 First Division goals before returning to his native North-east with Sunderland in 1974. However, it was not long before the popular Wearsider was back at Upton Park, re-signing for £80,000 in October 1976. Once again, he led the scorers' list with 24 Second Division goals in 1978/79, winning an Adidas Golden Boot Award in the process. Although offered a new contract, his amazing career again retraced its steps when he returned to Roker Park for the second time in the summer of 1979 and won another Second Division Championship medal. He moved on to Carlisle United in 1980 and was back in London again for 1982/83, still scoring for Chelsea. He then returned to his beloved North-east as player-coach for Sunderland and enjoyed a fairytale return to Upton Park by helping the Wearsiders to a shock 1-0 win. Pop was appointed manager of Carlisle United, but later relinquished the post and played part-time for Gateshead in the Northern Premier League. Pop made history at Carlisle when, during a spell as player-manager, he turned out against Shrewsbury Town in a Second Division fixture at the age of 39 years and 321 days in September 1985! After finally retiring from playing he continued in the game as a coach with Carlisle, Sunderland, Manchester United and Leeds United, where he performed sterling service in Youth development at Elland Road before the club almost went out of business due to their dire financial position under the Risdale regime. He left Leeds in May 2004 along with manager Eddie Gray following the fallen giant's plunge from the Premiership. Pop was back at Upton Park as Tony Cottee's special guest for the Carling Cup tie against Southend United in September 2004.

Career record

Played	League		FAC		LC		Europe		Total	
	App	Gls	App	Gls	App	Gls	App	Gls	App	Gls
1970-71	14	3	0	0	0	0	0	0	14	3
1971-72	42	9	4	1	10	4	0	0	56	14
1972-73	42	28	2	0	2	0	0	0	46	28
1973-74	22	7	0	0	1	1	0	0	23	8
1976-77	30	14	2	0	0	0	0	0	32	14
1977-78	37	9	3	2	1	0	0	0	41	11
1978-79	40	24	1	1	1	1	0	0	42	26
TOTAL	**227**	**94**	**12**	**4**	**15**	**6**	**0**	**0**	**254**	**104**

whenever called upon. In December 1928, he underlined his goalscoring ability in a record 13-2 Football Combination victory over Fulham reserves at Upton Park by scoring five times against the west Londoners, as did fellow-forward Johnny Campbell. But still he failed to secure a regular first XI place, a situation that prompted his move across London to Brentford in February 1931 (where he won a Third Division Championship medal and scored 32 goals in 124 League apps). George later became a member of Hammers' scouting staff, retiring from his position in 1971. A former lorry driver, George began his career with St Peters Albion before joining the Magpies and ended his career with Hearts after leaving Brentford in 1935.

ROBSON, Keith — 1974-76

Born: Hetton-le-Hole, Northumberland, 15.11.53
League apps: 68 (13 goals)
Cup apps: 19 (6 goals)

LIKE HIS NAMESAKE George, this aggressive forward was signed by Hammers from Newcastle United. A skilful, but temperamental, player who had his fair share of flare-ups with opponents and referees, he figured in both of the club's successful Cup runs of the mid-1970s, but missed the 1975 FA Cup Final versus Fulham. He made up for that disappointment the following year, gaining a European Cup Winners' Cup runners-up medal and scoring Hammers' equaliser in the Brussels Final versus Anderlecht. His spectacular goal versus Eintracht Frankfurt in the 3-1 Semi-final, second-leg victory at Upton Park clinched a memorable 4-3 aggregate win over the Germans to book West Ham's ticket to the Heysel Stadium. Transferred to Cardiff City in August 1977, he played 21 games for the Bluebirds before moving on to Norwich City in February 1978. After three seasons at

Carrow Road, where he was a team-mate of fellow ex-Hammers Alan Taylor, Graham Paddon and John McDowell and scored 13 goals in 65 First Division games, Keith transferred to Leicester City where he scored one goal in 12 appearances before being loaned out to Carlisle United to pair up with his old West Ham mate and namesake, Bryan "Pop" Robson for a spell. Returning to East Anglia after a short time playing in Hong Kong, Keith became involved in local football with Wroxham, Norwich Busmen and Corinthians while working full-time at the Impress Metal Packing Co near his home in East Anglia. Interestingly, before he left West Ham, Robbo had a taste of the exotic when he went on loan to Team Hawaii in their only NASL campaign. The club had simply shifted from San Antonio to the mid-Pacific and crowds at the Aloha Stadium, Honolulu ranged from 1,800 up to almost 13,000. Still a regular visitor to Upton Park, Keith likes nothing better than a pint in the West Ham United Supporters Club before games. Old habits die hard!

Keith Robson

ROBSON, Mark — 1992-93

Born: Stratford, London, 22.5.69
League apps: 47 (8 goals)
Cup apps: 4 (1 goal)

AN EXCITING WINGER who fulfilled a life-time dream when he signed for his local club on a free transfer from Tottenham Hotspur in August 1992. He proved he had fully recovered from a long-term knee injury by playing a starring role in West Ham's 1992/93 promotion-winning campaign. He scored eight League goals himself and set up many others for Clive Allen and Trevor Morley with his pinpoint crosses. He played mainly on the right flank, but blond-haired "Robbo" could also shine on the left, where he would invariably cut inside to shoot. Although slightly built, he was not afraid to run at opponents and torment them with his tricky ball skills. Made his Hammers debut in a pre-season friendly at Leyton Orient (July 31, 1992) and did enough to earn a one-year contract. His First Division debut came as substitute at Barnsley (August 16, 1992) and he missed just two other games thereafter. Mark signed a new contract prior to the 1993/94 season but, after just one start and two sub outings in the Premiership, he was bitterly disappointed to find himself out of the first team reckoning. He was reportedly in tears when he heard from Billy Bonds that West Ham were prepared to let him go to Charlton Athletic to fulfil his wish for regular first team football. Robbo reluctantly moved to the refurbished Valley in November 1993 for a bargain £125,000. Despite being born only a corner kick away from Upton Park, and training with Hammers as a schoolboy, Mark's pro career started at Exeter City in December 1986. After 26 League games for the Devon club, a £50,000 move to Spurs brought him back to London in July 1987. But he was limited to just three starts and five sub outings at White Hart Lane, so he gained first team experience in loan spells with Reading (seven League apps), Plymouth Argyle (seven League apps), Watford and Exeter City (11 apps, two goals) before Tottenham manager Terry Venables released him. A true East Ender, the chirpy cockney enjoys coaching youngsters in his spare time and managed local boys' side Senrab to a number of honours. Mark spent four years with Charlton and scored 11 goals in 123 appearances at the Valley before being snapped up on a free transfer by Third Division Notts County in the summer of 1997. Playing as a winger, midfielder and just behind the two strikers, Mark had a wonderful first season at Meadow Lane and was a major reason why the Magpies ran away with the Third Division Championship with a haul of 99 points! Having scored the goal that clinched Notts the title and scored four times in 33 appearances, the 1998/99 season was less productive due to injury and he made just four appearances in Division Two. He did have a spell with Wycombe Wanderers where he made a further four appearances. Hanging up his boots in October 1999, Mark returned to West Ham soon after his retirement as coach to the youngest of our Academy hopefuls and then moved over to Charlton when a full-time vacancy became available. He then became coach to the Under-19s at the Valley.

ROBSON, Stewart — 1987-91

Born: Billericay, Essex, 6.11.64
League apps: 69 (4 goals)
Cup apps: 14 (2 goals)

THIS FORMER ENGLAND Under-21 captain's promising career was blighted by injury, and Hammers rarely saw the best of him following his expensive £700,000 move from Arsenal in January 1987. A wholehearted midfielder who never gave less than 100 per cent, Stewart's talent remained unfulfilled at Highbury where he underwent surgery for a serious pelvic injury even before he arrived at Upton Park. John Lyall hoped "Robbo" would emerge as his driving force in midfield

Mark Robson

but he missed too many games through injury. He made his debut at Coventry City (January 24, 1987) – the club he would later join from West Ham – and after 18 League appearances in his first half-season with Hammers, Stewart played 37 games in 1987/88 and won the Hammer of the Year award. But he then featured in only 14 more League games over the remaining three seasons of his time in east London. At one stage, he was sidelined for more than a year with a pelvic injury that required three operations and long rehabilitation at a London physiotherapy clinic. Yet Stewart underlined his courage by returning in glorious style for a League Cup Fifth Round replay at Derby County in January 1989. He continued to be dogged by injury, though, with a virus and knee problems adding to his miserable time with Hammers. His last outing was as sub at Watford (January 12, 1991) before Billy Bonds gave the robust Robson the chance to make a fresh start with Coventry City. Robbo initially went to Highfield Road on loan, but did enough to earn a contract with the Sky Blues who snapped him up on a free transfer. Revitalised, Robson was appointed club captain by manager Terry Butcher and finished his first season there as Player of the Year. But the injury jinx struck again in 1992/93, when he was restricted to just 15 League matches and he played only the first match of 1993/94. Yet it was all so different for Stewart as a youngster. A pupil of Brentwood Public School, he captained England Youth and made his Arsenal debut, aged 17, ironically at Upton Park (December 5, 1981). Although very competitive in midfield, Robbo could also adapt to the full-back or central defensive positions when needed, and even played in goal twice for the Gunners (without conceding a goal) when Pat Jennings was injured! Rated one of the best young prospects in the country by former England manager Bobby Robson but, typical of his bad luck, had to withdraw from three full international squads due to injury. After being forced to retire from the game due to injury in the mid-1990s, Stewart took up coaching and worked with the backroom staff at Wimbledon and then for Middlesbrough and Tranmere Rovers in a consultancy role before joining Southend United as a coach in February 2003. Following the departure of manager Rob Newman from Roots Hall in April 2003, Stewart was put in temporary charge of the Shrimpers and oversaw a 1-0 home win over Leyton Orient in his first match at the helm. He was the latest of a long line of ex-Hammers who took up managerial posts with the Essex club, which include Ted Fenton, Bobby Moore, Kevin Lock, Frank Lampard senior, Alvin Martin and Paul Brush.

Stewart Robson

ROBSON, William — 1933

Born: Southwick, County Durham, 1906
League apps: 3

A FORMER SUNDERLAND Boys star, this fine full-back spent his formative years in Wearside junior soccer – most notably with Castletown St Margaret's in the United Churches League. A miner by trade, he progressed to his coal works side, Hylton Colliery, competing in the Wearside League. His performances there drew the attention of Derby County who signed him as a pro. It was via the Baseball Ground that he arrived at Upton Park in the summer of 1933 after six seasons, but only 13 League appearances with the Rams. Making his Hammers debut in the opening match of the season versus Bolton Wanderers at Upton Park, he played in the following two matches, away to Brentford and Plymouth Argyle respectively, to complete his hat-trick of first team appearances. Joined Reading in the close season of 1934 and scored one goal in 134 League games at Elm Park. Bill died in Oxford (August 11, 1960) aged 54.

ROSENIOR, Leroy — 1988-92

Born: Balham, London, 24.8.64
League apps: 53 (15 goals)
Cup apps: 12 (4 goals)

A POWERFUL STRIKER whose goals did much to keep Hammers in the top flight at the end of 1987/88. Leroy began his career with Fulham in 1982, making his League debut for them at Leicester City (December 4, 1982). He played 54 League games, scoring 15 goals, before moving to Queens Park Rangers for £50,000 in the summer of 1985. But he made only 38 League appearances (eight goals) and nine Cup appearances (two goals) before returning to Craven Cottage in 1987 for another 30 matches in Division Three that yielded 20 goals. John Lyall had tried, unsuccessfully, to bring several leading strikers to Upton Park in the difficult winter of 1987/88 before Rosenior answered the call after scoring 40 goals in 111 League and Cup appearances altogether for Fulham. The £275,000 signing, who was particularly strong in the air, arrived relatively unknown to Hammers' fans but made an immediate impact, alongside the unsettled Tony Cottee, by scoring the winner on his debut versus Watford at Upton Park (March 19, 1988). He added another four First Division goals in eight remaining games, including a vital double versus Chelsea that ensured survival in the final home match. The following season, with Cottee having left for Everton, Rosenior carried the burden up front. He topped the scorechart with seven League goals and eight more in various Cup competitions, but it was not enough to keep Hammers in Division One. Then the injury jinx struck Leroy in a big way. Persistent knee and Achilles injuries limited him to just four League starts under Lou Macari in 1989/90 and, worse still, just two sub outings the following season. With competition for places further intensified by the return of Frank McAvennie, and the signing of Trevor Morley and Jimmy Quinn, Leroy had loan spells with Fulham and Charlton Athletic. There was talk of him going to France to play for Metz, but he received an unexpected recall to First Division action at the start of 1991/92. His last appearance for Hammers came in the role of sub at Nottingham Forest (September 28, 1991). Leroy, whose family originate from Sierra Leone, Africa, finally settled at Bristol City, where he played first team football and scored eight times in 42 League and Cup appearances for the Ashton Gate club in 1992/93 as City finished 15th in the old First Division and Rosie scored a hat-trick in a 4-1 win over Brentford on the last day of the season! They were to be his last goals in the Football League as he virtually gave up playing to take up a coaching role at City although he did make four sub and two starts in 1993/94. He then managed the reserves and played for them at centre-half. After two years in charge of City's second string and a spell coaching Fleet, he was appointed manager of Gloucester City whom he led to the FA Trophy Semi-final. He then returned to Bristol City to take up the post of assistant director at their Academy where his son Liam was a promising youngster at the time (and later played for Fulham). The departure of Tony Pulis saw him handed his first taste of Football League management along with Tony Fawthrop and David Burnside. Rosie was later made first team coach under ex-Barnsley boss Danny Wilson with the Robins, but left in December 2001 to take over the reins at Merthyr Tydfil. Just a few months into the job, he was given the opportunity to take over at struggling Third Division Torquay United. One of only three black players in Football League management today, he completely turned round the Gulls' fortunes, leading them to promotion to the newly named League One in May 2004.

ROTHWELL, James   1910-14

Born: Crosby, Liverpool, Merseyside, 1888
SL apps: 88 (4 goals)
Cup apps: 11

JIM DIDN'T HAVE the happiest of debuts for Hammers, being in the West Ham team trounced 3-0 at Brentford (December 13, 1910), but luckily the scoreline was reversed in the next fixture versus Leyton at the Boleyn, which enabled Irons' new defender to settle into the side in the number 2 shirt. He missed only one match to the end of the season that saw his team finish a respectable fifth in the Southern League that campaign. He remained more or less a regular until 1913/14 when he played his last match at left-back in a 3-2 win at Southampton (February 14, 1914)

ROWLAND, Keith   1993-98

Born: Portadown, Northern Ireland, 1.9.71
League apps: 23
Cup apps: 5

SIGNED TWICE BY Harry Redknapp – initially at Bournemouth for whom he made his League debut versus Darlington (August 17, 1991). The slim left-back made 72 appearances for the Cherries, as well as spending one match on loan to non-League Farnborough Town (August 1990) and two on loan to Coventry City (both sub outings) in January 1993. In the summer of 1993, with Redknapp by then back at West Ham as Billy Bonds' assistant, Rowland earned a permanent move to the Premiership when Hammers signed him for £110,000 and Paul Mitchell for £40,000. He made his debut on the opening day versus Wimbledon (August 14, 1993), but his first season was punctuated by injuries and he found it difficult to hold down a regular first team place with the more experienced David Burrows having replaced Julian Dicks at left-back. Still, Keith underlined his versatility by moving into the left-midfield position on occasions, where his crossing ability led to a number of goals. Unfortunately, a broken leg – sustained in a tackle with Everton's John Ebbrell – ended his season prematurely in April 1993. At least Keith could look back on winning his first senior Northern Ireland cap versus Latvia in September 1993. The return of Julian Dicks in October 1994 meant that Keith once more had to fight for his first team place. Although Keith made only 12 first team appearances in 1994/95, he continued to be picked by Northern Ireland and made three more showings versus Canada, Chile and Latvia in 1995. Unable to oust Dicks, Rowland slapped in a transfer request, but it fell on deaf ears. His adaptable nature paid dividends when he was given the left-sided role in Hammers new look five-man defensive formation in 1995/96 and the friendly Ulsterman experienced a new lease of life. So much so, that West Ham turned down a reported £1 million bid from Premiership Champions Blackburn Rovers. "When I saw the headline '£1 million for a Ham Rowl', I thought it was an April Fool joke!" Keith commented at the time. The following season, he might have rued not making the move, though, as he was kept on the sidelines by Dicks and his fellow countryman Michael Hughes and he needed regular first team football to reclaim his place in the Northern Ireland team. Never one to let the side down when called upon, he netted his first ever goal for the club in the shock 1-1 draw at Newcastle in November 1996 and went on to complete 15 Premiership appearances that campaign as well as regain his position for his country. But in 1997/98, his career was at a crossroads and after just seven appearances that season he was transferred to First Division QPR along with club and country team-mate Iain Dowie in the deal that bought Trevor Sinclair to Hammers. Keith stayed three seasons at Loftus Road, making 60 appearances and scoring three times as part of the West Ham enclave that also included Tim Breacker and Ludo Miklosko. After a loan spell at Luton Town, he was given a free transfer to Third Division Chesterfield and made his last 14 League appearances scoring his final goal at Saltergate before dropping into non-League to join Martin Allen's Barnet in the Conference in March 2003. He switched to ambitious Ryman Premier side Hornchurch in July 2003 and teamed up with Old Irons team-mate Steve Jones at Urchins.
Northern Ireland caps: 1993 vs Latvia (sub); 1995 vs Canada, Chile, Latvia; 1996 vs Poland, Liechtenstein, Norway, Sweden, Germany; 1997 vs Ukraine, Armenia, Italy; 1998 vs Albania (with QPR); 1999 vs Turkey, Finland, Moldova, Germany, Canada, Republic of Ireland (19).

Keith Rowland

RUDDOCK, Neil   1998-2000

Born: Wandsworth, London, 9.5.68
League apps: 42 (2 goals)
Cup apps: 13 (1 goal)

TRULY A LARGER than life character, this renowned "hard man" defender actually started life as a striker with Millwall in 1986 and was one of a number of promising youngsters at the Den at that time, which included Teddy Sheringham. Signed for Hammers for a £300,000 fee in July 1988 after a fall-out with Gerard Houllier at Anfield and, after initial question marks over his fitness levels, Razor went on to have a storming first season in the claret and blue. Making his debut in the 1-0 win at Sheffield Wednesday on the opening day of the 1998/99 campaign, Neil settled in at the heart of Hammers' defence to play 30 times in League and Cup and added the final touch to an already lively dressing room! But let's start at the start. After failing to break through at Second Division Millwall under George Graham, the rookie striker who sometimes played on the wing was sold to Spurs for a nominal fee of £50,000 after scoring once in four appearances at the Den. Then, bizarrely, after two seasons and a solitary goal in 11 outings at White Hart Lane, he found himself transferred back to the Lions for £300,000 in June 1988. While he was away, Millwall had been promoted to the giddy heights of the First Division under the astute Graham, but there was to be no happy homecoming for the returnee. Despite scoring four goals in four games for the Lions, Neil found himself heading for the exit door at Cold Blow Lane for the second time when First Division Southampton tabled a bid of £250,000 to take him out of south London and down to the South Coast just eight months later in February 1989. The switch from the Den to the Dell and his subsequent conversion from attack to defence proved to be the change needed to finally kick-start his career as his infectious enthusiasm helped the previously struggling Saints move away from the relegation zone. Having found his true vocation – to stop rather than score goals – his game went from strength to strength. Three seasons as a Saint (although his disciplinary record suggested he was more of a sinner), during which time the Dell boys retained their top flight status and Razor racked up 138 senior appearances and proved he hadn't lost his penchant for getting forward by scoring 13 times, persuaded his old club Spurs to splash out £750,000 to take him back to London in July 1992. But after just one full season under Terry Venables at White Hart Lane, where he added another three goals and 50 appearances to his CV, Razor really hit the jackpot with a £2.5 million move to Liverpool in July 1993 after he'd fallen out with chairman Alan Sugar over the sacking of his hero Venables. During his early days at Anfield the rugged centre half enjoyed some of the best football of his career and reminded the Kopites of another former incumbent of that crucial position – Liverpool legend Ron Yeats. His fine form won him an England cap versus Nigeria in November 1995 to add to the ones he'd already won at Youth, Under-21 and B levels and complete a successful year that had seen him win his first medal at club level when Pool defeated Bolton Wanderers 2-1 at Wembley in the Final of the Coca Cola Cup. By 1998, however, he'd fallen out of favour with the Anfield hierarchy and was loaned out to First Division QPR in March 1998. His and Vinnie Jones's intimidating presence at Loftus Road saved the west Londoner's from relegation and, while the cash strapped Rangers management dithered over making a permanent offer, that wily old fox Harry Redknapp steamed in to throw "Hell Razor" a Premiership lifeline for a fee of £100,000 in the close season of 1998. The now near veteran defender had made 156 senior appearances and scored a dozen goals for the Reds. He soon made his imposing physical presence felt in the Hammers defence and contributed to the camaraderie that, in his own words, made the Upton Park dressing room "The best I have ever been a part of". But football clubs are run by boardrooms and not dressing rooms and Razor was on his way again in July 2000 to Crystal Palace in a move that suited all parties. As his wages at West Ham were appearance based, his 56 first team appearances (three goals) must have earned him a fair few bob and with no fee involved in his move to south London, he was able to negotiate a good deal with Palace. Immediately installed as club captain at Selhurst Park, Neil promptly took the young Palace players out on the town. Whether that episode hastened his departure from Palace is not recorded, but after making 26 appearances (three goals) in 2000/01, Neil was released by mutual consent in the closing weeks of a season that had been interrupted by a series of injuries and suspensions. Next stop was Swindon Town when he teamed up with his former Anfield boss Roy Evans to become player-coach with the Wiltshire outfit. But, although still an inspiration on the field, the move to the railway town signalled the end of the line for Razor's long and colourful first class career as he found himself increasingly isolated after new owners were appointed and sacked boss Evans. So his 19 League and Cup appearances and two goals for Swindon Town brought the curtain down on his roller-

RUFFELL, James   1921-37

Born: Doncaster, Yorkshire, 8.8.1900
League apps: 505 (159 goals)
Cup apps: 43 (7 goals)

ALTHOUGH JIM WAS born in South Yorkshire, he became an adopted East Ender after his family had moved south and played his early soccer with Essex Road School, Manor Park, Fullers, Chadwell Heath Utd, Manor Park Albion, East Ham and Wall End United before joining Hammers in March 1920. Apart from a brief spell with Aldershot, Jimmy served no other club during his pro career. His League appearances set a West Ham United record, which remained unchallenged until Bobby Moore surpassed it in 1973. Making his first appearance in Hammers' colours in a 3-0 victory over Port Vale at the Boleyn in September 1921, Jimmy's League and Cup appearances rose steadily in the early 1920s – as did his goalscoring record, despite having scoreless seasons in 1921/22, 1932/33 and 1936/37. It's doubtful if his career total of 166 in League and Cup will ever be surpassed by an orthodox winger. Inevitably capped by his country and a member of the West Ham team that contested the first Wembley Cup Final in 1923, the Hammers' management could hardly have foreseen what lay ahead when they plucked the diminutive outside-left from the works team of the Ilford Electricity Board! Chosen six times to play for England, he made his international debut versus Scotland at Manchester in April 1926, when even the dual threat of Jimmy and former West Ham star Syd Puddefoot in the England side could not prevent the Scots winning 1-0. There can be little doubt that had it not been for the very high standard of competition for the England left-wing spot at that time, with Cliff Bastin (Arsenal), Eric Houghton (Aston Villa) and Eric Brook (Manchester City) all in contention, our subject would have won many more caps. In addition to his half-dozen full caps, further representative honours bestowed on him included selection for the Football League versus Scottish League in 1926/27 and against the Irish League in 1928/29 as well as appearances in English Trial Matches against the North, South and Rest in 1927; The Rest versus England, 1927; and against the Rest and Lancashire in 1929 – matches in which players were playing for their international lives. A succinct assessment of Jimmy Ruffell's play was given in a book entitled *A Century of English International Football 1872-1972* by Morley Farror and Douglas Lamming: "Opponents learned to pay Ruffell the compliment of close marking; it was fatal to let him give full rein to his exceptional speed and flashing shots." His two decades at the Boleyn saw him form many notable left-wing partnerships, numbering among them fellow England internationals

Billy Moore, Len Goulden, John Morton and briefly, Syd Puddefoot, when the latter returned to West Ham in 1932. But if Jim had had to make a choice, it would probably have been the first-named, Billy Moore. Portraying perfectly the cigarette-card image of the professional footballer, complete with centre-parting in his slicked-back hair, Jimmy set a dashing scene as he tormented his opposing full-backs, often leaving them with muddied backsides as he cut in to score yet another goal. When he left West Ham in 1937, he chose to see out the remainder of his career with little Aldershot, and in a remarkable coincidence he played his last game for the Hampshire club in opposition to the same team that he'd faced 17 years earlier in his first game for Hammers… Port Vale! Jim became involved in the fish trade after he retired from the game he graced with such distinction and was also later a brewery representative and an Essex licensee. The last link with the 1923 FA Cup Final team was lost when Jim passed away on September 6, 1989. His death prompted the following tribute from someone who witnessed Jimmy's career at first-hand and who himself holds a unique place in Hammers' history, the late Jack Helliar: "I had the privilege of being a personal friend of Jimmy and his family and can categorically state that Jimmy was the finest winger ever to play for West Ham United – a legend. He will be sadly missed by all his friends and acquaintances throughout football for, as well as being one of the 'Greats', he was also one of the nicest people you could wish to meet. Always smart, a perfect gentleman." A theme reiterated by my father, George Hogg, who also saw Jimmy play before World War II: "He was always well turned out, well-groomed and very gentlemanly. He was the Trevor Brooking of his day, in that respect." Footnote: Jim's brother Bill was also on Hammers' books, but never made the first team and transferred to Nelson in 1927.

England caps: 1926 vs Scotland, Northern Ireland; 1928 vs Northern Ireland, Wales; 1929 vs Scotland, Wales (6).

Career record

Played	League App	Gls	FAC App	Gls	LC App	Gls	Europe App	Gls	Total App	Gls
1921-22	14	0	1	0	0	0	0	0	15	0
1922-23	33	6	9	1	0	0	0	0	42	7
1923-24	39	2	3	0	0	0	0	0	42	2
1924-25	42	9	6	3	0	0	0	0	48	12
1925-26	40	12	1	0	0	0	0	0	41	12
1926-27	37	13	3	1	0	0	0	0	40	14
1927-28	39	18	2	1	0	0	0	0	41	19
1928-29	37	20	5	0	0	0	0	0	42	20
1929-30	40	13	4	0	0	0	0	0	44	13
1930-31	37	13	1	0	0	0	0	0	38	13
1931-32	39	15	2	0	0	0	0	0	41	15
1932-33	8	0	0	0	0	0	0	0	8	0
1933-34	22	8	2	0	0	0	0	0	24	8
1934-35	36	20	2	0	0	0	0	0	38	20
1935-36	30	10	2	1	0	0	0	0	32	11
1936-37	12	0	0	0	0	0	0	0	12	0
TOTAL	**505**	**159**	**43**	**7**	**0**	**0**	**0**	**0**	**548**	**166**

Matthew was still unable to show enough consistency to satisfy Harry Redknapp and, in August 1995, he was sold to First Division Norwich City for £320,000 to embark on a fresh start in Norfolk. But his new start turned into a disaster when he was injured in his solitary senior appearance and had to be stretchered off when he tried to make a reserve team comeback against Hammers shortly after. Diagnosed with the dreaded cruciate knee ligament injuries, Matt didn't kick another ball in anger that campaign. The following season was almost as bad when, after two sub appearances, he was loaned out to Third Division Northampton Town where he at least got some match experience and scored four goals in 15 games for the Cobblers in 1996/97. In March 1997, Norwich cut their losses and sold Matt for £165,000 to First Division Oldham Athletic who were fighting relegation. His two goals in eight matches failed to prevent the Latics' plunge into Division Two and, with only 16 appearances and one goal to show for his efforts in 1997/98, Matthew decided to retire from the game at the age of just 27. Far from feeling sorry for himself, Matthew enrolled at East London University and gained a degree in Applied Sports Science in 2001 with the ultimate aim of becoming a PE teacher.

RUSSELL, John   1904-05

League apps: 16
Cup apps: 1

THIS FORMER EVERTON defender was on duty for the official opening of the Boleyn Grounds versus Millwall (September 1, 1904). Wearing the number 6 shirt, John helped Hammers win that inaugural fixture against their arch rivals 3-0 and stayed in the side for a 15-match run until losing his place to Dick Jarvis. He was back on duty for the final match of the season when Irons ended the campaign as they had began, with a 3-0 win.

RUTHERFORD, Jack   1933-34

Born: Nenthead, Cumberland, 6.11.1908
League apps: 33
Cup apps: 2

SIGNED FROM WATFORD (31 League apps) on the recommendation of former Hammers goalkeeper Ted Hufton, after the latter had joined the Hertfordshire club in the twilight of his career. Although Ted claimed the credit for sending Jack to Upton Park, it was Gillingham (44 League apps) who discovered him originally playing for Crawcrook in the North Eastern League while continuing to work as a coal miner. From the Kent club he transferred to Vicarage Road, and from there to the Boleyn to become regular first-choice keeper for season 1933/34. Jack made way for a new signing from Burnley, Herman Conway, the following Second Division campaign and, in June 1935, he joined Charlie Paynter's old home-town club, Swindon Town. Jack made 30 League appearances for Town between 1935 and 1937 and also had a spell with Dartford during that time. In 1937, he joined Hartlepools but played just four times there before making the short journey to Barrow in 1938, where he made 37 appearances up until the outbreak of World War II.

coaster career, which is probably best summed up by his recollections of his first meeting with new Liverpool manager Gerard Houllier: "I'd had some problems with him – we got off on the wrong foot on his first day at the club when he introduced himself to the players saying: 'Hello Michael, hello Robbie, hello Stevie Mac.' He came up to me and said: 'And what is your name?' so I replied: 'Have you been in a coma for 15 years?' That didn't go down too well and I think we both realised it would be best for all concerned if I moved on when West Ham came in for me." Nowadays Neil seems equally at home in TV studios as he was on the playing field and is becoming a celebrity in his own right with appearances on *A Question of Sport, They Think It's All Over* and *I'm A Celebrity – Get Me Out Of Here!*

RUSH, Matthew   1990-95

Born: Dalston, London, 6.8.71
League apps: 25 (3 goals)
Cup apps: 1

A STRONG, PACY right-winger who took some time to make the breakthrough at Upton Park after joining the club from school in July 1988. He signed pro in March 1990 and made his first team debut later that year versus Hull City in a 7-1 Second Division slaughter at Upton Park (October 6, 1990). Started only three games in the top flight in 1991/92, but opened his goal account with two headers in a home win versus Norwich City. His form in the reserves didn't escape the notice of Jack Charlton, though, who called Matthew into the Republic of Ireland Under-21 team on two occasions that season. Rush's days at Upton Park appeared to be numbered when he failed to feature in any senior matches in 1992/93. He joined Cambridge United on loan in March 1993, making ten appearances, and benefited from an 11-game stint with Swansea City a year later. Just when he seemed to be on his way, Rush's Upton Park career received a boost when he was recalled in the spring of 1994 and played ten Premiership games, scoring a vital goal in a home win versus Ipswich Town. After another extended run in the first team in 1994/95,

Matthew Rush

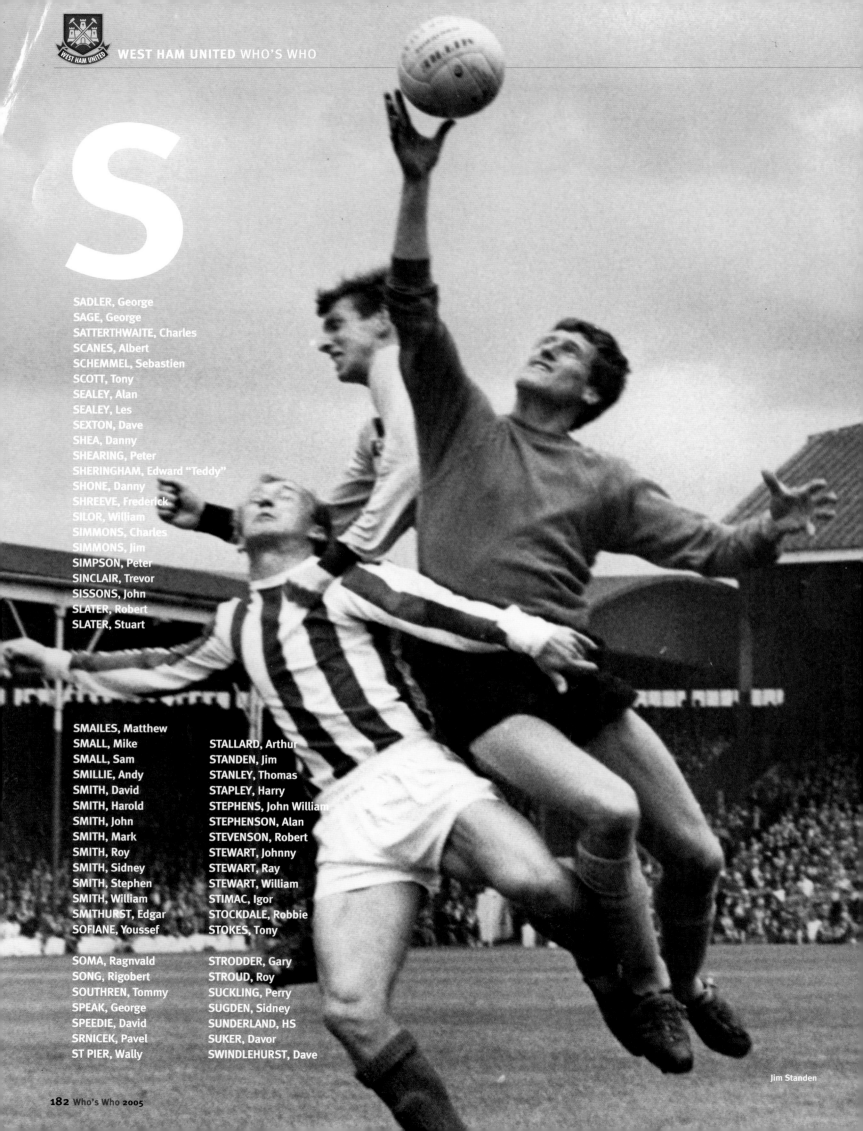

S

SADLER, George
SAGE, George
SATTERTHWAITE, Charles
SCANES, Albert
SCHEMMEL, Sebastien
SCOTT, Tony
SEALEY, Alan
SEALEY, Les
SEXTON, Dave
SHEA, Danny
SHEARING, Peter
SHERINGHAM, Edward "Teddy"
SHONE, Danny
SHREEVE, Frederick
SILOR, William
SIMMONS, Charles
SIMMONS, Jim
SIMPSON, Peter
SINCLAIR, Trevor
SISSONS, John
SLATER, Robert
SLATER, Stuart

SMAILES, Matthew
SMALL, Mike
SMALL, Sam
SMILLIE, Andy
SMITH, David
SMITH, Harold
SMITH, John
SMITH, Mark
SMITH, Roy
SMITH, Sidney
SMITH, Stephen
SMITH, William
SMITHURST, Edgar
SOFIANE, Youssef

STALLARD, Arthur
STANDEN, Jim
STANLEY, Thomas
STAPLEY, Harry
STEPHENS, John William
STEPHENSON, Alan
STEVENSON, Robert
STEWART, Johnny
STEWART, Ray
STEWART, William
STIMAC, Igor
STOCKDALE, Robbie
STOKES, Tony

SOMA, Ragnvald
SONG, Rigobert
SOUTHREN, Tommy
SPEAK, George
SPEEDIE, David
SRNICEK, Pavel
ST PIER, Wally

STRODDER, Gary
STROUD, Roy
SUCKLING, Perry
SUGDEN, Sidney
SUNDERLAND, HS
SUKER, Davor
SWINDLEHURST, Dave

Jim Standen

SADLER, George — 1946

Born: Whitwell, Northumberland, 7.5.15
League apps: 1

CENTRE-HALF GEORGE JUST qualifies for this directory, making the necessary one appearance in the 1946/47 season. Signed from Gainsborough Trinity, along with goalkeeper George Taylor, he had to be content with the solitary Second Division outing, there being a glut of defenders at the Boleyn at that time. They included veteran Charlie Bicknell, Arthur Banner, Steven Forde, Johnny McGowan and Ernie Devlin. George subsequently transferred to Southern League Guildford where he came under the managership of another ex-Hammer, Archie Macaulay. Hammers provided the opposition to the Surrey club at his benefit in 1954. George joined the Hammers prior to World War II, and served with his colleagues in the Essex Regiment Territorial Army and Royal Artillery. He also participated in all-in wrestling during the summer months.

SAGE, George — 1895-96 TIW

Born: Woolwich, London, December 1872

A WINGER WHO joined TIW after the break-up of the old Castle Swifts club in 1895. He played in the FA Cup tie versus Chatham and the floodlit friendly versus Old St Stephens (December 15, 1895). George gained a winner's medal in the West Ham Charity Cup Final against Barking.

SATTERTHWAITE, Charles — 1903-04

Born: Cockermouth, Cumbria, 1878
SL apps: 32 (13 goals)
Cup apps: 4 (5 goals)

A HIGH CLASS inside-left who joined Hammers from New Brompton (now Gillingham) for the start of the 1903/04 season. He was an immediate success in the claret and blue, scoring on his debut in the opening game of the season versus Millwall and finishing the campaign as Hammers' top scorer in Southern League matches with 13 goals to his credit. He met with equal success in Cup ties, scoring in all three qualifying rounds of the competition, including a hat-trick against Chatham, before his – and Hammers' – scoring run ended with a 1-0 intermediate round defeat versus Fulham. He also once scored four goals in a Southern League fixture versus Brighton. His fine form and consistency, in a season during which he missed only two Southern League matches, alerted other clubs and he transferred to Woolwich Arsenal in the following close season. In 1906, Charlie visited Hammers in their new home for a First Round FA Cup replay with the Gunners, and helped his new club to a 3-2 win assisted by two other ex-West Ham men, McEachrane and Bigden. Well-known for his thunderbolt shooting, he once broke the goal nets with one of his scoring efforts at Plumstead and in an Arsenal versus Sheffield United match he smashed a tremendous 25-yard drive which hit the bar, rebounded against J Lievesley, the Blades' goalie, knocking him clean off his feet, the ball ending up in the net. With Liverpool in 1900/01 (he was Reds' 12th man for their 1901 FA Cup visit to the Memorial Grounds), Charlie had an England trial in 1904/05 while with the Gunners, for whom he scored 21 goals in 61 League appearances between 1904 and 1908. His brother, S Satterthwaite, also played for Arsenal, 1907-10.

SCANES, Albert — 1909-10

SL apps: 3 (3 goals)

BERT WAS ONE of several number 9s drafted in to deputise for England international George Webb, whose business commitments often prevented him from turning out for Hammers. Two goals on his debut at Crystal Palace and a winning counter at Upton Park versus Northampton Town made the former Barking man the most successful by far of that season's understudies, but he wasn't retained for the following campaign and moved to Croydon Common for 1911/12.

SCHEMMEL, Sebastien — 2001-03

Born: Nancy, France, 2.6.75
League apps: 63 (1 goal)
Cup apps: 10

THIS EXCITING FRENCH Under-21 international right-back originally caught the eye of Glenn Roeder when he was across the Channel watching Metz as a scout for Harry Redknapp ahead of the Intertoto Cup Final between the two clubs in 1999. Roeder brought back a glowing report on the overlapping full-back and when Redknapp saw him at first hand he quickly made a mental note and eventually signed him on a loan deal in January 2001. He immediately filled in for the injured Trevor Sinclair at right wing-back and proved an instant hit in his Premiership debut in the 1-1 draw at Charlton in January 2001. Following Redknapp's shock exit, new manager Roeder had no hesitation in signing the all action Metz man on a permanent basis and showed a shrewd side to his nature by knocking the French negotiators down from their original asking price of £1.5 million to secure his services for a bargain £765,000! Virtually an ever-present in 2001/02 until a foot injury caused him to miss the last two games of the season, Seb had done enough to win the coveted Hammer of the Year award and duly received the trophy before the last home game of the campaign against Bolton. But that was as good as it ever got for the Frenchman with the flowing locks at Upton Park and if you believe the story of Samson and Delilah, you'd swear Sebastien, like his fabled counterpart, lost all his strength when he had his hair cut. Once shorn, Schemmel hardly resembled the player of the previous season and neither did his performances as Hammers plunged to the foot of the Premiership. A big fall out with Glenn Roeder, who had no time for his first signing as West Ham manager, followed and in an unsavoury incident, the unhappy Frenchman had to be escorted from the club's premises by security staff, following which he showed fans outside the ground a letter of dismissal issued to him by his employers. With trouble in his personal life as well, everything had gone wrong for the talented French star whose future at West Ham once looked so secure. Thrown a lifeline by his first boss Harry Redknapp at Portsmouth, Seb made 18 appearances for Pompey in 2003/04, but then fell out with Harry as well. As his options continued to recede, Hammers coach Peter Grant poured cold water on speculation that the player might return to Upton Park in October 2004.

SCOTT, Tony — 1959-65

Born: Huntingdon, Cambridgeshire, 1.4.41
League apps: 83 (16 goals)
Cup apps: 14 (3 goals)

AN ORTHODOX RIGHT-WINGER with a penchant for scoring goals. He joined the Upton Park groundstaff in 1957 after starring for Huntingdon Boys and St Neots Town, quickly making his way through the junior ranks and 12 appearances for England Youth. Tony had his scoring League debut versus Chelsea in 1960, going on to make over 80 senior appearances before transferring to Aston Villa for £25,000 and renewing his right-wing partnership with Phil Woosnam at Villa Park. He scored five times in 57 League and Cup appearances for Villa before joining Torquay United for £5,000 in September 1967. At Plainmoor he joined up with former Hammers team-mate John Bond and scored four goals in 87 League outings for the Devon club who were managed by another

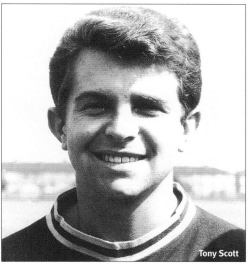

Tony Scott

ex-Hammer, Frank O'Farrell. In July 1970, Tony again joined up with "Bondy", who was then manager at Fourth Division Bournemouth with another former Hammer, Ken Brown, as his coach. Tony won a Fourth Division runners-up medal in his first season at Dean Court and scored six goals in 61 League matches for the Cherries before moving on to join Exeter City in June 1972. Scotty made another 51 League appearances for the Grecians and scored another two goals – his last in the League as injury forced his retirement in May 1974. He then had a spell working at Manchester City for his mentor, Malcolm Allison, as Youth Team coach at Maine Road.

SEALEY, Alan — 1961-67

Born: Hampton, Middlesex, 22.4.42
League apps: 107 (22 goals)
Cup apps: 21 (4 goals)

SCORER OF THE two goals that defeated TSV Munich in the memorable 1965 European Cup Winners' Cup Final at Wembley, his career plummeted after a freak pre-season training accident the same year. The players had organised an impromptu cricket match at the Chadwell Heath training ground. Sealey fell awkwardly over a wooden bench and sustained a broken leg. Signed from Leyton Orient in the exchange deal that took Dave Dunmore to Brisbane Road in March 1961, Alan was a frequent member of the Hammers' attack in the 1960s. Spotted originally by talent scout Eddie Heath and signed for Orient by caretaker manager Les Gore after scoring five goals in his first trial match, Alan joined Hammers in a somewhat unusual fashion. He arrived at Upton Park just after the departure of Ted Fenton and just before the appointment of Ron Greenwood as new team boss – actually being signed by chairman Mr Reg Pratt! He had been well schooled in the finer points of the game at Orient by master coach Eddie Baily (who went on to become West Ham's chief scout). Transferred to Plymouth Argyle in November 1967, Alan stayed only briefly at Home Park before ending his playing career with his then local club Romford in the Southern League. Alan took over the family business of distributing bookmakers' lists when he retired from playing. He was back at Upton Park for the Bobby Moore memorial match in March 1994, when the 1964 and 1965 Cup-winning teams returned for a night of nostalgia and to pay tribute to their former skipper. Sadly, Alan too passed away at the tragically early age of 53 in February 1996. The club responded to the death of one of its most popular former players by staging an emotive minute's silence before the home FA Cup tie versus Grimsby Town during which his goals against TSV were shown on the big screens in perfect silence. Alan's wife Barbara was an honoured guest at the 40th anniversary reunion and dinner hosted by Tony Cottee to commemorate West Ham's 1965 Cup Winners' Cup victory on May 20, 2005.

Left to right: Ron Greenwood, Alan Sealey, Albert Walker and Bill Jenkins

SEALEY, Les — 1996-97

Born: Bethnal Green, London, 29.9.57
League apps: 4

ALTHOUGH HE ONLY played four first team games for West Ham United, goalkeeping giant Les "The Cat" Sealey left behind an incredible impression on all at Upton Park and in the wider world of football, where he is remembered as a true legend among his profession. His sadly premature and untimely death on August 19, 2001, at just 43 years of age, stunned the game and left a void only his larger than life character could fill. The cousin of that other Hammers legend, Alan Sealey, Les had begun his career with Coventry City and played in goal for the Sky Blues when Hammers won through a thrilling two-leg League Cup Semi-final against them by 4-3 on aggregate in 1981. But after 178 appearances for the Highfield Road club, Les twice got to Wembley's famous Twin Towers with his next team, Luton Town, although he had to be content with a runners-up medal on both occasions in the 1988 Simod Cup and the 1989 Littlewood's Cup Finals. But The Cat got the cream eventually in dramatic fashion when, after 259 first team games for the Hatters, the self confessed mad-cap keeper was signed by Sir Alex Ferguson for Manchester United on loan to cover for injuries in March 1990. After being on the winning side in both of his two First Division outings for the Red Devils at the tail end of that 1989/90 season, The Cat watched in anticipation as one of the keepers he was understudying at Old Trafford, Scot Jim Leighton had a nightmare match in the 3-3 FA Cup Final draw with unfancied Crystal Palace at Wembley. An anxious Alex Ferguson, on the verge of the glory years, took a gamble and pitched Les into the fray of the Wembley replay. It became the fairytale to end all fairytales as The Cat kept a clean sheet and United won 1-0! Les was back on Wembley duty the next year too, but this time tasted defeat in the Rumblelows Cup Final against Sheffield Wednesday. His greatest triumph, however, was just around the corner when he emulated cousin Alan Sealey by helping United to a European Cup Winners' Cup victory over Barcelona in Rotterdam in May 1991. The signing of Peter Schmeichel, after Les had won three medals in a year and played 33 First Division matches and 20 in the Cups for the Reds, hastened his departure to Aston Villa in July 1991. Amazingly, after 24 games for Villa in addition to brief loan spells at Birmingham City (15 apps) and Coventry (two apps), Sealey was re-signed by Ferguson as cover for Schmeichel in January 1993! But there the fairytale ended and after just two Cup appearances, Sealey made an ill-advised stop-over at Second Division strugglers

Blackpool on another free transfer in July 1994. After nine appearances at Bloomfield Road, he jumped at the chance proffered by Harry Redknapp to join his boyhood heroes West Ham in November 1994! Now with his lifelong ambition of playing for the team he supported as a boy from the North Bank almost within his grasp, Les's day-to-day life at Upton Park and the Chadwell Heath training ground took on a new zest as he coaxed and cajoled the club's younger custodians (and the not so young) on the art of goalkeeping according to Les. Yet when the time came for him to make his long-awaited Hammers debut, it was surrounded by the most bizarre circumstances at Highbury in September 1995. With ten-man Irons behind to an Ian Wright penalty and their two allowed subs already on the field – an injury to John Moncur led to Les grabbing Keith Rowland's jersey and entering the fray supporting Iain Dowie in attack! The following March, however, an injury to Ludek Miklosko gave Les the chance to make a more orthodox debut against Newcastle United in the maelstrom of St James's Park in a Premiership clash featured live on Sky. With Kevin Keegan's Magpies buoyed up by the knowledge that a win would take them back to the top of the Premiership, West Ham were expecting a non-stop barrage on their goal from the Geordies' potent strike force, though not the black and white avalanche that was about to engulf them. But this was to be The Cat's finest hour. With Steve Potts sent off early on, Les's goal was under constant siege from the first minute to the last as Newcastle blitzed the Irons goal with an amazing 40 goal attempts, 27 of which hit the target with veteran Les saving 24 of them at a rate of one every four minutes to limit the score to a respectable 3-0 and produce the finest display of goalkeeping in West Ham's history. After the match Peter Beardsley claimed: "The one Les saved from Rieper was magnificent – world class. But he's got the best coach in the world there with Peter Shilton." While Shilts himself added: "Les was a little bit busy! He made nine or ten great saves." While the man himself said: "Now I've achieved everything in my career. I'm in the record books, I've played for West Ham United!" It seemed Les had little else to prove when he accepted a free transfer to little Leyton Orient along with Alvin Martin in July 1996. But he soon had the desired effect with six clean sheets in his 14 games before going back to West Ham in a straight swap for the great Peter Shilton, who wanted the opportunity to take his career total of appearances over the 1,000 mark with O's. Drawing on the lessons he'd learned from the great Shilts, Les now concentrated on coaching the goalkeepers at Chadwell Heath, but there was still one more full game in the

Premiership awaiting him at Blackburn Rovers and then, in a nice touch by Harry Redknapp, a last minute cameo in the last game of the season at Champions Manchester United as Les brought the curtain down on an amazing career in the Theatre of Dreams. As testimony to the excellence of his work as West Ham's goalkeeping coach up to the departure of Harry Redknapp, one needs to look no further than his protégé, Stephen Bywater. "Les is a top man," said the England Under-21 keeper just after his arrival. "He's lively and he's taught me a lot. I'm learning more and more from him all the time and I know I'm going to progress under his guidance." Before his departure from the coaching staff in June 2001, proud Les brought his sons Joe and George to Upton Park for their goalkeeping apprenticeships. Les once announced: "I think you're born to be a goalkeeper." If anyone was, he certainly was!

SEXTON, Dave — 1953-56

Born: Islington, London, 6.4.30
League apps: 74 (27 goals)
Cup apps: 3 (2 goals)

TRANSFERRED TO HAMMERS from Luton Town (nine League apps, one goal) in March 1953, he had learned his early soccer with Chelmsford City in the Southern League. Son of former professional boxer Archie Sexton, who fought Jock McAvoy for the British Middleweight title in 1933, Dave enjoyed a chequered playing career. A striker of some repute, he scored some valuable goals in his three years at the Boleyn but the only representative honour he won was playing for the FA versus the RAF in 1953. Moving to Leyton Orient in May 1956, he later had spells with Brighton & Hove Albion (where he was a member of their Third Division South Championship team and scored 26 times in 47 League apps) and Crystal Palace (27 League apps, 11 goals), where his playing career was ended by injury in January 1962. Dave's managerial career has since overshadowed that of his playing days. As a manager-coach he saw service with Chelsea (twice), Orient, Fulham, Arsenal, Queens Park Rangers, Manchester United and Coventry City. He was appointed assistant to England manager Bobby Robson in July 1983, and was later put in charge of the revolutionary new "Soccer School" and the Under-21 squad. His greatest triumphs in management were undoubtedly at Chelsea, whom he steered to an FA Cup win in 1970 and a European Cup Winners' Cup success over Real Madrid in 1971. He also led the Blues to runners-up spot in the First Division (1971/72). A feat he

Dave Sexton is beaten as Luton Town's Syd Owen heads clear

repeated at QPR (1975/76) and Manchester United (1979/80). Dave was head coach at Aston Villa in the 1990s and in 2002 he was appointed chief scout by England manager Sven Goran Eriksson. Dave then recruited ex-Hammers Ken Brown and Noel Cantwell, who sadly died in September 2005, as his assistants.

SHEA, Danny   1908-13/1920-21

Born: Wapping, London, November 1887
SL apps: 179 (111 goals)
Cup apps: 22 (22 goals)
League apps: 16 (1 goal)

WITH HIS IRISH ancestry and inquisitive nature in opposing penalty areas, Dan would have been a certain contender for the Republic of Ireland team had he been around today. Charlie Paynter discovered this brilliant inside-forward almost on the club's doorstep, playing Sunday morning football for the Builders Arms pub team in Stratford and also for Pearl United and Manor Park Albion in 1908. He progressed almost immediately to Hammers' Southern League side. A superb ball-player, hard to dispossess, he developed into a consistent goalscorer and became the leading light in West Ham's attack. His fine form didn't fail to catch the attention of Football League clubs, and after 166 Southern League appearances for Hammers, Blackburn Rovers duly broke the existing transfer record to take him to Ewood Park for £2,000 in 1913 – in a move that modern day benefactor Roman Abramovich would have been proud of – and saw Dan pocket £550 as his share of the fee. It proved to be a shrewd transaction on Hammers' part when, after winning two England caps and a First Division Championship medal while at Rovers (scoring 27 goals to help them to the title), he returned south during the war years to make a further 75 appearances in the claret and blue as a guest player in the hastily-formed London Combination. He also had spells with Birmingham, Fulham and Nottingham Forest in World War I and was in the side that defeated Everton in the Final of the Victory Shield. Although Danny went back to Blackburn with the cessation of hostilities to win further England honours in two Victory Internationals versus Scotland, like George Hilsdon, Harry Stapley and Syd Puddefoot before and after him, he returned for a second spell at the Boleyn. It proved to be an abortive reunion, however, for after 16 Second Division outings and a solitary goal to show for his efforts in 1920/21, he transferred to Fulham (107 apps, 24 goals) after a difference of opinion with the West Ham management in November 1920. The move saw him regain some of his old form, and he finished the following season as Cottagers' second top scorer with 11 goals. But he continued to move around, first joining Clapton Orient (33 League apps, eight goals) and later Coventry City (64 apps, 12 goals). Dan played out the last days of his chequered career with Sheppey United in the Southern League. Worked as a docker during World War I and after he hung up his boots, he was also a publican in later life. Described as: "An artful schemer and delicate dribbler at inside-right for many seasons. Had the knack of wheeling suddenly when near goal and unleashing a thunderbolt shot." Shea worked as a coach in Switzerland for the Winterthur club in Zurich and then with amateurs Woking in the late 1920s. Danny also played 36 war-time games for Fulham scoring 19 goals and he also played one game for Glasgow Celtic in January 1919 on loan. Such was his reputation, Celtic moved the legendary Patsy Gallagher to outside-right to

accommodate him for the game with Clyde at Parkhead. Former Fulham outside-left Peter Garigan was quoted in 1954 as saying: "At Fulham in 1920/21, I had as my inside-right one of the greatest ball artists who has ever played for England – Danny Shea. His manipulation was bewildering. He was the 'Prince of Partners', the intellectual footballer." An occasional visitor to Upton Park in later years, Danny Shea died at the age of 73 at Wapping, after being taken ill on Christmas Day, 1960.

SHEARING, Peter   1960

Born: Uxbridge, Middlesex, 26.8.38
League apps: 6

AN EXPERIENCED SENIOR amateur goalkeeper with Uxbridge, Hayes and Kingstonian, he played

against the last named for Hendon in the 1960 Amateur Cup Final at Wembley. Peter signed for Hammers after a spell on Spurs' books, making his initial League appearance versus Sheffield Wednesday at Hillsborough. He went on to make half a dozen First Division outings before returning to reserve duty. Began a grand tour of the West Country clubs when transferred to Portsmouth (17 League apps), later taking in Exeter City (86 League apps), Plymouth Argyle (24 League apps), Exeter again, Bristol Rovers and, finally, Gillingham (39 League apps). He assisted fellow ex-Hammer Andy Nelson at Charlton when the latter was manager at The Valley and also became a fully qualified referee. Peter had been forced to retire following injury at Bristol Rovers, but recovered to continue his career at Gills. He ran a Post Office at Maidstone in Kent for nearly 30 years after leaving The Valley.

SHERINGHAM, Edward "Teddy" 2004-

Born: Highams Park, London, 2.4.66
League apps: 33 (20 goals)
Cup apps: 3 (1 goal)

EDWARD P SHERINGHAM esquire, as Brian Clough used to call him. Yes, some player. Fifty-one caps for England, Division Two Championship Winners' medal 1988, League Cup runners-up medal 1992 Zenith Data Winners medal 1992, Charity Shield 1997, League Championship medals 1999, 2000 and 2001, FA Cup Winners' medal 1999, European Cup Winners' medal 1999 and Inter Continental/Cup Winners' medal 1999. Some player, some record. But surely, after a 20-year career in the game, too old for the rigours of this new-fangled Coca Cola Championship? Even that crafty cockney Harry Redknapp let him go at the end of 2003/04. Wrong! Thirty-eight-year-old vintage Sheri can still do it! At the end of the 2004/05 season, Teddy was sitting proudly at the top of West Ham's goalscoring chart with 21 vital goals without which Hammers' quest to return to the Premiership would already have been a pipedream. Yet that's exactly what the glittering prizes that lay ahead remained to young Edward as he graduated from his apprenticeship as a young Lion at Third Division Millwall in 1983/84 and scored the first of a record breaking total of 111 goals in 262 senior appearances at the Den. But with no appearances the following season and only a handful of games and no goals out on loan at Fourth Division Aldershot to show in 1984/85, the big-time must have seemed light years away for the young Lion cub who'd supported West Ham as a kid. But that's where Teddy's luck with managers first began. At Millwall he had George Graham, at Forest, Brian Clough, at Spurs, Terry Venables, and at Manchester United, Sir Alex Ferguson. Disciplinarian Graham soon taught the impressionable young striker to "forget the art gallery stuff" in favour of getting in the box to poach tap-ins. Millwall made a cool £2 million from the shrewd Scot Graham's teaching when they sold Teddy on to Nottingham Forest in July 1991. The glory days were all but over at the City Ground with the team and its messiah Brian Clough only a shadow of their former selves. Even so, Teddy enjoyed two trips to Wembley during his one full season on Trentside as a loser in the 1-0 Football League Cup Final defeat to Manchester United and a winner in the victory over Southampton in the Zenith Data Systems Cup Final. It was the last of the summer wine for Forest, who finished rock bottom of the first Premiership table, but not for Teddy, who didn't hang around long enough to take the chop with Forest, but instead headed for champagne days at White Hart Lane when joining Spurs in August 1992. The fee was £2.1 million and although Terry Venables had moved up to chief executive at Tottenham it would be naive to think that El Tel wasn't influential in the transfer. Later to star in Venner's Euro 96 side that lost so unluckily to Germany in the Semi-final at Wembley, the England coach included Sheringham in his *Terry Venables' Football Heroes* book published in 2001 enthusing: "Teddy is a top-flight goalscorer and an extraordinary goalmaker. He can score them from anywhere and make them from anywhere. Under me his attitude was faultless. He gave everything, was serious about the game, listened to what was said and took on board what he felt was useful to the team." Although there were no trophies or Cups won during his first spell in N17, there were 99 goals in 197 League and Cup appearances to keep the Spurs fans happy, until his £5 million move to Manchester United in July 1997 saw him go from hero to zero in their eyes. Little did they know that after four medal-laden years and another 44 goals in 153 first team appearances at the Theatre of Dreams, he would return for an extended encore at the Lane on a free transfer in July 2001. With 26 goals in 80 more League and Cup appearances still to flow from his talented boots, those same Spurs fans were delighted to welcome him back hot on the heels of his Footballer of the Year and PFA Player of the Year awards. Another free transfer followed in July 2003 when the persuasive charm of Harry Redknapp enticed Teddy down to the South Coast to assist in keeping Portsmouth afloat in the Premiership. And the Pompey chimes kept ringing as another ten goals from 38 League and Cup appearances ensured their survival. Teddy was voted Hammer of the Year in April 2005. Inevitably, he scored Hammers' first goal in the Premiership in a 3-1 win over Blackburn in August 2005!

SHONE, Danny — 1928

Born: Wirral, Merseyside, 27.4.1892
League apps: 12 (5 goals)

A STOCKY INSIDE-LEFT signed from Liverpool. Dan made a scoring First Division debut on the opening day of the 1928/29 season for Hammers versus Sheffield United at Upton Park. Although he almost managed a goal every other game in his 12 League appearances in the claret and blue, West Ham transferred the likeable Dan to Coventry City on January 2, 1929 in a double deal that also resulted in James Loughlin joining the Midlanders. He scored one goal in nine matches for City. He began his career with Grayson's in Division One of the West Cheshire League before signing for Liverpool as a pro in May 1921. He scored 23 goals in 76 League games for Pool.

SHREEVE, Frederick — 1908-11

Born: birthplace unknown, 17.12.1882
SL apps: 65 (4 goals)
Cup apps: 10

RIGHT-BACK FRED HAD the unusual distinction of scoring on his Hammers debut from that position. A known penalty-taker, his goal, which helped secure a 2-1 win over Northampton on October 24, 1908, probably came from the 12-yard spot. Formerly with Millwall, he went on to form a regular full-back partnership with Bill Taylor that season, ending up with 19 Southern League appearances to his credit. The following term saw him with a new partner in Bob Fairman, and he missed only one match to complete his most successful season at Upton Park. He began his career at Burton United and joined Doncaster Rovers for 1911/12. Fred's son Bert later played for Charlton Athletic and appeared for them in both the 1946 and 1947 FA Cup Finals.

SILOR, William — 1909-10

Born: birthplace unknown, 1887
SL apps: 6

PREVIOUSLY HAVING SERVED Eton Mission, Leyton and Norwich City (with whom he scored seven goals in 26 games in 1908/09). Bill made his first appearance in Hammers' colours in a 1-0 Southern League defeat at Exeter City on March 5, 1910, in the centre-forward position. Switched to the outside-left berth for his next outing versus Croydon Common, he remained there for a further four matches to bring his total appearances to a round half-dozen in the claret and blue.

SIMMONS, Charles — 1904-05

SL apps: 34 (8 goals)
Cup apps: 1

INSIDE-FORWARD "CHIPPY" SIMMONS was with West Bromwich Albion for six years before signing for Irons. "A wonderful ball player with a deceptive body-swerve. Would have won numerous England caps but for being a contemporary of the great Steve Bloomer." Apart from playing in the first-ever game at the Boleyn Ground, Simmons did likewise with West Bromwich Albion at the Hawthorns (October 3, 1900). Only one season with Hammers, Chippy began his career with Worcester Rovers.

SIMMONS, Jim — 1920-22

Born: Blackwell, Derbyshire, date unknown
League apps: 27 (1 goal)

SHARES A UNIQUE and, until now, unrecognised distinction with fellow early-century ex-Hammer, Billy Barnes: *both* signed for the club from Sheffield United, and *both* scored FA Cup Final goals for the Blades! Sometimes confused with a predecessor of the same surname, "Chippy" Simmons, who was signed from West Bromwich Albion in 1904, Jim was a nephew of the legendary Sheffield United goalkeeper Bill Foulke. Usually employed in the outside-right position, he realised every footballer's dream when he scored Sheffield United's first goal in their 3-0 1915 FA Cup Final victory versus Chelsea at Old Trafford. Billy Barnes had achieved the feat when he scored Blades' winner in the 1902 Final replay versus Southampton at Crystal Palace. Jim was forced to retire from the game before Hammers reached their first Final in 1923. Jim played for Blackwell Colliery before joining United in 1908 and he amassed 204 League appearances and scored 43 goals for the Blades up to his transfer to Irons in 1920.

SIMPSON, Peter — 1935-37

Born: Edinburgh, Scotland, 13.11.08
League apps: 32 (12 goals)
Cup apps: 4

PLAYED HIS FIRST game for West Ham in a 4-3 defeat by Norwich City in the first League match played at Carrow Road, following the Norfolk club's move from their previous ground, The Nest. Although he failed to get on the scoresheet on his debut, Peter gave a good return for the modest fee paid to Crystal Palace by Hammers for his services, being equally at home in any forward positions. He began his career with St Bernards, where he had two seasons before joining Kettering Town. Palace had signed him with four other players from Kettering in June 1929. He was the most successful of the quintet and scored six goals versus Exeter City in Glaziers' 7-2 win on April 4, 1930 and in all scored 153 League goals for the south Londoners in 180 games and was awarded a benefit match by them against the famous amateur club, Corinthians. He later transferred to Reading where he scored a more modest four in 19 outings in the Third Division South in 1937/38. A former shipping clerk who began his career with Leith Amateurs.

SINCLAIR, Trevor — 1998-2003

Born: Dulwich, London, 2.3.73
League apps: 177 (37 goals)
Cup apps: 29 (1 goal)

THE PURCHASE OF this multi-talented forward from QPR for £2.3 million plus Iain Dowie and Keith Rowland in part exchange in January 1998, represented one of the best value transfer deals struck in recent history by West Ham. Not only did Hammers get almost five years' sterling service out of a player who was equally at home as a withdrawn striker, wide on either flank or in central midfield, but when he left to join Manchester City after Hammers' fall from the Premiership they made a healthy profit on his outgoing transfer when receiving £2.5 million from Kevin Keegan's City. Lampooned by some fellow managers for signing him, Redknapp's judgment was proved to be spot on as the player thrived on a return to the Premiership and enjoyed a new lease of life away from the stifling atmosphere of Loftus Road, where his career had stagnated and was going nowhere. After scoring 21 goals in 190 appearances for the Hoops over five seasons, the England Under-21 international's time had run its course in west London and he was an immediate hit in the East End with seven goals in 14 Premiership matches to the close of 1997/98. Although born in London, Sincs was brought up in Manchester and the former FA School of Excellence pupil made his breakthrough into League football with Third Division Blackpool, making nine

appearances in 1989/90 when the seasiders were relegated to the Fourth Division. They were promoted back up to the new Division Two in 1991/92 and Trevor scored 16 times in 140 appearances over four seasons at Bloomfield Road until a £750,000 cheque took him to Shepherd's Bush. At Upton Park, Sincs continued to vindicate his manager's faith in his ability with a series of outstanding performances at wing-back during 1998/99, although preferring to play as a striker. It was his unselfish ability to fit any role asked of him that made him almost indispensable and would eventually open the door to the full England team. Conspicuous by his absence for the second half of the 2000/01 Premiership campaign due to a groin strain, it was more than a coincidence that his prolonged spell out of action coincided with Hammers' poor run of results in the closing stages of the season. In 2001/02, he missed just four League games and his consistent displays were noted by Tord Gripp, Sven Goran Eriksson's assistant, who'd made a number of scouting trips to England before the Swede officially took over as England manager in January 2001. Having previously been included in squads by Terry Venables, Glenn Hoddle and Kevin Keegan, Tricky Trev was fearful of being passed over yet again, but duly made his England debut in the 1-1 draw with Sweden at Old Trafford in November 2001. Having initially been left out of the original 23-man squad to go to the 2002 World Cup Finals in Japan and South Korea, the 29-year-old was then called up on standby after an injury to Kieron Dyer. Then, having waited until the England medical staff eventually passed the Newcastle star fit to play, Trevor opted to fly 8,000 miles home despite being invited to stay on with the squad until the tournament commenced. In a dramatic twist just a day after returning home, the withdrawal of Danny Murphy saw "Air Miles" Trev back on another flight to the Far East. In an amazing turnaround of fortunes, Trevor was selected as a sub for England's second match of the tournament – the 1-0 victory over old foes Argentina and, grabbing his opportunity after Owen Hargreaves' injury, became one of England's success stories as they progressed to an ultimately disappointing Quarter-final defeat to eventual Champions Brazil. Everything looked rosy when Sincs, realising that he could achieve his international ambitions at Upton Park where Sven Goran Eriksson had become a virtual season-ticket holder, signed a new, improved contract at the start of 2002/03. But relegation put an entirely different complexion on things and, in July 2003, he moved to his boyhood idols Manchester City for £2.5 million. Capped 11 times for England while a Hammer, things have not gone so well for him since his move to the City of Manchester Stadium, however. In fact, Trevor has only added one cap to that total since leaving Upton Park; a sub appearance versus Croatia in 2004. Sincs was even

openly criticised by his own manager Kevin Keegan in the national press over his poor form in 2003/04, saying: "Trevor has every right to be disappointed with what he had done. He is a much better player than what we have seen." QPR fans who witnessed his fantastic long-distance match-winning overhead kick against Barnsley

in an FA Cup tie would agree with that statement. As would Hammers fans who were at Upton park when he enacted an acrobatic 12-yard volley against Derby County on Boxing Day 2001. Ah, those were the days! Up to the end of 2004/05 Trevor had scored three goals in 43 League and Cup appearances for City.

SISSONS, John   1963-70

Born: Hayes, Middlesex, 30.9.45
League apps: 213 (37 goals)
Cup apps: 52 (16 goals)

BECAME THE YOUNGEST player to score in an FA Cup Final at Wembley and the second youngest to appear there (behind his Preston opponent of that May day in 1964, Howard Kendall). His career looked certain to rocket into the international arena the following year when he returned to the Twin Towers as a vital part of Hammers' victorious European Cup Winners' Cup-winning side. But despite numerous Under-23 appearances, Johnny never won a full cap. Originally an inside-left in his formative years with Middlesex and England schoolboys, he was successfully converted to outside-left by Ron Greenwood after making his senior debut versus Blackburn Rovers at Upton Park (May 4, 1963). One of the most feared wingers in the League when on song, his form inexplicably waned towards the end of his time at the

Boleyn. Transferred to Sheffield Wednesday, he made 115 League appearances (14 goals) for the Hillsborough club before moving on again to join forces with his former team-mate John Bond at Norwich. He managed only 17 games for the Canaries (two goals), however, and ended his League days with Chelsea, making a further 11 outings in 1974/75. John later emigrated to South Africa where he built up a successful motor products company of which he is now a partner. He suffered a big blow when his treasured 1964 FA Cup Winners' medal and 1965 European Cup Winners' Cup counterpart were stolen during a robbery at his home on the outskirts of Cape Town, South Africa. On a happier note, West Ham paid for John and his former team-mate "Budgie" Byrne to make a special 11,000-mile round trip from South Africa for the occasion of the Bobby Moore Memorial Match, in March 1994, when they were guests of honour along with their colleagues from those two Cup-winning teams. John has been in South Africa for 30 years now, after originally signing a two-year contract to play for Cape Town City. Although he played his last match at the age of 38, he still keeps fit by being a keen cyclist. He

entered the 65-mile Argus cycle race, a major event in the African sporting calendar that attracts 22,000 cyclists worldwide. In all, John pedals 150 miles a week to and from work and takes part in ten races a year. John was flown back to the UK by *Ex* magazine to attend a reunion dinner to commemorate the two Cup-winning feats of the mid 1960s in May 2005.

JOHN SISSONS
WEST HAM UNITED
OUTSIDE LEFT

Played	League		FAC		LC		Europe		Total	
	App	Gls	App	Gls	App	Gls	App	Gls	App	Gls
1962-63	1	0	0	0	0	0	0	0	1	0
1963-64	14	3	7	3	1	0	0	0	22	6
1964-65	38	8	2	1	1	0	9	2	50	11
1965-66	36	5	2	1	9	1	4	1	51	8
1966-67	35	7	2	1	6	3	0	0	43	11
1967-68	37	8	3	2	2	0	0	0	42	10
1968-69	32	4	1	0	2	1	0	0	35	5
1969-70	20	2	1	0	0	0	0	0	21	2
TOTAL	**213**	**37**	**18**	**8**	**21**	**5**	**13**	**3**	**265**	**53**

Back row, left to right: Bond, Standen, Moore, Hurst, Bill Jenkins, Brown. Front row: Burkett, Sissons, Byrne, Boyce and Bovington

SLATER, Robert   1995-96

Born: Ormskirk, Lancashire, 22.11.64
League apps: 25 (2 goals)
Cup apps: 4

THIS INDUSTRIOUS RED-HAIRED midfielder took the long route to Upton Park. Robbie's family emigrated to Australia when he was just 18 months old and, in common with most youngsters in New South Wales, he tried his hand at Australian rules football, rugby and cricket, although his favourite sport was surfing off Sydney's famous Pacific beaches. But it was at soccer that he caused waves, beginning his career with St George's. While playing for Sydney Croatia he represented Australia at the Seoul Olympics in 1988 and was spotted by a scout from Belgian giants RSC Anderlecht. He promptly packed a bag for Brussels and spent a year there learning the game among a legion of other foreign imports before crossing the border to sign for French First Division side RC Lens in 1990. It proved to be an inspired switch for the nationalised Aussie and he made 34 appearances at the Felix-Bollaert Stadium in 1991/92, scoring two goals – both vital strikes in 1-1 draws against St Etienne and AS Cannes. Making 81 appearances and scoring four times in three seasons in France's Le Championnat, Robbie also picked up a French League Cup winners' medal before finally making it back to England in a £50,000 deal to Blackburn Rovers to return to his native Lancashire in August 1994. He was just in time to participate in the most successful season in Rovers' proud history as, along with ex-Hammer Tony Gale, he was a member of the Blackburn first team squad that won the 1995 Premiership Championship by a short head from Manchester United. Eighteen League appearances that never-to-be-forgotten season entitled him to a medal along with Galey, on whose recommendation he joined Hammers for a £600,000 fee plus Mattie Holmes in part-exchange in August 1995. Robbie gave a good account of himself in his only season at Hammers and, while not tearing up any trees, always gave 100 per cent effort. He even managed a couple of goals, the first against his old club Blackburn in the 4-2 defeat at Ewood Park in December 1995, the second the only goal of the game against Nottingham Forest at Upton Park in February the following year. Transferred to Southampton for £250,000 in September 1996, the nomadic "Socceroo" made 30 League appearances for the Saints in 1996/97 and scored two vital goals which enabled the Dell boys to avoid relegation. The second of his two tallies was once again against his old club Blackburn in a vital 2-0 win on the south coast. Rovers had reason to feel aggrieved because the 39 times capped Australian international never got on the scoresheet for them! A hernia operation delayed his progress in 1997/98 and, after 50 League and Cup games for the Hampshire club (two goals), Robbie got the wanderlust again and signed for Wolves on transfer deadline day in March 1998 for a fee of £75,000. But his stay in the Black Country was destined to be short and after just seven appearances at Molineux his contract was cancelled after he cited family reasons for wanting to return home to his property in Lens in July 1998. In September 1998, Slater went back down under to sign for Northern Spirit of Sydney in the newly formed Australian Pro League.

SLATER, Stuart   1987-92

Born: Sudbury, Suffolk, 27.3.69
League apps: 141 (11 goals)
Cup apps: 33 (5 goals)

ONE OF THE most exciting products of West Ham's youth system, Stuart emerged as a first team star in the early 1990s but did not fulfil his full potential in claret and blue. Born and bred in the sleepy Suffolk countryside, the shy, unassuming youngster turned down the chance to join his local club, Ipswich Town, to sign up for Hammers as an apprentice in July 1985. Proved outstanding for the youth and reserve teams, scoring prolifically despite his lightweight build for a striker. He turned pro in April 1987 and John Lyall gave Stuart his first taste of the first team when he introduced him as an 89th minute sub versus Derby County in the First Division at Upton Park (October 3, 1987). After one other sub outing that season, "Chopper" featured in 18 games in Lyall's last season with the club, which ended in relegation. But under Lou Macari, Slater continued to blossom into one of the country's most exciting young prospects. In 1989/90 he established himself as a first team regular, playing 40 Second Division matches and scoring seven League and four Cup goals. The following season, under Billy Bonds, he had a number of outstanding games. His close control and neat ball skills brought many a match to life. Bonzo thought Slater was at his best playing wide on the left, but the player maintained his preference for an out-and-out striker's role, or a position just behind the front two where he could run at defenders. As word of Slater's pace and skill spread throughout the League, he became more closely marked and found it harder to make an impact, especially in front of goal. One of his three goals in 1990/91 came against Everton in a thrilling FA Cup Quarter-final tie under the Upton Park floodlights (March 11, 1991). Slater murdered the First Division side almost single-handedly with his penetrating runs down the left flank – an outstanding performance capped by his winning goal. Afterwards, Everton boss Howard Kendall told the press that Slater was worth £3 million. Now everyone had heard of the likeable lad who always let his football do the talking for him. The former England Under-21 international earned one "B" cap, as sub versus Switzerland at Walsall in May 1991. West Ham turned down a £2 million offer from Glasgow Celtic, but constant transfer speculation clearly had an unsettling effect on Stuart who failed to reproduce his breathtaking Everton display in subsequent matches. Indeed, after scoring versus Bristol Rovers (May 8, 1991) at the end of the promotion-winning season, he went a whole season – 41 League and 12 Cup ties – without scoring. When Celtic, by now managed by Stuart's agent, former Hammer Liam Brady, came back in for him with a £1.5 million bid in the summer of 1992, West Ham agreed to sell their most prized asset. The move may have been financially very rewarding for Slater, but the Glasgow "goldfish bowl" didn't suit his laid-back, quiet lifestyle. As Celtic's big-money buy, and with arch rivals Glasgow Rangers winning everything in sight north of the border, Stuart's performances came under close scrutiny from Parkhead fans and the Scottish media. His difficult 15 months at Celtic brought him only three goals and when his mentor, Brady, resigned amid a well-publicised boardroom battle, it was inevitable that Slater would soon follow. In fact, Stuart was pleased to go "home" – to Ipswich, where he had stood on the terraces and worshipped mid-1970s favourites such as Muhren and Thijssen. The £750,000 move, in September 1993, as well as taking him close to his family home, also reunited him with his first manager, John Lyall, as well as fellow former Hammers McGiven, Goddard, Whitton and Parkes. After 55 Scottish Premier League and Cup appearances for Celtic, Stuart started well with Ipswich in his first taste of the Premiership but in his second season (1994/95) Town finished rock bottom and were relegated to the First Division. In October 1996, after scoring four goals in 88 League and Cup appearances for Town, Stuart was given a free transfer to Premiership Leicester City. But after one month at Filbert Street and no first team games, "Chopper" joined First Division Watford on another free transfer. Relegated the following season, Stuart helped the Hornets back up the following season but, plagued by an Achilles tendon injury, Stuart was released by Watford manager Graham Taylor with just two weeks' wages and a free transfer after 37 appearances and one goal for the Vicarage Road club. Like the previous entry, Robbie Slater, Stuart packed his bags and headed for the sunshine soccer on offer in the new Australian Soccer League where he signed for Melbourne side Carlton before they went into liquidation. Back in the UK, Stu signed up for Forrest Green who were managed by Frank Greegan and after a short spell at Aberystwyth Town, followed him to West Super-Mare in the Conference South. In September 2004 the Seagulls were in financial trouble and accepting offers for any of their players in a fire sale at Woodspring Park. Stuart was certainly experiencing the other side of football's coin! In 2003 he had been coaching the Under-11s at Chadwell Heath on a part-time basis.

SMAILES, Matthew · 1929

Born: Lancaster, Lancashire, 25.3.1899
League apps: 7
Cup apps: 3

MADE HIS HAMMERS debut in the 8-2 thrashing of Leeds at Upton Park (when Vic Watson struck six goals against the hapless Yorkshiremen). Matt could hardly have hoped for a more memorable first appearance. Beginning his career with Annfield Plain in Northumberland, he then had two years with Blackburn Rovers (four League apps) before joining West Ham in 1928. According to his pen-picture in a 1928 club handbook, he was obtained as an understudy to Collins, Barrett and Cadwell, being equally at home in any of the half-back positions. Together with George Robson, Matt lodged with Jack Hebden and his family in Central Park Road, East Ham. He joined Coventry from Hammers where he played 11 games in the Third Division South. Moved to Ashington FC in August 1931.

SMALL, Mike · 1991-94

Born: Birmingham, West Midlands, 2.3.62
League apps: 49 (13 goals)
Cup apps: 10 (5 goals)

WHATEVER LIKABLE MIKE'S critics say about his somewhat ungainly style and difficulty in avoiding offside decisions, no one can take away one remarkable purple period in the club's traumatic 1991/92 relegation season – his first at Upton Park. Signed from Brighton & Hove Albion for £400,000 on the eve of the season, Small arrived with an impressive pedigree. In his only season on the south coast, he netted 21 goals (including one against Hammers at Upton Park) in Seagulls' promotion challenge, which ended in the Play-offs. And he showed immediate promise once in the top flight with West Ham. After making his debut against one of his former clubs, Luton Town (August 17, 1991), he went on to score 13 goals in an amazing 20-match sequence, including a notable winner at Arsenal. The flood of goals turned to a trickle after Christmas, although 18 League and Cup strikes in his first season at Division One level was very encouraging. Unfortunately for this powerful striker, his Upton Park career went downhill from then on. He was sent off in the opening match of 1992/93, at Barnsley, and – with recent arrival Clive Allen forming a new potent strike partnership with Trevor Morley – rarely got another chance. Low on confidence, and plagued by a long-term back injury, Small could not even guarantee himself a regular place in the reserves! He featured in just nine League games in the 1992/93 promotion term – his last at Notts County (March 13, 1993). West Ham tried to cut their losses and pave the way for the player to try his luck elsewhere after Mike had spent a brief loan spell at Wolves (for whom he scored at Sunderland). Billy Bonds even declared that Small could leave on a free transfer, but still there were no takers – except Charlton Athletic, who briefly took him on loan in 1993/94 – before his Hammers' contract expired. Mike began his League career with Luton, making three sub appearances in 1981/82, before going on loan to Peterborough United (two starts plus two sub outings) a year later. He then turned his attention to the Continent, playing in Belgium (Standard Liege), Holland (Twente Enschede and Go Ahead Eagles) and Greece (PAOK).

SMALL, Sam · 1937-48

Born: Birmingham, West Midlands, 15.5.12
League apps: 107 (40 goals)
Cup apps: 9 (1 goal)

SIGNED FROM BIRMINGHAM in the days before they had adopted the "City" and where he made six League appearances, Sam was an unselfish, hard-working centre-forward who served the club well, both before and after the war. Indeed, you could add "during" to that sentence, as it was Sam who scored the all important goal in Hammers' 1-0 Football League War Cup win at Wembley in 1940 versus Blackburn Rovers. Described in the club's 1939/40 handbook as "one of the nicest chaps in the game", he would have undoubtedly made an even bigger impression at the Boleyn but for the outbreak of hostilities. Transferred to Brighton & Hove Albion in March 1948, he made 38 League appearances without scoring for the Seasiders. Sam, who began his career with his local Bromsgrove Rovers club in the early 1930s, died in 1993.

SMILLIE, Andy · 1958-61

Born: Ilford, Essex, 15.3.41
League apps: 20 (3 goals)
Cup apps: 3

A SKILFUL, BALL-PLAYING inside-forward who had won a host of representative honours with Ilford, London and England Schoolboys before joining the Upton Park groundstaff in 1956. Signed pro in 1958 after adding three England Youth caps to his earlier honours. He made his First Division debut in December the same year versus Spurs at White Hart Lane. Andy refused the terms offered to him for 1961/62, and was subsequently transferred to Crystal Palace where he joined up with fellow ex-Hammers John Cartwright, Alf Noakes and George Petchey, and also Hammer-to-be Johnny Byrne. He scored 23 goals in 53 League appearances at Palace and later had spells with Scunthorpe (13 apps, two goals) and Southend (163 apps, 29 goals) before ending his League career with Gillingham (94 apps, seven goals). He then joined Folkestone Town in July 1971 and then Ferndale. Andy now runs a restaurant on the seafront at Southend – Smiley's.

Sam Small

SMITH, David · 1919

Born: Ayrshire, date unknown
League apps: 1

A RIGHT-WINGER WHO came from Stewarton and played in Hammers' first-ever League match versus Lincoln City at Upton Park on August 30, 1919 – his only appearance in the first team.

SMITH, Harold · 1927

Born: North Shields, Tyne and Wear, 10.3.1899
League apps: 1

DESPITE HAVING THE misfortune of attending a non-football playing school as a lad, Harry quickly made up for lost time in local junior football before graduating to Cullercoats, a senior amateur club. His performances there prompted Newcastle United to sign him as a full professional for the 1925/26 season. He subsequently made several appearances in Magpies' reserve side from the inside-left position prior to his transfer to Hammers the following season. One of a number of North-Easterners on the Upton Park payroll at that time, he made only one First Division outing in the 2-1 home defeat by Manchester United on October 29, 1927. Harry returned north to join Blyth Spartans in August 1928 and then had a spell with West Stanley.

SMITH, John · 1956-59

Born: Shoreditch, London, 4.1.39
League apps: 127 (20 goals)
Cup apps: 5 (2 goals)

ONE OF THE club's finest discoveries, plain John Smith was a major influence during the promotion season of 1957/58. The far from ordinary skills he exhibited that campaign will be long remembered at Upton Park. Joining the groundstaff in 1954 and signing full pro two years later, after he had won honours with East London, Middlesex and London Schoolboys, he went on to win England Youth and Under-23 caps while with Hammers. On the verge of full England international honours (he was twice named as reserve during 1959/60), his career took a downward spiral after he was involved in an exchange deal that saw Spurs forward Dave Dunmore arrive at Upton Park and John move in the opposite direction. After failing to make much impact at White Hart Lane, John played out the remainder of his career in the lower Divisions with Coventry, Leyton Orient, Torquay, Swindon (where he won a League Cup Winners' medal in 1969) and finally Walsall, where he was appointed manager, resigning in March 1973. He then managed Dundalk in the League of Ireland. John died at the tragically early age of 49 while managing a social club in Harlesden, north-west London.

SMITH, Mark · 1979

Born: West Ham, London, 10.10.61
League apps: 1
Cup apps: 1

A LAD WHO looked destined to follow in the tradition of a long line of Upton Park full-backs, he instead had a career of latent promise cruelly cut short by injury. A West Hammer by birth, he had won rave notices with Newham, Essex and London Boys, and was an England trialist before signing for his local club in October 1979. After skippering the youth team he made his initial senior appearance versus Southend in a 5-1 League Cup win at Upton Park (October 8, 1979) and his League bow versus Swansea (November 17, 1979) before the tragic termination of his career.

SMITH, Roy — 1955-56

Born: Rawalpindi, India, 19.3.36
League apps: 6

AN INSIDE-FORWARD OF some talent, Roy retained his amateur status for two years before signing full pro in June 1955. Although of English parentage he was born in India – a somewhat unusual location for a footballer. He played his early soccer with Woodford Youth Club when his parents returned to this country, and from there joined Hereford United before moving to Hammers. Making two League appearances in 1955/56 and a further four the following campaign, he then decided to emigrate with his parents instead of looking for another club after being placed on the transfer list by West Ham. He recommenced his League career in the early 1960s with Portsmouth where he contributed nine games and three goals towards Pompey's 1961/62 Third Division Championship triumph.

SMITH, Sidney — 1904-05

SL apps: 2 (1 goal)

INSIDE-RIGHT SID PLAYED in the last two matches of the 1904/05 season, making his debut in the 1-1 Boleyn draw with Portsmouth (April 21, 1904) and getting on the scoresheet with "Chippy" Simmons and Frank Piercy in the 3-0 win at Watford (April 25, 1904).

SMITH, Stephen — 1919-22

Born: Hednesford, Staffordshire, 27.3.1896
League apps: 27
Cup apps: 4 (1 goal)

IN DIRECT CONTRAST to his fellow winger and contemporary D Smith, Stephen had a good run in the first team during Hammers' initial League season, making 23 Second Division appearances in 1919/20. Formerly with Portsmouth, he made only one showing the following season, however, and three the next before transferring to Charlton Athletic in 1922. After three seasons at the Valley (90 League apps, eight goals) he joined Southend United (86 apps, 11 goals) in May 1925. He went on to have spells with Clapton Orient (seven apps, one goal) and Queens Park Rangers (25 apps, one goal) before signing for Mansfield Town in June 1929. The son of an English international of the same name who played for Aston Villa in the late 19th century. Like his father, Stephen was a left-winger who was renowned for the accuracy of his crosses and good passing ability. He passed away at Chichester, Sussex in 1980. In the 1986 edition of *Who's Who of West Ham United*, this player was erroneously listed as Sydney Smith and appears as such in other books about the club, but his correct name is actually Stephen Charles Smith.

SMITH, William — 1928-29

Born: Corsham, Wiltshire, 29.9.1901
League apps: 2

A WEST COUNTRYMAN, full-back Bill has often been confused with a colleague and namesake Harry Smith, an inside-forward who played for Hammers at about the same time. He played as an amateur for Casham in the Wiltshire League before joining Southern League Bath City (still as a member of the non-paid ranks) for a season-and-a-half. He then signed pro forms for Notts County (41 apps, four goals) and spent four years on Trentside until his transfer to West Ham in 1927. Bill died in 1990.

SMITHURST, Edgar — 1920-21

Born: Eastwood, Nottinghamshire, 5.11.1895
League apps: 3

MADE HIS FIRST team debut in a stirring 2-1 victory over Tottenham Hotspur at Upton Park on March 13, 1920 – one of Spurs' rare defeats in a season that saw them run away with the Second Division title with a record 70 points. Ed had another League appearance that campaign, in Hammers' concluding fixture at home to South Shields. Signed from Oldham Athletic in March 1920, right-winger Edgar made one more Second Division game in 1920/21 in the 1-0 defeat to Leicester City at Boleyn Castle before being transferred to Chesterfield for a fee of £100 in August 1921. Curiously nicknamed "Joe", his full name being Edgar Ishmael Smithurst, he had to wear a glove on the field to protect a bullet wound sustained at Ypres during World War I while in service with the King's Own Yorkshire Light Infantry. Having begun playing the game with Warmsworth FC, Doncaster West End and Doncaster Main Colliery he was a wartime guest for Southampton and Oldham. In fact, the reason he signed for the Latics was because of a particularly fine performance for them in a game against Blackburn Rovers on February 1st, 1919 at Boundary Park. The correspondent for the *Oldham Chronicle* was so taken by his display he wrote: "The wildest hopes of the most sanguine of the (Oldham Athletic) officials must have been exceeded by the form of the two men (the other was a centre-forward, Tommy Broad), especially Smithurst, the outside man. To see him flying down the wing, keeping a fine control of the ball and beating opponent after opponent, made one wonder what sort of a player was appearing in an Oldham jersey." At Chesterfield, "Joe" scored one goal in 14 games in Division Three North for the Spireites before transferring to Doncaster Rovers in February 1922.

SOFIANE, Youssef — 2003-

Born: Lyon, France, 8.7.84
League apps: 1
Cup apps: 1

BIG THINGS WERE expected of this French Under-18 international striker who impressed in pre-season games after Glenn Roeder signed him on a free transfer from French Le Championnat side AJ Auxerre in June 2002, but he failed to transfer that promise to the high demands of the Championship. Continually plagued by injuries, the 20-year-old endured a frustrating time at Upton Park although when on song he has been compared favourably

Youseff Sofiane

to Jermain Defoe with his snappy style around the box. Considered one of the most exciting prospects to emerge from France's renowned youth development programme in recent years, Sofiane made his First Division debut when coming off the subs bench in the 2-1 opening day win at Preston in August 2003 and kept his place for the next game versus Rushden & Diamonds in the 3-1 Carling Cup win at the Boleyn. After spending part of 2003/04 on loan to his former club Auxerre, Youssef again looked sharp in pre-season and was hoping to make a breakthrough in 2004/05. In September 2004, Youssef was loaned to bottom of League Two club Notts County under the proviso that he was ineligible in the Magpies' Carling Cup Second Round visit to Upton Park on September 21. In the event, County put up a fighting display befitting of the oldest club in the League as they went out by a 3-2 margin. Inspired by their performance they promptly won 3-0 at Rochdale the following Saturday! Young Youssef got on just after half-time, but what really caught the eye in the match stats was a hat-trick for a certain G Hurst of County. Closer inspection revealed that it was Glynn Hurst who did the damage in the number 10 shirt! It seemed that Sofiane was in good company at Meadow Lane, but he was back at Upton Park at the end of his month loan spell in October 2004. At the start of 2004/05 he was on trial at MK Dons.

SOMA, Ragnvald — 2001-02

Born: Bryne, Norway, 10.11.79
League apps: 7
Cup apps: 2

THIS SIX-FOOT-TWO-INCH Norwegian international seemed to have all the right credentials when Harry Redknapp eventually obtained his signature for a £800,000 cheque from his home-town club Bryne FK in January 2001. Ragnvald had made 50 First Division appearances and scored five times for the little Norwegian outfit between 1999 and 2000. Since making his debut for Bryne as a 17-year-old, he won the club's Player of the Year award in three successive seasons and had also accumulated 19 appearances for Norway's Under-21 team before breaking into the full squad. Making his Hammers debut from the bench during the closing moments of the epic 1-0 FA Cup win over Manchester United at Old Trafford, the versatile defender was left in limbo following the sacking of Redknapp as incoming manager Glenn Roeder didn't seem to hold him in as high regard as his predecessor. That certainly seemed to be the case as he made just two sub appearances in 2001/02 and just one start in the 7-1 defeat at Blackburn Rovers, his last in the Premiership. He did make one more outing in the claret and blue though, as a sub in the 1-1 FA Cup Fourth Round draw against Chelsea at Stamford Bridge in January 2002. Soma went back to Bryne for the 2002 season and made 11 First Division appearances and scored in the 4-0 victory over SK Brann in September 2002. Brann must have remembered that goal because in December 2003 they signed him up for Norwegian First Division football and, after making his debut in April 2004, he went on to make 25 appearances during the 2004 season.

SONG, Rigobert — 2001-02

Born: Nkenlicock, Cameroon, 1.7.76
League apps: 24
Cup apps: 3

A VERY EXPERIENCED Cameroon international defender with over 30 full caps to his credit when he

Tommy Southren

SOUTHREN, Tommy — 1950-54

Born: Southwick, Sunderland, 1.8.27
League apps: 64 (3 goals)
Cup apps: 2

ALTHOUGH A NORTH-EASTERNER by birth, this speedy outside-right played most of his early football in Hertfordshire junior competitions after his parents had moved to Welwyn. Signed from the quaintly-named Peartree Old Boys, Tommy joined the pro ranks in 1949 and gained a first XI place a year later. A member of Hammers' reserve team that won a unique Combination Cup and League double in the 1953/54 season, he also represented the London FA versus Berlin FA the same campaign. He joined Aston Villa at Christmas 1954 and had four years at Villa Park, playing 63 League games and scoring six goals before moving to Bournemouth, where he played 64 Third Division games scoring 11 times. Since the publication of the last *Who's Who of West Ham* in 1994 we are sorry to announce that Tommy Southren passed away on May 10, 2004 aged 76. Since his death more light has been shed on his early career however, and makes interesting reading now. Few of the 25,000 crowd who witnessed Tommy make his West Ham debut in a thrilling 5-3 defeat at the Boleyn Ground in September 1950 on the right wing as a replacement for flu-victim Eric Parsons would have realised he was first discovered at the age of 13 by the famous Arsenal secretary-manager George Allison. It was 1941. The Southren family had just moved south from Sunderland to Welwyn Garden City, Hertfordshire. Tommy was one of 22 schoolboys chosen for a Ministry of Information film called *The Team*. His role in the film: a greedy little street footballer who, hanging onto the ball too long, muffs a certain goal by miskicking and falling down. George Allison, also in the film, tells the lads about the value of teamwork and all ends well. During the film-making young Tommy impressed the man from the London glamour club with his football ability. Allison suggested he should sign amateur forms for Arsenal. Tommy, eyes wide with awe, said "yes please sir". Three years rolled by and the war dragged on and although Tommy answered two or three letters from Mr Allison, he still thought it was nothing but a wonderful dream. He joined the navy and having little time for anything else but seamanship decided to forget his ambitions of becoming a professional footballer. "I never did think I was good enough," he recalled. Demobbed, he joined a Welwyn Club, Peartree Old Boys, then he was spotted by a West Ham scout and the dream that started on celluloid way back in 1941 became reality. Signing for Aston Villa for a £10,000 fee on New Year's Eve 1954 (the transfer deadline day back then) after receiving a call from Hammers manager Ted Fenton requesting that he should meet with him and Villa chief Eric Houghton before midnight at Euston Station to clinch the deal. Rushing from a New Year's Eve dance at Welwyn, Tommy just made it! Tommy was 12th man for Aston Villa when they defeated Manchester United 2-1 in the 1957 FA Cup Final at Wembley. But there were no subs in those days!

SPEAK, George — 1914-15

Born: Blackburn, Lancashire, 7.11.1890
SL apps: 13

YET ANOTHER IMPORT from Midland League Gainsborough Trinity, George started out with native Lancashire clubs Clitheroe Central and Darwen, and had a trial with Liverpool before joining Grimsby Town in May 1911. After making a mere four Football League appearances for the Mariners, the stocky left-back made the short journey across Lincolnshire to join Trinity in July 1913 and spent ten months there before transferring to Hammers in May 1914. Beginning the 1914/15

season as West Ham's first-choice left-back, he lost his place after four matches and did not regain it until the end of March to make 13 Southern League appearances in all. He made three wartime outings the next season, but played most of his football during the conflict as a guest of Preston North End and joined the famous Lancashire club permanently for a £25 transfer fee in March 1919. He'd risen in value considerably by the time of his transfer to Leeds United in July 1923, joining the Yorkshiremen for a substantial £250 after 65 League appearances for PNE. His career ended on a winning note at Elland Road when he picked up a Second Division Championship medal in 1924 before retiring the following year. Died March 10, 1953. George was given the following testimonial in Doug Lamming's excellent *Who's Who of Grimsby Town* – "Capital back, quite fearless, kicking an admirable length and placing to advantage. A believer in direct methods, George was a little apt at times to take undue risks. Described as 'a bundle of pluck and energy'." He made 28 League appearances for Leeds.

SPEEDIE, David — 1993

Born: Glenrothes, Scotland, 20.2.60
League apps: 11 (4 goals)

ONE OF THE most controversial and unpopular players to ever wear a West Ham shirt, this fiery little former Scottish international striker certainly made his mark in an 11-match loan spell towards the end of the 1992/93 promotion season. A temperamental character who had more than his fair share of disciplinary problems throughout a long and turbulent career, "Speedo" was never going to win any popularity polls around Upton Park. The fans couldn't forget how he had antagonised them in his previous days with Chelsea in particular. Their anger towards Speedie was never more clearly illustrated than the abuse he received following two bad misses late on in the home game versus arch rivals Millwall, which ended in a 2-2 draw. Afterwards, manager Billy Bonds, who stuck by his loanee with typical honesty and integrity, personally apologised to the player for the hostile treatment he received from the terraces. All credit to Speedie, because no one could question his commitment to helping Hammers towards the top flight – despite all the stick he received. He scored twice versus Leicester City and also grabbed the winner versus Bristol Rovers, but the highlight of his stay came on the last day of the season in what proved to be his final appearance for the club. He netted the opening goal in the 2-0 victory versus Cambridge United (May 8,

arrived at the Boleyn for £2.5 million from Liverpool in November 2000, after falling out of favour with Liverpool boss Gerard Houllier. Redknapp's first defensive signing in the wake of the mind-boggling £18 million move of Rio Ferdinand to Leeds United and, compared to that fee, it could be claimed we got Rigobert for a song. Certainly the fans soon made one up for him with the inevitable renditions of "We've only got one song" a frequent feature at Upton Park. Captain of Cameroon, he first came to the notice of the wider football world during the 1994 World Cup Finals in the USA when, at just 17 years old, he became the youngest player to be sent off in the history of the finals. He also starred at France 98 and led them to victory in the 1999 African Nations Cup when he scored the match-winning penalty in the shoot-out versus Nigeria in the Final. Having previously made 38 appearances at Anfield, where he arrived for £2.7 million from Italian side Salernitana in January 1999, the tough tackling right-sided defender was obviously no mug and he proceeded to prove the point with Man of the Match awards against Aston Villa and Leicester City while continuing to represent his country to lead them to qualification to the 2002 World Cup Finals in Japan and South Korea. But he would be back on mainland Europe by that time following his loan transfer to FC Koln in September 2001 and Glenn Roeder's signing of Tomas Repka. No stranger there, he'd made 123 appearances for FC Metz in the French Le Championnat between 1994 and 1998, having started with Tonnerre Yaoundi. It was not a good time to be at the Mungersdorfer Stadion, however, and Song's 16 appearances couldn't prevent Koln slipping out of the Bundesliga at the end of 2001/02, six points adrift of safety. In 2004/05 Rigobert was with top Turks Galatasery.

1993) that clinched promotion from Division One by the narrowest possible margin – just one goal difference over third placed Portsmouth. Even the fickle fans hailed Speedo a hero that day! In fact, David enhanced his more pleasant reputation as something of a lucky promotion charm. For he had been prominent in getting Blackburn Rovers promotion to the top flight at the end of the previous season (1991/92) – but was then discarded when chairman Jack Walker and new manager Kenny Dalglish joined forces to rebuild the club at the expense of millions of pounds. After his spell with Hammers, Speedie moved on to Leicester City in 1993/94, when he contributed 12 vital goals to Foxes' promotion charge back to the Premiership – albeit missing the glorious Play-off Final versus Derby County due to injury. Speedie began his long career with Barnsley and also had stints with Darlington, Coventry City and Liverpool. Capped ten times for Scotland, Dave had amassed 175 goals in 611 League and Cup games before injury ended his career in 1994 while with Leicester. Joined City's coaching staff for a time and later became an agent.

SRNICEK, Pavel — 2004

Born: Ostrava, Czech Republic, 10.3.68
League apps: 3

A VASTLY EXPERIENCED Czechoslovakian international goalkeeper who ousted his great friend Ludo Miklosko from the national side and played for the same club side – Banik Ostrava in his homeland. Pavel made two full and one sub appearance for Hammers in 2003/04, coming on in unusual circumstances in the latter against Millwall after Stephen Bywater had been sent off at the New Den. Signed from Portsmouth on loan for extra cover in February 2004, Pavel spent eight seasons at Newcastle United between 1990 and 1998, where he racked up 188 appearances before being given a free transfer back to Banik Ostrava in the summer of 1998. He was soon back in the Premiership with Sheffield Wednesday in November 1998 and made 52 League and Cup appearances for Owls before being given a free transfer to Italian Serie A club Brescia in June 2000. He made 32 appearances in three seasons there before being signed by Portsmouth manager Harry Redknapp in June 2003 and made three League appearances and one League Cup outing at Fratton Park before arriving at the Boleyn. He has made 49 appearances for the Czech Republic and was very popular with the Geordie fans during his time at Gallowgate.

ST PIER, Wally — 1929-32

Born: Beacontree Heath, Essex, birthdate unknown
League apps: 24

WEST HAM WERE tempted to accept an offer from Sunderland for Syd Puddefoot because they had an option on a promising young goalscorer from Chatham, once the Kent club were out of the FA Cup. They duly went out – 9-0 at Sunderland! – and Stallard signed pro for Hammers. Syd stayed, too, and Arthur scored a vital debut goal in a 3-2 Boleyn victory over Millwall, deputising for Puddy (April 14, 1913). He had to wait until towards the end of the following season before claiming a regular first team spot for the last 11 matches of 1914/15, when Puddefoot switched to inside-right allowing Arthur the number 9 jersey. The result was a sensation as Stallard took over the goalscoring mantle of his hero. He hit seven in 11 Southern League fixtures and it seemed Hammers had unearthed another major find to rank alongside Harry Stapley, George Webb, George Hilsdon, Danny Shea and Puddefoot himself. The horrors of World War I were to deem otherwise, however, and despite scoring 17 times in just 23 wartime fixtures to underline his rich promise, Arthur Stallard was destined to die for his country during the conflict… falling on the battlefield in France on November 30, 1917, just seven months after scoring his last goal for Hammers.

STALLARD, Arthur — 1913-15

SL apps: 13 (8 goals)

A RESERVE TEAM centre-half who spent most of his playing days as understudy to Jim Barrett, but went on to serve West Ham United for 47 years as chief scout to become the greatest star-finder in the club's history. Among his many discoveries, with the help of his vast scouting network, were the legendary trio of Moore, Hurst and Peters… but back to the beginning. His first amateur club was Eagle Park, but Wally arrived at the Boleyn from Ilford in April 1929 after selection for Essex County, the Isthmian League and FA XIs. He made his First Division bow at right-half versus Leicester City at Upton Park the following October, numbering four senior outings that campaign. The most appearances he managed in any one season was seven. It was when he retired from playing and was appointed chief scout by his manager and good friend Charlie Paynter that he found his true forte. Beginning as a steady trickle, the flow of talent he brought to the club reached its crescendo in the 1960s and 1970s, and was evident in all Hammers' Cup triumphs over that period. Given a well-deserved testimonial evening in May 1975 (when many of his "finds" turned out to play), Wally retired the following year after a lifetime of loyal service. Wally passed away in 1989.

STANDEN, Jim — 1962-67

Born: Edmonton, London, 30.5.35
League apps: 179
Cup apps: 57

AN EMERGENCY SIGNING from Luton Town after Hammers' regular keeper Lawrie Leslie had suffered a broken leg, he performed with such distinction that he made the first XI spot his own. Kept out of the side by brilliant Welsh international Jack Kelsey at his first club Arsenal, Jim was also forced to understudy another international, England's Ron Baynham, at Kenilworth Road. All this reserve duty ended at Upton Park, however, and Jim took part in the club's dazzling Cup success of the mid-1960s. An accomplished cricketer, he also won a Championship medal with Worcestershire and topped the first class County bowling averages with 64 wickets at an average of 13 runs during the same period. In all, Jim took 313 wickets for Worcestershire between 1960 and 1970. Apart from a brief comeback,

Jim lost his place with the signing of Bobby Ferguson from Kilmarnock in 1967 and went off to play for Detroit Cougars in the US Professional League. After returning to England for the 1969/70 season at Millwall, he played eight games for the Lions before signing a two-year contract at Portsmouth while continuing with the bat-and-ball game. He made 13 appearances for Pompey before hanging up his boots. Jim settled in Camberley, Surrey, where he had a sports shop, but later returned to the USA. He was coaching goalkeepers at Fresno University, California in 1986 and now lives in California where he works for a Honda car-leasing firm. Jim was delighted with the reception he and his mid-1960s colleagues received when they returned to Upton Park as guests of honour at the Bobby Moore Memorial Match in March 1994. Jim's 1965 European Cup Winners' Cup medal was up for auction at Christie's in October 1994 valued at between £4,000 and £6,000. Just before the auction, Jim explained: "I'm not desperate, hard-up or on the breadline. I simply want to raise some money for a real estate deal." In May 2005, Jim was flown back to the UK to take up his invitation as a VIP guest at a special dinner to commemorate those Cup successes of the mid-1960s by West Ham *Ex* magazine.

STANLEY, Thomas — 1920

A LEFT-BACK SIGNED from Liverpool, "Digger", as he was nicknamed by the Anfield fans, made only one appearance for Hammers – in a 2-1 defeat at Stockport County. An experience shared by fellow debutant Viv Roberts, who also made his solitary Second Division appearance in that encounter with the Cheshire club.

STAPLEY, Harry — 1905-08

Born: Tunbridge Wells, Kent, 29.4.1883
SL apps: 71 (39 goals)
Cup apps: 4 (2 goals)

IT WAS CONSIDERED something of a coup when this famous amateur accepted an invitation to play for West Ham – borne out when he scored the only goal of his debut match versus Portsmouth (December 23, 1904). A schoolmaster in private life, he played for Manor Park Albion, Bromley, Norwich CEYMS, Reading and Woodford Town before joining the Hammers. Harry resisted the lure of professionalism throughout his distinguished football career and set a goalscoring record unique in the history of the game. Somewhat slightly-built for a centre-forward, he nevertheless topped Hammers' scoring lists for three successive seasons in the old Southern League and his subsequent transfer to the then

Jim Standen

Jim Standen is watched by team-mates (left to right) Eddie Bovington, Martin Peters, Eddie Presland and Bobby Moore saving a shot from Liverpool's Chris Lawler (right) with Ian St John closing in

Second Division Glossop saw him lead the Derbyshire club's goalscoring charts for a further seven consecutive campaigns – a performance largely overlooked in the record-books. Capped for England as an amateur international before World War I on ten occasions: versus Ireland, Holland, Wales, Belgium and Germany in 1908; and versus Ireland, Holland, Belgium, Switzerland and France the following year. He added to his total in 1919 when he made a brief return to Hammers and won further caps versus Sweden and Holland in the Olympic Games. He once scored five goals in a match for his country. His duties as a school teacher prevented him from playing in midweek matches at distant destinations, such as Plymouth Argyle and Bristol Rovers, but his signing was thought to have been a major factor in the club allowing George Hilsdon to join Chelsea. A brother, W Stapley, also played for West Ham but not in the Southern League side. He, too, also joined Glossop, having previously been with Dulwich Hamlet. Harry's career also took in King Charles Higher Grade Schools XI, Reading reserves and Reading amateurs. Was also a Berks and Bucks Senior Cup winner and represented West Berks League. He scored 67 goals in 135 League games for Glossop but was never selected for a full international although, during the seasons when he was Glossop's leading scorer, England called on eight different centre-forwards. Before moving to Derbyshire, Stapley was a schoolmaster at Woodford. He went to Glossop to become the private tutor and personal cricket and football coach to sons of Sir Samuel Hill-Wood Bt. (the family associated with Arsenal). Henry was particularly successful as a cricket coach – three of his pupils in the Hill-Wood family later going on to win blues at Oxford and Cambridge. As the years passed, he was taken more into Sir Samuel's confidence and served as private secretary when he became an MP for the High Peak constituency. He also served as his employer's nominee on the board of various local companies. Harry died at Glossop on April 29, 1939.

STEPHENS, John William   1947-48

Born: Cramlington, Northumberland, 13.9.19
League apps: 22 (6 goals)
Cup apps: 2 (1 goal)

ONE OF TWO footballing twin brothers who played for East Cramlington and Leeds United before the war, Bill suffered what must be the fastest-ever injury to a club player in a competitive match when he broke his left leg five seconds after the kick-off of an Eastern Counties League match at Bury St Edmunds (April 22, 1949) – his second leg-break in successive seasons. He was shaping up well at centre-forward before his first mishap in 1947/48 when he made 23 first team appearances (scoring seven times). Bill had only one more senior showing after that and was transferred to Cardiff City in December 1950, but he never made the League side at Ninian Park. Originally signed by Charlie Paynter from the manager's own home-town club, Swindon, where he had scored 25 times in 47 matches. Bill died in 1974.

STEPHENSON, Alan   1968-72

Born: Chesham, Buckinghamshire, 26.9.44
League apps: 108
Cup apps: 10 (1 goal)

Alan Stephenson

A COSTLY ACQUISITION from Crystal Palace who tried in vain to make the number 5 shirt his own. Despite an impressive pedigree that included seven England Under-23 caps, he largely failed to solve the problems at the heart of Hammers' defence, which had prevailed from the time of Ken Brown's departure. Nevertheless, he still managed over a hundred senior appearances – mostly alongside Bobby Moore – and never lacked endeavour. After a period on loan to Fulham, during which he played ten times for the Cottagers in 1971/72, he was eventually transferred in the close season to Portsmouth for a fee of £32,000, where he logged another 100 senior outings up to 1974. His best years were undoubtedly at Palace as his 185 League and Cup appearances bear testimony. Stephenson went to South Africa in the close season of 1975 before returning to Orient as coach. He left the game to become a licensee.

STEWART, Ray

1979-90

Born: Stanley, Perthshire, Scotland, 7.9.59
League apps: 345 (62 goals)
Cup apps: 86 (22 goals)

RAY BECAME THE most expensive teenager in British football when John Lyall signed him from Dundee United for £430,000 in August 1979, but it proved money well spent. Although the young defender was uncapped when he joined Hammers at the age of 19, within two years he had won an FA Cup winners' medal, scored in the League Cup Final and completed the notable achievement of being capped by Scotland at every level. The latter period of his 11-year stint at Upton Park was severely hit by injury, but Raymond – West Ham's undisputed "Penalty King" – certainly earned his place in Hammers' Hall of Fame. A product of Errol Rovers in the Dundee Sunday Boys' League, he turned down offers from more glamorous clubs, such as Glasgow Rangers, to join his local team, Dundee United, in May 1973. Encouraged by manager Jim McLean, he developed into one of Scotland's most talented defenders, showing maturity far beyond his tender years. He captained Scotland Under-15s to a 1-0 victory over England at Wembley – the first of his five unbeaten appearances at the famous Empire Stadium. Ray's first team debut for the Terrors came just six days before his 17th birthday, in 1976, at Celtic's Parkhead. Playing in midfield – a role he filled on numerous occasions – he was asked to mark a certain Kenny Dalglish! Ray enjoyed his three seasons as a pro at Tannadice where he made 41 Scottish Premier League appearances and scored five goals, but the club needed to sell its best assets. McLean turned down an original £175,000 bid for Stewart by the east Londoners, plus an improved offer, and it was with extreme reluctance that McLean finally gave permission for Hammers to sign Stewart. Many youngsters would have been daunted by the prospect of leaving their family home in the Perthshire countryside for the challenge of life in the big city of London, but

Ray settled immediately. He made his West Ham debut in a League Cup, Second Round (second leg) tie at Barnsley (September 4, 1979) alongside Billy Bonds in the centre of defence. He was used in midfield for his home debut versus Sunderland (September 15, 1979), when the Upton Park faithful were impressed with the new signing's toughness in the tackle and his ability to fire ferocious shots from long distance. West Ham were in the Second Division then, but the good times were just around the corner and Stewart was at the heart of the club's success in the early 1980s. He was top scorer in the 1980 FA Cup run, scoring a couple in the Fourth Round win at Orient and the dramatic penalty winner versus Aston Villa in the Quarter-final at Upton Park. Ray's coolness under pressure – there was only a minute left – and his deadly shooting – invariably relying on power rather than placement – established him as one of the most successful spot-kick specialists in the country. Ray underlined his versatility again by playing in the centre of defence (in place of the injured Alvin Martin) in the epic Semi-final replay win over Everton at Elland Road and, of course, played his part in the 1-0 FA Cup Final triumph over Arsenal. Ray's first season in east London went like a dream, and the fairytale continued in 1980/81. Hammers romped to the Division Two title with a record points haul. "Tonka", as Ray was affectionately known to the fans, missed only the home clash with Grimsby Town and, in March 1981, returned to Wembley to face First Division Champions Liverpool in the League Cup Final. Once again the unflappable Stewart showed nerves of steel as he ran up and placed his right-foot shot past Ray Clemence for the last-gasp penalty equaliser in front of 100,000 fans. Liverpool went on to win the replay at Villa Park, but no one could deny Ray his moment of glory. His knowledge had also been enriched by the experience of European football and then, as a reward for consistent performances at club level, the first of his ten full Scottish caps versus Wales at Swansea (May 16, 1981). Ray believes that his best game for his country came later in that Home International series – a 1-0 win over England at Wembley. He earned seven senior caps under Jock Stein, the former Celtic

supremo, but is sure it would have been more but for his fracas with Mark Hateley, which resulted in both players being sent off in an Under-21 international at Hampden Park in April 1982. The incident almost certainly cost him a place in Scotland's squad for the 1982 World Cup finals in Spain. It was not until after Stein's death that Ray – who admitted that he was occasionally critical of some of Stein's coaching methods – received a recall, playing a further three matches under Andy Roxburgh. On the domestic front, Ray continued to enjoy life with Hammers. Promotion to Division One brought out the best in him. He rose to the challenge magnificently, scoring ten League and three Cup goals. Ray thrived on responsibility and whenever Alvin Martin was absent, he assumed the captaincy with ease and a deep sense of pride. A natural leader, he was also prominent throughout the club's best-ever First Division campaign of 1985/86, finishing third top scorer with six – behind Frank McAvennie and Tony Cottee – as Hammers ran Merseyside giants Liverpool and Everton to a photo-finish at the top. Although high on the all-time appearances list at West Ham, Ray would probably have topped 600 in the League but for the injury that almost threatened his career and severely restricted his appearances in his latter years with the club. Lyall's team were fighting a losing battle against relegation when, in the first half of the game at Derby County (January 14, 1989), he suffered an agonising injury – rupturing two of the four ligaments around his knee, including the main anterior cruciate ligament. Ray wouldn't listen to the medics who warned he may never play again. Instead, he called on his most determined characteristics to rebuild his shattered knee via a long and lonely rehabilitation programme. Some 14 months had passed when Ray made his first tentative comeback bid, in a reserve fixture at Arsenal (March 10, 1990). He played seven Combination League games in just a month, but it was too much too soon. A second operation was needed before another comeback attempt followed at the start of 1990/91 – his testimonial season at Upton Park. A hamstring strain added to Ray's frustration but he refused to throw in the towel and did at least manage to

Ray Stewart left, celebrates with Paul Allen, Geoff Pike, Alan Devonshire and Billy Bonds after the 1-0 1980 FA Cup Final victory over Arsenal at Wembley

WEST HAM UNITED
RAY STEWART

play a small part in Hammers' promotion campaign. New manager Billy Bonds recalled Ray for a vital Second Division match at Brighton (April 10, 1991) and he made four more League appearances as well as coming on as sub in the ill-fated FA Cup Semi-final versus Nottingham Forest at Villa Park. Ray Stewart's last-ever game for West Ham United was in a 1-1 draw versus Charlton Athletic at Selhurst Park (May 4, 1991). He didn't feel much like joining in the promotion celebrations, though. At 31, the normally ebullient Scot was saddened by the news that he would be released on a free transfer. When no playing or coaching offers materialised in the south, he returned to Scotland and joined St Johnstone. Initially signing as a player (he scored three times in 17 Scottish Premier League appearances in 1991/92), Ray also worked in a coaching capacity with the reserves and, making use of his extensive list of contacts and energy in the PR field, took up the community officer's role at McDiarmid Park. Hammers fans of the 1980s will no doubt remember Ray best for his unrivalled penalty record. He successfully converted 76 spot-kicks and missed only ten. Quite remarkable. It must be said, no West Ham player from the boys of 1986 has worked harder at management than Ray and he has served a tough apprenticeship north of the border, where being the boss requires a very much hands on approach. After cutting his teeth with his local side St Johnstone, he then took up the position of coach to Second Division Stirling Albion and actually made two

appearances for them in 1994/95. After fluctuating fortunes and a shock win over Aberdeen in the Scottish Cup, Ray moved on from Annfield to take over at Livingston in a similar capacity before becoming manager there. Next stop after Livvy, and far removed from capital city Edinburgh, was a post at little Forfar Athletic where Ray had been for two years until being sacked in November 2004. In late October 2004, Ray had got the Station Park outfit nicely placed mid-way in the Scottish Division Two table and said at the time: "It's not about paying the mortgage. I'm pretty self-sufficient now,

but football is part of my life. It isn't about money, it's about being part of something I thoroughly enjoy and building a team from scratch." An enthusiastic member of the West Ham team in the six-a-side London Masters tournaments over the years, Ray also likes to participate in occasional Boys of 1986 get-togethers and official club functions when his workload permits.
Scotland caps: 1981 vs Wales, Northern Ireland, England; 1982 vs Northern Ireland, Portugal, Wales; 1984 vs France; 1986 vs Republic of Ireland, Luxembourg; 1987 vs Republic of Ireland (10).

Career record

Played	League		FAC		LC		Europe		Total	
	App	Gls	App	Gls	App	Gls	App	Gls	App	Gls
1979-80	38	10	8	3	8	1	0	0	54	14
1980-81	41	5	3	1	9	2	6	1	59	9
1981-82	42	10	2	0	5	3	0	0	49	13
1982-83	39	8	1	0	6	3	0	0	46	11
1983-84	42	7	4	1	5	1	0	0	51	9
1984-85	37	6	4	1	4	0	0	0	45	7
1985-86	39	6	6	1	3	3	0	0	48	10
1986-87	23	4	3	0	3	0	0	0	29	4
1987-88	33	4	2	0	0	0	0	0	35	4
1988-89	6	2	2	0	1	1	0	0	9	3
1990-91	5	0	1	0	0	0	0	0	6	0
TOTAL	**345**	**62**	**36**	**7**	**44**	**14**	**6**	**1**	**431**	**84**

STEVENSON, Robert
1898 TIW

Born: Barrhead, Scotland, 10.5.1869

PREVIOUSLY WITH WOOLWICH Arsenal, whom he captained, Stevenson was the first big-name player to appear for the Ironworks. He had turned out for Old Castle Swifts in 1894/95 but went home to Scotland after the break-up of that club. He returned to play for Irons in 1895/96. Installed as club captain, he filled a number of positions in Ironworks' first season including full-back and centre-forward.

STEWART, Johnny
1895-97 TIW

Born: Newcastle-upon-Tyne, 1872

A HALF-BACK, JOHNNY played for Old Castle Swifts before joining new club Thames Ironworks in 1895/96. He appeared in Irons' FA Cup tie against Chatham and played out of position in the forward line (where he acquitted himself well) in all the West Ham Charity Cup matches, gaining a winners' medal.

STEWART, William
1899-1900

Born: Coupar Angus, Scotland, 11.2.1872
SL apps (TIW): 16

SIGNED FROM LUTON Town. His debut for TIW was versus Reading (March 1, 1900). A wing-half, he played in the last 16 matches of the season as captain but didn't reappear for 1900/01.

STIMAC, Igor
1999-2001

Born: Metkovic, Croatia, 6.9.67
League apps: 43 (1 goal)
Cup apps: 9

AN EXPERIENCED CROATIAN international defender signed from Premiership rivals Derby County for £600,000 in September 1999, after being put on the transfer list at Pride Park. He loved to play in the typical European role as sweeper, and was a tough-nut defender first and foremost who had many a run in with Hammers players prior to joining the claret and blue cause – most notably John Hartson, who was sent off for a clash with the then Rams' defender in the spring of 1998. Igor made his West Ham debut in the 1-0 win over Watford at Upton Park when Stuart Pearce suffered his first leg-break. After that, Igor became an indispensable component of the Hammers rearguard in the absence of the England legend. He was the subject of controversy soon after joining when, after playing against Osijek in the First Round of the UEFA Cup, he was deemed to be ineligible after being sent off on his previous European appearance five years earlier with Hajduk Split. He was compelled to miss the Second Round tie against Steaua Bucharest before becoming another victim of the Upton Park injury jinx which kept him out of action for eight weeks. He was back to score a rare goal in the 2-2 draw against Newcastle United at St James's Park in January 2000 and more or less held his place for the rest of the season with some sound displays as Hammers finished ninth in the Premiership. The 2001/02 season was destined to be Igor's, and the man who signed him Harry Redknapp's, last season at Upton Park following on from the disappointment of his country's failure to qualify for Euro 2000, when he and team-mates Davor Suker and Slavan Bilic were powerless to see Croatia through. Having begun his career with Cibalia Vinkovci in the old Yugoslavia in the late 1980s, Igor transferred to NK Hajduk Split and made 18 appearances (two goals) in 1990/91 before heading for Spanish Primera Liga Cadiz CF in 1992/93, during which he made 32 appearances.

But Cadiz went down and the following 1993/94 campaign he made 30 appearances and scored four times, but the club finished rock bottom of the Spanish Second Division! So Igor went back to Hajduk and scored twice in 21 appearances in 1994/95 before moving on to Derby County for a fee of £1,570,000. Igor was capped 47 times by Croatia and returned once more to play for Hajduk Split in 2001/02, making 11 appearances and scoring two goals! Igor is now head coach at Hajduk.

STOCKDALE, Robbie
2003-04

Born: Redcar, Yorkshire, 30.11.79
League apps: 7
Cup apps: 2

THIS ENTHUSIASTIC YOUNG right-back signed on loan from Middlesbrough in October 2003 helped to create a couple of bits of quiz-night trivia in his short stay at the Boleyn. Firstly, his arrival ensured that he was the first player to have played for West Ham who had played for both England (at Under-21 level) and Scotland at full international level and when Robbie and his Hammers captain Christian Dailly were joined on field by the substitute appearance of Don Hutchison in the 1-0 Upton Park defeat to Stoke City on December 9, 2003, it was the first time in their history that Hammers had fielded three Scottish internationals in one match – so there! A capable if not outstanding defender, Robbie made his debut in the claret and blue in the 0-0 draw against Cardiff City at Niniah Park in October 2003 and was on duty a few days later for the unlucky 1-0 Carling Cup defeat versus Spurs at White Hart Lane. The reason for Robbie's dual international record is because his grandparents are both Scottish and, of course, he was born in England. Robbie was picked for his first Scotland appearance by manager Berti Vogts for the friendly with Nigeria in April 2002 and has since added three more to his total. Robbie has had his fair share of injuries during his time on Teesside and was put out on loan to First Division Sheffield Wednesday in August 2000. He played six times for the Owls and on returning to the Riverside from east London in January 2004 he again found himself leased out to Rotherham the following month. And a good job he was too! For Robbie made a major contribution to Ronnie Moore's Merry Millers staying in the First Division with his tough tackling and resolute defending. He marked the last of his 16 appearances at Millmoor with a stunning goal in the 3-0 win over Burnley to ensure safety. Robbie signed for the Yorkshiremen in the summer of 2004 and returned to Upton Park in September when the Reds went down 1-0.

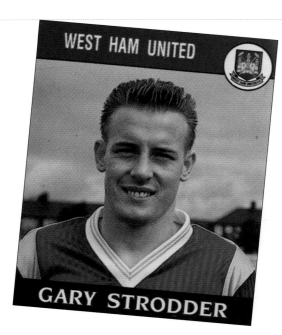

WEST HAM UNITED
GARY STRODDER

STOKES, Tony
2005-

Born: East London, 7.7.87
Cup apps: 1

LIKE HIS YOUTH team colleague Hogan Ephraim, Tony made his eagerly awaited first team debut when coming on as substitute in the 87th minute of the 4-2 Carling Cup victory against Sheffield Wednesday at Hillsborough on September 20, 2005. Tony, who joined the club at the age of 11, prefers to play as a link man rather than as a main striker where he can give full rein to his creative ability.

STRODDER, Gary
1987-90

Born: Mirfield, Yorkshire, 1.4.65
League apps: 65 (2 goals)
Cup apps: 14

A TALL, SLIM central defender with closely cropped hair who was originally signed by John Lyall as cover to help solve an injury crisis in the 1986/87 season. "Strodds" arrived from Lincoln City (where he played 132 League games after making his debut versus Wigan, August 28, 1982) at a cost of £150,000, after fellow central defenders Alvin Martin and Paul Hilton both suffered injuries. He made his First Division debut in the number 5 shirt at Chelsea (March 21, 1987), and found himself in the first team reckoning again for much of the following season when Tony Gale became the next long-term casualty. He made only another 23 first team appearances over the next two seasons before Billy Bonds sold him to West Bromwich Albion for £190,000 in August 1990. Gary established himself as a first team regular at the Hawthorns and scored nine times in 166 appearances for the Baggies between 1990 and 1995 before accepting a £145,000 transfer to Notts County in July of that year. Gary hit another ten goals in 148 appearances for the Magpies to prove once again that he didn't just concentrate on his defensive duties – a handy plus point for any defender as managers love an unexpected goal from that department! A short loan spell to Rotherham United (three apps) was followed by a permanent move to little Third Division Hartlepool United for a £25,000 fee in February 1999. Struggling near the foot of the table at that time, with the help of old pros like Strodds and Peter Beardsley, Pool made a steady improvement over the next few years and when Gary finally left them, after adding another 67 appearances to his impressive career total to join Unibond Premier outfit Guisley for the 2001/02 season,

Tony Stokes

they were in a lot better shape than when he joined. Gary's father, Colin, played for Halifax and Huddersfield Town in the early 1960s.

STROUD, Roy — 1952-56

Born: West Ham, London, 16.3.25
League apps: 13 (4 goals)

BORN WITHIN EARSHOT of the West Ham ground, Roy's parents moved to Hounslow when he was a youngster, and it was in the county of Middlesex that he made a name for himself, playing for London and Middlesex Boys before being selected for England Boys in the outside-right position. During the war years, he gained invaluable experience with Arsenal and Brentford while still retaining his amateur status. This was rewarded when he won the first of 11 England caps in 1948. He later toured the Continent, Iceland and the Far East with Hendon, the Athenian League and Middlesex Wanderers XIs. Making his Second Division debut in April 1952 versus Notts County, Roy eventually took the professional plunge in November the following year, by this time playing at centre-forward. Injuries restricted his early progress and were to prove a bugbear throughout his time at Upton Park. Roy joined Southern League Chelmsford City in 1957, but his injury jinx followed him to New Writtle Street and, after sustaining a broken leg, he decided to retire from the game – returning to his former trade in the grocery business.

SUCKLING, Perry — 1989-90

Born: Leyton, London, 12.10.65
League apps: 6

A GOALKEEPER BROUGHT in by new manager Lou Macari on loan from Crystal Palace who played six consecutive Second Division games in 1989/90 as cover for the injured Phil Parkes. Unfortunately for Perry – an East Ender – four of those games ended in defeat so Macari turned instead to unknown Czech keeper Ludek Miklosko. It left Suckling to move on for another loan spell, this time at Brentford. Perry arrived at Upton Park in December 1989, making his debut in a home defeat by in-form Oldham Athletic (December 16, 1989), shortly after enduring the nightmare experience of being on the wrong end of Palace's 9-0 First Division crushing at Liverpool. Perry, who also played for Hammers at Ipswich, Leicester and Plymouth as well as at home versus Barnsley (the only time he finished on the winning side) and Hull, began his career as an apprentice at Coventry City. He moved on to Manchester City and gained ten England Under-21 caps before transferring to Selhurst Park in 1987. After making nine appearances on loan at Griffin Park, Perry was given a free transfer to Watford in July 1992 and went on to complete 46 appearances at Vicarage Road before joining Doncaster Rovers on another free transfer in August 1994. He made another 35 appearances at Belle Vue up to the end of 1995/96, when he left the country to pursue a career as a player-coach in South Africa. When Perry first joined Hammers during Lou Macari's reign, his arrival elicited an amusing observation from that great old character Jack Hellier who, with his son John, used to print and edit the club's programmes and also act as Press Officer at Upton Park. On hearing of his signing for the first time Jack came out with the dry comment: "It's Perry Mason we need to sort this lot out!"

SUGDEN, Sidney — 1902-03

Born: Battersea, London, 1880
SL apps: 1

"A WONDERFULLY DASHING player with a splendid turn of speed and a deadly shot. But not a good team man," centre-forward-cum-inside-forward Sidney Sugden was so described by a contemporary reporter. He played just one game for West Ham, in the 3-1 Memorial Ground victory over Watford (October 18, 1902) at number 9. He began his career with Ilford before the turn of the century, and was so keen to remain an amateur he declined an offer from those giants of the Victorian/Edwardian eras, Aston Villa. He changed his tune when he joined Nottingham Forest, however, and signed pro for the Trentside club in 1903/04 when he became their top scorer with 13 goals in 27 First Division matches. His form faltered the next season when he drew a blank in 12 outings and he returned to London to join Queens Park Rangers (January 14, 1905). After making a big impact with Rangers (65 Southern League apps, 23 goals, plus two FA Cup apps), he transferred to their near-neighbours Brentford where he stayed for three seasons before transferring to Southend United for 1909/10 (22 games, five goals) who were languishing near the bottom of Southern League Division One. There was an interesting story behind Syd's solitary match for Hammers, which came about as a result of William Davidson's dispute with the West Ham management. Davidson left the club in a hurry, John Farrell, his deputy, was unfit and Sugden, then playing for Ilford, volunteered to fill the spot.

SUNDERLAND, HS — 1899-1900 TIW

SL apps: 1

PLAYED HIS SINGLE Southern League (Division Two) match in the 2-0 defeat at Bristol City (December 2, 1899). Previously with Gravesend United and Millwall, the latter with whom he played 12 Southern League games in 1898/99.

SUKER, Davor — 2000-01

Born: Osijek, Croatia, 1.1.68
League apps: 11 (2 goals)
Cup apps: 2 (1 goal)

PEDIGREES DIDN'T SEEM to come much better that that of Croatian international striker Davor Suker who Harry Redknapp captured on a free transfer from Arsenal in July 2000, but paid a king's ransom in wages. Having scored 11 times in the 14 starts allocated to him by Arsene Wenger during his year's contract at Highbury, it looked like the deal of the new millennium when the Gunners didn't extend the prolific hitman's contract and Harry got his man. But perhaps the perceptive Wenger knew something that Harry didn't – like the injury-prone goalscoring legend was past his sell by date! Even a dramatic late leveller in the 2-2 Boleyn draw with Champions Manchester United in his and Hammers third game of the season couldn't disguise the fact that this once great striker was more likely to spend more time in the referee's book, on the bench or in the treatment room than he would in the scoring charts for West Ham. With two caps for Yugoslavia before the breakdown of that proud country's identity and another 63 for Croatia in which he scored an amazing 43 goals, Davor helped his country to the Quarter-finals of Euro 96 in England and also won the coveted Golden Boot at the 1998 World Cup Finals in France. He was top scorer with six goals in the tournament in which he and team-mates Slaven Bilic and Igor Stimac helped the Croats to third place overall. With a list of clubs resembling an encyclopedia of European football reading: NK Osijek, 1985-89 (91 apps, 40 goals); Dynamo Zagreb, 1989-91 (60 apps, 34 goals); Sevilla, 1991-96 (153 apps, 75 goals); Real Madrid, 1996-99 (86 apps, 38 goals); and Arsenal, 1999-2000 (22 apps, eight goals) – was it any wonder that Harry was impressed. But the bare statistics at the top of this entry tell their own story and Davor continued his extraordinary journey across Europe in search of goals and yet more glory to link up with TSV 1860 Munich for 2001/02 in the Bundesliga where he managed another four goals in 14 games, including a brace in the 4-2 victory over Borussia Monchengladbach in the final game of the season at the Bokelberg Stadium. In 2002/03, he managed just one more goal in 11 Bundesliga appearances against Arminia Bielefeld in a 3-1 win at the Olympia Stadium.

SWINDLEHURST, Dave — 1983-85

Born: Edgware, Middlesex, 6.1.56
League apps: 61 (15 goals)
Cup apps: 10 (2 goals)

A STRIKER IN the Hurst/Cross mould, his signing for a substantial fee from Derby County did much to minimise the effect of the latter's departure from the Boleyn. A Palace youth team-mate of Alan Devonshire in the early 1970s, their reunion at Hammers proved a fruitful one after a gap of some ten years. It was after scoring 73 goals in 237 League games for the Glaziers that he moved to Derby in 1980. A similar scoring ratio for the Rams impressed manager John Lyall sufficiently to bring him to Upton Park. A series of injuries kept him out of first team contention, and he was eventually transferred to Sunderland in 1985. Big Dave got off to a good start at Roker with two goals against Grimsby Town, but he soon found himself in a struggling side. Scoring 11 times in 72 appearances, Sunderland were preparing for their first ever season in the Third Division when he left for sunnier climes to join Anorthosis of Cyprus in July 1987. In March 1998, he was back in London with Wimbledon's "Crazy Gang" and at the tail end of the season they won the FA Cup against Liverpool at Wembley, but there was no glory for Dave, just two First Division appearances and no goals as he moved on to Fourth Division Colchester United before a loan spell later in the season saw him notch another goal in four outings for Colchester's relegation-avoiding rivals Peterborough United in what must have been a risky loan deal! That goal for Posh was his last in the League as he then embarked on playing and managerial roles at non-League Bromley and Molesley while coaching at local schools. In 1998, Dave returned to his first club, Crystal Palace, to take up a coaching appointment in the Selhurst Park outfit's Youth Academy and was promoted to reserve team manager in 2001.

T

TARICCO, Mauricio
TATE, Isaac "Hal"
TAYLOR, Alan
TAYLOR, Archie
TAYLOR, Frank
TAYLOR, George
TAYLOR, Tommy
TAYLOR, William
TERRIER, David
THIRLAWAY, William
THOMAS, Mitchell
THOMPSON, A
THORPE, Percy
TIHINEN, Hannu

TINDALL, Ron
TIPPETT, Thomas
TIRRELL, Alfred
TIRRELL, Patrick
TODOROV, Svetoslav
TONNER, Arthur
TRANTER, Walter
TRAVIS, Don
TRESADERN, Jack
TUCKER, Ken
TURNER, Charlie
TURNER, Cyril
TYLER, Dudley

Alan Taylor

TARICCO, Mauricio — 2004

Born: Buenos Aires, Argentina, 10.3.73
League apps: 1

AN ARGENTINIAN UNDER-23 international, this combative midfielder with an attacking bent was signed on a free transfer from Spurs on November 18, 2004 and made his debut in the explosive local derby at Millwall two days later, but was substituted early in the match due to injury. Ipswich Town signed him as a 21-year-old from Argentinos Juniors for a £175,000 fee in September 1994. Having an Italian father enabled the English-speaking Mauricio to play in England without a work permit under EEC rules and after taking a season or two to settle down in East Anglia he quickly became a favourite with the Tractor Boys to win the club's Player of the Year award in 1996/97. Despite being naturally right-footed, he made the right wing-back position his own and liked nothing better than taking on opponents and pushing forward at any opportunity for a crack at goal, scoring against Reading, Stoke and local rivals Norwich City to prove the point. Such was his progress at Portman Road, Premiership giants Spurs had no hesitation in laying out £1.8 million in December 1998 after he'd made 170 appearances and scored seven times for Town. The versatile, tenacious tackling Taricco took the step up in his stride, but began to fall foul of referees as the temperamental side of his character began to surface under the extra pressures of the Premiership. He showed signs of putting the disciplinary problems of 2001/02 behind him when he became a regular at White Hart Lane, playing on the right or left side of midfield with equal effect. In six years at Tottenham, he added another 156 League and Cup appearances to his career total and had scored another two goals up until the end of 2003/04. Alas, his Hammers career was destined to last a mere 27 minutes when the unlucky Argie tore a hamstring during his debut at Millwall in November 2004. When Mauricio realised he would be sidelined for up to two months, he sportingly offered to terminate his contract rather than be a burden on the club's finances. His decision prompted manager Alan Pardew to proclaim: "This is one of the most honest acts from a player I have experienced in all my years in the game."

TATE, Isaac "Hal" — 1927-29

Born: Gateshead, Tyne & Wear, 28.7.1906
League apps: 14

YET ANOTHER SIGNING From Newcastle United, Isaac impressed the West Ham management with his safe handling while keeping goal for the Magpies against Hammers. Known as "Ike" to his colleagues, he joined the Geordies at the age of 18 and had three years at St James's Park before arriving at the Boleyn as understudy to the great Ted Hufton. His quest for regular first team football led to his transfer to Doncaster Rovers. Better known as "Hal", he made 127 Third Division South appearances for the Belle Vue club between 1929 and 1934.

TAYLOR, Alan — 1974-79

Born: Lancaster, Lancashire, 14.11.53
League apps: 98 (25 goals)
Cup apps: 25 (11 goals)

THIS SPEEDY WHIPPET-LIKE striker made the transition from Fourth Division Rochdale in true Roy of the Rovers fashion, appearing in the 1975 FA Cup Final within six months of his transfer. Once rejected by Preston, he had drifted into non-League soccer with Lancaster and Morecambe before Rochdale gave him his chance. But as a West Ham player he hit the headlines. It was Alan's deadly finishing that got Hammers to Wembley. He scored twice in the Sixth Round victory over Arsenal at Highbury, poached another brace in the Semi-final replay versus Ipswich Town at Stamford Bridge, and did the same again in the Final against fighting Fulham. Although he played in the 1976 European Cup Winners' Final versus Anderlecht in Belgium, his style of play made him very susceptible to injuries, which restricted his first team outings. Transferred to Norwich City in August 1979, he later joined Cambridge United after a spell with Vancouver Whitecaps. He was given a free transfer by Hull City at the end of 1983/84 and then back in the claret and blue for a different cause with Burnley in June 1984. Later he had a brief spell with Bury before making an amazing return to Division One with Norwich City in 1988/89. He was running his own milk round franchise at Scarning, Norfolk in the early 1990s. Alan, who scored 86 goals in 332 League matches for his eight clubs between 1973 and 1989, changed his vocation when he ploughed his savings into a new business venture in Norwich when he opened Taylor's News in 1994. In May 1995, Alan took part in a 20th anniversary celebration match of the 1975 FA Cup win between Fulham and West Ham at Craven Cottage and there were distinct feelings of déjà vu as Fulham's goalkeeper Peter Mellor allowed history to repeat itself when letting Billy Jennings' shot through his legs for a carbon copy of Alan's first goal for West Ham in 1975! "Sparrow" as he was nicknamed at Upton Park, along with 1975 team-mates Billy Bonds, Tommy Taylor, Mervyn Day, Keith Robson, Kevin Lock, Patsy Holland, Billy Jennings and Wembley sub Bobby Gould, eventually went down 2-1 to their Fulham counterparts (who had Tony Gale guesting at number 5) in the match staged to raise cash for the Fulham 2000 Fund. Nowadays, Alan is often seen back at Upton Park on match days as a guest of the club and is an enthusiastic attender of any official functions organised by Hammers and was indeed prominent at the official launch of the previous *Who's Who of West Ham* book in November 1994.

TAYLOR, Archie — 1906-09

SL apps: 63
Cup apps: 7

ARCHIE JOINED HAMMERS at the age of 25 from London rivals Brentford, making his Southern League debut versus Bristol Rovers at the Boleyn (October 15, 1906). Although that match was lost 1-0, the tough-tackling former Bristol Rovers and Bolton Wanderers left-back helped to tighten the defence of a Hammers team that finished a creditable fifth in the Southern League First Division that season. Archie moved to his home-town club Dundee in March 1909, but later returned south to join Barnsley where he filled the number 2 spot in the 1912 FA Cup Final for the Yorkshire club who defeated West Bromwich Albion 1-0 in a replay at Bramall Lane, after a 0-0 draw at Crystal Palace. Later managed York City. He started with Dundee East Craigie as centre-half in the side that won the Dewar Shield, Forfarshire Cup and East of Scotland Cup and also produced James Sharp of Arsenal.

TAYLOR, Frank — 1899-1902

SL apps (TIW): 14 (1 goal)
SL apps (WHU): 12 (4 goals)
Cup apps: 1 (1 goal)

THE YOUNGEST PLAYER in Thames Ironworks' last Southern League team, Frank took over the left-wing spot following the tragic death of England international Tom Bradshaw on Christmas Day, 1899. Tipped by the writer of the club's handbook to become "one of the finest outside-lefts in the kingdom", the former Harwich man served the old Ironworks and the new West Ham well enough, without rising to those somewhat rashly predicted heights.

TAYLOR, George — 1938-56

Born: Wigan, Lancashire, 21.3.20
League apps: 115
Cup apps: 3

ONE OF CHARLIE Paynter's many signings from Midland club Gainsborough Trinity, the career of goalkeeper George at Upton Park was spent mainly as understudy to Ernie Gregory, although he did make 38 appearances in 1954/55 when the latter missed the whole season through injury. It was his reliability as a deputy that made Hammers reluctant to release him. His sound displays aroused the interest of other clubs, but every time he was set for a move, Ernie was injured and George had to step in to fill the breach. He was nearing the veteran stage when he eventually left the Boleyn, seeing out his playing days with Southern League Sittingbourne. George died in October 1983 at the age of 63. In addition to his first team matches, George played 231 times for the reserves.

TAYLOR, Tommy — 1970-79

Born: Hornchurch, Essex, 26.9.51
League apps: 340 (8 goals)
Cup apps: 56

TOMMY TAYLOR

HIS ARRIVAL FROM near-neighbours Orient in October 1970 for a hefty fee, plus Peter Bennett as part of the deal, solved a long-standing defensive problem for Hammers. Tommy had caught the attention of a number of clubs in his auspicious start with the Brisbane Road outfit, during which time he helped the O's to promotion from Division Three and also captained the England Youth team. He was on the verge of full international recognition after winning no less than 13 Under-23 honours while with Hammers, albeit some of which were permissible under the ruling that allowed over-age players in the team. An integral member of the side that brought Cup success to Upton Park in the mid-1970s, he returned to his former club in the summer of 1979 after losing his place to Alvin Martin. He later became youth coach for Charlton Athletic, after a spell in Belgium with Antwerp. He then spent three years in New Zealand football management before returning to fill a coaching post with Football League newcomers Maidstone United in 1989. Appointed Youth Team manager at Cambridge United in 1993, Tommy was promoted to first team boss in 1995, but was only in charge at the Abbey Stadium for a year when he accepted an offer from Orient chairman Barry Hearn to fill the hot seat at Brisbane Road. Like many before and since, Tommy found it a thankless task managing the O's and, after five years of trying to get

them out of the Third Division, he ended his association with the club in 2001, declaring: "Barry Hearn is the best chairman I've ever worked for." He then took charge of another struggling Third Division Club, Darlington, whose wealthy chairman George Reynolds harboured grandiose ambitions to turn the little Feethams outfit into another Newcastle in the soccer-mad North East. "That was never realistic with players earning as little as £150 a week," Tommy told the West Ham retro magazine *Ex*. Tommy left the Quakers in October 2002 and, after helping out at Nationwide Conference Club Farnborough Town towards the end of 2002/03, he accepted the manager's job in May 2003 at the John Roberts Ground. Things didn't work out too well at Boro, however, and Tommy was then reported to be working in the West Indies! In November 2004 he was appointed boss of Kings Lynn.

his way at White Hart Lane (where he was third choice left-back when Billy Bonds came in with his half-million pound offer), the gangling Thomas made 35 First Division appearances in his first season for Hammers. But they were difficult days at West Ham. Against a background of unrest on the terraces, where the fans were revolting against the club's ill-fated bond scheme, the team's miserable performances on the field culminated in relegation. As an out-of-form ex-Spurs player, the critics saw Thomas as an ideal scapegoat. He played just three more League games in 1992/92 (when Dicks was suspended) and never made the first team again after appearing versus Crewe Alexandra in the League Cup tie at Upton Park (September 23, 1992). Despite the club's efforts to try and recoup some of the money they paid for Thomas, there was little interest in him outside Luton, whose manager David Pleat initially took Thomas on loan before finally agreeing to buy him outright at a cut-price £50,000 in March 1994. Pleat was in his first spell as Hatters' manager when Thomas joined the club from school and made his League debut – ironically, at Upton Park (January 4, 1983). And Pleat's first signing when he became manager of Tottenham, in 1986, was... Mitchell Thomas. He made 157 League appearances for Spurs and played left-back in the team defeated by Coventry City in the 1987 FA Cup Final. Altogether, Mitch made 340 League and Cup appearances in his two spells with Luton (six goals) before joining Burnley in July 1999 where he made another 112 League and Cup appearances before being released by the Clarets in summer 2003.

Career record

Played	League		FAC		LC		Europe		Total	
	App	Gls	App	Gls	App	Gls	App	Gls	App	Gls
1970-71	30	1	1	0	0	0	0	0	31	1
1971-72	42	0	4	0	10	0	0	0	56	0
1972-73	37	3	2	0	2	0	0	0	41	3
1973-74	40	0	2	0	2	0	0	0	44	0
1974-75	39	0	7	0	3	0	0	0	49	0
1975-76	42	2	0	0	5	0	9	0	56	2
1976-77	36	0	2	0	3	0	0	0	41	0
1977-78	42	2	3	0	0	0	0	0	45	2
1978-79	32	0	0	0	1	0	0	0	33	0
TOTAL	**340**	**8**	**21**	**0**	**26**	**0**	**9**	**0**	**396**	**8**

TAYLOR, William — 1906-09

Born: Tyneside, date unknown
SL apps: 63
Cup apps: 7

BILL MADE HIS Southern League debut for Irons in the 1-0 home defeat versus Bristol Rovers (October 15, 1906). He made only four appearances that season, but made the left-back position his own over the next two years before being superseded by Bob Fairman.

TERRIER, David — 1997

Born: Verdun, France, 4.8.73
League apps: 1

FRENCH UNDER-21 INTERNATIONAL who was snapped up on a free transfer from FC Metz in July 1997. Joining Hammers on a three-year deal, a get out clause was inserted into the contract stipulating that the stylish central defender could depart by mutual consent after a three-month trial period. "I haven't come here for the money, I want to experience English football and hopefully enjoy success," insisted the 23-year-old, adding: "I hope to stay for the entire term of my contract." Terrier made 31 French Le Championnat appearances in 1996/97 for Metz and played a major role in his side's UEFA Cup run, which was finally halted by Newcastle United. He made only one brief appearance for West Ham however, when he came on as a sub late in the 2-1 opening day victory over Barnsley at Oakwell in August 1997. After spending an unhappy six months at Upton Park, he joined Newcastle in January 1998, but never made a first team appearance during his six months on Gallowgate. It seemed a strange predicament for someone who'd been selected on 15 occasions for France at Under-21 level and played 127 League games for Metz, where he was a team-mate of Rigobert Song. In 1999/2000, David played 26 times for Nice and between 2001 and the end of 2003/04 he'd made 78 appearances for Ajaccio in Corsica.

THIRLAWAY, William — 1921-23

Born: New Washington, County Durham, 1.10.1896
League apps: 36 (2 goals)
Cup apps: 3

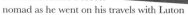

AN OUTSIDE-RIGHT SIGNED from Unsworth Colliery, Billy made 33 Second Division appearances in 1921/22. But a subsequent loss of form saw his first team outings reduced to just two in 1922/23 and a solitary game the following season – his last as a Hammer. He then joined Southend United where he made seven appearances at the beginning of 1924/25 in Division Three South. He then became a soccer nomad as he went on his travels with Luton Town, South Shields, Birmingham (23 apps, one goal), Cardiff City (March 1927), Tunbridge Wells Rangers (July 1930) and Unsworth Colliery (August 1931).

THOMAS, Mitchell — 1991-94

Born: Luton, Bedfordshire, 2.10.64
League apps: 38 (3 goals)
Cup apps: 9

ARRIVING FROM RIVALS Tottenham, as an expensive £500,000 replacement for injured crowd favourite Julian Dicks, Mitchell always had a lot to prove to Hammers fans. He started reasonably well in the left-back spot and within weeks of making his debut versus Luton Town (August 17, 1991) – his first club – the tall, slim defender delighted the Upton Park faithful by scoring the winner… against Spurs! He was also on target versus Crystal Palace and Oldham Athletic and even after Dicks returned, in January 1992, Thomas kept his place by switching to midfield. After losing

THOMPSON, A — 1903-04

SL apps: 10 (1 goal)

ARRIVING IN MID-SEASON from Middlesbrough, centre-forward "Thommo" had to wait until his third match in the claret and blue before scoring what proved to be his only goal for the club in the 4-1 Boleyn win over Wellingborough Town (January 30, 1904). He was a colleague of Chris Carrick and Frank Piercy at Boro. Scored two goals in three outings for the Teessiders in 1902/03.

THORPE, Percy — 1933-34

Born: Nottingham, Nottinghamshire, 18.7.1899
League apps: 3

AN EXPERIENCED RIGHT-BACK who had represented Nottingham Boys before graduating to League standard with Blackpool (113 League apps, five goals), Reading (72 League apps) and Sheffield Wednesday (103 League apps), captaining the former and latter. He made his trio of Second Division appearances in quick succession versus Bolton Wanderers, Brentford and Plymouth Argyle at the start of the 1933/34 season. Having also represented Sutton Town and Connahs Quay and Shotton either side of his spell with Blackpool, Percy went on to play twice for Accrington Stanley and once for Port Vale after leaving Hammers.

TIHINEN, Hannu — 2000

Born: Keminmaa, Finland, 1.7.76
League apps: 8
Cup apps: 2

OF ALL THE players Harry Redknapp signed and all the players he wanted to sign during his seven turbulent years as manager at West Ham, this is the player he should have made sure he signed above all others. Known as "The Iceberg" in his native Finland, Hannu began his career with the KePS Kemi Club in 1995 and scored ten times in 48 matches for the little Finnish outfit before signing for the country's top dogs HJK Helsinki in 1997, where he won the Finnish Championship in his first year and the domestic Cup the following season. After racking up an impressive 65 League appearances and scoring another eight goals in his three seasons at the Finnair Stadium, where he also got his first taste of Champions League football, he moved on to join Norway's Viking FK in 1999. Despite scoring on his debut on the opening day of the 2000/01 season in the 4-1 defeat at SK Brann and picking up a domestic Cup runners-up medal in October 2000, The Iceberg was destined for the Premiership when Hammers enacted something of a coup by bringing him to Upton Park on loan during the Scandinavian close season. He arrived just in time to take part in the epic FA Cup run up to the disposal of Manchester United at Old Trafford in January 2001 and, a few days later, a superb last-ditch goal-line clearance in the 0-0 Upton Park Premiership draw with Spurs alerted the mass West Ham support that here was a very special player indeed. But, alas, the West Ham board couldn't or wouldn't stump up the million or so that the Stavanger club required and Hannu was jetting back to the frozen wastes having left Hammers a tantalising glimpse of the sort of defending that only Rio Ferdinand had displayed in recent history. Back in Norway, Tihinen promptly helped Viking to win the Norwegian Cup by scoring one of the goals in the 3-0 Final win over Bryne FK. But having added another 34 Norwegian First Division appearances and two goals in 2001 and 2002 to the 25 appearances (three goals) he made before his loan spell with Hammers in 2000, The Iceberg was soon shifting again. With a host of continental clubs vying for his signature, crack Belgians RSC Anderlecht won the race in the summer of 2002 and Hannu settled in quickly in Brussels with 24 appearances and three goals towards the winning of the Belgian First Division title in his first season. He also featured in all eight of the Belgians' UEFA Cup ties, which ended in 3-2 Quarter-final defeat to Panathinaikos. Now linked to Milan, Anderlecht were determined to hold on to their sought-after central-defender par excellence, who underlined his worth still further as one of the most persistent performers in the 2003/04 Champions League scoring a vital winner against Lyon in a short but exciting European adventure. Back at West Ham on July 31, 2004 for a pre-season friendly visit with RSC Anderlecht, the commanding Finn shed further light on his all too brief Upton Park career: "My three months with West Ham were wonderful," he reflected, "it was very difficult to leave, and not my decision. I understand that Viking Stavanger wanted a lot of money for me but it was so nice to be at West Ham. It would have been nicer to stay. I am sure I will enjoy this visit." He did too, the match was a thrilling 4-4 draw, with Anderlecht winning 5-4 on penalties!

Hannu Tihinen

Ron Tindall

TINDALL, Ron — 1961-62

Born: Streatham, London, 23.9.35
League apps: 13 (3 goals)
Cup apps: 1

A STOCKILY-BUILT CENTRE-FORWARD who had a great goalscoring record with his first club, Chelsea. After a humble beginning as an office boy at Stamford Bridge, he went on to score 68 times in 160 first XI appearances for the Blues and won representative honours for the Football League versus League of Ireland. Ron arrived at Upton Park in November 1961 as part of the exchange deal that took Andy Malcolm in the opposite direction, scoring three goals in 13 outings that season. A first-class cricketer, his commitments to Surrey in their fight for the County Championship clashed with the start of the 1962/63

campaign. When they were finally resolved he decided to transfer to Third Division Reading to ensure regular first team soccer. After serving the Elm Park outfit well, he moved on again to Portsmouth in 1965, where he successfully converted to a defensive role. He made 162 League appearances for Pompey before taking up coaching appointments at Fratton Park, which culminated in him becoming general manager for the start of 1970/71. One of his first signings for the south coast club was former Hammer and cricketer, goalkeeper Jim Standen. The scorer of 5,000 runs and taker of 150 wickets for Surrey in the late 1950s and early 1960s, Ron left football for a time to manage a golf club at Waterlooville, Hampshire. He later emigrated to Australia and was made director of coaching for Western Australia after settling in Perth at a place called Wembley! Ron organised coaching programmes for the 107 sports officially recognised by Western Australia, a state that is ten times bigger than the UK. Ron also spent many years as assistant manager of Australia's Under-18 side before taking control as technical director at the Australian Ministry of Sports and Recreation. The author of several books on soccer coaching, he formed the coaching foundation of Western Australia in 1999. Now retired down under and living with his wife of 46 years, Anne, at Carrambine on the outskirts of Perth, it's ironic that his lifetime's work contributed to Australia inflicting their first ever defeat on England when the Socceroos won 3-1 at Upton Park in 2003.

TIPPETT, Thomas — 1933-35

Born: Gateshead, Tyne and Wear, 13.7.1904
League apps: 27 (10 goals)
Cup apps: 1

A GOALSCORING OUTSIDE-RIGHT who progressed through a number of Tyneside junior teams before turning pro for Craghead United in the North-Eastern League. It

was only apt that this former blacksmith should sign for Hammers after spells with Doncaster Rovers (31 League apps, four goals), Rochdale (70 apps, 47 goals), Port Vale (39 apps, 11 goals) and their Potteries neighbours, Stoke City. An all-round sportsman, his direct style of wing-play made him an able deputy for England international Johnny Morton. Tommy wrote himself into the record books at Rochdale when he scored six goals against Hartlepools United in a Third Division North fixture April 21, 1930.

TIRRELL, Alfred — 1913-15

Born: Desborough, Northamptonshire, 7.2.1894
SL apps: 7

A FULL-BACK TRANSFERRED to Upton Park from Peterborough City (South Eastern League) during the close season of 1913. He made his debut on February 28, 1914 at Crystal Palace (2-1), his only appearance that season. Played six Southern League games in 1914/15. Alf turned out a few times during the war, mostly in 1918/19 when he was the most regular player with 30 appearances. He was still with the club when peacetime soccer resumed in 1919, but didn't play in any first team matches that year. Alf transferred to Luton Town in the close season of 1920 and played in over 120 Southern League and League games (six goals) up to the end of 1924/25.

TIRRELL, Patrick — 1908-09

Born: birthplace unknown, 1885
SL apps: 13 (1 goal)

SIGNED FROM SOUTHERN League rivals Northampton Town, Pat had the pleasure of scoring one of the goals that enabled Hammers to defeat his former Cobblers team-mates 2-1 at Upton Park on October 24, 1908. Operating with equal efficiency at either right or left-half, he got stuck on 13 appearances that season, his last as an Iron. He arrived at Upton Park during the close season of 1908. Already fully experienced having made 95 Southern League appearances for Northampton Town. Before Northampton he had a short spell at Kettering. At Northampton he was a team-mate of Herbert Chapman, who later managed Arsenal, and of James Frost, who preceded him at Upton Park by a couple of months. Tirrell played six times against Hammers between 1905 and 1908, four times as a half-back. He turned out 14 times in Southern League games for West Ham in 1908/09 but was part of a huge clear-out at the end of that season. In May 2002, medals and memorabilia belonging to the player's family were put up for auction at Sotheby's.

TODOROV, Svetoslav — 2000-01

Born: Lovech, Bulgaria, 30.8.78
League apps: 14 (1 goal)
Cup apps: 3 (1 goal)

THIS 23-TIMES CAPPED Bulgarian international striker was signed for a bargain £500,000 fee from his home-town club Liteks Lovech in January 2001. Making his debut as substitute in the 3-0 defeat at Liverpool the following month, "Toddy" scored his first goal for Hammers after coming off the bench again in the 3-2 Upton Park Sixth Round FA Cup defeat to Spurs in March 2001. He scored his only Premiership goal in the 2-1 reverse against Middlesbrough at the Riverside in the last fixture of 2000/01, just after the departure of Harry Redknapp and the introduction of Glenn Roeder as caretaker boss. But after making just two starts and four sub appearances as well as an outing in the League Cup, the unsettled little Bulgar signed again for Harry Redknapp's promotion challenge with First Division Portsmouth. A neat finisher with a good touch, Toddy contributed 26 goals towards Pompey's First Division Championship success and made many more for his colleagues. Svetoslav sustained a bad knee injury just prior to the start of the club's first Premiership season and, following an operation in the USA, missed all of the 2003/04 season apart from a brief sub appearance at Anfield. Harry Redknapp stuck by him, however, and after missing out on Euro 2004, the player was hoping to make a complete recovery in 2004/05. Beginning his career with Bulgarian First Division Club Dobrudzha Dobrich in 1996/97, where he scored twice in 12 appearances, he was then snapped up by Second Division Champions Liteks Lovech and scored 37 times in 71 League matches over four seasons for his local team. Originally came to England for a trial with Preston North End, but was spotted by a Hammers scout and ended up at the Boleyn Ground instead.

TONNER, Arthur 1933

Born: Glasgow, Scotland, 1913
League apps: 1

ORIGINALLY A GOALKEEPER in schools soccer, he was converted to full-back by his first junior club, Stafford, in the Tradeston and District League. His move to St Anthony's – who had earlier provided forward Hughie Mills – led to his discovery by West Ham and his eventual move south. An apprentice sawyer before signing pro forms for Irons, he helped to cut down Forest in his only first team outing in the 5-2 Upton Park win over the Nottingham men in September 1935. He then returned to Scotland with St Mirren, but came back south to make 41 appearances for Swindon Town before joining Swansea Town in 1939.

TRANTER, Walter 1897-99

Born: Middlesbrough, Teesside, 1875
SL apps (TIW): 20

SAID TO HAVE "rushed in where others feared to tread", Wally was left-back in the Thames Ironworks team that won the London League Championship in 1897/98, losing only one match in the process. A good story was told of his carrying off, in "error", the Dewar Shield amid high spirits at the League's presentation concert to honour the triumph. Appointed club captain, the Middlesbrough-born defender led Hammers to the Second Division Championship of the Southern League, but surprisingly threw in his lot with the top section with Chatham the following season. He returned to the Memorial Grounds for 1900/01, although there is no record of his appearing at senior level for the new club, West Ham United. Later went to play in Northern Ireland for a Belfast club.

TRAVIS, Don 1946-48

Born: Manchester, Greater Manchester, 21.1.24
League apps: 5

ANOTHER CENTRE-FORWARD, DON holds the unique record of being the only Hammer to score four goals on both his reserve and first team debuts. To chart his amazingly chequered career we must go back to 1940, when he played for the first of his 12 clubs while still an amateur at the age of 15… Blackpool. His apprenticeship with the Seasiders was disrupted when he was called up for National Service with the Army in 1944, serving as a gunner in the Royal Artillery. It was around this time that he played for Plymouth Argyle, and was saddled with the nickname of "Sailor" after being wrongly reported as being in the Navy by the local press! He made his initial appearance for West Ham in a Combination match versus Chelsea Reserves in September 1945, and scored his first quartet. No sooner had Charlie Paynter signed him for Hammers than he was whisked away and posted to Scotland with his unit, where he made guest appearances for St Mirren and Cowdenbeath. It was while on leave in February 1946 that Don made his first team bow against… Plymouth Argyle. Apart from Don's feat of again scoring four, the match threw up another Hammers' record, winger Terry Woodgate scoring a hat-trick in seven minutes. He also scored again the following match versus Portsmouth, seemingly saving it up for the Navy towns! A long post to the Middle East followed and, on his return, he found competition for the number 9 shirt from Sam Small, Frank Neary and Bill Stephens. Despite making another four Second Division appearances and scoring heavily for the reserves, he was somewhat surprisingly transferred to Southend United at the end of 1947/48. He played only once for the Essex club, however, before beginning a transfer trail across northern England, taking in spells with Accrington Stanley (71 League apps, 35 goals), Crewe (36 League apps, 11 goals), Oldham (113 League apps, 60 goals), Chester (99 League apps, 45 goals) and Oldham again. He returned south for one last taste of glory with Southern League Yeovil in 1959, being in the side that performed a giant-killing on his old employers, Southend. But his travels were still not over as he played for Southern League Trowbridge Town and Western League Dorchester Town after leaving Huish. Don Travis played five times for West Ham during the transitionary, regionalised Football League South tournament, scoring seven goals in 1945/46. These are not recognised in official Football League records, however. Standing six feet three inches tall and with a physique to match, Don served six League clubs and scored a total of 154 goals in 325 matches. He began his career at Moston Fields,

Manchester Schoolboys, Ferranti FC and Goslings FC. His older brother, Harry, played for Oldham in World War II and was Bradford City's top scorer in 1935/36.

TRESADERN, Jack 1919-24

Born: Leytonstone, London, 26.9.1890
SL apps: 6
League apps: 144 (5 goals)
Cup apps: 16

DESPITE THE INTERVENTION of two world wars, the first of which badly interrupted his playing career and the second his managerial progress, Jack Tresadern eventually made his mark in both spheres without gaining the honours his talents fully deserved. "Tres", as he was popularly known, joined Hammers from Barking in 1913 after helping that club win the London Senior Cup and South Essex League in 1911/12. Represented Essex and London and in 1912 scored one of the goals by which Barking defeated Brentford 3-2 in the London Challenge Cup. A former cashier with a firm of London ship repairers, he later ran a poultry farm in Essex. He began life at Upton Park as understudy to the great Tommy Randall in the left-half position. Although small in stature, his lack of physical attributes did not prevent him being commissioned to the Royal Garrison Artillery during World War I, along with future team-mate George Kay. Indeed, after the war and when he had won a regular first XI place, his robust play prompted his trainer and mentor Charlie Paynter to remark that it must have been Jack who inspired the maxim: "The bigger they are the harder they fall!" In his youth, Jack captained his school team and also appeared in West Ham's English and Corinthian Shield XIs under Harry Earle, the father of famous Hammer, Stan Earle. He had a trial with Southend United but elected to stay an amateur to join Barking. Jack's finest hours as a Hammer came in season 1922/23, when his sterling displays in Irons' promotion to the First Division and winning through to the first Wembley Cup Final, gained him well-deserved international recognition against Scotland. Jack had one of his rare off-days versus the Scots, however, and although England managed to draw the match at Hampden Park 2-2, Jack often recalled ruefully afterwards: "I was the best player Scotland had on the field." Even so, his off-colour performance against the Scots did not stop his inclusion in the England side that defeated Sweden in Stockholm the following month in a match when team-mate Billy Moore scored one of the goals in a 4-2 victory. In October 1924, Jack swapped clubs when he transferred to Burnley before joining Northampton Town as player-manager, where he played with former Hammer colleague Percy Allen at the County Ground. Incidentally, it was around this time that Jack's career was running parallel with the aforementioned George Kay, who had managed Southampton and later bossed Liverpool. In fact, it could be claimed the pair were the forerunners of the now famous West Ham managerial academy. Jack later held the reins at Crystal Palace, Spurs (who gained promotion to the First Division under his guidance) and Plymouth Argyle. It was at the latter port of call that Jack Tresadern stood his greatest test of character… and came through with flying colours. When he took over at Home Park war clouds were already gathering on the horizon, but it would have been hard for anyone to imagine the extent of the devastation the forthcoming blitz was to have on the fortunes of Plymouth Argyle. It is now a recognised fact among football folk that had it not been for the efforts of "Tres" in somehow seeing the club through that nightmare transitional season of 1945/46, and convincing the Football League legislators that the game was still a viable proposition at Plymouth, the Argyle would not be in existence today. It is said Jack had to literally scour the dockyards and local Leagues on many occasions that campaign to raise a side. After saving the Pilgrims, he later managed three Southern League clubs, Chelmsford City, Hastings United and Tonbridge – the latter of whom he was serving when he suffered a heart attack at his home in the town on Christmas Day, 1959, and died the following day at the age of 67.

England caps: 1923 vs Scotland, Sweden (2).

TUCKER, Ken 1947-57

Born: Poplar, London, 2.10.25
League apps: 83 (31 goals)
Cup apps: 10

KEN'S CAREER HAD a sensational, if somewhat unusual, beginning in that he scored a hat-trick on his debut versus Chesterfield at Upton Park in October 1947, and then did not score again for another four years (in 14 appearances during that period). A fast, powerful winger signed from Finchley, his scoring exploits in the reserves (73 goals in 191 matches) finally won him regular first team recognition in 1955/56. His success when scoring 15 in 37 appearances was due largely to his decision to change from part-time to full-time training. Ken transferred to Notts County in March 1957, and later joined the enclave of ex-Hammers at Margate. He became a newsagent and then a licensed victualler when he retired.

Ken Tucker

Dudley Tyler

TURNER, Charlie 1938-39

Born: Athlone, Republic of Ireland, 1911
League apps: 11

WEST HAM SIGNED this experienced Republic of Ireland international centre-half from Southend United for extra defensive cover following the retirement of Jim Barrett. Although he was mainly the understudy to Dick Walker during his two seasons at Upton Park, he was capped five times by the Republic of Ireland over the same period to add to the nap hand he had already gained while with the Shrimpers. In the summer of 1939, Charlie transferred to Hartlepool United and after World War II he returned to Ireland to manage League of Ireland club Shelbourne. He left Irish football to join Stalybridge Celtic and then moved to Leeds United before teaming up with Southend in the close season of 1935 and played 110 League and Cup matches for the Shrimpers.

Republic of Ireland caps: 1937 vs Norway (twice); 1938 vs Czechoslovakia, Poland; 1939 vs Hungary (5).

TURNER, Cyril 1919-21

Born: Berkshire, date unknown
League apps: 7 (1 goal)

THIS RIGHT-BACK MADE his Hammers debut versus Stoke City at the Victoria Ground on September 27, 1919. He was on duty again versus the Potters in the return fixture at the Boleyn Ground the following week, when a 1-1 draw went some way to avenging the earlier 2-1 defeat on the Staffordshire club's enclosure. The legendary Syd Puddefoot was Hammers' marksman on both occasions. It was Cyril who was the unlikely goalscoring hero in the next match, however, when deputising at centre-forward for "Puddy" (who was either injured or, more likely, on international duty) he scored the only goal of the game against Grimsby Town at Blundell Park.

TYLER, Dudley 1972-73

Born: Salisbury, Wiltshire, 21.9.44
League apps: 28 (1 goal)
Cup apps: 1

SIGNED FOR £25,000 – a record at the time for a non-League player – largely on the strength of his performance against Hammers for Southern League Hereford during their historic FA Cup run of 1971/72. His rise to stardom was even more remarkable, taking into account a "hole in the heart" operation while he was still a junior player. Dud's brief sojourn at the Boleyn was made memorable despite the shortness of his stay. His return to Edgar Street and his former club was sweetened when they celebrated their newly-won League status with a thrilling FA Cup victory over West Ham in 1973/74 (after a draw at Upton Park). He retired from the game after sustaining an ankle injury in 1977. Dud scored 11 times in his 131 League games for the Bulls and still lives in Hereford working as a sales manager based in Banbury.

C. TURNER (Half-back)
Born at Athlone, Ireland
Previous Club: Southend United
1 Season at West Ham
Height: 5ft. 11in. Weight: 11st. 7lb.

U-V

UNSWORTH, David

VAN DER ELST, Francois

Francois Van der Elst

UNSWORTH, David   1997-98

Born: Preston, Lancashire, 16.10.73
League apps: 32 (2 goals)
Cup apps: 9

THIS POWERFULLY BUILT defender was signed from Everton for £1 million in August 1997 and was sold on for a cool £2 million profit after just one season at the Boleyn to Premiership rivals Aston Villa in July 1998. In a sensational saga, David stayed at Villa Park for just two weeks before returning to Everton for another £3 million fee without kicking a ball in anger for Villa! At least Hammers saw more of him than their claret and blue clad counterparts as he considerably tightened up the left-side of the defence with his strength in the air and on the ground. He also added his weight to attack on numerous occasions and got on the scoresheet in wins over Crystal Palace and Chelsea. Although Hammers fans were largely sorry to see him depart, it was obvious following his brief spell with Villa that his heart belonged at Goodison where he went on to appear in more Premiership matches (304) than any other Everton player up until he signed again for Harry Redknapp at Portsmouth on a free transfer to stay in the Premiership in July 2004. Something of a penalty expert with 23 successful conversions for the Toffees, David was awarded a solitary England cap against Japan at Wembley in 1995 to add to his total of six Under-21 caps. He returned to the Twin Towers the following year as a member of the Everton side that defeated Manchester United 1-0 in the FA Cup Final and added a Charity Shield Winners' medal the following August. Dave joined up with Hammers' Championship rivals Ipswich Town in February 2005 on loan and signed for Sheffield United in the summer.

VAN DER ELST, Francois   1981-83

Born: Opwijk, Belgium, 1.12.54
League apps: 62 (16 goals)
Cup apps: 8 (3 goals)

MOST REMEMBERED FOR his stunning performance against Hammers in the European Cup Winners' Cup Final for Anderlecht at the ill-fated Heysel Stadium in 1976. West Ham signed their tormentor-in-chief and architect of their defeat for £400,000 from New York Cosmos six years later (January 1982). His appearance for the Belgians that night versus his club-mates-to-be (although he could hardly have realised it at the time) was the first of a unique hat-trick of appearances in successive seasons in the Final of that competition. "Frankie" was on the losing side versus Hamburg in 1977 and a winner again the following year versus WAC Austria. Also in the Anderlecht team that won the UEFA Super Cup versus Liverpool in 1978, Francois was an automatic choice for his country until his move to the States. His form at Upton Park saw him resurrect his international career, however, culminating in his appearance in the 1982 World Cup in Spain (where he had two outings as sub). He made his Hammers debut at Brighton (January 16, 1982) and, after five goals in the second half of that campaign, he contributed a useful nine League and five Cup goals as West Ham climbed to eighth position in the 1982/83 First Division. Considered by many to have been one move ahead of many of his colleagues at the Boleyn, it's doubtful if the brilliant Belgian would have returned to his own country with Lokeren so soon if his family had been able to settle here. After two full seasons playing for Lokeren, Francois suffered a very bad injury when he broke a leg and tore ligaments, forcing him to retire at just 31. After playing snooker with Ray Stewart in his time with Hammers, Francois got the idea of opening his own snooker club and now runs Snooker Palace in Opwijk, Belgium. He also visited Upton Park in 2003/04 on a trip to England with a group of his regular customers and still rues the day he left West Ham.

David Unsworth

W

WADE, Don
WADE, Reg
WADE, William
WAGGOTT, David
WAGSTAFFE, George
WALDEN, George
WALFORD, Steve
WALKER, Albert
WALKER, Charlie
WALKER, Dick
WALKER, James
WALKER, Len
WALLACE, J
WALLBANKS, Fred
WANCHOPE, Paulo
WARD, Elliott
WARD, Mark
WARD, TG
WATSON, George
WATSON, Lionel
WATSON, Mark
WATSON, Victor
WATTS, Ernest
WAUGH, William T
WEALE, Robert
WEARE, Arthur J "Jack"
WEBB, George
WEBSTER, Joe
WEBSTER, Simon
WELDON, Anthony
WHITBREAD, Adrian

WHITCHURCH, Charlie
WHITEMAN, Robert
WHITTON, Steve
WILDMAN, William
WILLIAMS, A
WILLIAMS, Gavin
WILLIAMS, Harry
WILLIAMS, Rod
WILLIAMS, William
WILLIAMSON, Danny
WILKINSON, F
WILSON, Arthur
WILSON, Ron
WINTERBURN, Nigel
WINTERHALDER, Arthur
WINTERHALDER, Herbert
WOOD, Edward John "Jackie"
WOOD, Jimmy
WOODARDS, Dan
WOODBURN, John
WOODGATE, John Terence
WOODLEY, Derek
WOOLER, Alan
WOOSNAM, Phil
WRAGG, Doug
WRIGHT, George
WRIGHT, Ian
WRIGHT, Ken
WRIGHT, P
WYLLIE, Robinson "Bob"

Nigel Winterburn

WADE, Don
1947-50

Born: Tottenham, London, 5.6.26
League apps: 36 (5 goals)
Cup apps: 4 (2 goals)

A MAKER, RATHER than taker, of goals, this inside-forward was born near the Tottenham ground. It was West Ham who signed him as a pro, however, after he had played for Spurs' juniors and Edgware Town. Prominent in Army football, he made his Second Division baptism in 1947/48 versus Fulham after his demobilisation. An all-round sportsman, he also played on the wing on occasions. Moved to Bedford Town after his service with Hammers.

WADE, Reg
1929-32

Born: Ilford, Essex, 1907
League apps: 32
Cup apps: 1

SIGNED PRO FOR Hammers in 1929, after gaining an FA Amateur Cup winners' medal with Ilford in that year's Final versus Leyton at Highbury. Taking the step up to professionalism in his stride, he made his First Division debut in the left-back position in a 4-1 victory over Liverpool at Upton Park (January 18, 1929). His best run in the first team was in 1930/31 when he made 28 appearances. He transferred to Aldershot in 1932 and made 186 League appearances for the Shots, scoring one goal. He also had a spell with Millwall whom he joined from Barking in 1925, but failed to make the first team.

WADE, William
1929-32

Born: Jarrow, Northumbria, 22.3.1901
League apps: 16

SOMETIMES CONFUSED WITH his namesake and contemporary, fellow full-back Reg Wade. Bill was a big, beefy defender who came to Hammers from Preston North End, where he'd made 139 League appearances. He had previously played as an amateur for Smith's High Docks, Bertram (in the South Shields Combination) and Jarrow (in the North Eastern League). Mainly a reserve at the Boleyn, he returned north to join the newly-formed Wigan Athletic in 1932. Bill passed away at South Shields on August 23, 1958.

WAGGOTT, David
1908-10

Born: birthplace unknown, 1885
SL apps: 10 (3 goals)
Cup apps: 1

SIGNED FROM WEST Stanley (North Eastern League) after having previously had experience with Wednesday (then without the Sheffield prefix). Made his Southern League bow for Irons in a 1-0 Boleyn Castle defeat versus Crystal Palace in his normal inside-left position, but the following season he made his last two appearances at outside-left.

WAGSTAFFE, George
1909-10

Born: Bethnal Green, London, 1887
SL apps: 3

FORMERLY WITH SOUTH Weald, Hammers signed this well-built centre-half from Norwich City. Making his debut in a 4-2 reverse at Luton, he went on to make a trio of outings that season. Moved to Doncaster Rovers, then a Midland League club, in the close season of 1910.

WALDEN, George
1911-12

SL apps: 2

GEORGE WAS AN amateur throughout his career who made occasional appearances in West Ham's South Eastern League XI and made two showings in the Southern League versus Watford (March 11, 1914) and Brentford (March 27, 1914). A right-winger with Clapton, he played in the Spotted Dog club's victorious FA Amateur Cup Final-winning team versus Bishop Auckland in 1915.

WALFORD, Steve
1983-87

Born: Highgate, London, 5.1.58
League apps: 115 (2 goals)
Cup apps: 14

A £165,000 BUY from Norwich City, where he had proved his pedigree in over 100 League appearances, at the beginning of 1983/84. Steve settled in well at left-back. Once on the Upton Park staff as a junior, he broke into League football with Spurs in 1975/76, but played only two League games at the Lane. Followed manager Terry Neill to Arsenal in 1977 and gained experience in all defensive and midfield roles while clocking up almost 100 League and Cup outings with the Gunners. A very economical player, he used the ball with telling effect and stunned his team-mates by scoring a spectacular only goal of the match versus Everton at Goodison Park (August 29, 1983) in only his second game for Hammers. He went on to perform consistently well in 129 League and Cup games in the old First Division until losing his place to George Parris midway through the club's most successful season to date – 1985/86. He had loan spells at Huddersfield Town (where he played in Terriers' record 10-1 Second Division defeat versus Manchester City, (November 7, 1987), Gillingham and West Bromwich Albion before being given a free by West Ham. In 1989, Steve joined the Lia Sun club of Hong Kong, but after playing in Turkey he returned to the UK with Wycombe Wanderers. In March 1992, he joined Wealdstone on loan.

Steve Walford

Probably the most successful of all the "Boys of 86", Steve was on the verge of becoming a black cab driver when Wycombe Wanderers manager Martin O'Neill, a former playing colleague at Norwich, invited him to join the Adams Park outfit as youth development officer in 1993. It was the beginning of one of the most successful partnerships in football as the pair guided Wycombe into the Football League and then continued their success at Leicester City by winning the League Cup twice (1997 and 2000) reaching another Final in 1999 and keeping the Foxes in the Premiership against an increasingly unstable financial background. The two managerial wizards then revitalised sleeping Glasgow giants Celtic out of their slumber and from the shadow of Glasgow Rangers to once again dominate the Scottish scene. Not to mention reaching a UEFA Cup Final along the way!

WALKER, Albert
1932-37

Born: Little Lever, Lancashire, 4.2.10
League apps: 162
Cup apps: 12

THIS STOUT-HEARTED DEFENDER began his playing career amid humble beginnings in his native Lancashire during the late-1920s.

Signing amateur forms for Southport after progressing from his school side to Little Lever United in the Bolton and District League, Albert spent just over a year at Haig Avenue before making an exciting move to First Division Bolton Wanderers. Alas, his initial taste of the big-time with Wanderers, already well-served at full-back by Haworth and Finney, was a brief one. Twelve months later, he had exchanged the wide open spaces of Burnden Park for the more cramped confines of Barrow's Holker Street in the old Third Division North. But again it was only a short stay, for with Barrow unable to pay his wages and after scoring 11 times in 72 League games, Albert could hardly refuse when Hammers scout Ned Liddell arranged for him to travel south to join West Ham for a bargain fee in the summer of 1932. Newly-relegated to the Second Division, Hammers struggled at the start of 1932/33, as the previous season's disastrous form began to spill into the next. Changes were called for, and the likable Lancastrian made his debut in a 5-2 victory over Oldham Athletic at Upton Park to begin a memorable partnership with Alf Chalkley. After six seasons' sterling service with Irons (he was an ever-present in the side that finished third in the Second Division in 1934/35), the former engineer returned north in 1938 to sign for Doncaster Rovers, where he made 40 League appearances. But after spending the war years in the National Fire Service, he moved back south to join Colchester United – then the talk of the football world for their daring FA Cup exploits as a Southern League outfit. Albert linked up again with former West Ham and England wing-half, Ted Fenton (then in charge at Layer Road and later to succeed Charlie Paynter as Hammers' manager in 1950). In 1952, Ted duly asked Albert to join him at Upton Park as coach to the Metropolitan League side. Coming up through the ranks as he had done as a player, he took charge in turn of the Eastern Counties League XI, the reserves in the Football Combination and was finally attached to the first team. Albert retired in 1980 after 34 years combined service as player and coach. He passed away in April 1993, aged 83.

WALKER, Charlie   1936-39

Born: Nottingham, Nottinghamshire, date unknown
League apps: 110
Cup apps: 8

RECKONED IN THE club handbook for 1938/39 to be one of the best left-backs ever to don the claret and blue, Charlie was signed from Arsenal in 1936 after finding his first team opportunities limited at Highbury by the outstanding presence of England captain Eddie Hapgood. He had no selection worries at Upton Park, and soon settled down to form a memorable full-back partnership with Charlie Bicknell. Indeed, the pair missed only two matches between them in the last pre-war season of 1938/39, and were on duty at Wembley in June 1940 when West Ham annexed the Football League War Cup. Charlie played in all but one of the ties leading up to that triumph and went on to compete in 38 further war-time fixtures before signing up for the RAF. He returned after an extended tour of duty in the Far East in time to participate in the first peacetime season of 1945/46 in the 22-club Football League South, which comprised pre-war First and Second Division clubs. He played in 21 of that season's fixtures, but after appearing in an exciting 3-3 draw versus Wolves at Molineux, departed to join the club he had left to sign for Arsenal before the conflict, Kent League Margate Town, as secretary-manager – under the proviso that he could play for the Kent club as long as his League rights were retained by West Ham.

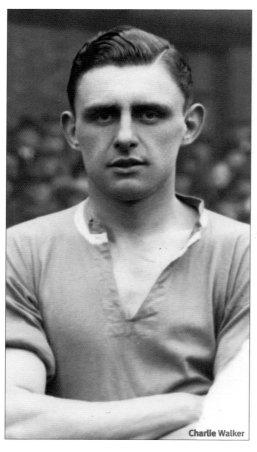

Charlie Walker

WALKER, Dick   1934-53

Born: Hackney, London, 22.7.13
League apps: 292 (2 goals)
Cup apps: 19

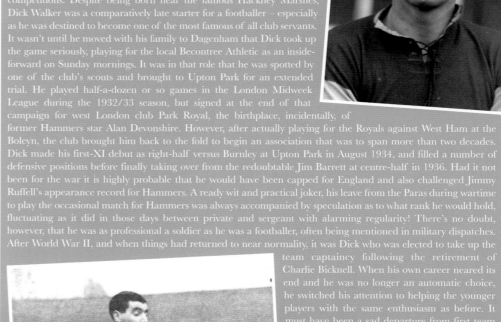

A NAME INDELIBLY written into the history of West Ham United in an association that spanned three decades and almost 600 matches in all competitions. Despite being born near the famous Hackney Marshes, Dick Walker was a comparatively late starter for a footballer – especially as he was destined to become one of the most famous of all club servants. It wasn't until he moved with his family to Dagenham that Dick took up the game seriously, playing for the local Becontree Athletic as an inside-forward on Sunday mornings. It was in that role that he was spotted by one of the club's scouts and brought to Upton Park for an extended trial. He played half-a-dozen or so games in the London Midweek League during the 1932/33 season, but signed at the end of that campaign for west London club Park Royal, the birthplace, incidentally, of former Hammers star Alan Devonshire. However, after actually playing for the Royals against West Ham at the Boleyn, the club brought him back to the fold to begin an association that was to span more than two decades. Dick made his first-XI debut as right-half versus Burnley at Upton Park in August 1934, and filled a number of defensive positions before finally taking over from the redoubtable Jim Barrett at centre-half in 1936. Had it not been for the war it is highly probable that he would have been capped for England and also challenged Jimmy Ruffell's appearance record for Hammers. A ready wit and practical joker, his leave from the Paras during wartime to play the occasional match for Hammers was always accompanied by speculation as to what rank he would hold, fluctuating as it did in those days between private and sergeant with alarming regularity! There's no doubt, however, that he was as professional a soldier as he was a footballer, often being mentioned in military dispatches. After World War II, and when things had returned to near normality, it was Dick who was elected to take up the team captaincy following the retirement of Charlie Bicknell. When his own career neared its end and he was no longer an automatic choice, he switched his attention to helping the younger players with the same enthusiasm as before. It must have been a sad departure from first team football for Dick when he made his last Second Division appearance, before one of the lowest crowds ever to assemble for a League match at Upton Park, versus Plymouth Argyle in February 1953. Hammers lost 1-0, but Dick turned in his usual immaculate performance, earning the respect of every one of the 8,000 in attendance. It was to be another four years before he hung up his boots completely, continuing to chalk up another 200-plus appearances for the reserves and "A" team until the end of 1956/57. He was given a well-deserved testimonial match in October 1957. Dick became coach to Dagenham and later a full-time member of Spurs' scouting staff for many years. His later life was an unhappy one, beset as he was with ill-health, which required him to spend long spells in hospital. His death, in February 1988 at the age of 75, represented a sad demise for a man whose greatest legacy was the help he gave to young players making their way in the game.

Career record

Played	League		FAC		LC		Europe		Total	
	App	Gls	App	Gls	App	Gls	App	Gls	App	Gls
1934-35	3	0	0	0	0	0	0	0	3	0
1935-36	2	0	0	0	0	0	0	0	2	0
1936-37	27	0	2	0	0	0	0	0	29	0
1937-38	32	0	1	0	0	0	0	0	33	0
1938-39	38	0	5	0	0	0	0	0	43	0
1945-46	0	0	4	0	0	0	0	0	4	0
1946-47	34	0	1	0	0	0	0	0	35	0
1947-48	39	1	1	0	0	0	0	0	40	1
1948-49	40	1	1	0	0	0	0	0	41	1
1949-50	39	0	2	0	0	0	0	0	41	0
1950-51	33	0	2	0	0	0	0	0	35	0
1951-52	4	0	0	0	0	0	0	0	4	0
1952-53	1	0	0	0	0	0	0	0	1	0
TOTAL	**292**	**2**	**19**	**0**	**0**	**0**	**0**	**0**	**311**	**2**

WALKER, James · 2004-

Born: Sutton-in-Ashfield, Nottinghamshire, 9.7.73
League apps: 13
Cup apps: 4

AN UNDISCOVERED GEM of a goalkeeper hidden away in the lower divisions for ten years, Jimmy Walker at last took his place on the big stage when picked to play in West Ham's Carling Cup Third Round tie against Chelsea at Stamford Bridge in October 2004. The experienced Walker signed on a free transfer, after 476 senior appearances for little Walsall in divisions Three, Two and One, took his opportunity with both hands and earned himself a permanent place in West Ham folklore by putting in a magnificent performance against the Russian backed millionaires of SW6… and, of course, saving that penalty from Frank Lampard. Although Hammers lost 1-0, after outplaying Chelsea's overrated stars on the night, Jimmy's superb stop made him the toast of east London and a serious contender for Stephen Bywater's number 1 jersey. The display from a man who had to take his own kit home to wash in eight of his 11 eventful seasons at Walsall's tiny Bescot Stadium was even more remarkable given the pampered lives of his overpaid opponents and delivered a breath of fresh air to a game turned stale by money madness. Those old enough to remember were left recalling another legendary Hammers goalkeeper who started his illustrious career at Walsall – world-record £565,000 signing from QPR, Phil Parkes, who a certain James Walker used to study from the terraces of Walsall's former ground Fellows Park as a youngster. Graduating to a YTS contract with Notts County in 1989, Jimmy was actually a Nottingham Forest fan in those days due mostly to the fact that Peter Shilton was between the posts for Cloughie's men, which didn't go down too well at Meadow Lane! And he was soon off to Walsall without playing a single game for County. Walker first came to the notice of Hammers when playing in the Worthington Cup Second Round, first-leg clash at the Bescot Stadium in September 2000 when Jermaine Defoe came off the bench to score his first ever senior goal for West Ham, which enabled Irons to win 1-0. Jim was also on top form in the Upton Park return that ended 1-1 and thought he'd seen the last of Irons for a while. But in January 2001, the Boleyn boys were back in the Black Country for an FA Cup Third Round tie at the Bescot that had all the hallmarks of a giant-killing. It was Hammers who went through again however, with a double from Freddi Kanoute and a Frank Lampard strike securing a 3-2 win, but the scoreline was no reflection on the performance of the Saddlers keeper. In 1994/95, Walsall finished runners-up in Division Three with the third best goals-against record in the division and in 1998/99, another second-place finish earned them promotion to the First Division, but were relegated after only one season. In 2000/01 they were back again thanks to Walker's heroics in the Second Division Play-off Final against Alan Pardew's Reading in a 3-2 victory at the Millennium Stadium, Cardiff. Something of an expert at saving penalties, his save from the 12-yard spot was the major factor in Walsall's shock FA Cup win at Charlton Athletic in 2001/02 and he made another vital save in a penalty shoot-out in the FA Cup at Reading in 2002/03 to once again thwart Pardew's men. Another injury-time save from Gary McAllister of Coventry City led to comparisons with the great Gordon Banks who, coincidentally, was the guest speaker at Jimmy's testimonial dinner to commemorate his ten years at Walsall. It was Jim's shut-out in the First Division clash at Upton Park in March 2004 that probably clinched his dream move to Upton Park as his magnificent display denied the Hammers in a 0-0 stalemate. Perhaps Pards thought it better to have him on your side than against! Although voted Walsall's Player of the Season and winner of the Save of the Season award in 2001/02, Jimmy has only one winners' medal (from the Play-off Final) and no international caps to show for his 12-year career so far, but he does have a lot of clean sheets!

WALKER, Len · 1900-01

SL apps: 1

LEN MADE ONLY one Southern League appearance for West Ham, playing at inside-left in the 2-0 defeat at Bristol Rovers' Eastville enclosure (November 24, 1901). He joined Brentford in 1903.

WALLACE, J · 1901-03

SL apps: 17 (3 goals)

THIS INSIDE-FORWARD MADE his initial Irons appearance in the 3-0 defeat at Reading (November 23, 1901) in the number 8 shirt. It was the only Southern League game he played that season. The following term he switched to the inside-left berth and had a 16-match run in the first team in which he scored three goals, the most notable of which was the only goal of the match versus Spurs at the Memorial Grounds. He joined Luton Town with Billy Barnes during the close season of 1904.

WALLBANKS, Fred · 1935

Born: Wigan, Lancashire, 14.5.08
Cup apps: 1

ONE OF THE six famous footballing brothers who played League soccer in the 1930s and 1940s, Fred had a brief but unusual sojourn at Upton Park, making his solitary first team appearance in an FA Cup tie. An aspiring left-half with his local Chopwell Boys while at school, the versatile Lancastrian converted to the centre-forward position when he went to live in the north-east, and enjoyed success in that role with Spen Black and Whites and later Consett in the North Eastern League. His next port of call was with legendary amateurs Crook Town, with whom he gained further experience as an inside-forward in the Northern League before signing pro forms with Bury. After a spell with Chesterfield, Fred went back to non-League fare with Scarborough, where his 34 goals in one season again attracted League clubs. Bradford City duly signed the young sharpshooter, but converted him to the full-back berth where he made 15 League appearances for City. By now a recognised utility player, he travelled south to join West Ham in December 1934, and made his first appearance in the claret and blue against Brighton reserves at Upton Park two days before Christmas in a 4-0 win. The following month, Ted Fenton was injured in a home Third Round FA Cup tie with Stockport County, and Fred was drafted into the side at right-half for the replay after the Cheshire club's shock 1-1 draw at the Boleyn. Worse was to follow at Edgeley Park, with Hammers being dumped out of the competition in true giant-killing fashion. It was Fred's first and last senior outing and at the end of the season he transferred to Nottingham Forest where he made eight League appearances. One of six footballing brothers: James Wallbanks played for Norwich City, Northampton Town, Wigan Athletic, Millwall and Reading; Horace Wallbanks for Aberdeen and Luton; Harold Wallbanks for Fulham, Southend United and Workington Town; and John Wallbanks for Barnsley, Chester and Bradford City; while an adopted brother, surname Harvey, also played for Barnsley.

WANCHOPE, Paulo · 1999-2000

Born: Heredia, Costa Rica, 31.1.76
League apps: 35 (12 goals)
Cup apps: 10 (3 goals)

Paulo Wanchope

BRILLIANT, BUT ERRATIC is the best way to sum up this unpredictable Costa Rican international striker. From a famous footballing family in his homeland – his father is a former player and his two brothers are stars in Costa Rica – Paulo came to England when Derby County paid CS Herediano £600,000 for his signature in March 1997. He scored 28 times in 83 appearances for the Rams before Harry Redknapp laid out £3.5 million for his services in July 1999, seeing him as a perfect partner for Paulo Di Canio. Making his debut in the Intertoto Semi-final, first-leg against Dutch side Heerenveen at Upton Park the same month, Paulo was unlucky not to mark his bow with a goal, but got the only goal of the return match to open his account. Also on target in the 3-1 win in the second-leg of the Final at Metz and the 3-0 UEFA Cup First Round, first-leg win over NK Osijet, Paulo's signing looked an astute bit of business at that stage. Although no one could criticise his goals record in his one season at Upton Park, he infuriated the Upton Park faithful by missing twice as many goals as he actually scored and the £3.65 million move to Manchester City suited all parties. He got off to a dream start at Maine Road with a hat-trick on his debut against Sunderland. A regular in the Costa Rica team that qualified for the 2002 World Cup Finals in Japan and South Korea, he found himself on the transfer list despite ending 2000/01 as City's leading scorer. That particular squall blew over, however, and the awkward, gangling striker has endured under the managership of Kevin Keegan into the new era at the City of Manchester Stadium and figured strongly in City's battle against relegation in 2003/04, weighing in with four vital goals in the last three games of the season to keep the Blues in the Premiership. At that stage he had scored 29 times in 75 senior appearances in four years at City. In August 2004, Paulo made a £500,000 move to Spanish Primera Liga side Malaga where he had made 25 appearances scoring six times by the end of the 2004/05 season. But in a sad postscript to his stay in Spain, in June 2005 Paulo was begging any English club to save him from his racial hell on the Costa del Sol. A disillusioned Paulo claimed: "I've seen racism in almost every stadium in Spain. It's a shame that referees haven't abandoned a few games because of it. That would have set an example and cut the problem off at the root. What has upset me most have been the insults in my own stadium. It all got too much for Wanchope after a match against Real Betis when the abuse was also aimed at his family. He jumped into the crowd and hit the fan responsible.

WARD, Elliott 2004-

Born: Harrow, Middlesex, 19.1.85
League apps: 14
Cup apps: 1

THIS HIGHLY-RATED YOUNG defender was expected to break into the first team during 2003/04 until a back injury ended his season before it had even started. A close pal of Anton Ferdinand, Elliott trained with his local club Watford as a youngster and first turned out for Hammers' reserve team as a 15-year-old schoolboy in 2000/01. Graduating through the ranks of the West Ham Academy, he signed a new deal in July 2004 after turning in some impressive displays for Hammers' second string over the seasons. He gave a good account of himself in his long-awaited senior debut in the 2-0 Carling Cup victory over Southend United at the Boleyn in August 2004, when he kept his head as the Shrimpers kept Hammers' rearguard under almost constant siege in the second half until a second goal made the game safe. Certainly one to watch for the future. Elliott's brother Darren, who is six years his senior, plays in defence for Hammers' big rivals Millwall and the two came face to face in the hard-fought 1-1 draw between the Irons and Lions at Upton Park in April 2005. Elliott proved his worth further when he forged an impressive partnership with Anton Ferdinand at the heart of Hammers' defence as the club returned to the Premiership.

WARD, Mark 1985-89

Born: Prescot, Lancashire, 10.10.62
League apps: 165 (12 goals)
Cup apps: 38 (2 goals)

A BARGAIN SIGNING from Oldham Athletic in the summer of 1985, Mark cost only £225,000 initially, plus £25,000 more after his 25th appearance. A diminutive, though very competitive, right-winger, the tenacious "Wardie" made his debut at Birmingham City (August 17, 1985) and went on to play a prominent part in Hammers' most successful-ever First Division season. Although never a regular goalscorer himself, his ferocious shooting made him especially dangerous from set pieces, while his crosses created plenty of chances and goals for strikers Frank McAvennie and Tony Cottee. Mark made many of his runs from deep positions and showed a willingness to work back in support of his full-back – usually Ray Stewart. But after McAvennie left for Celtic

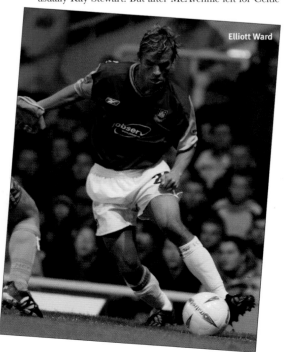

Elliott Ward

Mark Ward

in 1987 and Cottee joined Everton a year later, Ward, too, became unsettled, particularly when West Ham were relegated at the end of 1988/89 and manager John Lyall got the sack. It was not long before Mark – sometimes fiery on the field – clashed with new manager Lou Macari. Their dispute came to a head in October 1989 when Wardie missed the team coach travelling to Aston Villa for a midweek League Cup tie and the PFA was called in to mediate. Although Mark resumed his place in the side for a handful of games, he was determined to get away from Upton Park. His last appearance for the club came at Ipswich Town on Boxing Day, 1990. Four days later, he was back north making his debut for Manchester City after new Maine Road boss Howard Kendall had agreed a £1 million-rated swap deal that took Ian Bishop and Trevor Morley to Upton Park. Ward was only with City for 18 months and 55 League matches, though, before he was on the move again – this time back to his native Merseyside to join Everton for £1.1 million. Ironically, Wardie had been overlooked by the Everton management while on Goodison's books as a schoolboy. He drifted into non-League football with Northwich Victoria, who sold him to Oldham for £10,000 in July 1983. Now Everton were paying 100 times that figure to bring him back to Goodison! Two-and-a-half seasons on and Mark had lost his way at a club in turmoil. Ambitious Birmingham City signed him on loan in March 1994 to help boost their Second Division promotion bid. He played nine League games for Barry Fry, who saw enough in the little scouser to splash out £500,000 on him the following August. An inspirational figure at St Andrews, Fry made the diminutive scouser the lynchpin of his Third Division Championship-winning team of 1994/95 when he also picked up an Auto-Windscreen Shield medal after City had defeated Carlisle United at Wembley. Wardie enjoyed a brief spell

as player-coach with Blues before moving on to Huddersfield Town in March 1998, after scoring eight times in 82 appearances for Brum. Playing a vital role in central midfield for Town, the club's nickname – the Terriers – suited Mark down to the ground as he galvanised the midfield to ensure McAlpine's men avoided the drop into Division Two. After his eight crucial appearances for Town, he then signed for Wigan Athletic on non-contract terms in September 1996 and ended his League career at Springfield Park with another handful of appearances. But, following a short spell with Northwich Victoria, again his urge to continue playing was so great it took him halfway across the world for spells in Hong Kong and Australia and then, after returning home for a stint in Altrincham, who promised him a managerial post that failed to materialise, he was off to colder climes – Iceland – to play for Valur Reykjavik in the Icelandic Premier League. For someone who hadn't even been to London until he joined West Ham, Mark must have felt he was almost as seasoned a traveller as Alan Whicker! Mark then found himself deep in Rugby League territory playing for Unibond Premier League Champions Leigh RMI. He began the 2000/01 season in the Conference as player-coach at Hilton Park but severed his ties in December 2002.

WARD, TG 1901-02

Cup apps: 1

USUALLY A CENTRE-FORWARD, this player made his solitary appearance for Hammers in the infamous 2-1 FA Cup defeat versus Grays at the Memorial Grounds (November 16, 1901), playing on the right-wing. Joined West Ham from Ilford (September 14, 1901).

WATSON, George · 1932-35

Born: Forest Gate, London, 1907
League apps: 33
Cup apps: 5

GEORGE BEGAN HIS football career as a bustling centre-forward with his local junior side, Wycliffe Albion, scoring 69 goals for that club when they won the Forest Gate and District League Championship. Despite this success, it was when George joined his next club, Abbey Langthorne Works team, that he realised his true ambition – to be a goalkeeper! Proving to be as efficient at stopping goals as he had been at scoring them, he came to Hammers as an amateur during the 1929/30 season and, after being sent back to Ilford to gain experience, was signed as a pro. Given the unenviable task of replacing Ted Hufton after the latter had transferred to Watford following Hammers' relegation to Division Two in 1932, George did well in his initial season as a first team regular and was in the side that reached that year's FA Cup Semi-finals. A good swimmer, he won the "White" Cup for the Hammers' club championship three years running. George died in 1991.

WATSON, Lionel · 1905-08

Born: Southport, Lancashire, 1881
SL apps: 76 (26 goals)
Cup apps: 4 (1 goal)

LIONEL JOINED HAMMERS with Harry Hindle and Fred Blackburn from Blackburn Rovers (in the close season of 1905) in an Edwardian version of Billy Bonds' triple transfer swoop of more recent times. Watson had a good scoring record with the Lancastrians prior to moving south, scoring four goals in 14 First Division games in 1904/05 and was Rovers' leading scorer with 16 tallies from 31 starts in 1903/04. He maintained a similar scoring rate at Upton Park after making his debut there versus Swindon Town (September 2, 1905). An infant prodigy who had won three soccer medals before the age of ten, he began his career in earnest with Southport Central. Later moved to Manchester City, but retained his amateur status while with the Mancunians. A great practical joker, he signed pro with Blackburn.

WATSON, Mark · 1996

Born: Birmingham, West Midlands, 28.12.73
League apps: 1

THIS SIX FOOT three inch striker was playing for Sutton United in the Diadora (Isthmian) League Premier Division when he hit a purple patch towards the end of the 1994/95 season. Scoring two goals in four successive matches against Carshalton Athletic (twice), Bromley and Purfleet, the news filtered through football's grapevine and soon the scouts were flocking to Gander Green Lane to check out this new goalscoring sensation whom Sutton had plucked from the obscurity of local soccer. One of them was a West Ham scout and soon the bemused youngster was on a flight to Australia after Hammers had splashed out £50,000 to Sutton and included him in their 1995 Centenary Tour down under – after Mark had finished the season with 16 goals for United and not 60 as has been recorded elsewhere! An instant hit in Oz, Mark must have had to pinch himself as he lined up alongside Don Hutchison to make a scoring debut against Western Australia in a 2-2 draw under the brilliant lights of Perth's Wacca Stadium, less than a month after playing for non-League Sutton. Rubbing shoulders with household names such as Tony Cottee, Martin Allen, John Moncur, Les Sealey, Tim Breacker, Kenny Brown, Matthew Rush, Danny Williamson and Frank Lampard senior, Mark featured in three of the four tour fixtures with an itinerary that took in Perth, Melbourne, Sydney and Brisbane in eight days and gave a good account of himself. But the following season must have been an anti-climax for Mark as he spent almost the entire term in the reserves, where he finished as top scorer by a country mile with 15 goals in 24 Combination matches and three in eight Capital League games. He finally made his Premiership debut in the penultimate game of the season at QPR, who needed to win and hope that other results went their way to stay up. Coming on as sub for the injured John Moncur in the 77th minute he might have just got his 15 minutes of fame with injury-time as Hammers slumped 3-0 and Rangers went down anyway. Having been loaned out in September 1995 to near neighbours Leyton Orient for whom he scored in his solitary sub appearance with a spectacular overhead kick to equalise in a 1-1 draw at Plymouth Argyle, then Cambridge United (four apps, one goal) in October 1995 and finally Shrewsbury Town in February 1996 where he made one Second Division outing. In May 1996, almost a year to the day he'd joined, Mark left Hammers to sign for Second Division Bournemouth as part of the deal that saw Steve Jones go in the opposite direction for his second spell at Upton Park. An ankle injury hindered his progress at Dean Court and his two goals in 17 senior outings for the Cherries were scant reward for some persistent performances despite his injury. Freed during the summer of 1997, he drifted back to the non-League scene and joined Welling United in August 1997. After playing four senior matches for the Kent club he returned to Sutton United in March 1998 and, none the worse for his adventures, found his scoring boots again to bag 11 goals in 35 matches during his second spell for Sutton. In May 2000, he signed for conference side Woking for £8,000 but after only scoring once in 13 games he moved on to Chesham United and then Aldershot Town in March 2001. In August 2002, he rejoined Sutton for a third time in the Ryman Premier and then jumped ship again to join Lewes in November 2003.

WATSON, Victor · 1921-35

Born: Girton, Cambridgeshire, 10.11.1897
League apps: 462 (298 goals)
Cup apps: 43 (28 goals)

OF ALL THE great centre-forwards who have worn the number 9 shirt for West Ham United over the years, Vic Watson stands out as the finest. Spotted playing for Wellingborough Town having earlier turned out for Girton, Cambridge Town, Peterborough and Fletton United and Brotherhood Engineering Works, he was duly signed for a £50 transfer fee in March 1920, to give cover for leading scorer Sydney Puddefoot. Vic later became as big a star as the man he was to replace so dramatically when the latter signed sensationally for Falkirk. Scoring on his first team debut from the inside-left position versus Port Vale at Upton Park in September 1921, he was a former Army sergeant instructor during World War I. Vic even played three games at outside-left over the Christmas holiday fixtures before claiming the centre-forward spot when Syd moved north of the border. From then on, the goals and honours followed thick and fast, with his 22 League goals being largely responsible for Hammers' promotion to the First Division, and five counters in the FA Cup contributing likewise to the club's appearance in the first Wembley Cup Final during that doubly-memorable 1922/23 season. Capped for England versus Wales and Scotland, he had no trouble keeping up his scoring rate in the First Division, notching over 200 goals during nine seasons in the top flight. The highlight of those gala years came on a rain-lashed afternoon in an unforgettable 8-2 thrashing of Leeds United at Upton Park (February 9, 1929), when Vic scored six times against the hapless Yorkshiremen. Inexplicably over-looked by England, still the selectors remained unmoved, but a club record 42 First Division goals the following season saw him back in an England shirt in 1930. The six-goal blast against Leeds apart, Vic scored four goals in a match on three separate occasions, and tallied an astonishing 13 hat-tricks during his

LAMBERT & BUTLER'S CIGARETTES

Hammers' career. Transferred to Southampton in 1935, where he scored on his debut versus Swansea Town (August 31, 1936) and 14 times in 37 League and Cup games. He had one season with Saints before retiring to grow tomatoes and cucumbers in his native Cambridgeshire – after a brief spell as trainer-coach with Cambridge City after the war – no doubt to the accompanied relief of defences throughout football. Described by a contemporary scribe: "Dashing centre-forward whose tactic was to persistently harass the opposing defence." Vic died on August 3, 1988 at the age of 91.

England caps: 1923 vs Wales, Scotland; 1930 vs Scotland, West Germany, Austria (5).

Career record										
	League		FAC		LC		Europe		Total	
Played	App	Gls	App	Gls	App	Gls	App	Gls	App	Gls
1920-21	9	2	0	0	0	0	0	0	9	2
1921-22	37	12	3	1	0	0	0	0	40	13
1922-23	41	22	9	5	0	0	0	0	50	27
1923-24	11	3	0	0	0	0	0	0	11	3
1924-25	41	22	6	1	0	0	0	0	47	23
1925-26	38	20	1	0	0	0	0	0	39	20
1926-27	42	34	3	3	0	0	0	0	45	37
1927-28	33	16	2	0	0	0	0	0	35	16
1928-29	34	29	5	1	0	0	0	0	39	30
1929-30	40	42	4	8	0	0	0	0	44	50
1930-31	18	14	0	0	0	0	0	0	18	14
1931-32	38	23	2	2	0	0	0	0	40	25
1932-33	35	23	6	4	0	0	0	0	41	27
1933-34	30	26	2	3	0	0	0	0	32	29
1934-35	15	10	0	0	0	0	0	0	15	10
TOTAL	**462**	**298**	**43**	**28**	**0**	**0**	**0**	**0**	**505**	**326**

Vic Watson

WATTS, Ernest — 1903-04

SL apps: 25 (1 goal)
Cup apps: 4 (1 goal)

JOINED HAMMERS FROM Reading, but prior to his time with the Berkshire club he served Notts County in the Football League. Made skipper of Irons in the 1903/04 season, the last at the Memorial Grounds and also his with the club, as he joined New Brompton for 1904/05. A sterling centre-half and an ex-soldier, Watts played for the Royal Berkshire Regiment Cricket XI and held an RHS certificate for life-saving. Took part in the North versus South match of 1903.

WAUGH, William T — 1922

Born: Bedlington, Northumberland, date unknown
League apps: 6

PREVIOUSLY WITH AMATEUR side Bedlington United, this right-back made his Second Division baptism for Hammers in a 2-1 defeat versus Leicester City at Filbert Street (January 14, 1922), and went on to complete half-a-dozen League appearances in the claret and blue.

WEALE, Robert — 1925-26

Born: Troedyrhiw, Wales, 9.11.1903
League apps: 3

A FORMER WELSH Schoolboy international, this tricky outside-right filled the place vacated by Bill Edwards in the London Combination side when the latter stepped up to the first team. Signed from his home-town team, Troedyrhiw, Bob was later given a taste of First Division football, but after marking up his debut versus Notts County (October 10, 1925), made only two further League appearances before joining Swindon in June 1927. His form must have improved dramatically at the County Ground, for in December 1928 Southampton paid a club record fee of £1,000 to take him to The Dell. Despite scoring a hat-trick soon after his arrival, he failed to live up to expectations, however, and after a dispute over terms and making 48 League and Cup appearances, scoring ten goals, he decided to move back to his native Wales with Cardiff City in August 1930. But he didn't stay long at Ninian Park,

playing for Boston Town and Guildford City in 1931, before moving on to Newport County in 1932, making 26 League appearances, and the next year he was in North Wales with Wrexham, where he had 23 League outings. He continued life as a soccer journeyman, playing for Glentoran in 1935 and Bath City the following year. His younger brother Tom also played League soccer before the war with Cardiff City and Crewe. Bobby died at Merthyr Tydfil in 1970.

WEARE, Arthur J "Jack" — 1936-38

Born: Newport, Wales, 21.9.12
League apps: 58
Cup apps: 2

A FINE CUSTODIAN whose youngest brother, Len, made 524 League appearances between 1955 and 1969 for Newport County. Jack began his career with Lovells Athletic before signing pro forms for Wolves in the 1933/34 season, from where he joined Hammers. A healthy 35 Second Division outings in 1936/37 were followed by a further 23 in 1937/38. But the following season the agile Welshman lost the first team spot to Herman Conway and Harry Medhurst, who each made 21 appearances in the last pre-war League programme. After the war, Jack played a further 141 games for Bristol Rovers and had a short spell with Barry Town (six Southern League apps) before retiring in May 1951 to let young Len carry on the family trade of football. Jack joined the RAF for his wartime service and reached the rank of sergeant as well as becoming a qualified physical training instructor. During service in the UK he played as a guest for Bournemouth, Bristol Rovers, Hibernian and St Mirren. While with Saints he played in the side that defeated Glasgow Rangers in the Scottish Summer Cup at Hampden Park 1-0, having beaten Greenock Morton in the Semi-final who included Sir Stanley Matthews and Tommy Lawton in their line-up. Later during the conflict he was posted to India where he met up with his former Hammers team-mate, full-back Charlie Walker. The pair were selected to play for England versus Scotland (the selectors didn't realise Jack was a Welshman!) at Irwin Stadium, New Delhi and, after the game, were presented with trophies by Lord Louis Mountbatten, then Vice-Roy of India. In 1952, he emigrated to South Africa and worked for a food processing company in Estcourt Natal. In 1957 he applied for a job in Rhodesia (then Salisbury)

and was a production manager there until he retired in 1987. Jack was living in Harare, Zimbabwe in 1994.

WEBB, George — 1908-12

Born: Poplar, London, 1887
SL apps: 52 (23 goals)
Cup apps: 10 (9 goals)

RIGHTLY REVERED AS the first West Ham United player to win a full international cap for England, centre-forward George was selected for his country versus Scotland and Wales in 1911 – a busy year for the famous amateur in terms of representative honours. "Amateur centre-forward and a power in the land in the pre-1914 era. Fast, had a great shot while hefty physique made him even more redoubtable." So described by a football historian from a later era. Honoured at English Amateur international level in 1910 versus Switzerland, five times the following year versus Wales, Belgium, Germany, Holland and Denmark, and Holland in 1912. He joined team-mate Danny Shea and George Kitchen in representing the Southern League versus Irish League in 1911. Born and bred in the East End of London, he first showed his talent with his Shaftesbury Road School side before graduating to the local Ilford Alliance and then on to the renowned Wanstead club. Attending a pre-season trial match at Upton Park in August 1905 at the age of 18, he impressed sufficiently to be given a run out in the reserves versus Reading, but had to wait another three years for his full Southern League debut, when he scored the only goal of the match against the then powerful Leyton side at Upton Park. The stepson of George Hone, an early administrator of TIW and a director of West Ham, he was well connected in business circles as a toy manufacturer and freemason. He hung on to his jealously-guarded amateur status throughout his career, even after an ill-fated taste of Football League soccer with Manchester City, whom he joined in July 1912 and played for in their two opening games of the season – both 1-0 wins away to Notts County and deadly rivals Manchester United. While out of the side injured, Webb

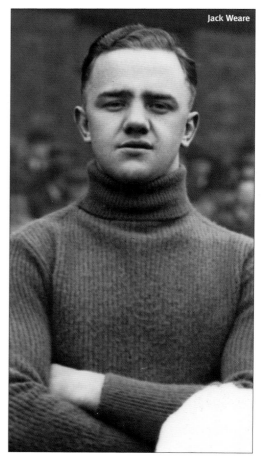

Jack Weare

was horrified to learn that a transfer fee had been paid for his services and promptly "resigned" from City. Not only was there a cash payment, but the deal also led to the first ever meeting between the two sides, a friendly being staged at Upton Park in November 1912. City won 4-2. Despite his reluctance to relinquish his amateur status and a tendency to put his business interests before football, George impressed many of the "old school" by refusing to allow the lure of professionalism to weaken his Corinthian spirit and it came as a great shock to all at the Boleyn Grounds when he died of consumption at the age of 28 in March 1915.

England caps: 1911 vs Wales, Scotland (2).

WEBSTER, Joe — 1914-20

Born: Nottingham, Nottinghamshire, 1883

A GOALKEEPER WHO had served the club from Southern League days, he made two Second Division appearances as deputy for Ted Hufton, versus Huddersfield Town and Port Vale respectively at Upton Park in season 1919/20. He joined Hammers from Watford in 1914 and played in the first 17 fixtures of 1914/15. In 1912/13, Watford were fined by the Southern League authorities for failing to forward Webster's name at the start of the season. He was a colleague of the famous Spurs and England international, Arthur Grimsdell, in his Watford days. Began his career with his local club Ilkeston and had three years' active service in France in World War I when he played for the "Footballers Battalion". Re-joined Hammers after the Armistice but went back to Watford as trainer after one season. He died in Northampton on October 15, 1927.

WEBSTER, Simon — 1993-96

Born: Earl Shilton, Leicestershire, 20.1.64
League apps: 15

THIS COMMANDING CENTRAL defender was still anxiously awaiting his first team debut for Hammers 16 months after joining the club from Charlton Athletic for £525,000. His absence from the senior side had nothing to do with form – only a cruel injury blow. "Webbo" had been with Hammers for just 14 days in July 1993 when he suffered a broken leg in a pre-season training accident involving Julian Dicks. It was the second time in his career that Simon had had to battle back from a broken leg, having suffered a similar injury while with Sheffield United. He had arrived at Bramall Lane in March 1988 from Huddersfield Town, who collected a £35,000 fee, having previously signed him for a mere £15,000 from Tottenham in February 1985. The former White Hart Lane apprentice appeared in three first team matches, making his Spurs debut versus… West Ham at Upton Park (January 1, 1983)! How unlucky Simon would love to be playing Premiership football there again. He did manage a comeback in April 1994, playing 12 Combination matches until the end of the season. But he was still troubled by the leg in pre-season friendlies and his frustration was compounded early in the 1994/95 season when his ankle had to be plastered. While on the long road to recovery, Simon spent his spare time taking A-level human biology with a view to becoming a physiotherapist. After a frustrating and courageous 22-month battle for full fitness, Simon confounded medical opinion by making his long awaited West Ham first team debut as he came on as a late substitute in the 2-0 victory over Blackburn Rovers at Upton Park on April 30th 1995. During his long, lonely fight for fitness, Simon had become the forgotten man of Upton Park, but after a brief loan spell at Oldham Athletic, his recovery seemed complete. A series of stirring performances at the heart of the Latics defence helped to turn around the Boundary Park club's season

Simon Webster

after they'd achieved only one win in 12 matches prior to his arrival. Battling Simon helped steer the Lancastrians away from relegation to the Second Division with four wins being recorded in his first five appearances. It all proved to be a false dawn, however. Even though he got on as a sub for Hammers' last five games of 1994/95 to help them steer clear of relegation as well, most notably with his heroic rearguard display in the final minutes of the last game of the season in the 1-1 draw that deprived United of the Championship, Simon was finally forced to retire from the game in November 1996. But showing tremendous fortitude and after a brief spell playing for St Albans City, Simon went on to qualify as a physiotherapist after years of studying at the University of East London. In August 2000, he was appointed as one of the part-time West Ham United academy physios and was now Simon Webster Bsc (Hons) MCSP SRP and then in 2003 he was promoted to first team physio. It represented a tremendous achievement in overcoming adversity to build a new career in a separate field and let's face it, no one should know more about injuries than Simon.

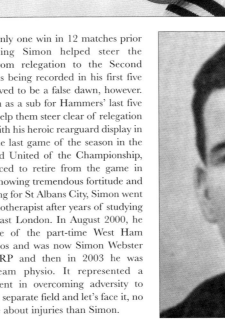

Tony Weldon

WELDON, Anthony 1931-32

Born: Croy, Inverness, Scotland, 12.11.1900
League apps: 20 (3 goals)
Cup apps: 2 (1 goal)

TONY WELDON BEGAN his career with Scottish junior side Kilsyth Rangers before moving on to Airdrieonians for the princely sum of £5 in December 1924. At Broomfield Park he succeeded in turn two full Scottish internationals in Willie Russell and Hughie Gallacher, until a thumping £2,000 transfer to Everton in March 1927. His partnership with fellow compatriot Alex Troup made a major contribution to the Toffeemen's League Championship success the following year. In June 1930, he was on his travels again when a £1,000 fee took him to Hull City, where he made 31 League appearances and scored six goals, before joining West Ham in 1931. He battled bravely on Hammers' behalf in 20 League appearances during the disappointing 1931/32 campaign. In the following close season he moved on again, this time to Welsh side Lovell's Athletic, serving his by now customary year's stint, then transferring to Rochdale in the summer of 1933. The following summer, he joined Dundalk as player-coach, and, late in 1934, was appointed player-manager of Bangor (Northern Ireland), thus becoming one of the few players to play for clubs in England, Northern Ireland, Scotland, the Republic of Ireland and Wales. Incidentally, Tony was the father-in-law of former Leeds United centre-forward Jim Storrie. Tony scored 13 times in 74 League and Cup appearances for Everton.

WHITBREAD, Adrian 1994-95

Born: Epping, Essex, 22.10.71
League apps: 10
Cup apps: 4

ARRIVED FROM NEWLY-RELEGATED Swindon Town in August 1994, just after the start of the season, in part-exchange for the beleaguered Joey Beauchamp, who was relieved to be heading for the Wiltshire club without even making a competitive appearance for Hammers. For this powerful central-defender it was a case of returning to his east London roots. Adrian began his promising career with near-neighbours Leyton Orient, whom he had captained at the age of 21 and made 125 League appearances prior to his £500,000 transfer to Swindon in July 1993. With the veteran Alvin Martin and Steve Potts already occupying the central defensive positions at West Ham, Adrian started the 1994/95 term on the subs bench. He got on for the last 21 minutes of the opening home game versus Leeds United (August 20, 1994) and made his first full appearance in the 2-0 League Cup, Second Round second-leg, win over Walsall at Upton Park (October 5, 1994), collecting the sponsor's Man of the Match award in the process. With an abundance of central defenders at the Boleyn, Adrian found first team chances few and far between and following a successful loan spell at Portsmouth commencing in November 1995, Adrian eventually joined the Fratton Park club in October 1996 for a fee of £250,000. In four years on the south coast the commanding central defender made 145 senior appearances and scored three goals for Pompey before being loaned to Luton Town (13 apps) and then Reading who he finally signed for in February 2001. He made 37 first team appearances at the Madejski Stadium before going on loan to Exeter City in January 2003, where he made a further seven League appearances. Now assisting Martin Allen at Brentford.

WHITCHURCH, Charlie 1944-46

Born: Grays, Essex, 29.10.20

Adrian Whitbread

CHARLES JOINED HAMMERS from Portsmouth as an amateur left-winger in the 1944/45 season, after beginning his career with Ford Sports before World War II and making guest appearances for Charlton and Southend United during the conflict, signing pro the following summer. Although he had left Upton Park for Spurs before full League football was resumed in 1946/47, he was a regular member of the side that competed in the Football League South tournament during the first post-war season of 1945/46. After scoring twice in eight appearances for Tottenham, the former English Schoolboy international moved on to Southend United, where he scored a further five times in 17 outings for the Shrimpers before bowing out of League football in 1948. Employed at the Ford Motor Company in Dagenham, he continued to play for their works team until he emigrated to Canada in 1951. Charlie passed away in July 1977 in Michigan, USA, where he was involved in rocket research with General Motors.

WHITEMAN, Robert 1909-15

SL apps: 136 (3 goals)
Cup apps: 10

IN COMMON WITH George Wagstaffe, Bob also served South Weald and Norwich City, and was by far the most successful of several signings made by Hammers from the Norfolk club. Counting his ten FA Cup outings and four appearances in the first wartime season, he made exactly 150 appearances for the club. A fine total for the times, and nearly all from the right-half berth. Described as "a consistent performer, a good interceptor with no frills". Played locally for Manor Park Albion before joining South Weald.

WHITTON, Steve 1983-86

Born: Plaistow, London, 4.12.60
League apps: 39 (6 goals)
Cup apps: 7 (2 goals)

ALTHOUGH HE WAS born in the East End of London and played for Newham Boys, Steve decided he would have a better chance of advancement with Coventry City than a London club, signing apprentice for the Midlanders in April 1977. Signed as full pro the following year, he duly made his First Division debut versus Spurs in 1979. A flankman of great power and pace, he really came into his own in 1982/83, and was the Highfield Road club's top scorer with 12 goals in 38 League matches. He signed for Hammers for £175,000 in the summer of 1983, making his first team bow in the initial fixture versus Birmingham City. Steve had a period on loan to Birmingham during the 1985/86 season and joined the Blues for £60,000 in August 1986, playing 95 League games and scoring 28 goals before moving on to Sheffield Wednesday in March 1989 for £275,000, where he played 32 times, scoring four goals. In January 1991, he teamed up with former manager and coach John Lyall, and Mick McGiven, at Ipswich Town in a £150,000 deal. Steve made 130 League appearances for Town and scored 23 goals before joining Colchester United in March 1994 for £10,000. Steve was destined to become something of an institution at Layer Road after the U's fans forgave him for missing penalties in the first two matches! Revelling in the role of player-coach with the little Essex club, Steve soon made up for those misses with some long-range specials

Steve Whitton

STEVE WHITTON
WEST HAM UNITED

and a last-gasp goal at Cambridge United that put the U's into the Third Division Play-offs at Wembley in May 1998 and promotion to Division Two. Stepping up to take over as manager in 1999, after scoring 24 goals in 138 senior appearances, Steve worked minor miracles keeping the garrison town club in the Second Division while on a shoestring budget and it must have come as a big shock when he was relieved of his post.

WILDMAN, William 1906-08

Born: Liverpool, Merseyside, 1883
SL apps: 39
Cup apps: 2

BILL PLAYED TWO seasons with his local Queens Road team before joining Everton. He had four seasons at Goodison Park but made only two League appearances during that time before signing for Hammers in 1906. Missed just one match in his first season at Boleyn Castle playing at right-back, but an unfortunate injury sustained in the second match of the 1907/08 season versus Spurs effectively ended his career in the claret and blue.

WILLIAMS, A   1895-97 TIW

SIGNED FROM DARTFORD, he was equally at home playing at full-back or centre-half and appeared in the club's first ever FA Cup tie against Chatham.

WILLIAMS, Gavin   2005

Born: Pontypridd, Wales, 20.6.80
League apps: 10 (1 goal)

WIDE-MIDFIELDER GAVIN HAD served two of the most famous "giant-killing" clubs in the game in Hereford United and Yeovil Town before his record-breaking £250,000 move from the Football League new boys to Hammers in December 2004. After serving a tough two-year YTS apprenticeship with Hereford, the young Welshman was offered a pro contract with the newly-relegated-to-the-Conference Bulls in the summer of 1998, having already made his first team debut in an FA Cup Second Round replay against Colchester in December 1997, which the Edgar St outfit won after a penalty shoot-out. He went on to score 31 goals in 134 appearances for United before an acrimonious move to Conference rivals Yeovil in the close season of 2002. The transfer was a red rag to the Bulls, but turned out to be the right one for the ambitious youngster as he was almost an ever-present as the Glovers ran away with the Conference title to claim a Football League place for the first time in their 110-year history. Having won every Player of the Year award and scoring 21 times in his 104 outings for the famous Huish side, Gavin jumped at the chance of stepping up to the Championship with Hammers and made an impressive debut in the 3-2 victory over Nottingham Forest on Boxing Day 2004 at Upton Park, after coming on as a 77th-minute sub for Luke Chadwick. Called up for the full Welsh International squad to face Hungary in February 2005, an injury prevented him from any involvement in the 2-0 friendly win over the Magyars at the Millennium Stadium, but he later joined team-mates Carl Fletcher, James Collins and Danny Gabbidon in the Welsh side.

WILLIAMS, Harry   1951-52

Born: Salford, Lancashire, 24.2.29
League apps: 5 (1 goal)

DISCOVERED BY MANCHESTER United during an England Youth trial game, he spent a little under a year at Old Trafford without playing in the League side. Harry left them to join Cheshire League Witton Albion, where his exploits aroused the interest of West Ham. After scoring heavily for the "A" team and Combination side, the young inside-forward was drafted into the first XI for his debut versus Rotherham at Millmoor in October 1951. He made another four appearances that season and scored a goal versus Southampton, that being the sum total of his Second Division outings for Hammers. Transferred to Bury in 1953, and from there to Swindon Town the following year.

WILLIAMS, Rod   1937-38

Born: Newport, Wales, 2.12.1909
League apps: 9 (5 goals)
Cup apps: 1

THIS ROBUST CENTRE-FORWARD cracked five goals in nine Second Division appearances for West Ham in the 1937/38 season underlining the availability of goalscorers in those days. Previously with Reading, he made his initial appearance in Hammers' colours in a 0-0 draw with Coventry (November 13, 1937) at the Boleyn after signing for £4,000, and proved an able stand-in for

Sam Small. In the summer of 1938, he transferred to near-neighbours Clapton Orient, and was O's top scorer with 17 goals in 1938/39. Before joining Reading, Roderick, as he was christened, played for Sutton United, Epsom Town, Uxbridge Town (with whom he represented the Athenian League), Crystal Palace (as an amateur), Norwich City (106 goals for reserves) and Exeter City, where he scored 36 goals in 1936/37.

WILLIAMS, William   1922-26

Born: Leytonstone, London, 1905
League apps: 34 (7 goals)
Cup apps: 9 (1 goal)

BILLY BECAME THE youngest-ever full professional when he signed for Hammers in 1921, at the age of 15, from Fairbairn House Boys' Club. A former England Boys star, he made his Hammers debut versus Blackpool at Bloomfield Road and scored in a 3-1 defeat (May 6, 1922) – his only Second Division appearance in the claret and blue. In March 1925, he made another entry into the record books as a member of the party that embarked on a trip to Australia. Returning home in September after several Test matches down under, the experiment brought the following comment from the club's 1925/26 handbook: "Has had a unique experience for so young a player, having had a glorious time in Australia since April last, where he has been finding the net frequently. We hope that continuous football has not affected his efficiency." The writer's fears may not have been altogether groundless, as Bill only made a further 14 first team outings before his transfer to Chelsea in 1927. After one year at Stamford Bridge, he became a free agent in amateur football and, among others, served Dartford, Guildford and Dagenham. Eventually retiring at the age of 40, he went into the haulage business and later ran a tobacconist and confectioner's shop in Ilford. Billy eventually retired to live at Frinton-on-sea and passed away there on March 8, 1994. The club was informed of his death by his grand-daughter, Miss Lisa Gordon, of Harold Hill, who showed club historian John Helliar a fascinating collection of pictures depicting her grandfather's career. The oldest photo was taken in 1919 and recorded the impressive catalogue of success by Billy's school football team, Central Park School of East Ham, which held the Dewar Shield – the trophy presented to the winners of the London Schools' Championship. In 1917/18 and 1918/19 they also won the Robert Cook Cup, which was competed for by Essex Schools. During this period they had also won the Bethell Shield on four occasions, in addition to three times winning the White Cup. So Billy came to West Ham as something of a schoolboy prodigy.

WILLIAMSON, Danny   1994-97

Born: West Ham, London, 5.12.73
League apps: 51 (5 goals)
Cup apps: 7

THE FIRST YOUTH product at Upton Park to score on his home debut since Tony Cottee (1983) when he netted the first versus Southampton (May 7, 1994) in the final game of the 1993/94 season. This promising midfielder had made his first team bow a week earlier, as sub in a 2-0 victory at Arsenal, and also impressed in a midweek goalless draw at Queens Park Rangers. A schoolboy star for Newham and Essex, Danny gained experience earlier in the 1993/94 season during a 13-match loan spell with Third Division Doncaster Rovers, making his League debut versus Lincoln City (October 9, 1993). Having realised his ambition of playing for the team he supported as a boy when he lived but a hefty goal-kick's distance from Upton Park, it was an injury to John Moncur that finally won him a place in his favoured position of central midfield. Danny, one of the few home-grown talents at cosmopolitan Green Street, responded with some

exhilarating performances that even brought claims for international recognition from some quarters. Recalled into the side to play Bolton at Burnden Park after being dropped earlier in the 1995/96 season, he capped a marvellous display with a wonderful solo goal towards a 3-0 away win. Having signed a contract that tied him to West Ham until 2000, big things were expected from the exciting midfielder in 1996/97 but his season was decimated by injuries, which sidelined him for three quarters of the campaign. There was shock and disbelief when Everton risked a £2 million fee to take him to Goodison Park in the summer of 1997, when it was clear the player was injury prone. In the event, Danny only made 15 League appearances on Merseyside in 1997/98 and never played another first team game. He was forced to retire in 2000 at the criminally early age of 27. As they say, a footballer's career can be short.

WILKINSON, F   1905-06

SL apps: 14 (2 goals)
Cup apps: 1

A SLIGHTLY-BUILT OUTSIDE-LEFT, "Snowball", as he was affectionately known by early-century Hammers fans, was a steal from Second Division Manchester United who had put a £150 fee on his head but had to let him go to West Ham as they, as a Southern League club, were not bound by Football League rules. He began his football life in the puritanical surrounds of St John's Sunday School team, which won the Walter Spencer Challenge Cup and thus Wilkinson became the owner of his first football medal. In 1902, he signed for Manchester League club Newton Heath as an amateur and won a runners-up medal with them. He signed pro for Manchester United but was allowed to join Hull City who were at that time playing friendly matches, so again no fee was due. But when Hull joined the Second Division of the League they could not afford the £150 United wanted. So the former pattern maker at an iron foundry fittingly joined the Irons. Snowball soon saw familiar faces at the Boleyn Ground, including the famous Fred Blackburn who was his wing partner and an old adversary in a Lancashire Cup Final. A former sprint champion, his speed served him well during his 15 Southern League appearances during 1905/06.

WILSON, Arthur   1932-34

Born: Newcastle-upon-Tyne, Tyne & Wear, 6.10.08
League apps: 29 (14 goals)
Cup apps: 6 (2 goals)

YET ANOTHER MEMBER of the considerable north-east England enclave that assembled in increasing numbers between the wars at Upton Park. A Geordie by birth, Arthur was a talented inside-forward who liked a crack at goal. His early honours included selection for both Newcastle and Northumberland Boys, and he was with Newcastle United Swifts before being snapped up by his local club – Scotswood – when he left school. He then made the long trip south to sign pro forms for Southampton, where his fine form and 12 goals from the wing-half and inside-forward berths in 65 League and Cup appearances attracted the attention of West Ham's management and an invitation to Upton Park for a fee of £500. Making his initial Irons appearance versus Swansea Town at the Vetch Field on the opening day of the 1932/33 League campaign, he went on to score a creditable 15 goals in 33 League and Cup games that season. Arthur later joined Chester and in November 1937 he joined Wolverhampton Wanderers where he stayed until January 1939 when he transferred to Torquay United. A member of the side that reached the 1933 FA Cup Semi-final versus Everton at Molineux, it was Arthur's vital goals against Spurs and Manchester United after the 2-1 Cup exit to the Blues that saved

Hammers from relegation to the Third Division South by just one point! A situation that makes the team's recent trials and tribulations seem a lot less serious!

WILSON, Ron — 1946-47

Born: Sale, Cheshire, 10.9.24
League apps: 3

A USEFUL PLAYER who could fill any of the defensive duties, but was most at home at wing-half. He made his debut in the troubled 1946/47 season, which saw the resumption of normal League matches for the first time since 1938/39 and Hammers fighting off the threat of relegation to the Third Division South. Although he was retained for the following season, Ron did not appear for the First XI again. Afterwards coached Hornchurch and Upminster, Aveley and Barking. A keen photographer, Ron was the club's unofficial "snapper" during his time at Upton Park. Along with the previous entry, Ron was one of the club's oldest surviving players in recent years.

WINTERBURN, Nigel — 2000-03

Born: Nuneaton, Warwickshire, 11.12.63
League apps: 82 (1 goal)
Cup apps: 12

WITHOUT DOUBT ONE of the finest defenders of recent times, England international left-back Nigel arrived at Upton Park for a bargain £250,000 from Arsenal in June 2000 with the biggest haul of honours of any player in the club's 105-year history to that date. Having won a medal or reached a major Final in all except three of his 13 success-laden seasons at Highbury, it would have seemed he had nothing left to achieve in the game and that his time at Upton Park might serve as a precursor to his retirement. But Winterburn soon proved the sceptics wrong as he went about his duties with all the enthusiasm of a young professional, but with the benefit of 17 years of top-level experience behind him. The result was an immediate tightening of a previously porous defence and an improvement in professional discipline that bore all the hallmarks of more than a decade of success at Highbury. Making his Hammers bow in the season's opening fixture against Chelsea at Stamford Bridge, Nigel went on to play in 33 of the 38 League matches and even had the audacity to score the only goal of the game against Leeds at Elland Road! Invaluable in the run to the FA Cup Sixth Round, it was obvious that "Iron Man" Nige had a season in him yet – and then some! Thinking that 2001/02 would be his last season, manager Glenn Roeder drafted in £900,000 Slovakian international Vladimir Labant as his long-term replacement, but it soon became clear in the 1-1 draw at Spurs that the costly Slovakian wasn't up to the task and found himself being substituted by the man he was meant to replace! The situation led to Nigel volunteering to play on for another season at reduced pay to resolve the problem. With 31 League appearances in 2001/02, the tough-as-teak defender would probably have taken his Hammers appearances to over the 100 mark in all competitions if it hadn't been for sustaining a broken wrist in February 2002/03, which meant he missed the closing games of the season and Irons' inexorable slide into the Nationwide. But what a player! His success at Highbury, where he won a Premiership medal in 1997/98, Division One Championship medals in 1988/89 and 1990/91, FA Cup winners' medals in 1993 and 1998, League Cup winners' medal in 1993 and a European Cup Winners' Cup medal in 1994 and scored 12 times in 590 matches, was in direct contrast to his early career when he was shown the door by both Birmingham City and Oxford United before making the grade with Wimbledon after suffering the indignity of a free transfer from Oxford. After scoring eight goals in 182 appearances for Dons between 1983 and 1987,

Arsenal boss George Graham had seen enough to take him to Highbury for £407,000 as an early piece of the Gunners jigsaw that was completed two years later when the First Division Championship came to Highbury for the first time in 18 years.

WINTERHALDER, Arthur — 1906-07

Born: Oxford, Oxfordshire, 1885
SL apps: 10 (5 goals)
Cup apps: 2 (1 goal)

STRANGE AS IT may seem, Arthur was no relation to his namesake Herbert Winterhalder and the fact that these two players with such unusual names played on the same stage within a year of each other seems to be just another of the amazing coincidences thrown up in the history of the game. A pupil of Oddessa Road School who represented West Ham Schools XI in February, 1899, Arthur made a sensational Southern League debut on the left wing when he scored a hat-trick versus Spurs at the Boleyn (December 29, 1907) and almost emulated the feat of Billy Grassam six years earlier who went one better and scored four on his debut versus Gravesend (September 1, 1900). Even so, with Ken Tucker (versus Chesterfield, October 4, 1947) and Tudor Martin (versus Newcastle, September 9, 1936), Arthur goes down in Hammers' history as one of only three players to score that dream of all forwards – a debut hat-trick. Arthur also signed off his West Ham career with a goal, in a 4-1 Upton Park victory over Southern League Champions Fulham on the last day of the season 1906/07. So ended his short, but sensational, sojourn as an Iron. Footnote: Don Travis scored four goals in his debut for Hammers in a 7-0 League South victory versus Plymouth Argyle at bomb-damaged Upton Park (February 16, 1946). Terry Woodgate also hit a seven-minute hat-trick in the same match, but these feats are not recognised in official football League records due to the regionalised, temporary nature of the competition.

WINTERHALDER, Herbert — 1905-06

Born: Kettering, Northamptonshire, 1880
SL apps: 12

GRAMMAR SCHOOL EDUCATED Herbert preceded his unrelated namesake to the Boleyn Grounds by some 15 months, but the two wingers' West Ham careers overlapped into the same season in 1906/07, although they never appeared in the same team. A fact that saved contemporary football reporters from a deal of potential confusion! After making a name with his school side, young Herbert signed for Kettering Athletic in 1895, a junior team competing in the Kettering Combination, and later amateur forms for Kettering Town, with whom he won a Midland League Championship medal during his three-season stay with the Poppies – his home-town club. His form there attracted the attention of Sheffield United for whom he signed and stepped out in 13 First Division matches. At Bramall Lane, Herbert was a team-mate of Fred Milnes, the famous amateur full-back who also served Hammers briefly. Herbert made the long journey to Plymouth to assist the Argyle in their first season of 1903/04. In 1904, he joined the ill-fated Wellingborough Town who folded in 1904/05 after suffering from lack of funds. Our subject succinctly summed up his season there to "Rambler" of the *East Ham Echo* in August 1905: "The least said about Wellingborough, the better. It was a disastrous year right through, financially and otherwise." Making his Southern League bow in a 2-1 home defeat to Luton Town (September 16, 1905), Herbert went on to make ten appearances that season playing at centre-forward and on both wings, but had to wait until the next season and his last match in the claret and blue to score his only goal for the club – in a 1-1 draw at the Crystal

Palace (September 29, 1905) during Glaziers' second season at the famous old venue. Herbert's father was a jeweller from the Black Forest area of Germany and when he retired from playing Herbert ran a photographic and art shop in Kettering for some 40 years until his death in September 1946.

WOOD, Edward John "Jackie" — 1937-49

Born: West Ham, London, 23.10.19
League apps: 58 (13 goals)
Cup apps: 3 (2 goals)

AN OUTSTANDING OUTSIDE-LEFT with an eye for scoring goals, this colourful character was also a great practical joker who, along with Dick Walker and "Big Jim" Barrett, symbolised the happy spirit that existed at the Boleyn in the late 1940s. Born and bred in West Ham, Jack was connected with the club as a youngster, but as there was no youth policy in those days, he went into amateur soccer with Leytonstone – winning an England cap in the process. Having signed pro in 1937, Jack's career, like so many other players of his generation, was badly disrupted by World War II when called up with the Essex Regiment Territorials in 1939. He returned for the 1945/46 season, and made a fair total of first team appearances in the immediate post-war years to add to the ten already gained before hostilities, although by this time he had converted to inside-forward. In October 1949, he transferred to Leyton Orient, where he made a further ten League appearances.

WOOD, Jimmy — 1930-35

Born: Royton, Lancashire, date unknown
League apps: 63 (13 goals)
Cup apps: 1

THIS SPEEDY OUTSIDE-RIGHT gave six seasons of loyal service to West Ham without ever being able to lay claim to a regular First XI place. After learning the basics of the game with Crompton Albion in the Oldham Amateur League, he signed pro forms for Hyde. He left Hyde for a season and went to Bournemouth, but returned to his first pro club before transferring to Hammers in July 1929. The highlight of his career with West Ham must have been his inclusion in the team that did battle with Everton in the FA Cup Semi-final at Molineux in 1932/33. Drafted into the team as a replacement for the injured Tommy Yews, he turned in a fine display as Irons went down 2-1 and unluckily missed out on Wembley. In June 1935, Jim transferred to Crystal Palace, and scored four goals in ten matches.

WOODARDS, Dan — 1907-21

Born: East Ham, London, 18.11.1886
SL apps: 109 (3 goals)
Cup apps: 14

A PRODUCT OF local junior football, Dan was an outstanding wing-half at the height of his career, winning the nicknames of "Dapper Dan" and "Beau Brummell", because of his well-groomed appearance. He assisted Plashet Lane School when they won the East Ham Shield and in 1904 was playing for East Ham Excelsior before moving on to St Ethelburgas. He first joined West Ham in 1905 but made no first team appearance, waiting until March 23, 1907 before making his Southern League debut versus Brighton. He played for Hastings in 1908/09 but returned to Upton Park in 1910. Still on the staff when Hammers joined the League in 1919, having played in 180 games including wartime, he was still playing for and coaching the reserves. In later years, the Boleyn Ground bore testimony to his fastidious nature when he was appointed club groundsman. The Luftwaffe rearranged his

WOODGATE, John Terence — 1939-53

Born: East Ham, London, 11.12.19
League apps: 259 (48 goals)
Cup apps: 16 (4 goals)

ANOTHER LOCAL PRODUCT, this flying forward was equally at home on either wing. Actually making his Second Division debut before the war versus Bradford Park Avenue on Good Friday 1939, Terry won a regular place in the first team after the conflict, having served for more than six years in World War II with the Essex Regiment and Royal Artillery. The experience he had gained guesting for many clubs during the wartime period kept him in good stead for the Second Division campaigns that followed. But first he caused a sensation by scoring a seven-minute hat-trick versus Plymouth Argyle in a Football League South fixture at Upton Park (February 16, 1946) and thus emulated Syd Puddefoot's feat of World War I. He became a regular in Hammers' post-war Second Division side and was ever-present in 1950/51. Able to perform on either wing with equal efficiency, he was an asset not least for his welcome input of goals. However, the emergence of Harry Hooper and Malcolm Musgrove as regular first-team contenders prompted his transfer to Peterborough United in March 1954. After hanging up his boots he took over a public house in March, Cambridgeshire. Sadly, Terry passed away at the age of 62, in April 1982.

Terry Woodgate

Career record

	League		FAC		LC		Europe		Total	
Played	App	Gls	App	Gls	App	Gls	App	Gls	App	Gls
1938-39	4	0	0	0	0	0	0	0	4	0
1945-46	0	0	4	0	0	0	0	0	4	0
1946-47	41	5	1	1	0	0	0	0	42	6
1947-48	38	7	2	0	0	0	0	0	40	7
1948-49	38	9	1	0	0	0	0	0	39	9
1949-50	29	4	2	2	0	0	0	0	31	6
1950-51	42	12	2	0	0	0	0	0	44	12
1951-52	38	8	3	1	0	0	0	0	41	9
1952-53	29	3	1	0	0	0	0	0	30	3
TOTAL	**259**	**48**	**16**	**4**	**0**	**0**	**0**	**0**	**275**	**52**

handiwork in August 1944, however, when a VI landed on the south-west corner of his beloved Boleyn pitch. Dan was the only person at the ground when the rocket exploded and caused a huge crater on the field. He was said to have been badly shaken by the blast and indignant at the damage done to his finely manicured playing surface. Hammers had to play all their matches away from home while emergency repairs were done, but amazingly, won nine consecutive matches, then lost 1-0 to Spurs on their return to Upton Park in December – despite Dan's efforts to restore the coveted greensward to its former glory.

WOODBURN, John — 1919-20

Born: Darvel, Scotland, date unknown
League apps: 4

A RIGHT OR centre-half signed from Hurlford, he made his Second Division bow in a 1-0 victory over Birmingham at St Andrews on October 25, 1919. Completed a quartet of League appearances that season before being transferred to Peterborough and Fletton United.

WOODLEY, Derek — 1959-62

Born: Isleworth, Middlesex, 2.3.42
League apps: 12 (3 goals)
Cup apps: 1

AN EXTREMELY FAST flankman who had won England Schools honours (he holds the record for scoring the fastest goal ever recorded at the old Wembley Stadium versus Wales in 1956/57) before joining Hammers. While still on the groundstaff he added six England Youth caps and an FA Youth Cup runners-up medal to his earlier triumphs and looked set for a big future. Two goals on his League debut in October 1959 versus Luton Town did little to dispel that view, and it was something of a surprise when he eventually left Upton Park. Former Hammers' manager Ted Fenton swooped on the eve of the 1962/63 season to take Derek and his colleague Mick Beesley to Southend in a dual transfer. Derek left the Shrimpers (after scoring 24 times in 181 League and Cup games) for Charlton (three apps) in 1967, only to return to Roots Hall four months later to make another nine appearances. He finally finished his League career at Gillingham in 1970 where he scored nine times in exactly 100 appearances. In July 1971 he signed for Folkestone Town.

WOOLER, Alan — 1973-75

Born: Poole, Dorset, 17.8.53
League apps: 4
Cup apps: 1

SIGNED BY HAMMERS from Reading in August 1973 after beginning his career with Southern League Weymouth, Alan was given the unenviable task of taking over Bobby Moore's number 6 shirt at Upton Park. After a spell with Boston Minutemen in the North American Soccer League in 1974, he moved to Aldershot and made over 200 League appearances for the Hampshire club.

Derek Woodley

WOOSNAM, Phil — 1958-62

Born: Caersws, Montgomeryshire, Wales, 22.12.32
League apps: 138 (26 goals)
Cup apps: 15 (3 goals)

THE ORIGINAL "WELSH WIZARD", Phil was a footballing genius who almost single-handedly controlled Hammers' destiny from the inside-right position in the immediate post-promotion years, and was the first Hammer to play for the principality since Wilf James in 1932. A relatively late starter, he did have one game for Manchester City as far back as 1952, after moving to Maine Road for trials while still retaining his amateur status. Woosie's talents were evident at an early age and he graduated from Montgomeryshire Schoolboys through to Wales Schoolboys to Youth international honours at the time he won a scholarship to Bangor University reading physics. While at college, he won the first of eight amateur caps versus England at Bangor in 1951. He also captained the varsity side to the Welsh Universities' Championship. Outside of campus he played his early soccer with Wrexham, Peritus, Manchester City, amateur Sutton United and Middlesex Wanderers. Graduating with a BSc degree, Woosnam joined the Royal Artillery as a second lieutenant to complete his national service, during which time he played for the Army XI with Maurice Setters (WBA) and Eddie Colman and Duncan Edwards (Manchester United). Phil's career really took off at Leyton Orient although he continued to teach at Leyton County High School. It cost Hammers a then club record fee of £30,000 to persuade O's to part with their star performer in November 1958, and he made his debut versus Arsenal at Upton Park the same month. Phil relinquished his teaching career just before his move to Hammers, and although he had signed pro forms with O's, it wasn't until he had joined West Ham at the age of 26 that he was free to concentrate on the game on a full-time basis. Few players can have crammed so much into their lives at such an early age, although he was relatively old to be embarking on a first-class soccer career. He was chosen for Wales on 15 occasions during his four years at the Boleyn, having already won one cap while at Brisbane Road and also represented the Football League. The arrival of Johnny Byrne in March 1962 seemed to hasten Phil's departure, which to many appeared premature, the pair's link-up in Hammers' attack having become the highlight of the London scene by the time of his move to Aston Villa. He gained another two caps and scored 23 goals in 111 League matches while with Villa. In 1966, Phil emigrated to the States to take up the post of player-coach to Atlanta Chiefs, who won the North American Soccer League two years later under his guidance. He was then appointed commissioner of the League and since then probably did more to further the game in the States than any other single person. The staging of the 1994 World Cup Finals in the USA has seen much of Phil's groundwork come to fruition and in his role as a soccer marketing consultant based in Atlanta, he must have been one of the proudest spectators at the tournament. The ironic thing is that Woosie nearly didn't go to the USA at all, as he explained at the World Cup: "I wanted to continue my playing career in Division One and one week after agreeing to join Atlanta Chiefs, Tommy Docherty asked me to join him at Chelsea. I hadn't signed anything with Atlanta, but I had given them my word and I stuck to it. But more than once I moaned 'Why didn't you come in for me earlier' at Chelsea." American soccer chiefs will be thanking their lucky stars and stripes that the Blues delayed.

Wales caps: 1958 vs England; 1959 vs England, Scotland; 1960 vs Northern Ireland, Republic of Ireland, Scotland, England; 1961 vs Northern Ireland, Spain, Hungary, England, Scotland; 1962 vs Northern Ireland, Brazil (14).

PHIL WOOSNAM

WRAGG, Doug — 1956-59

Born: Nottingham, Nottinghamshire, 12.9.34
League apps: 16

THIS POPULAR WINGER was spotted by Hammers playing in the "Star" Youth Final at Wembley in 1953, and was duly signed pro in June the same year. Doug was prominent in schools football and played for Nottingham and England Boys. He was also a fair boxer, being a former Hyson Green and England representative in his native Nottinghamshire. His career benefited enormously when he was demobbed from the

Army in 1955 and able to return to full-time training. After proving himself a capable first XI deputy and nearly seven years with Hammers, Doug was transferred back to his home county via Mansfield Town in March 1960. In 1960/61, he was Stags' leading scorer with 11 goals in 33 games and had hit two in 13 League appearances in 1959/60. He later moved on to Rochdale and then Chesterfield, before going out of the League with Grantham. Nicknamed "Oily" by the fans, Doug was in the Fourth Division Rochdale team that battled through to the Final of the 1962 League Cup and played in the first match of the two-leg Final versus Norwich City at Spotland, which the East Anglians won 3-0 and the Final 4-0 on aggregate. Doug enjoyed his most consistent spell at Spotland and scored 14 times in 103 League appearances for Dale. His time at Chesterfield was touched by tragedy when he was a passenger in the car crash that claimed the life of his colleague Ralph Hunt. Doug scored four times in 17 League appearances at Saltergate and also had two outings in the League Cup. Doug was employed by a subsidiary of Raleigh, making car seat covers at Bilborough, Nottinghamshire.

WRIGHT, George — 1951-58

Born: Ramsgate, Kent, 19.3.36
League apps: 161
Cup apps: 9

AN EXCELLENT FULL-BACK signed from Southern League Margate, after beginning his career with Ramsgate Athletic and then Thanet United, who gave good return for a small transfer fee. His debut versus Hull City at Boothferry Park in September 1951, was the first of a remarkable appearance total for Hammers. A great servant, the nearest George got to international honours was when he was selected for an England "B" Trial XI versus Olympic Trial XI at Highbury in 1952, although he also turned out on two occasions for the Football Association versus Cambridge University and then represented London in the Final of the 1958 Inter Cities Fairs Cup versus Barcelona. After playing eight times in the 1957/58 promotion season, George transferred to near neighbours Leyton Orient, where he made 87 League appearances, making an unfortunate debut when he put through his own goal versus Bristol Rovers in August 1958. Leaving in 1961 for Gillingham, he ended his League career at the Kent club with four more appearances. George then went back to finish his career with Ramsgate Athletic in the summer of 1963. George ran his own cabinet-making business in Kent for many years, but sadly passed away in September 2000. He will always be remembered, though, as the man who tamed the great Sir Stanley Matthews. It happened before a full house in the Third Round of the FA Cup when West Ham were paired with the great Blackpool team of that time. Then in the Second Division, Hammers' first choice left-back Noel Cantwell was out injured and the job of marking Matthews was given to George who was then in the reserves and had put in a transfer request. The game was only three minutes old when Blackpool took the lead through... Matthews! The wizard winger, never a prolific scorer, turned up unattended to sidefoot the ball in at the far post. Yet, despite that storming start, that was as good as it got for First Division Blackpool. With George virtually shutting out the Matthews threat, West Ham went on to triumph 5-1 with Vic Keeble scoring a hat-trick and John Dick netting two. But the Man of the Match was George Wright!

WRIGHT, Ian — 1998-99

Born: Woolwich, London, 3.11.63
League apps: 22 (9 goals)
Cup apps: 3

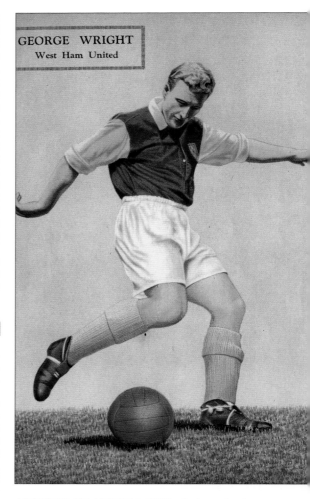

GEORGE WRIGHT
West Ham United

ANOTHER EX-ARSENAL STAR who it was hard to imagine in a West Ham shirt after achieving legendary status at Highbury. But not only did he wear it, he wore it well and by the end of his season-long stay had the West Ham fans firmly among his admirers. And rightly so, for despite his wealth and fame, Wrighty never gave less than 100 per cent effort in the claret and blue. He got off on the right foot by scoring the only goal of the opening day Premiership clash with Sheffield Wednesday at Hillsborough in August 1998 and never looked back. Showing remarkable fitness and application for a player in the veteran stage of his career, the England international striker scored another all-important goal in the 1-0 Upton Park victory over Southampton in October to add to the brace he'd scored in the previous month and was ready to rumble, as he might have put it. As they would be with his former Arsenal colleague Nigel Winterburn a little later, the Hammers fans were left wishing Wrighty had been in their team when at the peak of his powers, if this is what he could achieve when supposedly on the wane. The most prolific scorer in Arsenal's history with a total of 185 goals in 288 matches, Ian had won 31 England caps when he arrived in Green Street and added another two against Luxembourg and the Czech Republic before he left. He'd scored nine goals for his country before announcing his retirement from international football in February 1999, following the departure of England boss Glenn Hoddle. Brought up on the same south London estate as his Arsenal team-mate, the late David "Rocky" Rocastle, Ian was a plasterer and labourer when spotted playing for local side Greenwich Borough by Crystal Palace manager Steve Coppell and joined the Eagles in 1985. In six seasons at Selhurst Park he forged a successful strike partnership with Mark Bright and the pair became a headline writer's dream as they scored over 100 goals between them. His highlight with Palace was the 1990 FA Cup Final versus Manchester United at Wembley

Ian Wright

when he came off the bench to score two stunning goals to take the game to a replay. Signed by George Graham for £2.5 million in September 1991, Ian quickly proved it to be money well spent when he scored on his debut in a League Cup tie at Leicester and then helped himself to a hat-trick against Southampton at the Dell three days later! In 1994/95, Wrighty scored in each tie of every round up to the Final of the European Cup Winners' Cup against Real Zaragoza in Paris and for the fourth season in a row was Arsenal's top scorer. Ian claimed most of the game's top honours in eight seasons at Highbury, being a member of the Gunners sides that won the FA and League Cups in 1993, The European Cup Winners' Cup in 1994 and the Premiership Championship and FA Cup double in 1998. But let's not forget his Full Members Cup medal with Palace in 1991! Forced out of action for three months by a bad cartilage injury in his first and last season with Hammers, he bounced back in April to score against Spurs in a 2-1 win at White Hart Lane with an exquisite lob over the keeper to finish the season as top scorer. On leaving Hammers, Ian had short spells with Burnley and Celtic. He finally retired in early 2000 and has since concentrated on his career as a TV celebrity with his own Friday night chat show.

WRIGHT, Ken   1946-49

Born: Newmarket, Suffolk, 16.5.22
League apps: 51 (20 goals)
Cup apps: 1

AWARDED THE DISTINGUISHED Flying Cross for his heroic deeds during the war while in the RAF, Ken joined West Ham from Cambridge City as an amateur, but signed pro forms in 1946. A forward with an eye for goal, he maintained a good scoring ratio during his four seasons at the Boleyn. After penning a tribute to Ken via the Vintage Claret feature in *Hammers News* magazine in 1994, the author received a letter from the subject's wife, Kathleen Wright, thanking him for the article on her late husband. She also informed this author that Ken rejoined the RAF shortly after giving up professional football due to a knee injury. He then became a flying instructor with Bomber Command.

WRIGHT, P   1914-15

League apps: 10 (1 goal)

MAKING HIS FIRST appearance in the 2-1 home win over Gillingham on the opening day of the 1914/15 season at outside-left, he scored his only goal in a 4-1 win over Bristol Rovers at Upton Park (October 24, 1914) when Leafe, Bailey and Burton also got their names on the scoresheet.

WYLLIE, Robinson "Bob"   1956-57

Born: Dundee, Scotland, 4.4.29
League apps: 13
Cup apps: 2

A SCOTTISH CUSTODIAN who began with junior side Monifieth Tayside FC before transferring to Dundee United. His displays at Tannadice were impressive enough to send Blackpool over the border seeking his signature as a deputy for Scottish international George Farm. He played 13 First Division matches for the Seasiders up to his transfer to Hammers in May 1956. Required to do a similar job at Upton Park – this time as deputy to Ernie Gregory – it was an unlucky 13 in League matches again for Bob, as he moved on to Plymouth at the end of 1956/57, playing five times there before finally settling down for a lengthy stay at Mansfield Town.

Ken Wright in action against Cardiff City at Upton Park with Eddie Chapman in background

Y-Z

YENSON, William
YEOMANSON, Jack
YEWS, Thomas Peace
YOUNG, John "Jack"
YOUNG, Len
YOUNG, Robert

ZAMORA, Bobby

Bobby Zamora

YENSON, William   1902-04/1908-09

Born: Kingston Bagpuize, Oxfordshire, 1880
SL apps: 50
Cup apps: 7

ANOTHER EARLY-CENTURY IRON who made an FA Cup Final appearance, albeit a losing one, after leaving the confines of the Memorial Grounds. Bill swapped his defensive duties for an attacking role on his departure to Bolton Wanderers, lining up in the centre-forward position for the Lancastrians in their 1904 Cup Final meeting with Manchester City at the Crystal Palace after scoring two of Trotters' goals on the way to the Final. City's 1-0 victory (inspired by the legendary Billy Meredith) prevented what would have been a remarkable hat-trick of winners' medals gained by players with West Ham connections: Bill's appearance having been preceded by those of Billy Barnes for Sheffield United in the 1902 Final at Crystal Palace (Billy joined Hammers the following season) and goalkeeper Hughie Montieth's appearance in Bury's record-breaking win of 1903, also at the famous London venue. Bill later came back to the capital to play for Queens Park Rangers and returned to Upton Park when he re-joined Hammers for the 1908/09 season. The "Sportsman" pen-pictures of the 1904 FA Cup Final teams included: "Yenson came from West Ham at the beginning of the present season. Originally a full-back he was tried for Bolton at 'half' then falling in the centre-forward position. He is scarcely an orthodox centre, but a robust and useful player, fond of throwing his weight about and worrying the full-backs." Bill had captained Rangers when they won the Southern League Championship in 1907/08 and made 26 appearances in 1908/09 before returning to Irons. But he didn't stay long, moving to Croydon Common where he made 36 appearances and scored two goals in 1909/10. "A tall, well-built player although a trifle slow at times. He played some excellent games for the Hammers."

YEOMANSON, Jack   1947-50

Born: Margate, Kent, 3.3.20
League apps: 106 (1 goal)
Cup apps: 5

AN IMMEDIATE PREDECESSOR of George Wright, both at Margate and West Ham, it was Jack who set the high standards for his successor to follow. It would be a toss-up between these two fine full-backs to find who gave Hammers the best service; certainly Jack's 106 League appearances, spread over four seasons, were invaluable in helping Hammers through the tricky postwar period. And he did achieve something his replacement never managed… he scored a goal!

YEWS, Thomas Peace   1922-33

Born: Wingate, County Durham, 28.2.1902
League apps: 332 (46 goals)
Cup apps: 29 (5 goals)

WITH JIMMY RUFFELL on the opposite wing it was small wonder that centre-forward Vic Watson claimed all Hammers' goalscoring records during an era of wing-service unsurpassed to this day. Vic headed countless goals from Tommy's runs along the touchline and crosses from near the corner-flag – a ploy nicely summed up by manager Charlie Paynter when he once commented: "Tom could pick a fly off Bill's eyebrows!" Scorer of a near half-century of goals himself

Jack Yeomanson

during his 330-odd appearances in the claret and blue, he made many more goals than he scored. Signed by Hammers for a fee of £150 from Hartlepool United in the club's Cup Final year of 1923, he also had other talents, being a "rag-time" pianist of some note. His renditions were very much in demand during frequent Continental tours in those happy days. After ending his playing career with nearby Clapton Orient in the mid-1930s (he joined the O's in 1933, but made only three League appearances), Tom became an engineer at Briggs Motor Bodies. At the time of his death, in August 1966, Tom was a chargehand at the Ford Motor Company.

YOUNG, John "Jack"   1922-33

Born: Whitburn, Tyne and Wear, 1895
League apps: 124 (3 goals)
Cup apps: 14

A DASHING LEFT-WINGER who converted to full-back with considerable success. Signed for a sizeable – for those days – fee of £600, his switch of positions brought the following comment in Jack's pen-picture in the programme for the 1923 FA Cup Final: "He played for Southend United at outside-left, and went to Upton

Career record

	League		FAC		LC		Europe		Total	
Played	**App**	**Gls**	**App**	**Gls**	**App**	**Gls**	**App**	**Gls**	**App**	**Gls**
1923-24	12	1	0	0	0	0	0	0	12	1
1924-25	33	1	6	1	0	0	0	0	39	2
1925-26	32	1	1	0	0	0	0	0	33	1
1926-27	39	8	3	0	0	0	0	0	42	8
1927-28	42	11	2	0	0	0	0	0	44	11
1928-29	41	10	5	3	0	0	0	0	46	13
1929-30	41	3	4	1	0	0	0	0	45	4
1930-31	37	7	1	0	0	0	0	0	38	7
1931-32	23	2	2	0	0	0	0	0	25	2
1932-33	32	2	5	0	0	0	0	0	37	2
TOTAL	**332**	**46**	**29**	**5**	**0**	**0**	**0**	**0**	**361**	**51**

Park as a forward; but he displayed his aptitude as a defender, and well-earned the position he now occupies." By the mid-1920s, ill-health had eroded his First Division appearances, and he played his last game for West Ham at Elland Road versus Leeds (September 19, 1925) before transferring to QPR. In 1929, he joined Accrington Stanley. After retiring from playing due to ill-health, Jack continued his links with the game by scouting for Liverpool, whose manager George Kay was his former captain at West Ham. Jack's daughter, Miss Dorothy Young, still lives in the same house that her parents occupied when her father returned to his native town of Whitburn, Tyne and Wear, and was the guest of honour of West Ham United when entertaining Newcastle United in February 1993. She later donated the original shirt that Jack wore in the 1923 FA Cup Final to the club. Jack was made team captain with QPR and became something of a penalty expert at the Bush – scoring 12 times in 91 League and Cup appearances for Rangers. On retiring he ran a farm near Sunderland. Jack passed away in 1952 at the age of 57.

YOUNG- LEFT FULL BACK.
WEST HAM UNITED. F.C.13

YOUNG, Len   1934-35

Born: West Ham, London, 23.2.12
League apps: 12

A FORMER ESSEX Schools player, Len was a well-built centre-half who had two seasons at Upton Park as understudy to Jim Barrett. Locally-born, he was one of the club's many captures from Ilford. Transferred to Reading, he was still playing for the Berkshire club in the old Third Division South after the war (26 apps), and later joined Brighton & Hove Albion (eight apps), where he retired from playing in 1949.

YOUNG, Robert   1907-09

Born: Swinhill, Lanarkshire, Scotland, 1886
SL apps: 42 (1 goal)
Cup apps: 2

BOB MADE HIS Hammers debut versus Spurs at left-half but, being something of a utility man, filled all the defensive berths with the exception of goalkeeper during his two years at the Boleyn Ground. Joining Hammers from St Mirren at the beginning of the season in which his former Saints team-mates were destined to reach the Final of the Scottish Cup at Hampden Park versus Celtic, the 21-year-old set about establishing himself in Irons' Southern League side to finish the term with 33 appearances to his credit. First team outings were scarcer the following season, however, and a 6-3 defeat at Norwich (December 12, 1908) signalled the end of his career in the claret and blue, in which his only goal was scored versus Norwich (April 4, 1908). Transferred to Middlesbrough, he stayed on Teesside until 1910 when he joined Everton for a massive (for those days) fee of £1,200. Quite a transformation for someone who didn't play any football until he was 17. He had been a keen athlete and won several half-mile races. Turned out for Swinhill Hearts and Larkhall Thistle before joining Saints.

ZAMORA, Bobby   2004-

Born: Barking, Essex, 16.1.81
League apps: 57 (16 goals)
Cup apps: 2 (2 goals)

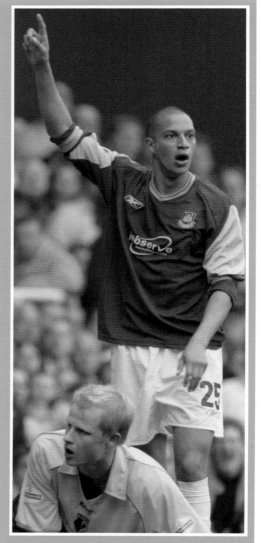

A LIFELONG HAMMERS fan who was born in the same Barking stronghold that also produced club legends Sir Bobby Moore and Sir Trevor Brooking, Bobby Zamora has so far failed to follow their footsteps into Upton Park's Hall of Fame. Hoping to kick-start his career after a frustrating spell in the Premiership with Spurs and a switch to his boyhood heroes as part of the £7 million-plus deal that saw Jermain Defoe depart for White Hart Lane in January 2004, Bobby still had to hold down a regular place in Alan Pardew's plans over a year later and had seen proposed moves to Crystal Palace and Stoke City come to nothing. But it had all been so different at his second club Brighton & Hove Albion, whom he had joined from Bristol Rovers for a £100,000 fee after just six sub appearances for the Pirates, succeeding in a brief loan spell in which he scored six times in six games for the Seagulls. His goalscoring continued unabated following his permanent move to the south coast in August 2000 and his 31 goals in all competitions were a major contribution to Albion's Third Division Championship success in 2000/01. Honoured by his fellow professionals with a place in the PFA's Third Division team, he amassed a grand total of 77 goals in 130 appearances in all competitions for the troubled Second Division club before Spurs manager Glen Hoddle splashed out £1.5 million for his signature in July 2003. Yet his one moment of glory with the north Londoners came at Hammers' expense when he scored the only goal of his 18-match Spurs career to dump the club he left as a youth-team hopeful seven years earlier out of the Carling Cup after a fiercely contested Third Round tie at White Hart Lane in October 2003. Scoring the winner on his debut in a 2-1 win over Bradford City at Valley Parade in February 2004, the inevitable "Bobby Dazzler" headlines were again in evidence later that month when he scored the only goal of the match against Cardiff City at the Boleyn and he ended the season with five goals in 20 appearances in his first season "back home". A superbly skilful and mobile striker when firing on all cylinders, there was evidence that Bobby was happier playing away from the pressures of Upton Park in 2004/05, as his two strikes at Wolves in mid-January seemed to confirm. But, come the hour, come the man and Bobby finally delivered the goods as he scored three goals in the Play-off Semi-finals against Ipswich to shoot Hammers into the Play-off Final showdown with Preston North End. At the Millennium Stadium, Cardiff, it was Bobby's goal that ensured Hammers' passage back to the Premiership.

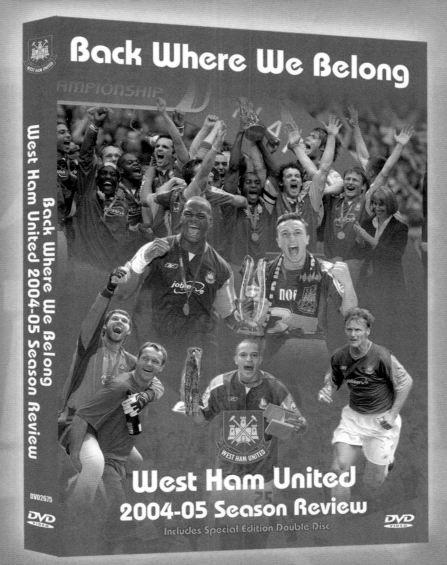

ACKNOWLEDGMENTS

Like any project of this scale and detail, many people have contributed to the final completion of this, the third edition of the *Who's Who of West Ham United FC*. I would firstly like to express special thanks to the CEO of Profile Media Group David Ellingham, who backed the venture with that most important ingredient – hard cash! Also former West Ham star Tony Gale for his penetrating foreword; the editor of West Ham retro magazine *Ex*, Tony McDonald, for his permission to use material from the 1994 centenary edition and the loan of many invaluable photographs; also *Ex Magazine* archive editor Terry Connelly for his unsurpassable knowledge on the past players of West Ham and his unstinting help and encouragement during the three-year haul to publication in addition to the loan of many pictures and snippets of information gleaned from his many contacts among the subjects of the book, and the interest of his sons Eamon, Aidan and Euan; Kirk Blows, whose insightful introduction would be hard to beat (definitely five stars Kirk!); fellow Hammers historian John Northcutt, who unselfishly offered invaluable assistance despite having to halt work on his own Who's Who project because of the emergence of this tome; Steve Blowers of *Hammers News* for his many helpful pointers on the whereabouts of ex-Hammers around the world, his privately produced handbook for 1997/98 and his indispensable players lists; club photographer Steve Bacon for providing player pics up to the letter "D", despite being seriously incapacitated by diabetes; West Ham lensman Kieran Galvin for acting as a timely and very professional substitute for Steve; Fred Loveday and Denis Lamb for their help on the 1986 and 1994 editions respectfully; Kelly Miller (nee Harkins) of *Hammers News* for her patient response to my many requests for help; my son Christopher who, despite having to live surrounded by enough programmes, magazines, newspapers and books to seriously compete with the British Library, was a constant source of support and practical help; also his close friends Robert Balcombe, Lee Coleman and Peter Sell who helped considerably (thanks lads!); special thanks also to Gary Bird, Allan Hambly and Andrew Baker of Newham Council; my sales bosses at Profile Media Group Eddie Thomas and Kevin McCarthy (who actually gets a mention in Bobby Ferguson's entry) and work colleagues Grant Levy, Tal Sidi and Ian Henderson for scanning the internet; the editorial and production teams, led by Eddie Taylor – head designer Simon Marriott, Laura Fell (for the daunting task of keying in some 224,000 words and deciphering my often unintelligible handwriting!), Liverpool fan Chris Gerrard for his help with Neil Mellor's biog, Robin Castle and Chris Deary for accessing Soccerbase for many details and their Chelsea Magazine

editor Lee Berry; picture researcher Osha Mason and Gordon "Eagle Eyes" Beveridge for his sterling efforts in checking a mountain of facts and figures and copy settings, likewise Stephen Mitchell for his endless patience in a similar role, Salome Davis for scanning pics, Richard Lee and Janine Singh for extra design work and also Owain Jones for editorial help, Lorraine Rollo and Terry Seward of Programme Master for providing much-needed progs and promoting the book, Elizabeth Hodgson and Cate Langmuir for encouragement and practical pointers; Tim Crane for giving up his lunch hours to bring in his unsurpassable collection of West Ham trade cards for scanning; also Brian Taylor for his cigarette cards and Stephen Marsh for the same; the late Jack Helliar and his son John; late lensman Albert York for his "tunnel shots"; Richard Austin for pics from the 1994 edition; ex-*Hammers News* men Danny Francis and Ben Sharratt; Cliff Moulder of Mpress Ltd for allowing us to use the aerial shot of Upton Park and also Charles Dickinson of the same company for his assistance; Debra Hollis for sourcing George Webb's date of birth and her encouragement; Eileen Gunn for information on Lee Boylen of Canvey Island, non-League newspapers and general support; special thanks to Sue Masters; also to Jenny Doucy of West Ham United FC (for her help with the biog of John Burton); Steve Shiv Sohal for his reminiscences of his time at Bobby Moore's soccer school at Forest School, Snaresbrook, Essex where Bobby was, according to Steve, a pioneer of the Kick Racism Out of Football campaign – although preceding the coining of that phrase, Bobby took Steve (who was the only Asian in the class) and his pal Barry Gibbins under his wing; cheers also to Christopher Seltzer, Liam Curry, Mike "Black Cabbie" Wilson, Huddy and Wattsy; former *Recorder Sport* West Ham journo Trevor Smith for his five decades of Hammers coverage; also to Huw Jenkins for internet promotions; thanks are also due to my old pal Geoff Thompson for several football books; I would also like to thank my good friends John Mayo, Dave Galpin, Richard Goodhew, Hugh Barr (despite the fact that he's a Charlton fan), Michelle, Geoff Brodie, Barry Nunn and Brian Read for putting up with me for the duration of this project! And also my three daughters Mandy, Sandy and Dulcima. Thanks also to Chelmsford Hammers Ben Snr and Terry Orwell. Finally, many thanks to the board of West Ham United and chairman Terry Brown in particular for allowing us to use the club's official crests without any charge and all the players of West Ham United over the past 105 years!

For Val, George, Maisie and Jean.

photograph: Andrew Baker

1904-2004

100+
YEARS

The Boleyn Ground